FANNY KEMBLE

By J. C. Furnas

FANNY KEMBLE

Leading Lady of the
Nineteenth-Century Stage

A Biography by

J. C. FURNAS

The Dial Press
New York

Published by
The Dial Press
1 Dag Hammarskjold Plaza
New York, New York 10017

Manufactured in the United States of America
First printing
Design by Francesca Belanger

Library of Congress Cataloging in Publication Data

Furnas, J. C. (Joseph Chamberlain), 1905–
    Fanny Kemble : leading lady of the nineteenth-
century stage.

    Bibliography: p.
    Includes index.
    1. Kemble, Fanny, 1809–1893.   2. Actors—
Great Britain—Bibliography.   I. Title.
PN2598.K4F87   792'.028'0924 [B]   81-9849
ISBN 0-385-27208-1   AACR2

For Dutchy's Lady

ACKNOWLEDGMENTS

THIS BOOK is indebted for research facilities first and foremost to the Princeton University Library; then to the New York Public Library and the New York Society Library. Other libraries whose help is most gratefully acknowledged include: The Bobst Library of New York University; the Boston Public Library; the Bowdoin College Library; the British Library; the Butler Library of Columbia University; the Colby College Library; the Cornell University Library; the Dartmouth College Library; the Duke University Library; the Folger Shakespeare Library; the Haverford College Library; the Houghton Library, Harvard University; the Huntington Library, San Marino; the Indiana University libraries; the Knox College Archives; the Lenox Library Association; the Library of Congress; the National Library of Scotland; the Newark Public Library; the Perkins Library of the University of North Carolina; the Pierpont Morgan Library; the Philadelphia Free Library; the Rutherford B. Hayes Library; the Stockbridge Library Association; the University of Illinois Library; the University of Kentucky Library; the University of Pennsylvania Library; the University of Rochester Library; the State University of New York libraries; the University of Texas Library; the University of Vermont Library; the Yale University Library.

Among museums and cognate institutions just as gratefully thanked: the Boston Athenaeum; the Brooklyn Museum; the Chicago Historical Society; the Cincinnati Historical Society; the Eleutherian Mills Historical Library; the Garrick Club; the Georgia Historical Society; the Historical Society of Pennsylvania; the Iowa State Educational Association; the Massachusetts Historical Society; the Museum of the City of New York; the Boston Museum of Fine Arts; the National Portrait Gallery, London; the National Portrait Gallery, Washington; the New-York Historical Society; the Pennsylvania Academy of the Fine Arts; the Rhode Island Historical Society; the Rosenbach Museum and Library; the St. George's Society; the Theatre Collection, Harvard University; the Theatrical Collection, University of Bristol; the Victoria and Albert Museum; the Walter Hampden-Edwin Booth Collection, Players Club; the White House Collection.

Individuals thanked for generous help include: Michael Balfour; Malcolm Bell, Jr.; Dewey Benefield; Constance Cummings; Edward C. Darrin; the late Marryat Dobie; Leon Edel; Dorothy Marshall; Sir Geoffrey and Lady Meade; Virginia Murray; B. N. Nightingale; Eleanor Ransome; Eugenia Rawls; Martha Saxton; John A. Scott; George E. Shambaugh, Jr. And most of all—and most gratefully—Fanny Kemble Wister.

Nancy van Itallie of The Dial Press has been a skillful midwife.

IT IS TWENTY-FIVE YEARS since my first reading of Frances Anne Kemble's *Journal of a Residence on a Georgian Plantation* led me to look closely into her career and character and consequently yearn to find time and opportunity to write a full biography. All that while several photographs of portraits of her looked down on me in my office. Now I can look up at them and say, "Miss Kemble, for better or worse, I have been and gone and done it."

Note that I say "Miss Kemble." In this book I usually refer to her as "Fanny," as did her family and early public. This was convenient for me and by no means disrespectfully meant. But I sometimes wonder what may happen to me if some night I dream of her and, forgetting myself, call her Fanny to her face. She may very well think that, since she never laid eyes on me before, I hardly know her well enough for that, and I flinch to think of the snubbing she would inflict. Yet I'm not sure I would agree. Maybe I do know her pretty well after twenty-five years of hope and about four years of research. And she proved to be a lady worth knowing.

CONTENTS

FANNY KEMBLE

I like biography better than fiction myself; fiction is too free. In biography you have your little handful of facts, little bits of a puzzle, and you sit and think, and fit 'em together this way and that, and get up and throw 'em down and say damn, and go out for a walk, and it's real soothing, and when done, gives an idea of finish to the writer that is very peaceful. Of course it's not really so finished as quite a rotten novel; it always has and must have the incurable illogicalities of life about it. . . . Still, that's where the fun comes in.

—Robert Louis Stevenson

I

Footlight Patricians

THE DEATH she would choose, Frances Anne Kemble decided in
1839, would be to "break my neck off the back of my horse at a full
gallop on a fine day."[1] The young horsewoman who thus wished to
die with her boots on had already been a successful actress, a sought-
after social lioness, and a conspicuous author. At the time she was
also an unlucky, unsuccessful wife and affectionate mother. Presently
she would be a browbeaten divorcée and, after her fashion, an auxiliary feminist; then a powerful witness against black slavery and, also
after her own fashion, a brilliant autobiographer.

Her skill in the saddle lowered her chances of getting her wish.
Not until fifty-odd years later did she die of a stroke in her bedroom.
But that formula bubbling up in her young womanhood—sun in the
sky, wind in the face, animal energy at full tilt in exultant rhythms,
and then sudden annihilation—conveys the essential Fanny Kemble
better than any phrases whittled out by a biographer a century and a
half later.

Henry James, who knew her very well in her last twenty years,
called her "the first woman in London . . . a deep, rich human nature."[2] The more he saw of her, the greater his delight and respect.
Not that she was merely warm and winsome. Her tongue could flick
off skin at fifty yards. Her printed strictures on slatternly southern
belles left marks. But most people coming within her gravitational
field felt the integrity and goodwill underlying most of her doings
and sayings, and whether as slim, twenty-year-old stage star or gray-

3

headed grandmother, no taller but much thicker, she was very easy to remember. American and British diners-out, fellow actors, theater managers, lady novelists, minor and major poets, Yankee handymen, Swiss mountain guides, and former slaves all bore witness about her, always pungent but usually, though sometimes grudgingly, admiring.

The ingredients blending into this notable woman were, as it stands to reason, out of the common. Her great-granddaughter, Frances Anne Kemble Wister Stokes, recalls how in the dining room of the Pennsylvania country house she was reared in, "hung five portraits of the Kemble family, all . . . . Shakespearean actors. Two were by Sir Thomas Lawrence, and one by Sir Joshua Reynolds. All the Kembles were beautiful, and we loved them. They presided magnificently over the room."[3] Fanny Kemble's aunt, Mrs. Sarah (Kemble) Siddons, was the English-speaking world's most august tragedienne. Her performance of Lady Macbeth, William Hazlitt wrote, was "something above nature . . . almost as if a being of a superior order had dropped from a higher sphere to awe the world with the majesty of her appearance. Power was seated on her brow, passion emanated from her as from a shrine."[4] In slightly different terms her brother, Fanny's uncle, John Philip Kemble, was almost as awesome. His stately handling of Hamlet and Coriolanus invoked, wrote "Christopher North" (John Wilson), "a sense of the sublime, like some strain of magnificent music."[5] A much younger brother, Charles, Fanny's father, was matchless in roles of gallant charm. Other Kembles filled smaller but valued niches in the British and American theaters. Sister Elizabeth (Mrs. Whitelock) had her apprenticeship in London, then went adventuring in America and prospered well enough to come home and retire comfortably; years later Fanny's hostess in Baltimore would recall Mrs. Whitelock's thrillingly lovely stage voice. Brother Stephen was a provincial manager and actor of real talent in Edinburgh and Newcastle. Since the offspring of these and following generations of Kembles tended to turn actors, the name persisted in lights or at least in many a cast of characters from the time of George III to that of George VI. As if to symbolize the tradition, the family genes endowed most of them—Fanny included—with the Kemble nose, a shapely but emphatic beak with a curiously elongated tip.

"Damn it, madam," protested Thomas Gainsborough when making studies for his famous portrait of Mrs. Siddons, "there is no end to your nose!" [6]

Fanny also inherited her aunt's preternaturally large eyes, subject of the only recorded conversation between the two. Small Fanny had committed one of her frequent breaches of discipline, and Aunt Siddons was asked to bring her stern stage presence to bear. She took the child on her knee and, having reared several of her own, doubtless read her lines very well. But, though Fanny seemed attentive to that voice the merest whisper of which enthralled thousands of grown-up Londoners, all she said when her cue came was "What beautiful eyes you have!" [7] But it may be biologically misleading to ascribe all the loveliness of Fanny's own great brown eyes—enhanced, as Sir Thomas Lawrence noted while drawing her, by double eyelashes—solely to the Kemble line. The eloquently deep black eyes of Fanny's mother, Mrs. Charles Kemble, née Marie-Thérèse De Camp—she was born in Vienna in the empress-queen's time—were also vastly admired during her thirty-odd years on the London stage. Leigh Hunt, liberal poet-journalist, abandoned his usual astringency to celebrate Miss De Camp's "striking features . . . beautiful figure . . . rich profusion of hair." [8] The influential *Blackwood's* magazine called her "that dangerous yet unwicked witch" with a "motion that was itself music . . . gliding and floating and flying." [9] And she was not only a remarkable dancer practically from babyhood, but also a renowned singer of light music, farce-comedienne and able play-carpenter of original as well as adapted scripts.

With a mother like that Fanny hardly needed the Kemble reference to account for her pungency on stage and off. The three Kembles of the dynasty's greatest days—Sarah, John, and Charles—could with some fairness be described as Olympianly great but (except when acting Lady Macbeth, Coriolanus, or Mercutio) somewhat pedestrian personalities. The word would be less applicable to Marie-Thérèse's progeny, Fanny least of all.

In 1832 Fanny and her father came to America to earn dollars to mend the family's shaky finances. One of the most amiable friends they made there was Gouverneur Kemble, an affluent industrialist-politician of Knickerbocker descent crossed with British gentry, who introduced himself on the cordial assumption that anybody with his surname was somehow kin. His great friend, Washington Irving, called him "one of the noblest beings that ever was created,"[10] and the hospitality of his family manor house in the Jersey hills and his own country house up the Hudson was deservedly famous, causing that patrician *arbiter elegantiae,* General Winfield Scott, to describe him as "the most perfect gentleman in the United States."[11] Fanny thought him "a nice man, with a remarkably fine face," and Charles and he got on well talking ancestors. "We are an old family," Fanny was led to believe, "but the direct line is lost after Charles the Second."[12]

That is, it was thought their forebears, like Gouverneur Kemble's, had been the Kembles of Herefordshire (maybe a Wilshire branch), staunch Cavalier gentry and Catholics; indeed a Kemble in holy orders, the Venerable John, died a brave martyr on the scaffold in 1678. Roger Kemble, actor-manager and founder of the dynasty, duly came from the west country, was reared Catholic and sent three of his sons for a Catholic education in France. But Roger, like his father, was a hairdresser before taking to the stage—neither trade consistent with gentle ancestry. Yet the romantic—and dramatic—values of Cavalier boots and ruffles and martyrs gallant under the ax appealed to the playacting Kembles—and to their hopes of upward social mobility. Clinging hazily to a claim of such descent, Mrs. Siddons and Charles Kemble visited the Venerable John's grave, and on the great silver trophy given Charles when he retired from the stage in 1840 were engraved the Herefordshire Kembles' arms: "Sable on a bend ermine three leopard heads caboshed." Nothing known to the Royal College of Arms justified this implicit claim. On the contrary, Roger seems to have failed to establish it, for, being "unwilling to bear Armorial Ensigns without due authority,"[13] he procured from the Crown a new blazon for him and his descendants, similar to but tactfully different from the Herefordshire family's. Whether Fanny was aware of this rather lame piece of ostentation in Roger Kemble, gentleman, of Kentish Town in the Parish of St. Pancras, I do not know.

In any case, whether or not Roger partook of genuine gentrice, he spent much of his professional life playing the role of the stage urban gentleman who was focus of most of the comedy and much of the tragedy of the theater of the eighteenth century. Tall, patricianly handsome, graceful and leisurely in movement, he looked and behaved the part and somehow passed its traits and the accompanying stage presence on to John, Sarah, Stephen, et al. Without that it might have been harder for him and later for them, standing on his emerging shoulders, so to speak, to reach the enviable level of acceptance that enabled granddaughter Fanny to be so surefooted in society.

How notable the Kembles' social leap was is hard to appreciate now when acting is so nearly clear of the onus once attached to it, and the social stratification of England, though still a thing to reckon with, is much less rigid. Well into the eighteenth century, English law kept up the medieval presumption that stage players, Gypsies, and vagrants were all "masterless men," hence social mavericks dangerous to the public peace and subject to harsh penalties for merely existing, let alone making a living from fly-by-night entertaining of their betters. Common sense modified this stupid convention but not adequately or consistently. Formal exceptions originating in Elizabethan times favored chiefly the semipermanent theatrical companies of London under direct royal or noble patronage. In Roger Kemble's day that meant the two Theatres Royal (Drury Lane and Covent Garden) supplemented by the Haymarket. Informally, certain precarious itinerant troupes in "the provinces," "the country," got along by wheedling or bribing temporary leave to perform out of capricious town councils or constables. "Strollers," the general name for such adventurers, had much the same connotation as the law's "rogues and vagabonds."

Strollers' lives were usually sordid, often disheartening. Only superior troupes had a horse and cart to carry crucial bits of scenery and a few indispensable props. The actors probably walked from town A, where a sulky justice of the peace had threatened to jail them, to town B where, the year before, the actress doing "second business" had carnally coaxed the constable to look the other way. With luck the landlord of The Blue Dragon let them use his assembly room, but were he too bitter about a similar troupe who had sneaked away recently owing him twenty shillings rent, a local barn was all they could hope for. The plays that the audience—a scattering of bored local gentry and wide-eyed tradesmen—got for their money were slovenly, corrupted, mercilessly cut, rantingly performed perversions of Shakespeare, Otway, or Rowe plus the later crime melodramas and la-sir comedies. Between acts some member of the company danced or sang a song. A certain amount of greasy but gaudy finery was reserved for the principals; the minor characters' costumes were varying combinations of whatever garments anybody had available.

On the march such a troupe must have looked like refugees from a lingering catastrophe. Small wonder that staid society, having forced dislocation on them, deplored their presence even when Puritan scruples against playacting were not involved. Nor was their ill repute altogether unjustified. Many such strollers were no better than their looks and law and public opinion implied. Visits from Thespis' cart often meant unpaid tavern scores and petty swindles. In Hogarth's engraving "Strolling Actresses Dressing in a Barn" the playbill identifies the leading lady as "Mrs. Bilkvillage." Her strumpetish half-nakedness suggests another cogent reason for the players' bad name among the steady-paced in Hogarth's time and later. There was a certain affinity between the theater and commercialized copulation. Ever since the rowdy, bawdy Restoration of 1660 had begun letting women play the female stage-roles that hitherto boys had taken, a strong odor of the brothel had clung to histrionics. The gay, pretty women whom managers recruited for the companies under royal patronage in London were more or less assumed to be accessibly looselived. The girls who hawked oranges among the patrons were more so and cheaper. A hundred years later in the larger, more formally designed theaters of London in the Kembles' heyday, the upper galleries were acknowledged resorts of whores seeking custom.

The Theatre Royal, Covent Garden, where Fanny Kemble made her triumphant debut in 1829 at the age of nineteen, then managed by her father for the stockholders, was subject to that reproach. Ten years later Thackeray could still write, "A man that . . . has been behind the scenes of the Opera, or has even been to the theatre and looked up to . . . the second tier of boxes, must know that the *Harlot's Progress* [one of Hogarth's series of social-warning prints] is still by no means concluded."[14] And note "behind the scenes." As the England of the eighteenth century gradually replaced *Moll Flanders* with *Pamela,* a yearning for self-respect stirred among actresses. By Fanny's time certain reputations, such as Mrs. Siddons's, were unassailable. Yet well into the nineteenth century the statistical presumption that an aspiring actress—let alone the ballet girls[15]—was approachable in irregular terms was a good bet. And when all that held good of "His Majesty's Servants" in the metropolis, better repute could hardly be expected among bedraggled women-strollers.

When strolling entailed such risks of hunger, jail, and cold shoulder, it is strange that this hole-and-corner profession attracted able persons. Many of the recruits who kept it going were endogenous, children of stroller parents taking such risks for granted and absorbing with their mothers' milk—administered between mama's quick changes to play first the heroine's waiting woman and then her long-lost sister—the actor's arcane belief that this strange way of making a living is rewardingly special. Hence the high likelihood that actors' children will also be actors. Further, from outside the profession came stagestruck youths and maidens, some experienced as amateurs, emulous of the strollers' reverberating skills. Sometimes this histrionic urge—real enough, however hard to define or account for—seized a promising youth of anomalous background and in spite of all parents and parson could say, he was off with the raggle-taggle-strollers-O![16] Such infusions of fresh blood of quality cannot have been too rare, else the strolling industry would never have survived the harsh Act of 1737 that, while renewing the privileges of the Theatres Royal, forbade playacting for gain outside London. The way round that was ingeniously sneaky: the Act did not forbid musical concerts. Most strollers could sing or play an instrument, more or less. So they advertised musical programs at the usual admission scales and threw in "free" dramatic performances. Local authorities winked at the subterfuge consistently enough to keep the more tenacious companies going.[17]

Such troupes gradually stabilized on regular "circuits," a week or two in Bath, say, then Bristol, then Gloucester, and local publics learned to look forward to their arrival. That encouraged local capital to build more or less licitly licensed theaters like the great London houses in everything except size, affording circuit-companies permanent seating, lighting, and stock scenery. Hence there grew up a far-flung provincial stage industry the upper strata of which gave actors a tolerable if often still precarious living. Admirers of *Pendennis* and *Nicholas Nickleby* will recognize it in full bloom. It became the training ground for talent of London quality. York's admiration of the lovely Mrs. Greenroom's heart-wringing performance of *Isabella* might bring up a scout from London and presently a favorable offer from Drury Lane or Covent Garden. At the same time improved highways and coaches enabled the great names of the London stage to reap handsome sums from summer tours of the provinces supported by the members of the company permanently fixed in each successive town, which was, of course, the origin of "the star system."

That—in a rather earlier phase—was the kind of show business in which Fanny's grandfather flourished after years of strolling; in which her aunts and uncles learned their trade and gained positions of varying stature. Though that world had not treated Roger Kemble badly in the long run, he did not think well of it as a calling. He forbade daughter Sarah to marry an actor; she did it anyway.[18] He sent son John Philip to Douai with the priesthood in view. He apprenticed son Stephen to an apothecary. He procured son Charles a place in H.M. Post Office; an ungracious attitude but consistent with the trend toward upper mobility that went along with the downward-trending Kemble nose.

Fanny Kemble never knew her grandfather Roger. He and his formidable wife died years before she was born. Her Aunt Sarah she saw on the stage only once, when after some years of retirement the great lady contributed her presence to a benefit.[19] The child remembered only "a solemn female figure in black, and the tremendous *roar* of public greeting which welcomed her."[20] Niece sometimes referred to aunt with equivocal reverence as Melpomene—the classic Muse of tragedy, in which character Reynolds depicted her in her best-known portrait. It appears that her social presence owed more to serenity than to vivacity. Tom Moore, fashionable diner-out and rhymester, recalled sitting between "Mrs. Siddons and Lady Castlereagh. . . . I heard for the first time the voice of the former transferred to the normal things of this world . . . in her most tragic tone,—'I do love ale dearly.' "[21] Maria Edgeworth, second only to Jane Austen in the matter of Regency women, said that "Mrs. Siddons was awfully dull, except when she got upon her own profession."[22] Yet Samuel Rogers, cultivated banker and connoisseur of celebrities, no man to suffer bores gladly, esteemed her highly, and something about her stirred Sir Thomas Lawrence, her time's most valued portrait painter, into strange emotional capers.

Her influence on Fanny was partly rhetorical—her readings of Shakespeare and Milton were fine training for niece's susceptible ear—and partly minatory, for Melpomene's decline into thwarted inanity may have increased Fanny's misgivings about the family profession. Years later she told how depressed she had been by "the vapid vacuity of my aunt Siddons's life . . . her apparent deadness and indifference to everything, which I attributed (unjustly, perhaps) less to her advanced age and impaired powers than to what I supposed the withering and drying influence of the overstimulated atmosphere . . . in which she had passed her life." And just before the grand old lady died: "What a price she has paid for her great celebrity! . . . The cup has been so highly flavored that life is absolutely without savor or sweetness to her now."[23]

Mrs. Siddons herself told Rogers that after she retired she often found herself thinking, "This is the time I used to be thinking of going to the theatre; there was the pleasure of dressing, then of acting, but it is all over now."[24] It is readily seen how this end of a great career heightened Fanny's reluctance to pursue the traditional Kemble destiny. Add her dismay every time they cast her in one of Melpomene's outstanding roles. After Mrs. Siddons died, when they told Fanny she would have to do Lady Macbeth in the provinces,[25] it made her feel, she said, "as if I were standing up by the great pyramid of Egypt to see how tall I am . . . *the* Lady Macbeth will never be seen again! I wish just now that in honor of my aunt the play might be forbidden . . . for the next ten years."[26] In a manner of speaking, however, she had already played the role. One of the Kemble colleagues was Charles Young, a genial principal actor much at home in the Kemble household. It amused him to teach big-eyed Fanny, still a toddler but obviously sharp as a tack, to declaim bits from Shakespeare, such as Lady Macbeth fresh from wielding the daggers and telling her already bloody-handed husband, "My hands are of your color." That grisly line came out of the child: "My handth are of oo tolor." Years later when Fanny was playing Lady Macbeth in good earnest, Young was behind the scenes watching as she smeared her hands with red paint before her entrance, laughing and telling her: "Ah ha! My handth are of oo tolor!" One may assume that whereas her niece chuckled, Melpomene would not have. No chuckler she.

Nor was John Philip Kemble—"the noblest Roman of them all" or "Black Jack" depending on the public's mood, anyway the second pillar of the Kemble fame. Regally beaked, tall and so rich in stage presence that they said he seemed too big for any room he entered, he was even deeper than his renowned sister in the good graces of the few thousand who made up Regency London's *élite*—the intertwined households of great noblemen, wealthy gentry, and the occasional legal, clerical, literary, and histrionic talents whom they delighted to honor. David Garrick, king of the London stage in the preceding generation, seems to have been the first to cross the gulf to semiacceptance as a result of his intelligence and great personal charm. But he could never have managed it unless a certain potential had not already existed. Both ingredients, personableness and opportunity, were necessary. Sarah Siddons's success probably came of her haunting, formidable beauty combined with patently great integrity. John Philip's welcome to his betters' tables was in a different idiom: Thanks to his father's mistaken ambitions for him, he had had a gentleman's schooling at Douai, good French and Latin at command, intelligence enough to dabble creditably in criticism and poetizing— and he was an able tosspot.

In the London of the Prince Regent and Richard Brinsley Sheridan, the ability to swill down quantities of port—or claret as fashion shifted—was as necessary to fine gentlemen as wearing silk stockings below one's knee breeches. In his last years John Philip's wife—former actress Priscilla Hopkins, daughter of the Drury Lane prompter—had him near teetotaling. For most of his career, however, he drank bottle for bottle with famous fashionable topers, and yet, though drink is a notorious risk for actors, it seldom affected his stage performances. Offstage was another matter. Sober, he was somberly if interestingly taciturn in company. Full of wine, he held forth at vast but apparently entertaining length on acting and his own genius; later in the evening he might be found breaking all the glasses in an obscure tavern, or haranguing the fishmongers at Billingsgate at 5:00 A.M. and going home with a fine turbot under his arm as a gift for Priscilla, or picking fights with Covent Garden costermongers in the shadow of his own theater. None of that put off his eminent friends—Lawrence the painter, Sir Walter Scott, and the like, for the arts; the Earl of Guilford, the Earl of Essex, the Earl of Northumberland who, when Covent Garden burned down, lent him ten thousand pounds toward rebuilding and then made it a gift.

Through his part-ownership of Covent Garden he ably entrenched himself as chief producer of the British theater as well as its most renowned actor. But shifts in public taste toward more spectacular—hence expensive—productions undermined whatever economic soundness the house had ever had. The fire closed that chapter; but to open another more disastrous one Kemble and his associates rebuilt it on an even greater scale which meant higher operating costs. The consequent financial woes wore down even Kemble's resourcefulness. Having secured himself one thousand pounds a year—then a comfortable income—safe from creditors, he made a present of his share of Covent Garden to brother Charles and, full of years, fame, and odd ailments, retired to Switzerland. There, according to Rogers, who disliked him, he was jealous of the attention paid to Mont Blanc. Fanny knew him only as a venerable figure who once came to London on Covent Garden business: "White hair and beautiful face . . . an expression of the most benign dignity."[27] There is a Kemble Street, rather down-at-heel now, in the neighborhood of Covent Garden. The

Kemble's Head is a pleasant little pub on the corner of Long Acre and Bow Street.

In 1795 John Philip Kemble's drinking cast him in an unrehearsed scene from *Tom Jones* that, at another time, might have kept Fanny Kemble from ever existing. To be fair, this lapse was not characteristic of him even in his cups. Marie-Thérèse De Camp, twenty-one years old and dewily bewitching, was then a chief ornament of the company he headed at Drury Lane. That evening he was too drunk to remember that he was stably married and in no case a roaring womanizer. He forced his way into Miss De Camp's dressing room, grabbed and tousled her in spite of her cries, and—fortunately before worse happened—desisted only when people rushed in. Fifty years earlier that would have made gleeful gossip without much consequence. By 1795, however, public distaste for such behavior, even in the Alsatia of the theater, made some redress advisable in view of the lady's unblemished reputation. Kemble put into the London newspapers a statement calling his behavior "very improper and unjustifiable" and declaring Miss De Camp's "conduct and character irreproachable."[28] The giggling and joking died down; Thérèse's unflappable behavior even increased the wide esteem in which she was already held. She resumed adding piquant charm to Drury Lane's stage bill of fare.

But its company contained another Kemble—Charles, last of the brood, eighteen years John Philip's junior and standing in a semifilial relationship. When his job in the post office palled on the tall, handsome boy, he developed the family urge to act. John Philip, as executive head of the tribe, forbade it. The natural consequence was that Charles went barnstorming on his own just as John had years earlier when Roger forbade him to quit Douai for the stage. In time John relented and secured Charles a good opening in London. He was a slow starter but stubborn and malleable. Eventually varied experience among able performers made him a highly polished professional in secondary and some principal roles. His skills of personation so blossomed that even William Macready, a great but peevish tragedian who disliked him, called him "a first-rate [actor] of second-rate roles." [29] Here was the perfect drunken Cassio, the most effective Laertes, the most winning Bassanio, the suavest Charles Surface; and many found him admirable in Hamlet and Romeo too.

So popular a performer was often cast opposite the delicious Miss De Camp. Presently they were determined to marry. There was little against it. Both were self-supporting. Intermittent childbearing would be no hindrance; the female fashions of the day enabled gravid actresses to go on performing until fairly near term. But John Philip had the bad taste again to play heavy father and forbid the marriage. The rest of the clan appear to have supported him. Emotions ran high. They tried the old ploy of cool-off delay: wait until Charles's thirtieth birthday and then, if you're still of the same mind . . . So, on big brother's say-so, Charles, already a talented grown man, actually waited five years and so did Thérèse. Then the family had to keep their bargain. And who gave the bride away at St. George's, Bloomsbury? Why, stately old Coriolanus-Hamlet himself, duly lending the weight of the chief of the Kemble name.

It was a strange story, not quite as bizarre circa 1800 as it would have been circa 1900 but still making one wonder how the participants viewed one another in so slippery a context. Was it fear of risking loss of John Philip's patronage that secured the young folks' obedience? Was John Philip guilty, maybe subliminally, of jealousy? Since Mrs. Siddons was still queen dowager, how much did her views—whatever they were—have to do with it? Did Charles and Thérèse faithfully observe the condition that for five years they should meet only professionally? There is reason to believe that Thérèse was restless about it off and on and Charles steadier. How much did daughter Fanny know of this curious prelude to her coming into the world? That her autobiographies fail to mention it is understandable. But backstage gossip being the same in her time as in ours, odds are high that she had more than an inkling; that may account for her scant mentions of John Philip. Yet he continued to have a strong hand in inadvertently shaping her life. Had he not saddled Charles with Covent Garden, that great gilded barn stuffed with perplexities, litigations, heartaches, and frustrations, Fanny might never have gone on the stage. So she would probably never have seen America; never made that sorry marriage there; never got so immersed in Shakespeare that he came to overshadow even horses, water in motion, and mountains among the glories of her private cosmos.

One may also wonder how much Fanny knew of her aunt Ann Kemble[30] (Curtis), who alone among Roger's children failed to make it safely upward. Her story is more Defoe than Fielding. She too tried the stage but went lame (cause unstated) and the man she married proved to be a bigamist. Drifting into shady courses, she presently emerged giving juicily ballyhooed lectures on sex problems (with living models) to mixed audiences at a "Temple of Health" operated in London by a notorious Dr. Graham who billed her as "Mrs. Siddons's youngest sister." Before she turned to this dubious expedient, friends of hers had advertised for contributions to set her up in the needle-work and artificial-flower business on the pretext that, though "repeatedly solicited for relief . . . [Mrs. Siddons] has flatly refused her."[31] Eventually she reappeared in the public press as getting shot in the face by the pistol of a customer in a disorderly house; what she was doing there was not explained. The rest of her life she wrote hack fictions under the pseudonym "Ann of Swansea" to supplement annuities of twenty pounds each paid her by Mrs. Siddons and John Philip on condition that she stay far from London. That did not discourage her from using their names to bait the circulars with which she sought subscriptions for her works.

Like most who knew him, Fanny was very fond of her father. She also admired the lifelong zeal with which he kept refining the spoken subtleties of emphasis and pacing that Shakespeare demanded, and was loyally distressed by the way his struggle to keep Covent Garden afloat embittered his middle years. Yet she seems to have regarded herself as primarily Thérèse De Camp's daughter and in spite of the overshadowing Kemble connection, particularly proud to be so. That mother of hers, Fanny wrote, looking back after forty years,

> [though having] no specific gift in such perfection as the
> dramatic talent of the Kembles, had in a higher degree
> than any of them the peculiar organization of genius. To

the fine senses of a savage rather than a civilized nature,
she joined an acute instinct of correct criticism in all matters of art, and a general quickness and accuracy of perception, and brilliant vividness of expression. . . . Had she
possessed half the advantages . . . which she and my father labored to bestow upon us, she would . . . have
been one of the most remarkable persons of her time.[32]

Nor was this daughterly hyperbole; it was the judgment of a witness
who knew personally and had taken the measure of scores of certified
powerful celebrities.

Fanny might also have described her as even more show-busi-
nesslike than the Kembles. They were all at least adolescents when
breaking in. She was a child prodigy. Her parents were a French
army officer, Georges De Camp (some said his real name was Fleury),
and a Swiss girl said to come from a farm background, but there were
other hints of the stage; anyway her solid Swiss-style piety fits the
first reference better. At the instance of a British nobleman whom he
knew in Vienna, De Camp took his wife and baby Thérèse to London,
hoping to develop there his ambitions toward music and the graphic
arts. He did not prosper. Tuberculosis carried him off after he had
begotten four children. His widow's only substantial asset was the
eldest girl, dark-eyed and miraculously graceful. At six she was dancing Cupid in an opera ballet, then had leads in a troupe of children
doing little French plays. Therein she drew notice from the Prince of
Wales (soon Prince Regent, eventually George IV), who made a pet
of the sparkling little creature and often took her to amuse his mor-
ganatic wife, Mrs. Fitzherbert. Instead of making her an intolerable
spoiled brat, this seems to have immunized her as much as any Kemble against awe of persons of impressive rank.

To the French she spoke at home she somehow added superb
command of English and enough voice training for professional purposes. Both the matter and manner of her speech was her daughter's
pride: "The truth of her intonation, accents and emphasis, made her
common speech as good as a play . . . the Shakespeare . . . and
Milton of Mrs. Siddons [had] every word underlined and accentuated,
lest [she] omit the right inflection . . . my mother could no more

have needed such notes where to speak *true*, than she would a candle to have walked by noonday."[33] At eighteen she had emerged from the ruck of promising young aspirants by the swaggering vivacity with which she played Captain Macheath in a sexes-reversed version of *The Beggar's Opera;* the elegance of her legs in knee breeches was probably no handicap. The sauciness that she took to such roles once led a captious woman friend in the profession to say of her work as the Page in *The Follies of a Day* that she "acted the impudent little wretch so well, I was quite angry with her."[34] She was just as chipper in petticoats playing the singing chambermaid, the avatar that so affected John Philip. None ever questioned his praise of her virtue. For all her stage coquetry, and the sleazy mores of the greenrooms she had to frequent, London seems universally to have acknowledged that her untouchedness was genuine. She was imbued with her Swiss forebears' rigid Protestantism and most Sundays saw her at London's Swiss chapel, the minister of which was a close friend.

Such a connection was not the usual thing for either party. In other contexts Thérèse was what her times called "an original." She loved to fish. Whether the fish bit or not, she had the true joy in standing or sitting, rod in hand, float in the water, hope persistent. Whatever the neighbors of her country retreat said or thought, there she was at every opportunity. If it began to rain, she went on fishing and let her clothes dry on her back. When low in her mind—and she was moody—she worked up storms of rearranging furniture so drastically that sometimes Charles, returning late, had reason to think he had got into the wrong house. She never explained these seizures nor did any who knew her expect explanation. None of it came of the romantic fallacy, already strong then, of nonconformity as a good in its own right. She merely did, with a sort of canny innocence, what made sense for her at the time. This quality enchanted one of her son's Cambridge cronies who visited the Charles Kembles' London house long after she had retired from the stage: "I never met anyone whose education and circumstances have been necessarily artificial with so young a heart and such birth-freshness of feeling and thought."[35]

Fanny called her "a frank, fearless, generous and unworldly

woman." Indeed, daughter's account of mother sometimes might be self-description. Thérèse had "a fine and powerful voice . . . was a capital horsewoman . . . talked better, with more originality and vivacity than any Englishwoman I have ever known."[36] And in both, "vivacity" could mean an inordinate pungency. Thus when Thérèse first saw a well-known artist's portrait of Charles as Macbeth, she was incapable of saying merely that it disappointed her: "A fat, red, round, staring, *pudsy* thing! . . . bless my soul . . . how could he miss . . . the Kemble jawbone! Why, it's as notorious as Samson's!"[37] On her death in her mid-sixties a newspaper obituary by somebody who must have known her paid tribute to her charm and fast-stepping intelligence but added that though "in private society she was most excellent company . . . the spice of satire, and sometimes of ill-nature . . . rendered her conversation always pointed, though not always agreeable."[38]

Fanny had much of that. In certain other details the two were different: Thérèse's young figure was exquisite, Fanny's merely good. She was a fine and original cook; Fanny faulted her for not passing that on: "All I learned from her was a detestation of bad cookery."[39] She also felt that her mother was more rigid about the emotional demands of one's first communion than less exacting minds required. But Fanny did not fault her for a misjudgment that could have been an emotional disaster. At sixteen Fanny's complexion was lovely. Her small sister Adelaide (alias "Totty") contracted smallpox, then an endemic hazard that often permanently scarred the face. As Totty's case gave no signs of disfigurement, Thérèse deliberately infected Fanny with the same presumably attenuated organism as a better way than vaccination to a safe, lifelong immunity. In terms of the state of knowledge at the time, it made some sense. But it was a wrong guess. Fanny had a severe case that, though leaving no scars, slightly muddied her skin for life. She could still pass in stage makeup under the soft gaslight of late Regency theaters and be pretty under wax candles in ballrooms. But in full daylight. . . . And there was always Totty unmarred and beautiful. Many a girl could never have forgiven.

Thérèse and her brother Vincent—also very good-looking—developed smallpox in the same round, and whereas his blooming cheeks, like Totty's, went undamaged, she came out scarred. It mattered less because she had already retired, but it was a severe penalty for poor immunological luck brought upon herself by a woman who was, by all accounts, wildly attractive. Did her Bible-based piety let her see this as somehow deserved? One almost hopes so; maybe such tacit, half-primitive feeling was what helped her and her damaged daughter take it not too badly.

The reason why Thérèse had hung up her buskins some years earlier was that she had gained too much weight to play saucy young things any longer. Her daughters too eventually found themselves thickening as middle age approached. John Genest, historian of the British theater, a contemporary who said of Thérèse that "no person understood the business of the stage better,"[40] thought it a pity she could not reconcile herself to matronly parts and so keep one of London's finest talents active. The only time she did so was when, at fifty-five, she played Lady Capulet to Fanny's Juliet the first night. But she found plenty to do after retiring: she advised Charles in his battles with creditors, shareholders, actors, and the sheer uneconomic bulk of Covent Garden; supervised Fanny's and doubtless Charles's professional wardrobes; chaperoned Fanny and counterbalanced her chronic skittishness; occasionally gave acting lessons to aspiring novices; endured the large and small vagaries of her sons; cooked; kept up with her fishing. . . .

The third De Camp sibling, Victoire, making good use of her authentic French, became a governess-teacher in a select girls' school near London. Through Thérèse's good offices handsome brother Vincent—Leigh Hunt said he was even prettier than Mrs. Charles—had small parts at Drury Lane but carved himself no great place there. In the Theatre Royal, Bath, he prospered for a while, married a local heiress, but marital troubles led to a separation and his emigrating to America. There, as "Mr. De Camp from the Theatre Royal, Drury Lane" he got fairly well imbedded in the American theater. The fourth of the De Camp brood, Adelaide, was Thérèse's loyal right hand in the shaping of the Charles Kemble family. As a high-spirited girl she had done well in uncle Stephen Kemble's provincial company in the north country. But then she and the son of a rich Yorkshire squire fell in love and wanted to marry. The squire wanted no she-stroller for daughter-in-law, broke up the match, disowned the boy, and packed him off to India. That unhappy ending must have been the more bitter for Adelaide because her best friend, Stephen Kemble's beautiful daughter Frances—the first "Fanny Kemble"—had triumphantly married the young fellow she wanted, grandson of Sir Richard Arkwright, plebeian inventor of pioneer textile machinery, whose father was considered the wealthiest commoner in England. As Mrs. Arkwright she lived happily ever after, singing old ballads like an angel to entertain herself and the elegant friends thronging to the elaborate estate over which she presided—one of the few country places that Charles Kemble, who had little taste for nonurban sur-roundings, positively liked to visit.

Instead of being embittered, however, Adelaide left the stage and turned companion-aunt-confidante-balance wheel for Thérèse's household. Humorous, outspoken, loyal, "Aunt Dall" sustained the day-by-day rhythms of which Thérèse was the potentially explosive source of energy. When Fanny and her father toured the provinces, she kept them and their affairs right side up as traveling supervisor. She kept a firm hand on her flibbertigibbety niece: after doing Juliet at Weymouth, Fanny fainted offstage. On reviving, she wanted to go and cut midnight capers on the sea beach, for sand and surf were things she could never resist; but "thinking I had had enough of emotion and exertion, [Aunt Dall] made me go in and eat my supper and go to bed, which was detestable on her part, and so I told her, which she didn't mind in the least."[41] Former professional though she was, she went out front to see Fanny act only once, because she could not bear to see this girl she loved so dearly suffering under stage sorrows and dangers. Forty years later Fanny called this aunt of hers "the only person I can think of who . . . fulfilled Wordsworth's conception of 'Those blessed ones who do God's will and know it not.' "[42] Charles and Fanny had special reason unstintingly to cherish her memory, for in effect she got herself killed in the line of duty looking after them in a strange land across the sea.

II

"Cette Diable de Kemble"

THE COVENT GARDEN PLAYBILL for Fanny Kemble's first public performance ran:

JULIET by Miss Kemble
(Being her first appearance on any stage)

It was technically but not actually true. For she had first been professionally behind footlights almost twenty years earlier, some months before she was born. On October 4, 1809, at the reopening of the rebuilt Covent Garden, Mrs. Charles Kemble, seven months pregnant, sang Lucy in *The Beggar's Opera*. Two nights later she played the Widow Bellairs in a farce, *Who Wins?* Then she—and Fanny-to-be—deserted the stage until well after the child was born on November 27, 1809.

The reason almost certainly was that during both performances the audience had rioted violently and it was felt that such commotions were unsuitable to Thérèse's delicate condition. These great "O.P." riots marked the Kembles' return to the magnificent new Covent Garden. For sixty-seven successive performance nights the tumult persisted. The consequent strain on the Kembles, Thérèse included, though she was no longer present onstage, should please believers in prenatal influences. How better account for the ups and downs of Fanny's turbulent life to come? She might well have been born with the O.P. birthmark.

O.P. stood for "old prices," and the riots expressed public resentment against the decision of Covent Garden's management, personified in John Philip Kemble, to raise admissions to the new theater to cover increased costs of capital and upkeep. Week after week a well-organized anticlaque danced an "O.P. war dance" in the pit while volleys of orange peels and abuse smothered the actors' stubborn efforts to perform what the playbills doggedly announced night after night. The storm was no respecter of persons. The first night even Mrs. Siddons's majesty as Lady Macbeth did not damp determination to break up the show. Charles Kemble, though personally more popular than his high-chinned brother, was hooted when he slipped during a fencing scene. As the O.P. movement gained momentum, John Philip and Mrs. Siddons got out of range, leaving the nightly ordeal to minor members of the company, sometimes including Charles. But eventually it was John Philip who had to make the grudging capitulation that, helped by the mob's own weariness of uproar, ended this strange episode. Riots in theaters were by no means unknown in the British theater in those days. But these were uniquely long-lasting.[1]

Thérèse had already borne Charles two sons. The first died early. The second, John Mitchell Kemble, was two years Fanny's senior. Fanny was born in Newman Street half a mile from Covent Garden on the fringe of the Soho district then only beginning its slide into today's seediness. In after years Fanny remembered a nursemaid and making mud pies on a recumbent tombstone in some churchyard. The matter of who was in charge of her must have been confused, because in 1813–15 her parents were making provincial tours to get Charles out of the rut of supporting roles. Then at the age of five the perky little creature was entrusted to Charles's handsome sister, Mrs. Thomas Twiss, whose girls' school at Bath was well regarded. Here again Roger's progeny had gravitated upward. In 1815 few British schools can have had a former actress as headmistress; nor did actresses usually marry such scholarly gentlemen as Twiss, a barrister learned in classical tongues and Shakespeare. One son became a general in the Indian Army; another was a member of Parliament and man-about-town. The three tall, studious daughters taught in the school and trained the pupils in deportment and ladylike accomplishments by example as well as precept.

A while ago writers of "girls' stories" made great play with pitiful little neglected things all tears and defiance of harsh treatment when sent away to school. Willful little Fanny, indubitably a handful, should have hated this exile to a hothouse of conventional decorum. But perversely she loved her beautiful aunt and the stately sisters and, though she learned little, gratefully absorbed Bath, which still retained much of the liveliness of the most famous English watering-place of the eighteenth century; Fanny's Bath was almost precisely the same as Jane Austen's. Here too she first encountered Shakespeare when the son of a nearby country estate put on *Macbeth* in his elaborate puppet theater. And here she played her first dramatic role. The Twiss son destined to be a general, then a gigantic lad studying military engineering, had a drawing-room stunt of enacting bits from Sheridan's melodrama, *Pizarro,*[2] in which the hero dashes across a stage-bridge holding his small (stage) son high in the air. Needing a prop-child, John Twiss picked up Fanny as the smallest person at hand to be breathlessly flourished about. Twenty years later matters were reversed. Her size—or lack of it—was a minor professional flaw.

One gathers that the Twiss establishment spoiled her; she would hardly have objected. A year of it doubtless sent her home as engagingly bumptious as ever. Thus one day François Joseph Talma, a very great French actor, came to call at the Kembles' new lodging in Covent Garden—they moved often, for Thérèse was a shifter of quarters as well as furniture—and found nobody home but a maidservant and six-year-old Fanny holding her hand. Drolling with the child in his best English, Talma told her to tell her father that Talma, the great French tragedian, had been there; could she remember that? The child said oh, yes, and added rapidly that her father was a tragedian too, and so was her uncle, and the baby upstairs who was always crying must be one. . . . Talma recounted this to the Kembles, who were vastly amused. Possibly, however, not this incident alone but a succession of such bits of ingenuous forwardness persuaded the family council that it might be as well again to try sending her away from home.

Talma's call and the subsequent choice of a French school for Fanny betokened that the final overthrow of Napoleon had restored the English Channel to its function of highroad instead of military barrier breached by smugglers only; and that the old, uneasy but invaluable cultural interaction between Britain and France had resumed almost as if Trafalgar and Waterloo had never been fought. In terms of miles Mme. Faudier's well-considered school in Boulogne was nearer than Bath to London. The differences in folkways were both stimulating and emotionally risky. Parents today might hesitate to transfer a high-strung child of seven into an alien environment uninsulated. In Regency times they had fewer such notions. Fanny would come back speaking French—an accomplishment expected in a girl meant to be a well-received lady, as well as fitting for a daughter of Thérèse, whose native tongue it was, and of Douai-educated Charles Kemble. Gratifyingly, French became Fanny's second language. She spoke it so well that the nobly born French novelist Pauline Marie Armande Aglaë called her the only non-French person she had ever met whose accent was flawless.

Otherwise the child's needs were not well served. *Chez* Faudier lacked the geniality of *chez* Twiss. When Fanny was an old lady in faraway Pennsylvania she recalled how, shut in a garret as punishment for one of her frequent delinquencies, she climbed out on the roof; and when a passer-by warned Mme. Faudier that one of her little charges was skipping about up there, she said: "Ah, ce ne peut être que cette *diable* de Kemble!"[3] Next time they tried the cellar, with minimal results; for minatory discipline they even took her to see a criminal guillotined in the public square. Fortunately it was all over before Fanny and escort got there. Had she seen the knife come down and the head drop into the basket, it might well have left lasting emotional damage. But with "cette diable de Kemble" one should not discount a high level of psychic resistance. In certain kinds of situations she wept as readily as was then looked for. Individuals' distress roused in her passions of generous pity. When playing high-tension roles, she sometimes carried their cooked-up emotions off-stage and took overlong to simmer down from Bianca's or Isabella's revulsions or sorrows. But she was also as tough as befitted the granddaughter of strollers, and the harshness of these schooldays apparently did little permanent harm.

In between capers and punishments her nimble mind absorbed enough of what the school offered to win her a disproportionate number of the prizes awarded at the end of the school year. And now and again straitlacedness relaxed into another sort of education. In addition to the daily ritual of two-by-two, close-order promenade along the street *en crocodile* that then passed for exercise in girls' schools, the pupils were taken on weekly half-holidays of spontaneous rambling and larking in the bucolic valley back of town or on the cliffs or down on the dunes by the sea. The old lady in Pennsylvania specifically mentioned how energetically they harried the local rabbits "who—haunted and rummaged from their burrows in the hills of coarse grass by a pitiless pack of schoolgirls—must surely have wondered after our departure, when they came together stealthily with twitching noses, ears, and tails, what manner of fiendish visitation had suddenly come and gone, scaring their peaceful settlement on the silent, solitary seashore."[4]

Fanny's early preference for turf instead of pavement underfoot and hills in the distance instead of windowed walls eventuated in an abiding love affair with mountains and the sea. This could be an example no more significant than most of the proto-Victorian cult of nature as embodied in Wordsworth ("The sounding cataract haunted me like a passion") and Byron ("Roll on, thou deep and dark blue ocean, roll!"). Journal-keeping, letter-writing young ladies and their high-waisted, high-minded swains dutifully labored it. Fanny's long paragraphs about woods and fields unmistakably reflect it. In parallel conformity with her time she also wore stays and rode a sidesaddle. But note qualitative differences: Just as she rode that sidesaddle better than most, her observations and descriptions are unusually rich. Elaborate as the literary fashion may have been, from her words usually emerged a valid sense of being there and a sharp sense of the pleasure she felt, no less genuine for her having trained herself to feel it. And maybe Thérèse appears here too. One reason why the Charles Kembles moved so often was that she could hardly endure any dwelling submerged in London's grime and claustrophobic weather; and green vistas and clean watercourses were the breath of life to her—and to the elder daughter whom she conditioned to set great store by unobstructed sky and handsomely arranged chlorophyll.

When Fanny came home from Boulogne, it was to one of her mother's anti-London gestures: she had installed the family in suburban Craven Hill, beyond the northern edge of Kensington Gardens. For a century the area has been indistinguishably London; then, it had views of growing crops and clusters of trees near and far. Modern transport was still undreamed of. The Kembles could not afford horses or daily coach hire, yet this otherwise cozy retreat was two and a half miles from Covent Garden. Even well-to-do Britons then still retained the use of their legs. The City magnate who kept his own carriage might still walk some such distance from his West End house to Lombard Street when weather suited. But that was by daylight. Charles Kemble's homeward walk followed his evening's stint at Covent Garden, ungodly late and worse lighted the farther he went. The stage-door man then rented loaded pistols to homeward-bound actors at two shillings a month. How often Charles thus armed himself for his dismal trudge I do not know; but that he consented to an arrangement that made it often necessary shows how fond he was of his family and how seriously he and they all took Thérèse's crotchets. Presently he rented a pied-à-terre, half a house in Soho that Fanny particularly valued because they said it had once belonged to "wicked Lord Lyttelton."[5] Thence Fanny went to her arduous, dull music lessons under an exacting teacher in Russell Square. She much preferred soaking her ten-year-old soul in the galloping rhythms and breathless doings of *Marmion* and collaborating with elder brother John Mitchell in staging standard plays with the miniature theaters and cardboard characters then so popular among children.

This life was much preferable to that *chez* Faudier. Aunt Dall imposed lessons but they were hit-or-miss and Fanny often managed to get into duly punished trouble. Conceiving herself ill used, she planned to drown herself in a pond near Craven Hill but decided instead to run away to London and, like a true Kemble, go on the stage. Soon brought back, she was put on bread and water for a week with daily incarceration of some hours in a garden outhouse; whenever anybody came near enough to hear, she sang loudly to show defiance of authority. She considered revenging herself on her unsympathetic elders by doing away with little Totty, then five years old, of whom she was sisterly fond. Totty's death, while distressing her parents, would do her the favor of sending her straight to heaven. Fanny had been told that the berries of the privet bushes in the garden were poisonous, never to be eaten; suppose she left a few where Totty might find and sample them. . . . But "I never did poison my sister, and satisfied my desire of vengeance by informing my aunt of my contemplated crime."[6]

Maybe in consequence of this her parents presently tried sending her away to school again. Paris this time—a school kept in an elegant former mansion off the Champs-Élysées by a cultivated Englishwoman who, in spite of stiff Protestant-Evangelical piety, greatly admired John Philip Kemble; an engraving of him as Coriolanus had the place of honor in her drawing room. Her pupils, mostly British, acquired not only polished French and the usual ladylike music, dancing, drawing, "use of the globes," and so on, but also heavily English-flavored religion as prophylactic against the insidious Catholicism of France. Each Sunday the girls were deployed for Church of England service at the British embassy chapel, then went to a French Protestant service at a nearby *temple,* and sometimes a third service at one or the other again in the evening. Written reports on all those sermons; morning and evening daily prayers . . . Such intemperate formalism should have put a temperament like Fanny's off religion for life. Bult her mother's impressive Swiss piety had been good preparation for Mrs. Rowden's version. Fanny grew up able to laugh at the memory of those sermons and yet retain a lifelong commitment to religious feeling.

Among her schoolmates, chiefly daughters of gentry, she made no close friends—that would come later—but got on well enough with all. She learned the ballroom dancing that would be the joy of her young life, became a skilled seamstress, had sound elementary training for her rich contralto, learned Italian and some Latin, made a gradually kindling acquaintance with the stately sonorities of Corneille and Racine—good preparation, she found later, for intimacy with Shakespeare, different as the two poetic-dramatic idioms were. Indeed she was first touched with Kemble fire when acting in the school's staging of Racine, startling herself and apparently others by suddenly getting histrionically airborne.

Other formative experiences in Paris were extracurricular. In those days, of course, Byron's reputation for profligacy combined with the melodramatic nihilism of his vastly popular works to confound him with the devil in many minds—an identification that he seemed almost to court. That his works were often high-class poetry had less to do with his renown than the effluvia of black mass and festering sin clinging to his handsome person. Lively pupils like Fanny at schools like Mrs. Rowden's had heard of him enticingly in their elders' whispers. Taboo led, of course, to prurient curiosity. One evening an elder pupil passed Fanny a contraband volume of Byron open at the first page of "Parisina," his juiciest treatment of eroticism. At once aware what it was, Fanny gulped down the forbidden lines well into the first sequence and then carried the book off to hide it for a safer opportunity. Between her precaution and the school's schedule she did not get back to it before the owner retrieved it. Whether she had read as far as the lovers' voluptuous, incestuous embracings is doubtful. But even so, "the small, sweet draught which I sipped in that sleepy school-salon atmosphere remained indelibly impressed upon my memory"[7] and led to an unduly mordant influence from the Byron phenomenon on her young soul for years to come.

France itself provided more wholesome cross-influences. Mrs. Rowden's Protestant quasi-convent, admitting the outside world only in the shape of carefully screened teachers, kept France at arm's length. But the Charles Kembles had good friends in Paris; Fanny stayed *en famille* with one or another such French household during her brief vacations. Better still Charles sometimes timed his vacations to coincide with hers. His easygoing temperament made him the ideal father to show a growing daughter the best of the Paris he knew well; those were "pleasant days of joyous *camaraderie* and *flânerie!*—in which every thing, from being new to me, was almost as good as new to my indulgent companion."[8]

This was not yet the Paris that Haussmann created for Napoleon III, all boulevards and uniform-height facades. Before those sweeping demolitions and vista-creations it was a much less homogeneous city, the eighteenth and even the seventeenth centuries often meeting the eye and stirring up the mind. But its post-Waterloo gaiety and style had Britons and their womenfolk—plus, of course, Scandinavians and Germans and Spaniards—flocking there for high living and pungent entertainment in much the same spirit as would their children under Louis Philippe and their grandchildren under the Third Republic. Father and daughter dined at the famous Trois Frères Provençaux, ate ices on the boulevards, explored the popular theater—partly business for Charles, always looking for French pieces to adapt—delighted in the burlesques[9] then developing a new stage idiom. Fanny particularly relished *Les Anglais pour Rire,* which lampooned the "traveling English, to whom the downfall of Bonaparte had opened the gates . . . to carry amazement and amusement . . . by their wealth, insolence, ignorance, and cleanliness."[10] Decades later she would use such an approach in a farce written to amuse her old age about the tourists infesting her beloved Swiss mountains.

A charming pair strolling into the Variétés or the Porte St.-Martin—a six-foot-tall, almost exquisitely handsome gentleman giving his arm to a small, high-colored, high-stepping girl with huge brown eyes, both merrily and affectionately enjoying themselves. Fanny and her father early formed a habit, seldom flawed, of getting on well. Yet never, as it might today, did this comradely intimacy blur the line between generations. To their offspring Mr. and Mrs. Charles Kemble were invariably "sir" and "ma'am."

Three years at school without ever going home were good preparation for the inordinate amount of time that Fanny would spend alone in later life. When her father came to fetch her home in the summer of her sixteenth year, she feared, or said she did, that she might fail to recognize her mother. There was no need. Thérèse was relaxing in an almost complete escape from the city—a country cottage at Weybridge twenty miles southwest of the center of London between two running-to-seed country estates. Charles had a rented house on Soho Square and came down weekends by stagecoach. Happily letting herself go, Thérèse was gardening, trying to make drinkable wine out of the grapes in the arbor, cooking, sometimes fishing in the little river all day. The children, Fanny falling right in with them for all her new accomplishments, ran more or less wild in the countryside.

The two boys naturally liked it. For Totty, now ten years old, it was rather perplexing; years later she told Annie Thackeray, elder daughter of the great novelist, that she had particularly hated the fishing because her mother took her along to bait the hooks with live worms or minnows. Fanny's tomboyishness—she never took to dolls at all—sent her following John Mitchell, now a tall schoolboy, into scratch cricket and pistol-practice, doing better in the second. But her most grateful memories were of rambling and scrambling on the gorse-covered hills and of joining her mother's fishing. It was not all harmony. Thérèse objected strongly to the girl's irrepressible squeals when she had a bite, which threatened to frighten off further prey. But the sport grew inordinately on Fanny. Years later in the Berkshires she had sternly to ration herself to one day's fishing a week. She too was repelled by the use of live bait. But gritting her teeth, she impaled worm or minnow herself, though she usually had a boatman with her, because it would be unfair to impose that grisly necessity on another. And when fishing with another woman, she baited for both, though "if I were a man, nothing could induce me to marry a woman whom I had seen bait [a] hook with any thing more sensitive than paste."[11]

Neither at Weybridge nor in Soho Square during the winter was her formal education advancing. Gratefully exploiting this gap, she began to cultivate a lifelong habit of prolix, sometimes poignant versifying and reading hungrily in any direction that beckoned. One led toward the then fashionable Germans (in translation) among whom de la Motte's *Undine* and Goethe's *Wilhelm Meister* were to exert disproportionate influence on her, more particularly the latter. Two thirds of it is a dismaying if rather bloodless denunciation of the typical actor's life as Goethe saw it. Gulped down raw by this restless descendant of great actors who all still carried the scars of strive-and-succeed, it may account for much, though not all, of Fanny's subsequent low opinion of the stage as a calling. Whenever as girl or woman she explains to friends or herself her dim view of theatrical things and persons, one gets echoes of Goethe's hero summing up,

after his disastrous experiences with Melpomene and Thalia and their
shoddy mortal exponents, thus:

> It is impossible to describe how ignorant actors are
> of themselves, how boundless are their pretensions. . . .
> Each would not only be the first, but the sole hero, he
> endeavors to exclude all competitors, and does not see that
> even with their assistance, he can hardly accomplish any-
> thing important. Each one fancies that he is original, and
> in spite of his appetite for novelty, he can scarcely quit
> the old and well-remembered track. With what untiring
> zeal do they oppose each other; and they are often kept
> together by the narrowest of views of interest—by the
> most contemptible feeling of self-love . . . secret cal-
> umny and shameful slander keep incessant jealousy alive
> among them. They are either dissipated or foolish in their
> habits.[12]

Goethe has the hero's intellectual friend suggest that this analysis
would apply more or less to many persons outside the theater. But of
its pertinence to the world Fanny had heard discussed among her
nearest and dearest ever since she was born she seems to have had no
doubts.

The consequences of that damage—if damage it was—were in
the future. At the time her desultory exploration of exotic books
tended to get a previously rather cloistered mind better into tune
with its times. Discipline for the body was something else. Mrs.
Rowden's system had done nothing for Fanny's posture. To Thérèse,
whose lithe carriage had been as famous as her eloquent eyes, slouching and lounging were practically treason. Fanny's going-on-sixteen
dignity was affronted by various posture cures, the strangest of
which, a backboard with steel shoulder braces and a collar held by a
rod behind the head, made her look, she said, like "a young woman
walking about in a portable pillory."[13] As last resort they called in
a sergeant in the Foot Guards known for applying to young ladies the
posture-cure methods used on recruits in the barracks yard. Thanks
to him the rest of her life Fanny was flat-backed and erect—specially
important for one so short destined for the stage. When a candid
friend told her that she looked like Mrs. Siddons through the wrong

end of opera glasses, it was a backhanded compliment but it did mean she was making the most of what inches she had.

Thérèse also tried to form Fanny's promising voice. Here the familiar mother-daughter conflict may have interfered. Both were, Fanny said later, "of exceptional impatience of disposition and irritable excitability of temperament," and it is more than surmise that, for all the deep affection between them, they had their jangly times. Thérèse's musical ear was exquisitely sensitive and her tongue, as already noted, had the authority of an electric cattle-prod: "I used to practice in her sitting-room, and I think I sang out of tune and played false chords oftener, from sheer apprehension of her agonized exclamations." Whereas Totty's "high, sweet, true little voice"[14] responded promisingly to her mother's severities, maybe partly because the younger's less quirky (though by no means wishy-washy) disposition was not so nearly cognate. In time sound development of that "true little voice" made Adelaide Kemble a renowned opera star and the second of Charles Kemble's daughters to keep Covent Garden afloat when it was foundering.

Yet when Fanny's time came, it was Thérèse's abrasiveness about false emphasis, awkward gesture, mawkish turns of voice that, for all their clashings, made Fanny's Juliet a triumphant launching of her theatrical career. One hardly regrets that her voice never got as far as Totty's. Fanny intemperately enjoyed such great singers of her day as Pasta and Malibran and worshiped Weber because he wrote *Der Freischütz* and *Oberon*. But in view of her distaste for any stage and contempt for most of the roles she acted, one cannot imagine her happy among operatic plots, characters, and stagecraft often inferior to even those of the dramatic vehicles she scorned. She liked to tell of lovely Louisa Brunton, Thérèse's quondam colleague, who, in the middle of a gripping scene, would whisper to her fellow actors: " 'What nonsense all this is! Suppose we don't go on with it.' "[15] As an operatic principal Fanny Kemble might well have decided suddenly that what is too silly to be said shouldn't be sung either and walk off stage. Or if she didn't, it would have been only that no Kemble could conceivably commit such a histrionic sin.

Before Thérèse gave up, however, Fanny's voice had training

enough to give her a valuable skill at singing winningly for her own and others' entertainment. She sang all through a tremendous storm at sea and, when the captain complimented her on such intrepid behavior, said she did it to assuage her terror. She sang when galloping hell-for-leather along stormy beaches. She sang to her own piano accompaniment when stark lonely as a young wife marooned on a stuffy country place outside Philadelphia. She sang her lungs out tramping among the Alps in middle age.[16] And—in quite another set of contexts—she found it socially useful to be able to sing much better than most lady guests in the drawing rooms of the great houses of Britain.

Thérèse's hand in shaping her elder girl—so far as "shaping" fits so adventitious a growth—may help explain the prevalence of women among those whom Fanny relied on. She could and did make excellent friends with men of stature. She fell disastrously in love at least twice. But as developing girl and then woman she came to look chiefly to her own sex for the affectionate tutelage and influential examples that most burgeoning organisms require, even those destined to be notably independent. Her seventeenth year brought her the longest and maybe most rewarding of these relationships.

John Philip's widow returned to England after he died. One of his great friends, the Earl of Essex, lent her Heath Farm, a country house attached to his estate in Hertfordshire. There, until country life grew too boring, she played elegant gentlewoman on the tidy income from her husband's nest egg. For a while her retired sister-in-law, Mrs. Whitelock, lived with her but this minor Kemble's ways were rather too boisterous for her hostess's strong sense of *comme il faut*. Occasional guests worked out better—the Charles Kembles, for instance—and momentously for Fanny sometimes their visits coincided with those of Harriet St. Leger, a gentlewoman-spinster of thirty whose prominent Anglo-Irish family were close friends of Mrs. Siddons and John Philip.

Harriet's style was curious though not unprepossessing. She was tall, fine-boned, spare almost to emaciation, with great shining gray eyes and a flyaway grace of motion set off by her eccentric dress. In that day of cumbrous finery she always wore a scantily cut dark riding habit, boots from a men's bootmaker and a plain black beaver hat. "All the emptyheaded men and women in the country prated incessantly about these inoffensive garments,"[17] complained a sympathetic friend and neighbor. Refinements kept it from being mere tomboyism grown up: "It was difficult to find cashmere fine enough . . . or lawn clear and exquisite enough for her curious collars and cuffs."[18] Within this rather fey exterior was a sober, conscientious mind given to amateur metaphysics and theology, outdoorsiness and animals. A surviving letter of hers to Cecilia (Siddons) Combe, Melpomene's youngest daughter, is a cross section of her personality; it begins with comment on a pudding recipe, asks for copies of Cecilia's husband's latest lecture, glances witheringly at "Liberal Tories" in Ireland, and describes her way of allaying political anxieties: "I cut down trees, I play with my dog [her family bred a famous strain of retrievers], I dig, I carry potatoes to the donkeys, I listen to the music of the mind."[19] Then off she goes lengthily but coherently discussing whether the goodness of God is immanent in His creative powers.

A twelve-year gap in age was no bar to immediate, deep affection between this free-spirited eccentric and Thérèse De Camp's brash daughter. Indeed the gap may have furthered the quasi–tutor-pupil relation between Fanny and her "Plato in petticoats"[20] as, lifting a line from George Farquhar's *The Inconstant,* she called Harriet. Their first days at Heath Farm went in a rush of talking and walking in Lord Essex's grounds, and talk and reading most of the night in the bedroom they shared.[21] When the end of Harriet's visit parted them, they pledged each other to write often and at length. And so they did for the next fifty years, oftener and longer because though Fanny paid a few visits to Harriet's family seat, Ardgillan Castle, they met in person rather seldom. For most of the time Fanny was in London, or touring the provinces, or in America, Italy, Switzerland. . . .

Into those letters Fanny put what now seems disproportionate response to Harriet's suggestions and queries about moral and religious questions. Today the picture of this brace of gentlewomen, one very young, the other still young in our terms, swapping comments on the efficacy of an intimate sense of God's mercy in defusing the problem of evil does seem strange. Keep in mind, however, that this was thirty years before Darwin published and that Regency times saw not only the Brighton pavilion and the prize ring, but also infiltration of British society, well into its upper strata, by the Evangelicalism that took soul-searching as a duty. This heightened whatever religious bent a given amateur had and led to awareness of moral problems otherwise likely to be swept under the rug. Susceptibility naturally varied widely among individuals. Only a minority of ladies, still fewer gentlemen were affected. At its worst it turned out such chill female pharisees as Thackeray's Sophia Alethea Hobson Newcome. But some of its other fruits (at its best and widest) were the freeing of the black slaves in the West Indies and social service work as a lay career, which in turn did so much for feminism. To Fanny particularly, the religious frame of reference gave not only badly needed comfort in her seasons of dire trouble but also the fellowship of many persons whom she valued and who were good for her on both sides of the Atlantic. Further, it is pleasant to see how innocently her letters to Harriet skip from I-danced-all-night-how-glorious! to diamonds-in-my-shoes-when-I-play-Portia to, next paragraph, what-you-say-about-divine-grace-is-very-helpful.

After Harriet went home to Ireland, Fanny was much on her own at Heath Farm. Mrs. John Philip, though determinedly prim and proper, seems to have had small notion what to do about her beyond family civility. Fanny lived much in the open and read avidly, beginning with the unfinished business of exploring Byron. She says she absorbed his poems one day and Jeremy Taylor's homilies the next *en sandwich.* No doubt Taylor's doctrine was good for her soul and his burly eloquence good for her sense of style; but consider the contrast with *Manfred* and *Cain*—those glowing examples of solipsism mixing agnosticism with blasphemy and misanthropy. This immersion in Byron would have horrified Mrs. John Philip had she got wind of it. Fanny herself may have been uneasy about it. Her long, otherwise pellucidly candid letters to Harriet do not, so far as available record shows, mention this growing passion.

This secret vice, which is about what she felt it to be, surfaced on her return from Heath Farm to London as an announced ambition

to be a writer. It was not altogether *outré*. By 1827 a bright girl of
good character could contemplate that career as she could not have
two or three generations earlier. For this real if still begrudged opening she and many other scribbling girls and women had to thank the
"blue stocking"[22] element that came into notice early in George II's
time. Its typical member was Hannah More, indubitably a lady as
well as the learned, pious, prolific author of produced plays, a highly
regarded novel of manners and Evangelistic morals, and numerous
tracts of the same flavor. In *Vanity Fair* Thackeray would travesty
her "The Shepherd of Salisbury Plain" as "The Washerwoman of
Finchley Common" by Lady Emily Sheepshanks. Not all these pen-
wielding women were so fusty. The *Evelina* novel of Fanny Burney
(d'Arblay) still sets up tingles of fun, yet did not disqualify her for a
post as gentlewoman at the royal court. Anne Radcliffe's "gothic"
novels of the same vintage begot several generations of highfalutin
nonsense eagerly read. . . .

Such ladies constituted more effective hints of women's potential
than the antics of Mary Wollstonecraft—though, for better or worse,
she too was an able writer. The brilliance of Jane Austen and Maria
Edgeworth was reinforced by contemporary acceptance of lesser talents—Mrs. Barbauld's, Mrs. Opie's, Lady Morgan's. . . . By the
time Fanny's ambition bloomed, some hundreds of more or less clever
women dissatisfied with being relegated to childbearing, servant
scolding, pauper patronizing, and one or another level of social chatter had set sail on this course. For a significant number it also meant
bread and butter in the cupboard in spite of disastrous marriages to
drunken, incompetent, or unscrupulous men. Several of Fanny's
friends lived that dismal story. Here was a real stroke for protofeminism—female brains and spare energy conspicuously coping where
lord-and-master was feckless or vicious.

It would long be unthinkable for women to enter law, medicine,
or architecture, or to attend professional art classes. Except in such
eccentric sects as the Quakers, they were also unthinkable as religious
chiefs. But writing could be done at home—quietly, that favorite
word of the Evangelistic mind—without rubbing elbows with male
fellow-trainees. In fact, writing was as yet hardly a profession as such.

Most published novels, verses, criticism were written by those with independent incomes or primary careers at the bar or in the universities or the church or in salaried journalism. The minority dependent wholly on book writing for livelihood usually had so slim a time they were scornfully lumped in a starveling community called Grub Street.

Yet for all such pen-and-ink victories the woman writer never quite won her war while the nineteenth century lasted. The first edition of her maiden novel circa 1820 was likely to have only "By a Lady" on the title page. The Brontë sisters chose to appear as Acton, Ellis, and Currer Bell. Mary Ann Evans plowed ahead as George Eliot. Today married women writers often retain their maiden names, but then it was quite the other way: Mrs. Gaskell, Mrs. Craven, Mrs. Humphrey Ward, et al. As late as 1885 W. S. Gilbert's "singular anomaly, the lady novelist" was still suspect among most men and unadventurous women. She had probably taken to scribbling because she lacked the good looks or anyway charm to qualify her for a real woman's privileges. She was gaunt, harried, peevish, and graceless. That stereotype had overcome such occasionally contradictory data as Lady Caroline Lamb, pretty and (to be courteous) unstable daughter of the Countess of Bessborough, who published a competent if ill-advised novel based on her relations with Byron; and Mrs. (Caroline) Norton, one of Sheridan's three ravishingly beautiful daughters, novelist and editor, cursed with a dog-in-the-manger husband, handsomest woman in London society, one of its most amusing raconteurs, and a good friend of Fanny's.

Fanny's hopes of publishing may have been better based than those of many other ambitious girls, because Kembles, both sexes, had reason to take print as an adjunct to their profession. John Philip did pamphlets debating aspects of Shakespeare with established critics, and a volume of verse that, though watery, rhymed and scanned well enough. He and Charles published dozens of cut-down, expurgated "acting versions" of Shakespeare and adaptations of French, Spanish, and German plays—chief resource of the Regency manager needing new scripts. Mrs. Siddons published well-received analyses of Shakespeare. Several of Thérèse's adaptations (one, *Smiles and Tears,* was based on Mrs. Opie's novel, *Father and Daughter,* with la-sir comedy interpolated to relieve the mawkishness) were published; their sprightly and chewy dialogue shows how well she had got the hang of English.

So Fanny's plan to write a historical novel about Françoise de Foix, a romantic, harried figure from the sixteenth century whom she had met in a book at Heath Farm, was not thought absurd by her family. When, after drafting, she decided to make it a play about the lady, no Kemble need have been surprised. When she read the end product to them, there was no tactless astonishment, merely pleasure; even Thérèse allowed it merits. Between that draft and the version eventually published came polishing and rearranging, but even in that first form it was probably a credit to a girl of seventeen. It was also absurd for her at that age to summon from the vasty deep these overweening emotions—raging jealousy, middle-aged concupiscence, revulsionary treason, and carnal lust. James Spedding, one of brother John Mitchell's scholarly cronies at Cambridge, liked the rhetoric and pacing but mistrusted these "darker passions . . . reflected from Shakespeare—I do not believe that she is a whit more familiar with than you and I, who know them out of the Bard of Avon, and Walter Scott, and Don Juan . . . as for anything else we are as innocent as lambs unborn.."[23] Mentioning *Don Juan* was nearest the mark. Fanny had soaked up Byron to considerable purpose. It is clear in the characters' slashing brutalities and the texture of the verse they spout—not as good as run-of-Byron, of course, but recognizably school-of . . .

For example, here are the lustful lines that this girl, hardly dry behind the ears, gave Louise of Savoy, the villainess whom she eventually played herself (with bitter misgivings about both script and role) when Covent Garden staged *Francis the First* in 1832:

> Now out upon this beating heart, those temples
> That throb and burn; and this crimson glow
> That rushes o'er my brow; now, by this light,
> I had not dreamed so much weak womanhood
> Still slumbered in my breast.

The family's favorable view of *Francis the First* led to an offer from John Murray, a name already potent in publishing, to pay well for publication rights. In those days people bought the texts of plays to be read like novels or the verse narratives then popular. Shelley, Byron, Sir Henry Taylor, and Robert Browning used the dramatic form with little or no thought of stage production. And the name Kemble on a title page might well rouse profitable interest.

At an elegant dinner party a year after Fanny's triumphant stage debut, her mother gave the guests "a long history of her daughter, who was a most extraordinary child, and quite unmanageable," she said, but was now "quite altered and reformed in disposition,"[24] presumably quieted down by success and hard work. Fanny, too, retrospectively describing herself as adolescent, used such adjectives as "difficult and troublesome . . . vehement and excitable, violently impulsive." Relief from her freakishness came through a suggestion from Mrs. Henry Siddons, actress and charming widow of the only son of Melpomene's who turned actor. A merely tolerable performer, then a rather fumbly manager, he had done one outstanding thing— married Harriet Murray, leading lady of his company in Edinburgh. Her brother William, the leading man, was, Fanny thought, "one of the most perfect actors I have ever known." On Siddons's death William took over as actor-manager, and much more successfully. Edinburgh proudly called Harriet "our Mrs. Siddons"; actually she was at her best only in a narrow range of roles suiting her delicate style. But in them she was irresistible: "a sweet and most engaging countenance . . . voice exquisite . . . demure playfulness. . . . Men, women, and children . . . inevitably *fell in love* with her."[25]

It was the beginning of "the happiest year of my life"[26] when this delightful lady invited Fanny to a long visit in Edinburgh. She stayed and stayed, developing a classic schoolgirl crush on her hostess, meeting a wide range of stimulating people, falling utterly in love with the place. She had found an urban situation that did not keep her from spreading her wings. The rest of her life, whenever she mentions the place in a letter, the very ink lights up: "I send my love to dear dear Edinbro'."[27] "Beautiful Edinburgh . . . delightful to me above all places I ever saw." And a statement sure to impress anybody acquainted with the local weather: "I love the very east wind

that blows over the streets of Edinburgh." The place was as free as it
was handsome: "I had the utmost liberty . . . at early morning have
often run up and round and round the Calton Hill, delighting . . .
in the noble panorama on every side. . . . I walked down to the
sands at Porto Bello and got a sea bath, and returned before breakfast,"[28] glowing, toes hardly touching the pavement.

During such a visit to a local fishing village on a stormy day,
the waves breaking over the end of the pier made her eager to go
meet them on their own terms. She knocked at a cottage to ask
whether a boat could be got. A large, fair-haired, barefoot fishwife
summoned her menfolk. They swaddled the little lady in tarry garments, bundled her into their boat, and out they went into a formidable hurly-burly. In ten minutes Fanny was remarkably seasick and
begging to be taken back. The Valkyrian fishwife welcomed her with
kindly laughter and a solid friendship ensued. Three years later when
Fanny came back to Edinburgh an acclaimed actress, one of her first
concerns was to drive to Newhaven to knock again, no longer the
plainly garbed child-woman but "in all the starlike splendor of a lilac
silk dress and French crepe bonnet . . . my dear fish-wife stared
 . . . mouth and gray eyes wide open . . . in the next [moment].
 . . . 'Ech, sirs! but it's yer ain sel' come back again at last!' "[29]

Even today Edinburgh conveys a stern, venerable but all-alive
elegance that makes it Europe's most remarkable chief town, or
maybe second only to Venice. In 1827 it lacked most of today's suburbs, and no railroad occupied the castle-dominated ravine between
the Old Town's medievalism and the New Town's Regency stateli-
ness. Many of its ladies still went to evening parties in sedan chairs.
The stone of the New Town's masonry retained sharp-cut edges. The
Theatre Royal, however, one of the very first gestures toward escape
from the Old Town, had been built and licensed in 1767 as a parallel
gesture toward lifting the Scottish stage into cultural recognition.
Until then it had been the usual provincial hole-and-corner affair, for
Scotland's moral disapproval of playacting was only very gradually
disintegrating. In that new respectability the Kembles had played a
role. In 1784 the General Assembly of the Church of Scotland, a
great social as well as religious occasion, coincided with Mrs. Sid-

dons's playing at the Theatre Royal. Her prestige was so high, her
character so highly esteemed, that many of the delegates, ministers as
well as laymen, left its sessions in midafternoon to secure places for
her performance. The Kirk of Scotland changed its schedule to accommodate that of a playactress—a landmark in Scottish cultural history. In the 1790s Stephen Kemble's management brought in
gentlemanly and impressive brother John Philip as well as sister Sarah
again. Her son Harry's incumbency has been noted. Less directly,
Walter Scott's vast admiration for Mrs. Siddons had as much or more
to do than his warm approval of the Murrays with persuading Edinburgh's best people of the virtues and importance of the playhouse.
Nor did it hurt that he and other leaders of the community found
John Philip good company and an able consumer of claret. Thus it
was that as niece of Melpomene, cousin of her late son, protégée of
her much admired daughter-in-law, young Fanny had ample social
access to the good talkers and eminent minds of what still called itself
the Athens of the North.

Among these new older friends were the brothers Combe, bachelors both. George, a middle-aged lawyer, was well into a second
career writing and lecturing to spread the gospel of the new "science"
of phrenology, the early-nineteenth-century precursor of psychoanal-
ysis. His much younger brother Andrew, a well-established physician, shared this work. George was dry and solemn, "tall,
puritanical, dissenter-looking,"[30] said acerb Mrs. Charles Eastlake
who, partly on religious grounds, scorned phrenology. He was, however, as Fanny would find, a very helpful man to tie to. Andrew was
"given to mirth, especially with children,"[31] and so thin as well as
tall that Fanny and he joked about his clothes being all that held his
bones together. It was no less a joke because he knew, and soon so
did she, that his emaciation came of the "consumption" (tuberculosis)
that sometimes forced him to drop his practice and seek health in
milder climes. Fanny and he hit it off wonderfully. They agreed in a
formal written bond drawn up by one of the cubs in George Combe's
law office that at age sixty-five she would return to Edinburgh, dead
or alive, and the doctor, dead or alive, would do the same, to have
another dance together. Within twenty years he was dead. When

Fanny reached the age of sixty-five, she was in America battling the ills of advancing age alone in a remodeled but cramped farmhouse—a situation dreary enough to cause her bright young grandson to say she reminded him of Tennyson's jilted Mariana wasting away in her Moated Grange. Fanny had kept her and Dr. Combe's bond. It is now among her papers in the Library of Congress. One wonders if she got it out to remember with on her sixty-fifth birthday.

As Dr. Combe drove house to house on his rounds, Fanny often sat in the gig beside him, a privilege that her hostess also allowed her daughters unchaperoned. Far away in London Thérèse took alarm and filed expostulations. Fanny seems to have protested that the man was some twelve years her senior and had no designs on her. Both statements were true but her mother was wary in such matters. Her uneasiness about the doctor did not subside until three years later when Fanny, returning from dancing all night, "found my darling Dr. Combe" come to see her on his way to Italy. "If I had not been so tired I must have made a jump at his neck. . . . He brought me a letter from Mr. [George] Combe, whom I love only one step lower."[32] She made sure that Thérèse met him; and had the satisfaction next day of finding them coming sociably together, thick as thieves, to fetch her from riding school.

It was George, not Andrew, to whom she wrote occasional letters discussing Shakespeare, merely tucking in messages to "the dear Dr.," fretting about his health with an affection inconsistent with a more than comradely relation. Presently George married Melpomene's handsome youngest daughter Cecilia, loyal companion of her old age. Before he proposed, he actually inspected her head for the bumps that would show whether her mental and moral proclivities were what he wanted in a wife. This probably did not strike merry-minded Andrew as funny. Both these intelligent, able, and responsible men believed wholeheartedly in the tenets of phrenology—that the surface irregularities of the skull so reflect the functions of the brain beneath that they define individual temperaments; and that society could use phrenological findings so to guide education, vocational choices, and medicine that the world would be a beautifully harmonious place. This belief in that variety of enticing nonsense was then shared by thousands of other cultivated, well-meaning Britons and Americans.[33]

Fanny's fondness for the Combes and Cecilia (a dutiful believer) could not persuade her altogether to accept these teachings. In 1837 she suggested airily that George study her new baby's head as "the most approved model of skulls"[34] and joked about her opportunity to phrenologize a Pennsylvania convention of which her husband was a member. But by 1846, during babble about phrenology at her sister's dinner table in Rome, she confessed that "I remain suspended between belief and incredulity."[35] By 1870 she complained that the Combes' books on hygiene were marred by their emphasis on phrenology as "solution of all the mysteries of human existence . . . as I was never able to get beyond a certain point of belief . . . it was agreed . . . that my brain was deficient in the organ of causality"; and that, though George always phrenologized Cecilia's servants for suitability before she hired them, "her lady's-maids were quite as inefficient, her housemaids quite as careless, and her cooks quite as fiery-tempered and unsober as those of 'ordinary' Christians."[36]

Thérèse's uneasiness about Dr. Combe might have been allayed—rather disturbingly—had she known of a strong counterforce consisting of Harry Siddons, Jr., Melpomene's grandson. At twenty he was in the romantic process of preparing to seek his fortune in India, where an uncle was high in the service of the East India Company. Had she been on hand, Thérèse would probably have spoken sharply about a callow youth who, however promising and handsome, was only beginning a hazardous career with no resources but one uncle, two hands, and whatever luck came his way. His mother, however, paid small heed while he and Fanny "walked and talked and danced and were sentimental together after the most approved cousinly fashion."[37] Whether that was policy, negligence, or lack of attention—after all, Harriet Siddons was both leading lady of an important theatrical company and manager of a busy household—one cannot know; in view of her generally exquisite tact, the first is likeliest. Anyway, the lad's departure preceded any serious understanding; only he had "Fanny" engraved on his sword blade before he sailed. The affair lost momentum, of course, with every day of his shaking down in India. Years later she met his widow and heard how vainly the newly affianced pair had scraped and scrubbed to get those five letters off that sword.

Two years after leaving Edinburgh, Fanny told Harriet St. Leger that she and Mrs. Harry Siddons were the only two persons whom she called *friends*. Thérèse surmised that "our Mrs. Siddons's" serenity masked an actually tumultuous spirit. If so, Fanny never saw the mask slip. The lady seems to have been a classic catalyst, effecting change without itself being affected. Under her stabilizing, smiling care Fanny was a demonstrative sycophant. She wore a sash of Mrs. Harry's over every dress she donned. She picked a sprig of fragrant myrtle daily for her idol to wear. The idol acquiesced but encouraged nothing. Idolatry was not permanent. After acting Juliet herself Fanny found Mrs. Harry's reading of the role "comparatively cold . . . [not] the passionate young Italian girl."[38] But unquestionably this gracious woman blended with the austere charm of Edinburgh into an atmosphere highly growth-promoting. One result was further widening of the girl's religious bent. Not that Mrs. Harry preached at her or required religious gestures beyond decorous household prayers, church on Sunday—no more than Fanny had at home, less than at Paris. But somehow the unruffled assurance with which Mrs. Harry went about her complex concerns seemed to imply large, good things, an inner sense of integration with God and his works. She might have been the unwitting mother superior of a religious order composed of herself and one novice.

Rising health of soul made Fanny swear off Byron in much the frame of mind of an addict renouncing opium: "A great effort . . . [for Byron's works] stirred my whole being with a tempest of excitement that left me in . . . mental perturbation impossible to describe." Now acutely aware that "the noble poet's glorious chanting of much inglorious matter did me no good," she eschewed reading him for two years. Then she found that, though "all the noble beauty . . . remained," there was no more "power of wild excitement."[39] Nowadays those terms are slightly comic. In a high-strung girl of eighteen 150 years ago they carried their own seriousness. Ironic comedy came a while later when Thérèse read Moore's life of Byron and decided the poet had been shamefully maligned by envious foes and a despicable wife; whereas Fanny would allow no such whitewashing: "I cannot at all agree with Mr. Moore that upon the showing of his own works Byron was a 'good man.' If he was, no one has done him such injustice as himself." Things grew so hot that Fanny had to renounce all discussion of that "despondent, defiant questioning, murmuring, bitter, proud spirit."[40]

This reversal of the usual senior/junior position is the tastier for the dead seriousness of both; each usually showed a sense of humor. There was a postscript years later when Lady Byron—who totally lacked humor—consulted Fanny, a cordial acquaintance, on whether she should grace a new edition of Byron's works with a preface meant to reduce their harmful effect on youth. Fanny tried to get out of advising but finally pronounced that such a step was probably needless, for circa 1850 young folks might well be less susceptible to such toxins. She thought Lady Byron "talks more than I do," she told Harriet St. Leger, "perhaps that will seem to you incredible,"[41] and it irked her that the solemn creature portentously urged her to "be something *to the People* . . . bring your talents to bear upon their welfare."[42] But she also thought her efforts to get women stirred up in others' behalf were constructive and liked her for having fastidiously stayed out of the further reaches of controversy about her strange husband.

Providence is inscrutable. Fanny's reward for so scrupulously kicking her Byron habit was to be fed, unwilling but plucky, into the hopper of show business; and eventually to have a journalist characterize her as "the female Byron."[43]

III

'*Miss Kemble*
Called for the Stage!'

AFTER HER URBAN IDYLL in Edinburgh, Fanny resumed her niche in the Charles Kembles' often eventful household. Little about the younger children appears before 1830. Presumably Miss Totty was growing. Of young Henry one knows only that he once got lost in London streets, and that when asked what he wished to be when grown, he replied: "he would be '*a gentleman and wear leather breeches.*' "[1] But now much crowds in about elder brother John Mitchell. At Dr. Benjamin Malkin's august grammar school at Bury St. Edmunds, he had already acquired a sort of eventual fame in a scuffle that broke the nose of a schoolmate, William Makepeace Thackeray—hence the novelist's prizefighter profile. At the time, however, more attention went to John's winning an "exhibition" (a partial subsidy) to Cambridge University. This hint at mental prowess set his father planning for him to go the bar after the university and in due course become lord chancellor. After all, Lord Lyndhurst, son of John Singleton Copley, once a mere Colonial portrait-painter, had managed that; why not a scion of another representational art? And Charles's son, who had a full share of the family good looks, would be grand presiding in wig and robes over the House of Lords.

At the university his mental promise got him into a mutual admiration society of undergraduates calling themselves the Cambridge Conversazione Society but better known as "the Apostles" because they numbered twelve and took themselves very seriously. They included Alfred Tennyson (for a while), Arthur Hallam, Edward

47

FitzGerald, Richard Monckton Milnes (Lord Houghton), a couple of archbishops-to-be. (More recent members have included Bertrand Russell, Lytton Strachey, Roger Fry, Guy Burgess.) For Fanny these youths' visits to her parents' house meant several important lifetime friendships. Both at Cambridge and later, Thackeray kept up affectionately with Jacky Kemble in spite of the broken nose. Some affinity between Jacky and his namesake-uncle appears in a letter of young Thackeray's advising a cousin going to Cambridge to stay out of debt, avoid dinner parties, and go see John Kemble who "(particularly when he is drunk) will give you the finest advice on these and other moral and religious points."[2]

A certain waywardness was developing. Jacky neglected to keep up with the university's scholastic formalities. He toyed with a truculent utilitarian radicalism: "His speeches [at Apostles meetings] never had the insipidity due to lack of prejudice,"[3] said the biographer of the early Apostles. He had a try at law but regardless of his father gave it up to prepare to take holy orders in the Church of England. These recurring changes dismayed Charles, almost a third of whose professional salary of twenty pounds a week went to support the young student. But off John went to Germany to study theology. In time his consequent intimacy with the language and its history made him an important pioneer researcher into the germs of Anglo-Saxon. Fanny rather approved of his veering into religion; but she also resented his thus adding to the family's troubles, which were already vexing enough because of a gathering storm over Covent Garden.

Soon after her return from Scotland late in summer 1829, things grew black. The theater was plastered with notices of a forced sale of whatever assets it contained, and her father, as stockholder, was personally sued for debts contracted before his taking over. It occurred to Fanny, not for the first time, that she should relieve her parents of supporting her by turning governess—that first resort of the Regency/Victorian young lady forced to earn a living. Her French, music, and piety were more than adequate for the work, but it was not a valid scheme. The fifty pounds or so that she probably cost her father annually was insignificant relative to his potential liabilities.

Nor can one imagine Gypsyish little Fanny, tagged with a theatrical background, managing to keep a prunes-and-prisms governess's place in a staid middle-class family. But she wrote about it to her father, who was touring in Ireland, and showed Thérèse the letter. In the same mail to him went her mother's advice to let the matter go without comment until he got back.

Next day mother asked daughter with no special emphasis whether she thought she had stage talent. Daughter said she had no idea. Mother suggested that she learn and enact for her some well-known role. Daughter chose Portia, then and later her ideal woman. Mother cued her through it and said now try something showing deeper passions, try Juliet. Fanny, discovering a talent for quick study, learned and auditioned Juliet for this best friend and severest critic. The critic made no comment whatever, but soon after Charles returned she made Fanny go through it for him. Afterward neither parent said more than very nice, my dear, a reticence that made the girl go sit on the stairs out of earshot and weep bitterly. Presently Charles secretly concealed in a dark box at Covent Garden an elderly friend whose judgment he trusted and had Fanny do her Juliet again on the empty stage ostensibly to see how that gilded white elephant's huge spaces suited her voice. Out there alone she was "completely carried away by the . . . wonderful play, I acted Juliet as I do not believe I ever acted it again, for I had no visible Romeo, and no audience to thwart my imagination."[4] Charles's friend's verdict was "Bring her out at once." And there it was. The role destiny chose for Fanny Kemble was not Rebecca Sharpe or Jane Eyre but Juliet. In a last hope of making shore, the Kembles bent on the only sail still left in the locker.

Fanny had been drafting a new verse play set in medieval Italy. She already suspected, however, that to go on writing would be rather a luxury, and she was too young and altogether too decent to feel any touch of Iphigenia in her parents' decision to put her on the stage. Nor was the possibility of following the family trade wholly unanticipated. Before going to Edinburgh she had rather jauntily told Harriet St. Leger: "They are in sad want of a woman at both the theatres. I've half a mind to give Covent Garden one." Soon she was quoting her father: " 'There is a fine fortune to be made by any young woman, of even decent talent, on the stage now.' " But when the clouds lifted a little he retreated, saying, like a true son of Roger, that "he should be sorry to see me adopt that career."[5] Now the worst was besieging the stage door. To Fanny's mind Covent Garden was a vast smoldering fire consuming her parents' peace of mind and hopes of security, but if they wished her to dance on those embers in case she might prove a phoenix, dance she would and wince as little as possible.

Both Charles and Thérèse decided to appear with her in what, under the circumstances, certainly were supporting roles. Romeo was one of Charles's most applauded parts, but now fifty-two, he considered himself too old to handle it anymore; so he cast himself as Mercutio, whom he had never played before. The venture was wildly successful. This aging veteran's reading of Romeo's witty, debonair, and dashing kinsman was a landmark in theatrical history like his sister's Lady Macbeth and his brother's Coriolanus. For Romeo they considered young Henry, extremely good-looking at the age of fifteen. Reluctantly he learned the part but played it so ridiculously badly that Charles, Thérèse, Aunt Dall, Fanny, and Henry went into fits of laughter and gave the scheme up. What to do about Henry remained an intermittent perplexity the rest of his life, but the one thing none ever suggested again was making an actor of him.[6] Thérèse broke her retirement to do Lady Capulet, Juliet's mother. She was already at the formidable task of turning an utterly inexperienced girl into an actress in three weeks of morning rehearsals. Both survived it, and the arrangement was emotionally sound. On the evening of October 5, 1829, when Aunt Dall launched Fanny out of the wings on her cue, it was no stage mother but a real one—and an utterly trusted dramatic coach to boot—waiting to embrace her in the glare from the lights and the roar of greeting from the pit.

> I ran straight across the stage, stunned with the tremendous shout that greeted me . . . the . . . flooring of the stage feeling as if it rose up against my feet; but I got hold of my mother and stood like a terrified creature at bay. . . . I do not think a word I uttered during that

> scene can have been audible; in the next . . . I began to
> forget myself; in . . . the balcony-scene, I had done so,
> and for aught I knew, I was Juliet; the passion I was ut-
> tering sending hot blushes over my neck and shoulders,
> while the poetry sounded like music to me as I spoke it.[7]

From out front it looked like this to T. Noon Talfourd, a well-
known barrister moonlighting as journalist-critic-playwright: The
house was agog at the notion of seeing Miss De Camp again and
charmed by the idea of veteran parents playing second fiddle to their
unfledged daughter

> . . . known to be of high literary endowments though
> educated without the slightest view to the stage as a
> profession. . . . The interest was almost too complicated
> to be borne with pleasure; and when Kemble [as Mercu-
> tio] bounded on the scene, as if he had cast off all his
> cares and twenty of his years . . . there was the keenest
> enthusiasm we have ever witnessed. Similar feeling
> greeted . . . Mrs. Kemble; but our hearts did not breathe
> freely until the fair debutant [sic] herself had entered,
> pale, trembling, but resolved, and found encouragement
> and shelter in her mother's arms . . . the first act did not
> close until . . . every spectator . . . was electrified by
> the influence of new-tried genius . . . the illusion that
> she was Shakespeare's Juliet came so speedily upon us, as
> to suspend the power of specific criticism . . . her eyes
> are full of a gifted soul . . . she . . . moves with such
> dignity that it is only on recollection that we discover she
> is not tall. . . . She treads the stage as if she had been
> matured by the study and practice of years.[8]

Tom Moore, Regency Britain's parlor laureate and poetical
diner-out, was there and thought Fanny "a girl of wonderful promise."[9] Young Thackeray was there, "much delighted with her";[10] in
their mutual middle age he reminded her how, in those giddy days,
he and his cultivated young cronies " 'were all in love with you.' "[11]
Even Leigh Hunt, no man to go with the crowd, allowed her "a very
handsomely-formed and expressive countenance, a promising sym-
metry of figure . . . a clear and good voice"; praised the originality
of her interpretation: "She appears to have an inclination to think for

herself . . . this . . . first attempt . . . may be accounted the most
favourable on record." [12] Seeing her again in Juliet a week later, he
objected to her overdeliberate handling of a few lines—a Kemble
habit—but otherwise "we recollect no part of her performance that
we could wish altered. Her tones in the balcony scene . . . touch
the heart like deep sorrow." [13]

At the rousingly happy family supper afterward Fanny found at
her plate a tiny jewel-studded watch. She named it Romeo, put it
under her pillow, and went to sleep on it, "a blissful girl." Next
morning Washington Irving, a close family friend and great favorite
of hers, called to congratulate them all. She ran to him, new toy in
hand like a child, and "putting it to his ear with a most mischievous
look of affected surprise, he exclaimed, as one does to a child's watch,
'Why, it goes, I declare!' " [14]

The public's joy in her carried Juliet through thirty-one alter-
nate-evening performances—a long run in those days. Covent Garden's creditors drew in their horns, for her success eventually cleared
off thirteen thousand pounds of the liabilities. The Charles Kembles
could breathe again. Every night Fanny was billed the box office was
mobbed and London's most elegant young men fought for places in
the pit (today's "stalls" or "orchestra," with only mere benches to sit
on) where they could bask in this incandescent young person's immediate glow. There were Fanny Kemble teacups and handkerchiefs
with her picture on them, Fanny Kemble prints in all the stationers'
shops. *Francis the First* sold out eleven printings. But Thérèse made
sure that none of it went dangerously to the head. The pit was as
near as those young fellows got. Fanny was forbidden the greenroom—the performers' traditional clubroom where new scripts were
aired, casting worked out, gossip swapped, stage calls awaited, and
where gentlemen dropped in to size up and make acquaintance with
pretty young actresses. Fanny awaited "Miss Kemble called for the
stage!" in her own dressing room under guard of Aunt Dall or her
mother. This standoffishness must have led to some backbiting, but
I find no hint of it in the scores of theatrical memoirs of the time.
Some of Fanny's fellow performers disliked her and said so, but not
on these grounds.

In several other respects her stage career was outrageously atypical. It was wildly unorthodox, for instance, for her parents, wise in the business, to dream of bringing out in Juliet or any other demanding leading role this teen-age neophyte whose maiden season should have been limited to small bits—the way her father, mother, and almost everybody else had begun. To take that risk before the most exacting audience in London was madness. With Covent Garden tottering, the penalties of failure would have been catastrophic. Had Fanny not risen to the occasion, not even the Kembles' popularity could have stifled the giggles and hisses that would have spelled shipwreck. As it was, her parents' presumption—or faith in her—and her own integrity and latent talent enabled her to start at the very top and, seldom taking secondary roles, remain a sought-after leading lady whenever she found it useful. For another unlikely twist, she became a successful actress through going on the stage to help her family, not because of the usual constructive self-esteem and sense of narcissistic adventure. Thérèse mentioned with wonder to young "Dicky" Milnes that Fanny showed small sign of being directly elated by her success until she learned from Charles how rapidly the debts were being cleared off.

Strangest of all, though Fanny was woman enough to feel the thrill of what was happening, the longer she worked behind footlights, the lower fell her opinion of the family trade. Within weeks of that glowing debut she told Harriet:

> You say [acting] is a very fascinating occupation . . . it does not appear to me so . . . it carries with it drawbacks enough . . . as . . . antidote to the vanity and love of admiration which it can hardly fail to foster. The mere embodying of the exquisite ideals of poetry is a great enjoyment, but . . . controlling the very feeling one has, in order to manifest it in the best way . . . [is distasteful]. . . . As to the mere excitement proceeding from the public applause . . . I do not think I shall ever experience it. But should I reckon too much upon my own steadiness, I have the incessant care and watchfulness of my dear mother to rely on.[15]

To supplement that defense Fanny was including in her nightly prayers—how many suddenly successful young women nowadays pray reg-

ularly between toothbrush and pillow?—a fervent plea for the Lord's
help in keeping herself free of the theater's potential evils.

A remarkable reaction to becoming the toast of London before
one's twentieth birthday!

Her salary, thirty pounds a week, was a handsome income in
1830. With her new affluence came riding lessons, which probably
went far to reconcile her to the exacting process of role study, rehearsal, fittings, and performances involved in expanding her repertory. Soon a star pupil at Captain Fozzard's famous riding academy,
she "rode tame" mounts too restive for other lady pupils, and when
the Duchess of Kent brought her ten-year-old daughter Victoria to
inspect the school with a view to lessons, Fozzard chose Fanny to
demonstrate his methods. (The next time Fanny saw the girl she was
a pretty little queen giving the Speech from the Throne in Parliament
with a touchingly admirable purity of diction.) For a lady to ride
astride was then unthinkable, so this was all sidesaddle, one knee
straight with foot in stirrup, the other hooked round the pommel;
the long skirt of the habit muffled all indecorous hints of bifurcation.
The squarer the rider's seat, the easier the skewed weight was on the
horse, but at best the arrangement was a makeshift making special
training for the animal desirable;[16] and it required unusual suppleness and sense of balance if the lady was not to look absurd at the
trot. Fanny had those qualities but considered herself inadequate in
the subtle skills with the reins that riders call "good hands." Nevertheless she was immediately mad about riding, counting on it much
of her life for joy and health and the exorcising of blue devils.

She seems to have had a premonition of hippophilia, having declared that she wouldn't care go to to heaven unless she could be an
"angel on horseback."[17] She did not, however, develop the horsiness
(in a pejorative sense) that sometimes afflicts equestriennes. This fits
with a surmise of mine that, though based on merely internal evidence, I think well of: To some extent she may have formed herself
on Scott's most charming heroine, Diana Vernon of *Rob Roy*. This
was probably not conscious, but once one thinks of it, there it is—
Fanny's temperament scenting affinity and looking to it for definition

and systemic bent. The reader first meets Diana in a mannish riding costume putting a big black mare over a gate and overwhelming the narrator-hero with gleeful chatter. She is lovely and shrewd, casually independent and, relative to the conventional heroine of the day, charmingly perverse. She rides and shoots on equal footing with her boorish cousins, reads ancient and modern languages with her learned cousin, yet is by no means either a frumpish blue-stocking or a horse-godmother, rather a white-skinned brunette with a dimpled chin, sparkling dark eyes, and tiny hands and feet. She says she is "accustomed to mind nobody's opinion but my own" and complains that because she is a girl, "I would be shut up in a mad-house if I did half the things I have a mind to."

Barring the tiny hands and feet, there is a great deal of Fanny Kemble there. She read Scott as everybody else did then. *Rob Roy* came out when she was nine years old—ample time for her to absorb Diana before her emotional gristle turned to bone. She certainly considered Diana special: seeing Covent Garden's stage version of *Rob Roy* in 1832 she commented, "Miss Inveraretie was a cruel [that is, cruelly inadequate] Diana, but who would not be?"[18] And a competent ear for style can hardly miss the strong likeness in point of view, rhetorical bounce, and ingratiating energy between Di Vernon's cascading protests and descriptions and Fanny's exuberant autobiographies and letters. When Scott first met Fanny, he complimented her on the way she sat her horse. I like to think he had his Diana Vernon in mind at that moment. As child, girl and woman, Fanny was too solid to be wholly accounted for in terms of "role models." But in following her story one keeps glimpsing in the shadows behind her Thérèse De Camp, Harriet St. Leger, Harriet Murray Siddons; and for all that they never existed, Undine, the water sprite, the "nixie" dangerous for human men to marry, and Diana Vernon, impatient horsewoman. They make a formidable group. The adjective often applies to Fanny also.

With her new money Fanny bought her father a horse to ride in the park with important friends and acquaintances. Totty got the beautiful guitar for which she had been yearning. For Thérèse the tangible result of her daughter's triumph was the famous drawing of

Fanny inscribed "To Mrs. Charles Kemble/Sir Thomas Lawrence."
The story behind it: Lawrence, draftsman-prodigy son of a country
innkeeper, was discovered young, sent to London for training, and
rose briskly to fame and prosperity. He became the successor to Reynolds as the man by whom fashionable London most wanted to be
portrayed. It followed that he did conspicuous actors partly as pro-
motion, partly because lithographs and engravings from such portraits sold well. He painted Mrs. Siddons and John Philip Kemble
several times each. That entangled him with the family, particularly
its women. Very likely he was twitchily in love with Melpomene, for
he was a bachelor given to ephemeral affairs. Just as probably nothing
substantial came of it. Instead, as intimate of the household that her
presence pervaded, he successfully courted her pretty daughter Sarah.
After a while, with the emotional shiftlessness that marred his life,
he discovered that it wasn't Sarah but her younger sister Maria, also
pretty but in another way, whom he couldn't live without. Somehow
Melpomene and the girls, whose dispositions were as different as their
looks, Maria turbulent, Sarah wistful, worked it out his way. But
both sisters were "delicate," meaning threatened by tuberculosis.
Maria died first, on her deathbed pledging Sarah never to marry Lawrence. In a few months Sarah made sure of keeping her word by
dying. The nineteenth century could show no finer example of gentlewomen driven by unfortunate love into "fatal decline."

Understandably this miserable affair caused Mrs. Siddons to
break with Lawrence. But now here he was, sixty years old, again
fluttering toward the Kemble flame by stopping Charles on the street,
saying he heard that his daughter's debut was preparing and might
he, for old times' sake, call and wish her luck? Easygoing Charles
said yes. Lawrence's personal charm—part of his portrait-foundry
equipment—soon had him playing solicitous godfather for Fanny
who, of course, reminded him poignantly of other days. He helped
Thérèse choose styles and colors for costumes for Fanny's new roles.
He went to her performances whenever possible and each time sent
her a written criticism that she found very helpful. And, of course,
he was to do her portrait as Juliet. It was a highly finished preliminary drawing for that which he gave Thérèse. As basis for lithograph

and engraving, in various degrees of quality, some deplorable, it sold widely throughout the English-speaking world.

Mrs. Siddons, now quite feeble, was apprised of the renewed relationship. Dining at Charles's one day, she asked how the portrait was coming along—and then said abruptly that when she died, she wanted Lawrence to join Charles carrying her to her grave. Lawrence wept on hearing of this. He never had the privilege, for he died first—suddenly, before the portrait had reached the canvas-and-oils stage. Before dying he had mentioned to Thérèse how much his drawings of Fanny had come out looking like Maria. Some months later Fanny, examining Lawrence's studies of her two dead cousins, burst out in her journal, "Oh that man! . . . whose wanton and heartless duplicity planted the death that conquered them both!"[19] As an old lady thinking back over Lawrence's unctuous powers of insinuation, she surmised that his death might have been for her a lucky escape: "I was a very romantic girl, with a most excitable imagination . . . a very dangerous fascination was added to my sense of gratitude. . . . I think it not at all unlikely that had . . . I [continued to sit] to him . . . in spite of the forty years' difference in our ages . . . I should have become . . . the fourth member of our family whose life he would have disturbed and embittered."[20] Awareness of the poignancy of this emotional puzzle was what made Fanny write to cousin Cecilia, then Mrs. Siddons's companion: "In case your Mother should not have heard . . . you had better prepare her for the news of the death of Sir Thomas Lawrence . . . you may save her in some degree the shock which I fear the intelligence must give her."[21]

This strange episode was only one side effect of the decision to put Fanny on the stage. Her success at once opened glittering social opportunities, and her parents had no reason to deny her the world of resounding titles, fine feathers, and late hours. Charles particularly, but Thérèse too in great measure, was already well received in elegant drawing rooms, so they could take it in stride when their daughter's new fame brought a never-ending trickle of invitations to Lord and Lady Thisandthat's dinner, ball, garden party . . . with a card for Miss Kemble included by no means casually.

Fashionable dinners presented no strains to anybody whose

tongue wagged as readily and trenchantly as Fanny's, whose social confidence was solidly based on acquaintance with persons who mattered in Edinburgh and *chez* Charles Kemble. Indeed she considered that the conversation at her father's dinner table, featuring pithy Thérèse and often spiced by clever notables from various walks of life, was more amusing than most of what one heard in the great world. Nor did it hurt that she had, as she once told George Combe in his own phrenological jargon, "a very comfortable self-esteem."[22]

At Lord and Lady Thisandthat's, once the gentlemen left their wine and "joined the ladies" for tea in the drawing room, cards were usually available; younger guests tended to prefer music. So the young Countess of Lyonesse would sing some not too difficult operatic airs accompanied on the pianoforte by the Honorable Arabella Saltire-Chevron. If Lord Alfred Martlet, second son of the Duke of Vair, had a tolerable tenor voice, he might sing duets with Lady Scutcheon. Much time and effort and many guineas to music masters had gone into drilling such accomplishments into these girls. Now came the rewards in admiration from eligible young patricians who might marry them if dowries and settlements could be satisfactorily worked out; and never mind the seldom brilliant quality of their music, they often looked winsome while performing. Among such amateurs Fanny's at least semiprofessional voice and capable piano work were much in demand. She was always more than ready to play and sing, particularly enjoying the traditional Scottish songs that she had made her own while in Edinburgh. Sometimes she had to do duets with Tom Moore, whose pseudo-Irish ballads persist in collections of songs your grandparents knew and were then the favorite musical agenda for such evenings. Fanny's only objection to singing with him was that she had to take vexing care lest her robust contralto drown out the little great man's sentimental chirpings.

The fashionable balls were sheer joy. She never got enough dancing. She sometimes thought that, if she had to perform in public, she should have trained as a dancer instead of an actress. Actually, though the potential skill was probably there and the performances of Taglioni, Fanny Ellsler, and other such great dancers of her time delighted her, she could hardly have stomached the prurient overtones of the Victorian ballet. But the ballroom was different—a world very dance-minded in a ceremonious way where dancing was not only a pleasure but an indispensable means of interaction between the sexes. After Waterloo the Napoleonic empire's favorite "quadrille"— a stiffly designed but lively square dance going back to Louis XIV's time—crossed the Channel along with Poland's energetic mazurka and polonaise, and the Germans' alarming waltz in which He actually put His arm halfway round Her and His hand between Her shoulder blades. These innovations overshadowed but did not altogether suppress the old English dances like the Sir Roger de Coverley (a cousin of the Virginia reel), so there was no lack of variety to keep Fanny's toes busy during the whirling, half-breathless, bright-eyed hours that often stretched into spring sunrise at one or another great London house.

"If I am a little tired with acting," Fanny told Harriet, "why, a night's dancing soon sets me right again." She likened herself to the girl in the German folktale who danced her stockings off her feet. She inveighed against the stupidity of Londoners who went to three or four balls in a night, wearing out their horses en route, when if they concentrated on one, they might be dancing all the time. She was still ecstatic at the end of her second season: "Such shoals of partners! . . . such perfect music! such a delightful floor! Danced till the day had one eye wide open, and then home to bed . . . Broad daylight!"[23]

All under chaperonage, of course. Thérèse never relaxed the rules of the time. Such solo flights as Fanny enjoyed in Edinburgh were out of the question in larger, tougher London. Fanny went nowhere unless under escort of Charles, Thérèse or Aunt Dall. No substitute would suffice. Because nobody else was available and brother John was thought inadequate, Fanny could not go to William IV's coronation in 1830, for which noble friends had got them places. She took it all well, even getting fun out of the contrast between her parents as chaperons:

> At half-past two, though the carriage had been ordered
> . . . my father told me he would not "spoil sport," and
> so angelically stayed till past four. . . . the best of fa-

thers, the most affectionate of parents, the most benevolent of men! There is a great difference between being
chaperoned by one's father [and by] one's mother [who]
poor dear! never flirts, gets very sleepy and tired, and
wants to go home before she comes; the former flirts and
talks with all the pretty, pleasant women . . . and does
not care till what hour in the morning—a frame of mind
favorable to much dancing.[24]

IV

Youth like
Summer Morn

IN A LONDON or New York theater of our time a production as popular as this *Romeo & Juliet,* with Fanny enchanting and Charles dazzling the town, would run for months eight times a week. They did
things differently then, for it was a far narrower amusement market.
The management of Covent Garden followed the prevalent method—
keeping up a star's draw by presenting him or her in a series of
standard vehicles in a repertory allowing several changes of bill a
week. The consequent widening of role experience was valuable for
the performer in contrast to the lucrative but stagnant practice of
playing the same thing over and over until receipts drop below the
profit point. Yet it was also a heavy strain to get up one long, exacting leading part after another and keep lines and business packaged
together in one's head for instant use. Theoretically a veteran would
hardly need rehearsal to go on in *Douglas* last night, *George Barnwell*
tonight, *The Rivals* tomorrow night. In practice, however, there was
much fumbling, ad-libbing and substitution of violent action for the
script's original values.

As a Kemble, however, Fanny was allowed no such fudging and
had to assimilate seven famous, highly emotional roles in six months.
That all seven were among Mrs. Siddons's great successes was no
coincidence. London wanted to see how Melpomene's little niece wore
her aunt's impressive buskins. Shrinkingly she dreaded the inevitable
comparisons. Add a general dread that, as project succeeded project,
the luck would run out, the pitcher go once too often to the well.

. . . In any case the scripts would hardly have been new. For generations the British stage had been working up a fund of tragedies, melodramas, farces, comedies, and operas (light pieces with songs interpolated) to display leading actors in. There were new plays written by literary parsons (the Reverend Dr. Edward Young; the Reverend John Home; the Reverend H. H. Milman, friend of the Kembles); men-about-town (Major General John Burgoyne); bluestocking ladies (Miss More, Miss Mitford, Miss Baillie); aspiring hacks (George Colman, George Lillo); actors and actresses (David Garrick, pretty Mrs. Inchbald, part of whose charm was an engaging stammer that never plagued her on stage) and were successful enough to swell the canon. A fat supply of further items came from adapting French, Spanish, and presently German plays. Yet contrary to today's assumptions newness in a script was, though an advantage, less than major. What Londoner and provincial alike looked for in the playbill posted up in the public house were the names of the chief performers—if familiar, good; if not, rousing curiosity—then the titles of the well-worn pieces in which they sought to please with conventional or maybe innovational handlings of material everybody had already witnessed dozens of times. Our attitude toward opera is a fair analogy. Sometimes a new opera does make a place for itself but attention dwells chiefly on how the new tenor sings *I Pagliacci*. The true opera-buff no more minds hearing *La Bohème* again than a track-and-field fan objects to seeing the 220-yard hurdles listed among the events.

The backbone of this theatrical canon was Shakespeare, in cutdown, sometimes added-to, usually expurgated versions that nevertheless retained most of the great scenes and three-dimensional characters in which leading actors could spread themselves. The Jacobean Philip Massinger was sometimes mined for scripts reworked for Drury Lane or Covent Garden. So were later, fumbly imitators of the great Jacobeans—Otway, Southerne, Rowe, et al.—names now familiar only to students. Some of the resulting so-called tragedies, actually lurid melodramas, Fanny's contemporaries played to shreds. Invariably these scripts employed blank verse. Only overt comedy spoke prose. Any drama with a tinge of seriousness had to wheeze along in iambic pentameter—a noble verse form when strong, watery when not—because Shakespeare, Ben Jonson, and Massinger had used it. The convention was so powerful that Mrs. Siddons, they said, spoke in blank verse when instructing a servant. So sinewy a writer as Farquhar floundered into blank verse (not improved by being printed as prose) whenever a character in one of his plays uttered a serious thought.

In this canon comedy, sometimes briskly amusing, often highly actable, came from Farquhar, Sir John Vanbrugh, Henry Fielding, Sheridan . . . and, as novelties appeared, several lesser hands. There was also a swarm of standard one-act farces for "afterpieces"—which may need explanation. Management usually followed up the imposing play—say Mrs. Siddons in *Venice Preserved* or Edmund Kean in *Richard III*—with a short melodrama or boisterous or satirical farce.[1] The tragedian of the evening in a provincial troupe might change costume and reappear to great applause as Sir Gullible Giggle. The titles of these *digestifs* give their tone: *High Life Below Stairs, Miss in Her Teens, The Devil to Pay* . . . This elder and not very reverend theater has left us only a few traces, chiefly moribund catchwords: whoever today speaks of Mrs. Grundy refers, usually unwittingly, to a character in Thomas Morton's *Speed the Plough*. Lady Bountiful is a bit part in Farquhar's *The Beaux' Stratagem.* Call a womanizer a Gay Lothario and you are back in Rowe's *The Fair Penitent.* Simon Pure is from Mrs. Susannah Centlivre's *A Bold Stroke for a Wife.* Mrs. Malaprop mangled words in *The Rivals,* which is distinguished among the above by not being quite dead yet.

Obviously this was largely an actor's theater. Tastes were already shifting and lower social strata growing more influential in the audience; hence spectacle and action for its own sake, always a temptation to producers and performers, was ominously diluting the elder stage. The *trompe l'oeil* scene painter, the simulated battle scene with cannon going off and toy fleets engaging among ingeniously wiggly waves, trained animals, particularly horses, varied the fare at even the Theatres Royal. For a generation after Fanny's debut, however, the primary function of the stage remained, albeit in lessening degree, that of showcase for talents parading before self-appointed expert admirers. Acting techniques reflected this. In each well-known script a first-class performer exploited certain "points"—crucial lines given special emphasis or striking bits of stage business that the actor and the house learned to look forward to. When he reached one of these—say Hamlet's "The play's the thing" threat—his pause for acknowledgment and the house's roar of loyal applause coincided to the satisfaction of all. Developing talents borrowed and tried to handle such points just as Kean or Miss O'Neill did. A minor actor who fouled up one of the leading man's points was well advised to make himself scarce. The technique led into "attitudes": the heroine bidding the hero farewell would half freeze in the most graceful phase of her gesture and hold it while the audience applauded tearfully.

Very tearfully if all was well. In return for loyal interest the customer expected an emotional orgy. All the old tricks of declamation—this theater was almost as declamatory as that of ancient Greece—the overwrought stage business, shrieks, swoonings, leapings, tense posturings were meant to rouse tears or fears. In Garrick's or John Philip Kemble's time, even in that of William Macready and Edwin Forrest, a prominent leading lady expected every other man in the pit to blubber aloud when she was hauled off to prison. Yet she also expected him to retain enough sense of where he was—not in Venice or Seville but a playhouse—madly to applaud her for affecting him so strongly, shouting, waving his hat, stopping the show till she came back on stage to curtsy her thanks. When things went best, such a demonstration occurred six or seven times; and if the house did not thus "rise to her" on her first entrance, she was hurt.

A modern actor discussing emotional rapport or lack of it with an audience invokes residual traces of this collective intimacy. It made the customer as strong a factor as writer or actor in the pacing of a play, for performers came to manipulate and lean on it. Hence Fanny's dismay when Edinburgh's audiences proved "cold," unresponsive, because not given to London-style hullabaloo. She sorely missed being carried along by the booster effect of such outbursts of admiration. In 1833, when Philadelphia's audiences proved even colder, she explained at length:

> 'Tis amazing how much an audience loses by this . . .
> hanging back, even where the silence proceeds from un-

willingness to interrupt a good performance . . . an actor
. . . is deprived by that very stillness of half his power.
Excitement is reciprocal between the performer and the
audience . . . the very noise and tumult . . . [tend] to
heighten the nervous energy which the scene itself begets.
. . . besides . . . the physical powers of an actor require,
after any tremendous exertion, the rest and regathering of
breath and strength, which the interruption . . . affords
him.[2]

And this closeness to the customer was more than figurative. Not long before Fanny's time gentlemen influential with management were free not only to hang about backstage but even to sit, somewhat offside, in view of the house during performances. Thirty years later that custom had disappeared but most of the action was still played not within the modern box-set picture frame but on the stage apron before the proscenium arch flanked by boxes the occupants of which were practically on stage with the cast. Before electric lights the house lighting, though low enough in our terms, could not be dimmed. So the customer in the pit watching Hamlet and Laertes squabbling over Ophelia's grave also had a good view of the dowager Viscountess of Blazonry dripping tears on the rail of the stage box.

In some ways these conditions enhanced the actor by affording him or her a breath of the great days when *Hamlet* was written for a stage the scenery of which consisted largely of a placard reading Castle of Elsinore. It was still up to writer-plus-actor so to tear a passion to tatters and then fuse it back together that the customer would overlook anomalies and be airborne into illusion more gripping because it lacked substantial corroboration. Read that eerie line "Is this a dagger that I see before me?" as it can be read, and the auditor's response is God Almighty, there it is: "The handle toward my hand; come, let me clutch thee . . ." In her eventual career as reader middle-aged Fanny Kemble could make an audience see that dagger with no help whatever from stage, costume, or lighting—her only props a book, a lamp, and a voice.

Meanwhile in 1830—the year William IV came to his throne and the French put Louis Philippe on theirs and the first steam railroad opened for business—the management of Covent Garden put

Fanny over the jumps of the parts she had to play. The first hazard
was Belvidera, heroine of *Venice Preserved*. The only thing she liked
about that was the costume that Lawrence and Thérèse settled on for
her first entrance, a "Venetian patrician's black dress with white satin
puffs and crimson lining and rich embroidery of gold and pearl
. . . a black hat and white feather . . . with which . . . I was
enamored . . . feeling an unspeakable accession of dignity. . . . I
begged hard to be allowed to wear it through the tragedy, but this,
with some laughter . . . was forbidden."[3] The part she really liked
that year was Portia: "Juliet, with the exception of the balcony scene,
I act; but I feel as if I *were* Portia—and how I wish I were!" said the
budding protofeminist. Thérèse had let herself go on the costumes for
the heiress of Belmont. First dress "an open skirt of the palest pink
. . . shot with white and the deepest rose-color . . . like a gown
made of strawberries and cream. . . . third dress . . . white satin
. . . a most beautiful crimson velvet hat, . . . with one sweeping
white feather."[4] Fanny wore that when sitting for a miniature-painter
at Bath; a widely distributed engraving made from it was the worst
portrait of her ever to appear. Maybe it served her right for so ecstat-
ically describing those gorgeous clothes to austerely tailored Harriet
St. Leger.

On through the winter she triumphed in Arthur Murphy's *The
Grecian Daughter,* Edward Moore's *The Gamester,* Southerne's *Isabella*
(in which Mrs. Siddons had first swept London off its feet), August
Friedrich Ferdinand von Kotzebue's *The Stranger.* Fanny thought
them all more or less deplorable: Belvidera "a sort of lay figure in a
tragic attitude"; *Grecian* "flat, poor, and trashy"; *Stranger* "the quin-
tessence of trashy sentimentalism."[5] In later years she reproached herself for having been so harsh about them. To be fair, they merely
carried somewhat further the extravagance of plot and situation accepted in things like *King Lear.* Their difficulty lay in lacking the
depth of characterization and rhetorical brilliance of Shakespeare and
his greatest contemporaries. Nevertheless our great-great-grandfathers
loved what actors could do with these wild rages, persecuted wives,
daggers, conspiracies, swordplay, obsessive love-affairs, poisonings,
comic-strip mayhem, blabber-mouthed humor, and stages littered

with corpses. Nine out of ten were set in Italy or Spain where swash-bucklers named Antonio or Pedro always lacked surnames, and hero-ines whose names, like those of Cunard liners, ended in *ia* were mighty handy with knives. The tenth had a classic Greek or Roman setting. Typically it concluded with the stage direction "Enter Eura-sia, distracted," meaning gone out of her mind for grisly adequate if fantastic reasons; after spouting twenty lines of lunatic gibberish, she either stabs herself or dies of exhaustion.

There was particular cause for dismay in *The Grecian Daughter*'s special feature: The heroine, a nursing mother deprived of her baby, finds her royal father starving in prison and restores him to sudden vigor by administering what must have been the most stimulating mother's milk ever secreted; offstage, of course. Fanny's distaste for *The Stranger* was highly creditable; this German-sentimental monu-ment of mawkishness was a very early toying with the since familiar motif of more-to-be-pitied-than-censured, and the droopiness of the theme is more than matched by the implausibility of the plot. Yet it was a mainstay of the Regency theater, depicted more in wonder than in irritation by Thackeray: In Chapter IV of *Pendennis* Bingley's pro-vincial company is doing *The Stranger* with the lovely Emily Costigan (Fotheringay) as Mrs. Haller, the erring but redeemed-through-suh-huh-huffering wife:

"If a man were to say it is a stupid play, he would not be far wrong. Nobody ever talked so. If we meet idiots in real life, as will happen, it is a great mercy that they do not use such absurdly fine words. The Stranger's talk is sham, like the book he reads, and the hair he wears, and the bank he sits on, and the diamond ring he makes play with." And since Thackeray did not have to act in it, he could go on: "But, in the midst of all the balderdash, there runs that reality of love, children and forgiveness, which sets all the world sympathizing." That is one way, not the best, to say that *The Stranger* was a good tool for eliciting the sobs and tears that the public hoped for. In spite of her queasiness Fanny seems to have played Mrs. Haller acceptably or better. And a few times she gave Melpomene's sleazy but heavily charged roles such sympathetic energy that she spun her-self into genuine hysterics offstage.

*   *   *

Prominent London actors usually ended their major seasons in late spring and then toured the solidest provincial houses in summer engagements of some one to three weeks. Managers in Bristol, Manchester, Glasgow, and Dublin paid them well, which contributed gratifyingly to the retirement nest eggs they hoped to lay away. Late in May 1830, Charles and Fanny, looked after by Aunt Dall, took Fanny's repertory, Charles playing most of the leads, to Bath, Edinburgh, Glasgow, Manchester . . . Since it was still stagecoach times, they could not take a supporting company along; their minimal costume luggage was cumbrous enough. In each town the local company played the minor roles. It was assumed—sometimes correctly—that most professionals would be "up in" the supporting parts of *A New Way to Pay Old Debts, The School for Scandal, Henry VIII,* or whatever the visiting "stars"—the term goes that far back—chose to bill.

These provincial houses warmly emulated Fanny's London triumphs. In Edinburgh she made a new friend in Sir Walter Scott and was assured by Andrew Combe that her performance of the previous night was "transcendently beautiful." [6] After her first performance in Dublin:

> I was escorted back to the hotel . . . by . . . about two
> hundred men, shouting and hurrahing like mad. . . .
> they opened the carriage door and let down the steps
> . . . and helped [me] out, clapping and showering the
> most fervent expressions of good-will upon me and aunt
> Dall, whom they took for my mother. . . . formed a line
> on each side of me, and several . . . dropped on their
> knees to look under my bonnet, as I ran laughing, with
> my head down, from the carriage to the house. [7]

Obviously her distaste for the stage did not keep her from relishing such flattering absurdity. But this was not the high spot of the tour. She had reached that in a less frivolous context late in August.

The world's first steam railroad, between Manchester and Liverpool, had its final trial run then, and Fanny Kemble, whose family knew some of the scheme's backers, sat on the engine-driver's bench with George Stephenson, inventor-engineer-father of the project. Her delight in the experience gushes out of her account of it:

We were introduced to the little engine which was to drag
us along the rails. She (for they make these curious little
fire-horses all mares) consisted of a boiler, a stove, a small
platform, a bench, and . . . a barrel containing enough
water to prevent her being thirsty for fifteen miles. . . .
the reins, bit, and bridle of this wonderful beast is a small
steel handle, which applies or withdraws the steam from
its legs or pistons, so that a child might manage it. The
coals, which are its oats, were under the bench. . . . This
snorting little animal, which I felt rather inclined to pat,
was then harnessed to our carriage, and . . . we started
at almost ten miles an hour . . . without any visible
cause of progress other than the magical machine with its
flying white breath and rhythmical unvarying pace. . . .
[Returning] the engine . . . set off at its utmost speed,
thirty-five miles an hour, swifter than a bird flies (for they
tried the experiment with a snipe). You cannot conceive
what that sensation of cutting the air was . . . I stood
up, and with my bonnet off, "drank the air before me."
The wind . . . or perhaps the force of our own thrusting
against it, absolutely weighed my eyelids down . . . the
sensation of flying was quite delightful . . . yet strange
as it was, I had a perfect sense of security, and not the
slightest fear.[8]

Part of that may have come of being deeply impressed by the
man beside her on the bench. She told Harriet she was "most horribly
in love" with him.

He explained . . . the whole construction of the steam-
engine, and said he could . . . make a famous engineer
out of me, which, considering the wonderful things he
has achieved, I dare not say is impossible . . . his face is
fine, though careworn . . . though his accent indicates
strongly his north-country birth, his language has not the
slightest touch of vulgarity or coarseness. He has certainly
turned my head.[9]

In any case, Fanny shared with her father a sturdy interest in
technological advances. They had already explored the Thames Tun-
nel project under escort of Marc Isambard Brunel himself; Fanny's
impressionistic account of its gaslit out-of-this-worldness and respect
for the courage and skills of the men working on it is one of her best

bits of writing. Now in Lancashire she marveled at the textile mills and imaginatively remarked the anomaly that huge iron castings for bridges and steam engines were formed in "moulds of sand . . . inconstant, shifting, restless sand." During the next year's tour she, Aunt Dall, and Charles visited the great new breakwater at Plymouth. The boat trip out with the architect-engineer was rough, and as foul weather was working up they had almost at once to return, for even in the harbor capsizing was a strong possibility: "Shut my eyes that I might not see how we heaved, and sang that I might not think how sick I was; and so we reached shore and I ran up and down the steep beach . . . and the wind soon dried my light muslin clothes."[10]

Admiringly she told her journal that the breakwater was "a noble work. The daring of the conception, its vast size and strength, and the utility of the purpose were alike admirable."[11] Yet her fascination with ingenious power did not blind her to a rudimentary but commendably precocious sense of the social risks in inventiveness. She understood that some of the opposition to Stephenson's railroad came of unwillingness to see the landscape torn up: and left Manchester aware how "a child . . . confined in the hot oily noisy and confusing atmosphere of a manufactory [would yearn for] green fields and sunny paths."[12] A few weeks after her ride with Stephenson the reverse of that coin came violently uppermost. Charles, Thérèse, and Fanny were among the several hundred guests when the railroad line was formally opened. The lions of the day were the Duke of Wellington, the diplomatic corps, and delegations from Parliament. It terrified Thérèse when the makeshift coaches picked up speed. Fanny's exultation was diluted by having to persuade her mother that there was no danger. At a stopping point there was a rising tumult: the first railroad accident in history had occurred. William Huskisson, M.P., the government's financial expert, had got down to stretch his legs, strayed over on a parallel track, and was mortally mangled by a locomotive. As the train carrying the dying man neared Manchester, it was welcomed by a crowd of mill hands who hated Wellington and the Tories and had turned out in the rain to hiss and groan at them.

* * *

The man who tied up Huskisson's legs—so he did not bleed to death on the spot—was the Earl of Wilton, at whose country place, Heaton, a few miles from Manchester, the Kembles were staying. Lady Wilton's mother, the Countess of Derby, had been Elizabeth Farren, a fine comedienne and friend of the Kembles. Fanny thought Lord Wilton the model of an elegant, cultivated, patrician host— handsome, good-natured, versatile, playing his splendid pipe-organ just as well as he rode the horses of his own stud. The beautiful Lady Wilton was "extremely kind . . . petting me almost like a spoiled child, dressing me up in her own exquisite riding-habit and mounting me on her favorite horse"[13]—a sure way to Fanny's heart. To save time Fanny had to wear her first-entrance costume to dinner at Heaton, and the Wiltons and their other guests were indulgently amused to see the vivid little creature come sweeping gloriously in as long-trained and furbelowed Belvidera.

The company included a Baring heiress and her husband; some Hungarian nobility; two of the season's outstanding aristocratic beauties; Henry Greville, brother of Charles, the famous politician-turf-man-diarist, himself a noted diner-out very valuable to know. Here was the essence of the great British country house: splendid names, fastidious manners, go-as-you-please activity, and platoons of servants to keep it all going smoothly. In the old days at Weybridge Fanny had nibbled at that. The adjoining estate, Oatlands, had been leased by Lord Francis Leveson-Gower (later Earl of Ellesmere). Relations with his Kemble neighbors became cordial. Now as a person in her own right at Heaton, Fanny "walked and rode and sang and talked"[14]—four of the five things she liked most to do—and found herself valued by these people who took such a life for granted, the same who spent the other half of the year at the London balls and dinner parties that she already knew. Thenceforth for years she was a sought-after guest in such circles and, when Harriet questioned its value, was clear-sightedly frank:

> With regard to . . . "fine people," and liking their society. . . . They do not often say very wise or very witty things . . . but neither do they . . . poke their elbows into one's side (figuratively speaking) in their conversa-

tion. . . . my social position does not entitle me to mix
with . . . "fine people." My father's indolence renders
their society an irksome exertion . . . my mother's pride
always induces her to hang back. . . . We are none of
. . . us very keen tuft-hunters. But for these very reasons, if "fine people" seek me, it is a decided compliment
. . . my vanity is flattered. . . . I would rather pass a
day with Stephenson than with Lord Alvanley, though the
one is a coal-digger by birth . . . the other . . . the
keenest wit and one of the finest gentlemen about town.
But Stephenson's attributes . . . are his individually,
while Lord Alvanley's gifts and graces (his wit, indeed,
excepted) are . . . those of his whole social set.[15]

As to the comforts of great houses, she had already confessed, apropos
of a well-meaning but sadly simple country inn, "I have no fancy for
gypsying, and the greatest taste for . . . what I should call 'silver
fork existence' in general." Late in life she finally qualified this:

I have no doubt that [my parents] felt both pride and
pleasure in . . . my enjoyment of all the gay grandeur
and kindly indulgence. . . . I now . . . doubt how far
they were judicious in allowing me to be so taken out of
my proper social sphere. It encouraged my taste for . . .
a mode of life never likely to be mine, and undoubtedly
increased my distaste for the coarse and common details of
my professional duties . . . the sham splendors of the
stage.[16]

This spiral of aristocratic elegance took another turn when blue-
stocking Lady Dacre weighed in. Her husband, Baron Dacre—a very
old title—had been a utopian-minded intellectual and was now exploring German literature and philosophy. His lady was an admired
poetess and translator of classic Italian poets; her tragedy set in old
Saxon times was produced at Drury Lane;[17] her painting was better
than amateur, her sculpture still better; and in her sixties she was one
of Britain's finest horsewomen. At The Hoo, the Dacres' country
house in Hertfordshire, the acquaintance ripened into an intimacy
that had Fanny writing to Lady Dacre as "Dear granny." There too
the girl came to know some of the period's chief politicians: Earl

Grey, Lord Melbourne, Lord John Russell (later Earl Russell, Bertrand's grandfather).

Thence it was a short step to the famous Sunday breakfasts (early luncheons) given at his London house by Samuel Rogers, an eminent banker-poet who kept casting his nets for cultivated persons to notice and, if they proved amusing or forceful, continuing to invite them. At his table one fenced or chimed in with Lord Macaulay, Sir Henry Taylor, cultivated gentlemen-journalists such as the Reverend Sydney Smith, the renowned wit and diner-out whose jokes were sometimes as good as they were elaborate, and this or that rising poet or novelist. Rogers was also famous for his snakily savage tongue. His excuse was: "I have a very weak voice; if I did not say ill-natured things, no one would hear what I said."[18] Yet he did not resent his friends' ferocious jokes about the cadaverous appearance that made him look older and frailer than he actually was—for one example, when beds were scarce during an overnight stay in a country town, it was suggested that Rogers could be put up in the nearest graveyard.[19] And he was cryptically generous. "Borrow five hundred pounds of him and he'll never say a word against you till you want to repay it,"[20] said Thomas Campbell, the popular poet ("Ye mariners of England! . . ."). In this exacting company Fanny seems to have held her own. It was a stunning compliment when, years later during her marital crisis, Rogers, the most astringent of old bachelors, urged her to come into his elegant town house in St. James's Street as honored chatelaine-hostess.

Maybe one reason why Fanny got on so well with high-placed persons was that they roused no awe in her. Though she liked Lady Cork, for instance, she thus described her famous Saturday evenings: "Such rooms—such ovens! . . . fine folks and foul air! . . . we stood and sat, and looked and listened, and talked nonsense and heard it talked, and perspired and smothered and suffocated . . . did not get to bed till two o'clock." When Lord Melbourne—not yet confidant-pilot of the young Queen Victoria but already high in politics—asked to be introduced to her, her pert confidence to Harriet was: "If he likes, he shall be the decrepit old nobleman you are so afraid of me marrying . . . we dine with him Wednesday week, and I will write you word if the impression deepens."[21] She was even scornful about royalty—of a sort—in the form of the young Reverend Augustus Fitzclarence, rector of Mapledurham. His surname meant that, as everybody knew, he was one of the several bastards whom William IV (Duke of Clarence before he was king) begot on Dorothy Jordan,[22] a great comedienne of the Kembles' generation. Fitzclarence made himself conspicuous among Fanny's bodyguard, as Lawrence dubbed the youths who thronged the pit when she acted. Soon he was begging Charles to admit him behind the scenes to be near Fanny's magic presence. Only after he invoked his mother's old friendship with the Kembles did Charles grudgingly consent. All it got the reverend by-blow was a stiff introduction to "my daughter" and the privilege, which he did seem to value, of mooning at her as she skipped into her dressing room. Then at a ball one evening he found his chance and implored her to dance with him.

> [Fanny] had not the slightest objection . . . [but while dancing] I was unpleasantly struck with the decidedly irreverent tone of my partner's remarks. . . . seeing me exchange signs of amicable familiarity with some one across the room, [he] said ". . . Oh, your father. You are very fond of him, ain't you?" . . . And then followed an expression of his filial disrespect for the highest person in the realm, of such a robust significance as fairly took away my breath.

She told him to change his tone or take her back to her chair. He apologized and gave her "a short sketch of his life . . . [he was] not bred to the Church and had the greatest disinclination to taking orders . . . the navy being the career he preferred . . . but . . . in consequence of the death of a brother he had seen literally taken from on board ship and . . . compelled to go into the Church." He seemed to envy her " 'natural turn for religion' "[23] and asked her to write sermons for him, since he lacked the knack. When she laughed at him he said aggrievedly that her friend, the Honorable Mrs. Norton, had been thus helping him. What a pity that old Roger Kemble, only two decades gone, who had wanted coat armor he could clearly call his own, could not hear his granddaughter laughing in the face of a dynastic peer of Don John of Austria and the Duke of Berwick!

There were hazards, of course, in this subculture geared to take in its own glittering washing. The data are scanty but it is clear that in the spring of 1831, in her second season at Covent Garden, Fanny learned about that. The context mingled high life and histrionics. Leveson-Gower, the kind neighbor at Weybridge, had done an admired verse translation of Victor Hugo's *Hernani*. His sort of people were given to amateur theatricals. How amusing it would be to stage it with a caste of nobility and gentry and persuade dear little Miss Kemble to lend it special interest in the female lead, Donna Sol. Miss Kemble would be "excessively amused [though] it will take up a terrible deal of my time, for I am sure they will need rehearsals without end."[24] The first two performances at Bridgewater House, the author's family mansion in London, went so well that royalty asked for a third and round the project clustered all sorts of informal parties and visits here and there.

The fateful element was the leading man, Augustus Craven, son of a younger son of Baron Craven, and a renowned amateur actor. It amused Fanny to learn that she and he had already met: in her Paris schooldays she went to her first ball at a nearby pension for young gentlemen of whom Craven had been one. The conjunction was rather too propitious. Amateur theatricals were, as mothers of marriageable girls well knew, a fine way to "get young people together" in spite of the stiff restrictions then customary. Matters developed fast during a week at Oatlands with Craven among the Leveson-Gowers' guests. Thérèse was chaperoning, of course, but it was June in the English countryside and much bucolic activity set a tone favorable to close acquaintance and "serious consequences . . . an ephemeral love."[25]

The story pieces together in Fanny's journal. Here are host, hostess, and the young folks on "a charming, meandering ride"; and in the evening telling "terrifical ghost stories." They all go rowing with Lady Francis, Thérèse, and Fanny singing softly in time with the oars. Then Charles writes to Fanny that Covent Garden won't need her for a few more days and "in the evening Mr. [Craven] and I acted some of Racine's 'Andromaque' . . . then two scenes from

Scribe's pretty piece '*les premières Amours*' [*sic*]. He acts French capi-
tally,"[26] and also came up with ingratiatingly ridiculous puns in
French.

At this point something committing may have happened between the two, for back in London a few days later "Mrs. Jameson
came and sat with me. . . . We talked of marriage, and a woman's
chance of happiness in giving her life into another's keeping. I said
I thought if one did not expect too much one might secure a reason-
ably fair amount of happiness, though . . . the risk . . . was immense. I never shall forget the expression on her face . . . it has
haunted me ever since."[27] Anna Murphy Jameson wrote *The Diary of
an Ennuyée*, a much admired semiautobiographical novel recommending travel on the Continent as anodyne for heartbreak; but the heroine
dies of "a decline," whereas her creator lived on in a prolonged, toil-
some career as lady-litterateur. She had reason for dismay at the mention of marriage, for hers with a peevish, shiftless young lawyer was
calamitous. Now her fleetingly agonized expression followed by
pointed lack of comment were good preparation for the advice that
Aunt Dall gave a month later during the summer tour. Marriage
outside the profession, she pointed out, almost always meant leaving
the stage and " 'your position in society is both a pleasanter and a
more distinguished one than your birth or real station entitles you to.
. . . [That] probably would alter for the worse if you left the
stage.' " After this caution from a woman whose own hopes of marrying off the stage had been thwarted, Fanny "took up Dante, and
read about devils boiled in pitch, which . . . cheered my spirits very
much."[28] Soon she was writing to Harriet that Juliet could never be
an alter ego for her; the only thing Miss Capulet says with which
Fanny feels consonance is her misgiving about plighting her troth to
Romeo—"too rash, too unadvised, too sudden." Acting just now
seems very hard work but "easy work, if there is such a thing, would
not be best for me just now."[29] Riding out of Exeter one afternoon,
Charles and Fanny come on a Gypsy woman whose standard patter
about love, children, and crossing water also included a promise that
the end of Fanny's summer would be happier than its beginning.
"That may very easily be,"[30] said Fanny and gave her a shilling.

For Aunt Dall, burned child, reluctance to see Fanny marry

above her socioprofessional level may have been stronger than the actual situation called for. British nobility were slightly unstiffening about marrying actresses. An early crack in the dam came in 1728 when the Duke of Bolton married Lavinia Fenton, the charmer who created Polly Peachum in *The Beggar's Opera.* As generations passed, such marriages multiplied, very slowly, true, but the curve was upward. By Fanny's time every few years some peer or wealthy baronet grew so fond of an actress that marriage ensued. Several such marriages involved women whom Fanny's family knew: the great Eliza O'Neill, who married Sir William Becher, Bart.; Maria Foote, who, after acquiring three thousand pounds in a breach of promise suit against a wealthy lover, married the Earl of Harrington; Miss Mellon, a rather rowdy comedienne, first married Thomas Coutts, the great banker, and, after he died, the Duke of St. Albans, who made no objection to the great legacy-fortune that came with her. True, dowagers' heads were shaken and ungenerous jokes cracked in the clubs. It is significant that practically no such unions took place between peers' daughters and irresistible leading men. In sexual and cultural terms the flavor of King Cophetua was strong, unmistakably *de haut en bas.*[31] But to its credit Mayfair often swallowed beautiful women interlopers with little or no gulping, and their offspring were likely to be more or less accepted.[32] It was good practice for the approaching wave of titled Britons marrying American plutocrats' daughters—and fortunes.

Such precedents failed Fanny and Craven, however, for one crass reason: Those marriages had what this star-crossed pair lacked—ample income. Craven had little future beyond minor diplomatic posts at salaries far too low to support a wife in any manner conceivable in his social situation. His other assets were what one may assume to have been good looks, proper manners, and amusing ways. Doubtless Thérèse made the most of such practical shortcomings. How much did her and Aunt Dall's representations weigh with Fanny? And even supposing her residual levelheadedness failed her, Craven's zeal may have waned as practical counsel reared its ugly head among his people as well as hers. Anyway, the engagement, which obviously had been serious, somehow broke off, and Fanny took it hard, to judge from her journal six months later: "I think I should like to go to Oatlands once more—oi me, oi me—how changed it would appear for now all things are winter and when I was last there summer was in my heart."[33] In the middle of the following summer Charles and she are in Liverpool about to embark for America. They have been drawing packed houses and the approaching voyage should have supplied further mental distraction. But on a biting cold Sunday, when even chillproof Britons had to have a sitting-room fire in late July, the pangs of the old parting, whatever it had been like, came back: "I did not think there was such another day in store for me as this. I thought all that was past and over, and had forgotten the last drop in the bitter cup."[34]

Weeks later, after a long, rough voyage has landed her in a New World, she still has to take to versifying to relieve emotionally poignant harkings-back:

> What though a brighter sky bends o'er
> Scenes where no former image greets me,
> Though lost in paths untrod before,
> Here, even here, pale memory meets me.[35]

As to Craven, she did not yet know her luck. He secured a diplomatic post at Naples; presently came into a legacy of fourteen thousand pounds; on the strength of it married the clever, penniless daughter of a Breton noble house; went through the money instead of investing it for the adequate income it could have supplied; and eventually his wife had to support them both with chancy earnings from writing novels some of which were popular. In 1836, apparently before the money was gone, Fanny saw them in London: "Who do you think Adelaide and I went to dinner with last Friday? . . . the [Cravens] she sought me with apparent cordiality and I had no reason whatever for avoiding her. She is very handsome . . . [and] remarkably amiable, with the simple good breeding of a great French lady, and the serious earnestness of a devout Roman Catholic. They are going to Lisbon, where he is Attaché to the Embassy."[36] Apparently Mrs. Craven also greatly approved of Fanny. Thirty-odd years later she wrote a small book in praise of Fanny's first autobiography, which contains, most thinly disguised, the inconsequential little story of how Hernani and Donna Sol did not marry after all.

V

White Elephant, Red Ink

FANNY'S EMOTIONAL CRISES need not obscure those of the other Kembles. Toward the end of Charles and Fanny's first tour in 1830 John Mitchell became a cause for anxiety—no less acute because for a while the matter was kept from Thérèse. That was a year of revolutions or attempts at them, and John now wrote that instead of pursuing theology in Germany, he was in Gibraltar joining several of his Apostle friends in a certain General Torrijos' liberal plot to overthrow the royal Spanish government. He chose Fanny to be recipient of this news and warned her not to try to write to him in admiration, expostulation, or anything else.

The leader of the group was John Sterling, a notably brilliant Apostle who had made friends with Torrijos y Cia., picturesque exiles in London. The financing came largely from Robert Boyd, a young former Indian Army officer who, wishing to do something spirited with a legacy of five thousand pounds, had bought with part of it a surplus Royal Navy gunboat that might come in handy. Alfred Tennyson and Arthur Hallam went to the Pyrenees for liaison with Torrijos's adherents in the north. Theirs was immediate frustration. Sterling fell too sick to go filibustering but he smuggled Torrijos y Cia. over to the Continent, and Kemble, Boyd, and Richard Trench—later archbishop of Dublin—followed them on their own.

Motives were ingenuously impeccable, perseverance exemplary.[1] For months the British governor of Gibraltar looked the other way while the conspirators tried to set Spain on fire. Between episodes,

Trench told Fanny later, "they passed their time smoking and drinking ale, John holding forth upon German metaphysics . . . dense in
proportion as the tobacco fumes grew thick and his glass empty."
John's few letters home were turgidly optimistic but plans kept on
being thwarted and skirmishes fizzling out. "I would give anything
to see him," Fanny wrote to Harriet, ". . . but I fear to wish him
back among us. I am afraid that he would neither be happy himself,
nor make others so."[2] As the great day persisted in hanging fire,
Trench came home; then, after long delay, John shaved off the beard
he had sworn never to trim until Spain was free and returned to
London. Whatever air of comic opera the affair had vanished when
Torrijos, finally invited to leave Gibraltar, was captured and shot
with his whole entourage, Boyd included.[3]

John's return coincided with the rehearsals for *Hernani* that entangled Fanny with Craven; it was a season to remember. The night
after his arrival Fanny's agitation set her dreaming that "John had
come home . . . [I] flung myself out of bed to run downstairs . . .
and then I remembered that he had come home . . . I had seen and
welcomed him, which . . . I might as well have dreamed . . . and
saved myself the jump out of bed. I hate dreaming; it's like being
mad—having one's brain work without the control of one's will."[4]
John and she got on well enough but without close sympathy. When
he read in a newspaper in Munich that she was to go on the stage, it
made him feel, he said, "the sensation of a cold sword through the
heart"[5]—which ill became a descendant of two generations of actors
then living on the earnings of one. He married Natalie Augusta
Wendt, daughter of a professor at the University of Göttingen, who
proved an uncomfortable spouse, and lived on into his fifties, occasionally singing Spanish revolutionary songs after he had dined well.
His primary value lay, as previously noted, in important researches
into the mysteries of Anglo-Saxon. But he also zealously practiced
Freemasonry, edited the subsidized *British & Foreign Review,* and succeeded his father as Examiner of Stage Plays.

Younger brother Henry had got on well enough at Westminster
School and then in some polish-schooling at Paris. His good looks
and genial temperament made him welcome at the best balls and

parties. But the family were chronically uneasy about him. When they suggested Heidelberg to round him off, Fanny demurred, mistrusting his "sweet, affectionate, gentle disposition . . . easily led and persuaded . . . [he might] turn lord and master of some blue-eyed *fräulein* . . . and become a *dis*-respectable *pater familias* at nineteen." Charles declined to try Germany on another son, and because John's stay in Cambridge had been unsettling, Henry shied away from there. Late in 1831 it remained true that "Henry is too young and too handsome to be . . . lounging about the streets . . . a mere squanderer of time."[6]

He had once inclined toward the Royal Navy. But when an admiral of Charles's acquaintance offered to take him under his wing as midshipman, Thérèse, who had a horror of anything maritime, vetoed the scheme. Soldiering was proposed. Henry acquiesced, Thérèse withheld the veto. Again Charles's acquaintance included the right people: Lord Hill, commander in chief, and Sir John Macdonald, adjutant general. The queer old system of buying commissions— Humphrey Squireen, Esq., paying Lieutenant Spontoon to resign in his favor—still obtained. Under the auspices of Charles's Olympian friends an ensigncy came available. Purchase was financed by the £450 that John Murray paid Fanny for *Francis the First,* which she had put away for some special need. Resplendent in his new uniforms, Henry went to Ireland to join his regiment, which was presently ordered to the West Indies. Thérèse never saw him again; she died in 1838 before he returned.

Originally Fanny had earmarked her £450 to help pay damages in case a suit against her father brought by Charles Malloy Westmacott, editor of the *Age,* a scurrilous London weekly paper, went the wrong way. This takes us back to when horsewhips had more than one use and it was still conceivable for cabinet ministers to fight duels. Westmacott, persuaded that Charles Kemble was snubbing him—in view of the family's dislike of the press and of this particular editor's reputation, it may well have been true—was sniping at the Kembles and their theater. On the opening of Fanny's 1830–1831 season the *Age* ran a sneering commentary on her personal appearance and verses applying to her the term "doxy." Use of it (in the plural) was explicable as rhyme for "empty boxes" in the next line. But the word meant "thieves' whore" if it meant anything and the *Age* had already gone rather farther than even the sordid standards of the day allowed in describing her face as "deficient in dignity," her arms as "unusually red and coarse," her figure as "squat" and "judging from her mama's,"[7] likely to get worse as time went on. Charles gave Westmacott a beating with a walking stick.

It caused talk, mostly approving. When Fanny, who had not read the *Age,* learned what the provocation was, she confessed that, as she told George Combe, "could a comet from heaven have fallen on Mr. Westmacott, I should have been delighted . . . but I was sorry that heaven was pleased to make my father's arm the instrument of its justice."[8] To Harriet she said much the same, but added, "What does my poor, dear father expect, but that I shall be bespattered if I am to live on the highway?"[9] She promised herself that if Westmacott's threatened suit succeeded, she would turn over not only Murray's money, but also whatever she could get for a volume of verse she had in mind.

Actually nothing came of the suit. But henceforth, in view of how handy her £450 was for Henry, her attitude toward publication was peculiar. Her wish to become a professional writer never revived. But she did come more or less to assume that when she needed extra money for a special purpose, she need only show a newborn manuscript to a publisher and a substantial sum would shower down. In America that procedure got her into great trouble. But she never lost faith in it, to an extent that a hard-pressed hack would find exasperating.

In that eventful June of 1831, when Fanny played in *Hernani* and John Mitchell came back from Spain, Sarah Siddons died. She had long been failing. It was less a shock, public or private, than an occasion for contemplating her glorious past. Fanny "could not be much grieved for myself . . . I had but little intercourse with her, though she was always very kind to me." Gratefully she remembered the previous Christmas when Melpomene could still preside over a reunion of "her clan, more than three dozen strong; some of them so handsome, and many with a striking likeness to herself."[10] But the great woman was somehow always at arm's length. Fanny could say both that though this was "a great dramatic genius . . . off the stage [she] gave not the slightest indication of unusual intellectual capacity"; and with a touch of awe, "I wonder if she has gone where Milton and Shakespeare are, to whose worship she was priestess all her life."[11]

Her strong sense of her aunt's prowess suffused her when Covent Garden's management—in which Charles had only a minority voice—set Fanny doing Constance in Shakespeare's *King John*, another of Mrs. Siddons's greatest roles. They even made her a headdress like Melpomene's in the part. The girl was painfully aware that her immaturity made such a challenge doubly inadvisable. For Constance was no tear-jerking heroine of unidentified age like Isabella or Belvidera but a majestic great lady with charm as well as momentous troubles and the tongue of a royal fishwife: "I am horribly frightened; it is a cruel weight to lay on my shoulders." The actual performance so agitated her that she went psychogenically deaf and averred that she heard hardly a word she herself uttered even in Constance's violent diatribes, and then had a prolonged fit of weeping on her dressing room floor. Later she learned that it had gone swimmingly. Even Thérèse allowed, "You have done it better than. . . . any other girl of your age would do it."[12] Two days and she was recovered enough to repeat the role without emotional storms and giddily report to Harriet on that dinner at Lord Melbourne's: "I fell out of my love for our host (who, moreover, is absorbed by Mrs. Norton) and into another love with Lord——, who is one of the most beautiful creatures of the male sex I ever saw; unluckily, he is . . . neither as old nor as decrepit . . . as the nobleman I am to marry . . . so he won't do. . . . We are going to a party at Devonshire House to-night."[13]

Awareness of her handicaps, some irreparably physical, some psychological, some technical, heightened for Fanny certain strains familiar to actresses. Thus in her third season Covent Garden, probably hoping to exploit Mayfair's interest in an author of its own, cast Charles and Fanny in *Katharine of Cleves*, Leveson-Gower's blank verse adaptation of a French piece in which the famous Mlle. Mars had done great things. "A . . . melodramatic, pantomimic part that I have no capacity for," Fanny told her journal, ". . . neither in the first nor the last scene are my legs long enough to do justice to the lady." It went well, however. "My mother came down from her box and seemed much pleased with me." But "I was so tired I could scarcely stand" and the fashionable party that followed was so wearing that "I had a most wretched night . . . dreaming I was out in my part [forgetting her lines] and jumping up in bed, and all sorts of agonies." [14]

Fanny was also uneasy about adding Beatrice of *Much Ado* and Lady Teazle of *The School for Scandal* to her repertory for change of pace. She mistrusted herself in comedy as well as queenly parts; indeed she once said that she had never got the hang of comedy until, after she quit the stage altogether, her platform readings of Rosalind, Falstaff, Malvolio, et al. firmed up her touch. Thérèse, grooming her for Beatrice, once told her she was like the chief mourner at a funeral. That was probably coach's shock therapy, hard to reconcile with this girl already holding her own in the sprightly give-and-take of the great world. And in time she felt rather at home with Beatrice, if less so with Lady Teazle, and could get through hyperfrivolous Lady Townley (in Farquhar's *The Provoked Husband*) and the hypervivacious Bisarre (in his *The Inconstant*) more or less creditably. But her heart stayed with roles that—assuming she had to act—she could get her teeth into.

What that meant is clearer when one considers the only role she ever chose for herself outside Shakespeare—Camiola, heroine of Massinger's *The Maid of Honour*. It came to her notice through two cultivated and stage-minded clergymen. The Reverend William Harness gave Fanny a copy of Massinger's plays as newly edited by the Reverend Alexander Dyce, another friend of the family and an authority on the old drama. "Edited" with a vengeance! To fit Massinger for family reading and to guide actors fearing to offend, Dyce did for him what the immortal Thomas Bowdler had done a decade earlier for Shakespeare—cleaned him up by suppressing overt lewdnesses. Fanny, previously unacquainted with most of Massinger, was much taken with it, specially *The Maid of Honour*, the theatrical merits of which the blue pencil had not much harmed. The plot was another of those Italianate monstrosities, the leading male role morally grotesque, as Fanny soon realized. But the blank verse is temptingly crisp and one can see why she wanted to do the heroine. Mistress of a great fortune in her own right, Camiola lavishes devotion on the warrior-hero, only to be jilted for an importunate duchess. She puts him in his place first by publicly convicting him of dishonorable behavior, then, when he capitulates, spurns him by proclaiming herself the bride of Christ and taking the veil. Clear-minded and strong, she transcends the world of fumbling, lascivious men; Fanny's hankering for the role, like her admiration of Portia, was probably part of her inchoate feminism. She was persuaded it was the best acting she ever did, and the audiences seem to have agreed that though the play itself left them rather cold, she handled it very well.

The cuts that Dyce felt necessary were neither many nor long in this case—occasionally such lines as "Virgins of giant size are sluggards at the sport"; "Which of your grooms . . . ministers night physic to you?"; "Queens themselves . . . only aiming to feed their carnal appetites . . . in some kind commit authorized whoredom." Since Fanny was accustomed, like other actors, to much more drastic cleanings-up, she may never have bothered to check the unbowdlerized text to see what the reverend editor spared the audience and her. She had no quarrel with the principle of "purified editions" that enabled worthy old works to come down off dusty shelves. She told Anna Jameson that "sweeping these fine dramas clean is a good work that cannot be too much commended."[15] Thus *Venice Preserved* as Mrs. Siddons—and Fanny—played it lacked Otway's scenes between the dirty-old-man senator and the scornful courtesan in whose house the conspirators meet. The reading versions of Shakespeare that Fanny took over from Charles dropped Hamlet's sneering pun about "country matters"; the more specific stanza of Ophelia's song; Iago's pungencies about Othello and Desdemona; the nurse's fond leerings about baby Juliet's falling on her back.

The spirit of such surgery was stated well in the previous century when Garrick explained how he adapted that gem of grinning lewdness, William Wycherley's *The Country Wife;* "The most enter-

taining parts of this play, to the age for which it was written, are
precisely those which the purer taste of the present would reject
. . . judicious alterations have rendered it worthy the approbation of
the public."[16] Note that that was written three generations before
the little princess came to her throne to lend her name to "Victorian
prudery,"[17] a phenomenon very firmly established during the two
previous reigns. It was already part of Fanny's Regency matrix, and
throughout her long life her standards of stage decorum were stiff.
She vastly admired great dancers but deplored the inordinate display
of legs inevitable in the ballet. She was appalled by the enthusiasm
with which a West End audience, women as well as men, applauded
a French company in a farce, *Vert Vert,* in which a certain Mlle.
Déjazet played an adolescent boy in men's clothes, knee breeches, and
silk stockings. (She forgot—it's hardly possible she did not know—
that one of her own mother's first successes had been in such a
"breeches part.") And she was proportionately disgusted a generation
later by the right-up-to-there tights and very low bodices—only
slightly less candid than the current Playboy Bunny's uniform—that
went with Offenbach's travesty-operas and the *Black Crook* sort of
thing.

She was aware that cleaning up might go to absurd lengths.
Thérèse and she hooted on learning that Benvolio's joke about shirts
and smocks had to be cut from *Romeo & Juliet* because "body linen"
could not be mentioned before the refined audience of Bath. But not
even her growing reverence for Shakespeare tempted her to forbid Nice
Nelly to delete his grosser salacities from public performances. As to
censorship generally neither she nor Charles felt uneasy about his and
then his son's serving as Examiner of Plays—the official under the
Lord Chamberlain who passed on all play scripts produced in Britain
in order to bar anything imperiling morality or the public interest.
That power, and its necessity, was taken for granted.

In all this she was child of her time, of course. In a culture
committed to *tabu* on certain words—or objects—to throw them at
an audience makes for disproportionate emphasis and distorts dramatic values. Had Covent Garden allowed Camiola's waiting woman
to swear by her virginity, as Massinger wrote the part, or had the

comic-fop character assured Camiola that "I mean not to ride you," the dignity that Fanny valued in the role would have been irreparably impaired. Indeed only fanatic defense of a constitutional right to double entendre could deny that to excise many of Shakespeare's often rather lugged-in gamy touches does his plays little harm. It is true that to clean up Chaucer's "Miller's Tale" would be to destroy a masterpiece of lewd storytelling in joyous verse. But those prudish cuts unquestionably improved *Venice Preserved*.

In one way such surgery was part of a broader, long-established tradition. For some two centuries theater managers had been carving up or adding to august scripts—not only Shakespeare and Massinger, but also Wycherly, Mrs. Centlivre, et al.—to adapt them to given actors' styles or new kinds of staging or to eliminate what seemed to them—and often were—weak spots. Or it could be a mere matter of running time. Today's producers of Shakespeare usually cut him down to keep within our audiences' attention span. Fanny distrusted such tinkerings. She deplored Garrick's innovation, become standard practice, of hoking up the end of *Romeo & Juliet* with a pretentious funeral procession and was severe on thus meddling with one's betters.

The public's failure to warm up to *The Maid of Honour* kept Fanny from enlisting it as another strong item in her repertory. But earlier in 1831 she had added a good one, doing very well indeed by the role of Bianca, heroine of Milman's *Fazio,* a standard Italianate tragedy better written than most and not quite as absurd. The finale is, however, unfortunately typical: Aldabella, the local siren, has lured away Fazio, Bianca's husband. Resenting this, Bianca denounces him to the law for a great theft complicated by suspicion of murder. Her remorse when he is condemned to death moves her to beseech Aldabella to beg him off from the authorities. She refuses, Fazio is executed, Bianca denounces Aldabella as corrupting occasion of it all and succeeds in getting her sentenced to spend the rest of her life in a nunnery. Then Bianca dies of heartbreak, making the diagnosis very clear with her last words: "It breaks—it breaks—it is not iron." Curtain. Fanny once admitted that some time she would like to try playing "that naughty woman Aldabella,"[18] but she never did; and it was probably just as well. She did play an equally naughty queen a few times—Louise of Savoy in her own *Francis the First,* at Covent Garden that same winter. She was against doing so: "[I] would rather forfeit . . . a hundred . . . pounds . . . this play . . . ought not to be acted at all."[19] But she went along to keep peace in the managerial family.

Neither party to the dispute was wrong. The printed play had been widely read and rather admired. Curiosity to see it staged did fill the house a few nights with Fanny wisely letting beautiful, tall Ellen Tree handle the heroine while she imbued the villainous queen mother with smoldering energy. But even though Charles, a masterly play-doctor, had cut and rearranged it, the script did little for either lady. Almost at once Fanny was rewarded for being cooperative. Sheridan Knowles, an able actor-playwright, brought Charles a new comedy, *The Hunchback,* that proved to have a brilliant future. Its heroine, Julia, was the only leading role that Fanny ever "created," making the most of the rich variety of moods and emotions leading to its denouement. Julia's hunchbacked[20] guardian (whom Knowles played himself) proves to be her actual father, a nobleman, etc., etc. But for all her pleasure in letting herself go in a suitable part, Fanny was clearheaded about the script: "The plot is so confused and obscure that nobody to my knowledge (not even the author himself, of whom I once asked an explanation of it) was ever able to . . . give a plausible account of it. . . . a very satisfactory play to *see,* but let nobody who has seen it well acted attempt to read it in cold blood."[21] I have never seen it acted; but reading it does make me respect the flair enabling Charles and Fanny to see opportunity in it.

A particularly extensive repertory was needed, for an overseas venture was imminent. Covent Garden was still in danger from residual debt and internally from legal squabbles among its stockholders. As early as the *Hernani*-Craven affair the Kemble family council was weighing the advisability of touring America to gain money safe from creditors if the endless Chancery suits hanging over Charles should go the wrong way. The scheme had points. Less-distinguished actors had reaped golden harvests over there. So while miserable over Craven and

anxious about John Mitchell, Fanny also had gnawing at her the prospect of what she thought of as "that dreadful America . . . I do hate
the very thought of America."[22] Yet when Charles offered to go
alone, daughterly solicitude would have none of that; and on the
practical side, Fanny's acting opposite her father would more than
double chances of success in such a foray. By the end of 1831 she was
daydreaming about trouping America until her share of the winnings
reached ten thousand pounds, then returning to England, making the
round of the provinces, acting in London for a few nights of leave-
taking and then—glorious prospect!—farewell forever to the stage.
Mrs. Whitelock, Mrs. Siddons, and John Philip had thus retired on
a funded income in their declining years. Why shouldn't their niece
do so at an age when she could still do anything she liked?

Presently Charles's affairs were so threatening that he sold the
horse Fanny had given him because he could no longer afford its
upkeep.

> When from day to day [he] may be obliged to declare
> himself insolvent, [Fanny told her journal] keeping a
> horse does seem rather absurd. . . . From my earliest
> childhood this has been hanging over us . . . The house
> must go, the carriage must go, the horses must go. . . .
> It is pitiful to see how my father clings to that theatre.
> . . . Even today . . . he exclaimed, "Oh, if I had
> £10,000, I could set it all right again. . . ." My mother
> and I actually stared at this infatuation. If I had . . . a
> hundred thousand pounds, not one farthing would I give
> to the redeeming of that fatal millstone . . . we need not
> starve . . . as long as God keeps us healthy in body and
> mind, nothing need signify, provided we are not obliged
> to go off to that dreadful America.[23]

Five months later that was where Charles, Aunt Dall, and Fanny were
bound for what was planned to be two years. Thérèse; John, absorbed
in Anglo-Saxon; and Totty, now Miss Adelaide, a young beauty; were
left to ponder what would come of it all.

The first step was the farewell performance in London—*The
Hunchback,* June 22, 1832. Fanny's final curtain-call, all shouts and
waving hats and handkerchiefs, had her so teary that she could not

remember afterward whether she had made curtsies. But she knew she had thrown kiss after kiss to the house along with the flowers from her girdle. The men in the pit fought madly for them. Farewell to the old property-man and "my good, pretty little maid . . . sobbing by my dressing-room door" and to Covent Garden itself, "[which] my Uncle John built; where he and my aunt took leave of the stage, and I made my first entrance." [24]

Engagements at Edinburgh and Liverpool came before sailing to fatten the war chest. Rail service from London to Edinburgh did not yet exist but steam was already undermining the stagecoach with a new steamship service from Greenwich to Edinburgh's port of Leith. Salt water or not, Thérèse sailed thither along with the party to have another week with them, coming back the same way. From their window in Edinburgh Charles and Fanny watched the sailing of the return steamer, "moving fast . . . the dark smoky wake . . . warning us how soon it would be beyond the ken of our aching eyes." [25] Edinburgh's audiences were still less demonstrative than Fanny liked but they filled the house and it was reassuring that even *Francis the First*—Fanny now playing the heroine—went well enough.

Her beloved town afforded her the perking up that she needed. She saw much of the Combes and spent an afternoon sitting on the floor of George's phrenological museum with her lap full of skulls while he explained the significance of their irregularities. Among other old friends seen was "that enchanting old sweetheart of mine, Baron Hume . . . devoutly kissing the tip of my little finger. . . . These old beaux beat the young ones hollow. . . . Commend me to this bowing and finger-kissing. . . . be-Madaming, too, has in it something singularly pleasing . . . there's a hoop and six yards of brocade in each of its two syllables." [26] She developed a troop of three or four gentlemen to ride with her daily. On their last such outing, seeing a sprig of heather decorating Fanny's habit, they organized an order of knighthood devoted to her—badge a bit of heather—and pledged to meet and drink her health every fourteenth of July until she came back.

Two days later Charles, Aunt Dall, and Fanny were in Liverpool, going profitably through their histrionic paces and preparing for the great leap westward. Harriet St. Leger came over from Ireland to stay with them until they—and twenty-one trunks of costumes and props—sailed on August 1, 1832, in the American packet ship *Pacific* of the Black Ball Line, for New York City.

What sort of young woman was it whom family destiny thus sent to the New World for good or ill—and as it worked out, plenty of each? She was no conventional beauty. Ruefully she told how Harness, coming backstage after seeing her play Camiola, asked, " 'But do you contrive to make yourself so beautiful?' "; and how Emily FitzHugh's mother, Mrs. Siddons's intimate friend, said in affectionate exasperation, " 'Fanny Kemble, you are the ugliest and handsomest woman in London!' "[27] In America three years later young Robert E. Lee reported to a West Point classmate that though on stage Miss Kemble "surpasses any performer I ever saw [and] is beautiful," in the ballroom "she is next door to homely . . . I could not recognize her as the being I had so much admired."[28] The previous December in Philadelphia a local belle told her mother that people at a party had been disappointed when "instead of the graceful and elegant female they had seen on the stage, they beheld a dark complexioned, unhappy, diminutive little person who looked as if . . . studying the character of a witch."[29] One cause of this contrast was go-as-you-please Fanny's developing scorn for the protection then expected against weathering of women's skins: "With hair and eyes as dark as mine, a gipsy complexion doesn't signify, and I prefer burning my skin to suffocating under silk-handkerchiefs, sun-bonnets, and two or three gauze veils."[30] Next year at Newport Fanny Appleton, soon to become one of Fanny's best friends, who already thought her fascinating, nevertheless noted, "By exposure to the sun she is burned to a bright mahogany color and yet wears every evening a white muslin with bare neck and gloveless arms."[31]

Do not, however, think of Fanny as what the French call a *jolie laide*. The full chin balanced the Kemble nose. The mouth hinted both wistfulness and sauciness. The pose of the smallish head was charmingly alert. So far the data are reliable. Then discussion falters because during the first three decades, when presumably she looked

her best, photography did not exist, and when it came along, was
unfair to what age and trouble had left of the girl whom Lawrence
drew so fondly. She not only liked that drawing, she sensed in it a
tinge of Lawrence's talent for intimacy. It does not much resemble
most of her many portraits. But then they also are wildly inconsistent
among themselves. Though all are striking and most of them attractive—indeed some, in spite of Jeffrey, downright pretty—no two are
markedly alike except in the features mentioned above. She was half-
amusedly aware of this herself and once thought of never again letting
anybody try to "[paint] me as I am, which is any thing but what I
look like,"[32] a notable flash of cryptic insight. As for the clumsy
engravings from lithographs of the Lawrence drawing and the cheap
woodcuts of "Miss Kemble" in various roles that were in all the shops
and now clutter up theatrical iconography, any one is worse and less
reliable than any other.

No measurements survive but Fanny freely conceded that she
was stubby even for a time when five feet four was tall for a woman.
The only thing she liked about doing *The Grecian Daughter* was that
the heroine's high-waisted, long-line costume made her look taller.
Otherwise she had to fall back on the family fund of stage presence
and the noble, confident carriage that she owed to Thérèse and the
sergeant. Overweight crept up on her in middle age, as it did on all
the Kemble women, but until after the birth of her second child, her
waist was daintily slender. That does not imply lack of substance.
When her actor-cousin, John Kemble Mason, doing Romeo to her
Juliet, first picked her up on stage, he whispered to her, " 'Jove,
Fanny, you *are* a lift!' " She rather liked being called "the Shetland
pony."[33] Maybe her insistence on doing things her own way, as well
as her compact, surefooted style, suggested that nickname. Sometimes she mentioned another animal as worth resembling—a tigress
in the London zoo that she admired not for predatory disposition but
for liquid sureness of motion and integrated power.

For domestic cats she seems to have cared little. Large, beauti-
ful dogs she found irresistible. During those days with Craven at
Oatlands she encountered "a monstrous and most beautiful dog whom
I should like to have hugged, but that he looked so grave and wise

it seemed like a liberty." At Covent Garden a friend brought his Newfoundland backstage to see her: "His solemnity, when he was desired to keep still while the rehearsal [of *Francis the First*] was going on, was magnificent, considering the stuff he must have thought it."[34] In New York a Newfoundland puppy named Neptune so delighted her that his owner gave him to her. There are fates worse than to have been Fanny Kemble's Neptune or the handsome and devoted Irish setter whom years later she kept for her son-in-law.

About horses this ardent horsewoman seems to have been rather impersonal. That she was kind to her mounts goes without saying. But she was likelier to comment on a horse's gaits than on its disposition. There was one poignant exception: For some years toward the end of her marriage she owned and rode whenever possible a tall bay named Forrester (after the brother characters in her best play, *An English Tragedy*) that she loved dearly: "A capital horse . . . who grins with delight when I talk to him and pat him . . . high courage and good temper. I do not like to think what would become of me if anything were to happen to him."[35] Something did. Relations between her and her American husband, Pierce Butler, were grinding toward disaster and her despair was about as deep as his growing vindictiveness was mordant. Probably with economy as pretext but unquestionably out of sheer meanness he sold Forrester to a liveryman. Fanny sold a publisher a volume of her verses for enough money to buy Forrester back. But Butler was not long thwarted: the horse had a fall, dislocated a hip, and had to be shot.

In Britain Fanny rode decorously in company with friends or father or brother as escort. In America she often rode alone, which caused comment. In the country her near-isolation probably made escort hard to come by. Yet there may have been more to it. Her best remedy for "the blue devils," she said, was "violent bodily exercise, riding, or climbing up steep and rugged pathways."[36] And aloneness tended to become part of the tonic quality sought. During her breezy explorations of Edinburgh she had usually been alone. Now hear her on a bitterly cold evening in New York; she has been paying calls in a hired hack and comes out of the last house into rousing weather:

The keen cutting wind whizzed along the streets, huge masses of dark clouds, with soft brown edges, lay in the pale delicate blue of the evening sky. The moon was up, clear, cold, and radiant . . . a few men buttoned up to their chins, and women wrapped in cloaks, were scudding along . . . I determined to walk home, and bade the hack follow me. I walked tremendously fast, enjoying the fresh breath of the north. . . . How I do like walking alone; for this alone I wish I were a man.

And apropos a crowded steamboat: "There is no moment . . . when I would not rather be alone . . . feeling, as I often do, the society of even those I love a burthen."[37]

This preference for solitude blended with her love of water in motion. Heavy surf went straight to her head: "I feel *strong,* as I run by the side of the big waves . . . the same . . . wild excitement which thunder and lightning produce in me. . . . I have felt taller by three inches . . . [and] three times more vigorous . . . when running by the sea."[38] She shared the Romantics' passion for waterfalls but outdid most of them in fascination with merely lively streams: "A pool in a rocky basin, with foaming water dashing in and out of it, was a sort of trap for me,"[39] often forcing her to doff shoes and stockings. Sometimes she just walked in fully dressed and sat down. She might ascribe her soaking skirts to having slipped and fallen in but close acquaintances knew better. Undine the watersprite whom she read about at Heath Farm—dangerous to marry and systemically reflecting the vagaries of oxide of hydrogen—must be added to Diana Vernon as a literary phantom shaping Fanny Kemble. "Poor poor Undine, how often I think of her!"[40] she told her journal soon after the frustrating Craven crisis.

Yet she could also curb masterful whims. Back then the British chambermaid's early duty was to light a fire ready laid in the bedroom to take the edge off the chill before the occupant arose. The kindling blaze so attracted Fanny that she forbade maids to light fires for her, instead crept out of bed to do it herself and then huddled on the hearth watching the spread and growth of the flames and losing herself in the ensuing glow. That might immobilize her until half the morning was gone. So, calling on the self-discipline that Thérèse inculcated, she renounced fire lighting as she had renounced Byron, confessing, however, that she envied the servant who did it for her.

By itself that might show frivolous insensitivity to how it felt to be assigned by society to light fires for others on cold mornings. On the whole, however, her social imagination was better than that. Though, reared as and when she was, she could hardly conceive of having to live any considerable time without servants, she never left the cleaning of her birdcages to them. She said it was she who owned and enjoyed the birds, and it was unfair not to assume the consequent unpleasantness. When Elizabeth Fry, Quaker pioneer in solicitous penology, took young Fanny to join a party of ladies visiting Newgate prison to do the women prisoners good, the girl came away backhandedly dismayed. As Friend Elizabeth, with the best intentions in the world, gently exhorted these unfortunates, "their less excusable sister sinners of the better class" sat smiling opposite in a condescending row: "I hardly dared to look at the [women convicts] . . . I felt broken-hearted for *them* and ashamed for [me]."[41]

In Baltimore next year an acquaintance's account of the sweated wages and bad conditions in a factory he owned horrified her. She rejected his excuse that to treat his labor force better would so raise costs as to put him at disadvantage with competitors whose standards were comparable. Her denunciation of that attitude could have come from a Marxist—only at the time there was no such thing—infected with religion. She ended by laying it down that "happiness might and did exist most blessedly upon half the means which men spent their lives in scraping together. . . . My Father laughed, and said I was the last person in the world who could live on little. . . . I looked at my satin gown, and held my tongue, but still I was not convinced."[42]

Yet, for all the "irregular and passionate vehemence"[43] of which she quite justly accused herself, she could recognize a good case against herself and act on it. An example in a strangely archaic context: That fall in New York City she was dancing her slippers off at an evening party when she learned that another guest, the Reverend Dr. Jonathan Mayhew Wainwright, whom she had met and liked, had gone home when waltzing began because he could not countenance it by staying. This German innovation was frowned on by many who saw no harm in quadrilles and reels. Next day Wainwright came to call and read Fanny a courteous lecture about waltzing, making "perfectly good sense, to which I could reply nothing whatever . . . I promised him never to waltz again, except with a woman, or my brother"[44]—a genuine if petty sacrifice for a girl of twenty-two who loved waltzing almost as much as raspberry tarts or running water.

So sober a decision implies no lapse in her ebullience. In her first months in America youthful brashness called most of the tunes: "I wish somebody would explain to me every thing in this world that I can't make out . . . I wish I could make myself draw. I want to do every thing in the world that can be done."[45] She had a right to presume on her versatility. At this stage her compact person contained a frivolous dancer-till-daylight-doth-appear; a loyal disciple of walk-run-and-breathe-deep; a romantic blue-stocking scribbler; a quasi-tomboy who rode horses thought too powerful or high-strung for ladies; a stage professional who knew the show must go on at all costs; a member of a small but weighty clan well aware of its prestige; an anything-for-a-lark picnicker and diner-out; a self-dedicated seeker after religious truth; a biologically normal young woman made for involvement with the opposite sex and ensuing reproduction. . . . No wonder that artists had difficulty catching a likeness that would correspond with any other artist's version. They were heavily handicapped by the protean quality noted years later by Fredrika Bremer, a Swedish novelist-feminist then prominent in Britain and America. Miss Bremer had been having a heavy cold. Fanny, coming to call, said I do hope you are feeling well enough to have visitors. Oh, yes, my dear, Miss Bremer said, visitors permitted; only "I do not know that I ought to see *so many people as you are.*"[46]

VI

That Dreadful America

CIRCA 1830—just before steam began to take over on blue water—American-built, -owned and -officered square-rigged sailing packets dominated the mail, fast freight and passenger trades of the North Atlantic. Better designed, more stoutly constructed and more boldly handled than their European competitors, they were at once reliable and relatively fast. In terms of later expectation their speed was, of course, no great thing. Even these crack vessels averaged no better than four weeks westbound (against the prevailing winds) and three eastbound; whereas transatlantic steamers eventually got it down to five days. The contrast in size is also striking. The packets of the Black Ball, Swallowtail, and other American lines were structurally beautiful if not quite so fine-shaped as the long-voyage clippers soon became. But to us they would have looked alarmingly small. The Black Ball's *Pacific,* the Kembles' ship, was above average at 568 tons—only half again as long as today's harbor tug.

Doubtless the Kembles should have chosen the *Siddons* of the Dramatic Line, which also had *Garrick, Sheridan* and *Roscius.* But their need to reach New York at the start of the theatrical season put them into the *Pacific* where they were, as matters then went, very well off. Her captain, "a very intelligent, good-natured person; rough and bluff,"[1] was, Fanny learned to her surprise, only five years her senior. American packet-owners liked young officers inclined to carry sail in a style to turn a British seaman's hair white yet handling these ships' advantages so well that the underwriters allowed them specially low premiums. The *Pacific* lived up to American packets' reputation for generous eating and drinking and ornate quarters all velvet cushions and gilt mirrors. She even had a special "roundhouse" superstructure above the ladies' cabin as a sort of seagoing drawing room—particularly thoughtful because women passengers were few. Again, however, she offered little that those remembering the old *Queen Mary* or *Ile de France* would consider comfort. Sleeping accommodations, segregated by sexes, were in some respects no more commodious and certainly less sanitary than those of a representative penitentiary today.[2] The twenty-odd passengers sitting down with the Kembles for the first dinner aboard ("champagne, and desert [*sic*], and every luxury imaginable") were all "traders in cloth and hardware . . . counting-house men" except a "nice, young quiet thing,"[3] British-born sister of an Anglo-American merchant taking her home to Boston.

Despite all the good cheer Fanny was more or less in tears at dinner. For now that the die was cast, the ship out of the Mersey and headed downchannel, she felt as dismal as ever about encountering the uncouth America she had read of, target of Sydney Smith's notorious rhetorical question of a dozen years previous: "Who reads an American book, or goes to an American play, or looks at an American picture or statue?"[4] Fanny wouldn't have cared to visit America even had so doing not entailed acting in an alien and probably crude context. Though *The Tempest* was her favorite Shakespeare, she did not share the sense of brave new world then sending Britons—sharpshooting journalists and protosociologists by the score—to see what changing political and social rules might do for mankind generally and Britain particularly. Sadly she carried on board some carnations from the Liverpool hotel: "Dear English flowers! they will be withered long before I again see land, but I will keep them until I once more stand upon the soil on which they grew."[5] Next day, after reading one of Daniel Webster's speeches, she called the United States "this bragging big baby," and the day after found it strange to hear American passengers "speaking in English of the English."[6]

Most of the company had already made several crossings and knew how best to while away a month or so of isolation at sea. They organized into a seriocomic convivial society, each member given an absurd nickname, Charles presiding over the first meeting. One of the chief purposes was to drink a good deal, an activity in which Charles bore himself creditably. In those later hours the ladies saw little of the men but were welcome to the earlier parlor games, dancing on deck (weather permitting), singing old songs, public readings, occasional cards, and of course, conscientious promenades. Fanny began to find the *Pacific* an at least tolerable floating sample of its distant country of origin. The more singing and dancing, the likelier that her forebodings would lose their edge.

The process was hardly begun, however, when, once the ship was off soundings, head winds and heavy seas took over. Until then Fanny's experience with salt water had been only the steamer trip from London to Edinburgh and four Channel crossings. In later years, though she made many transatlantic voyages, she never got good sea legs. Now she and Aunt Dall were more or less prostrate belowside for ten days. Aunt Dall remained fairly miserable in any but the calmest weather. But about a third of the way across Fanny recovered enough to dip pen in ink. After dinner that day the captain seems to have prescribed champagne, all passengers "collected in the round-house . . . the sky darkened tremendously, the rain came pelting down, the black sea swelled . . . the ship scudded before the blast, and we managed to keep ourselves warm by singing." Then tea, some cards, and Fanny "dozed, and finally to bed. Bed! . . . Oh for a bed! a real bed! any manner of bed, but a bed on shipboard! And yet I have seen some fair things. . . . I have seen one lonely ship in her silent walk across this wilderness, meet another, greet her, and pass her, like a dream . . . [yet] I have left my very soul behind me. England, dear, dear, England! oh, for a handful of your earth!" [7] She must have said something like that in the *Pacific*'s mate's hearing. Months later, in New York, when the ship was in port again, he had a box of English earth delivered to Fanny at her hotel.

There is, of course, a whiff of Augustus Craven in that nostalgic geophilia. Yet her condition was unmistakably better. She felt robust enough, even in rough weather, to risk rereading Byron and declaimed pertinent passages from *Childe Harold* to her cabin mates.

The next Sunday was exhilarating: "The morning was brilliant; the sea bold, bright . . . flinging up a cloud of glittering spray round the prow," and Charles read the appointed day's service from the Book of Common Prayer to the company assembled aft under a tarpaulin awning. Fanny's genuine religious sense was never more becoming:

> It affected me much, this praying on the lonely sea, in the words that at the same hour were being uttered by millions of kindred tongues in our dear home; there was something, too, impressive and touching in this momentary union of strangers, met but for a passing day . . . perhaps . . . never to behold each other's faces again. . . . The bright cloudless sky and glorious sea seemed to respond, in their silent magnificence, to our Te Deum.— I felt more of the excitement of prayer than I have known for many a day.[8]

"The excitement of prayer"—an uncommon turn of phrase.

In the afternoon gulls came patronizing the ship and seaweed floated alongside, from the Gulf Stream, they said—tokens that the voyage was half accomplished. Under all plain sail with a fair wind the *Pacific* plowed buoyantly westward. After dark there were northern lights and phosphorescence in the wake: "Mercy, how strange it was! . . . Came back to our gipsy encampment, where, by the light of a lantern, we supped and sang sundry scraps of old song—at ten came to bed"[9]—and this time no severities about seagoing beds. Then a day of dead calm; then, the North Atlantic being itself again, a roaring gale that fetched Fanny on deck instead of trying to sleep belowside with "the ship pitching, bouncing, shuddering and reeling, like a thing possessed." Presently a great sea walked inboard, broached the ladies' cabin skylight and drenched everything in it. While Fanny tried to reassure poor Harriet Hodgkinson, the young English girl, she was herself "rather excited by this invasion" and regretting she had left the deck where "I wish to goodness I had been . . . [when] that spoonful of salt water was flung from the sea's boiling bowl."[10] Though there were still queasy moments, her new liking for maritime hurly-burly stayed with her while the *Pacific* struggled against head winds off the Banks, "dipped, and dipped, and dived down into the black chasm, and then sprang up again, and rode over the swelling surges like an empress. . . . I got cradled among the ropes . . . and enjoyed it all amazingly. . . . sad and solemn . . . but it stirred my spirits to ride over these huge sea-horses, that came bounding and bellowing round us."[11]

They spoke an England-bound ship in weather too rough for lying to. A note that Fanny hastily wrote to Harriet St. Leger was tied to a lump of lead and thrown as the vessels passed on opposite tacks but fell short. Fanny wept. It was also sad when a small land bird that took refuge on board died in spite of her ministrations; she had hoped to feed it back to strength and release it ashore. The last Saturday on board she was plaintively surprised to find that at supper though "I don't know one of the ship's company, don't care for some of them . . . have led a loathsome life . . . for a month . . . yet the *last* Saturday night seemed half sad to me." Next morning, thirty-two days out—not bad; a few winters previously the voyage had taken the *Pacific* seventy-two days—the anticipated landfall: "the wished-for line of darker element. . . . Hail, strange land! my heart greets you coldly and sadly! . . . I am home-sick before touching land."[12]

On Monday the "newsboat" came out to pick up British news-papers and word of mouth about what had been going on abroad a month earlier, for it was forty years too soon for the Atlantic cable, let alone radio. Then came the pilot boat and the bluff young captain "gave up the cares and glories of command and we danced an inter-minable country dance . . . sang all the old songs, laughed at all the old jokes, drank our own and each other's healths, wealth and prosperity, and came to bed at two o'clock." In the morning a harbor steamboat came out in fog and drizzle to take off the passengers. They cheered the *Pacific* as the steamboat cast off: "Poor ship! there she lay—all sails reefed, rocking in melancholy inaction, deserted by her merry inmates, lonely and idle. . . . I should like to return in that ship."[13]

That evening there was a final, highly convivial dinner in the Kembles' rooms in the American Hotel. Fanny was wistful: "Friends

of thirty days are better than utter strangers, and when these my
shipmates shall be scattered . . . there will be no human being left
near us whose face we know, or whose voice is familiar."[14] Actually
several of those shipmates were New Yorkers who kept up the acquaintance and were helpful in adjustment to the new country. But
that first inclement night Fanny had reason to feel dreary. Cholera
had struck New York, driving people out of town, and though the
threat had dwindled, potential theatergoers might not return in time
for the Kembles' engagement. Nor was the general situation jolly. It
was then much farther from Lands End to Sandy Hook than the three
thousand miles we now discount in terms of airplanes and trans-
oceanic telephones. That month under sail at sea had shown with all
the emphasis of battering head winds how far it was in terms of time
and chance. And now they were ashore, the Kembles had the notorious uncertainties of show business increased by their having to face
a strange land.

Misgivings proved pointless. The Kembles met sailing far
smoother than the Atlantic Ocean had afforded them. Box offices
showed no ill effects from cholera. Fanny thought New York's Park
Theatre "pretty . . . plenty of gold carving, and red silk."[15]—a
helpful contrast with Covent Garden's vastness that asked too much
of the voice and numbed the effect of facial expression. The Park's
owner-manager, formerly of Drury Lane, was prospering with high
salaries to lure over some of Britain's ablest actors. This annoyed London managers, for those returning from such lucrative forays across
the ocean usually looked for higher pay at home. But it was raising
the American stage's standards of performance, which needed it. According to Alfred Bunn, then manager of Drury Lane (incidentally
the original of Mr. Dolphin in *Pendennis*): "[Americans are] a singular
mixture of good and bad taste—good or they would not receive with
so much admiration our best talent; bad, or they would not countenance so much of their own indifferent talents."[16]

Charles opened the engagement with *Hamlet* supported by the
Park stock company. Fanny was kept under wraps for the second
night. Naturally interest was high in this further example of im-
ported stage aristocracy that had already included Kean and

Macready; now a Kemble! The New York *Evening Post,* the city's
most literate daily, called Charles's Hamlet "a picture of unaffected
courtliness . . . the gallant and the finished gentleman," and predicted that his example on the American stage would "raise and refine
its style."[17] It bothered Fanny that the house's applause was rather
tepid when her father made his first entrance but she soon discerned
that this audience had some of Edinburgh's tradition of reserve; at the
final curtain there was no question that things had gone well.

Next night she did *Fazio*—in which she was consistently impressive, of which she even rather approved. There were hazards.
Aunt Dall was uneasy because in the version used "I am to be discovered instead of coming on [that is, be on stage when the curtain rises,
not enter later after preliminary minor doings] and also because I am
not seen at first in what she thinks a becoming dress."[18] Worse, her
Fazio was to be a "washed-out man" with whom she had worked
before at home and thought depressingly incompetent. Rehearsals
showed that crossing the ocean had not improved him. He bungled
the stage business, got in her way, was shaky in his lines. But his
incompetence worked out for the best. On the great night up came
the curtain on Fanny in a dull costume seated with her back to the
house:

"The people did not know me, and would not have known me
for some time, if that stupid man had . . . gone on [with his part]
but . . . he stood stock still, looked at me, and then at the audience,
whereupon the latter . . . gave me such a reception as I get in Covent Garden theatre every time I act a new part." After this inadvertent showmanship Fazio went up in his lines and, too flustered to take
Fanny's whispered promptings so botched the first act that "I thought
the whole thing must necessarily go to pieces." But Fazio is not much
on stage in the latter acts, so Fanny could "move a little more freely,
[gather] up my strength, and set to work comfortably . . . the people applauded, I warmed . . . and got through very satisfactorily."[19]
Indeed she did. Her fiery glow—the wrath that Bianca heaped on
Fazio that night was probably genuine enough—completed the Kembles' opening victory. "Never . . . have we seen a more delighted
audience or heard more enthusiastic applause," said the *Evening Post,*
attributing to Fanny "an intensity and a truth never . . . exhibited

by an actress in America, certainly never by one so young."[20] Philip Hone, mayor of New York and—which by no means necessarily follows—leader of upper-class opinion, told his diary: "I have never witnessed an audience so moved, astonished and delighted . . . deafening shouts and plaudits."[21]

The third night's bill was *Romeo & Juliet.* It was thought best to have Charles do Romeo in place of the fumbler who had mangled Fazio and was originally to play Fanny's star-crossed lover. It was one of Charles's best roles. When he played it in Boston next year Fanny wonderingly admired his doing it "still most beautifully. . . . In spite of his acting it with his own child (. . . a manifest absurdity) the perfection of his art makes it more youthful, graceful, ardent, and lover-like—a better Romeo, in short, than the youngest pretender to it nowadays."[22] But, aware of his age, Charles had the common sense to dislike playing the part. Fanny was "sorry for the [displaced actor] . . . sorry for my father . . . sorry for the public, who [thus] lost his admirable Mercutio." But that evening he "acted Romeo beautifully; I looked very nice, and the people applauded my gown abundantly."[23] In due course she swept all before her in *The Hunchback.* The same methods and repertory that had rescued Covent Garden served equally well in America. The Kembles' instant popularity easily surmounted Fazio-Romeo's complaints to the press that he was ill treated. Patiently they let him try again in a role in *Venice Preserved* that, though extensive, called for little more than what Fanny called "stand-and-stare-and-start-and-scream"[24] acting.

For the next two seasons father and daughter, with Aunt Dall as bottleholder, consultant, and moral prop, were the prospering money-makers they had traveled so far to be. It was harder work than at home. At Covent Garden or Drury Lane even the most successful role played only alternate nights, leaving every morning and three evenings a week free in spite of rehearsals for future roles. In America the Kembles' several-week engagements meant five or six nights a week in an ever changing repertory:

> At each place we have to drill a new set of actors, and
> every night to act a different play; my days are passed in
> dawdling about cold dark stages, with blundering actors

who have not even had the conscience to study their parts,
all the morning. All the afternoon, I sort out theatrical
adornments, and all the evening I enchant audiences,
prompt my fellow-mimes, and wish it had pleased heaven
to make me a cabbage in a corner of a Christian kitchen
garden![25]

As time passed and things brightened, Fanny's intrinsic perkiness was
reviving. "A cheating German woman came [to the hotel] this morning with some bewitching canezous and pelerines: I chose two that I
wanted, and one very pretty one that I didn't, but as she asked a
heathen price for 'em, I took only the former—dear good little
me!"[26]

Gratefully she saw that, hard as he was working, the infusion of
fresh money and freedom from the burden of Covent Garden were
vastly benefiting her beloved father. After only ten days ashore he was
"wonderfully improved in health, looks and spirits; the fine, clear,
warm (hot, it should be called) atmosphere agrees with him." In
Philadelphia a few weeks later he spoke "of a great increase of absolute muscular vigour and strength; and when he said this, I felt that
my share of the unpleasant duty of coming hither was already handsomely repaid."[27] New York provided ample relaxation between theatrical chores. Convivial acquaintances—some old shipmates, some
gentlemen Britons settled there for business reasons, some Americans
calling on the famous Mr. Kemble as a social duty and discovering
his talent for friendship—were in and out all day. They walked him
all over their nervously energetic city. They took him across the river
to Hoboken—then a sylvan resort—for turtle-eating high jinks. They
dined him at cordially bibulous length, and when they trooped into
Fanny's drawing room to ask her to play and sing for them, she set
it down in her journal that Charles was no more and no less "how
com'd ye so"[28] than the others. She knew Charles had a good head;
even when, as did happen though seldom, he came on stage a bit
tipsy, his professionalism would bring him through. These hospitable
New Yorkers made up horseback parties including Fanny and a young
wife or daughter or two. On picnics to Hoboken or the Brooklyn side
of the Narrows everybody got tiddly on champagne and cherry

bounce and then went back to somebody's red-brick mansion up Canal Street way and danced and sang till all hours.

And just as in Paris, Charles was as good company for his daughter as for his whiskered and pantalooned cronies. In Philadelphia one evening he had dined out and returned to the hotel about ten o'clock suggesting a midnight walk: "I bonneted and booted and we sallied forth" over the Schuylkill to what is now West Philadelphia, then still somewhat woodsy:

> We sat down on a tree trunk . . . for upwards of a
> quarter of an hour without uttering a syllable. . . . We
> were disturbed by a large white spaniel dog . . . coming
> down from among the cedar bushes, [that] reminded me
> of the old witch stories. . . . We arose to depart. . . .
> The broken notes of a buglehorn came at intervals . . .
> from the opposite shore. . . . The moon threw our shad-
> ows on the lonely path. . . . The air was soft and balmy.
> . . . The world was still. . . . As we walked down Mar-
> ket street through the long ranges of casks [on the side-
> walks outside warehouses], the only creatures stirring,
> except some melancholy night-loving cat, my father said
> very calmly, "How I *do* wish I had a gimlet."—"What
> for?"—"What fun it would be to pierce every one of these
> barrels." For a gentleman of his years, this appeared to
> me rather a juvenile prompting of Satan . . . I laugh-
> ingly expostulated . . . he replied with much innocence,
> "I don't think they'd ever suspect me." [29]

Charles Kemble's enjoyment of being cordially treated had no flavor of social climbing. He was accustomed to taking a far more aristocratic society in stride. He laughed at the transparently spurious heraldry on the panels of certain American private carriages and the high proportion of titles—general, colonel, judge, and so on—among the men to whom he was introduced. Fanny concluded that "America will be a monarchy before I am a skeleton," and that most of the American women she met were as title-thirsty as an English banker's wife. Her perplexity about these women kept her aware of being in a strange land—the stranger for the language's being much the same and yet handled so differently, often so stridently by her own sex.

The women flocking up and down Broadway in the September sunshine were dressed "like French women gone mad" . . . [and] walk "with a French shuffle"[30] that she attributed to their French-made footgear; and to judge from the prices in the shops they fluttered into, they paid extravagantly for elegant little boots and the rest of their finery. The number of pretty women with implausible tiny waists was high but they seemed to fade early. The chief cause of that, pronounced this disciple of the Combes' hygiene, was not so much the climate or the overheated rooms that foreigners usually blamed, though those had a share, as early marriage and lack of exercise. The latter at least was a true bill. For most well-to-do New York women of that day "exercise" meant a daily hour or two driving in a carriage and a few times a week dawdling from shop to shop for half a mile of Broadway.

By Fanny's time this was cultural lag. Upper-class Englishwomen were considerably modifying such sluggishness by a good deal of walking not only to go somewhere nearby, but also as deliberate, recreational exercise; and they rode both in the parks and at country seats. In America Fanny was a sort of inadvertent missionary in these respects. Her insistence on riding whenever possible, becomingly and jauntily topped off by a visored riding cap that Lady Ellesmere had given her, combined with her conspicuous success on the stage to create a small bull-market in sidesaddles. Imitations of "the Kemble cap" appeared in millinery shops. " 'Tis quite entertaining," she wrote to Harness from Boston next spring, "to see how, before I have been a fortnight in a place, all the women are getting into riding skirts and up on horses. I have received ever so many thanks for the improved health of the ladies who, since my arrival, are horseback-mad; and I truly think a good shaking does a woman good in every way."[31] And this in spite of her indignation at the shortcomings of American horse-training. She found no mounts properly broken to the standard British gaits to which her style of riding was suited, and despised the omnipresent, peculiarly American gait, the "rack"—and an instrument of torture she thought it was.

This America that she was gingerly encountering had other cultural lags maybe understandable in a new and remote land but irksome for all that. New York had special backwardnesses. She allowed it a sort of Parisian charm with its tree-softened streets and briskly good-natured crowds. Charles and she both enjoyed its clear air—a relief from Britain's coal-smoky cities.[32] Yet there was no reservoir-and-aqueduct water supply, only wells more or less polluted. Most of the streets were unaccountably ill paved. The incalculable quantity of horse droppings fouling the street crossings in wet weather or blowing about in clouds in dry, was no more—or less—offensive than in London. But London had no hogs scavenging at large—a primitive arrangement persisting in New York well after Boston had suppressed it. That Fanny did not complain about this shows at least that she was not invariably captious about America. She made up for it by the severity with which she reproached New York hotels for failing to supply more than a very few private sitting rooms and bedrooms of some comfort instead of mere cells the bleakness of which assumed that patrons spent all but sleeping time in the bar, the dining room, or the public parlors. For British visitors, accustomed for a couple of generations to a certain privacy, this was annoying.

Boston's Tremont House and Philadelphia's Mansion House proved nearer reasonable standards. But she decided that America would never develop a decent hotel "if the servants are not a little superior to the Irish savages who officiate in that capacity . . . in the northern states."[33] The difficulty was that since native-born whites despised what they considered menial employment, the waiters, chambermaids, et al. staffing city hotels were in Fanny's time and well afterward mostly recently landed Irish, typically penury-numbed peasants unacquainted with the instruments and demands of urban civilization. Their tactless adherence to a traditionally mistrusted religion widened the consequent dichotomy, but it would have been a serious social lesion on secular grounds alone. Cognate feelings among Britons were as much part of Fanny's heritage as "God Save the King." In America people now as well-thought-of as Harriet Beecher Stowe and Mark Twain were among the millions unquestioningly sharing anti-Irish prejudice in classic form. The rest of her life on both sides of the water Fanny did the same. But at least she dwelt on the Irish in America less than on another consistent source of foreigners' complaints—the hordes and clouds of insects infesting America, city and country alike, between May 1 and October 1. Woven-wire screening did not yet exist. Except for "mosquito bars" shrouding the beds of some well-to-do southerners practically no protection was known. Horses and poultry and hogs kept flies hideously plentiful. Wherever lamps or candles were lighted, moths and flying beetles abounded. Bedbugs were less common than they had been a few decades earlier, when foreigners unwilling to be eaten alive slept on the floor, but were by no means unknown. And mosquitoes! They made Aunt Dall's life a misery and covered Fanny's arms with bumpy blotches. Neither could learn to take pervasive, chronic itching for granted. And in their rooms ants too came swarming "on the floors, on the tables, in the beds, about one's clothes; the plagues of Egypt were a joke to them. . . . Oh bugs, fleas, flies, ants, and musquitoes! . . . I sit slapping my own face all day, and lie thumping my pillow all night; 'tis a perfect nuisance to be devoured of creatures *before* one's in the ground; it isn't fair."[34]

A residual squeamishness about the theater and its people was another cultural lag. Fanny was puzzled to see that though the house was good when her father and she went to see J. W. Wallack in *The Rent Day,* there weren't twenty women in the dress circle, whereas in London the notion that ladies shouldn't "go to the play" remained vigorous among only Evangelicals and Dissenters. Certain well-placed New Yorkers entertained the Kembles; but the Reverend Dr. Wainwright (who cured Fanny of waltzing) could not ask them to his house. To meet them, he had to ask to be invited to a party where they would be; whereas in the Kembles' London several theater-buff clergy of good connections and unimpeachable standing—Harness, Milman, Dyce, et al.—were their close friends not only reciprocally calling and dining, but even coming backstage. Note too that Wainwright's parishioners were no thin-lipped knot of Methodists but high-chinned Episcopalians in a fashionable church. In New York the Kembles regularly attended his services. Charles thought his sermons powerful if not subtle and Fanny admired the intelligent clarity with which he handled the liturgy. But it must have been uncomfortable—though she never says so—to reflect that while in his

priestly capacity he could give them the vehicles of communion, the
social onus on their profession prevented them from crossing his private threshold.

New York City rewarded the Kembles handsomely in money,
gave them reason to feel well treated, afforded them cordial friends.
But it was no great wrench to pack up the props and costumes and,
leaving the ants behind, move on to their mid-autumn engagement
in Philadelphia. The wrench was in the logistics. The crow-flight
distance was eighty miles but the trip was wildly complicated just
then by a mixture of old and new technology. The game opened with
a steamboat from Manhattan to Perth Amboy and up the Raritan as
far as she could float. There they squeezed the traveler into one of a
procession of cramped stagecoaches lurching over atrocious roads to
the end of track of the first railroad to be built across New Jersey.
Since it still lacked steam locomotives, horses drew the bunty little
passenger cars to Bordentown. Thence another steamboat took them
down the Delaware to Philadelphia—ten hours Manhattan wharfside
to Philadelphia. The one excuse for this eclectic scramble was that
two generations earlier the same trip had meant two days on horseback or a day and a half more or less by boat plus a "stage wagon"
not daring to call itself a coach; or a week or two round by sea.

Fanny now first encountered the contrast between American
roads and England's post roads surfaced with John Loudon McAdam's
crushed stone; and the complementary contrast between the stately
British mail coach rumbling smoothly along and the Concord coach
that made what time its four horses could manage among the mud-
holes, interlacing ruts, odd boulders, and tree stumps that made obstacle courses of most American highways. Light and elegantly
strong, the Concord was a handsome thing when new and shiny. But
the design did not include springs, which would never take American
strains. The body was slung on heavy leather straps that absorbed
some shock but seldom enough, and its passenger-seating arrangements were torture for those of even average size.

This first time the Kembles had only fourteen miles of it but it
was enough to rouse Fanny into disapproval; the coach was a "mem-

orable black hole on wheels . . . shaped something like [a boat], the
sides merely leathern pieces removable at pleasure . . . in bad
weather . . . buttoned down to protect the inmates . . . the middle
[seat] having a movable leather strap by way of a dossier, lifts away to
permit the ingress and egress of the occupants of the other seats"
three abreast, nine in all jammed in plus hand baskets and cold-
weather wraps.

> For the first few minutes, I thought I must have fainted
> from the intolerable sensation of smothering. . . . How-
> ever, the leathers having been removed, and a little more
> air obtained, I . . . resigned myself. . . . Away wal-
> lopped the four horses, trotting with their front, and gal-
> loping with their hind legs: and away went we after them,
> bumping . . . jumping, jolting, shaking, tossing and
> tumbling, over the . . . cruellest, hard-heartedest road,
> that ever wheel rumbled upon. Through bog and marsh
> and ruts, wider and deeper than any christian ruts I ever
> saw, with the roots of trees protruding across our path,
> their boughs every now and then giving us an affectionate
> scratch through the windows . . . a half-demolished
> trunk or stump lying in the middle of the road lifting us
> up, and letting us down again. . . . Even my father's
> solid proportions . . . were jerked up to the roof and
> down again every three minutes.

Fellow sufferers included several pretty women whom the jolting did
not keep from chattering all the time in "the national nasal twang";[35]
one of them occasionally did stop talking to vomit out of the window.

The scenery, frowsy and stunted second-growth woods, was depressing.

> The few cottages and farm-houses . . . reminded me of
> similar dwellings in France and Ireland; yet the peasantry
> here have not the same excuse for disorder and dilapida-
> tion [sic]. . . . the same desolate, untidy, untended look;
> the gates broken . . . farming utensils sluttishly scattered
> about a littered yard . . . house-windows broken, and
> stuffed with paper or clothes; dishevelled women and
> barefooted, anomalous looking human young things.

> . . . none of the enchanting mixture of neatness, order,
> and rustic elegance . . . which render so picturesque the
> surroundings of a farm . . . in my own dear country.[36]

The zigzag rail fences—a rail fence rapidly weathers into a really remarkable ugliness—depressed her as a slovenly waste of materials and
made her long for the charm of English hedgerows. The fall coloring
lived up to all that she had heard about it; but morbid reservations
intruded:

> The colors of the autumnal foliage are rich and beautiful
> beyond imagination—crimson and gold, like a regal man-
> tle, instead of the russet cloak of our fading woods . . .
> [yet] its gorgeousness takes away from the sweet solemnity
> that makes the fall of the year pre-eminently the season of
> thoughtful contemplation. Our autumn . . . is mellow
> and harmonious . . . the brilliancy of this decay strikes
> one . . . as if the whole world were dying of consump-
> tion, with these glittering gleams and hectic flushes, a
> mere deception of disease and death.[37]

The steamboat on the Delaware, though roomy and fast, revived
her lively disgust with an American trait of that day that now sounds
to us as indecent as it seemed to visitors generations ago. Tobacco
chewing was very widespread among American men and most of
them regardlessly spat the resulting thick yellow juice wherever they
liked.

> Every place is made a perfect piggery of [Fanny wrote],
> street, stairs, steamboat, everywhere—and behind the
> scenes, and on the stage at rehearsal, I have been shocked
> and annoyed . . . by this horrible custom. . . . after a
> few hour's [*sic*] travelling in a steamboat . . . the white
> dress, put on fresh in the morning [is] covered with yel-
> low tobacco stains; nor is this very offensive habit confined
> to the lower orders . . . I have seen *gentlemen* spit upon
> the carpet of the room where they were sitting, in the
> company of women, without the slightest remorse.[38]

Indeed the New World promised to take much getting used to,
and the actuality was shaping up overclose to anticipations. Nor was
intermittent homesickness much help. Toward the end of their first
stay in New York, Fanny and her father strolled down to the Battery

between sunset and moonrise, and a lovelier light never
lay upon sea, earth and sky. . . . the modest violet
. . . of twilight . . . possessed the main sky wholly,
except where two or three masses of soft dark purple
clouds floated, from behind which the stars presently
winked at us with their bright eyes. The river lay as still
as death . . . tiny boats were stealing like shadows over
the water. . . . To-night, as I stood watching that sur-
passing sunset, I would have given it all . . . for a wreath
of English fog stealing over the water.[39]

"Souvent femme varie," Fanny's old friend, Francis I, wrote on a
window at Chambord. Soon after her journey through darkest New
Jersey Fanny was abandoning her view of its fall coloring as picturesque pathology and cordially rejoicing in it:

How call ye this the season's fall,
    That seems the pageant of the year?
Richer and brighter far than all
    The pomp that spring and summer wear.[40]

Beyond the normal changeability of women one reason for this change
of tone may have been her feeling that Philadelphia was better than
New York. Its municipal housekeeping was neater and, the year having gone beyond September mugginess, the climate was cooler. As
she walked to rehearsal on a crisp morning, "the pure, fresh, invigo-
rating air, and gay sunlight . . . the delightfully clean streets, and
pretty mixture of trees and buildings . . . caused me to rejoice.
. . . neatness, is carried almost to an inconvenient pitch . . . a
perfect phrenzy of cleanliness; and of a Saturday morning, early, the
streets are really impassable, except to a good swimmer."[41] Further,
Philadelphia had "a greater air of age. . . . The red houses are not
so fiercely red, nor the white facings so glaringly white . . . not so
new and flaunting a look. . . . New York always gave me the idea
of an irregular collection of temporary buildings, erected for some
casual purpose, full of life, animation, and variety, but not meant to
endure . . . a fair, in short."[42] America's lack of venerable buildings
continued to put her off. In Charleston, South Carolina, seven years
later she found "the lower streets, in all their dinginess and decay
. . . a refreshment. . . . I have had a perfect red-brick-and-white-

board fever ever since I came to this country . . . once more to see a house which looks as if it had stood long enough to get warmed through, is a balm to my senses, oppressed with newness."[43]

Horses for hire at the riding school were, however, no better than New York's: "poor half-broken dumb brutes . . . with their shuffling, rollicking, mongrel pace."[44] But there was a tolerably behaved gray up to Charles's weight and Fanny put up with other mounts as available, for riding was more and more, she wrote to Harness, "meat and drink and sleep to me, and . . . the best opportunity of seeing the country, which one never does well in a carriage."[45] Above the famous waterworks at Fairmont was country worth seeing—woods and vivacious little watercourses feeding into Wissahickon Creek. In that long ago October the trim little figure on horseback heading westward on Market Street every clement afternoon escorted by a handsome large man on a gray horse may have drawn more attention than Fanny Kemble on the stage of the Chestnut Street Theatre.

Not that her professional aspect was inconspicuous. For all its leaven of Quaker mistrust of worldly things, Philadelphia was a good show-town with its own playwrights and developing actors. Once the Kembles discerned that their audiences' relative undemonstrativeness did not mean disapproval, they had little to complain of. Again Charles opened the campaign and his meticulous Hamlet was well received. Then Fanny played meteor across the horizon next night in *Fazio* and Philadelphians scrambled for seats as gratifyingly as New Yorkers had. Her "symmetrical figure . . . flashing dark eyes . . . luxurious hair," recalled Charles Wikoff, an old scapegrace who was a flighty youngster in 1832, had "the audience half won before she essayed to act . . . when . . . she began to display her power . . . the spectators were transported with enthusiasm, and wept and applauded wildly . . . the town went Kemble mad. . . . I forgot everything else, law included . . . went about like one possessed."[46]

Just as they had in New York, crude engravings of the Lawrence drawing and certain other portraits of Fanny multiplied in shop windows. Thomas Sully, Philadelphia's renowned portraitist, came eagerly round. Background as well as reputation was propitious: his

English parents had been actors coming to Charleston soon after his birth, and he had been a pupil of Lawrence's in London. A pleasant man personally—"one of the few people here that I find pleasure in associating with," [47] Fanny said—he had a pleasant family to match, and Fanny made good friends with his young daughters. He did an admirable portrait of Charles as Fazio, and many a night was out in front making flying sketches of Fanny as Bianca or Julia or whatever role was billed that night to work up into the various oil portraits of her that survive. She also formally "sat for" most of them, but the one that was engraved and several times used as frontispiece of a book of hers was done merely from memory and such fugitive sketches. Fanny had her usual misgivings about these projects. "I do not feel very sanguine about it," she said of one of his last efforts, "for Sully's characteristic is delicacy rather than power, and mine may not be power, but it is certainly not delicacy." [48] Yet she probably enjoyed the sitting in company she liked as she once had sitting for Lawrence, and certainly the Sullys' friendship was valuable at a time when Philadelphia's hospitality to the Kembles as persons, unlike New York's, was not proportionate to its enthusiasm for them as actors.

A few men of standing came round to make acquaintance with Charles; that was about all. A minor reason may have been that the Chestnut Street company supporting the Kembles included old Vincent De Camp, Thérèse's handsome emigrant brother. He had come to see them in New York soon after they arrived. But Philadelphia had long been his professional base and here he now was in secondary comedy roles—Orlando in *The Honeymoon,* Lord Trinket in *The Jealous Wife* . . . No harm in that, any more than in the presence in supporting casts at the Park Theatre in New York next season of John Kemble Mason, Fanny's cousin and quondam Romeo, who was trying his luck in America too. [49] But over the years Philadelphia had picked up rather a gamy flavor from Vincent De Camp to supplement that of his already dubious profession. A contemporary chronicler who knew him well and rather liked him, and admired his handling of "eccentric comedy," said that "as eccentricity was his *forte* . . . so were his personal traits . . . they rendered his social intercourse at times obnoxious. He was captious and fretful . . . a child of larger growth."[50] There is no evidence that relations between him and his sister Adelaide and his niece and his brother-in-law were uncordial. A rather unctuous letter from him at the Pennsylvania Historical Society indicates that, having retired from the stage and gone into the dairy business near Mobile, Alabama, he has sent Fanny (and her husband) a pair of pregnant dairy cows for their farm outside Philadelphia in the late 1830s; that he wants sister Victorine to come to America to live with him; and that, dairying not being profitable, he is thinking of trying his luck in the Texas that was so much in the public eye at the time.[51] Not a prepossessing profile on the whole, and a social mentor coaching the Kembles on how to get as well accepted in Philadelphia as in London would have told them to pay Uncle Vincent to be their advance man in Patagonia. Walnut Street was not open-minded about such family connections.

Nevertheless the Kembles' good breeding effected one crack in the ice toward the end of their first engagement: "A Mr., Mrs., and young Mr. [Biddle], called upon us . . . the only inhabitants of this good city, who have done us that honour,"[52] that is, made a welcoming gesture as a family social unit. A week later the Biddles had the Kembles to dinner—the first feet-under-the-mahogany hospitality they had been offered. Fanny found their style of dining acceptable and had the sense to welcome this breach of looking-askance. Word that the Biddles,[53] no less, had countenanced the Kembles' existence seems eventually to have compensated for Uncle Vincent, for before their second engagement was over, certain other august Philadelphian families asked them to large parties. Yet it was never the complete breakthrough to the sort of status they were used to at home. Biddles and Willings, acknowledged patricians, might do as they liked, but old John Francis Fisher, equally august, remained proud of his parents' refusal ever to allow actors in their home, not even the Kembles or so certified-gentlemanly a figure as William Macready. At the time Fanny held her fire about this attitude but when publishing her indiscreet journal some years later loaded it with a blistering note:

> There is no town in Europe where my father could fix his
> residence for a week . . . without immediately being
> sought out by those best worth knowing. . . . during a

month's residence in Philadelphia, scarcely a creature
came near us . . . as regards myself, I have no inclination
. . . to speak . . . but it gave me something like a feeling of contempt . . . for the good taste of the Philadelphians. . . . I can only attribute the want of courtesy we
met with in Philadelphia, to . . . that very small spirit
of dignity which is always afraid of committing itself.[54]

Once the barrier was breached for him, "young Mr. Biddle"
haunted the Kembles' quarters at the Mansion House, bringing
Fanny masses of flowers or gadget-toys in a rather callow devotion
that afforded her good-natured amusement. On Christmas it was a
workbox obviously so costly that Charles ordered Fanny to return it.
She persuaded him to relent not because she wanted the thing but to
spare the boy's feelings. Had Thérèse been on duty, she might have
sent him packing as a nuisance whose parents were probably unaware
of his antics. But as the workbox episode showed, neither Aunt Dall
nor Charles was of that severe school of duenna.

In New York a young English professional musician of some
cultivation generously named Francis Henry Fitzhardinge Berkeley
had recommended Charles Kemble to get in touch with a Philadelphia crony of his, Pierce Butler, an accomplished amateur flutist and
theater-buff, whose social position in Philadelphia was heavily but-
tressed by expectations of great wealth. Four days after Fanny startled
the town in *Fazio,* Butler came calling. "A pretty-spoken, *genteel*
youth enough . . . drank tea with us and offered to ride with me.
He is, it seems, a great fortune,"[55] Fanny told her journal, being no
better than most at knowing when their fate has come upon them.

In previous letters Berkeley had given plenty of reason to go
making the Kembles' acquaintance. He described Charles as "the best
and most finished actor you have ever seen" and was ecstatic about
Fanny as Bianca: "The workings of her fine face and the subdued and
intense passion which she brings forth with the eye of Fire is only
met with once in a man's life." Soon he has met her personally and
reports that she persists in calling

a male fowl a Cock and her ambulatory pedestals legs.
. . . In conversation she is very free but highly educated

and accomplished . . . she puts you out of countenance
by cursed apt quotations . . . if you show any French,
she kills you with [quoting] Racine, if Italian knocks you
down with Dante—Rather blue!! but mind, not obtru-
sively so. . . . In person she is pretty . . . large hands,
large arms: never mind, you will fall in love with her—
for she is right lovely to look upon . . . her voice low,
soft and beautiful. Off the stage rather swarthy, with her
face all expression, a pleasant, agreeable, well bred girl.[56]

Some while later, as Fanny returned glowing and merry from a
junket into the country, she again found the pretty-spoken youth
with Charles; he stayed to dinner. In addition to young Biddle's flowers others kept turning up almost daily with a card "from a *Friend,*";
Fanny and Aunt Dall surmised that, this being Philadelphia, the
giver was a very shy Quaker. The Kembles went back to New York
for their second engagement. The first evening of their return to Philadelphia for the second booking, Butler called. Three days later he
rode with Charles Kemble and Fanny and stayed to dinner. He kept
turning up at the riding school when Fanny was there trying out
mounts with a view to suiting Aunt Dall and herself better. He confessed to being the flower-sending Friend. Young Biddle too stayed
much underfoot. Fanny never says so but it must have caused talk
that one day she rode (duly chaperoned) with a scion of the great
name of Biddle and the next with one of old Major Butler's grandson-
heirs. But soon after Christmas the relative standing of the two was
clear. The ailing southern lady downstairs in the Kembles' hotel,
with whom Fanny had made great friends, began to discuss how nice
it would be if Butler, not Biddle, proposed marriage. When, the last
day of 1832, the Kembles left to play Baltimore and Washington,
Biddle said his good-byes the previous evening. At four o'clock of a
winter morning Pierce Butler went down to see them off on the
steamboat.

Steamboat to a railroad across the peninsula between the Delaware and Chesapeake bays; another down the Chesapeake to Baltimore. This railroad had a steam locomotive that whisked them along

at sixteen miles an hour but its passenger cars were less comfortable than those of that wonderful Mr. Stephenson's operation. The Baltimore theater where the Kembles expected to appear lacked supporting actors, had meager scenery and a manager tottering into bankruptcy. Charles, veteran trouper, made a satisfactory deal with the other house. The engagement prospered, but Fanny had a poor opinion of this southern-flavored boomtown still so crude that she couldn't ride because no sidesaddle was anywhere available.

On to Washington in an "exclusive extra"—a privately hired Concord coach—over roads too like New Jersey's to a rambling, rattle-trap hotel and a primitive, tiny theater. The national capital's empty distances and sporadic buildings struck the Kembles as absurd—the usual European visitor's reaction. But official Washington crammed into the miniature theater in the spirit summed up by Mr. Justice Joseph Story of the U.S. Supreme Court writing to his wife: "the Chief Justice [John Marshall] and myself . . . attended . . . the theatre to hear Miss Fanny Kemble. . . . She played with great propriety of manner, feeling, and power. I have never seen any female acting at all comparable . . . She is so graceful, that you forget she is not very handsome. In Mrs. Haller she threw the whole audience into tears. The Chief Justice shed them in common with younger eyes." And there survive verses that the old gentleman wrote in her honor ending:

> Go, lovely woman, go! Enjoy thy fame!
> A second Kemble, with a deathless name![57]

The following year when the Kembles were playing Boston and Story was teaching at the Harvard Law School and making no bones of his joy in Fanny's performances, an impertinent student asked him how he reconciled that with his staid profession and austere principles. "I don't try to," he answered. "I only thank God that I am alive in the same era with such a woman."[58]

The Kembles were presented to President Andrew Jackson; met Daniel Webster and Edward Everett; and here was Washington Irving, as much Fanny's favorite uncle as in London. He treated her in the same spirit when they met again in New York and Fanny confessed her distaste for her profession:

> I . . . complained of the little leisure it left me for study
> and improving myself, for . . . occupations congenial to
> me. . . . "Well," he said, "you are . . . seeing men and
> things . . . seeing the world . . . acquiring materials
> and . . . observations and experiences and wisdom, and
> by and by, when with fame you have acquired inde-
> pendence and retire . . . you will begin another and a
> brighter course with these matured powers. I know of no
> one whose life has such a promise in it as yours."[59]

This flattering and reassuring council made Fanny feel, she said, "almost hopeful." Note that Irving apparently took it for granted that marriage was not for her. Maybe he was apprehensively aware that soon after the Kembles returned to New York, Pierce Butler turned up there without any known pressing reason for leaving whatever affairs he was attending to in Philadelphia.

It was true that this Pierce Butler was "a great fortune," potentially at the time and actually a few years later. All Philadelphia knew that on the death of an elderly aunt he would be heir to a considerable amount of city real estate, some hundreds of acres of good farmland in several parcels and, far larger in extent, value, and revenue, his grandfather's plantations in Georgia's famous Sea Islands. Nor were the farmlands negligible. Eventually sold to developers, two of those parcels comfortably endowed several of his descendants.

In certain such ways that grandfather, Major Pierce Butler, was an ancestor worth having. He was third son of an Irish baronet of an illegitimate branch of the Earls of Ormonde. That made his progeny an unusual thing, Americans sprung from genuine Old Country nobility. He came to America as officer in a British regiment during the French and Indian War. After the war he resigned his commission, had the luck to marry a Charleston heiress—a Middleton—and went into planting and politics in South Carolina. In the Revolution he was in the rebel legislature. As a delegate to the Constitutional Convention and then a fiercely conspicuous U.S. senator, he came to know Philadelphia, bought property there, and made it his head-quarters. Gradually he transferred his wife's interests—and her many black slaves—from South Carolina to the newly exploited Georgia coast. Periodically he went south to keep an eye on his holdings but day-by-day operations were left to a conspicuously capable superintendent he employed.

The major's impressive wealth made it easier for Philadelphia to stomach his peremptory manners and the savage temper that, gossip said, his wife had cause to regret. The couple's southern background was no hindrance; Philadelphia's first families had "many ties of both friendship and intermarriage . . . in Virginia, Maryland and South Carolina."[60] Of his three daughters only one married, and she without his consent. Her husband Dr. James Mease, also Protestant Irish in origin, was a dabbler in politics and port-physician of Philadelphia. After becoming son-in-law of the wealthy major, he took to progressive farming and amateur science, being active in the renowned Philosophical Society, but his relations with his crusty father-in-law were never cordial enough to secure him the capital he would have liked. Mrs. Mease seems to have had her own crustiness. She so despised the several conventional religious sects that bulked large in Philadelphia that she was called, doubtless justifiably, an atheist. She allowed no Bible in her house and permitted her children to attend only the Unitarian church on the sardonic if recognizable grounds that "little or no religion was preached there."[61]

On the major's death in 1822 his grandsons became his eventual heirs (after his daughters' deaths) on condition that they change the surname to Butler. Thomas, the eldest, taking this as the affront to his father that the major probably intended, pledged his brothers to reject the condition—and the handsome legacy. Pierce saw fit to break this pledge after Thomas died, and when the estate fell in to him shared equally with the third brother, John.

That made both young fellows of wealth, once the aunts were to die. John made a brilliant marriage: pretty Gabriella Manigault Morris, granddaughter of Gouverneur Morris, the Hudson Valley statesman; her middle name linked her to Charleston aristocracy. He also was conspicuous in the local elite militia, otherwise, according to a fellow Philadelphia patrician, "a mere idler . . . . a hard, selfish, profligate fellow, totally without education or intellect . . . [but] the manners of a gentleman & . . . great taste in dress, house & equipment."[62]

Brother Pierce was much the more popular of the two. S. Weir Mitchell, Philadelphia's eminent physician-novelist and pioneer in psychiatry, recalled that Pierce "always fascinated my youth on account of his singular personal beauty and a certain refined charm of manner. He had the perfect amiability of a selfish man."[63] Soft-spoken and calm-eyed, under middle size . . . the best portrait of him that I know shows a not positively handsome but prepossessing person with the air of a well-fed fox. A close friend of Fanny's called him "pleasant looking . . . very quiet and gentlemanlike . . . showed intelligence and a spirit of minute inquiry."[64] Women usually took to Pierce—a confirmed ladies' man but not coarsely obvious about it. In 1832 the town was sure that he would soon be engaged to Emily Chapman, the reigning belle. Fanny, unaware of that, knew only that the lovely Miss Chapman was one of the sights of the day. Only years later did loosened tongues let her know that Pierce's conduct toward Emily after he met Fanny had been "most cruel and dishonorable."[65]

Unlike John, the complete drone, Pierce had at least studied law enough to gain admission to the bar. In 1832 the drone of ample independent means was rarer in America than in, say, 1900. Even though a young man inherited enough in good mortgages to marry and enjoy himself on, he was expected to follow some business or profession or at least go through the motions. This example of Max Weber's "Protestant work ethic" caused remark among Britons used to London's many comfortably situated young men of good family never getting round to going into banking or good works or politics or diplomacy and yet being consistently invited to the balls where Fanny, among others, danced with them. The Kembles had no way of knowing that the Butler brothers' idleness was exceptional, and not quite the thing. Hence, though Pierce's pursuit of the Kembles to New York and Boston may have raised eyebrows among Philadelphians, it can hardly have seemed out of the way to Charles that when this affluent youth wished to follow a girl he had his eye on, no commitment to office or courts prevented him.

Pierce had certain explicit accomplishments. He was well established among Philadelphia's amateur musicians, and though American-reared, rode well enough to become Fanny's prime escort—indeed a great deal of their courtship was on horseback. In the light of eventualities, however, it was ominous that Fanny, used to the Cambridge Apostles and Rogers's breakfast guests, needed to warn a friend seven months before her marriage that Pierce was "a person of little cultivation but strong natural sense, extreme truth and straightforwardness of character."[66]

Different characteristics emerged from the phrenological profile that George Combe worked out when, during his lecture tour of the States in 1840, he spent the day with the Butlers. Phrenologists listed the "traits" that bumps on the skull were supposed to reveal and scored the subject on the size of each, the larger the stronger the trait. Combe's findings, presumably made after exploring Pierce's head, may have masked shrewd insights under phrenological patter: Pierce scored *Large* on Amativeness (eroticism), Philoprogenitiveness (love of offspring), Concentration, Self-esteem, Love of Approbation; *Rather Large* on Adhesiveness (persistence); Combativeness, Destructiveness, Sensitiveness, Firmness . . . A *Very Large* rating on Benevolence failed to justify itself in the long run but at the time may have politely distracted Pierce from the rest. By then Fanny's skepticism about phrenology was developing well. Yet, though she mentions the Combes' visit to Butler Place in her letters home, she says nothing about Combe's examining Pierce.[67] One need not read too much into omissions that may be inadvertent. As between Mr. and Mrs. Pierce Butler, however, the fat was already hot in the fire and there was much uncomfortably recognizable in that description of the major's grandson as notably Amative, Philoprogenitive, Self-esteeming, Persistent, Combative, Destructive . . .

VII

Man Is Fire

IN THE SPRING of 1833, after sparring for months, Charles Kemble and a Boston manager came to terms. On the wings of renewed success in Philadelphia[1] and New York the Kembles boarded the overnight steamboat from New York to Providence. As the vessel nosed into the sound, Fanny's antennae registered better things. She liked the roomy, well-managed craft. She did not, as they said she might, feel queasy during the twenty minutes of open sea off Point Judith. The highway over which an "exclusive extra" took them to Boston was unexpectedly good. The city's approaches showed the neat dwellings and dooryards that New Jersey had signally lacked. She liked the Tremont House, then the nation's best hotel. The Tremont Theatre was satisfactory, the company the ablest she had ever worked with outside London, its women's average of good looks the highest she had ever seen; she was specially struck by the lovely young Mrs. Barrett who did Ophelia to her father's Hamlet.

Blue devils still hovered: "How desolate and cheerless this constant changing of homes is. . . . 'There is no rest for the wicked;' and truly, I never felt so convinced of my own wickedness as . . . since I have been in this country."[2] But there was a rousing welcome from the Hodgkinsons, their old shipmates from the *Pacific,* and they took her riding next day in beautiful weather. The goose was hanging high even though the objective of the ride was the new pride of the Bay Area's heart, the sylvan Mount Auburn cemetery out beyond Cambridge. At the time few emblems of mortality yet marred its beauties. Fanny did not know then that the place would be part of her life. Pierce Butler would court her there and in little more than a year Aunt Dall would be a tenant for all eternity.

After the rawness of Baltimore and Washington, the standoffishness of Philadelphia, and the garish jostling of New York, Fanny found Boston "one of the pleasantest towns imaginable. The houses are like English houses; the Common is like Constitution Hill; Beacon Street is like a bit of Park Lane; and Summer Street, now the [horse] chestnut trees are in bloom, is perfectly beautiful."[3] When visiting Britons thus remarked resemblances to London, upper-crust Bostonians, who tended to be overtly or cryptically anglophile, always purred happily. Further, Fanny told Harness in a gay letter, Boston was the most blue [harboring cultivated literary women] town in the Union as well as the most aristocratic; granted "the society is a little stiff."[4] But that was more observation than complaint. Cordially received, the Kembles cleared the social barrier hardly aware it was there.

The Hodgkinsons, well entrenched in the right quarters, must have helped there. Further effective were letters of introduction to the right people from Boston's own Edward Everett, calling them "distinguished and amiable strangers,"[5] and Sir Charles Vaughan, then British minister to Washington, to George Ticknor, eminent professor of languages at Harvard: ". . . the distinguished support of the English stage Mr. Charles Kemble & Miss Fanny Kemble. . . . Mr. Kemble you perhaps saw when you were in London, but Miss Kemble is a new luminary . . . an authoress as well as an actress . . . her play has at once placed her high in the literature of our country."[6] So the Kembles were immediately asked to a party at the Harrison Gray Otises to follow Fanny's opening in *Fazio*. The social verdict was most favorable. Anna Quincy, daughter of the president of Harvard, "could hardly believe that this delicate, subdued, *shadowy* creature was the Bianca who had been exhibiting such power . . . Mr. Kemble is . . . very much of a gentleman and very little of the actor about him. Miss Kemble drops the character of actress entirely. . . . We were . . . very agreeably impressed."[7] And so also were, apparently, the Wards, the Crowninshields, the Appletons, the Parkmans, the Everetts[8] and other pillars of Beacon Hill and Cambridge who entertained these gracefully cultivated visitors. Some who had been somewhat put off the first evening by Fanny's "subdued manners" later found her "very animated and pleasant, disposed to meet people half way," which Martha Ward, writing to her father, attributed to "her not having [acted] last evening, and feeling quite rested."[9]

In the theater it was New York and Philadelphia all over again, only the public warmed up sooner. "You say we have the Kemble fever on us," Martha Ward advised her father early in May. ". . . Boston people are very ardent and enthusiastic, and when they admire a thing, they admire it with all their heart and soul."[10] Thus to find a volatile enthusiasm in Boston of that day (or this) is strange; but it is a great tribute to Fanny's stage presence that any such notion occurred to a Boston girl. "It is delightful," quoth Fanny, forgetting she disliked the stage, "to act to audiences . . . so pleasantly pleased with us." She could see out of her window the theater box-office being mobbed every morning. Every night a mass of Harvard students came in from Cambridge to crush into the pit to adore her. Many came an hour early to line the street between hotel and stage door just to glimpse her as she passed. Henry Lee, then a pattern youth, wrote sixty years later:

> I scarcely ever go by the Tremont House without gazing once more at the windows of her room, in the superstitious hope that her radiant face may shine forth. It seems but yesterday we were all youths and maidens hanging round Tremont Place to see her mount Niagara—a horse I rode henceforth, on holidays, and in vacations, because she had been on his back. . . . Every young girl who could sported Fanny Kemble curls.[11]

One Brahmin schoolgirl, Sarah Perkins, stole daily into the hotel to hang a fresh bunch of flowers on the doorknob of Miss Kemble's room. One morning Fanny lay in wait, pounced out, and caught her, laughing and blushing, and made her a lifelong friend, confidante of some of her most intimate troubles.

Among the few not altogether bowled over had been ex-president John Quincy Adams who, seeing Fanny perform in Washington, had told his wife rather grudgingly that "Fanny Kemble [passes] for a great Beauty and a great Genius, both of which, with the aid of Fashion and Fancy, she is."[12] Now at dinner at the Parkmans one evening he found Fanny placed beside him and on her other side Daniel Webster. Both statesmen made the mistake, obviously with courteous intentions, of trying to talk Shakespeare with Sarah Siddons's niece. Webster drew first fire by saying that for all its theatrical virtues, the writing in *The Hunchback* was nothing like as good as Shakespeare's. Fanny replied as crisply as ever a naughty girl of twenty-two did to an august orator-lawyer-politician of fifty-odd that, after all, Shakespeares did not grow on every bush. Adams stepped into the breach, saying that he worshiped Shakespeare but for all that, *King Lear* was "ludicrous . . and Romeo and Juliet childish nonsense,"[13] and that he considered all "[Desdemona's] misfortunes as a very just judgment upon her for having married a 'nigger.' "[14]

That attitude in a great elder statesman who spent much of his latter years harassing proslavery elements in Congress will astonish only those unfamiliar with the private racisms of many who opposed black slavery. Fanny "swallowed half a pint of water, and nearly my tumbler, too, and remained silent."[15] Adams's diary shows him trying to make amends by mentioning Fanny's poems "but she did not seem inclined to talk of them . . . appeared chiefly to pride herself on horsemanship—She said she had rode that morning about thirty miles, and leaped over many fences and stone walls."[16] But things went better some days later when Adams brought elderly Washington Allston, Boston's most revered painter, to call on the Kembles. Fanny was charmed, and one may assume that the ensuing cordial chat did not deal with either Shakespeare or "niggers."

Comparable jarring marred an occasion to which she had eagerly looked forward—meeting the Reverend Dr. William Henry Channing, focus of the Unitarianism then subduing Yankee Calvinism and infiltrating the Northeast generally. He was fruitfully known to such intimates of Fanny's as the Combes and Harriet St. Leger; and ranked with Niagara Falls and Daniel Webster's forehead as things that British visitors always sought to see. In spite of an almost dwarfish body and chronic illness, he became a charmingly iconoclastic conscience for the Yankee soul—the sort of part that Emerson played for the next generation. With Fanny, introduced by Catharine Sedgwick, New England's chief bluestocking, he made the same mistake as Adams. Candidly admitting that his growing disapproval of the stage had long kept him out of theaters, he suggested that the best parts of Shakespeare, say the dagger scene in Macbeth, would lose little by being merely well declaimed before private audiences, which would shield The Bard and his best class of admirers from the distortions and pollutions inevitable on the stage.

Fanny soon knew Channing better, vastly admired him, and owed her eventual embracing of Unitarianism—her own version, of course—as much to him as to Philadelphia's W. H. Furness; and his writings on black slavery left deep marks in her life. But at this time this proposal left her "a little stunned," and eloquently she relieved her mind in her journal:

> The very cleverest men . . . talk the greatest stuff imaginable about actors and acting. . . . What! take one of Shakespeare's plays bit by bit . . . destroy the marvellous unity . . . to make patches of declamation! If the stage is evil put it away . . . with . . . those writings which properly belong to . . . nothing else. . . . [but] the effect proper and natural to a fine dramatic conception [cannot] be preserved . . . without the assistance of distance, dress, scenic effects,—all the appertainings that the author has reckoned upon to work out his idea." [17]

Thirty years later, if Fanny looked back through her writings and came on that passage, she must have laughed heartily at herself—a thing she was given to. For precisely what Channing had proposed and she so scorned—the reading of Shakespeare with no help from the traditional stage trappings, indeed with no trappings at all, not even actors—was exactly what she had made her second and highly lucrative and vastly satisfactory career.

Cordial, quasi-homelike Boston gave Fanny several lasting women friends—Catharine Sedgwick, Sarah Perkins, Fanny and Mary Appleton—but out of the pack of eager Boston youths with whom she danced and chatted none suggested what might have been a wise course for her—a Boston marriage. That would have settled her in surroundings she found amenable among people inclined to recognize her sound qualities. Such a match would have been a nine days' wonder, of course. But Louisburg Square could hardly have been stiffer than Walnut Street proved to be about one of its own marrying even an unsullied and cultivated actress. Indeed in the shadow of the sacred codfish the auspices might have been a touch better. But Boston's young men were probably soon aware that Fanny was already deep in what was then called "a previous attachment." Three days after the Kembles reached Boston she came in from a midday ride, having stopped to buy flowers to wear on stage that night, to find in the Tremont House's public parlor her father chatting with Pierce Butler.

Immediately he was underfoot. "Quite a beau of hers," Martha Ward told her father. "He rides with her, walks with her & waits on her most devotedly."[18] When the Hodgkinsons took the Kembles on horseback to Bunker Hill and Fresh Pond—a bit of topography that delighted Fanny—Pierce was included. When they went to the sea beach toward Lynn, as yet undignified by an amusement park, Pierce was included. To the Blue Hills, ditto. . . . In New York Pierce and Fanny had already been riding unchaperoned. On one balmy afternoon they took the ferry to Hoboken and rode up the Stevens bluff above Weehawken: "New York lay bright and distinct on the opposite shore, glittering like a heap of toys in the sunny distance . . . far up on the other side the river rolled away among shores that, even in this wintry time of bare trees and barren earth, looked gay and lovely in the sunshine." Jogging homeward through sunny woodlands, they got discussing "the difference between religion as felt by men and women,"[19] and it may have been much to Pierce's advantage that Fanny found this son of a petulantly freethinking mother able to discuss what William James would eventually call the will-to-believe. Pierce Butler was not essentially stupid. But the available bits and pieces indicate that under his quiet, well-collected surface he was smugly arbitrary.

Now in Boston they had other unchaperoned rides. Years later

Fanny so specifically associated Mount Auburn with her young happiness that anybody seeking the locus of their troth-plighting should
look there first. Sometime in May 1833, the fire-eating Irish adven-
turer's grandson and the west-country stroller's granddaughter became engaged.[20] Word of this filtered back to Philadelphia. "The
whole world is talking," Julia Kean wrote to her mother from Ball-
ston Spa. ". . . we shall probably see this celebrated actress placed
in one of the most elegant establishments in our country and leading
the circle which now scarcely deigns to notice her."[21] There was less
animus, and more common sense, in a letter that Walter Stirling, an
old friend of Mrs. Siddons's, wrote to a Philadelphian friend who had
asked guidance in re Fanny: "Her character is above question . . .
she is a perfect lady . . . but she is troublesome and self willed
. . . despising all authority and advice . . . since infancy she has
been the source of perpetual annoyance and anxiety—I am sure [her
parents] will be glad when she is married but I pity the poor man
. . . especially if he is so amiable a person as you think
Mr. Butler."[22] Stirling also thought that Fanny's acting was amateurish and overrated, quoting Melpomene in indirect confirmation,
and implied that Thérèse's difficult temperament had been a trial for
Charles. As it turned out, her parents were the last people to rejoice
when Fanny married; and as years passed, "amiable" was no word for
Pierce Butler.

There was no question of marrying soon. Though the Kemble
nest egg was growing, it needed another full season to reach its
goals. Charles and Fanny planned further to exploit their popularity
in the Northeast, then, in winter, go down to New Orleans, a famous
show-town where a long engagement would mean rich profits and get
them away from the worst of the cold. Then back to the Northeast
with the spring. By mid-1834 Fanny might be allowed to marry and,
as Aunt Dall knew was inevitable in marriage outside the profession,
leave the stage. Meanwhile the 1832–33 season was fraying out. They
would go junketing to Niagara Falls and over into Canada, covering
at least part of the cost with brief engagements in Albany, Montreal,
Quebec. Pierce would return to Philadelphia, attend to his neglected
affairs, and join the party in upper New York State.

Until then Fanny was not to lack amusing escort. In the Hudson
River steamboat northbound on June 30, 1833, somebody introduced
her to a celebrated Briton also going sightseeing—Edward John
(sometimes John Edward) Trelawny. He was a striking figure even
before one knew his story: deeply tanned, which then meant either
outdoor livelihood or exotic adventure; a nose no Kemble need have
scorned; bright blue eyes and, at forty years, still tree-tall and
sinewy. Any theater would have hired him to play Oriental princes
and bandit chiefs.

> A savage . . . in some respects [Fanny soon wrote] . . .
> a giant for strength . . . yet with the most listless indo-
> lent carelessness of gait . . . as if he didn't know where
> he was going, and didn't much wish to. . . . a wild
> strange look. . . . mouth . . . remarkably mild and
> sweet . . . voice is extremely low and gentle. . . . never
> profanes [his hands] with gloves, but wears two strange
> magical looking rings;—one . . . made of elephant's
> hair. . . . Occasionally, in his horror of one class of prej-
> udices, he embraces the opposite ones.

When a sudden thunderstorm soaked her light summer gown, Trelawny solicitously took her below to dry out by the boiler fire, "talking the while. . . . Mr. [Trelawny] is sun burnt enough to warm
one . . . with a look." Throughout the trip upriver, as the magnificent scenery streamed by and the pulsing forward urge of the engines
throbbed underfoot, she found this genuine descendant of a long line
of Cornish aristocrats "agreeable to talk to."[23]

It was he who had taken charge of Shelley's drowned body recovered from the Gulf of Spezia and spectacularly burned it on the
beach, at the last moment snatching the heart from among the siz-
zling coals. He had seen much of Byron in Italy and gone with him
to aid the rebel Greeks—the fashionable romantic cause of the day—
among whom he had held key guerrilla commands; and married the
barely nubile daughter of a partisan chief and brought her to England, where she died, leaving a baby daughter. He was much more
than willing to talk about his remarkable past. And not least because
it involved Byron, Fanny "to hear did seriously incline." He showed

her a letter to himself from Claire Claremont, Byron's mistress who
had borne him a son; for Trelawny she seemed to be a sisterly confidante. Fanny thought the letter notable only for unfeminine concision
and wondered whether he "gave it me . . . on that account . . . or
because it contained allusions to wild and interesting adventures of
his own."[24]

There were plenty of those. Two years previously, as if Byron,
Shelley, and Greek guerrilla-heroes were not enough, Trelawny had
anonymously published a book, *Adventures of a Younger Son,* that,
though issued as a novel, was widely taken as autobiography. Since
the narrator depicted himself as smuggler, deserter, and traitor, he
might well wish to stay unidentified, but he never got round to de-
nying that the "I" of the book was Edward John Trelawny. Specifically "I" told of enrollment as midshipman in the Royal Navy in the
middle period of the Napoleonic wars; of skipping ship in India,
taking up with the dashing Dutch captain of a French privateer and
commanding a schooner for him in sea fights against Chinese, Malay-
sian, and British vessels. On land "I" fought tigers, elephants, natives, and other local fauna; admired his captain's secret plantation on
a tropical island worked by liberated slaves; rescued and married a
lovely Arab girl of thirteen. She went privateering with him as a sort
of child-bride supercargo, was poisoned and died. Heartbroken, "I"
made his way home and resumed the life of a well-born, hard-up
gentleman.

In the *Pacific* Fanny had dipped into *Younger Son* but left no
opinion of it. She may not have reached the latter chapters where, as
an expert on Trelawny says, he makes himself out "a repulsive character . . . even by the standards of the age."[25] She cannot have
known—the truth did not come out for a century—that most of the
lurid goings-on in the book never happened. About Byron and Shelley Trelawny is less suspect, but the seriousness with which he and
his *Younger Son* were taken makes him one of the world's most successful liars. It was not true at all that he deserted from the Royal
Navy in romantic disgust. Instead he was prosaically discharged into
civilian life in the usual fashion back home in England instead of
exotic India. He did see some sea fighting in the Indian Ocean and

the East Indies but under Royal Navy colors. The freebooting, jungle perils, beautiful girls, etc., etc., were all moonshine. Lady Anne Hill, who first went into this, estimated the ratio of truth to fiction as 1/10.[26] Even the style is bogus, aping that of *Tom Cringle's Log,* an admired series of overwritten sketches of high jinks in the West Indies running in *Blackwood's* at the time when Trelawny was begetting his *Younger Son.*[27]

He lived on into the 1880s rather unstably, refusing to wear socks, edging toward vegetarianism, making a marriage that broke up, publishing recollections of Shelley and Byron to revive old glories, always picturesque. In old age he sat for the grizzled sea captain in John Everett Millais's episodic painting, "The Northwest Passage." In London in the 1840s when he frequented the same drawingrooms, Fanny saw a good deal of him. At his death Algernon Charles Swinburne who, like many, took this synthetic swashbuckler at his own estimate, gave him verses unworthy of so capable a poet:

> Worldwide liberty's lifelong lover,
>   Lover no less of the strength of song,
> Sea-king, swordsman, hater of wrong.

On the way to Albany the Kembles stopped over to visit Gouverneur Kemble's estate at Cold Spring opposite West Point. Trelawny was encouraged to wait for them and take the same steamboat northward two days later. At Albany he went along to see the falls of the Mohawk at Cohoes and, when transport back to Albany failed them, hired a skiff and rowed them back downriver. By the time they left Albany by rail for Schenectady, he was established as one of the party. "I am glad of it," Fanny wrote. "I like him."[28] So, one assumes, did Charles. Trelawny was writing to an old friend: "I should particularly wish you to know Fanny Kemble . . . an admirable musician, Poetess, and altogether a Lady."[29] On the canalboat from Schenectady to Utica he entertained them by reading aloud from *Don Quixote.* A less self-centered man might have hesitated to do that in presence of three professional actors, one of whom sometimes read for the British royal family. But they took it well: Fanny commented that "he reads . . . with very marked emphasis. . . . a strong sense

of humour, as well as poetry."[30] It was merry and leisurely taking the air on the deck of the smooth-sliding boat; the only
responsibility was taking care to duck at the traditional warning
shout of "Low bridge!" Trelawny soon felt well enough acquainted to
show Fanny a journal he was keeping, and she enjoyed accusing him
of being smitten by the impulsive, pretty attendant of the ladies'
cabin, advising him to marry her and settle down in bucolically romantic peace on a Mohawk Valley farm.

That Fanny was having a high old time is unmistakable. Cold
Spring had been richly pleasant. Gouverneur Kemble's boat had met
his kinfolk and wafted them over to the left bank where his country
place harmoniously coexisted with his cannon foundry that made ord-
nance for the U.S. Army; one was famous for hospitality, the other
for efficiency. From the veranda

> through various frames which [Kemble] has had cut
> . . . among the plantations [plantings of trees] around
> the lawn, exquisite glimpses appeared of the mountains,
> the little bay, the glorious Hudson itself, with the grace-
> ful boats for ever walking its broad waters, their white
> sails coming through the rocky passes, where the river
> could not be detected, as though they were sailing
> through the vallies [sic] of the earth.[31]

Charles and Aunt Dall half dozed in veranda chairs as befitted
their years but Kemble and his brother William had Fanny stirred up
by a promise of waterfalls on the property. They took her through
the foundry, all shut down for Sunday, and then climbing, climbing,
hearing water in the depths of a ravine until "a silver thread of gush-
ing water . . . ran like a frightened child across our way. . . . At
length, we reached the brown, golden-looking stream"—which so
enthralled Fanny that she insisted on following it up to the falls instead of taking a parallel path. That meant wading the stream several
times, which delighted her; so did the pool from which it issued fed
by three separate falls. Her passion for running water had her "in
perfect ecstacy . . . an uncontrollable desire seized me to clamber up
the rocks by the side of the fall." The Kemble brothers laughed at
her but there was no opposing this compact nixie. Gouverneur stayed

at the pool with her handbag, parasol, and bonnet; William under-
took to guide her up "over the ledges . . . nothing but damp leaves,
and slippery roots of trees for footing. At one moment . . . I swung
over the water by a young sapling . . . by which I recovered footing.
. . . I was soaked through with spray . . . had no hold. . . . With
my head bowed against the foam . . . I was feeling where next to
tread." William Kemble tried to haul her up through the fall by one
hand but flubbed the first try because, as John Mason had observed
on the faraway stage of the Theatre Royal, Bath, Fanny weighed more
than she looked. On the second try he

> drew me up beside where he was sitting, on the edge of
> the rocks, in the water. . . . standing on the top . . .
> in the midst of the rushing brook, I wrang [*sic*] my hand-
> kerchief triumphantly at [Gouverneur down below] . . .
> literally dripping from head to foot,—no Naiad ever
> looked so thoroughly watery, or could have taken more
> delight in a ducking. . . . we presently all met on the
> dusty highway . . . and laughed very exceedingly at my
> soaked situation.[32]

What would those languid, bedizened Broadway belles have said
had they seen Juliet-Bianca-Julia cutting such capers? Or the cautiously reared young matrons of Philadelphia?

Pierce kept tryst at Utica, bringing along half a dozen silver
forks that were welcome because American public tables then supplied only two-tined iron ones. Trelawny's presence may not have
surprised him; he had probably been told of it by mail. But the
juxtaposition has given rise to the notion that Charles invited Trelawny along in hopes that his renowned charm would win Fanny away
from Pierce. Possible, of course, but the deliberateness implied is not
like Charles Kemble. True, there was the potential of a triangle sce-
nario: Trelawny smitten and hovering, Pierce stubbornly holding his
own, Fanny hesitating between them. A touch of support for this
view is found in a letter from Trelawny to Fanny, probably in spring
1834, enclosing a friend's translation of Goethe's *Der Erlkönig* and
saying: "I shall not willingly die till I have heard you sing it. . . .

I cannot at this instant think of any thing else worth living for"; [33] and from Mrs. Jameson's telling Ottilie von Goethe, after encountering Trelawny in 1857, "If he loved anyone it is Fanny Kemble who appears to be his *ideal* of womankind." [34] A mildly flirtatious glow may well have worked up. But that it got close to Fanny's emotional chemistry is doubtful. She showed signs of mistrusting his habit of hyperbole and in any case knew he was almost double her age and lacked the man-to-tie-to quality that had had her half in love with another famous man in his forties, George Stephenson.

And if Trelawny did feel irresponsible hankerings, he had very probably been made aware that the young Philadelphian soon to join the party was the best man who had already won. The situation, if any, was subtly expressed in a short sequence, as if out of a pretentious French movie shot when they all went to see the famous Trenton Falls the day after Pierce arrived. Fanny and he were wandering beside one of the smaller, less emphatic cataracts. Fanny said she was tired; Pierce was lifting her up to seat her "on [a] fallen tree, when we saw Mr. [Trelawny] coming slowly towards us. He stopped and spoke to us, and presently passed on: we remained behind talking and dipping our hands into the fresh water." [35] Nothing there; only maybe there was. Fanny's having set down so trifling an encounter could mean that subliminally she felt tactical significance in it.

At least once Pierce seems to have poked at Trelawny unnecessarily. One day in the coach, after Charles and Trelawny had been debating the merits of Edmund Kean's acting—a ticklish subject among Kembles—Pierce saw fit to recount for Fanny incidents out of Trelawny's book, the whole of which he said he had greatly enjoyed. In Trelawny's presence, mind. It makes one grin to think of the Younger Son thus hearing garbled versions of the discreditable and yet fictitious past he had invented for himself being retailed in good faith—or was it?—by a third person who might like having the author sound like a brutal, unscrupulous opportunist. Things were queerer still when Pierce, making a conspicuously special effort, procured a copy of *Younger Son* for Fanny; and when Trelawny reached over ostensibly to see what it was, Pierce "snatched it away . . . saying . . . he was sure he would not like [it]." We do not know whether Fanny now read it all. But anyway here was a bit that would have attracted Henry James. Fanny's diary goes right on, very Fannyish:

> We got out and walked whenever the horses were changed. At one place . . . I saw a meek-eyed, yellowish-white cart horse, standing with a man's saddle on his back. The opportunity was irresistible, and the desire, too; I had not backed a horse for so long; so I got up upon the amazed quadruped woman's fashion, and took a gallop through the fields, with infinite risk of falling off, and proportionate satisfaction.[36]

Fortunate horse! But so short an assuagement of so large a craving. That for running water, on the other hand, was being fed full. After that perpendicular surfeit at Cold Spring, Fanny had met the Mohawk's plunge over the bench at Cohoes where "the foam looked very nice and soft, and thick, and cold: I longed to be in the middle of it."[37] And now Trenton Falls. They were almost as eagerly viewed by tourists as Niagara—"were" because long ago the Niagara and Mohawk Power Company obliterated most of its wonders by damming the gorge of West Canada Creek to generate electricity. Its specialty, no competition for Niagara's majestic scale and single-view composition, was successive cataracts of differing shape and fall as if the designer were giving samples—good-size ones too, no niggardly miniatures—of most of the various schools of waterfall. In between these set displays the waters leaped, roared, and glittered in various colors derived from those of the underlying strata, and threw up evanescent rainbows—a sort of hydraulic three-ring circus of chaotic beauty. No fairy godmother could have provided anything nearer Fanny's heart's desire. She expressed an almost frenzied delight—heightened, no doubt, by being in love—and then blended the best of her sense of natural beauty with her sense of divine immanence:

> We rejoined the whole party, sitting by a narrow channel, where the water looked like ink. Beyond this our guide saw it was impossible to go. I was for ascertaining this by myself; but my father forbade me. . . . I was thirsty, and the guide having given me a beautiful strawberry and

a pale bluebell, that he had found, like a couple of jewels, in some dark crevice of the rocks, I devoured the one, and then going down to the black water's edge, we dipped the fairy cup in, and drank the cold, clear water. . . . Oh fair world! oh strange, and beautiful, and holy places, where one's soul meets one in silence, and where one's thoughts arise with the everlasting incense of the waters from the earth which is *His* foot-stool, to the heavens which are *His* throne. It grew dark long before we reached Utica: half the way I sang, the other half I slept, in spite of ruts five fathoms deep, and all the joltings of these evil ways. Tomorrow we start on our way to Niagara, which [Trelawny] says is to sweep Trenton clean from our memories.[38]

He recommended Niagara personally. He said it was the only thing that he, far-ranging intimate of poets, man of battles and jungles and tropical dawns, had ever seen that did not disappoint him. That makes Edward John Trelawny probably the only man ever large enough to pat Niagara Falls approvingly on the head.

Off they rolled, lurching, creaking, swaying, at one point experiencing that ineffably bumpy invention, the corduroy road—surfaced with crosswise tree trunks of more or less the same diameter—every log another jolt as the wheels struck it. They laughed over that and over the soaking they got when a gusty thunderstorm demonstrated the uselessness of leather coach-curtains. They even got round to laughing over what looked momentarily like a serious matter: One morning as they stopped for breakfast at a village tavern, the driver, making a dashing arrival as stage drivers liked to, cut his wheels too sharply in rounding to, and the coach crashed on its side.

Fanny was under Charles, half-smothered by his bulk but neither was worse than bruised. Trelawny was momentarily stunned. Instinctively Pierce had clambered topside as the coach went over and had only a scratched finger. Aunt Dall, however, had a badly cut-up head and was bleeding profusely. The tavern people carried her inside and Trelawny, almost immediately alert again, applied a proper field dressing while Fanny rallied round with hot and cold water and smelling salts. While the coach was getting righted and patched up, "we, bound up, bruised, and aching, but still very merry, sat down to breakfast. . . . seeing it was no worse, we thanked God, and devoured."[39]

At Niagara Trelawny's I've-been-here-before guidance was superb. Fanny was proud of having been taken three times under the thundering curtain of the main fall, barefoot for safety, greedily stultified by the tumult and momentum. Ecstatic, she considered Trenton "the most beautiful, and Niagara the most awful . . . terrible loveliness . . . the impulse to jump down seemed all but irresistible. . . . But for the strong arm that held mine fast I think I might very well have taken the same direction as the huge green glassy mountain of water that was pouring headlong into . . . what no eye can penetrate." Then "the impression of awe and terror . . . completely wore away . . . its dazzling brightness, its soothing voice, its gliding motion, its soft, thick, furry beds of foam, its veils and draperies of floating light . . . made it the perfection of loveliness . . . akin to the 'perfect love' which 'casteth out fear.' "[40]

Her readiness to quote Scripture and her Nature-instigated rhapsodies were, of course, stigmata of her time. But she got so much pith, force, and grace into them that their emotional validity is unquestionable. And even as nixie she was discriminating. In those days, before locked canals bypassed the St. Lawrence's several sets of rapids, one "shot" them rather hazardously in open boats of special design. Fanny felt none of the excitement she had expected: "Instead of shooting down long sheets of running water . . . we were tossed and tumbled about and shaken up and down in the midst of a dozen conflicting currents . . . which break the whole surface into short pitching waves, and dance about in frantic white whirligigs, like . . . the bad nuns' ghosts in [*Robert le Diable*]." And at Quebec, which she thought sternly charming, "we went to visit two fine waterfalls . . . but of course to us just now there is but one waterfall in the whole world."[41]

How Aunt Dall and Charles felt about Fanny's engagement remains a matter of surmise. It probably changed as circumstances did. For the first months Charles doubtless found Pierce's society gentlemanly enough. Apparently without misgivings Aunt Dall somewhat relaxed chaperonage in his favor. But in the winter of 1833–34 Fanny's elders had other food for thought. The party's growing assets made more stringent the question of what Charles's creditors might do to his earnings when he brought them home, or to any income from investments in America remitted to him in England. They seriously discussed a scheme—a favorite of Aunt Dall's—to renounce Britain as too risky and settle down on the income from their American gains modestly and cheerfully in some nice corner, in France, say, as John Philip had done in Switzerland. There Thérèse, Aunt Dall, and Charles could enjoy the retirement that their failing health and advancing years deserved. Fanny, free of the vexations of acting, could go on with the writing that others besides her family thought promised well.

Yet as it grew clearer how seriously smitten Pierce was, it may well have crossed their minds that Fanny's part might change. Regardless of her father's tenuous resources, Mrs. Pierce Butler would be taken care of for life. But there was much to be said—or if not said, turned over in the tacit mind—against it. Marrying an American would mean virtual expatriation and was a disturbing notion besides. In Aunt Dall's view her marrying at all was not too advisable. Brother John Mitchell passed on to Fanny the sort of misgivings that word of the matter had roused in him and others: "Do let me know, dearest Fan, when this terrible affair of marriage is to be . . . much righteous indignation has been excited . . . they say . . . that when you have a house and a nursery to look after, you will leave off writing plays." And with the pomposity that he could never quite drop: "However, dearest girl, you will be happy if your husband only knows how to value you."[42] It was uncomfortable to have to decide so important an issue without getting Thérèse's shrewd and pungent counsel firsthand, but that was impossible. As Americans went, Pierce was presentable and there was enough eighteenth century—not to mention nineteenth and twentieth—in Charles and Aunt Dall for a most considerable fortune to carry weight. And the girl was certainly fond of him.

Not long after they reached "an understanding" and word of it got abroad, ground for uneasiness appeared. Charles Hodgkinson came to Aunt Dall and Charles to warn them, how explicitly one cannot know, that Pierce's "early career of profligacy" made him an unfit match. They passed on to Fanny these intimations of immorality but one wonders how emphatically, how tactfully? "I was in love," Fanny explained long afterward to the Sedgwicks, and "paid little heed to . . . cautions . . . at second hand."[43] The match held. In October 1833, after the Niagara tour gave the pair ample opportunity to meet under trying conditions, Fanny told Anna Jameson, "I shall not return to England, not even to visit . . . certainly never to make my home there again . . . rejoice with me that there is a prospect of my leaving [the stage] before its pernicious excitement has been rendered necessary to me."[44] This must mean that marriage at the end of the 1833–34 season was definitely planned. The emphasis on Fanny's quitting the stage may have its own significance.

The trip to New Orleans was not made. Hindsight hints that it may have been a pity. Had Fanny had a good look at the particular black slavery of that sugar-based, quasi-West Indian subculture with its stratum of free *gens de couleur,* unsavory quadroon concubinage, and French-Colonial sangfroid, all floating on the sweatiest and most dehumanizing kind of gang slave-labor, her already lively distaste for the "peculiar institution" might have sharpened until it ruptured her engagement to a suave young man whose chief potential resource was slavery. As it was, the Kembles' second season was confined largely to New York, Philadelphia, Boston. One assumes—direct evidence is scanty—that Pierce was with them much of the time.[45]

Aunt Dall's physical emergency may have been what ruled New Orleans out. The doctors blamed the head injury received when the coach turned over for a gradual degeneration of the nervous system. Toward spring she was paralyzed below the waist and having convulsions. Toward the end of the Kembles' second Boston engagement, further bookings were canceled to allow Fanny to devote herself to her aunt: "My first lonely watching by a sickbed, and I feel deeply the sadness and awfulness of the office . . . [after the final Boston performance] the phlegmatic Bostonians seemed almost beside themselves . . . they shouted at us, they cheered us, they crowned me with roses. Conceive . . . . the shocking contrast between this and the silent sick-room, to which I went straight from the stage."[46] From the sickroom Fanny wrote broodingly to George Combe about the blow that loss of Aunt Dall's "unwearied kindness and devotedness" would be to her and even worse for Charles and "my poor mother."[47] A week later, as the pain was somewhat receding, Adelaide De Camp died. "Her last words . . . after a night of angelic endurance . . . were, 'Open the window, let in the blessed light.' "[48]

They buried her in a lot that Fanny bought in Mount Auburn near where she and Pierce had often dallied. For years afterward she insisted that she wished to be buried there herself by the side of the shrewd, plucky, dearly beloved old lady and asked Boston friends to be sure the plot was properly tended. "I have almost cried my eyes out for the last three months," she told Anna Jameson ten days after the funeral, "but that is over now. I am working again [in New York] and go about my work feeling stunned and bewildered."[49]

Bewilderment probably had a hand in subsequent events. Adelaide De Camp's incapacity and death could not have come at a time worse for Charles and Fanny. Her sober canniness was unavailable when crucially needed. The record is so fragmentary that piecing the story together is like reading only every fifth line of a memorandum. It is unmistakable that even before Aunt Dall died—though not before the fatigues and anxieties consequent on her illness had clouded the others' judgment—the chief issue was drawn. Pierce was single-mindedly pushing for marriage in May as planned the previous year. Fanny inclined that way chiefly because she was in love; less weightily but recognizably because marriage would free her from the stage. As the actuality approached, Charles grew dubious. His basic attitude toward Pierce is not known. They had been much together without overt frictions. But there was Hodgkinson's warning, and Charles certainly knew enough of men's world to understand that Pierce's decorous smoothness might mask much that would dismay Fanny.

Besides, the clan's economic situation had changed. In their second season the takings had been, though worthwhile, less than those of 1832–33, which was almost inevitable once they ceased to be novelties. Fanny's share, some thirty-five thousand dollars, was earning good interest in the New Orleans banks that someone had recommended. But some twenty thousand dollars of Charles's share had been entrusted to Nicholas Biddle's Bank of the United States, the deservedly respected keystone of the American financial system, which was succumbing to President Jackson's plans to smother it after the election of 1832. How many cents on the dollar would come out of it was anybody's guess, none optimistic. Fortunately—this is dim but necessarily implied—Charles had somehow learned that his creditors would make no trouble for him on his return. One would like to know whether Pierce was one of the council of war consisting otherwise now of only Charles and Fanny that made the decision that Fanny announced to George Combe in mid-April 1834:

"I shall continue my labors for another twelve months either there [Britain] or here . . . I hoped to be free from a profession that has always been irksome . . . but . . . I have good cause."[50] Within two weeks of Aunt Dall's funeral a return to Britain was decided on. Jubilantly Charles told Harness that Fanny and he were booked home late in June on a famously fine packet, the *United States:* "How happy Fanny's friends will be to see her once more before she is married, won't they? The legitimate drama will have another chance, I hope, of resuscitation; and we shall both at least take leave of the British stage in a manner worthy of the house of Kemble!"[51] Sadly Fanny wrote to Harriet that "the sole care of my father, who is deeply afflicted . . . and charge of every thing, devolves on me now."[52]

Plainly Pierce was to wait a year or so while Fanny completed her parents' old-age security fund. Had this plan been carried out, distance and postponement might have spared Fanny the miseries that her marriage brought. Pierce Butler had already waited long to claim his bride from the toils—in both senses—of what he eventually showed himself to consider her flyblown profession. And stubborn though he was, he was hardly the man to wait another year for a girl three thousand miles away too busy to marry him.

The experiment was never tried. Pierce, whose manipulative skill was high when his heart was in it, managed a thin-edge-of-the-wedge compromise that he can hardly have taken seriously but Fanny did. While the Kembles played their delayed farewell engagement in Philadelphia, it was decided that Fanny and Pierce would marry and have a semihoneymoon in the intervals of the farewell booking in New York. Then Fanny would sail for home with her father while Pierce waved a wistful farewell. Her account of this absurd arrangement is a pathetic or maybe willful failure to understand how unreal it was. It also hints at the kinds of pressure that Pierce had brought to bear and the strain they had put on whatever goodwill Charles bore him:

> A ray of sunshine is parting my stormy sky. Pierce has behaved *most* nobly, and my father most kindly—surely it is most noble to confess an error to a person whom you do not like and whom you feel has committed an injustice toward you.[53] We are together again the whole day long and on Saturday next before sailing for New York, we shall *be married.* . . . Pierce has promised me that this shall not interfere with my departure or the discharge of my duties to my father, and relying implicitly . . . on his word, I could not resist his entreaties to be his wife before I gave myself up to those chances which might never have suffered him to call me by that name. I cannot tell whether I have done for the best . . . he implored me so that I do not believe I had much power of thought . . . I think seventeen happy days snatched on the very brink of bitterness and parting not to be denied to one who has followed my footsteps for a whole year with a hope which he now beholds defeated.[54]

Thus the news reached the Sedgwicks in the Berkshires. Next day Catharine Sedgwick, who usually spent winters with brother Theodore in New York, was writing to her English blue-stocking friend, Mary Russell Mitford: "I admire and love [Fanny Kemble, who is] soon to be married. Butler is a gentlemanly man, with good sense and amiable disposition, infinitely her inferior. Poor girl, she makes a dangerous experiment; I have a thousand fears for the result."[55]

Six days later at Christ Church, Philadelphia, "the venerable Bishop White"[56] married Frances Anne Kemble and Pierce Butler, Mrs. John Butler matron of honor. A large and inquisitive crowd massed outside the church; another serenaded the newlyweds late that evening at their hotel. Next morning steamboat and rail—fellow passengers on the boat reported the bride wept all the way to Burlington—to New York to play out a contracted-for week at the Park Theatre. Fanny's contribution to Charles's benefit was to play Lady Freelove in Thérèse's standard farce, *The Day After the Wedding,* about a fractious bride brought to heel by a clever husband. But her final farewell to the American stage took place the following night in Philadelphia in a farce of Mrs. Inchbald's carrying on the joke, *The Wedding Day.* Back in Philadelphia? Yes. At some time during the promised seventeen days Pierce had played whatever emotional ace was up his sleeve and turned the arrangement upside down. Fanny made over to Charles full life-interest in her thirty-five thousand dollars to compensate him for lack of her collaboration and stayed in America.

Philadelphia did not quite get the situation straight. An account in Rebecca Gratz's letter to her sister in the South was probably nearer than most:

> She had consented to another year's labour for her father . . . when the time arrived, her lover, who was prevented by a law suit from leaving the country, could not bear to part with her, without first securing her hand—and when married, could not consent to the separation or to her continuing in the stage—her father was angry at losing the aid of her professional talents, considered himself wronged and deceived . . . since which it is reported that the Miss Butlers [Pierce's surviving aunts] have granted an annuity to her Mother, which secures her from any disappointment her daughter's retirement might have occasioned, and thus the good and talented Miss K is rewarded for her filial piety, and it is believed she will be a very happy wife. . . . The Butler family receive her very cordially.[57]

Sailing home alone, with his well-beloved and indispensable daughter exiled in marriage and his well-beloved and invaluable sister-in-law dead and buried, and his and his wife's interests only marginally served, Charles had reason to feel "wronged and deceived." So did Thérèse, to judge from a letter of Lady Dacre's to John Murray:

"[Fanny] cannot be so wrong toward her parents; as in all quarrels *both* are to blame . . . and there are two violent tempers . . . we are pretty well assured." [58] It certainly would have roused Fanny's violent temper had she known that Walnut Street believed Pierce's aunts had in effect bought her off from her father by endowing her mother. Much preferable was the emotion that came over her twenty-odd years later when she tried for the young Sedgwicks "a short sketch of the circumstances of my engagement . . . my heart failed me . . . it seemed to me too sad." [59]

VIII

Love, Honor, and Obey

WHEN LETTING Sarah Perkins know that she was about to marry,
Fanny warned her schoolgirl friend no longer to "imagine me . . .
as Fanny Kemble running along Chelsea Beach—or dipping her feet
in Jamaica Pond—but sober Mrs. Pierce Butler with a ring on her
third finger . . . and all the grave cares of matrimony."[1] That phase
did not set in until after a stay in Newport where Fanny was reported
"very gay, waltzing and gallopading most gracefully."[2] But then the
new Fanny Butler was to set up housekeeping at Butler Place, the
old major's larger farm six miles north of Philadelphia's Market
Street. Thérèse's daughter looked eagerly forward to "a garden, greenhouse, and dairy . . . to each of which I intend to addict myself
zealously."[3] But the painters and carpenters refitting the place—
probably set to work on short notice when the marriage finally crys-
tallized—had months yet to go. The rest of the year the newlyweds
spent as guests of the John Butlers in their new town house in Philadelphia.

One knows little of Fanny's relations with the beautiful Mrs.
John, except that they had little in common and seem not to have
quarreled. Sometimes they are mentioned as paired ornaments of a
dance or dinner. As to John Butler, the only person I have found who
had a good word for him was the fellow officer who wrote home to
his wife when he died in the Mexican War. Fanny's only comment
on her brother-in-law expressed annoyance because, aware of her name
for dashing horsemanship, he spurred up hell-for-leather when riding

with her. She seems rather to have liked Dr. Mease, her father-in-law, but saw little of him. While waiting for Butler Place to become habitable, she professed herself content studying manuals of house-keeping, trying to master double-entry bookkeeping—at Pierce's instance?—and consulting with cabinetmakers and upholsterers. She told Anna Jameson, "My pets are a horse, a bird, and a black squirrel, and I do not see exactly what more a reasonable woman could desire."[4] Sarcasm, of course, for at that very time she was immersed in fair-copying for publication the catch-as-catch-can diary she had kept during her first year in America. And that was not only an arduous task, it was the second-greatest mistake she ever made. This project occasioned fierce quarrels between her and her new husband. Henceforth in this disastrous marriage Pierce seldom had the right of a dispute. This time he did; whereas Fanny had been and still was too young and headstrong to understand how very inadvisable such publication would be.

Her original reason for arranging to publish was admirable. It had troubled her that Aunt Dall received from the Kembles for whom she did so much only food, lodging, and what pin money Charles could spare her; beyond that her resources were nil. Now Charles's anticipated retirement would straiten his resources. How nice it would be if Aunt Dall had a modest nest egg bringing in a few shillings a day as interest and available for emergencies. Suppose sale of Fanny's diary to an American and then a British publisher would bring in one thousand pounds. Some time that first winter stateside she contracted with Henry C. Carey, chief of Carey & Lea, Philadelphia publishers of, among others, Thomas Carlyle, Washington Irving, and Sir Walter Scott, for publication rights for twenty-five hundred dollars. Soon after marrying, she completed a parallel arrangement with John Murray, the London publisher who had brought out *Francis the First*. Now Aunt Dall was dead; the primary reason for publishing was gone. But the agreement with Carey & Lea stood and, happy thought, the money could go to Aunt Victoire who, having only her meager salary from that girls' school, could surely use it.

By early summer Carey had enough copy to begin setting up.

Late in November, while at John Butler's, Fanny reported to Harriet, "I toil on, copying my Journal, and one volume of it is already printed; but now that the object . . . is gone, I feel rather disgusted with the idea of publishing it all. . . . It seems to me a mere mass of trivial egotism . . . mere trash, but I have sold it."[5] This revulsion may mean more than the distaste for a piece of writing that often troubles the writer going back over it. For several months the journal project had been a fulminating *casus belli*. For in Pierce's view her text contained so much "unfit for the public eye"[6] that it should not be published at all. He is said to have tried to persuade Carey to withdraw it but the letter of the bond was insisted on. As it was, Carey had waited a year for delivery, and the sooner the thing appeared after Fanny's retirement, the better it could exploit her theatrical renown and conspicuous marriage.

So Pierce, deploying his new rights as husband to protect his wife from the consequences of brashness, began to censor her copy. That soon nudged her from annoyance into exasperation. "Any curtailment," he recalled in his own behalf fourteen years later, "greatly irritated her; she opposed the slightest alteration. . . . Every sentence . . . was stoutly defended, and my suggestions made her very angry."[7] Understandably these harsh squabbles made her sick of her "mere trash"; but she was not prepared to let anybody, not even the husband she had promised at the altar to obey, order her to omit this or tone down that. In the end she did knuckle under many times. In the published text Pierce's victories are marked with squads and platoons of asterisks and suspension points like crosses on battlefields. But every such victory had brought blood and tears. Reverse the usual formula: During the battle of the book she and he began to understand each other rather too well. It was not at all like what she had told Anna Jameson she assumed her marriage would be like: "no fairyland of enchantments . . . [but] rest, quiet, leisure to study, to think, and to work, and legitimate channels for the affections of my nature."[8]

One darkening November evening came a crisis. Fanny packed up and walked out of John Butler's house. The note she left asked that her things be turned over to whomever she sent for them and her pet bird be given to Rose, Sully's daughter. A twenty-dollar bill was to cover any petty debts. These gestures smelled of burning bridges. But three hours later she returned, went to her room, lay down without undressing, and slept until morning. There followed a gingerly patching-up but apparently it implied no valid readjustment. In the next ten years that would be the story again and again and again.

At year's end Butler Place was ready. They moved out there on December 31. On January 3 whatever hopes that the New Year and the new environment would alleviate matters disappeared. For that day the New York *Commercial Advertiser* came out with:

MRS. FANNY KEMBLE BUTLER.

This spirited and popular lady seems to have placed herself in rather an awkward predicament. It has long been understood that . . . her travels were written out and placed in the hands of London and Philadelphia publishers. Several months ago, we . . . announced the book as . . . shortly forthcoming. . . . [It] would have been had the fair traveller been forthgoing to England—at the time she expected . . . certain it is, that the American edition has been suppressed . . . rumors say, that the orders to suppress the London edition, until the revised substitute should be received, did not reach the British capital soon enough. At all events, portions of the lady's printed journal are said to have been received both in this city, and in Boston, and the tone of her remarks upon some of the most respected citizens by whom she was kindly received and entertained, but ill corresponds with the polite attentions bestowed . . . we shall not repeat them—although it will be seen by one of the extracts that she very civilly informs her readers that "next to a bug, a newspaper writer is her disgust" . . . as those fellows who were fawning about her, praising her beauty, and puffing her performances, are very great humbugs, we marvel that she made the exception. The New York audience too are well paid for applauding her to the skies. She and her father were "CASTING PEARLS BEFORE SWINE!" [9]

Then on another page under the headline "DIARY OF A LADY" were two thousand-odd words from the journal as it went to Carey & Lea before Pierce turned surgeon.

Chatter about a leak from England was protective coloring. The Philadelphia printshop was certainly the source, and one of the printer's devils probably the culprit. That is fairly clear in a letter from Fanny to Carey exculpating persons to whom Pierce or she had shown galleys in confidence. Anybody acquainted with publishing, then or now, must be tempted to wonder whether those leaks from Fanny's raw text to the press were inadvertent, for the tumult that their appearance created was very good for eventual sales. The suspicion is, however, probably ill-founded. So grave a breach of faith does not fit with the Carey firm's reputation for scrupulous behavior, such as paying royalties to foreign authors then unprotected by American copyright law. Note also that the two phrases picked out as most outrageous were, as it happened, among those that Pierce deleted or modified before proofs were sent to the Murray firm to set from; thus, his amended version said nothing about bugs, merely, "A newspaper writer is my aversion," and nothing at all about pearls before swine.

That gave Pierce more reason to grind his teeth when he saw these indiscretions, which he thought safely erased, in cold type in public where they could cause the greatest uproar. And they did. Presently Fanny wrote to John Murray that "the wrath of the natives is excited to such a pitch that I can only promise the second volume [final version in printed sheets] *if I live*. The newspapers here have opened like a pack of hounds upon the matter."[10] Such rueful jokes were all very well. But what a destroyer of hope for eventual harmony at Butler Place this stroke of bad luck must have been.

Carey's eagerness to publish Fanny's view of America came of the same circumstances that made it inadvisable for her to do so. Foreign visitors' accounts of what-I-saw-in-America had long exasperated Americans. Much of that was, of course, hypersensitivity, an unbecoming side effect of a surviving Colonial inferiority feeling. Other versions of this eventually appeared also in Australia and New Zealand. Britain was still patently and tactlessly elder, wealthier, more cultivated, less crude. There were two responses, both unfortunate: Too many Americans defiantly denied those facts; a certain number shamefacedly accepted and then exaggerated the disparities.

That is, soon after Yorktown one kind of American began to protest too much, maintaining that American ships, cities, cuisine, poets, novelists, public buildings, fighting men, schools, governments, morals, and so on were as good as—indeed often better than—the Old Country's. Hence the Fourth of July orator "letting his eagle scream" about the degeneracy of Europe and the United States's mission to show the world the way to peace, justice, and equalitarian affluence. Such judgments being largely emotional, it mattered little that the case was good only for ships and maybe forms of government, but devout belief in the whole list was reassuring. The minority attitude, commonest among the well-to-do, some of whom had been abroad, granted a general inferiority but suggested wistfully that they and their likes were exceptions; that certain small social groups up the Hudson, in Tidewater Virginia and Charleston, Philadelphia, and Boston, qualified for level footing with British gentlefolk. Thus James Fenimore Cooper, whose opinions of his fellow countrymen after he spent a while in Europe were, to say the least, violently unfavorable. The first sort were outraged when British visitors printed it that American tobacco-spitting was inexcusable, American hotel-cooking deplorable, and American inquisitiveness about personal matters unendurable. The second sort, conceding all that, were devastated when the same British visitors described Hermanus Patroon's great estate, pride of Dutchess County, as a nice enough little country retreat—the writer meant no harm, it had just not occurred to him that anybody would think the place notable—and smiled patronizingly at Hiram Powers's boneless statuary.

Pepper was added when, in the 1820s, British radicals began to recommend American democratic-equalitarian reforms. Manhood suffrage, disestablishment of religion, abolition of flogging in the army, blurring of social castes, divorce on grounds less lurid than adultery were among American innovations leading radicals to look across the Atlantic for leads toward freedom and justice. Returned doctrinaires preached emigration to America as a land of politicosocial as well as economic dreams come true. In classic reaction—equal in force and opposite in direction—conservative-minded Britons found it advisable to visit the States and publish at home accounts transparently meant to deter those thinking of either emulation or emigration. In 1835, the year Fanny's *Journal* was published, Charles Dickens's Tony Weller proposed to ship Mr. Pickwick off to America eventually to "come back and write a book about the 'Merrikins as'll pay all his expenses and more, if he blows 'em up enough." Eight years later Dickens followed this advice himself not once but twice, bearing down harshly in both *American Notes* and *Martin Chuzzlewit.* Some of the eminent players of this game openly confessed such a purpose. Mrs. Frances Trollope's preface to her *Domestic Manners of the Americans* (1832) piously renounced commenting on "the democratic form of the American government," only to acknowledge a page later that she wished "to show how greatly the advantage is on the side of those who are governed by the few, instead of the many"; and to describe the alternative as "the jarring tumult and universal degradation which invariably follow the wild scheme of placing all the power of the State in the hands of the populace."[11] A few years later Captain Frederick Marryat admitted that in writing his conspicuous book on America "my object was to injure democracy"; and he hoped it would be read "by every [British] tradesman and mechanic; pored over by milliners' girls . . . thumbed to pieces in every circulating library," to discourage emigration among the lower classes.[12]

Yet this was no conspiracy of propagandists. It was merely that Britain's ruling groups disliked favorable reference to American politicosocial experiments, whence publishers assumed that well-established people would like to read about how bad things actually were in the States. Unsympathetic observers had no trouble selecting large and small shortcomings for unfavorable contrast with British ways. When books thus begotten were at all conspicuous, they were also published in America. For further impact, the great British reviews, which were widely read in America, usually covered them exhaustively with extensive quotations from the nastiest passages, and American newspapers eagerly reprinted them. And reading them made for bad blood among a people already trained to be anti-British

by recent memories of the War of 1812 and school textbooks presenting anglophobia as patriotism.

Both the newspaper borrowing from British reviews and the
American publisher bringing out the travel commentaries of Basil
Hall, Mrs. Trollope, et al. were symptoms of the chronic cultural
colonialism mentioned above—a thing still lively among us. Because
the book- or newspaper-reading American was culturally insecure, he
was itchily inquisitive about outsiders' sneering comments, and also
gratified in an I-told-you-so way as well as outraged to learn once
more that listeners seldom hear good of themselves. It insulted America, his papers told him, to print that Americans spent too much
time slouching in and out of barrooms and were too fond of blowing
the national horn. Both observations were true, but thenceforward
"Basil Hall" was a hissing and a byword. In the same year as Fanny's
landing in New York, Mrs. Trollope supplied special fuel for such
feeling: "I would infinitely prefer sharing the apartment of a party of
well-conditioned pigs to [the cabin of a Mississippi steamboat]";
"Mr. Jefferson is said to have been the father of children by almost
all of his numerous female slaves"; one "never heard Americans con-
versing without the word DOLLAR being pronounced," [13] wild swings
that made the lady title-holder until 1839, when Captain Marryat
weighed in.

Fanny was aware of these monitory precedents. She marveled at
the persistent execration of Mrs. Trollope and was glad not to have
read her book, which excused her from discussing it. Long before she
began to prepare her journal for print, she wrote soberly to George
Combe about the inadvisability of speaking "before one has had time
to reflect" and assured herself that, though she could never approve
of spitting on the carpet and voting by [secret] ballot, "most of my
other prejudices are melting away . . . Americans are decidedly not
Hottentots . . . I have found many things to like and a few people
to love." [14] Yet her original reluctance to go to "that dreadful America" at all very probably reflected her familiarity with the reviews'
steady abuse of the place and with some of its most intemperate de-
tractors— Tom Moore, for instance, whose verses about the young
nation still blister the page; and Sydney Smith, whose personal ad-

juration to her on one of her earlier returns to America from England was: "Be brave, my dear Lady, hoist the American flag, barbarize your manners—dissyntax your language, fling a mantle over your lively spirits & become the first of American women."[15] It was peevishly assumed that her book on America leaned heavily on previous unfriendly accounts. A caricature of the episode of the overturned coach showed spilling out of her baggage books marked "Hall," "Trollope" and a trunk labeled "Fidler's Tour"[16]—plus a slang dictionary. So even though what she published did not include certain things that the newspapers said it would, she was destined to the same pillory as Mrs. Trollope; and she should have known that would happen.

Fanny wrote better, true; had no ax to grind; was more intelligent; and even when American crudities outraged her, fairer. But plenty remained for the hounds to give tongue about. The reader already knows she was severe about tobacco-chewing and -spitting; was scornful of not only American horses, but also American riders; was annoyed, as Britons often were, by the nasality of some and the un-English quality of most kinds of American speech; described American women as sluggish and vapid; found most American hotels slovenly managed. . . . In those and many other points her strictures coincided with those of previous observers about Washington's being only a rough sketch of where a city may be some day,[17] and the other inevitability about American men's drinking habits.

Little of that was unjustified, certainly not the last. Fanny was on firm ground as to American men's taking brandy "in a way that would astound people of any respectability in England." She ascribed their being the very worst judges of wine in the world, always excepting Madeira, which they have in great perfection" to

> the total loss of all niceness of taste consequent upon their continual swallowing of mint julaps [*sic*], gin slings, brandy cocktails, and a thousand strong messes which they take *even before breakfast* . . . a practice as gross in taste, as injurious to the health. . . . Bar-rooms . . . in the theatres, in the hotels, in the bath-houses, on board the steam-boats. . . . [Yet] though the gentlemen drink

more than any other *gentlemen,* the lower orders here are
more temperate than with us. . . . . a drunken man on the
streets is comparatively rare.[18]

Mrs. Trollope would never have written that last sentence. But
in those and many other observations Fanny's indiscretion was culpa-
ble. Had she been writing a letter home, there would have been no
harm; but in public print, she was sure to get American backs up.
Broadway's store personnel lacked the stylish deference that one ex-
pects of London shopmen; American wild violets lacked the scent of
their English cousins; American fruits were large and beautiful but
lacked the flavor of English pears and peaches ripened against walls.
American oysters were grotesquely larger than British.[19] And Fanny
should have been sent to bed supperless for letting memories of the
Household Troops put too much English on her description of a militia parade on the anniversary of the British evacuation of New York
fifty years earlier:

> We have had firing of pop-guns, waving of star-span-
> gled banners (some . . . the worse for wear) infantry
> marching through the streets, cavalry (oh Lord! what de-
> licious objects they were,) and artillery prancing among
> them, to the infinite ecstacy and peril of a dense mob.
> . . . O, pomp and circumstance of glorious war! . . .
> some had gloves, and some had none; some carried their
> guns one way, some another; some . . . "shocking bad
> hats" with feathers in them. . . . Discipline, order, a
> peculiar carriage . . . may all be the attributes of such
> miserable creatures as . . . receive wages for their blood.
> But for free Americans! why should they not walk crooked
> . . . if they don't like to walk straight![20]

And to compound her poor judgment, the latter part of that was
written a year or so after the event, when presumably she was better
adjusted to American ways and things.

One part of her knew better. After a few days in New York she
thought the rampant Britishness of some of her transplanted countrymen a "matter of amusement. How we English folks do cling to our
own habits, our own views, our own things, our own people; how,

in spite of all our wanderings . . . like so many Jews, we never . . . fail to . . . laugh at and depreciate all that differs from that country, which we delight in forsaking for any and all others." In her case one can say—as one cannot of the Marryats, Trollopes, and dozens of others—that there was no ill will involved, only brashness at worst; but a sort of destiny may have been at work. The day before landing, as the *Pacific* lay becalmed off Long Island, she half anticipated discord:

> The day was heavenly, though intensely hot, the sky utterly cloudless . . . I do not love a cloudless sky. They tell me that this is their American weather till Christmas; that's nice, for those who like frying. Commend me to dear England's soft, rich, sad, harmonious skies . . . the misty curtain of silver vapour that hangs over her September woods at morning, and shrouds them at night:—in short, I am home-sick before touching land.[21]

She was, after all, only twenty-two and had never before been anywhere but France under insulated conditions. But that is no excuse for her poor taste in printing her diary's ungracious account of the dinner party with which the Philip Hones quasi-formally welcomed the Kembles to New York. The younger daughter of the house, Fanny granted, was "beautiful; a young and brilliant likeness of Ellen Tree; with more refinement, and a smile that was . . . a whole focus of sun rays." Beyond that, "the dinner was plenteous, and tolerably well dressed, but ill served . . . not half servants enough . . . neither water-glasses nor finger-glasses. . . . After dinner we had coffee, but no tea, whereat my English taste was in high dudgeon." The piano at which she played and sang for them was "a tiny, old-fashioned, becurtained cabinet piano stuck right against the wall, unto which the singer's face was turned, and into which [the] voice was absorbed."[22] The several other guests were gaily caricatured. In print the identities of host and guests were masked by blanks. But that, as a scholarly commentator has said, merely set New York readers playing a game of fill-in-the-blanks.

Though ruefully touched by Fanny's praise of his lovely daughter, Philip Hone was justifiably hurt and disappointed. He told his diary—a rich repository of the lore of old New York that, unlike Fanny's, never saw print until well after his death:

> If she is . . . . at all concerned for her good name as a lady . . . it must be a "sorry sight" to see herself thus served up to the public gaze in all the . . . hasty conclusions from erroneous impressions in which the diary of an imaginative youthful Traveller in a Country in which all things are new and untried may be supposed to abound. . . . the remarks . . . on the private habits of the persons who received her and her Father kindly . . . are all in bad taste. . . . [such] publication now that she has become the wife of an American Gentleman and is to remain with us [is] injudicious in the extreme.[23]

He was the worse chagrined because in several previous meetings he had liked Fanny and been defending her against those disliking her on first acquaintance.

> Allowance should be made for the peculiarity of her situation, just arrived among strangers . . . the object more of curiosity than of affection. . . . She talks well, but will only talk when and to whom she chooses . . . has an air of indifference and nonchalance . . . an ungracious manner of receiving . . . those who desire to pay her attention. . . . But now is her time to make friends if she wants them.[24]

Three years after her *Journal* appeared—unhappily for all but Carey & Lea—Mrs. Pierce Butler, escaping the summer heat at a fashionable hotel at Rockaway Beach, encountered Hone at the evening dance. He sat down beside her to say that "I was happy to renew my acquaintance . . . and danced with her . . . she said to me with great earnestness and solemnity, and much agitated: 'Mr. Hone, I cannot express to you how happy you have made me . . .' The tear which stood in her flashing, expressive eye convinced me that this highly gifted woman . . . possesses that warmth of heart which I thought I had formerly had the sagacity to discover."[25] What a pity one can't be there to see fifty-eight and twenty-eight thus solemnly skipping through a quadrille of reconciliation!

*   *   *

The excerpt-greedy press never bothered, of course, to balance Fanny's indiscretions and sporadic injustices with the high ratio—far higher than Trollope's or Hall's—of American ways and things that she liked, often saying so at generous length. She was delighted with the tasteful development of Hoboken; the majestic, fast, and well-managed Hudson River steamboats; the scenery of the Hudson Highlands; shad in season, and the venerable Madeiras that emerged from good private cellars. Further, she admired William Cullen Bryant's poems (one wishes she had not also liked Nathaniel P. Willis's!), the dashing efficiency of American volunteer fire companies; New York's public bathhouses, more numerous and convenient than London's; the gentleness with which Americans handled draft horses, another strong contrast with Britain. American carriage-makers could not match the elegantly light, strong barouches and broughams at home, but New York's hackney coaches for hire were cleaner and better handled than London's.

Particularly welcome was the almost extravagant deference with which men treated women in the streets, public conveyances, churches, and hotel parlors. Within reason a woman could go practically anywhere alone with no risk of unpleasantness—except for that filthy spitting. One Sunday evening walking with her father up Broadway to Canal Street by bright moonlight, when half New York was also out strolling, "I thought the crowd a more civil and orderly one, than an English crowd. The men did not jostle or push . . . or tread upon one's feet . . . or crush one's bonnet into one's face, or turn it round on one's head, all which I have seen done in London streets. . . . the young men . . . invariably made room for women to pass . . . many . . . took the segar from their mouth, which I thought especially courteous." A few evenings later, crossing to Hoboken,

> the steamers . . . from the city, were absolutely thronged with a cheerful, well-dressed population abroad, merely for . . . pleasure and exercise. Journeymen, labourers, handicraftsmen, tradespeople, with their families, bearing all in their dress and looks evident signs of well-being and contentment, were all flocking . . . into the pure air, the

> bright sunshine, and beautiful shade of this lovely place.
> I do not know any spectacle which could give . . . an
> Englishman . . . a better illustration of that peculiar ex-
> cellence of the American government—the freedom and
> happiness of the lower classes.[26]

And presently she learned that though the men behind shop counters might be, by British standards, "seldom civil," at least "they do not rob you . . . [or] lie to you. . . . any question you ask, with regard to quality . . . will be answered without any endeavour to impose upon you." She reinforces that with the Pennsylvania farmer who, when she asked when the eggs he was offering for sale were fresh laid, answered "without an instant's hesitation, '[these aren't] the *very* fresh ones, *we eat all those ourselves.*' "[27]

This streak-of-lean, streak-of-fat quality may be one of the things making her book so entertaining. Add the flashes of wit and frequent passages of downright good writing. Charles Francis Adams, who had met Fanny in Boston, represented responsible opinion of its merits: "A singular compound of good sense, high feeling and strong expression with coarseness, trifling and eccentricity . . . much of the truth she tells will touch the sensitive . . . far more than the severest censure."[28] But that was in a private diary, not public print. What he meant by coarseness may be guessed from young Edgar Allan Poe's earnest review in the *Southern Literary Messenger;* it objected to Fanny's writing the slang of the boarding school and the greenroom, such as "dawdled," "gulped," "walloped," "pottered," and her mentioning once or twice that Charles and his guests were somewhat tipsy. He also faulted her "dictatorial manner," explaining that "a female, and a young one too, cannot speak with the self-confidence which marks this book, without jarring somewhat upon American notions of the retiring delicacy of the female character." Yet he commended the "sound sense and unwelcome truth" of much of her comment, admired the book's "vivacity of style, beautiful descriptions . . . forcible ob-servations," detected no "deliberate disposition to misrepresent," and called it on the whole "one of the most attractive (as it is one of the most original) [works] recently issued."[29]

The august *North American Review* dwelt less on Fanny's brisk vocabulary, saying merely that "in correctness of taste and maturity of judgment she is singularly deficient." Further censure was loftily good-natured: "the sort of work that might have been looked for from a 'clever girl' as the author repeatedly described herself, educated in the greenroom . . . in immediate contact with the not very strait-laced morals, and still less rigid manners of the children of Thespis . . . but . . . full of real talent, and influenced in the main by correct principles and good feeling." (Come, come, Fanny's manners were formed in very good English society and, as has been seen, she had very little to do with the greenroom's social aspect.)[30] Then the sound technical comment that "her prose is . . . just what it should be for a work of this kind, natural and colloquial, sometimes to excess but constantly enlivened by pointed and felicitous turns of language, and rising, when the subject requires it, into eloquence."[31]

It took time for the magazines to get such chiding and praise into circulation. Meanwhile the newspapers, yapping on the scent originating in the Philadelphia printshop, made Fanny's book a pre-publication *succès de scandale*. "The newspapers, whose editors she dislikes, abuse her and hers without mercy,"[32] Fitz-Greene Halleck, popular poet and convivial wit, wrote to his sister. Charles Francis Adams also understood it that way. Across the Atlantic the *Edinburgh Review* justifiably likened Fanny's "declarations against the Press-gang" to the sort of impulse "under which foolish and fearless school-boys provoke a nest of hornets."[33] Even after the actual book appeared, nobody pointed out that it did not contain the fatal "bug" reference. It might as well have, however, for Pierce had left in several other slurs on newspapermen equally provocative. For Fanny had brought along from overseas a lively form of the aversion to the press strong in the British middle and upper classes; and doubtless the Westmacott affair especially sensitized her. Even in those simpler times such an attitude was inadvisable for actors. But the farthest she ever went toward cooperating with the press was occasionally to contribute some of her verses.

Her book made sure of war to the knife by disdainfully contrasting the social standing of American newspapermen with that of their English counterparts: "Except where they have been made political tools, newspaper writers and editors have never, I believe, been admitted into good society in England. . . . young men here . . . too often . . . accept this very mediocre mode of displaying their abilities." Then: "I do solemnly swear, never again with my own good will, to become acquainted with any man in any way connected with the public press. . . . utterly unreliable people . . . their vocation requires that they should be so."[34]

Whether adequately expurgated or not, the published *Journal* sold handsomely—eight hundred copies the first day at Wiley and Long's New York bookstore, for instance. And thousands on thousands who never saw the book discussed and denounced it.

> The city is in an uproar, [Catharine Sedgwick wrote to her niece, Kate] Nothing else is talked of . . . in the counting houses . . . and Wall Street . . . people seem to think that there never was such *ingratitude!*—that coming as the Kembles did beggars to this country & leaving the stage enriched, Mrs. B. should dare to say a word against us—This is arrant nonsense—they gave at least an equivalent. . . . Nobody went to the theatre to do them a favor. . . . But I do wonder that two years after—after having married an American & being two years older she should deliberately publish it . . . shows a want of tact judgment & good sense. I am very sorry she has done it tho' I expect it will appear much worse to those who do not know her than to us.[35]

Lewis Clark, a friend of Fanny's and editor of the *Knickerbocker Magazine,* summed up for Henry Wadsworth Longfellow in Paris: "She tells a great many rough truths. . . . Some critics have treated her book with contempt . . . some have . . . sided with her, but all have lamented that, for her own sake, the author should ever have published it."[36]

The irresponsible reaction inevitably spread beyond its origin in the papers. Soon on sale in the bookstores was *My Conscience!: Journal of Fanny Thimble Cutler,* wife of Fierce Cutler, swaggering, drawing the longbow, riding roughshod. Also *Outlines Illustrative of the Journal of F—— A—— K——,* a dozen elaborate caricatures captioned from the *Journal* text, showing Fanny petting dogs as large as herself, de-

vouring oysters the size of bedpillows, and so on, culminating in
"Tableau Vivant . . . by the whole Stage Company" of the party
sprawled in the road when the coach overturned. Also *Fanny Kemble
in America* by "An English lady four years resident in the United
States,"[37] forty-eight pages of scurrility deriding Charles Kemble as
only a third-rate actor, scolding Fanny's text for never mentioning
how much she owed her mother's training, accusing Fanny not only
of assuming distaste for acting to attract notice but also of getting
tipsy with the men at the dinner table after dessert and frequenting
the society of stable boys. As for Pierce, some satirical verses included
hinted that he had been drunk when he proposed to her. Lucy Markoe
Kinney, a prolix Washington journalist, denounced Fanny's "ingratitude of the darkest die [sic]. Coming to this country without a
dollar in her pocket, [she] made a handsome independence, married
a fool of fortune . . . discovers the disposition of a spoiled child
. . . expressed unqualified aversion to the freedom of the press";
Pierce, she pronounced "greatly to be pitied . . . sorely will he re-
pent."[38] By midsummer the Bowery Theatre staged a burlesque
called *Bugs: Big and Little,* in which a she-character, Fanny Journa-
liana (played by W. F. Johnson, a knockabout comedian from Boston) performed high jinks on foot and on horseback so successfully
that it was several times repeated. Four years later the *Journal* was
still so much on the public mind that it was worthwhile for T. C.
Haliburton, a well-received Canadian humorist of the day, to lead his
latest effort, *The Letter Bag of the Great Western,* with a travesty of the
seagoing opening of Fanny's book.

It is easy to imagine how Pierce felt about being Fierce Cutler
publicly pitied for having married the wife whom he now saw pillo-
ried behind footlights. Nor did the British reaction help much. The
Edinburgh Review said good-humoredly that the book had "all the
freshness, confidence, and indiscretion of an interrupted correspondence . . . more like thinking aloud than anything or personal history we ever expected to see in print."[39] But the London *Times* had
long since picked up the leaks in the American papers and professed
itself unable to believe that "these passages ascribed to Miss Fanny
Kemble can proceed from the pen of that accomplished lady. Extrav-

agance without fancy, coarseness without humour, exaggerated phraseology without talent . . ." That gave the British a hotly followed lead. The *Athenaeum:* "one of the most deplorable exhibitions of vulgar thinking and vulgar expression that it was ever our misfortune to encounter,"[40] and then accusations of ingratitude to the American press and public. The *Quarterly Review* ran seventeen pages of scolding for this "work of very considerable talent, but . . . of exceeding bad taste"[41] and explained at condescending length how life behind the scenes coarsens and overstimulates, hence Fanny "ought not to be measured by the standard of those more delicate young persons whose mental complexions have not been *bronzed* by the alternate sun and breezes of the stage, the greenroom, and the box-office." Only the last paragraph recommends the "solid good sense, and sound principles . . . at the bottom of the whole work."[42] The consensus among those who mattered—and bought books—is clear in the successive verdicts rendered by Princess Victoria (not yet queen) reflecting first, one assumes, what her preceptors said about the book, then later her individual response: "very pertly and oddly written . . . not well bred . . . many vulgar expressions . . . full of trash and nonsense which could only do harm"; but a few days later she is reading on and on: "It amuses me . . . some very fine feelings in it."[43] In spite of ourselves we *were* amused.

In private close friends defended it ably. Catharine Sedgwick: "It is like herself . . . glorious faculties, delightful accomplishments, immeasurable sensibility, and a half a hundred little faults."[44] Lady Dacre told John Murray that "the depth of thought, the vigour of the writing, the high tone of poetry in her descriptions . . . make her work piquant and enchanting. . . . One sees her *own self,* with . . . her great qualities and her faults in every page." But the most robust rebuttal came from Francis Head, Waterloo veteran, pioneer mining explorer in South America, and in his latter years able man of letters, who, so far as I am aware, did not know Fanny personally: "She has been most unkindly and unjustly treated by the reviewers. . . . People say she is vulgar! So was Eve, for she scratched whatever part of her itched! . . . everything is vulgar nowadays . . . It is vulgar to say you are hungry or thirsty, that you perspire. . . . Poor Fanny Kemble has fallen a victim to this tyranny. Her book is full of cleverness, talent, simple-heartedness, nature, and nakedness."[45]

That complaint that "Victorian prudery" was out of hand well before Victoria reigned over it puts the finger on a quality of Fanny's, usually but not always becoming, that reminds one she was born in the days of sedan chairs and port wine. Throughout her life she retained a strong savor of that eighteenth century in which both her parents were reared. Margaret Armstrong's *Fanny Kemble,* the elementary biography of her, published forty years ago, was deservedly successful but should not have been subtitled *A Passionate Victorian.* By then Hollywooden abuse had already perverted the adjective; and the noun was anachronistic.

The pluck—or foolhardiness—or impudence—with which she nailed her colors to the mast well before the book appeared was all her own, however. In one of the essay footnotes tucked into her *Journal* after the explosion in the newspapers she told Americans:

> Such an unhappily sensitive public surely never existed in the world. . . . I live myself in the daily expectation of martyrdom. . . . if you express an unfavourable opinion of anything [in America], the people are absolutely astonished at your temerity. I remember . . . a lady saying to me once, "I hear you are going to abuse us dreadfully; of course, you'll wait till you go back to England . . ." I assured her I was not in the least afraid of staying where I was, and saying what I thought at the same time.[46]

One wishes that this beleaguered young woman could already have read what the *Atlantic Monthly* said of her *Journal* twenty-eight years later in reviewing her remarkable book about black slavery: "the dashing, fragmentary diary of a brilliant girl . . . crackled and sparkled with *naïve* arrogance. It criticized a new world with the amusing petulance of a spoiled daughter of John Bull. It was flimsy, flippant, laughable, rollicking, vivid . . . often with airy grace, often with profound and pensive feeling."[47]

That is why the *Journal* bobs up so buoyantly from among its companion books about America. Its mother wit and engaging readability were, however, no help at all in its writer's immediate life-to-live—with Pierce Butler in particular and most of Philadelphia.

IX

The Creaking Door

PLEASE IMAGINE, for the record is sketchy, the fluctuating bitterness that the *Journal* occasioned between husband and wife, sometimes dwindling through weariness, then flaring up again as fresh reviews or reports of gossip came in. It did not promise well that, though dismayed, Fanny remained unrepentant, and that in general she failed to follow the sound advice that Washington Irving gave when he heard she planned to marry: "So . . . you are . . . to be married and settle in this country . . . you will be told . . . that living in it is like living in England . . . nothing of the sort; which need not prevent you from being very happy here if you make the best of things as you find them . . . don't become a creaking door." And he told her of a friend of his who brought an English bride to America; she "worried and tormented his and her own life out with ceaseless complaints and comparisons . . . such a nuisance that I used to call her 'the creaking door.' "[1]

Aside from the *Journal* the vibrations from creaking were soon destabilizing. When Butler Place, fresh painted and new furnished, was finally ready, and Pierce installed Fanny in what he and Philadelphia thought of as a country estate, the temptation to creak—or at least let trivialities encourage creaking—heightened. During the renovation Fanny had several times explored on foot some neglected, hence more interesting, recesses of the acreage. But actually settling in there stirred up contrasts. Not that she yearned for a great nobleman's Heaton Place. Even Gouverneur Kemble's famous and charming establishment had not been like that. But in her world "country estate" meant a large, ivy-gabled manor house, say, an ornamental water in the distance, a studiedly informal flower garden tended by forelock-pulling gardeners who also managed the walled kitchen-garden. Butler Place was a tenant-farmed, revenue-producing hundred-odd acres distinguished from dozens of other such operations nearby only by reservation of its major dwelling for the owner's use. This was a standard pitched-roof, stone-built box of an eastern Pennsylvania farmhouse practically unshaded and shielded by distance only from the dust of the Old York Road a stone's throw away. The weedy grass was mowed only twice a season; most of the time, Fanny said, it looked like a poor crop of hay. The barn, stables, and other farm buildings grouped aside were the only relieving features of a flat and monotonously if richly fertile landscape. Years later Fanny recalled for a grandson how a British visitor answered a Philadelphian who asked "how [Butler Place] compared with an English country house . . . [he] was obliged to reply that it was like a second rate farm house in England, not like an English mansion or estate at all—which I believe it was supposed in Philadelphia to be." [2] Country estate! For the first months Fanny's letters were headed "The Farm, Branchtown." Only after long attrition did she raise that to "Butler Place, near Philadelphia."

As occasion served, she attempted improvements: flower beds, a greenhouse, a double row of sugar maples to grow up as screen between house and so-called highway, citrus trees in tubs kept in the greenhouse in winter and set out in summer. Fairly soon Willis Gaylord Clark, a local young man of letters, reported that the Butlers "exist in the finest style. In summer you can see the lovely English taste of Fanny in the embellishments . . . withindoors all is comfort and opulence. Butler's cellar defies criticism." [3] But at first relatively little could be done because the property was still under control of the Butler estate for the benefit of Pierce's surviving aunt. He and his problem bride lived there only by grace and favor until the old lady saw fit to be gathered to her fathers. And even after Fanny had had five years to develop the place, Cecilia Combe, visiting there, wrote of "a nice day [spent] with Fanny Butler at their cottage in the country." [4]

Fanny's exotic conception of the benevolent duties of a lady of the manor was unwelcome. American society had no niche for such a person. She was thinking, in English terms, of setting rosy-cheeked little clodhoppers in pinafores and smocks poring over hornbooks and slates at Lady Bountiful's knee in a whitewashed thatched cottage: "I offered to teach the little children of my gardener and farmer, and as many of the village children as liked to join them . . . my benevolent proposal excited . . . a sort of contemptuous amazement . . . the village school . . . for which they were obliged and willing to pay . . . fulfilled all their desires . . . my gratuitous education was sniffed at. . . . These people and their children wanted nothing that I could give them."[5]

She blundered again on a certain Fourth of July when, recalling how Lord Bountiful's birthday often meant a daytime rustic festival, she put on an alfresco dinner for the thirty-odd members of the farm families from Butler Place and its satellite York Farm across the road. It included hearty country victuals and plenty of wine and beer. The children enjoyed it but their elders, mostly local Quakers who, by that time, were stiff teetotalers, ate uncomfortably and touched nothing alcoholic. One of them remonstrated with Fanny for thus making them waste a fine working day in unavailing idleness. As to Lady Bountiful's traditional duty—anticipating today's social worker—of "visiting" to alleviate and uplift local poverty, it startled Fanny to find that Branchtown had "no *poor* . . . in the deplorable English acceptation [*sic*] of the word . . . [true, it had] comparatively poor people . . . toiling for their daily bread; but none who could not get well-paid work or find sufficient bread . . . helpless, hopeless pauperism . . . was unknown. . . . 'visiting' . . . poorer neighbors . . . would have struck [them] as simply incomprehensible . . . though their curiosity might . . . have been gratified"[6] She did not rashly conclude that America in general lacked hopeless cases, but she had learned that among Pennsylvania Quakers in the country was no place to look for them.

That dainty picture of herself as tutelary, ruffled-aproned inspiration of the dairy also failed to materialize. Twice weekly a supply of home-churned butter came to the Butler kitchen. Fanny was unaware that dairy and pastures were leased to the tenant on shares against which the household quota was charged. To her the sight of all those cows grazing the middle distance suggested butter churned fresh daily. She mentioned it to the Quaker farmer's daughter who operated the dairy: "Fresh butter every morning! who ever heard the like? . . . The young woman was quiet and Quakerly sober, in spite of her unbounded astonishment . . . but when, having exhausted my prettiest vocabulary . . . as I thought, not quite without effect, I turned to leave . . . she followed me to the door with . . . 'Well . . . don't thee fill theeself up with the notion that I'm going to churn butter for thee more than twice a week.' " [7]

Forty years later she made comic capital of these defeats. For all her high-handed dignity in many matters, she relished jokes on herself—in retrospect anyway—one cannot know how far exasperation stifled amusement over the Quaker farm-girl. She was bone-lonely at Butler Place because "between five and six miles of hideous and execrable turnpike . . . almost dangerously impassable in winter made driving into Philadelphia an undertaking that neither love, friendship, nor pleasure—nothing but important business or duty—reconciled one to. The cross roads in every direction were . . . muddy quagmires, where, on foot or on horseback, rapid progress was equally impossible." Even before moving to the country she had found Philadelphia town life jejune: "You can have no idea of the intellectual dearth and drought in which I am existing." And now in warm weather at Butler Place:

> Though people occasionally drive out and visit me and I
> occasionally drive in and return their calls, and we . . .
> at rare intervals, go in to the theatre, or a dance, I have
> no friends, no intimates. . . . Were I living in Philadel-
> phia, I should be but little better off . . . the materials
> for good society exist, yet all the persons whom I should
> like to cultivate are professionally engaged . . . have no
> time, it seems, and but little taste for social enjoyments.[8]

One gets the impression that Pierce was at least nominally dabbling in politics or law and, the roads being so bad, often stayed overnight in town, presumably at brother John's.

Eventually Fanny had good, fast friends in Philadelphia: the

Reverend Dr. William H. Furness, a great Unitarian light; his son, Horace Howard Furness, who became a great Shakespearean scholar; Sidney Fisher, patrician keeper of an invaluable diary of Philadelphia gossip; the Sullys aforesaid; Mary Fox, mistress of Champlost, the country place across the fields to eastward; and fruitful acquaintance with such as Lucretia Mott, the gently formidable Quaker chieftainess of abolitionism and, in the next generation, Dr. Silas Weir Mitchell, physician-novelist. But those connections took years to build and signified little as to general acceptance of Pierce Butler's Gypsyish wife. She herself wrote that whereas in Boston mental cultivation was an asset, and in New York money was socially ingratiating, in Philadelphia the dominant factor was, as a Philadelphia matron assured her, probably with undue emphasis, "birth, to be sure."[9] In her case that was one strike, no matter how gentlemanly Charles was, and add the little matter of Uncle Vincent. The second strike was her inadvertent interference with the orderly arrangement that had affianced Pierce Butler to the lovely Miss Chapman. The third was her deviant behavior—sunburn, horse-mindedness, tendency to speak up sharp as a man—topped off by her publishing that extraordinary book. Indeed, since she was also an actress, a fourth strike in a game where three is out, it is strange that Chestnut Street behaved as flexibly as it did. The Butler connection was weighty, however, and Fanny's personality sometimes attractive even in Philadelphia terms. She might have been ostracized but was not; instead was considerably if not altogether neglected.

On New Year's Day, 1835, when she took over at Butler Place, she was four months pregnant, which did not tend toward smooth living apart from troubles over the *Journal*. Pierce's account drawn up fourteen years later was defensive but probably reliable: Fanny "frequently [expressed] regret at having married me, and a desire for release . . . to return to her native country. I looked upon these expressions as merely perverse fancies, to be dispelled by the birth of her child; and I sometimes assured her that if she continued in the same mind after that event, I would not oppose her wishes, supposing that I should hear no more about it."[10] During his absences his willful wife was safe enough in bucolic isolation. She had several house-servants (on a basis of rather rapid turnover, for the American servant problem was deservedly notorious) and the farmer's household were within call. She was safe from molestation if not from purse-lipped talk when riding unescorted in the staid, dreary countryside over or rather through the fetlock-deep byroads. All winter she rode in spite of old wives' and doctors' misgivings, and ever after maintained that horseback exercise was good preparation for childbed until very near term. Subsequent female troubles, definite but not disabling, she laid to having resumed riding too soon afterward. In May 1835, apparently with no great difficulty, she gave birth to a blue-eyed daughter so unlike herself that, she told people, the effect was that of a Gypsy who had stolen a child. They named her Sarah, presumably after Pierce's mother, though there was also Melpomene.

She found nursing the baby a delight. Writing a novel in her old age, she described that part of being a mother as "alone sufficient in its exquisite happiness to atone for the misery of the most miserable marriage."[11] But for all that, within two weeks of the birth she was writing to Sarah Perkins that though maternity has rewards, children are likely to prove grave disappointments as they grow up. Within a few weeks more she was demanding that Pierce carry out his promise to let her go home now that the child was born: " 'I am weary of my useless existence; my superintendence in your house is nominal . . . you will suffer no inconvenience from its cessation . . . procure a healthy nurse for the baby . . . provided she is fed, she will not fret after me. Had I died when she was born you must have taken this measure, and my parting from her now will be . . . as though she had never known me, and to me far less miserable than at any future time.' "[12] In what fashion or on what terms Pierce welshed on the promise we cannot know. But it was hardly conceivable that any at all conventional-minded husband of that day would have honored it. Contemporary notions of the morally indissoluble ties (even stronger than legal ones) between husband and wife, wife and child, and parents and offspring were hickory-stiff and would have been so had Pierce himself been less unbending. The notable thing here is that Fanny felt so trapped that she proposed giving up the baby while that would still do a minimum of emotional harm. At least she felt like that on that desperate day. Otherwise she was for the rest of her life a consistently devoted mother tragically reluctant to contemplate any such severing of ties. The readiest explanation, whatever its worth, is a season of postnatal depression.

She had yet to confide in anybody about the war over the *Journal*. But there had been general hints or what biographers' hindsight picks up as hints that her marriage was the greatest mistake of her life—even premarital indications that marriage, particularly the kind in which people then put their social hopes, was not for her. Some years previously she had told Harriet, "I do not think I am fit to marry, to make an obedient wife, or an affectionate mother . . . I think I should be unhappy and the cause of unhappiness in others." That statement was more notable than it would have been a hundred years later, not only for originality but also for an ominous clearheadedness. After the Craven episode, just before going to America, her views of marriage were bristlingly analytical: As to "the necessity of one's husband being clever. *Ma foi je n'en vois pas la nécessité*. People don't want to be entertaining each other all day long; *very* clever men don't grow on every bush, and *middling* clever men don't amount to anything." [13] Isolated at Butler Place, she could hardly afford to recall those remarks she had thrown off at a London dinner only a few years past; and her new situation does seem a disproportionate penalty for having obviously felt, though refraining from saying, that she could be quite clever enough for two.

It is possible but very difficult to conceive of a happily married Fanny Kemble, for it is even more difficult to imagine a husband capable of harmony with her. In view of her special temperament the odds that she could ever have made a good choice were low. Her high self-sufficiency would have required that hypothetical Him to add to erotic attraction and great integrity a tact nearer angelic than human. Young Craven would never have done at all. Young Butler, weighing in when her biological needs were high and her impatience with acting had had five years to grow—with the prospect of another year before she could call her soul and person her own—was not much better.

It was, of course, bad luck for Pierce too that he had ever encountered Fanny. He would much better have married Emily Chapman, lived softly on inherited means, begotten a family of Main-Liners-to-be, tomcatted discreetly off and on, aged into a fixture at the Philadelphia Club—an ego (not in Freud's sense) insulated under his own rooftree. His judgment in pursuing her as potential wife was as bad as hers in taking him for husband. Even before conjugal rifts turned him neglectful and then sulkily vindictive, he had been in and out of her orbit for eighteen months, ample time to learn about her quick impulses and sparkly mental crotchets. Maybe he saw her in *Katharine & Petruchio,* the cut-down *Taming of the Shrew* that the Kembles sometimes used as afterpiece, and developed a daring wish to master this volatile girl. Probably he made the mistake of confusing Fanny with the many well-brought-up American girls he had seen throwing their weight about before marriage in a fashion that bemused Europeans and then, after marriage, turning into docile, quiet model spouse-mothers. In any case, to be blunt about the major flaw, Pierce Butler was a fool to insist on marrying above himself. Not technically: the Butlers' bloodlines certainly carried more prestige than the Kembles' and his wealth came of relatively "old money." But he lacked the quality Fanny had that, for lack of a better word, is called "class"—the suppleness and latent keenness, as in good steel, evident in this girl whom he wheedled into marrying him in contravention of her family interests. It was unfair but inevitable that, of the two, she suffered more from their shared blunder.

As the first year wore on, concealment from others began to slip. Pierce goes on business to Boston; Fanny, giving him a letter for Sarah Perkins, hopes that "should another opportunity occur . . . my little Lord and Master may be better inclined to suffer my company." Late the next spring Sarah became engaged to a Cabot; Fanny advised her to make sure that her husband seriously followed some absorbing profession: "As you are wealthy and stand in no need of support . . . it will require character in him to follow laborious study for its own sake, & you to urge him to pursuits which will take some of his time away from you . . . idleness in this country can in no way be dignified, graceful or respectable."[14] Can one doubt that this experienced matron of eleven months had Pierce's desultory law-yering in mind? For years this relation with the girl who had hung flowers on her doorknob was of high value for both. Sarah often stayed with relatives in Burlington, New Jersey, where the steamboat feeder for the New York railroad put in, and it was a great day when she could come spend a night or two at Butler Place; Pierce, with whom she got on well, met her at the Philadelphia wharf. The New York Public Library's celebrated Berg Collection has two tiny packets of dried flowers—lilies of the valley, violets, etc. says Sarah's label-ing, but now so desiccated that only a botanist with a microscope could be sure—cherished because one happy afternoon Fanny picked them for Sarah in the Butler Place garden.

Pierce's arbitrariness about the *Journal* set Fanny groping toward the protofeminism of the 1830s. That was inadvisable for the wife of a Philadelphia patrician. Worse, Fanny now grasped with dismay what had not really come home to her before—that black slave labor was the prime source of Pierce's expected wealth.[15] In the turmoil of falling in love, deciding to marry, and fighting the battle of the *Journal,* she had apparently failed to take in the full dimensions of that economic lesion. Actually, until reaching America, she either had no strong feeling against slavery or left no hint of it. Except Elizabeth Fry, her acquaintance included few of the antislavery zealots who had just brought about emancipation of the slaves in the British West Indies. In Baltimore she had been only "amused" as her aris-tocratic hostess described the family slaves as "the best and most faithful servants in the world. . . . 'our house,' 'our family' are the terms by which they designate their owners." Yet abstract reprehen-sion of slavery had probably rubbed off on her from such Evangeli-cally inclined friends as Harriet St. Leger and such reformers as the Combes. It shocked her when the free black steward from the *Pacific,* asking for a pass to see the Kembles act, had to specify the gallery because blacks could sit nowhere else in American theaters. She was distressed when a New York acquaintance told of slave floggings he had witnessed and when she learned that in most slave states to teach a slave to read or write was illegal: "So great is the dread of insurrec-tion . . . that they are kept in the most brutish ignorance. . . .

Oh! what a breaking asunder of old manacles there will be, some of these fine days; what a fearful rising of the black flood."[16] And when in Boston she made friends with Catharine Sedgwick, she was stepping fatefully and in the end most creditably into the antislavery current.

Boston is not the key there. Bostonians of the stratum that the Kembles met were not necessarily antislavery. Beacon Hill relied on slave-grown cotton for dividends from the outlying mills. Its sons sometimes took charming brides from the affluent southern families who summered at Newport and other northern resorts. Its temperamental revulsion from the wilder-eyed abolitionists was strong and made it hard for less shrill antislavery voices to get a hearing. (Much the same was true of New York and Philadelphia, each of which supplied the slave economy with quantities of dry goods, hardware, and, it followed, financing.) But even on Tremont Street certain conscience-troubled sober heads deplored slavery in terms fervid enough to develop whatever unfavorable impression of the "Peculiar Institution" Fanny landed with.

Though well received in Boston and New York, Catharine Sedgwick hailed from neither city. This handsome middle-aged spinster was the literary-intellectual leading edge of a notable Yankee clan, the patrician Sedgwicks of Berkshire County in far western Massachusetts. She was America's best-known woman novelist with a sideline of how-to-improve-oneself pamphlets. The novels are queerly dull reading now but better than much of what Britain's bluestockings were then publishing and they still interest scholars as early efforts to handle American regional backgrounds in fiction. For some generations Sedgwicks and their contemporary kin had ornamented and steered the legal, social, intellectual, and to some extent economic destiny of the Massachusetts upcountry previously known only as the scene of the Reverend Jonathan Edwards's white-hot sermons on original sin and Daniel Shays's Rebellion against the hegemony of Beacon Hill. Well off but not rich, balancing between the austere and the flexible, the Sedgwicks were looked up to as by natural right. Most of the men, a confusing number of them named Theodore, were lawyers. As Yankee gentry of the same order if not the same wealth, they intermarried with Appletons, Lowells, Parkmans, and knew everybody who amounted to anything, particularly in good works and reform movements, from Cape Ann to Hartford to Pittsfield. Their traits were real if not too wide cultivation, low-keyed articulateness, conscientious grasp of social problems, and deep appreciation of the beauties of their cool, mildly mountainous surroundings in the Berkshire country.

Before her marriage Fanny had seen much of Catharine Sedgwick in New York, and it was important for her later life when Catharine persuaded her to visit the Berkshires in the late summer of 1835. Undine fell in love with "the Valley of the Housatonic, locked in by walls of every shape and size, from grassy knolls to bold basaltic cliffs. A beautiful little river wanders singing from side to side in this secluded Paradise, and from every mountain cleft come running crystal springs to join it; it looks only fit for people to be baptized in (though I believe the water is used for cooking and washing purposes)." She also fell in love after another fashion with Sedgwicks generally: "almost the only [Americans] among whom I have found mental companionship."[17] She particularly took to Charles Sedgwick, the incumbent legal chief, and his wife Elizabeth (née Dwight, a fine old Connecticut Valley name) who kept a small girls' school of high reputation in the family house; and their charming young daughter Catharine; and young Charles who presently branched off into New York State; and she already knew Theodore III, the New York City lawyer. His and Catharine's link with home was the steamboat upriver to Albany, thence by stage across the hills to Stockbridge and Lenox. Fanny often took that route. She unreservedly liked these people. They had minds and spoke them; they rambled gaily and played amusing games and knew how to be disrespectful about the high and mighty.

Among them a mild early version of women's-rights sentiment and a sturdy hatred of black slavery were part of what cultivated people of goodwill lived by. At the time that presumption was deceptive. Many of their friends and kinfolk shared neither attitude. But round their tea table of evenings or during their long walks to points of scenic interest, they took right thinking on such matters for granted in a fashion that Fanny found dangerously attractive. They were probably crucial in her shift toward visceral antislavery conviction. We do not know the tenor of the "long and vehement treatise against Negro slavery"[18] that she wished to include in the published *Journal*. She reluctantly omitted it because Pierce insisted that would bring out a mob to burn Butler Place down—which, in view of some antiabolitionist measures taken by Philadelphian hoodlums, was not altogether fantastic. In mid-August 1835 Fanny was still rather coolly ironical about slavery and its foes and friends, writing to John Murray:

> Northern people pursue the emancipation plans with all the zeal of folks who have nothing to lose by their philanthropy and the southerners hold fast by their slippery property like so many tigers—the miserable blacks are restricted every day within narrower bounds . . . there will I fear be a season of awful retribution before right is done the unfortunate wretches. Our property lies principally in Georgia; if we are ruined I think I will come to England and take up my old trade.[19]

But she seems to have come back in the fall from Sedgwick country to Philadelphia and her second winter of stagnation with Pierce, evolving toward positions and emotions sure to widen the fluctuating rift.[20]

The following spring (1836) the last of the old major's daughters died and Pierce became full owner of the estate. Presently, much to his credit Philadelphia felt, and so it was, he made over a half interest in the plantations to brother John; there was plenty for both. Since the major's death the Georgia properties had been managed by the son of the original supervisor. His able handling of rice, cotton, and slaves made famous profits; otherwise the beneficiaries eight hundred miles away had paid little heed. Now that the Butler brothers were in full possession, however, it was less easy to look the other way about Pierce's situation. Heretofore he had merely derived some of his livelihood from resources created for his aunts by slavery. Now he was an out-and-out slaveholder.

Fanny's uneasiness about that was now sharpened by an enlarged pamphlet contributed to the controversy over slavery by her revered friend Dr. Channing. As benign leader of American Unitarianism, he was a national leader of immaculate reputation, and his *Slavery and Emancipation* made quite a stir. Unlike most northern-reared opponents of slavery he had lived for a substantial period in the South and, pondering that experience, come up with an original solution for the problem that at least showed he believed in people's essential goodness. He avoided the abolitionists' usual mistake of abusing slaveholders from afar, which, while it fostered self-righteousness, did not help the slaves at all. Instead of depicting slaveholders as ruthless brutes, Channing attributed to them a genuine desire to get rid of slavery—a certain number of them actually shared that—and the goodwill to apply as remedy gradual amelioration of the slave's condition. Let Northerners cease plumping for draconic emancipation by fiat and begin persuading the South to treat its slaves better and better, allowing them more and more freedom and responsibility on the job, educating and adjusting them to growing self-respect . . . until, in effect, the whole system would wither away and an eventual legal emancipation be mere formal recognition of a socioeconomic *fait accompli.*

For all the stir, few agreed that any such program was practical. Most opponents of slavery thought it too sanguine about the owners. Those who were culturally committed to the notion of blacks' essential racial inferiority thought it absurdly hopeful about both slaves and owners. But Fanny's veneration for Channing helped her to be persuaded. His sermons in print and her occasional meetings with him had already led her to consider herself a Unitarian; so far as he had a religious affiliation, Pierce was already one. Now she hoped to try Channing's scheme on Pierce's human property. Before his aunt died, Pierce had told her that whereas cotton lands in Georgia's Sea Islands were getting exhausted, farther west in Alabama were

> wild lands . . . where anyone possessing the negroes necessary to cultivate them, might . . . realize an enormous fortune; and asked, jestingly, if I should be willing to go thither. I replied, in most solemn earnest, that I would . . . if we might take that opportunity of at once placing

our slaves upon a more humane and Christian footing.
. . . Though the blacks may not be taught to read and
write . . . no law . . . can prevent one from . . . teaching them all . . . that personal example . . . can teach.
. . . I would tell them that in so many years I expected
to be able to free them, but that those only should be
liberated whose conduct . . . during that time would
render their freedom prosperous to themselves, and safe to
the community.

Forty years later she recalled "the amazement and dismay, the terror
and disgust, with which such theories . . . filled every member of
the American family with which my marriage had connected me; I
must have appeared to them . . . . a mischievous madwoman."[21]

Off and on Fanny had suggested, and Pierce apparently had not
peremptorily ruled out, a visit to Britain to introduce him to her
family and friends, and, one surmises, to assuage her homesickness.
Now that rather more than half the Butler fortune was at their command, such a trip was practical indeed. But now also the scheme
conflicted with a pressing need for Pierce and John to go south and
get responsibly well acquainted with their fine new properties. That
would require months. It seems never to have occurred to Mrs. John
that she might go along, but Fanny's new hopes for slavery made her
think she should. The best accommodations on the Butler's Island
plantation were, however, a rattletrap cottage that the supervisor used
when in residence; at Hampton Point the major's old mansion was
sadly dilapidated and the other rather more habitable dwelling no
great thing, unsuitable for a delicately reared wife, even less so for a
baby. As further complication Pierce had been chosen a delegate to a
state constitutional convention to meet in the spring of the next year.
He could work that in after leaving Georgia to avoid the warm-
weather malaria season that sent all whites able to do so fleeing from
rice plantations. But it would prevent his going abroad until far into
1836. It was determined that Fanny would go to England over the
winter with baby Sarah and an admirable nursemaid recently recruited—Margery O'Brien, intelligently trainable, responsible, soon

warmly attached to Fanny as well as Sarah, almost everything that people, Fanny included, thought Irish Catholics could not be. Then Pierce would come fetch them when the convention was ended.

This separation after only thirty months of marriage was hardly a hardship for either party, though doubtless each sometimes tried to feel that it was. In step with her unpopular ideas on slavery, Fanny's protofeminism was heating up. Not long before coming to America, she had set down her notion of "a well-assorted marriage" in terms that Pierce, in a very mellow mood, might have tried to tolerate: it should be "like a well arranged duet for four hands; the treble, the woman, has all the brilliant and melodious parts, but . . . the harmony is with the bass, which really leads and sustains the whole composition . . . without which the treble for the most part *runs to tune* merely, and wants depth, dignity, and real musical importance."[22] Pierce's stern treatment of her *Journal* and herself had long since spoiled any such civilized prospect of symbiosis. Now, blending her claustrophobia in marriage with the hints of women's rights then floating in the air, she developed a position then markedly radical. Years later, seeking to show the court how heinous her attitude had already become, Pierce accurately formulated it: "She held that marriage should be companionship on equal terms—partnership, in which, if both partners agree, it is well; but if they do not, neither is bound to yield—and that at no time has one partner a right to control the other."[23]

To that, of course, no husband of the 1830s aware of his rights as master of the house and his duties as his wife's guardian-owner could possibly subscribe. In this fall of 1836 Pierce seems to have hoped that months away from him, vulnerably on her own, would wean her from this heresy acceptable in neither law nor custom. And Fanny may have hoped that months of self-exile in Georgia would persuade him of the barbarity of subjecting her to a sugar-coated form of domestic slavery. Anyway she would be better off among family and friends in England than rattling round in wintry isolation at Butler Place. She took Sarah and Margery for a happy month with the Sedgwicks; then, on November 1, 1836, Mrs. Pierce Butler, baby and nurse, sailed from New York for Liverpool in the packet *South America,* 616 tons, R. Waterman, master.

The New York *Mirror,* the town's nearest approach to a literary weekly, saw her name in the shipping news and wafted her homeward half-jeeringly but also half apologizing for the furore about the *Journal:*

> Gone, dear Fanny, gone at last! Yes, the beautiful Juliet, the proud Lady Constance, Bianca, Julia, and the clever authoress of the "Journal," all sailed in the person of Mrs. Butler. . . . What with her playing, scribbling, riding and marrying, she has been as much talked about as a comet! . . . From the silent manner of her departure, we fear there is a settled coolness between her and our republican publick. She will now . . . have horses that gallop with the proper foot foremost, shopkeepers that measure her linen and ribands in respectful silence, audiences that know when to applaud. . . . Well, peace go with her! if she is not as good as we at first deemed her, she is better unquestionably than she has the credit of being now. . . . As to her book—a first perusal threw us into a proper passion. . . . Since that period we have crossed the ocean and had time to reflect and . . . we regard Mrs. Butler with much more philosophical indulgence. . . . We, Mrs. Butler, the sensible portion of the community . . . we forgive you.[24]

Fanny probably never saw that gratuitous harking back to issues already dead.[25] But one wonders whether, if she had, she would have noticed the implicit assumption that she was never coming back—erroneous, of course, yet a hint she might profitably have followed.

The *South America* gave Fanny one of the roughest of her many transatlantic crossings—twenty-seven days even though making the usually more favorable eastbound passage. The ship sprang her mainmast and could not carry normal sail. The heavy seas made it necessary to batten down even the cabin skylight, which meant foul air and dimness. When Fanny persuaded the captain to clear the skylight, a huge wave smashed in and flooded everything below. Nurse Margery did a good deal of praying, probably to Saint Paul, certainly to Saint Christopher. How the baby took it is not recorded. At one point Fanny was so sure the ship was foundering that she experienced what she took to be the drowning person's total-recall review of her past life.

Only at the end of November was the ship warped alongside in the dock at bustling, sordid Liverpool, giving Fanny the unwinding, long-breath-drawing, muscle-relaxing sense of being once again among fellow countrymen and one's own ways. For all the fifteen-odd years she spent in America, she never managed acclimatization, literally or figuratively, not even in her beloved Berkshires, let alone in alternately torrid and tooth-chattering Philadelphia. She was always as English as a Christmas pantomime, only not so vulgar. Yet she had mixed feelings about this repatriation, for her being a married woman at a time when marriage was strong as death made it dampingly temporary. Consciously or unconsciously she had to assume that she would some time go back, even that Pierce would, as was arranged, come to fetch her. London was "more beautiful, more rich and royal, than ever. . . . but we shall never desert America and the duties that belong to us there, and I should be the last person to desire that we do so . . . henceforth England and I are 'Paradises Lost' to each other,"[26] she wrote to Anna Jameson, then in Canada trying to get some validity or at least practicality into her own difficult marriage. But the serene conjugal attitudes that Fanny thus promised herself postulated something that never again came to pass.

Charles Kemble's house on Park Place received the three apparently with no trace of the strains that Fanny's marriage had set up. Family news was good. The Crown had recently installed Charles as Examiner of Plays at a comfortable salary. Fanny was in time for his grand farewell stage appearance. She was proud of the wit and charm with which he still played Benedick, and if she felt a pang at not being behind the footlights as Beatrice playing up to his extraordinary virtuosity, she did not bother to write it down. Brother John was established in the country juggling Anglo-Saxon roots. Thérèse was a semi-invalid harassed by the ailments of old age—including some mental failings—but she had the country amenities that she so loved, spending most of her time in the cottage in Surrey that Mrs. Whitelock had bequeathed her; there she died late in 1838 when Fanny was back in America. Adelaide was all beauty, charm, and wit and her voice had developed so promisingly that a career in opera was seriously planned. Elder and younger sister were not always harmonious, but nine tenths of the time they were loyally close. Fanny's misgivings about the operatic project reflected both her chronic mistrust of anything to do with the stage and the solicitous admiration she felt for this gracious young woman who had once been little Totty:

> I appreciate . . . all the feelings . . . prompting her to the choice of . . . her profession; but I also think she is unaware (which I am not) of the necessity for excitement, which . . . influences that have surrounded her from childhood have created . . . for which she is no more answerable than for the color of her hair. . . . She possesses some of the intellectual qualities from which the most exquisite pleasures are derived. But she will not be happy in this world; but, as nobody else is, she will not be singular . . . and in the exercise of her uncommon gifts she may find a profound pleasure.[27]

The Park Place house, full of Kembleish talk and British comforts, was a valuable contrast with Butler Place. One symptom of Fanny's consequent well-being was that, whereas writing anything purposeful had come hard in Branchtown, here where she belonged the literary impulse vigorously revived, and she was busily drafting *An English Tragedy*. Social life too was off and running. The London that had so petted Miss Kemble did not neglect Mrs. Pierce Butler. Never mind the disappointing reception that Britain gave her *Journal*, never mind her ceasing to be an active stage celebrity, Rogers, the Ellesmeres, Lady Dacre, et al. picked up just where they had left off. Dinner on dinner, country house after country house welcomed the returned wanderer. Among new close friends were Lord and Lady Lansdowne, and the celebrated Miss Berrys, whose evenings included pretty much everybody worth talking to or about. In later life Fanny was serenely proud of having been "one of the youngest members of that pleasant society . . . of wit, wisdom, experience, refined taste, high culture, good breeding, good sense and distinction."[28] On the less pleasant side she readily held her own in a social duel with Lady

Holland, a hostess renowned for brilliant dinner parties and manners roughshod with ruthless egocentricity. People said that it was worth eating a little dirt of the hostess's providing to get to those dinners. Fanny, however, who already knew many such people, made it plain that she did not relish the flavor even when eaten off Holland House's elegant dinner services. From her account of her skirmishes with Lady Holland on the few occasions when she was prevailed on to sit at the same table, one learns that, on due occasion, Mrs. Pierce Butler could be a female—and very female too—porcupine.

Toward spring she sometimes felt that "the turmoil and dissipation of a London life, amusing as they are for a time, soon pall . . . in my diminished relish for them . . . I am growing old." At the age of twenty-seven! But high spirits too kept cropping up in a fashion seldom experienced at Butler Place. In a letter that it would be a shame to paraphrase, she tells Harriet of a good time at Bannisters, the FitzHughs' modest, serene country place near Southampton, where once Melpomene had been more or less a member of the family:

> These overflowing spirits of mine come of a gallop of fifteen miles . . . with dear Emily [FitzHugh] over breezy commons and through ferny pinewoods, and then coming home and devouring luncheon as fast as it could be swallowed. . . . If my letter is all "sound and fury, signifying nothing," how can I help it? That rather ill-conducted person, Ninon de l'Enclos . . . said her soup got into her head . . . I should be loath to suggest any [comparison] between myself and that wonderful no-better-than-she-should-be [but] beyond all doubt my luncheon has got into my head, though I drank nothing but water with it. . . . However that may be, I wish you would speak to Emily (you needn't bawl though you are in Ireland) and tell her to hold her tongue and not disturb me . . . add her to the cold ride and the hot lunch in the list of causes of this crazy epistle.[29]

Within a week the breathless girl who wrote that was in Liverpool awaiting whatever reckoning was to follow nine months' respite from being a wife, much longer than had been planned. The conven-

tion to which Pierce was committed had been twice postponed, the
second time to the fall; he had spent the whole winter in Georgia. In
late spring, however, there was nothing to prevent his fetching wife
and child home. Yet he did not impulsively book himself on the next
packet. Cautiously he made homiletic inquiries preliminary to reunion with the woman and child whom he had not seen since the
preceding November. After the necessary weeks at sea his letter
reached Fanny in the family fastnesses in London. She replied in another letter that must not be paraphrased:

> My dearest husband: You ask me if this separation
> has not strengthened our affection and our value for each
> other? If it has endeared me to you I ought to be grateful
> . . . it has led me to reflect upon some passages of our
> intercourse with self-condemnation, and a desire to dis-
> charge my duty to you more faithfully. . . . Yet do not
> mistake me; you ask . . . how I like my independence,
> and whether I remember how vehemently and frequently
> I objected to your control . . . part of my regret . . .
> arises from the *manner* of my resistance, not the fact itself.
> . . . Neither my absence from you, nor my earnest desire
> to be again with you, can make me admit that the blessed
> and happy relationship, in which we stand to each other,
> is any thing but perfect companionship, perfect friend-
> ship, perfect love. For the existence of these, justice must
> also exist; and there is no justice in the theory, that one
> rational creature is to be subservient to another. . . . dear
> Pierce, upon what ground should you exercise this control
> over me? Is it because having full power to withhold the
> gift, I freely gave myself to you, to add as much by my
> fellowship as I could to your happiness? Is it because you
> are better than myself? I am sure you will not say so,
> whatever I may think. Is it because you are more enlight-
> ened, more intellectual? You know that is not so, for your
> opportunities have not been the same. Is it because you
> are stronger in body? . . . If . . . you do not admit and
> respect the rights of your wife, how comes it that she is
> at this moment an independent agent, having been so for
> upwards of six months, with the precious charge of your
> darling child, and the free and generous use of your
> means. . . . I would rather hear you acknowledge a prin-

ciple of truth, than enjoy the utmost indulgence that your affection could bestow upon me.[30]

Soon after digesting that daunting response to a husband's hope that his wife now better understood her status, Pierce, probably almost as much puzzled as irritated, let his lady know he was on his way to fetch her home. Dutiful logistically at least, Fanny took herself, baby, Margery, and accumulated uneasinesses to Liverpool and waited, and waited, and waited for Pierce's ship. Persisting contrary winds were keeping all incoming vessels far out in the Irish Channel. Wearying of Liverpool, she settled her small household in a tiny beach resort up the coast—and waited. Charles's doctor had ordered him to "take the waters" at Carlsbad, Adelaide had gone along to look after him and pursue some musical concerns, and they could not return in time to bid Fanny a proper farewell. She hoped that after some sightseeing in London and some country visits, Pierce and she could go spend some time at Carlsbad. But those wearisome winds had used up too much of the time available. The convention was now definite for early October. When the wind changed and Pierce landed, they had only ten days for a rushed stay in London, two days at Bannisters, two at The Hoo and back to Liverpool for the early September sailing of the packet *St. Andrew.* On what terms Pierce and Fanny met I do not know. But a certain chemistry must have come about. Nine months later she bore him a second daughter whom they named Frances. In the family she was usually called Fanny or Fan. In this text, to avoid confusion with her mother, she will be Frances only.

This third crossing may have been the worst Fanny ever had: for thirty-seven days she hardly left her berth, which at least spared her much to do with the dully vulgar other women passengers. On landing, she, the redoubtable pedestrian, was so run down that a mere quartermile forced her to rest on a park bench before struggling back to the hotel. No wonder that next year, when the British steamers *Sirius* and *Great Western* made Atlantic crossings, first ever under steam all the way, in eighteen and sixteen days respectively, making

New York within a few hours of each other, the chatelaine of Butler Place was delighted. She learned soon that one could be as seasick in a steamer as in a sailing packet. But at worst steam meant fewer days of misery; and otherwise: "Oh! . . . what joy this intelligence gives me! It seems at once to bring me again within reach of England and all those whom I love there . . . and speed and certainty with which letters will now pass between these two worlds . . . is a thing to rejoice at exceedingly."[31]

After some days in New York Fanny was recovered from the *St. Andrew* enough to get on home, soon thence to Harrisburg for the long-deferred convention. She seems now to have found a temporary serenity. Had the roughly savage voyage had a purgative effect on her emotions? or was this a hormonal quirk consequent on pregnancy? Anyway she cordially admired Harrisburg's beautiful situation on the broad, isle-studded Susquehanna; relished the large trout that it supplied; liked the delegates from the back-country districts. She was learning; a few years earlier their tobacco-chewing and neglected boots would have put her off from relishing their dry common sense. She was even trying to modify or at least question the subjective assumptions that made it hard for her to turn subordinated wife:

> A woman should be her husband's dearest friend [she tells Harriet, thinking out loud on paper], but friendship is a relation of equality, in . . . perfect respect for each other's liberty . . . that sort of marriage, if it exists at all . . . is, I suspect, uncommon . . . I am not sure that marriage ever is, can be or ought to be, such an equality. . . . A woman should . . . love her husband better than anything else on earth except her own soul; which . . . a man should respect above everything else on earth, but his own soul; and there, my dear, is a very pretty puzzle for you, which a good many people have failed to solve . . . perhaps, you have chosen, if not the wiser and better part, at any rate the safer and easier [that is, spinster-hood].[32]

Still playing wise woman (age twenty-seven) Fanny now counsels Sarah Perkins—whose engagement has broken up; she is now about to marry another eligible youth:

> Since my own marriage . . . I have reflected on it as I
> should have done before it. It has been my fortunate lot
> to marry a man whom I can both respect and love, but
> from the inconsiderate manner in which I engaged myself
> to him, had the result been different, I should have ac-
> cused no one but myself, & as it is I feel like some blind
> or drunken person . . . preserved by the merciful inter-
> ference of Providence.[33]

Which, being translated, signifies: "It reassures me when I tell others
I continue to respect and love Pierce Butler; some day it may be true
again, maybe it is true now in some buried fashion; but if it ever
becomes unmistakable that I can no longer do either, it will be my
own stupid fault for letting him persuade me to marry him." It was
at this point that she had found it helpful to write again to George
Combe that "though a person of no brilliancy of intellect, [Pierce's
moral faculties] are strong and excellent."[34]

By now this sequence is familiar: intervals of unstable equilibrium alternating with episodes of exasperation. It did not improve
matters that Pierce was going rheumatic—a complaint likely to further bad temper—unusually early in life. Yet both seem to have kept
up appearances well. Soon after they returned to Butler Place from
Harrisburg, Anna Jameson came visiting on her way home to England and reported to her great friend Ottilie von Goethe, that Fanny
was "brimful of genius, poetry and power and eloquence, yet is an
excellent wife, an excellent mother, and an excellent manager of a
household—no easy matter in [America], where no one will *serve,* but
if well paid, may condescend to *help* you . . . I like Pierce Butler
very much—more than I expected. It was difficult to please me in a
husband for Fanny."[35] That Pierce favorably impressed anybody so
jealous for Fanny's well-being as Mrs. Jameson, again confirms his
magically ingratiating quality. Within a couple of months, however,
things were so sour that husband and wife were again communicating
formally in writing: wife thus:

> You will oblige me by taking immediate means for
> my return to my own family. . . . I will never be subject
> to rudeness and ill manners from any one. . . . I will not

> return to the farm . . . but . . . remain here, at the
> corner of Chestnut and Eighth Streets [John Butler's], or
> go to an inn. . . . If you do not choose to take these
> steps, I have my watch and gold chain . . . which will
> get me sufficient money to go home in some manner or
> other. . . . There is abundance of time for me to reach
> England before my confinement; and if you will hereafter
> appoint means for your child's being brought over to you,
> I shall . . . observe them.[36]

But several months later the flames have subsided, and she has returned to "the farm"—is sitting on the veranda at Butler Place too near her confinement to risk going to church in Germantown, planning out in her mind the upcoming season's improvements to the grounds and watching toddler Sarah "zigzagging like a yellow butterfly about the lawn . . . Margery mounting guard . . . with such success as you may fancy a person taking care of a straw in a high wind."[37]

The new baby arrived on sister Sarah's birthday, a coincidence that their sardonic mother professed to think showed "an orderly, systematic, and methodical mode of procedure . . . creditable to me." In August Mr. and Mrs. Pierce Butler took the babies and their nurse to the great and fashionable summer hotel at Rockaway Beach on Long Island. The hotel's cramped quarters and lack of privacy gave Fanny's reined-in emotions something else than personal perplexities to let fly about:

> The beach is magnificent . . . the broad open Atlantic
> . . . breaking in one white thunderous cloud. . . . The
> bathing would be delightful but for the discomfort and
> indecency of the non-accommodation. . . . two small sta-
> tionary dressing-huts on the beach . . . one is compelled
> to disrobe . . . in the closest proximity to any other
> women who . . . come out of the water or go into it at
> the same time. . . . the beach at bathing time is . . .
> thronged with spectators, before whose admiring gaze one
> has to emerge all dripping, like Venus, from the waves,
> and nearly as naked; for one's bathing dress clings to one's
> figure.[38]

All that means that American resorts lacked the "bathing machines" that enabled ladies to get wet decorously on British beaches.
They were boxy miniature dressing-rooms on wheels. The lady got
in, stripped, donned the full-length shift that she went into the water
in. A horse harnessed to the contraption then drew it into waist-deep
water, the lady opened the door, and soused herself up and down in
the waves, got back in and dried off and dressed while the reattached
horse drew her back on the beach. Even had Rockaway Beach teemed
with bathing machines, however, Fanny would still have objected to
the hotel bedrooms, "small and furnished barely as well as a common
servant's room in England," and to the "perpetual presence of a crowd
of strangers . . . [nothing] but the benefit which I believe the children, as well as myself, derive . . . [induces] me to endure it."[39]

That picture of an early American effort to create a beach resort
would have fitted well into the *Journal*'s tactlessnesses. So would
Fanny's diatribes the preceding winter about

> the present deleterious custom of warming close and
> crowded [railroad cars] with sheet-iron stoves, heated with
> anthracite coal. No words can describe the foulness of the
> atmosphere, thus robbed of all vitality by the vicious
> properties of that dreadful combustible, and tainted be-
> sides with the poison emitted at every respiration from so
> many pairs of human lungs. . . . an attempt to open a
> window is met by a universal scowl and shudder.[40]

So would her explanation of why, when in New York, she walked for
exercise instead of riding:

> It is not thought expedient that I should be stared at alone
> on horseback; being stared at alone on foot, apparently, is
> not equally pernicious . . . I am . . . trudging round
> the Battery every evening to the edification of the ex-
> tremely disreputable company who (beside myself) are the
> only haunters of that lovely lung of New York . . .
> should I ever become a sickly, feeble, physically good-for-
> nothing . . . woman, I shall certainly not be singular in
> this free and enlightened republic where (even more than
> else where in the world) singularity appears to be dreaded
> and condemned above any or all other crimes, sins, and
> vices.[41]

But she did not stay docile about orders against riding unescorted in cities. Philadelphia often saw Pierce Butler's much discussed wife riding alone. When, saying she wished to get to know the city better, she announced her intention thus to explore Philadelphia's wharf district, Pierce warned her that "a lady going there on horseback and alone, would attract great, if not rude attention, and cause unpleasant remarks . . . [and] she replied by a few disdainful words, about my regard for what people said, dashed off, and took her ride along the wharves. . . . one of the many instances of perverse self-will, in which she delighted,"[42] wrote her much tried husband telling the world his undeserved woes.

In the fall of 1838, after some four years of failure to remain in any tolerable emotional adjustment, Fanny made her strongest suggestion yet that they abandon the hopeless game. Pierce was staying in Philadelphia, she at Butler Place:

> You are now again relieved from my presence . . . take my advice and casting aside your regard for appearances . . . make some arrangements by which in future to be freed from it altogether. . . . I believe you do not yourself think the state in which we live when on good terms . . . one of very intimate companionship or confidence; nature has . . . rendered the sympathy and communion of others totally unnecessary to you; and, were it otherwise, you are here in the midst of your own people . . . your own country. . . . the case is the very reverse with me. . . . In part this is my own fault; for I married you without for a moment using my own judgment or observation to ascertain whether . . . we were likely to be companions and fellows to each other. . . . the sentiment which drew us together is waning and perishing away. . . . There is, however, one tie by which I am bound to you, that of utter dependence upon your means, and, therefore, of necessity, upon your will. Such a bond . . . though borne by many women, must needs be irksome to one who has the least feeling of pride: how doubly irksome then to me, who have had and still have the means of perfect independence . . . in the exercise of a distasteful profession . . . but . . . unfettered by the very odious restraint of obligation without affection.

. . . could the society of two infants and my servants
atone to me for that which I habitually enjoyed in my
own country, I might not complain of the mental solitude
in which I live. If hitherto, however, my want of cheer-
fulness has dissatisfied you, I fear it may do so yet more
. . . since my last confinement, I have been suffering
. . . from painful and exhausting indisposition . . . the
loss of my health will not tend to improve my spirits
. . . therefore, I think your comfort will probably be increased by your absence from me.

These considerations . . . induce me to propose
that we may henceforward live apart; my discontents will
then no longer vex you, nor the restraints to which I am
now subject, gall and irritate me.[43]

Today the upshot of so firm a statement of so good a case for
reciprocal cutting of emotional losses would have been at least a decorously arranged legal separation giving Fanny custody of the children
with an ample allowance for her and their support and arrangements
for Pierce to see them often. In view of his sensitivities there might
have been conditions that Fanny stay off the stage and publish nothing of which he disapproved. Or outright divorce with similar arrangements would be just as likely. But this was 150 years ago when
society was reluctant to see put asunder what God had joined together. It even had a feeling of positive moral obligation to make
God's formula work as He had conceived it—dominant husband di-
recting, subordinate wife loyally obeying, progeny affectionately pat-
terning themselves on these models. It was positively wrong to wish
oneself away from one's husband, for it was a sacred, God-sponsored
union; almost wicked even to wonder what life would be like free of
his interferings. For all her gropings toward feminism, Fanny can
hardly not have felt the drag of these presumptions. They were in the
air she had always breathed. One senses that in the subservient terms
in which her gestures toward reconciliation are sometimes couched.

Though the laws of several American states were already not
illiberal about divorce, the culture lagged far behind the law. Though
legally possible, divorce was not really a social practicality in Philadelphia or anywhere else, cropping up only in markedly scandalous

contexts. Nor was legal or informal separation much more acceptable. That Fanny suggested it may mean that for her it was slightly—only slightly—less shocking a notion than for her more parochial husband. At home in London she knew women who had managed to struggle away from calamitous husbands without losing the social countenance of those they valued. Her analytical habit of mind sometimes afforded her useful crosslights on arbitrary institutions. For Pierce, however, tampering with marriage was unthinkable at this stage of his troubles. Besides, separation, let alone divorce, would amount to admitting not only that he had been stupid about wife choosing, but also that, having chosen, he was not master enough in his own house to correct or tread her down. Since he also genuinely loved his baby daughters, to retain their mother was convenient. Her occasional offers to leave him and semirenounce them he tacitly recognized as only counsels of hysterical despair.

Out of this tangle now came a strange double aberration. This couple who, hard as they tried, could not agree about black slavery or the nature of marriage, or the value of wide social relations, or anything else except that their marrying for love was a mutual misfortune now chose to defy all that and subject themselves to an isolation greater than that of Butler Place. It was Pierce's turn to spend the winter in Georgia. And this time Fanny, nurse Margery, and the babies would go with him.

X

Peculiar Institution

THE YOUNG PIERCE BUTLERS were to spend the winter on their estate in the Georgia Sea Islands. It sounds like an item from a Philadelphia society column circa 1926. A hundred years earlier, however, the Sea Islands' importance was economic, not recreational.

The couple's decision to make it a family party had a flavor of *credo quia impossibile.* Two years before the reasons for not doing so had been imperative. Now accommodations were no better and there were two babies to consider. Yet Pierce, usually wrongheaded, now drew the reverse conclusion. There is a hint that he hoped firsthand contact with slavery would reconcile Fanny to it. Also, tempted by one of those fragile, temporary reconciliations, he may even have told himself that having wife and children with him would relieve the loneliness down there among the Spanish moss. Certainly the decision was his, Fanny merely concurring. By now she no longer hoped responsibly to apply Channing's notions to the Butler slaves. Gloomily she anticipated "a whole manner of life repugnant to my feelings . . . the common comforts . . . are so little known [down there] that we are obliged to ship a freight of necessary articles of food. . . . Society, or the shadow of it, is not to be dreamed of . . . our residence . . . a half-furnished house in the midst of rice-swamps." [1] Slightly more buoyantly she told Sarah (Perkins) Cleveland that "whether I shall die of a yellow fever . . . [or] be shot at from behind a tree for my Abolitionism, or swallowed horse and all by an Altamaha alligator . . . [or] blown half way up to heaven [in a steamboat] on our way to Charleston are matters yet folded within the unopened chronicle of time." [2]

That was probably the sort of thing with which Pierce and John Butler had dissuaded her from going south in 1836. Now Pierce seems to have had misgivings of his own: "We are . . . departing [for Georgia] and not departing," says Fanny early in December. ". . . indecision and procrastination entering largely into the . . . disposer of my destinies . . . after a week or ten days more of doubt and darkness [Pierce may well] get up and be going [in] the . . . abrupt summons which invariably terminates these seasons of weary waiting." [3] A year earlier she might not have let her annoyance show so clearly. Nor would Pierce have so exposed the habit of vacillation that plagued him the rest of his life and actually, in the end, was the death of him.

It was already December 4, 1838. Not until two weeks later did he break through the cobwebs and get his party on board "the cars"—the new railroad from Philadelphia to Baltimore.

Their destination consisted of some thousands of acres of low-lying, nearly subtropical land in three parcels: Butler's Island and Hampton Point on St. Simon's Island were committed to large-scale, slave-worked production of rice at the former, at the latter the famous Sea Island cotton; the third parcel, Woodville, on what passed for high ground thereabouts, was used chiefly as retirement colony for superannuated slaves and summer refuge from malaria for the white man in charge. The sole reason for inhabiting the first two was profit. The only year-round denizens of Butler's Island were slaves and the black "drivers"—also slaves—who bossed them under white orders. During the summer "sickly season" whites went inland or stayed on high ground as much as possible. The health risk to the blacks was not quite as cold-blooded as it sounds. To some extent they resisted malaria better. But the difference was only relative, and the split year, involving prolonged lack of owner-supervision, often had deplorable social results. Throughout the South it was recognized that, other things being equal, the larger the plantations, the worse off the slaves; and that when the owner was considerably absentee and em-

ployed white overseers without close supervision, whether or not production suffered, the slaves usually did. Sea Island plantations were
large and the owners usually absent much of the year.

South Carolina's rice plantations had existed long enough to support a precarious but stylish subculture centered in Charleston and
Savannah. Down the Georgia coast no parallel had yet grown up.
Only decades earlier had Major Butler and other opportunists devoted
money and slave sweat to clearing brush and forest from these
swampy "islands"—actually a waterlogged flatland cut up like a jig-
saw puzzle by interlacing creeks—to plant long-staple cotton and
then, as it lost ground to the upland variety, rice. Each resulting
holding included crop-bearing swamp, fuel- and game-producing
woody jungle, water rich in fish, and, on the stretches of drier
ground, pasture. Typically each had rude barns for draft animals,
almost equally rude slave quarters, a sizable frame shack for an overseer, and, if it were a headquarters plantation, a rather more elaborate
dwelling for owner and family when in residence. But this edifice was
seldom as pretentious as the cotton-snobs' white pillared mansions in
the Yazoo Delta or the Alabama Black Belt. In winter the owner
families, soon linked by marriages of dynastic flavor, dined and jun-
keted back and forth by boat rowed by slave crews—they might as
well be in Venice, Fanny said.

Brunswick, near the Butler holdings, and Darien, still nearer
and smaller, were mere sites for a few churches, general stores, and
wharves for small vessels loading rice and cotton. The only link with
the outside world was a small steamboat coming through the sounds
from Savannah with mail, fancy freight, and the odd passenger. These
Georgia Sea Islands were an enclave all to themselves, a bundle of
slave-worked great manors lacking a dominant suzerain. All that held
them together—but it sufficed—was common economic purpose
strengthened by family ties.

The preliminary land-clearing had required a large labor force
and the new planter with so many new acres to exploit had ample use
for it. Rice particularly demanded large-scale organized effort to create and maintain the elaborate apparatus of dikes, ditches, locks, and
sluices needed for flooding and draining the rice fields. This was big-

gang slavery, unlike that of the thousands of much smaller cotton and tobacco operations to north and west. Plantations like Butler's Island supported and exploited black populations of several hundred; among the three Butler holdings the head count, including children, was well over seven hundred. Butler's Island was not, however, altogether typical. Its steam-powered rice mill, one of three such in the area, did custom processing for neighboring planters. Its owners had seen little or nothing of it for the fifteen years since the old major's death. Its able—meaning profitable—management had consisted of Roswell King, Jr., son of a cofounder of Darien who had helped the major organize his property. The antebellum South looked down on overseers. They had an often deserved bad name for base origin, misappropriations, mistreatment of slaves, and lewdness with slave women. But King was distinctly a cut above "overseer" within the meaning of the social statute, a well-connected local gentleman on terms of equal-footing friendship with the Butler brothers.

Relying on rules laid down by the major and the elder King, the son had made the Butler properties famous for production and discipline. Only the nearby owner-supervised Couper-Hamilton-Fraser plantations were better. Ten years previously King had written at the request of the *Southern Agriculturist* an article about this success. He attributed it to his insisting on a taut ship, forbidding visiting back and forth to other plantations, and strictly controlling the drivers lest they grow tyrannical. In the interests of health he assigned pregnant women to lighter field work,[4] maintained infirmaries in charge of slave nurse-midwives, added adequate high-grade proteins (salt beef, salt pork, salt fish) to ample rations of corn meal, and, instead of burdening women field-hands with cooking after their day's work, assigned old women to cook for all. He deplored the common reliance on mere

> overseers at low wages, perhaps more destitute of principle than the blacks; [who] do them more harm than the owners good . . . grind out good crops and in a few years break down the gang. Slave owners cannot be too particular to whom they trust the health . . . [lives] . . . and morals of . . . the sinews of the estate. A master, or an

overseer, should be the kind friend and monitor of the
slave, not the oppressor. . . . Slaves have a perfect
knowledge of right and wrong. When an equitable distribution of rewards and punishments is observed . . . they
will conform to almost every rule . . . laid down.[5]

The Butlers were now losing this faithful steward. King had
recently bought new land in the booming Alabama cotton country
and was taking thither a newly purchased gang of slaves of his own
to clear and plant. To replace him, the Butlers had hired an overseer
with a good reputation from serving under the Couper interests.
Fanny may well never have seen that article of King's. But she had
probably heard from Pierce enough about the man's principles and
abilities to persuade her that the slavery she would be seeing firsthand, though rather specialized, would show the "peculiar institution" at something near its best.

On December 20, 1838, the Butlers boarded "the cars." It was
December 30 when they reached their goal eight hundred-odd crow-
flight miles to south-southwestward. It might have taken no longer
in one of the coasting packets sailing more or less regularly from New
York or Philadelphia to Charleston or Savannah, the route that the
family's special supplies necessarily took. But in view of her last two
crossings Fanny probably wanted no more of the North Atlantic in
winter, and the likelihood of not only foul but notoriously dangerous
weather off Cape Hatteras ("graveyard of the Atlantic") particularly
in winter was sound argument for the alternative—an implausible
combination of inland-waterway steamboats, new-laid railroads, and
stagecoaches. It was safer, true, but in view of the flimsiness of certain bridges and the frequency of boiler explosions, not by much.
Several times along the way Fanny must have wished herself seasick
and terrified at sea along with the white flour, dried prunes, and
Madeira. Consider that the party included not only Fanny, Pierce,
and Pierce's sister (bound for Charleston), but also a toddler of thirty
months, a baby at the breast, and the invaluable Margery O'Brien.
One wonders how the diaper problem was solved. Time and again

Branchtown-to-Darien must have seemed like a classic case of you-can't-get-there-from-here.

The wooden trestle railroad bridges across minor streams between Wilmington and Havre de Grace looked so shaky that the nuisance of changing to a steam ferry across the Susquehanna, where no bridge yet existed, was welcome. From Baltimore to Portsmouth, Virginia, a fast Chesapeake Bay steamboat set them well forward overnight, but its internal economy gave Fanny a taste of the black servants' blend of good humor and slovenliness prevalent in most public and many private situations in Dixie. At Portsmouth, she wrote to Harriet, were "the first slaves I ever saw . . . poorly clothed; looked horribly dirty . . . a lazy recklessness . . . as they sauntered along, which naturally belongs to creatures . . . without responsibilities." At Suffolk out of the railroad car window she saw more examples of God's provision for Ham's descendants: "They seem full of idle merriment and unmeaning glee, and regard with an intensity of curiosity perfectly ludicrous . . . such whites as . . . are strangers. . . . my child leaned from the carriage-window, her brilliant complexion drew forth sundry exclamations of delight . . . one woman, grinning from ear to ear . . . drew forward a little mahogany-colored imp . . . and offered her to the little 'Missis' for her waiting-maid." [6]

Fanny may not have been aware that a few years earlier, only a few miles from Suffolk, paranoid Nat Turner's black believers had got some of their own back with an exultant spree of murdering any whites that came to hand. But she should have remembered that these were not her first slaves. Baltimore and Washington, where she had acted five years previously, were slave country, and a majority of the blacks she had then seen were slaves. Then, however, slavery had been only one of several matters rattling about in her head. The sluggishly unhealthy lives led by fashionable American women and the shortcomings of Irish "help" were also on her mind. Now the prospect of rubbing elbows with slavery in concentrated form kept that topic dominant. To reinforce that, she had promised Elizabeth Sedgwick to keep a diary (in letter form: "Dear Elizabeth . . .") of her experiences with topic A. Just before leaving Philadelphia, she had written to her as preface that an apologist for slavery [Pierce? or John?] had warned her against going south

> prejudiced against what I am to find there. I know not well how to answer. . . . I *am* going prejudiced against slavery. . . . Nevertheless, I go prepared to find many mitigations . . . much kindness on the part of the masters, much content on that of the slaves . . . you may rely upon the carefulness of my observation . . . certainly, on the plantation to which I am going, it will be more likely that I should some things extenuate, than set down aught in malice.[7]

A true Kemble, always able to quote Shakespeare to the purpose.

Southward from Suffolk the railroad took its passengers along the edge of the aptly named Great Dismal and into North Carolina's turpentine country of tall, gaunt pines. Then it petered out. Its human freight transferred to stagecoaches and entered on an irksome struggle to survive under makeshift, transitional conditions in a godforsaken part of the world. Stopping to eat meant inedible versions of hot biscuit—to Fanny "lumps of hot dough"—and dirt evenly distributed between the scrawny fried chicken and the garments of the black women serving. The track that the coaches more or less followed "lay . . . through swamps and was frequently itself under water" over corduroy so "dreadfully rough and unequal, that drawing a coach over it at all seemed perfectly miraculous . . . drivers in this part of the world deserve infinite praise both for skill and care; but the road-makers, I think, are beyond praise for their noble confidence in what skill and care can accomplish."[8] The bridge across the Neuse River was so rickety that in precaution the passengers were sent across on foot; when it did not fall down, the coaches followed empty and reembarked them. Next came ten miles of heavy going through deep sand to where the railroad resumed an existence so recent that this would be only the third time a train had gone over it.

There was no train waiting as there should have been, and the evening was winter-chilly. A solitary boxcar standing on the rails was the only hint of transportation. The passengers shivered in the coaches while round them gathered a small crowd of poor whites come to marvel at the expected steam carriage and willing to while away the time gawking at strangers. They had changed little in the hundred years since William Byrd II described their forebears in Lubberland. Fanny thought them the most "forlorn, fierce, poor, and wild-looking set" she had ever seen. "They wandered round and round us, with a stupid kind of dismayed wonder."[9] The passengers finally built a fire, held a council of war, and decided to seek food and shelter at a plantation said to be nearby. They loaded women, children, and luggage into the boxcar and recruited local blacks to push. This many-legged motive power had great trouble crossing two trestles consisting of only piles and rails with little footing between; but nobody fell in and in half an hour they all were enjoying a roaring fire of pine logs under "the Colonel's" patriarchal rooftree. This venerable widower welcomed the intrusion, set a bevy of black women preparing supper, gave the gentlemen homemade wine, let Fanny know he was a veteran of the Revolution and had known Washington—highly unlikely, unless he was pushing eighty—and when the train finally arrived, charged the party fifty cents each, a thumping price for that place and time, for "dirty water—I cannot call it tea— bad butter, and old dry biscuits."[10] As Fanny left, one of the black women let her know that at least three of her fellows were the colonel's daughters; whether by a single slave mother or not was unclear, but it seemed to be a matter of pride.

Before dawn the train clanked and wheezed to a halt in the outskirts of Wilmington, North Carolina, end of the line. The passengers had a long, stumbly walk in the dark to a hotel where the females of the Butler party drew the best available—one room with one bed, one cot, and one mattress on the floor. Wilmington seemed "ruinous, yet not old—poor, dirty, mean, and unvenerable in its poverty and decay." By afternoon, however, the world looked better. The steamboat for Charleston was clean and comfortable, the captain genial, and "after a most delightful walk . . . on deck, and comfortable tea, we retired for the night, and did not wake till we bumped on the Charleston bar on the morning of Christmas-day." A dismal way to spend Christmas—in a second-rate hotel—the better one had recently burned down—"half furnished, and not by any means half clean"[11] with doors and windows that wouldn't shut.

Fanny found she liked Charleston's down-at-heel dignity, its "genteel infirmity as . . . of a distressed elderly gentlewoman." In contrast to what she and so many other Europeans considered America's hyperconformity, "every house seems built to the owner's particular taste."[12] But the matter of black servitude would not stay submerged. By now Fanny expected "laziness . . . filthiness . . . inconceivable stupidity, and unconquerable good humour [from] the Dianas, Phillises, Floras, Caesars, et cetera, who stand grinning in wonderment and delight round our table." But she was not prepared to learn that the light-colored owner-manageress of the hotel was these blacks' legal proprietor. In the South's large towns slave-owning free blacks were not unusual, but nobody had warned her of that possibility. Every evening came "a most ominous tolling of bells and beating of drums" that reminded Fanny of frontier garrison towns in Europe until she learned it betokened Charleston's rigorous curfew and nightly militia patrol. After all, it was only twenty years since free black Denmark Vesey's aborted conspiracy of slaves had put the everlasting fear of arson and massacre into the South's most elegant town. "No doubt these daily and nightly precautions are but trifling drawbacks upon the manifold blessings of slavery," Fanny wrote to Harriet. ". . . still, I should prefer going to sleep without the apprehension of my servants' cutting my throat in my bed."[13]

It took the weekly steamboat to Savannah two nights and a day to thread through "cuts and small muddy rivers, where we stuck fast sometimes . . . a most dismal succession of dingy, low, yellow swamps and reedy marshes, beyond expression wearisome to the eye"—the sort of scenery Fanny would see a great deal of in the next five months. The well-managed hotel in Savannah afforded her the luxury of a warm bath. That night they boarded still another steamboat, tiny but clean and tidy; Fanny, Margery, and the babies had the miniature ladies' cabin all to themselves. Next morning their entrance into the great Altamaha River meant their journey's end was near. The channel wound between "low, reedy swamps, rattling their brittle canes in the morning breeze,"[14] and eventually there in the distance was Darien town, what there was of it. But a vessel lay at its wharf and nurse Margery cheered up because, she said, she had expected the utter end of the world; yet here were houses and ships and even steamboats!

The captain was still rounding his vessel to when a couple of smartly painted boats came swirling alongside, their black oarsmen shouting: "Oh, massa! oh, missis! oh, lilli missis! too glad to see you!" all broad grins and ecstatic whoops. These Butler boats, the smaller for the white folks, the larger for their luggage, were the eighth successive conveyance—nine if one counts the boxcar in North Carolina—that the Butler party had used since leaving their carriage at the railroad station in Philadelphia. Outer Mongolia would probably have been less inconvenient. One must admire Pierce Butler for managing thus to chivy his flock from railroad to hotel to steamboat to stagecoach and so on and so forth over and over again, babies crying, baggage going astray, carriages unavailable when worst needed, Fanny probably stonily silent, rain and darkness confusing everything—and all in the most lackadaisical and feckless region of the United States.

It was Sunday, nominal day of rest for slaves, so the whole population of Butler's Island was free to join the hurricane of welcome at the plantation wharf. On a weekday, however, the scene would probably have been the same, for neither the black drivers nor the blacks they drove could have been kept at work on this day of days in this walled-off little world where practically nothing ever happened:

> As we neared the bank, the steersman took up a huge conch, and . . . sounded out our approach. . . . the wharf . . . began to be crowded with negroes, jumping, dancing, shouting, laughing . . . clapping their hands . . . using the most extravagant and ludicrous gesticulations to express their ecstacy. . . . On our landing . . . the crowd thronged about us like a swarm of bees; we were seized, pulled, pushed, carried, dragged. . . . They seized our clothes. kissed them—then our hands, and almost wrung them off. . . . not until we were safely housed, and the door shut . . . we indulged in a fit of laughing, quite as full, on my part, of nervousness as of amusement. . . . Later . . . I attempted to take some exercise . . . but before I had proceeded a quarter of a mile, I was again enveloped in a cloud of these dingy dependents . . . . clamoring welcome, staring at me, stroking my velvet pelisse, and exhibiting at once the

> wildest delight and the most savage curiosity. I was
> obliged . . . to return home.[15]

Wildly disproportionate, hence food for thought. At the time
the best she could do with it was: "Their vehement professions of
regard and affection . . . reminded me of the saying of the satirist,
that 'gratitude is a lively sense of benefits to come.' "[16] Sound as far
as it went; but only Exercise I in a long, long series.

After nine days as tutelary goddess of Butler's Island: "The
strangeness of this existence surprises me afresh every hour. . . . I
[feel] like the little old woman whose petticoats were cut all round
about. 'O Lord a mercy, sure this is never I!' "[17] Even the intense
sunshine seemed almost alarmingly unnatural in January. Generally
the environment was a sort of frowsy, vegetation-choked Netherlands,
its swampiness half-tamed by dikes and ditches that discouraged
horseback riding, even extensive walking. For exercise Fanny took to
learning to row a light skiff; she found it boring even after attaining
some skill. For once she had too much water in her cosmos:

> A duck, an eel, or a frog might live here as in Paradise;
> but a creature of dry habits naturally pines for less wet.
> . . . "water, water everywhere"; indeed, in spring, the ov-
> erseer tells me, we may have to go from house to house in
> boats, the whole island being often flooded. . . . It is
> . . . in mere process of formation . . . [created by] a
> huge, rolling river, thick and turbid with mud. . . . The
> river wants *straining* and the land wants draining, to make
> either of them properly wet or dry.[18]

Yet this alien from a temperate zone and a culture that regarded
hothouses as tasteful luxuries was delighted by the variety, ever-green
character and extravagant vigor of the Sea Islands' flora on the jungly-
wooded far margins of the rice fields. She even managed to admire
the palmetto, the subtropics' least inspiring ornament, for anything
vaguely palmlike carried romantic connotations of languorous, poeti-
cally warm climate. Only far too much of Butler's Island's exotic
growth was shrouded and masked by the ubiquitous Spanish moss:
"Of all parasitical plants . . . the most melancholy and dismal

. . . dark grey drooping masses, swinging in every breeze like matted grizzled hair . . . a naked cypress with its straggling arms all hung with this banner of death [looks] like a gigantic tree of monstrous cobwebs."[19] This is lugubrious stuff and may well have made a minor contribution to the sense of oppression that these new surroundings often gave Fanny.[20]

Living conditions were quite as rough as predicted. The overseer-superintendent's ramshackle dwelling comprised three small and three much smaller rooms, two of the latter assigned to the overseer who was perforce temporarily a member of the family. Margery and the babies were established upstairs. The walls were of rough plaster; for locks the doors had only the pioneer's wooden string-latch; a small matter, Fanny noted, for nobody ever closed them anyway. Rather toothsome meals were prepared by a black man-cook in a dirt-floored, ineffably filthy shed separate from the dwelling, southern-fashion. Nobody had bothered to paint the house or plant shade trees. Most of the handsome orange trees that had once borne a beautiful minor crop for northern markets had been killed by an unusually cold winter some years previously. The scanty furniture had been put together by the plantation's slave carpenters with no attempt at elegance.

The house servants were in a state of mind and body to which the slave economy was used but for which an inconveniently fastidious rearing had not fitted Fanny. They were "generally barefooted, and always filthy both in their clothes and person . . . begrimed, ignorant, incapable poor creatures, who stumble about . . . in zealous hindrance of each other. . . . This unlimited supply of untrained savages (for that is what they are) is anything but a luxury. . . . Their ignorance, dirt, and stupidity seem to me as intolerable as the unjust laws which condemn them to be ignorant, filthy, and stupid." The young black woman assigned as housemaid was so noisome that "it is impossible to endure her proximity . . . I wait upon myself more than I have ever done in my life before."[21] Fanny nevertheless had the common sense to discern that whites were wrong in ascribing this smelliness to racial origin and making it a pretext for regarding their slaves as essentially inferior. She recalled having had the same difficulty with uncouth Irish peasants; and assured "Dear Elizabeth" that training in personal cleanliness, entailing a heightened self-respect, would keep blacks as inoffensive as their owners.

Pierce gave Fanny a sort of slave footman to fetch and carry for her, and luckily the choice fell on a youth named Jack—probably because he was rather too wispy in physique to make a good field-hand. Son of a recently dead head-driver, he had had slightly more familial stimulus than most of his peers; or, genetically, he had some of his father's unusual capability; anyway he was bright and reveled in the glory of looking after mistress. He warned her about snakes, quicksands, and the poisonous barbs of the large catfish that she occasionally hooked when she and he went fishing. Dutifully he tried to carry out her fruitless experiments in how best to put new-caught fish out of their flopping misery and in concocting pastes that would attract them as well as live bait. The better Jack and she grew acquainted, the stronger her opinion that, contrary to what the South and most of the North devoutly believed, blacks would be as clever and responsible as whites—not, after all, saying a great deal in most cases—if they had the same stimuli in rearing. Out there watching their floats in Fanny's particular little boat—she called it the *Dolphin*—they had long talks about all those things in the great outside world that she took for granted but were wonders to him. "His questions, like those of an intelligent child, [were] inexhaustible; his curiosity about all things beyond this island, the prison-house of his existence, [was] perfectly intense." But he was also, like the other slaves, "a stupendous flatterer, and . . . seems devoid of physical and moral courage. . . . in the midst of his torrent of inquiries about places and things, I suddenly asked him if he would like to be free. A gleam of light absolutely shot over his whole countenance . . . [then he] became excessively confused, and at length replied, 'Free, missis! what for me wish to be free? . . . me work till me die for missis and massa.' "22

The whitewashed walls of Darien's port area were within view to northward, but two arms of the river and a mile of swamp intervened; to get there required a several miles' pull in a boat. It caused comment among Darien's scattering of white ladies—the matrons and spinsters appertaining to the local banker and clergy and merchants—when the skiff running errands for Butler's Island sometimes had

Fanny rowing stroke for a black boatman at the after oar. The local ladies and Fanny had few sympathies anyway. A few necessary calls of ceremony—after all, the Butlers stood high in the local pecking-order—showed her that, by her standards, they were languid and rather slovenly in person, in household management, and in mind. Their drawling speech struck her as unworthy of ladies as well as whiningly unpleasant to hear, and it irritated her that her actually having a white nurse for her children was for them a source of incredulous, boringly prolix envy. (As for the slaves, they could not even conceive of a white woman doing such work; for a while they regarded Margery as Pierce's auxiliary wife.) Nor did they spare the head shaking about Fanny's outlandish attitude toward the blacks. One afternoon Fanny was being rowed home to Hampton Point from Butler's Island as a storm was blowing up. It was arduous going but the crew of eight oarsmen were "in great spirits . . . one . . . said something which elicited . . . general assent, and I asked what it was; the steerer said . . . there was not another planter's lady in all Georgia who would have gone through the storm all alone with them . . . i.e., without the protecting presence of a white man. . . . in the perfect confidence with which I go among them, they must perceive a curious difference between me and my lady neighbors . . . all [of whom] have expressed unbounded astonishment at my doing so."[23]

She liked the local white mullet and shad, the gorgeous sunsets and the vast sky overhanging the swamps, the plethora of remarkable birds, the venerable live oaks of Darien's sandy streets; but her particular pleasure lay in being thus rowed, alone or in company, through the intricate Altamaha delta by a boat's crew of robust blacks singing like melodious bullfrogs to keep the time right and lighten the task. "The tune and time they keep [are] something quite wonderful," said this quasi-professional musician, "such truth of intonation and accent would make any music agreeable." She detected the Scottish, French, English origins of some of the airs thus reworked and the occasional originalities of melody in others, such as

> . . . an extremely pretty, plaintive air . . . [with] but one line . . . repeated with a sort of wailing chorus—

> "Oh! my massa told me, there's no grass in
> Georgia." . . .
> [which was] supposed to be the lamentation of a slave
> from one of the more northerly states . . . where hoeing
> the weeds, or grass as they call it, is not nearly so severe
> as . . . in the rice and cotton lands of Georgia.[24]

Still other songs amounted to personal interaction of a muted, crypto-ironic tone, improvisations throbbing along with the swing of the oars:

> . . . alternate strophe and antistrophe of poetical descrip-
> tion of my personal attractions, in which my "wire waist"
> recurred repeatedly, to my intense amusement. . . . Occa-
> sionally I am celebrated as "Massa's darling" [much of the
> time this would have been irony indeed] and [Sarah]
> comes in for . . . the brilliant beauty of her complexion
> . . . the other day . . . our poets made a diversion
> . . . to the moral qualities of their small mistress. . . .
> "Little Missis Sally
> That's a ruling lady"

The significance was not lost on Sarah's mother. She was already uneasy lest a slave plantation's atmosphere of sycophancy mar her children: "I . . . saw . . . with dismay . . . [how the slaves] sprang to obey [Sarah's] little gestures of command. She said something about a swing, and in less than five minutes, head man Frank had erected it for her, and a dozen young slaves were ready to swing little 'missis.' "[25] Two generations earlier in his *Notes on Virginia* Thomas Jefferson pointed out that hazard as one of the slave-associated curses of southern society. But we can score an originality for Fanny here. Her comments on the slaves' boat-songs are among the first—so far as a pretty good knowledge of the literature will take me, I think the first—instance of a trained white musician taking American blacks' music seriously.

Among Darien's white oligarchy Fanny got on well with Dr. James Holmes, a northern-born and -trained physician usually called in for severe medical emergencies among the Butler slaves. He let

Fanny scold him about the evils of slavery—in which he professed to
believe as a practicality—and fought back but "lost nothing of his
courtesy or good-humor."[26] Years later his informal memoirs called
her a "hopeless monomaniac" on the subject, most unfair in her writings to those patterns of humane slavery, the Butler plantations. Yet
he was just as emphatic about the vigorous charm of this "elegant
and accomplished lady . . . I respected her highly . . . liked her
social, companionable, and even playful ways."[27] This demonstration
that two persons of goodwill, one in pantaloons, one in skirts, could
disagree on an overheated subject without lessening personal regard
is specially striking because early in her stay Fanny had looked into
the state of medical care at Butler's Island and been shocked right
down to the soles of her firmly planted feet.

Certain slave women had come to her with distressing, over-
graphic accounts of their gynecological troubles. Following up, Fanny
inspected Number One quarters (Butler's Island had three separate
"camps," that is, self-contained villages) to the "Infirmary . . . a
large two-story building . . . of whitewashed wood [containing] four
large-sized rooms." What windows were glazed were dark with dirt;
those unglazed were stopped with crude wooden shutters. The fire-
place chimney was huge and the fire relatively insignificant. The bet-
ter-off women patients were draped on wooden settles.

> [Those] too ill to rise . . . lay . . . on the floor, without
> bed, mattress, or pillow, buried in tattered and filthy
> blankets. . . . Here lay women expecting every hour the
> terrors and agonies of childbirth . . . others . . . groan-
> ing over the anguish . . . of miscarriages . . . some
> burning with fever, others . . . aching with rheumatism,
> upon the hard cold ground. . . . pray take notice [she
> told "Dear Elizabeth"] that this is the hospital of an estate
> where the owners are supposed to be humane, the overseer
> efficient and kind, and the negroes remarkably well cared
> for and comfortable.

Next day while trying to help control a woman patient in convulsions: "How much I wished that, instead of music, and dancing, and
such stuff, I had learned something of sickness and health . . . I

might have known how to assist this poor creature, and to direct her ignorant and helpless nurses."[28]

At least she was well grounded in cleanliness and order. She half cajoled, half ordered the attendants into attempting to clean up the prevailing foulness, going home "with my clothes covered with dust, and full of vermin, and with a heart heavy enough."[29] This depth of squalor needs placing in context. In that day sanitary conditions in institutions called hospitals were at best ill-conceived, because the relation of soap and water to infection and of fresh air, light, and comfort to convalescence were not understood. Neither Florence Nightingale nor Louis Pasteur had yet weighed in. Medicine was mostly pretentious guesswork, as much of it still is. Nursing was irresponsible fumbling even when alleviated by goodwill and discipline. And hospitals were largely for the lower orders. Persons of standing and resources were doctored and nursed at home, living or dying as the luck went. The typical concentrations of the ailing for mass-care were the seagoing sick bay, the postbattle army hospital, the emergency pesthouse, the monastery-founded sump called a hospital into which society drained diseased members of the urban proletariat. Fanny's slave infirmary was just another failure properly to provide for a stratum submerged even deeper than such groups as foremast hands, soldiers, and prostitutes. Given all that, however, the civic or religious impulse that created hospitals did carry overtones of solicitude and decency. And the lack of discernible effort toward even those qualities outraged Fanny no less because when she questioned those in charge, they hardly bothered to deny negligence.

When Fanny reproached the overseer for allowing such conditions, he said that soon after taking charge the year before, he had found the infirmary in poor shape and mentioned it to John Butler, then in residence, and to King. When neither evinced interest, he concluded it was "a matter of indifference to the owners, and had left it in the condition in which . . . it has been for the last nineteen years." So much for the representations in King's article. With unusual discretion Fanny seems not to have tried to badger Pierce into an inspection tour. She did make an earnest effort to get mothers with hospitalized children at least to keep them and their environment clean. When the notion seemed too strange for them to grasp, she rolled up her own sleeves and set examples, taking off the foul caps that kept the babies' crania verminous and dirt-caked, removing the filthier rags stuck to their lower parts, giving them the first all-over baths they had ever had. It must have caused immeasurable astonishment to see this buckra lady so employed even as demonstration of what she preached. Then she found that the healthier babies left in charge of elder siblings while mother did her regular field-tasks were not much better off. To back up her eloquence on the virtues of cleanliness Fanny offered a penny to each child-minder showing her a baby with a clean face and hands; and "this morning I was surrounded . . . by a swarm of children carrying their little charges on their backs . . . [with] shining, and, in many instances, wet faces and hands."[30]

Weeks later, thanks to her nagging at the overseer and probably Pierce too, she had "the pleasure of announcing . . . a variety of improvements to be made in the Infirmary. . . . a third story . . . added . . . [leaving] the ground floor . . . comparatively free for the most miserable. . . . to be furnished with bedsteads, mattresses, pillows, and blankets; . . . I feel a little comforted . . . some of my twinges will have wrought this poor alleviation."[31] But the twinges began again, sharp as ever, within a short time; when the family shifted quarters to the Hampton Point plantation, the less profitable and more neglected operation, she found the infirmaries there worse than Butler's Island's had been.

On certain large plantations elsewhere her efforts would have had some precedent. A planter's wife of unusual energy or sensitivity was not unlikely to constitute herself curator of the slaves' health, physical and sometimes moral. She dosed her husband's blacks, sat up with the critically sick, supervised the making of their garments, bullied wife-beaters into stopping it, made sure provisions were fairly distributed, sponsored "marriages." . . . "It is the slaves who own me," such a benevolent planter's lady told W. H. ("Bull Run") Russell of the London *Times*. "Morning, noon and night I am obliged to look after them, to doctor them, and to attend to them in every way."[32] But that sort of thing was less likely to come about in the rice country, for Ole Missis, as she was probably known, was absent much of the year. On the Butler properties, where no lady of the manor had been for a generation, if ever, it could have hardly begun at all. Fanny was in a special backwater where her imperative impulse to meddle in matters that nobody in charge had much reason to disturb was, in the inevitable opinion of Pierce and his staff, wantonly or at best misguidedly upsetting.

For Fanny was not being sarcastic when reminding "Dear Elizabeth" that these very Butler plantations were famous for humaneness, and with relatively good reason. Marriage of a sublegal, genially sanctioned sort, that is, a ceremoniously acknowledged shacking up, was encouraged; so was the local slave preacher. Butler slaves were very seldom sold away from the place, parent-and-children situations were never broken up. Well-behaved slaves were allowed to paddle round to Darien on Sunday to sell poultry and eggs they had raised, cooperage, and dugout canoes they had made, Spanish moss gathered as mattress- and pillow-stuffing. A former Butler slave testified seventy-odd years after Fanny's stay there that her family had been treated "very nicely"[33]—never hired off the place to work on the roads or bullied by the "paterollers"—the informal citizen patrols that beat slaves found straying without proper written passes. Pierce himself, on first coming down, had reduced women's field-tasks below those of men even when they could not plead pregnancy. In the rice-country's terms—or those of large-plantation slavery generally—all that was almost quixotically liberal. The Butler slaves' extravagant praise of their owners was not altogether sycophantic. And now here was one owner's alien wife rocking this creditable boat by acting ombudsman-partisan of the slaves as fiercely as if Butler's Island had been as shameless as one of those "nigger killing" sugar plantations in Louisiana.

How the slaves nudged Fanny into this role is clear in what went on one afternoon when she came ashore at the Butler's Island wharf at the hour when the women, their tasks finished, were fetching the overnight water supply in buckets. "What [they] do with it I can not imagine," she wrote, "for evidence of its ever having been introduced into their dwellings I saw none. . . . I exhorted them to go home and wash their children, and clean their houses and themselves, which they professed themselves ready to do, but said they had no soap. Then began a chorus of mingled requests for soap, for summer clothing . . ."[34]—items that she inevitably included in her next expostulatory interview with the plantation command. The hazards involved in thus becoming pipeline to Massa were apparent. Thus in the infirmary Fanny reproaches an ailing mother with an ailing baby for the child's filthy state; the reply is that working six days a week in the field does not leave enough time or energy to spare for keeping anything clean. Fanny passes this on to the overseer at dinner. Next morning she learns he has come early to the infirmary and flogged the woman not for having complained, he assured Fanny when she protested, but for having impertinently pleaded illness when ordered out to resume her daily task. Fanny probably made no effort to hide her disbelief. But after that, doubtless much to the overseer's relief, she chose to take most of her meddlings direct to Pierce.

Every fresh instance of a slave, usually a woman, bringing Fanny a complaint to pass on got her deeper into trouble. But not until Pierce read her book about it all twenty-four years later—I assume he did read it—could he have grasped the full extravagance of her crimes. There would have been an enormous explosion in 1839 had he known that she had explained to one or another of his slaves that she "had no ownership over them . . . that I held such ownership sinful, and . . . though I was the wife of the man who pretends to own them, I was, in truth, no more their mistress than they were mine. Some of them . . . understood me, more of them did not." Either way this was economic and domestic treason, only slightly mitigated in that she had not mounted a stump and made that apology to the whole black population of the island. It was almost equally subversive that

> I have seen many babies on this plantation . . . quite as pretty as white children. . . . when the very unusual operation of washing has been performed, the blood shines through the fine texture of the skin, giving life and richness . . . a species of beauty which I think scarcely any

body . . . would fail to acknowledge. . . . this very day
{I} stooped to kiss a little sleeping creature . . . on its
mother's knees. . . . The caress excited the irrepressible
delight of all the women present—poor creatures! who
seemed to forget I was a woman, and had children myself,
and bore a woman's and a mother's heart toward them and
theirs.[35]

Pierce and she did agree, however, in respecting and admiring
very black, very grave "headman" Frank, the chief driver. When both
owner and overseer were away—which could be overnight or days at
a time—he was completely in charge of punishments, provisions,
tasks, cultivation schedules. Fanny called him "Trustworthy, up-
right, intelligent . . . extremely well mannered, and, being respected, he respects himself. He is as ignorant as the rest . . . but
. . . always clean and tidy . . . {his} demeanor far removed from
servility." Betty, his "wife," kept their cabin clean and habitable, in
contrast to all others, and was "most active, trustworthy. . . . To
{her} excellent conduct . . . both the present and the last overseer
bear unqualified testimony."[36] That "last overseer" was King. Keep
him in mind in this context. Frank and Betty had a son named
Renty—of what name this was a corruption I can't guess—of a curiously assertive temperament. His markedly light skin and Caucasoid
features made Fanny comment privately to Pierce that she would
never have supposed him the son of two parents as black as Betty and
Frank. For all that, Pierce replied, guardedly begging the question,
he was their son.

    While winding up his local affairs, King visited his good friend
Pierce. Fanny found him personable, articulate and shrewd. On prod-
ding, this "man . . . {who} has passed his whole life among slaves"
said with courteous candor: " I hate slavery with all my heart; I consider it an absolute curse. . . . as for its being an irremediable evil
. . . that's all nonsense; for, as soon as people become convinced that
it is in their interest to get rid of it, they will soon find the means to
do so." He went on to praise the intelligence and loyalty of the
black slave engineer who operated the steam rice-mill, the matronly
black woman who managed the infirmary, and headman Frank who,
he said, "had quite the principles of a white man."[37]

His hatred of slavery did not, however, deter him from setting up a new slave-plantation that required transplanting scores of slaves away from their native place—a thing they considered calamitous even when it did not break up families. His willingness to make the best of slavery was further established when Fanny learned that early in his vice-regency at Butler's Island his respect for Frank had not kept him from appropriating Betty for as long as she suited his randy needs. Renty was the result. The Butler slaves knew all about it, and so, obviously, did Pierce. Such consequences of putting white men in absolute command over scores of black women were more or less taken for granted all over the slave states. Planters' and overseers' wives secretly—a few openly—deplored this side effect but had to accept it. Presently it came out that King's father had set him the example. Fanny pointed out to Pierce a light-colored, middle-aged driver who looked ungodly like King. "Very likely his brother,"[38] Pierce said, candid for a change. In time a couple of other instances of the fertility of father and son came to light.

Alone with the overseer one evening, Fanny got him discussing certain aspects of slavery. She learned that though he did not doubt its morality, he thought it inefficient and wasteful and was "decidedly in favor of free labor, upon grounds of expediency . . . the work of slaves . . . being compulsory, was of the worst possible quality and the smallest possible quantity . . . the charge of them before . . . they are able to work is onerous, the cost of feeding and clothing them very considerable." But Fanny already knew the economic flaw in that argument from economics. A "very distinguished Carolinian" (unidentified, probably an eminent Charlestonian) had said to her: " 'I'll tell you why abolition is impossible: because every healthy negro can fetch a thousand dollars in the Charleston market at this moment.' "[39] Dixie's capital was irrecoverably sunk in two things— land and black chattels, and nobody had the resources or the courage to start over again on any other basis.

Just before King left the Darien area, the overseer, Pierce, and he staged a little drama that might have been designed to show the callousness built into slavery and inevitably affecting slave owners. There was a slave named Psyche,[40] less filthy and feckless than most—"wife" of a steady, stalwart slave named Joe, mother by him of two small children kept relatively clean. As King's property, Psyche had lived and worked on Butler's Island during his incumbency. Now word of his moving to Alabama disquieted her. In spite of the Butlers' policy against splitting up families, he had a legal right to include her and her children in his Alabama-bound crew; he had done something like that in another situation some years previously at Hampton Point. Psyche had come confusedly to hope that between her long residence on Butler's Island and "marriage" to a Butler slave, she might now somehow belong to the Butlers. She asked Margery to find out how the matter stood.

Fanny asked the overseer who owned Psyche. He replied that, as a matter of fact, he did. King had offered to sell her and children to him because "they would be rather troublesome to him than otherwise down where he was going. . . . as I had no objection to investing a little money that way, I bought them"; but he had not bothered to tell Psyche. Relieved to hear it but still uneasy, Psyche besought Fanny to persuade Pierce to buy her. Before Fanny could take it up with him, here was Joe, Psyche's "husband," "in a state of frenzy . . . voice broken with sobs . . . reiterating his determination never to leave . . . never to go to Alabama, never to leave his old father and mother, his poor wife and children, and dashing his hat, which he was wringing like a cloth in his hands, upon the ground, he declared he would kill himself if he was compelled to follow [Mr. King]." When Fanny came on the scene, Pierce was calmly advising Joe "not [to] make a fuss about what there was no help for." Again Fanny went to the overseer. He explained that in token of friendship Pierce had made King a parting gift of Joe and he was to "go down to Alabama with his new owner the next day. . . . You will not wonder that the man required a little judicious soothing,"[41] Fanny wrote to "Dear Elizabeth."

She gave Pierce a very hard time, "appealed to him, for his own soul's sake, not to commit so great a cruelty . . . I cried . . . I adjured . . . all my sense of justice, and of mercy, and of pity for the poor wretch, and of wretchedness at finding myself implicated . . . broke in torrents of words from my lips and tears from my eyes!" In view of Fanny's powers of transmitting synthetic passions across footlights, this tempest of genuine outrage must have been formidable. It is a tribute to Pierce's powers of resistance that "he gave me no answer whatever . . . the intemperate vehemence of my entreaties and expostulations perhaps deserved that he should leave me . . . without one single word of reply; and miserable enough I remained."[42]

That evening the overseer came in to work on accounts. Fanny, who had been unable to eat all day, asked had he seen Joe since the storm. " 'Yes, ma'am; he is a great deal happier than he was this morning.' " King had reprieved him because "he did not wish to be bothered with any niggers . . . who were to be troublesome." The overseer had not bothered to tell Fanny of this happy turn of events but he "supposed" Psyche knew of it. Fanny, almost as embittered as relieved by these crassly callous doings, went all next day without a word from Pierce about it. She reckoned up the cash value of all her rings, necklaces, and brooches, doubting that the whole would come to the price of so superior a slave as Psyche plus her children, then reminded herself that she had once had and doubtless retained earning ability on the stage. That Pierce would let her resume acting was wildly unlikely. But in this rush of emergency feeling she ignored that. That evening she implored the overseer never to sell Psyche or her children without first giving her the refusal. Very sorry, ma'am, he said; being unaware that "you entertained any idea of making an investment of that nature . . . I would willingly have sold the woman to you; but I sold her and her children this morning to [Mr Butler]."[43]

And there it was. "Though [Pierce] had resented my unmeasured upbraidings . . . though he had, perhaps justly, punished my violent outbreak . . . by not telling me of his humane purpose, he had bought these poor creatures, and so, I trust, secured them from such misery in future. I jumped up and left [the overseer] still speaking, and ran to find Mr. [Butler] and thank him." As well she might. In fiction this gracelessly kind concession would have been first step toward an eventual harmony. Such a *casus pacis* might have been lubricated by Pierce's preening of himself for having thus shown that he could be a kind master not only to slaves—all Georgia already

knew he was that—but even to a wife. Only this star-crossed couple
were not characters in fiction. No gains in rapport ensued. Fanny's
comment at the end was: "Think, [Elizabeth], how it fares with
slaves on plantations where there is no crazy Englishwoman to weep,
and entreat, and implore, and upbraid for them, and no master willing to listen." [44]

Later, making fast friends with old John Couper, semiretired on
his famous Cannon Point plantation, she learned still more about
King as model plantation-manager. The old gentleman had observed
the father and then the son for years as neighbors, and his unfavorable
opinion of them and their methods made Fanny reflect that "the owners . . . living in Philadelphia, [had been] perfectly contented to
receive a large income from their estate without . . . caring how it
was earned." Blame for that past history lay far more on the major's
daughters, of course, than on the Butler brothers. But Fanny was no
longer disposed to give Pierce much moral leeway. Nothing in the
tragicomedy of Psyche neutralized the antibodies forming in her inner
depths one evening when a delegation of women field-hands came to
complain to Pierce of overwork:

> Mr. [Butler] seemed positively degraded in my eyes as he
> stood enforcing upon these women the necessity of their
> fulfilling their appointed tasks. . . . setting forth . . .
> as a duty, their unpaid, exacted labor! I turned away in
> bitter disgust. I hope this sojourn among [his] slaves may
> not lessen my respect for him, but I fear it; for the details
> of slavery holding are so unmanly . . . that I know not
> how any one with the spirit of a man can condescend to
> them. [45]

Once she did allow that Pierce could not be expected single-
handedly to reform so deep-rooted an abuse; but that lacked pertinence: "Born and bred in America, how should he care or wish to
. . . ? and, of course, he does not; and I am in despair that he does
not; et voilà . . . a happy and hopeful plight for us both." When a
mother of ten was flogged for neglecting her task in order to bring a
complaint to Fanny (the neglect, not the complaint, was formally the
offense), Fanny threw in Pierce's face "the brutal inhumanity of al-

lowing a man to strip and lash a woman . . . to exact from her toil
. . . to maintain in luxury two idle young men. . . . I said I
thought female labor of [this] sort . . . and corporal chastisement
such as they endure, must be abhorrent to any manly or humane
man. Mr. [Butler] said he thought it was *disagreeable,* and left me to
my reflections."[46] She half hoped, half feared lest she never be "allowed to return . . . these very conversations and discussions are
considered dangerous, and justice and freedom cannot be safely mentioned but with closed doors and whispering voices."[47]

Toward mid-February Fanny told Harriet with pleasure that she
and the children were moving to Hampton Point where "I shall be
able to ride again . . . better in mind, body, though not estate, for
my long unaccustomed exercise."[48] Six weeks on Butler's Island had
put her through six years' worth of dismaying discoveries and searing
emotions. She now hoped that the other plantation would be a change
for the better in further ways. They made the fifteen-mile trip in the
eight-oared boat. Pierce steered; Margery, small Sarah, and seven-
month-old Frances maintained royal dignity while oarsmen extempo-
rized songs praising Psyche and the malodorous housemaid, Mary,
who, along with Fanny's Jack, made up the retinue.

As the old major's original seat and first economic success (in
cotton), Hampton Point was locus of the Butler prestige. But Fanny's
change for the better was tempered by recent developments. Rice had
put Sea Island cotton's nose out of joint; further, the sandy soil that
had served so well for a while was half-exhausted; and nobody had
seriously tried to revive commercial orange-growing. The plight of
the major's once impressive (in Sea Island terms) house was symbolic.
It was falling apart, its habitable elements barely sufficing for the
overseer and his wife, ousted from their usual quarters to make way
for the owner and family. It was not worth repairing, for the Altamaha, gnawing away at the shore, was already much too close. A
new, rather modest dwelling under construction was not yet ready.
Nor was the house that the family took over exactly what a northern
builder would have called finished: "The staircase is open to the roof,
and the roof, unmitigated by ceiling, plaster, skylight, or any immediate shelter . . . presents . . . the seamy side . . . of the

wooden shingles. . . . The windows and doors, even when professing
to be shut, could never be called closed; and on one or two gusty
evenings, the carpet . . . heaved and undulated by means of a stream
of air from under the door, like a theatrical . . . ocean."[49]

Doing what she could with it, Fanny had the slave carpenter
make a plain pine table and settee furnished with cushions that she
fashioned herself and stuffed with Spanish moss; strewed books and
flowers round; and for the slaves not old enough to remember the
higher comforts of the old major's household, these innovations

> [seemed] the adornings of a palace. . . . often in the eve-
> ning, when . . . I sit writing . . . the door of the great
> barn-like room is opened stealthily, and one after another,
> men and women come trooping silently in, their naked
> feet falling all but inaudibly on the bare boards as they
> betake themselves to the hearth, where they squat down
> on their hams in a circle, the bright blaze . . . the only
> light of this half of the room, shining on their sooty limbs
> and faces. . . . watching me writing at the other end of
> the room. . . . I very often take no notice of them at all,
> and they seem perfectly absorbed in contemplating me.
> My evening dress probably excites their wonder and ad-
> miration no less than my rapid and continuous writing,
> for which they have sometimes expressed compassion, as
> if they thought it must be more laborious than hoeing;
> sometimes at the end of my day's journal, I look up and
> say suddenly, "Well, what do you want?" when each
> black figure springs up at once, as if moved by machinery;
> they all answer, "Me come say ha do (how d'ye
> do), missis;" and then they troop out as noiselessly as they
> entered, like a procession of sable dreams, and I go off in
> search, if possible, of whiter ones.[50]

At first she relished the contrasts between Island and Point.
"After . . . the rice-swamp, where the Altamaha kept looking over
the dike at me . . . it is pleasant to be on *terra firma* . . . and know
that the river is . . . below its banks, and under my feet instead of
over my head." The nearness of the ocean was a great thing: "Last
night . . . I felt weary, and went out into the air. . . . The scene
just beyond the house was beautiful; the moonlight slept on the broad

river, which here is almost the sea, and on the masses of foliage of
the great Southern oaks . . . and the measured rush of the Atlantic
unfurling its huge skirts upon the white sands of the beach (the
sweetest and most awful lullaby in nature) resounded through the
silent air."[51] She loved the spring luxuriance of bloom and new leaves
in the tangled woods cumbering those sandy acres not yet cleared.
The proximity of the ocean meant waters too choppy for the sit-and-
wait kind of fishing, but also a plenty of fine oysters, huge shrimp,
and even more and better fish than Butler's Island afforded. The St.
Simon's mutton, from sheep grazing salt pastures very like France's
famous Prés Salés, she thought just as delicate even though the black
butcher had no notion of how to cut conventional saddles, haunches,
and so on. Fanny herself, shrinkingly exploring with a butcher knife,
had to mark the carcass out for him.

And, as she had hoped and yearned for, at Hampton Point she
could ride. Available were a mare with foal, another that had just
foaled, and a powerful stallion named, heaven knows why, Montreal,
used as carthorse but apparently also saddle-broken. With true feminist feeling for encumbered mothers, she chose Montreal, necessarily
without his permission; and very probably he had never known a
sidesaddle.

> No sooner did he feel my weight, which, after all, is mere
> levity and frivolity to him, than he thought proper to
> rebel . . . and otherwise demonstrate his disgust. . . .
> opposition . . . aroused the Amazon which is both natu-
> ral and acquired in me, and I made him comprehend that,
> though I object to slaves, I expect obedient servants
> . . . spur and whip . . . with a judicious combination
> of . . . pats on his great crested neck, and endearing
> commendations of his beauty, produced the desired effect.
> Montreal accepted me as inevitable, and carried me very
> wisely and well.[52]

Almost daily the great horse with the small, trim guiding spirit on
his back, followed by Jack carrying saw and hatchet, went improving
into negotiable bridle paths the cattle tracks that wound through the
woods. The way Missis tamed that Montreal horse must have caused

talk in the quarters. Two generations later the younger King's daughter dwelt at length on the shamelessness of Fanny Butler's brazenly riding that stallion when the very word was one no lady would pronounce! Very likely the Darien ladies did whisper among themselves about that. At times our great-grandmothers' genius for prudery outdid itself. But then Fanny was sometimes a little rough-and-ready for the slave quarters. In 1864 Colonel T. W. Higginson encountered some freshly emancipated slaves from St. Simon's Island and asked the women if they remembered Mrs. Butler. Indeed they did; she rowed a boat, and rowed it well too; and one, turning shyly away with a hand up to her face, recalled that she "used to stop and pull up she stock'n's-an'-garters *anywhere*."[53]

The slaves of Hampton Point showed a much higher proportion of light skins than those of Butler's Island. Pierce offhandedly attributed this to its being less isolated; that is, more whites lived nearby or visited it. A more decorous consequence of its situation was the proximity—just across the next arm of the river—of Couper's seat, Cannon Point, already mentioned above. Though well along in years, its renowned owner, tall, blue-eyed, Scottish-born son of a minister, was still importing exotic flora of possible economic potential for his experimental garden, and still celebrating thunderstorms by exulting in the uproar as he marched round and round the verandas of his comfortable house. His elder son, Dutch-trained in dike- and ditch-engineering, was viceroy–part-owner of the great Hopeton plantation a few miles upriver. The son's viceroy on his Hamilton plantation on St. Simon's was his brother-in-law, John Fraser, former captain in the British Army. In spite of successful growing of sugarcane, that slave-killing crop, as well as long staple cotton and rice, these three operations seem to have come as near decent treatment of their blacks as was consonant with the institution of slavery. Couper had strong feelings on the subject and made them stick. It helped too that the Couper dynasty had relatively malaria-free residences on St. Simon's, hence were seldom absentee.

Ann (Couper) Fraser was a gracious matron educated in Charleston and "formed" (as they then said) by some years of London society before she brought her husband home to the Sea Islands. Fanny and

she were soon on cordial terms. Fraser was an able gentleman candidly giving Fanny further details about the younger King's ironclad
and regardless rule on Hampton Point. At both Hamilton and Cannon Point an Old World flavor was nostalgically strong; the atmosphere rather cultivated; the cooking admirable; all better than the
haut monde of Darien. Fanny even felt a personal contrast

> [between] the worthy canny old Scot . . . and his quon-
> dam neighbor, Major [Butler] . . . the Scotch tendency
> of the one to turn every thing to good account, the Irish
> propensity of the other to leave every thing to ruin, to
> disorder, and neglect; the careful economy and prudent
> management of the mercantile man, the reckless profusion
> and careless extravagance of the soldier. The one made a
> splendid fortune and spent it in Philadelphia. . . . The
> other has resided here on his estate, ameliorating the con-
> dition of his slaves and his property . . . a useful and a
> good existence.[54]

With Couper too she could, even more cogently than with Dr.
Holmes discuss topic A:

> [Couper] has spent so much of his life among [black
> slaves] . . . and apparently so successfully. . . . yet
> . . . it is impossible . . . perhaps, for these very reasons
> . . . for him ever to contemplate them in any condition
> but . . . slavery. He thinks them very like the Irish, and
> instanced their subserviency, their flattering, their lying,
> and pilfering. . . . I can not persuade myself that in both
> cases . . . these qualities are not in great measure the
> result of their condition. . . . he considers the extremely
> low diet of the negroes one reason for the absence of
> crimes of a savage nature among them. . . . But in this
> respect they certainly do not resemble the Irish.

And so on in all courtesy and mutual hope of understanding, Fanny
adds trenchantly: "It must not be forgotten that on the estate of this
wise and kind master a formidable conspiracy was organized among
his slaves. . . . We rowed home [from Cannon Point] through a
world of stars, the steadfast ones set in the still blue sky, and the
flashing swathes of phosphoric light turned up by our oars and keel
in the smooth blue water. It was lovely."[55]

Lovely, but the suppurations of slavery kept oozing up through the occasional amenities. Wherever Fanny went on Hampton Point, even if she stayed in the house, here were slaves, mostly women, calling, "Oh, missis!"—smothering her with tales of prolapsed uterus, rheumatism, ailing babies, or just begging sugar or rice to vary the monotonous rations or ends of cloth to eke out the allowance of coarse textiles for clothing. Fanny called on the dressmaking lore she had learned in Paris and extended by mending costumes, to concoct frocks for some of the women, one of them so tall that she had to stand on a chair to measure her. She had long been sewing coarse layettes in hopes that use of them would effect some change in baby care. Since a willing ear is bound to be mercilessly exploited, the tide of complaints rose ever higher: "I almost wish I was back again at the rice-island; for, though this is in every way the pleasanter residence, I hear so much more that is intolerable. . . . [the slaves'] condition does not appear to me . . . susceptible of even partial alleviation as long as the fundamental evil, the slavery itself, remains."[56]

A disheartening end to the Channing doctrine. Though such despair made doing so illogical, she was unable to refrain from passing much on to Pierce. In time he put his foot down:

> Whether he is wearied with the number of . . . supplications, which he would escape but for me . . . or whether he has been annoyed at the . . . pitiful and horrible stories of . . . the former rule of Mr. [King] . . . though their expression may be silenced by his angry exclamations . . . "Why do you listen to such stuff?" . . . "don't you know the niggers are all d——d liars?" . . . I do not know; but he desired me this morning to bring him no more complaints . . . as the people had hitherto no such advocate, and had done very well without, and I was only kept in an incessant state of excitement with all the falsehoods they "found they could make me believe." How well they have done without my advocacy . . . I see with my own eyes . . . I must return to the North . . . this is no place for me . . . I was not born among slaves, and can not bear to live among them. . . . Perhaps, after all, what he says is true . . . I am only preparing more suffering for them whenever I leave.

> . . . perhaps, too, he is afraid of the mere contagion of
> freedom . . . my way of speaking to the people . . . the
> human consideration I feel for them . . . makes my inter-
> course with them dangerously suggestive. [The Butler's
> Island overseer] once . . . hinted to me [that] my exis-
> tence among slaves was an element of danger.[57]

The overseer would have thought so twice over had he known
what came of it when Aleck, a bright and personable young slave
waiting table at Hampton Point, begged Fanny to teach him to read.
She knew that was illegal but also that several elder slaves at Hampton Point, including London, the black preacher, of whose influence
Pierce approved, had somehow learned. Nobody knowing Fanny
could conceive of her refusing. "I mean to do it. I will do it," she
announced to "Dear Elizabeth." "Unrighteous laws are made to be
broken." Then an amusing technicality occurred to her. Since she was
a married woman, *"femme couverte"* in the eyes of the law, her husband
was liable for crimes she committed: "My fines must be paid by my
legal owner . . . the first offense . . . is heavily fined, and the second more heavily, and for the third, one is sent to prison. What a
pity it is I can't begin with Aleck's third lesson, because going to
prison can't be done by proxy, and that penalty would light upon the
right shoulders!" After that vision of Pierce Butler jailed for the
moral crime of slave-owning compounded by marriage, she cut another legalistic caper:

> I . . . won't tell Mr. [Butler] any thing about it. I'll
> leave him to find out, as slaves, and servants, and children
> . . . do; then, if he forbids me, I can stop—perhaps be-
> fore then the lad may have learned his letters. I . . .
> perceive one most admirable circumstance in this slavery.
> . . . No slave's testimony avails against you. . . .
> I haven't much more than a week to remain in this blessed
> purgatory; in that last week perhaps I may teach the boy
> enough to go on alone when I am gone.[58]

Whether in that hope or to resist Pierce as arbitrary master, she
did include Aleck in some of the letter-learning lessons she gave small
Sarah, who was nowhere near as eager as the slave boy to profit by

them. In further token nibbling at the roots of slavery she had Jack
spread word that when their daily "tasks" were done, youngsters on
field work might volunteer to do landscaping chores for Missis at
actual cash wages. Fanny's resources were slim and the hour-rate mi-
croscopic, but here was legal tender acquired outside the system. The
first day she had three volunteers, soon two more; later even one of
the drivers came to pick up a little cash. In other parts of the South,
where owners sometimes allowed slaves to go live in town and do
wage work on their own, paying master a weekly sum as a sort of
rent for one's own person, the anomaly would not have been so striking. But in the Sea Islands it would have been, if on any scale at all,
thought subversive; certainly Fanny meant it to be.

Yet had Pierce known, he might not necessarily have interfered.
He seems not to have positively approved of slavery, merely taking it
as a fact of life in Dixie to be adjusted to as profitably as might be
while making minor humane gestures off and on. A few years later
Fanny's Jack contracted some sort of grave illness and Pierce took him
with him up to Philadelphia for treatment; he died there but not for
lack of the best available care. And Fanny herself once told of how
solicitously Pierce had supported and encouraged a very old man slave
whom she saw him taking for a walk.

During the final week or two one senses another of those false-
dawn slackenings of tension, or maybe just tacit agreement to stay off
thin ice as much as possible. Pierce falls sick while spending time at
Butler's Island; Fanny has herself rowed fifteen miles thither and fifteen miles back several times to look after him. On his return: "I was
much delighted. . . . it is getting much too late [in the year] for
him to remain in that pestilential swampy atmosphere . . . I want
him to see my improvements in the new wood paths."[59] That might
be any bright little wife. She is amused by his account of the masterly
malingering of a Butler's Island slave woman faking pregnancy long
past any plausible term. He tells her as much as he knows about the
long ago aborted slave rising at Cannon Point. They ride together,
Pierce on Montreal, Fanny on one of the mares. His trouble managing Montreal is little worse than Fanny's with Miss Kate, who doubtless also took a dim view of sidesaddles. Departure being imminent,
they pay farewell calls at neighboring plantations.

One understands this relationship only halfway if seeing it as two distinctly incompatible dispositions swindled by biochemistry into double handcuffs forged by their generation's views on marriage. That is sound as far as it goes. But there was also a fluctuating emotional consonance distracting them off and on from recognizing how hopeless a failure their marriage was. Doubtless, sometimes when there was no pressing reason for slavery to make a third at dinner, or when the presence of guests constrained the pair to behave as if nothing were wrong, leading them afterward to hope to do the same for themselves alone; or when Fanny was rather less bit-in-the-teeth than usual or Pierce not quite so stern about whatever she said or did— whatever had originally made them both seek marriage flickeringly prevailed again. And that, each in his or her own way, both were lovingly fond of the two little girls—a bond both conjugal and parental. Not until much more bitter water had gone under the bridge, almost washing away its foundations, were the children victims of a vindictive rivalry.

The temporary respite described above was gradually flawed by Pierce's chronic procrastination, the more irksome because Fanny dreaded both the hazard of malaria and the effect of the coming muggy weather on the little girls' health—and complexions. In March she tells "Dear Elizabeth": "We can not stay here much longer; I wonder if I shall come back again! and whether, when I do, I shall find . . . one idea of a better life in these poor people's minds." Some weeks later: "We shall not leave . . . so soon as I expected; we can not get off for at least another week." [60] On April 13 she takes what should be her last ride with Jack; four days later she is still there. . . . It must have been nearly May Day when the Pierce Butlers, returned from their Sea Island estates, arrived home at their country place on the Old York Road.

Some time that spring, probably before the above-described détente, there had been a really notable explosion ably exploited nine years later in Pierce's narrative of the indignities to which Fanny subjected him. It probably had nothing to do with procrastination, rather with some clash over slavery or plantation policy: "She resolved to leave me; packed up her trunks, left the children on St. Simon's Island, without saying a word to them or the nurse, and came to the plantation near Darien to go away in the steamboat; as it happened, no boat was to start for three or four days; for two days she shut herself up in a room, lay on a bed, and refused to eat or drink, because it was my food she would have to eat."[61] This is an aggrieved, hostile witness, but it does sound like Fanny in this phase of her unsentimental education.

How Pierce got her back to Hampton Point and in what frame of mind is lost to us. Though details would be welcome, they are not necessary to understanding. This dress rehearsal for eventual disaster was a simple consequence of Pierce's bad judgment. There had never been any reason to hope that exposing Fanny to the actualities of slavery, even on an allegedly model plantation, would reconcile her to it, or, by sympathetic analogy, to subservience to himself.

XI

A Sea of Troubles

VERY PROBABLY the Butlers returned from Georgia by sea, Savannah or Charleston to New York.[1] After only a few weeks at Butler Place things were so bad that Fanny again resorted to beseechingly defiant letters:

> It might seem indelicate to urge upon you the sacrifices I have made, and the trials I have embraced, in marrying you; yet . . . I must speak of the change in my situation, as I feel it. I have left my country . . . I have national attachments so strong as to amount to prejudices; and the customs, habits, and even the lovely outward face of my country haunt me . . . this you may . . . class with the phantoms of a diseased mind; however . . . regard it with thoughtful compassion, or with uncomprehending contempt, this is what I feel. . . . I have renounced all the pleasures of society . . . while you care not in how profound a seclusion you live. . . . We are not all made up of affections—we have intellects—and we have passions . . . as for retorting . . . "What need of intellectual converse, have you not an affectionate husband and two sweet babies?" You might as well say to a man who told you he had no arms—Oh! no, but you have legs.[2]

The last week in May she let Pierce know that she planned to sail June 13 in the *Great Western* (one of those trail-breaking transatlantic steamers) for England to support herself there by returning to the stage. All next day, filled with doings for the children's mutual birthday, Pierce did not comment. That night Fanny absented herself from the conjugal bed, leaving in her stead another position paper reproaching him with fouling up her attempts at freedom and—more mordantly than before—with responsibility for their plight: " 'You can never repair the injury you have done me in marrying me. . . . I will not remain here to be your housekeeper, your child's nurse, or what you make me, that is still more degrading and revolting.' "³ Internal evidence from both sides hints that since returning from Georgia, Pierce had spent many nights in Philadelphia. As he often pointed out, with Fanny in this haughty and obsessively teary mood, Butler Place was uncomfortable; there is also a trace of suggestion that he was philandering, as was likely enough. As for the "degrading and revolting" aspects of the situation, shamed resistances are easy to imagine, complicated by Fanny's possible reluctance to risk a third child.

Charles and Elizabeth Sedgwick had visited Butler Place soon after Frances's birth and in spite of their open hostility toward slavery got on well with Pierce and vice versa. Both Sedgwicks noted that all was not well. Charles thought Fanny spoke to her husband in an unwifely fashion and Pierce's mannerly charm had the usual effect on Elizabeth. During a second visit, after the return from Georgia, Elizabeth invited confidences while driving into Philadelphia with Pierce. She accepted his plea that he had " 'exiled himself, in a measure, from his home, his wife and his children, because his coming always made [Fanny] unhappy . . . [her] greeting consisted in tears and sobs and sleepless misery.' "⁴ So now, after the *Great Western* threat, Fanny's perplexed husband took his troubles to these committed intimates of his wife's who also seemed to approve of him: " 'Yourself and your husband,' " he wrote to Elizabeth three days after the birthday, " 'are the only persons to whom I dare speak of my misery . . . she sees in you . . . what we often speak of, the attainment of perfect and rational happiness in married life.' "⁵

His pleas for advice and help buoyed up the accompanying two-thousand-odd words of complaint and self-justification. The whole letter shows that when his heart was in it, Pierce Butler was a cogent special pleader. It helps one understand how he persuaded Fanny into that snap-judgment marriage for which she bitterly blamed herself and was now also blaming him. His brief contained some flat misrepresentation: it was not true that " 'for nearly three years after our marriage we were never apart; no separation, not even of a day . . . until she went with Sarah to England' "; nor that " 'my own family are as little aware of [these disagreements] as persons who never heard our name,' " unless Mr. and Mrs. John Butler were always struck deaf and blind whenever Mr. and Mrs. Pierce Butler stayed with them. But he was truthful and fair testifying that Fanny's " 'care and management of our children are admirable.' " [6] And his general case, however disingenuous, was no worse skewed in his favor than was to be looked for in a husband of 150 years ago unwilling and probably unable to believe in his wife's long-growing and now deep-seated revulsion from marriage as he—and his society—conceived it. He was not insincere in assuring the Sedgwicks that

> I have done all that deep love for a wife, the strongest affection for my children, and an earnest desire to secure peace and happiness for myself . . . dictated. . . . deep, true, free, and well tried love . . . caused us to marry. . . . yet her life is passed in . . . constant tears. . . . she has taken up the idea that she has become indifferent to me. . . . With all but me she is rational at all times. . . . Oh! how anxiously I have tried to soothe and calm this perturbed spirit. . . . Sometimes argument would lead to disagreement and throw her into that state when reason leaves her . . . at one time I restrained myself from ever expressing an opinion before her; she then complained that I never told her my thoughts or feelings, and even silence worked upon her to madness. . . . She is undermining her health by this constant gloom and weeping . . . the tone of her mind . . . is sickly and unnatural. . . . if there be not some cure made now of this disease of the mind, . . . when at last she does perceive the true nature of it . . . it will then be incurable. [7]

From any responsible clinical point of view, he had ruined his case for mental impairment with: "With all but me she is rational at all times." As if sensing that, he left these confident suggestions of pathology and turned to more personal matters:

> She says she is not happy, and as I evidently am not, a separation had better take place . . . she talks of a separation as if we had entered into partnership to carry on some small retail business, and not the great business of life—the lives not only of ourselves but of our children. If two marry, and have no children; if love dies, and dislike grows up; if respect changes into disgust; if tempers are unsuited . . . if the happiness of both can be secured by dissolving that tie which has been formed by such holy vows . . . why, let them part. But such are not we. If we are not happy together, more unhappy would we be apart. And . . . are we not more bound to consider our children than ourselves? And what would our children not lose by being bereft of their mother's guardian care? What could I do with two little motherless children? And would Fanny be happy parted forever from these darling children, earning her own support by public show, even though . . . among her own family and friends? . . . She . . . asked me if I would allow her either of the children? I know not what to do. . . . If she persists in going, and I am unable to restore reason by my own endeavours, I will try to induce her to take the children and go to see you before leaving the country. If she will agree to do this, I shall feel quite safe; and know that she will come back to me better and happier.[8]

Such assumptions that papering over cracks for the children's sake is advisable persist into our own time. Less familiar is the assumption of both parties that given separation, the matter of who gets the children is His to decide. At the time the salient detail was that the Sedgwicks took Pierce's side, led by Elizabeth as Pierce's confidante. She had not yet seen the journal Fanny kept for her in Georgia, with its explicit account of the disgust with which seeing Pierce as slaveholder had inspired his wife. Officiously Elizabeth wrote at once to Pierce: " 'Try to recollect that she is diseased, and treat her soothingly and compassionately, as you would if she were sick with an ordinary malady.' "[9] This was Pierce's reward for sharing his concerns with her. Whether he or Elizabeth first suggested it, both now called up Thérèse De Camp's ghost to account for Fanny's inability to simmer down into a proper wife and mother. For toward her death in 1838 at the age of sixty-four—a longish life for the time—Fanny's mother's behavior seems to have accentuated the pungencies of her personality. At worst it was probably some degree of senile decay; likelier just a marked example of the wise old doctor's dictum: "People don't change as they age. They just get more like themselves."

Obviously Fanny had acquainted Elizabeth with the family's understandable anxiety about Thérèse, hence this piece of solicitude: "My dearest Fanny,

> I have been exceedingly distressed by a letter . . . from your husband, informing me of your dreadful purpose of leaving him. . . . I am pleading for yourself as well as for him and the children . . . the more I have turned over in mind the subject of your troubles . . . the stronger . . . my conviction, . . . that your mind is positively and greatly diseased. . . . do you think, my dear Fanny, that with all that calmness of exterior, [Pierce] has not suffered deeply, intensely? . . . I should not be surprised if the catastrophe which now threatens him . . . were to prove, ultimately, a death blow . . . if he is indifferent to you, whence comes this racking misery? My dearest Fanny . . . you inherit, undoubtedly, from your mother, those morbid tendencies which poison and spoil all . . . even if you still persist in your belief, that you are a wronged and injured woman . . . I do not think [such feelings] afford the slightest justification for your leaving your husband. You have undertaken to be his wife, and . . . the duties of that relation; and, whatever you may think of your marriage contract, as a legal form, you must regard yourself as pledged in the sight of heaven to fulfil what you have undertaken. . . . You have no right . . . to deprive your husband of his children, even with his consent. . . . suppose that your husband permits you to take [Sarah], can you enjoy her when she reminds you constantly of what he has given up? . . . My poor, dear Fanny, my precious, almost idolized friend, do let

> me persuade you that your mind is diseased. How can you
> do this great iniquity and sin against God? . . . come
> and pass some time in Lenox; come directly. . . . let na-
> ture's sweet influences minister to you.[10]

Charles Sedgwick backed this up with a much shorter letter of similar tenor beginning: " 'Do not leave your husband, I pray you, for God's sake.' " It was indefensible thus to try to persuade a person in Fanny's frantic state of mind that she was skirting insanity. Fortunately she was emotionally robust enough to stand the strain; she showed no signs of ever heeding this amateur protopsychiatry. Nevertheless, such poignant representations, the stronger for her deep affection for and trust in the Sedgwicks, seem to have shaken her; maybe in one compartment she was ready to be shaken. No more was heard of the *Great Western* and she seems actually to have told Pierce that she would "endeavour" to adjust to her situation. For he quickly followed up the Sedgwicks' flank attack with this lofty adjuration that Fanny " 'not say that you will endeavour to overcome the morbid state of your mind . . . say I will do it, and like a drunkard who dashes forever from his lips the bitter cup that has brought wretchedness on himself and his family, you should summon strong resolution, and never again allow yourself to fall into that state in which reason leaves her seat.' "[11]

He ventured on further cautions as to " 'the fate of your unfortunate mother' " and assured her that

> my affection for you . . . can never cease. . . . you
> have it in your power to make me unhappy, to cause my
> home to be distasteful to me, and to force me away from
> you and my children—but you cannot make me cease to
> love you. . . . If sobs and tears are my welcome . . . if
> I am left to lie alone in my bed, while you pass the night
> on the floor absorbed in grief, it can hardly be expected
> that I shall find my home a cheerful one, nor can it be
> wondered at if I should sometimes absent myself from a
> home where gloom so often prevails. . . . drive from
> your mind the false and base idea that you have become
> indifferent to me. . . . Oh! my wife be wise![12]

His point about tears need not be unfairly discounted. A recent scholarly essay on Fanny is justified in saying, "The ease with which Fanny could cry was as marked as the ease with which she could laugh, and certainly did nothing to help her relations with her husband."[13]

Observe how sorry Pierce felt for himself because Fanny preferred the floor to his conjugal couch. In 1839 it was no facile decision, however, for a whipsawed soul to have to admit such repugnance to sleeping with the man to do so with whom, society said, was a duty to God, him, and the children. This situation was so bleak and lonely, in fact, that in spite of her Kembleish conviction that whatever she chose to do was probably right, Fanny was half-persuaded that her position was morally and socially untenable. There her religious-mindedness may have undermined her. The Sedgwicks appealing to "whom God hath joined" were validly reverent, hoping to be children of God in the same sense as Fanny. Their tenacious (if Unitarian) notion of the holiness of marriage and the sanctity clinging about offspring arraigned her before some of her own sensitivities.

And the circumstances of that summer favored yet another ill-defined truce. Pierce's rheumatism—never forget it, its part in these frictions may have been substantial—was sending him to "the hot springs" in what is now West Virginia. Two generations later they were the basis of elaborate resorts but then were so hard to get to that it was inadvisable for Fanny and the children to go along. That left Fanny at Butler Place free of his irritating presence. She never learned even halfway to tolerate torrid American summers; this one sent her wandering barefoot in her nightgown up and down the garden paths in hopes of some vestige of coolness at three in the morning. In early August it was a relief to follow the Sedgwicks' cordial advice and go to Lenox for two months of cool peace and gradual restoration of buoyancy. The children flourished, the Sedgwick clan were charming, stimulating and solicitous—and Fanny's already promising love affair with the Berkshires was unmistakably becoming a prime factor in her personal life. She could lick her wounds to some purpose

> while my eyes wander over the beautiful landscape. . . .
> my mind is filled with the great treasure of love . . .
> bestowed upon me . . . God knows how devoutly I thank
> him for this blessing . . . so far above my deserts. . . .
> In seasons of self-reproach and self-condemnation it is an

> encouragement and a consolation . . . to reflect that no-
> ble spirits have loved one—spirits too good and too noble
> . . . to love what is utterly base and unworthy.[14]

Such noble spirits could certainly be named Sedgwick in spite of their dismay over her disruptive impulses; or St. Leger; but by now it was inconceivable that anybody named Butler was qualified.

Pierce seldom learned from experience. Even before he went off to "the springs," he had been contemplating another winter in Georgia. It was John's watch on deck but maybe he wanted that mild winter climate for his rheumatism. That made some sense. But in view of the dance Fanny had led him before, it was either stupid or stubborn to plan tentatively to take wife and children along again. For sweetener, one gathers, he half promised that in the fall of 1840—a year ahead—they would all spend some months in Britain; he took care to mention this to the Sedgwicks. In early December Butler Place was closed and the family went to stay with the John Butlers as preliminary to going south. A dismal prospect for Fanny. She had no more hope of effecting anything among the slaves and dreaded a second dose of catch-as-catch-can travel

> in the middle of winter, with two young children . . .
> not very safe rail-roads . . . perhaps less safe steam-boats
> . . . half savage country. . . . We shall find, no doubt,
> our former animal friends, the fleas and alligators; the
> first, swarming in the filthy negroes' huts; the last, expa-
> tiating in the muddy waters of the Altamaha . . . none
> of them will have forgotten us . . . the alternative is to
> remain here alone; and as it is possible to live on the plan-
> tation with the children, I am going.[15]

Only she didn't. She never saw the Sea Islands again. Pierce fell sick—complaint unidentified, maybe rheumatic—and languished for weeks at his brother's while Fanny grew less and less enchanted with being nonpaying guest of persons with whom she had so very little in common. Had Pierce's condition been serious . . . But even he claimed for it a mere irksome incapacitation. Fanny's attitude hints that she suspected recurrence of his old procrastination now encouraged by aches and pains not uncommon among Philadelphians in winter. In any case, early in January of what must have seemed an inauspicious new year, she formally submitted to the sufferer a letter enclosing a proposed letter to her father that harked back to those fateful weeks in 1834 when it was a toss-up whether Pierce and she would marry:

> My dearest Father, I little thought at the time of my marriage, that the proceeds of my professional exertions would ever be *necessary* to my comfort, and yielded them to you . . . with no . . . desire but that they had been more. . . . [Now] the small income . . . from that sum . . . would greatly contribute to my positive comfort and that of my children . . . I find myself and my children living upon Mr. John Butler; I have neither home nor servants of my own; and as far as I can ascertain from my husband, whose sole reply . . . is that this matter is his business, he cannot afford to place me . . . in any other situation. I have determined . . . to resume my profession . . . if you have not borne in mind your promise . . . that the money I gave . . . you at my marriage should revert to me hereafter . . . do so henceforth; for indeed I know not what my need of it may be.[16]

The intent to resume acting probably disquieted Pierce more than this request to see the reversion confirmed. This effect the covering letter addressed to him probably confirmed:

> I have determined . . . I will no longer be dependent upon you. . . . I *can* no longer rely upon you. My comfort and happiness are as you say your business, but, as like most of your business, you neglect them utterly, I will so far see to them myself, that I will no longer submit to live upon your relations . . . I can obtain . . . for myself, a home, no matter how poor . . . where I might live with my children in decent privacy and by myself. . . . you are regardless of the dearest interest of your children; you have subjected them to . . . pernicious moral influences.[17] . . . I will live thus no longer.[18]

In 1840 not every distressed young wife could threaten not to go home to mother but to earn her own way on the stage. The effect here was highly irritant. It is plain that for all his early delight in

Fanny as actress, Pierce was sensitive to the low repute of acting and that whenever Fanny raised that specter, he outwardly wriggled and inwardly snarled and came to terms. At this point, for instance, John and he actually pulled themselves together and went south to their planterly duties, leaving wives and children at home. Though it would have been logical for Ella Butler and Fanny to keep each other company in town, Fanny had made it so clear that she wanted no more such dependency that she and faithful Margery were allowed to reopen Butler Place. Fanny told Harriet:

> [I] have resumed the monotonous tenor of my life, which
> . . . residence in town had interrupted, not altogether
> agreeably . . . [I am] teaching Sarah to read, and sliding
> through my days in a state of external quietude . . . not
> always . . . allied to content. . . . When the children's
> bedtime comes, and their little feet and voices are still,
> the spirit of the house seems to have fallen asleep. I send
> my servants to bed, and in spite of assiduous practicing,
> reading, and answering of letters, my evenings are sad in
> their absolute solitude. . . . I have taken vehemently to
> worsted-work . . . and . . . am going to read Gibbon's
> "Decline and Fall of the Roman Empire"—I mean to
> make a regular schoolroom business of it.[19]

The occasional jostlings that breached this respite from dwelling with a fractious husband and crass in-laws in a wide house were more or less unpleasant. Fanny felt obliged to discharge Margery O'Brien, the faithful, the uncomplaining, who dearly loved her small charges and Fanny too. The cause was that this devout Catholic was surreptitiously teaching Sarah the Hail Mary and heaven only knew what further Romishness. Once before Fanny had had to caution her against such zeal:

> The proselyting spirit of her religion was, I suppose,
> stronger than her conscience, or rather, was the predomi-
> nant element in it . . . upon this ground alone I am
> satisfied . . . she should have left me, for though it
> would not mortally grieve me if hereafter my child were
> conscientiously to embrace Romanism, I have no desire
> that she should be educated in what I consider erroneous
> views upon the most momentous of all subjects.

The parting was friendly. Fanny would have kept Margery on as personal maid with no responsibilities for the children, only "we have reduced our establishment, and I have no longer any maid of my own, therefore I could not keep her."[20] Instead Margery presently married, had a dreadful time with her husband, took the step, extreme for the time generally and heinous in her Church's view, of obtaining a Pennsylvania divorce and was pretty much ostracized in consequence. Some years later Fanny was doing what she could to help her in illness and hard luck. Her immediate successor—then successors—in the nursery at Butler Place were fresh landed Irish girls insufficiently acquainted with toothbrushes and so on.

In that same March Charles Follen, a self-exiled German scholar-gymnast who had become a valued voice in Boston's Unitarian-plain-living-and-high-thinking antislaveryism, was one of a hundred-odd passengers dying horribly when the steamboat *Lexington* burned in Long Island Sound. Fanny had much admired him and was shocked and grieved. Two weeks later came distressing news that her father's failing health had led him to resign as Examiner of Plays in favor of son John Mitchell, whose editorship of the *British & Foreign Quarterly* was precarious because its financial backer had died. Charles had been trying spas in Germany and Bohemia and climate in Italy. Adelaide went with him not only to look after him, but also to pursue the training of her highly promising voice under German and Italian tutelage. That was why neither had been at Thérèse's deathbed the previous fall. Fanny was understandably anxious lest her father too die before she saw him again. Even though the new steamers were making the mails swifter and more reliable, it was still irksome to be cooped up in a winter-bound farmhouse two or three weeks away from news of such potential.

The cooping up was relative. As spring came on, Fanny could ride more, and to judge from Sidney Fisher's diary it greatly agreed with her. At Wakefield, the Wisters' country place, he encountered her "on horseback and alone. She is very independent and rides about constantly unattended. . . . Never saw her look so well. Her costume was becoming and peculiar. A green cloth riding habit . . . a *man*'s waistcoat with rolling collar, yellow & gilt buttons, a calico shirt collar . . . over a black silk cravat tied sailor fashion, with a man's hat and veil. . . . a beautiful horse highly groomed." [21] One gathers that though Fisher was unaccustomed to the semimasculine character of English women's riding costumes, he found this version highly attractive. On Saturdays Ella Butler and her two children might do their family duty by driving out to visit. Probably more to Fanny's taste was a five-day house party including Mrs. Robert (Mary Appleton) Mackintosh, her new (and anti-American) husband, and Mary's charming sister Fanny (soon to be Mrs. Henry Wadsworth Longfellow), both high among Fanny's Bostonian friends. For these and a few others Butler Place was a tight fit but no less jolly for that. Fanny's account of it to Pierce sounds as if the effect was emollient; it began, " 'My dearest Pierce,' " and ended, "I grieve to hear of your low spirits, though 'tis some relief to me to think that I am not now near you to wear and harass you." [22]

He had reason for low spirits. His trip down to Georgia had been such an ordeal that Fanny congratulated herself on having been spared sharing it. Beyond Washington the Butler brothers had found the winter roads so bad that the stagecoach could make only eight miles in four hours and finally was forced to turn back because bridges were down and streams too swollen to ford. Then the ice clogging Chesapeake Bay was too much for the Norfolk steamboat. Now, however, having completed the struggle to reach Butler's Island and get his breath, Pierce had a stroke of luck. During Fanny's last stay in Lenox, Elizabeth Sedgwick had impressively assured her that his domestic troubles really had plowed Pierce up badly. She had not gone so far as to show Fanny his misery-laden, help-seeking letters. But now she saw fit to copy out and send Fanny extracts eloquent about his frustrations and heartburnings. Nursing his aches and pains in the swamps, Pierce must have been almost as startled as pleased to open a letter from Fanny and read:

> My dearest Pierce,
>   . . . I am almost in despair; I thought that once freed from the gloom and disquietude that my thrice un-happy temperament seems to throw over you, and alone with John in that favourable climate, you would have at least a temporary relief from pain and depression. Oh! my

1. Covent Garden Theatre.
(*From Doran,* Annals of
the English Stage, *Vol. III*)

2. The great Mrs. Siddons at age seventy-five, niece Fanny at age twenty-one,
painted by Henry Perronet Briggs. (*Courtesy The Boston Athenaeum*)

3

4

3. Caricature of John Philip Kemble as Henry V; the attached text ridicules his habit of pauses between words when reading his lines. (*Courtesy University of Bristol Theatre Collection*)

4. Thomas Sully's portrait of Charles Kemble in costume as Fazio. (*Courtesy Pennsylvania Academy of the Fine Arts*)

5. Adelaide Kemble Sartoris as drawn by R. J. Lane, Charles Kemble's close friend. (*Courtesy Sir Geoffrey Meade*)

6. John Mitchell Kemble, drawing by Savile Morton. (*From* William Bodham Donne and His Friends)

7. Marie Thérèse De Camp (Mrs. Charles Kemble) drawn by E. A. Page. (*Courtesy National Portrait Gallery, London*)

5

6

7

8

9

8.   Fanny Kemble's first appearance. (*Courtesy Phelps Players Collection, State University Library, Albany, New York*)

9.   W. M. Thackeray's caricature of Fanny and Charles Kemble as seen from the pit in Fanny's play, *Francis the First.* (*Courtesy The British Library*)

10.   Sir Thomas Lawrence's famous drawing of Fanny as Juliet, lithographed by R. J. Lane; the most widely reproduced and imitated portrait. (*Courtesy National Portrait Gallery, London*)

10

11. Fanny and Charles Kemble in *Henry VIII* at Covent Garden. Note close proximity of occupants of boxes to the stage, the low proportion of women among the spectators in the pit, and the several men with their hats kept on. (*Courtesy University of Bristol Theatre Collection*)

12. Fanny as Beatrice in *Much Ado About Nothing* as painted from memory and probably sketches made during the performance by Thomas Sully. (*Courtesy Pennsylvania Academy of Fine Arts*)

13

14

15

13. Thomas Sully's version of the offstage Fanny *c.* 1833. (*Courtesy Museum of Fine Arts, Boston*)

14. Fanny as Julia in *The Hunchback*, drawn from the orchestra by Asher B. Durand. This hairdo made "Kemble curls" fashionable for a season. (*Courtesy The Folger Shakespeare Library*)

15. Still another effort of Thomas Sully's to get Fanny adequately recorded with paint and canvas. (*Courtesy The White House Collection*)

16. Contemporary caricature of horseback incident described in Fanny's American *Journal*. Fanny is shown wearing the riding cap that was widely imitated in America as "the Kemble cap." (*Courtesy Lenox Library Association*)

17. Fanny, painted by Henry Inman as Mrs. Pierce
Butler, young matron-chatelaine of Butler Place.
(*Courtesy The Brooklyn Museum, Gift of Charles A. Schieren*)

18

19

20

18.   Pierce Butler. (*Courtesy New York State University Library*)

19.   Sarah and Frances Butler, drawn in London in the early 1840s by R. J. Lane. (*Courtesy National Portrait Gallery, London*)

20.   Fanny in middle age, provenance unknown. (*Courtesy Houghton Library, Harvard University*)

21

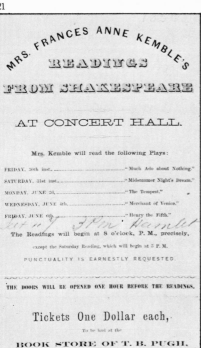

22

23

24

21. A typical program of readings to Fanny's Philadelphian public. (*Courtesy Baker Library, Dartmouth College*)

22. Fanny gave her good friend, Henry Wadsworth Longfellow, a season pass for two to her readings of Shakespeare. (*Courtesy Huntington Library*)

23. Mrs. Kemble reads Shakespeare by candlelight at the St. James's Theatre, London. (*From the* Illustrated London News, *August 10, 1850*)

24. Fanny in old age, photograph probably taken in England. (*Courtesy Lenox Library Association*)

dearest, what can be done for you? . . . go to Europe, to
Germany, and try the efficiency of those waters. . . . I
should too gladly see you go in the pursuit of health, and
that once cheerful and blessed equanimity of temper
. . . which was your most peculiar and fortunate possession. . . . God bless you, my darling dearest Pierce;
when you think of me—*if* you think of me—think of me
as one whose love for you has been a source . . . of pain
and agony, and now of bitter reproach; for oh! Pierce,
Elizabeth has written me some of the contents of that letter of yours . . . forgive me, my dearest, dearest Pierce,
if I have so bitterly cursed your existence. I cannot write
any more. I am blinded with crying.

Ever your own wife,
Fanny.[23]

    That generous outpouring implies not only goodwill but also
how deeply she could still feel about this inexplicably personable man
she married. Though the charm does not come well through the
available record, it was certainly there. In further evidence of it Elizabeth sent Pierce a sort of blessing on the reconciliation that she
hoped she had effected, apologizing for her "meddling" in terms leaving no doubt of her well-intended joy and giving a rather disingenuous account of how she had come to send Fanny those extracts. In
conclusion she hoped "that the present moment should be improved
for setting all matters right between you. . . . Even without any
personal interest in the matter I should most deeply lament the waste
of such rich, such abundant, such precious materials for happiness as
are in your hands."[24]

    Elizabeth Sedgwick was an open-minded, warmhearted, consci-
entious woman and her husband was all that too, plus a gracefully
ironic wit. Both treated Fanny as if she had been a well-beloved sister, and the very fact that the major's far from outgoing grandson
invited them into his most private affairs shows how cordially they
had made clear their good opinion of him. They seem to have taken
him for a worthy, likable fellow whose well-being they would have
wished for his own sake—and ten times more so because his destiny
involved Fanny's.

*　*　*

Fanny's new solicitude afforded Pierce gratifying behavior. She was docile when he proposed taking her and the children along for his summer soaking in "the hot springs," for, one heard, passable roads and habitable quarters now made it feasible; then she was readily reconciled when he decided to go alone after all, and soon—probably a good thing because prolonged absence might keep strains from building up again. There were sporadic, harmonious discussions of those plans to visit Britain in the fall. But then Fanny Ellsler, brightest rising star among dancers of the day, opened in Philadelphia in her first tour of America. Fanny thought her superb and an even better actress than dancer, giving the standard ballet roles genuine dramatic depth: "Her dancing is like nothing but poetic inspiration and seems as if she were composing while she executed it."[25] Even so her delight hardly matched Pierce's. He insisted on attending every performance and announced he would not leave town until her engagement finished. It must have been trying to sit beside him as he mooned over this bewitching creature much as he had mooned over another Fanny's performances six years earlier.

At this rate, his wife noted with irritation, he would not get away to the springs until early July. Then, just as the enchantress departed and left him free, he was called for jury duty that, he warned, might tie him down for six weeks. And he began to talk about possibly going to Georgia and—as usual—taking the family. . . . Yet he did not altogether rule out Fanny's going to Britain without him. He seems to have sympathized with her concern lest she never see Charles again and her hope that Adelaide and he would come home to meet her in London, or maybe she might join them in the Italy she yearned to see.

Having found it unhandily anomalous to be in London as "a widow bewitched" in 1835, Fanny was reluctant, however, to try it again; she even felt crosscurrents in her eagerness to see England once more: "Perhaps, dearest Harriet, it might be better for me not to . . . my roots are beginning to spread in my present soil, and to transplant them, even for a short while, might check the process."[26] Yet that did not mean she was infected with Pierce's indecisiveness. The likelihood that he would be immobilized until into September set her preparing to sail then. So, of course, he changed things once more. Jury duty or no, he was off to the springs; the trip to Britain, yes, yes, probably much later in the year. She and the chicks had better make a long, cool stay in the Berkshires with those admirable Sedgwicks. And when they rejoined him at Butler Place in October, sure enough, he was again talking Sea Islands for them all.

John Butler now did them all a great favor. Exercising his veto as part owner of Butler's Island and Hampton Point, he forbade Pierce ever to take Fanny there again on the ground, which even she felt tenable, that down there she was "a mere source of distress to herself, annoyance to others, and danger to the property." [27] With Georgia thus eliminated, Britain again became matter of preparations and vacillation. That ceased when within a few weeks came word that Charles Kemble was back from Italy and practically at death's door. Fanny must come as soon as possible. Before submarine cables and radio such a message was already two weeks old when received. Apparently Fanny's loyal alarm shook Pierce into decisive action. On December 1, 1840, in the fine new steamship, *British Queen,* New York to Liverpool, sailed Mr. and Mrs. Pierce Butler, their two very small daughters, and a new nursemaid, a hardheaded, plain-spoken young American woman—Protestant—named Anne Martin.

XII

Oh, to Be in England

FANNY'S FIRST CROSSING under steam was relatively calm. At Liverpool she received warning that Charles might not survive until she reached London; and that even if he did, his doctors would not let her see him, for it had not been possible to convey to him that she was on the way and the shock of unexpected recognition might carry him off. Actually, as though he sensed her imminence, he was better before becoming aware that she was in England. Having her at his bedside seemed to launch him on rapid recovery. The deep-seated affection between the two, different as their personalities and purposes were, may really have helped to bring him back from the threshold. Pierce rented a furnished house off Piccadilly and Charles was moved into it. There his convalescence was furthered by not only a loving daughter and engaging little granddaughters, but also by an affluent and by now well-reconciled son-in-law. As winter waned, Charles got well enough to urge the Butlers to entertain and even began dining out on his own. In early spring Adelaide, home from Italy to prepare for her operatic debut in London, joined the household, and Harriet St. Leger, whom Charles had known since her childhood, came over from Ireland for a long visit.

Pierce had planned to take his family home again after a few months. They stayed away two and a half years. John Butler, one assumes, kept an eye on the plantations, and funds thus derived from slave-grown rice honored his brother's drafts. John may have taken all this the better because it meant Fanny was far, far away. There

244

was some precedent for wealthy slave-owners thus settling abroad though they usually preferred Paris. Pierce's prolonged expatriation can be only partly laid to his usual inability to get into motion. On the positive side he was greatly enjoying himself and by summer 1841 leased a house in Harley Street, a new, stylish quarter not yet dominated by medical men. Outsiders were wrong, he advised Americans later, to think that Britons' reserve "towards those whom they casually meet . . . [means] they lack warmth and depth of feeling . . . let one go there with proper introduction, and he will see the icy surface at once dissolved, and hearts and houses open to him. Such was . . . my happy experience." [1]

That "proper introduction" he owed, of course, to his hairshirt of a wife. Her intimates and good friends welcomed her and by corollary the self-possessed husband of whom only a few had had a glimpse in 1836. These social contacts were heady stuff. Fanny's letters bubble with her pleasure in renewing choice old and acquiring new acquaintance among the sort of people whose engagements to marry were announced in the *Morning Post:* "We dined yesterday with the Francis Egertons [Lord and Lady Ellesmere]; tomorrow evening we have a gathering here with, I beg you to believe, nothing under the rank of a viscount, Beauforts, Normanbys, Wiltons . . ." [2] For the other school of accumulation: "Monday, Emily [FitzHugh] spends the evening with me, till I go to a party at Miss Rogers'; Tuesday . . . to the opera; Wednesday, we dine with the M———s, and go in the evening to Mrs. Grote's; who has a ball in the evening; Saturday, the opera again . . . pray don't say I am . . . neglecting my opportunities." [3]

Having sung at Buckingham Palace by request, Adelaide now moved another square toward full exposure of her talent by being asked to perform at a benefit for Polish refugees given by the Duchess of Sutherland at Stafford House, the other attractions being Rachel and Franz Liszt, a good friend of Adelaide's then in the brilliant beginning of his fame. The well-sifted audience consisted of what Fanny called

> our finest (and bluntest) people . . . in the great hall
> . . . with its scarlet floor-cloths, and marble stairs and

balustrades, and pillars of scagliola, and fretted roof of gold and white, and skylight . . . supported by giant gilt caryatides. The wide noble flight of steps and long broad galleries . . . with the sunlight raining down in streams on the . . . beautiful faces of the women, and the soft sheen and brilliant coloring of their clothes, and on perfect masses of flowers . . . in every niche and corner . . . one of the grandest and gayest shows you can imagine.[4]

The Butlers spent the third week in December with Lord and Lady Lansdowne at Bowood, a famous stately-home-of-England that impressed even small Sarah. Fanny took her for a run on the magnificent terraces and lawns and she said it was her idea of heaven "or that garden—I forget its name—that Adam and Eve were put into." Among the guests were old Rogers, Tom Moore, Macaulay, a sister of Lord Holland's, and Lady Harriet Baring. Several times the Butlers visited Worsley, the Ellesmeres' place, and The Hoo. The Duke of Rutland remembered to send a promised invitation to them and Adelaide to come to Belvoir after the holidays. The other guests were the Duchess of Richmond, the Duke and Duchess of Bedford, Lord and Lady Winchelsea "and a whole tribe of others whose names I forget," Fanny told Harriet, "but which are all duly set down in the butler's book."[5] Having rubbed elbows with such people as a girl, she could be flippant about them the rest of her life.[6] One wonders whether Pierce chimed in. Certainly, after Bowood and Belvoir, that even more stately mansion, he understood better why Fanny looked queer when Philadelphia thought Butler Place impressive.

In another gratifying context Pierce had the privilege of being brother-in-law to scintillant Adelaide Kemble. Fanny reported to Harriet that "she looks very well and very handsome . . . complains of the darkness of our skies and the dulness of our way of life . . . something completely foreign in her tone and manner, and even accent." Later: "The likeness between my sister and myself . . . is as great as our unlikeness. . . . Our mode of perceiving and being affected by things and people is often identical . . . we both often utter precisely the same words . . . as if one of us might save the other the trouble of speaking . . . [yet] she is a thousand times quicker, finer, keener, shrewder, and sweeter . . . and all my mental processes compared with hers, are slow, coarse, and clumsy." The Clarges Street house where they all lodged was full of professionals and influential friends come to gauge her singing powers: "She is singing most beautifully . . . love, longing, grief, and joy burst through . . . and light up her whole countenance with a perfect blaze of emotion . . . the tears stream down my face . . . I am obliged to run out of the room."[7]

Toward the end of that summer of 1841, as warm-up for her operatic assault on London, Adelaide went to the Rhineland under the wing of Liszt, he for piano recitals, she for operatic engagements. Since Charles Kemble was not yet up to travel, for propriety—and coincidentally for pleasure—a bevy of family and friends went along: Fanny, Pierce, the children (and Anne Martin); brother Henry on leave from soldiering; Mary Anne Thackeray, daughter of the provost of Kings College, Cambridge; Henry Fothergill Chorley, music critic and cultural man-about-town. Fanny found the country of Wilhelm Meister and Undine genial enough. But memories of the Hudson and the Berkshires blunted the renowned beauties of the Rhine; she was really quite American about it. And incorrigibly American Anne Martin, whose notion of an impressive river was probably something like the Delaware, sat in the steamboat

> looking at the shores, her brown eyes growing rounder and rounder, and her handsome face full of as much contempt as it could express, every now and then exclaiming, "Well, to be sure, it is a pretty river, and it's well enough; but my! they hadn't need to make such a fuss about it!" . . . I suspect [Fanny wrote], that Anne does not consider the baronial castles "of much 'count' " either. . . . I am rather disturbed at the little emotion produced in me by the romantic ruins . . . of the Rhine . . . I am losing much of my excitability; my imagination has become disgracefully tame . . . I find myself . . . chiefly intent upon when, where, how, and on what my children can dine.[8]

Actually she was then also intent on Adelaide's prospects. Her uneasiness lest the voice, sweet-true and elegantly trained though it was, lack the volume to fill Covent Garden was somewhat relieved by the singer's previous successes at La Scala, another huge cavern. Now the question of stage presence, which Kembles might be assumed to come by as naturally as Hapsburgs by the family chin, was settled when Fanny first saw Adelaide on stage—at Mainz in *Norma*. As the unhappy she-druid this Kemble handled the dramatic aspect of the role so well that Fanny regretted her commitment to opera, "mere uttering of sound and perpetual representation of passion and emotion, comparatively unmixed with intellect . . . she would . . . find in the great dramatic compositions of our stage, and especially in Shakespeare's plays, scope for her capacity which Italian opera cannot afford."[9] Soon Fanny would learn to her delight that her sister could also be a sparkling, nimble Susannah in *Le Nozze di Figaro*. Eventually, on November 2, 1841, Adelaide's Norma was a Covent Garden success of almost the same order as Fanny's Juliet twelve years earlier. The parallel went on: Her packed houses in that and other roles bade fair to pull the old theater again out of the red. As earnings piled up, she, like Fanny, hoped that a few years of it would make her financially independent, say three hundred pounds a year. And part of the plan was to make a tour of America. Fanny hoped that in a year or so Pierce and she would accompany Adelaide back to their own base.

Though Adelaide's sister got only reflected light from this triumph, she needed no glare of footlights to supplement the wit, charm, and style and talent for friendship that kept her spinning in London. Any impression that Pierce, as Philadelphia patrician, had that his marriage was a condescension cannot have survived after the Marchioness of Londonderry called one day to let Fanny know that Queen Victoria had asked the Duke of Rutland why Mrs. Butler had not been presented at a court "drawing room." That was ritual for the daughters of people who mattered and frantically sought by the mamas of others. For royalty itself to suggest it outside the usual course was unusual. "I would not go to the end of the street to see a drawing-room full of full moons," Fanny told Harriet. "But . . . under the circumstances it was certainly fitting and proper that I should go." She obtained permission from Pierce ("my supreme authority") and, shrinkingly aware she had already used up her allowance, ordered the requisite gown and feathers. At the ceremony fear lest her rented seven hundred pounds worth of diamonds go astray made her nervous. It made her more so that her briefing from her sponsor, Lady Francis Egerton, on what and what not to do was inadequate:

> I did all sorts of awkward things; but so, I dare say, do other people in the same predicament. One thing . . . if Her Majesty has seen me, I have not seen her; and should be quite excusable in cutting her wherever I meet her . . . I did not look at my sovereign lady. I kissed a soft white hand, which I believe was hers; I saw a pair of very handsome legs in white silk stockings, which I am convinced were not hers, but . . . attribute to Prince Albert . . . made a sweeping curtsy . . . and came away with no impression but that of a full-dressed confusion.[10]

Then she blotted her copybook by neglecting the confirming second step to royal acceptance, attending the Queen's birthday. That did not prevent Edward Everett, Fanny's old friend from Washington and Boston, then U.S. minister to the Court of St. James's, from presenting Pierce to the Queen at the next proper opportunity. Whether this was at his or Everett's instance, I do not know, but it outraged nurse Anne "when she heard that the ceremony consisted of going down on one knee and kissing the Queen's hand. She did not mind my doing it the least in the world."[11] But for a freeborn American man! It had also offended Anne's equalitarian sensibilities to be waited on by under servants when she dined, as befitted her status, with the upper servants at Bowood.

Mr. and Mrs. Pierce Butler in England managed most of a year outwardly more or less harmonious, withinsides jarringly irksome but not without affectionate intervals. Much of the time it looked as if transplanting Fanny to her native soil had proved salutary. Now, however, tremors were registering along the papered-over geological fault. The old vacillations were clouding over the matter of when they should go home. And the house in Harley Street, the carriage in which to pay those obligatory calls, the frequent entertaining, the paraphernalia needed for weekends in great country houses were straining even Pierce's handsome income. And his growing inability to pay heed to discrepancies between income and outgo was potentially more troublesome than his procrastination. As bills came in, including the ninety-seven pounds for her drawing-room gown, Fanny was again regretting not having reserved from her gift to her father enough to afford her at least the sort of pin money she had sought for Aunt Dall.

Again she felt impelled to fall back on her old resource—the pen. She was tinkering with an adaptation-translation of Alexandre Dumas's *Mademoiselle de Belle-Ile* that muffled the improper twist basic to the plot; maybe some manager would give her a couple of hundred pounds for it. She also contemplated a play picking up *The Stranger* where Kotzebue left off and working out the problem of what would happen between nobly forgiving husband and wife ever conscious of how noble that was; or maybe if she made a novel of it, R. H. Bentley's *Miscellany* would buy it. Or what about the long, journal-style letters that she had written to Harriet recounting that nightmare journey from Philadelphia to Georgia? She had scruples and doubtless fears about publishing the journal to "Dear Elizabeth," much as she might have liked to. She was, after all, married to the man whom it would make look pretty bad. But that lively narrative of American barbarism for which Pierce was not responsible . . . And that, of course, was what Bentley bought for a badly needed thirty guineas, making two long installments of it for readers by no means displeased to know of the squalor and fecklessness of this segment of the American economy.

Since it made backwoods and urban slavery out deplorable, Pierce can hardly not have been thoroughly annoyed. Already in a developing tactlessness of his own, he was carving himself out a London life apart from the cultivated, coronetted and upper-class creative circles of which his famous wife had made him free. Fanny saw fit to tell Sarah Cleveland:

> Sally & Fanny thrive phisically [*sic*] extremely well in
> their mother's earth & the former has grown an immense
> strapping girl with blue eyes and billows of light hair &
> manners that are like nothing else in the world but Bruen-

hilde's in the Niebelungenlied—My Husband so far as I
know is pretty well at least I judge so as from morning to
night he is out in search of amusement. . . . Day after
day passes without our exchanging a dozen words.[12]

"Amusements" is vague but for Pierce Butler in early Victorian London they cannot always have been confined to the London Zoo, high-
minded lectures at Exeter Hall, and study of the monuments in
Westminster Abbey.

The spring of 1842 revived aching old problems. Charles Kemble had celebrated his return to active health by again taking over
management of Covent Garden, and all too soon the backers' solemn
guarantees that he would incur no financial responsibility in case of
difficulty were to prove inadequate. Meanwhile the good effect on
him of return to professional concerns was gradually eroded by
mounting worries. Then there came intrusion of those intertwined
problems—slavery and wifely submission. Lydia Maria Child, a pillar
of William Lloyd Garrison's militant branch of abolitionism, had
learned of Fanny's "Elizabeth" journal and now asked leave to publish
parts of it as antislavery propaganda—for which end it would certainly have been effective. Fanny, of course, was inclined to say yes.
Pierce, doubtless still smarting from the relatively innocuous stuff in
the *Miscellany*, was, of course, sure to exercise his husbandly prerogative and say no. After all due wrangling they referred the issue to
Elizabeth. A couple of months later, steamship mails being better
but still slow, she replied duly advising against publication. She and
her clan were staunchly antislavery; ascribe this verdict to her respect
for the doctrine of wifely obedience. Anyway the slavery issue, and
the wifely-duty issue—that sheet anchor of morality and bone of contention *chez* Butler—had now followed the couple into Harley Street.
Pierce was bitter about the way this utter stranger to him, this infa-
mous Mrs. Child, had thus stirred up the old acrimony. In what he
saw as "a recurrence of [Fanny's] moral disease," she was now reverting to "the principle, always contended for, of doing exactly as she
chose. Having yielded [on arbitration of the question of publication]
she seemed to think herself specially justified in persisting on all others."[13]

In consequence Fanny reverted to her runaway reflex. She wrote

Pierce a note saying that if he wouldn't let her return to the stage for livelihood, he owed her a minimum living allowance until Charles's death gave her back her nest egg; packed up and took the train for Liverpool. Pierce followed by the next train, caught up with her as she was telling the manager of the hotel to book her on the next day's steamer for Boston. Pierce did all he could with the scandal that thus to abandon children and relatives would create; the dismay that her father and sister would feel; and for clincher "promised her that if she deferred her voyage until the next steamer only, and then was of the same mind, I would attend her to America, and thus save the exposure and pain to her family and myself . . . next day she returned with me to London."[14] Twice more that summer Fanny ran away from her stifling situation. Twice more, once the momentum of flight slackened, she was persuaded to return to what society and her glib-tongued husband insisted was her moral, indeed her religious duty.

All the while others' concerns impinged on the perplexed couple, involved them, and by obliging them to maintain decorum, probably helped them to maintain workable relations if they met at breakfast. Fanny's resilience was not yet exhausted. When Adelaide leaves London for a brief tour of the provinces, Harriet asks how Fanny will replace her society. "I presume with my own writing-table," Fanny replies, "and the carriage cushions, just as I do now . . . which is well enough. I am of too troubled a nature ever to lack excitement, and have an advantage over most people in the diversion I am able to draw from very small sources."[15]

Major diversion now came in a project of the Egertons': to stage *The Hunchback* with amateurs stiffened, not to say overshadowed, by Fanny as Julia—the first time she had set foot on a stage in eight years. Henry Greville was to play the romantic lead; most of the bits and walk-ons were "a pack of young Guardsmen"[16] and, if I read Fanny's memoirs aright, Pierce's aversion to footlights did not prevent his appearing in a secondary role. But as things worked out the professionals swamped the amateurs. The title role of Master Walter, the hunchbacked father, was given one of Fanny's august friends, Horace Wilson, professor of Sanskrit at Oxford and a noted amateur actor; but he fell sick, so Sheridan Knowles himself, who had "created" the role to Fanny's triumphant Julia in his own play eleven years since, was persuaded to take over. The vivacious supporting woman's role of Helen brought in Adelaide. The frivolous hairdo that went with the character proved a becoming change from her customary severe coiffure, and though she had never played a nonoperatic role before, to Fanny's joy "she acted Helen charmingly, without having bestowed the slightest pains upon it. Had she condescended to give it five minutes' careful study, it would have been . . . perfect . . . as it was, it was delightfully droll, lively, and graceful . . . proved her natural powers of comic acting to be very great."[17] Understandably the Egertons' elaborate toy had a great success. West End managers would have sold their souls to the devil to be able to send the printer such a billing as:

!!!For Three Nights Only!!!
THE HUNCHBACK

Master Walter	*Mr. Knowles*
Sir Thomas Clifford	*Mr. Greville*
Modus	*Mr. Butler*
Julia	*Miss Frances Anne Kemble*
Helen	*Miss Adelaide Kemble . . .*

and no need for the ghost to walk!

Miss Frances Anne's resumption of her career even in an amateur context was first ordeal and then anticlimax: The first night she was "so horribly nervous . . . that the chair shook under me while my hair was being dressed, . . . and the rustling of the curl-papers as the man twisted them in my hair almost drove me distracted, for it sounded like a forest crackling and rattling in a storm. After the performance, my limbs ached as if I had been beaten across them with an iron bar." But on stage "no recollections . . . of past times were awakened . . . I was fully engrossed by the endeavour to do the part as well as I could . . . the Julia of nine years ago did not once present herself to my thoughts."[18] And subsequently:

> Beyond doing it as well I could, I cared very little about
> it; it seemed a sort of routine business, just as it used to,

except for . . . its being amusement instead of business
. . . champagne and lobster salad suppers, instead of my
former professional decent tea and to bed—before twelve
o'clock . . . [after] our last representation of "The
Hunchback" [we] did not reach home till the white face
of the morning was beginning to look down the ends of
the streets at us.[19]

The parallels between the two sisters now extended further.
Marriage retired Adelaide at the height of her new renown; only her
case was less feverish than Fanny's. She was engaged to and presently
married Edward John Sartoris, a gentleman-about-town whose income, pushing five thousand pounds a year, was of the same order as
the whole Butler estate's and not subject to the ups and downs of rice
and cotton. He had a country place in Hampshire and twenty years
later was elected to Parliament from a Welsh constituency. About
that time Henry James made his acquaintance and thought him "as
good a specimen as you could find of a certain type of unprepossessing
Englishman, but I like him and he has always been very pleasant to
me."[20] That is about as definite a description of him as the data
supply; indeed when Adelaide announced the engagement, a mutual
friend wrote to Anna Jameson that she was

> in *utter* amazement . . . that *not* handsome, *not* ugly, *not*
> fat, *not* thin, *not* good, *not* bad, *not* pleasant, *not* unpleas-
> ant . . . thing I have seen for years and never yet learnt
> whether he had a father or a mother . . . that *man* Sar-
> toris (I hope he is positively that, bye the bye, but I never
> thought of him as of any particular *sex* even) . . . when
> I talked to A. about marrying a good man she could es-
> teem and not to marry him from any superabundence of
> the *belle passion,* I did not mean her to go as far as that.[21]

There are eventual hints that his desultory ways of amusing himself
led to neglect of his wife. Anyway at this early stage his very ample
means made it pointless for her to go on performing to accumulate
capital to live on. Late in November Adelaide did *Norma* for what
was taken to be the last time. Fanny, raptly admiring from the family
box, was bathed in tears.

For, having a talent for feeling two ways at once about the same matter, she was both relieved because another Kemble was freed of the hazards of footlights and dismayed because such glorious talent would never again delight the world: "It was terrible to me to see . . . that woman most dear to me, deliberately leave a path where the sure harvest is . . . an independent fortune, and a not dishonourable distinction . . . for a life where, if she does not find happiness, what will atone to her for all this that she will have left?"[22] Writing thus gloomily to Lady Dacre, Fanny made no analogies to her own scuttling of her independence for marriage, but the parallel doubtless occurred to both writer and reader.

Actually it was not quite Adelaide's last *Norma*. The packed houses welcoming every time she sang had not kept Covent Garden afloat and now came the inevitable crisis—more or less 1829 all over again, with the old familiar threat against Charles's personal solvency and well-being. Fanny was bitterly aghast:

> After all our remonstrating . . . against my father's again being involved in that Heaven-forsaken concern, and . . . the most . . . solemn assurances from those who advised him into it for . . . his name at the head of it that *no* responsibility or liability whatever should rest upon . . . him; and that if the thing did not turn out prosperously, it should be . . . immediately closed;— they have gone on, in spite of night after night of receipts below the expenses, and . . . suddenly . . . shut up shop, my poor father . . . personally involved for a considerable sum.
>
> This . . . is no medicine for his malady [lumbago]. I spend every evening with him. . . . he suffers less acute pain, but . . . lies silent, with his eyes closed, apparently absorbed in painful sensations and reflections. Yet, though he neither speaks to nor looks at me, he . . . certainly derives some comfort from my presence.[23]

In the approaching year Alfred Bunn was to take over Covent Garden for whatever he could make of its elephantine whiteness. Fanny proposed that meanwhile Adelaide and she should costar in dramatic pieces on the old stage to raise the back pay owed the actors,

clear up Charles's liability, "put a good benefit into his poor pocket
. . . [and] give rather a more cheerful ending to my sister's theatrical
career" with the additional attraction of "the pleasure and *fun* of acting with her."[24] The scheme had points. London was very likely to
flock to see how beautiful, glowing Adelaide handled nonsinging
roles—as to which Fanny had no misgiving—and Fanny's return to
professional work, under such appealing circumstances. But as it
worked out, Adelaide did the rescuing, such as it was, alone, going
on doughtily in opera without Fanny with very helpful financial results and winding up her professional life with a brilliantly successful
benefit.

One can take it for granted that, whereas Sartoris made no difficulty about Adelaide's doing a few weeks more in a good cause, it
was Pierce who prevented the costarring. There was no question of
Fanny's availability. Pierce had just postponed their departure until
spring 1843. But, one surmises, he was less concerned with the actors' unpaid salaries than with the effect a professional triumph might
have on his wavering wife. Letting her have a sniff of the old days in
that amateur *Hunchback* had been quite risky enough.

While seeking another house for the winter, Pierce moved his
establishment into the Clarendon Hotel at considerable expense. This
latest postponement was fifth or sixth in a year, or some such figure.
Things were so fuzzy and fumbly that even the principals could not
keep intelligible count. In June, when Fanny told Charles they would
soon go home, "neither he nor any one else appears to believe it."[25]
She told Sarah Cleveland that twice Pierce had canceled berths
definitely taken in homebound ships. Though enjoying herself off and
on in the England after which she had yearned, she also shrank from
the instability—emotional as well as financial—that prolongations of
their stay implied. Next spring Theodore Sedgwick, by now her
brotherly correspondent, wrote that people were talking about the
Butlers' inordinate stay abroad and attributed it to Fanny's known
predilections. Indignantly—and truthfully—she replied that "for a
year and a half past I have been perfectly wretched at our protracted
stay . . . and as often as possible have protested against . . . all the
consequences involved in it." Among minor consequences calculated

to exasperate a wife: Several times after she had exhausted herself "in the maelstrom of bills, parcels, packages, books, pictures, valuables, trumpery, rummaging, heaping together, throwing apart, selecting, discarding, and stowing away that precedes an orderly departure after a two years' disorderly residence,"[26] she had to bear the frustration of being told to reverse the engines, the return was canceled into some time next year.

Another result of postponements was the departure for home of Anne Martin, probably at her own instance; she seems to have done well by the children and Fanny and to have earned Pierce's good opinion. Now he took the opportunity to install a conventional governess as her replacement. This better suited the children's ages— Sarah was now seven, Frances five—than the care of a nursemaid alone, however kind. Amelia Hall, the young Englishwoman employed, seems to have had the requisite proper background and ladylike accomplishments. One cannot know how she felt about the prospect of presently going to America. The only substantial glimpse of her comes when, to Fanny's amusement, she swam into a great farewell party that the Butlers gave "in a most elegant black satin dress, with her hair curled in profuse ringlets all over her head"[27] at a time when the fashion was unobtrusive sleekness close to the skull. But Fanny was also regardful of a governess's sensitivities about status. During the few weeks overlap with Anne, Miss Hall dined with her employers—to the wonder of the Clarendon Hotel's staff. Only after Anne left did the newcomer dine with her little charges, for, by definition, she was a cut or two above nursemaids and should not be obliged to eat with any such.

How much of these troubles with Pierce Fanny divulged to her intimates is indiscernible. When publishing her letters, she made many excisions and burned the originals. Surviving uncut letters to Sarah Cleveland reveal a little. At least once, during this stay at the Clarendon, Fanny talked pretty openly with Charles Greville, who put it all down in his famous diary: he called her story

> a domestic tragedy without any tragic events . . . after
> wasting the best years of her life in something very like
> solitude near Philadelphia, with two children of whom

> She is passionately fond. . . . She has discovered that she has married a weak, dawdling, ignorant, violent tempered man . . . and that She has outlived his liking, as He has outlived her esteem and respect. With all her prodigious talents, her fine feelings, noble sentiments and lively imagination, She has no tact, no judgment, no discretion. She has acted like a fool, and he is now become a Brute . . . She is supremely and hopelessly wretched; She sees her husband brutal and unkind to her, ruining himself and his children by his lazy stupid mismanagement of their affairs . . . lives in perpetual terror lest their alienation should mount to such a height that their living together may become impossible, and that then she shall be separated from her children for whom alone she desires to exist.

After mentioning black slavery as one cause of dissension, he faults her for lack of discretion in handling the issue and goes on, perspicaciously enough: "Certainly one of the most remarkable women I ever saw, but one who never could have been happy in whatever condition of life she might have been placed. But her lot has been singularly unfortunate, and it would have been impossible . . . to do worse for herself than She has done." [28]

Some days later Greville discussed Fanny's plight with Adelaide, whose comments led him into

> how greatly [Fanny] has been the artificer of her own misery . . . want of taste, temper and judgment—overlooking the obvious and the natural duties of her condition while pursuing some imaginary or unattainable object, which what she dignifies with the name of conscience sends her in pursuit of. . . . A thousand times better . . . to have exchanged all her fine qualities for a few homely and useful ones; to have been unable to write journals, tragedies, and poems . . . been destitute of any grand aspirations after the emancipation and amelioration of her fellow creatures, but impressed with a sense of domestic duty and have studied the character of her husband for the purpose of improving it, and corrected the faults of her own in order to make him happy. [29]

There is a daunting summary of how Fanny's world felt about women's special obligations in marriage set down by one of London's best-placed men of the world, who was genuinely fond of Fanny in an avuncular way. His contemporaries saw such subservience as arising not merely from conjugal affection, which might or might not be deeply involved, but primarily from institutional duty and loyalty like those of a chief petty officer for the flag under which he has enlisted. This attitude, taken for granted by all sorts and conditions of Grevilles, was warning of how little Fanny could hope from public opinion if she and Pierce came to formal rupture. It also hints at the least hopeful aspect of her situation—her vulnerability to Pierce's threats to deprive her of the children altogether.

The occasion for escapade number 2 may have been Fanny's discovery that Pierce had seduced one of the maidservants at Harley Street. Whatever the reason, a violent spasm of resentment and despair sent her out of London to Kingston, whence she demanded money to keep her until the opening of the theatrical season. Pierce complied. In a few days Fanny had cooled off and returned. Pierce suggested that, to regain perspective, she take Sarah on a visit to Edinburgh and the benign influences of the Combes and Mrs. Harry Siddons. After some enjoyable weeks there Fanny wished to go to Liverpool, where Adelaide was performing. Lacking money for the trip and hearing nothing from Pierce, she borrowed fifty pounds. . . . Six months later, to his peremptory demands that she tell him who lent the money—probably the Combes, possibly Mrs. Harry— she was still refusing reply because of as she said in one of those in-house letters, " 'all the worst feelings of my nature,—pride, resentment, and a resistance which I conceived justified—to a demand, which I thought you had no right to make.' "[30] Then she rushed on past this minor squabble into sweeping expostulation:

> Our position is so *perilous* now . . . there is no possible concession of pride or resentment . . . I am not prepared to make for the sake of retrieving the past and averting the future. . . . the utter destruction of all our hopes, the deterioration . . . of our characters. . . . the remainder of our youth . . . lies before us . . . a home without

love, without peace, without virtue, whence we . . .
make haste to depart as from a place accursed. . . . Look
further . . . to age . . . the cheerless and fearful prospect . . . of two . . . who have thus wickedly wasted
every blessing. . . . Have we not youth . . . wealth—a
most fortunate social position—many friends who love us
and rejoice in our welfare—children—oh! Pierce!—Pierce!
I look at our children and tremble, lest God should strike
them for our sins . . . our abuse of all the benefits . . .
daily showered upon us. . . . my husband, oh, still my
most tenderly beloved husband, let us be wise before it is
too late! Show me wherein I have sinned . . . and mer-
cifully help me to amend . . . by that love which you
once had for me, by that unalterable love which I still
bear you . . . put away from your heart all evil thoughts
and feelings towards me. . . . Do not, for God's sake,
give yourself up to unworthy pursuits and pleasures; remember your children . . . do not . . . destroy our common life. . . . Before writing this to you, I prayed to
God to grant that I might speak to your heart as I have
spoken from my own.[31]

To which Pierce, well aware of what God and society meant the
relation of husband and wife to be, replied:

It is my most earnest desire to be reconciled . . .
[but] we had better not do so, unless our union is to be
permanent, and . . . our mode of life . . . different from
the past. This can only be the result of a clear understanding. . . . we have several times parted . . . and . . .
been brought together again by the strong bond of love
. . . but . . . after a short lull the same old grievances
have given rise to the same unhappy and miserable differences. . . . for the future. . . . either we must live
apart, wretched as such a life is for ourselves, and unfortunate and injurious . . . for our children, or we must
live on better terms. On my soul and conscience I have
done every thing in my power to make you happy and
contented. . . . The fault has been entirely your own
. . . perhaps . . . your misfortune more than your fault.
. . . If you will govern your irritable temper, and *if you
can consent to submit your will to mine* [author's italics], we

may be reconciled and may be happy. I firmly believe that husband and wife cannot live happily together upon any other terms. . . . I have made many concessions to you, you have followed your own will in almost everything, and neither your happiness nor mine has been secured. . . . *I desire nothing so much as a reconciliation with you provided it can be permanent.* [32]

To which Fanny, dodging the first condition and counterpunching the second:

I have already promised to *endeavour* to control my temper; to promise more . . . would be unwise and unwarrantable. . . . For your second condition . . . I am sorry to say that I cannot entertain this proposal for a moment. I consider it my duty *not* to submit my conduct to the government of any other human being; but, could I for a moment think of giving my conscience into any other hands than my own . . . though I love you better than any other living creature, my affection does not so far blind my judgment as to suggest you as fit for such a charge. . . . I am sorry you wrote me what you did, though when I had read but the first line, I was on the point of running to your room. [33]

Late that night face-to-face bitterness got her worked up to ringing for the hotel porter and ordering a cab for instant flight, no matter what the hour. After fruitlessly representing that there was only one more day until the shift into the new house, Pierce played his ace: "I then said to her, if she did quit the hotel in that disgraceful manner . . . I would, on the morrow, take the children to Liverpool, sail for the United States in the first steamer, and she should never see either of us again." [34] The cab was sent away. But next morning Fanny left the hotel for refuge with Adelaide in the house in Park Place that the Sartorises had taken. Pierce, governess, and children moved into the fine new house he had rented in Upper Grosvenor Street. For a week or so Fanny went there daily to have half an hour with the children.

Adelaide had been in Liverpool during escapade number 2 and was no stranger to this precarious situation. She did what she could to reconcile the sister she loved with the brother-in-law she liked. All she accomplished as go-between was a letter from Fanny to Pierce assuming that

> it is your determined resolution that we should separate . . . My sister leaves town on Monday. I shall not remain in her house. . . . you might [arrange for] . . . an entirely separate establishment, though in the same house. . . . we . . . have as little in common . . . as two people who had never seen each other till yesterday. This state of things appears perfectly agreeable, or at least endurable to you; it is not so to me. . . . it is utterly impossible that I should ever regard you with indifference . . . forget that you were once my lover [in 1840 this meant accepted suitor, not usually bedmate], and are my husband, and the father of my children. . . . my heart still answers to your voice, my blood in my veins to your footsteps; and if this emotion is to be one of perpetual pain . . . judge how little I am endowed by nature with a temperament fit to endure so severe and incessant a trial. . . . [in order] to avoid paroxysms of excitement . . . I propose an entire separation . . . if you still refuse me an entire reconciliation. . . . If, however, you will not consent that I should live under the same roof with my children upon these terms, I have but one alternative . . . to hire a lodging . . . in the same house as my father. . . . should I not receive an answer from you before Monday, I . . . . shall act accordingly.[35]

She also made it clear that in this case Pierce was obligated to give her a minimum living allowance, for she would have no dependence on relatives.

Before the Monday either despair or a change of inner climate sent Fanny knocking at the door of 26 Upper Grosvenor Street at midnight. Pierce opened it, for the servants were all abed. She came in with no explanation, went to bed in a hastily prepared room, and next morning entered on the emotionally absurd, necessarily traumatic for all, arrangement she had proposed, to which Pierce had not yet consented. Its only virtue was giving her access to the children, albeit at risk to their small psyches. Pierce and she slept, saw the children, breakfasted, lunched and dined separately. Mr. and Mrs. Butler answered invitations separately, and arrived and departed separately.

One wonders what Miss Hall, her new position sure to be affected somehow, thought of it all. It certainly caused talk among her employers' wide acquaintance. Among mediators volunteering, Mary (Appleton) Mackintosh who, like the absent Adelaide, loved Fanny and found Pierce eligible, succeeded in getting negotiations reopened. The crux of them was an ultimatum from Pierce responding to an offer of Fanny's to promise " 'compliance and obedience, in all things where my conscience does not forbid them.' " He began with a homily:

> Without obedience from a wife to her husband, it is utterly impossible to live happily together. The natural disposition of most women, which is gentle and yielding, leads them to . . . compliance towards their husbands, and to consult their wishes in most things . . . Unfortunately your natural disposition frequently prompts you to act in direct opposition to all my wishes . . . and with hostility to my interests, and . . . I am forced . . . to exact that obedience which a different spirit on your part would render unnecessary. . . . You now tell me, that compliance with my wishes, and obedience to my will in every respect, in which they do not interfere with the dictates of your conscience, you are . . . most willing to promise. . . . I fairly tell you that I shall expect and exact your promise to its entire extent. . . . I have twice separated myself from you[36] and been . . . once reconciled to you upon your own terms. . . . I have separated from you on principle, and . . . not from temper; and if we are now reconciled [and] you again oblige me to leave you, it will be for the last time.

Then he preached on the private conscience's unreliability in contrast to God's objective laws and stipulated that in future cases of conscience she follow advice from friends, the Sedgwick kind, presumably. Fanny replied briskly that that would be advisable but it would be " 'sinful in the highest degree' "[37] to let friends override her own judgments.

That could have been another sticking point. But stalemate was averted, for Pierce fell sick and Fanny, suddenly anxious about this man whom she still loved, sent a note beseeching leave to come to his room to look after him. . . . And still once more, to the astonishment of angels if not men, a new nudging toward mutual accommodation reached a point where each could try to believe. In the ratifying exchange of notes, Fanny: " 'I can promise . . . to *endeavour heartily* to do my duty better henceforward. . . . I am most unwilling that pride . . . should prevent my using every endeavour to conciliate you . . . I have been so often in fault toward you, that though I may not have much hope for the future, I have much regret for the past.' " Pierce in reply: " 'I am quite satisfied with the promises you have made me . . . adhere . . . to the spirit of them . . . [and] our reunion will be happy and lasting.' "[38]

Faces thus saved on both sides, the pair "lived together on good terms," Pierce averred years later, ". . . maintaining every relation of husband and wife"[39] for the three months preceding their sailing. Take that at full value and Fanny was lucky not to have the complication of a third pregnancy. But full credence may not be justified. By Fanny's account full conjugal harmony never revived after the explosion late in 1842. Available letters, published or unpublished, are scanty in this interval. The only likely pertinent passage, in a letter to Theodore Sedgwick responding to some expression of commiseration, is hardly blithesome: "To have to accept the conviction of the unworthiness of those we love must be even worse than to lay our dearest in the earth."[40]

Anyway Fanny did live in the Butler house for months, presumably seeing the children daily and gradually getting caught up in packing for departure. Their sailing date in early May remained firm. In mid-April their farewell party of two hundred-odd guests required six policemen to handle the crush and the crowd of curiosity seekers. The subsequent party for a more select list ate and drank much less per capita though they stayed until 2:00 A.M. The sadness inseparable from such occasions did, however, secure Fanny her last compliment from Sydney Smith, who wrote to her, "If I'm alive at all when you return—I shall most likely be paralytic in body and mind but come

& give one look at me, & I shall flash up for a moment & feel that some bright vision of other times is come back."[41]

Entertainments on that scale catered by the fashionable firm of Gunter's were expensive and Pierce Butler, the wealthy Yankee rice-planter, had so mishandled his affairs that he had to borrow substantial sums—from Harriet St. Leger and Adelaide Sartoris—to meet his final bills. He had, however, been businesslike enough to have his father-in-law sign a deed definitely providing that on his death Fanny's seven thousand pounds would revert to her. Aunt Victoire was now looking after Charles as Aunt Dall had done; and in her sister's tradition exhausted herself helping Fanny pack. Miss Hall took the little girls to a quiet beach resort near Liverpool to await their parents' presailing arrival. Fanny's last surviving note from Upper Grosvenor Street goes: "Charles Young . . . who dotes upon my children . . . went with them to the railroad. [Sarah] begged some of her grandfather's hair, but that he might not be told it was for her, for fear of grieving him. . . . Victoire, quite tired out with packing, is lying asleep on the sofa, and poor dear Emily [FitzHugh] sits crying beside me. Ever yours, Fanny."[42]

On May 4, 1843, after some twenty-nine months of overspending, domestic altercations, self-indulgence and shilly-shally, Pierce Butler actually managed to get his family on board a Cunarder homeward bound.

XIII

Impatient Griselda

HEAD WINDS all the way to Halifax did not seriously delay the ship. But in such weather a small steamer, particularly of the early paddle-wheel model, crank and unwieldy, was no place for poor sailors. Fanny had ten days of undernourished misery. The delight in heavy seas and high winds that Miss Kemble had learned to feel fourteen years earlier was missing, never again to appear in her score or so of later passages. This could be seen as a loss of receptivity as she passed the midpoint of her thirties. Yet in view of her progressive delight in the Berkshires and her awed wonder at the Alps when she met them during her forties, the point may not be well taken.

Her children fared better than their mother, "sick and sorry one hour, and flying about the deck like birds the next . . . little [Frances] *pervading* the ship from stem to stern like Ariel, and generally presiding at the officers' mess in undismayed she-loneliness." [1] Fanny was still very shaky when the ship came alongside at Halifax and correspondingly grateful when Samuel Cunard himself, Canadian pioneer of transatlantic mail-steamer service, came aboard to take her to his house for a few hours of respite. Two days later Elizabeth Sedgwick and daughter Kate were on the wharf at Boston, which was reassuring; and there was time to go out to Mount Auburn and lie on Aunt Dall's grave, whence "her example seemed . . . to rise in all the brightness of its perfect loveliness and self-denial. . . . her lovely virtues seemed to call to me to get up and be of good cheer, and strive to forget myself, even as perfectly as she had done. . . .

I am very sad," Fanny wrote to Harriet, "but far from out of courage." [2]

That was just as well. For the next two years Mrs. Pierce Butler would need and sometimes fail to find the special courage that keeps the sense of proportion acute and the moral head to waves created not by major issues but by arbitrary vexations. Consider the quarters that the family now occupied. Because there were few shots in the financial locker, Pierce had decided to rent Butler Place for regular revenue and install himself and brood in a Walnut Street boardinghouse in Philadelphia. Little Frances, whose very small memories of country living were idyllic, was articulately aghast. As for her mother: "My acquaintances," Fanny said, "assure me that I am very comfortable . . . I endeavor to persuade myself that my acquaintances are better judges of that than I. . . . It is . . . simply detestable." [3]

As of your grandfather's time, "boardinghouse" connoted the shirt-sleeved bookkeeper in the hall bedroom, the "home cooking" supper, and quarrels over the last pork chop . . . lower middle income shading into upper blue-collar. But in the presidency of Martin van Buren or John Tyler, Boston, New York City, Philadelphia had boardinghouses catering to upper-income types who now would have apartments at good addresses—high-paid business and professional men, well-endowed widows, well-established couples whose children's growing up made commodious houses no longer necessary, and (a thing foreign visitors always remarked) well-off young married couples postponing household cares, maybe even rearing a child or two in this sterile and straitened environment. These establishments had large, expensively got-up parlors, elaborate bills of fare though the cooking was seldom distinguished, goodish addresses, and scores of residents where the dingy downtown kind might have a dozen. In contrast to the parlors and dining room, the sleeping rooms were small and stingily furnished, for it was assumed, just as in the fancy hotel round the corner, that spare time was spent in the public rooms (including the bar) or one of the gentlemen's clubs beginning to spring up in cities in imitation of British models. For that matter, these acknowledgedly genteel boardinghouses were not unlike high-ticket pensions in Paris and Rome.

No doubt Chestnut Street felt that a proper red-brick-and-white-trim house of one's own was best. Yet little stigma attached to this alternative, for it could not be accused of being cheap, and as yet most Americans, even those with comfortable incomes, lacked the Briton's preference for all the privacy one could afford. So when her acquaintance assured Mrs. Butler that she was comfortable in Mrs. McPherson's well-reputed boardinghouse, it meant that Pierce had not impaired his or her dignity by installing her there. But Fanny disliked having no proper sitting room of her own, so she had to receive visitors in large, gilded rooms frequented by vapid, overdressed wives. Such circumstances clogged the working up of any such social life as she kept hoping Philadelphia would afford:

> I have received a great many morning visits, and one or
> two invitations to evening parties, but . . . I do not like
> to accept civilities which I have no means of reciprocating.
> . . . Had I a house of my own . . . I should not at all
> despair of gradually collecting . . . a society that would
> satisfy me. . . . Of the discomfort and disorder of our
> mode of life I cannot easily give you [Harriet] a notion,
> for you know nothing of the sort, and, until now, neither
> did I.

Presently her watch—maybe the one her father gave Juliet—and its chain, a gift from Harriet, were stolen from her dismal bedroom. When Harriet sent a replacement: "I think I shall sleep with it . . . so great will be my horror of having it stolen . . . in this wretched and disorderly lodging-house. . . . I am in perpetual misery lest I should have left any closet or drawer in my bed-room unfastened . . . a state of anxious and suspicious caution . . . as odious as it is troublesome."[4]

Then she had no horse,[5] and long walks in sticky summer heat, the alternative for exercise, were less enjoyable every day. Worse, the antislavery issue was threatening to revive. She became an admirer of the Reverend Dr. William Henry Furness, Boston-born and Cambridge-trained Unitarian minister of the congregation founded in Philadelphia by no less a person than Joseph Priestley. Furness was making trouble for himself by sermons against slavery—a topic that the controversy over the acquisition of Texas was then heating up. Philadelphia's Unitarians should have tended toward open-mindedness, yet some of them walked out on his conscience-stirring dicta; and others, "members of the church from its earliest establishment . . . very much attached to him . . . said if he would only give them notice when he intended to preach upon that subject, they would [stay away] . . . to which his reply not unnaturally was, 'Why, those . . . are precisely the persons who are in need of such exhortations!' "[6] He had been on good terms with Pierce's mother, that eccentric who admired Unitarianism for being nonreligious, and Pierce had inherited a respect for this man of goodwill who, though no Quaker, shared William Penn's spirit in Penn's "green country town." Fanny was not only uneasy lest Furness be deprived of his pulpit; in spite of this Furness-Mease nexus, she feared lest Pierce forbid her to take Sarah, now past her ninth birthday and sharp for her age, to a church where antislavery sermons were preached. And what her and Pierce's precarious relations needed least was more wrangling about slavery.

Even without that her mood was not sanguine. Condoling with Sarah Cleveland on the death of her young husband: "And yet sweet severing of love that has been true to the end is joy compared to the despair of seeing the end of love long forestall the end of life." And a month later: "When I consider my own position dispassionately it appears to me that my trials are what they are because of what I am. . . . my happiness so far as it centered on my deepest affections has been . . . destroyed forever—its very foundation from the beginning was rotten . . . bitter & terrible as this wreck has been to me—I have ever been forced to acknowledge that it was as inevitable as merited."[7]

Almost anything might produce jangling. When Frances fell downstairs and broke an arm, Fanny's insistence on rallying round was unbecomingly resisted. For the oncoming summer Fanny, never reconciled to the seasonal swelter of the Philadelphia area, wanted for her children beach coolness and sousings in salt water. But the fashionable shore resorts would cost too much for Pierce's new thriftiness. His substitute was Yellow Springs, a once smart but now rather run down small spa thirty miles west of Philadelphia near enough to the railroad to make weekend visits practical. Its focus was a copious, clear, very cold water source promoted as "the transparent spring"; but its greater feature was its iron-and-sulphur taste foul enough to get it considered highly health-giving. The patrons not only bathed in it but determinedly drank it.

The spring had for Fanny an Undinish charm. It was screened "only from earthly observers" by whitewashed walls "rising . . . to a discreet height. . . . No roof covers the watery chamber but the green spreading branches of tall trees and the blue summer sky, into which you seem to be stepping as you disturb the surface of the water. Into this lucid liquid . . . I give my chickens and myself, overhead, three breathless dips—it is too cold to do more"—55 degrees, F. the management claimed. Away from sun-cooked pavement and brick walls holding heat, the atmosphere of Yellow Springs was slightly less oppressive than the town's, and the fertile countryside, viewed from a tree-covered knoll behind the buildings, was "rich rolling country . . . yellow crops of grain running like golden bays into the green woodland that clothes . . . the tops and sides of the hills, the wheat, the grass, the oats, and the maize, all making different checkers in the pretty variegated patchwork covering of the prosperous summer earth . . . peaceful, plenteous, prosperous . . . comfortable to one's spirit and exceedingly pleasant to the eye."[8] She got hold of a horse and told Theodore Sedgwick that she had been "almost happy once or twice while riding over those hills . . . with no influences . . . but the holy and consolatory ministerings of nature,"[9] and was sorry to have had to leave abruptly after barely a month of healthily regular and relatively quiet existence.

That she had to leave, and abruptly, was her own willful fault. Her marked sense of privacy and joy in the bathing arrangements tricked her into demonstrating that a tempest in a teapot can be explosive. The bathing hours were: gentlemen before 10:00 A.M. and noon to 2:00 P.M. (dinner time); ladies 10:00 A.M. to noon. As the resort filled up with refugees from city heat, the ladies' two hours allowed no exclusive use of the spring for even short dips, so Fanny and her chicks were in the same proximity to others that had so irked her at Rockaway Beach. She took to coming just before noon, waiting till all others left, then going in and locking the door against the arriving men until she and the girls were ducked and reclothed. This high-handedness made the men complain to the manager, who complained to Pierce, who ordered Fanny to behave herself and observe the hours; in the right for the second time. Fanny persisted in misbehaving. Some men warned the manager that if she continued, they would force the door. When she refused to give in, Pierce, understandably furious, packed the whole family off back to Philadelphia. Fanny had not only shown deplorably bad manners, she had given Pierce opportunity to make her look dead wrong—which she was. Seven years later he asked the manager at Yellow Springs to write down his recollection of the affair to show the public what Fanny's husband had had to cope with.

After two weeks stewing in town Fanny, a nursemaid, and the children were sent to finish the hot season at an upcountry farm. It suited the children but Fanny was again feeling like the little old woman with the cut-off petticoats:

> We eat at the . . . table of these worthy people . . .
> with *two-pronged iron forks*. . . . the more sensible . . .
> eat exclusively with their knives. The farming men and
> boys come in to table from their work, without their coats
> and with their shirt-sleeves rolled up . . . my own nurse-
> maid, and the servant-of-all-work . . . and any visitors
> who may look in . . . sit down with us promiscuously to
> feed; all which, I confess, makes me a little melancholy.
> It is nonsense talking about positive equality; these people
> are sorry associates for me, and so, I am sure, am I for
> them.[10]

Toward the end of September there was a too short but bracing visit to Lenox and the Sedgwicks. On the way home the Butlers had some time in New York, where William Macready, the dominant English tragedian of the day, was opening a tour of America.[11] He had known Pierce in London. Now he gave his diary an outsider's view of the Butler marriage: "Dined with Pierce Butler, [William Cullen] Bryant, Mr. and Mrs. Longfellow. [Mrs. Butler] spoke admirably well, but quite like a man . . . a woman of a most extraordinary mind; what she said on most subjects was . . . the stern truth but what in the spirit of charity should not have been said in the presence of one . . . obliged to listen to it." [12] One assumes the subject was slavery or marriage, probably the former. Two months later Macready had a chat with Fanny and Catharine Sedgwick and, doubtless meaning well, told Fanny that "she did not do justice to the talents committed to her . . . she might in a country like [America] influence society." Fanny burst into tears. Presently Charlotte Cushman, a rising American actress then playing Macready's leads, a lady of rather dreary respectability currently in Fanny's confidence, told him that "Butler's feeling for [Fanny] was absolute aversion. . . . Mrs. Butler had written to her on her birthday that the only consoling reflection was that another year of wretchedness being gone, she was so much nearer its termination. . . . [Cushman] ascribes the unhappiness to his fickleness and instability; but I have seen enough to satisfy me that there has been enough . . . to drive a loving heart from home." And later after a confidential talk with Fanny he concluded oracularly that "both, as is always the case, are to blame." [13]

However that might be in the sight of an angelic jury on Judgment Day, a recent explosion had much redressed Fanny's situation by putting Pierce hopelessly in the wrong in a context more serious than the usurping of privileges at a one-horse spa. Somehow she found compromising letters to Pierce from a woman—unsigned. His story was he had put them away unopened, seals intact, and Fanny, searching his desk, had found them, broken the seals and read them; and their content did not show that he had actually gone to bed with the lady. That last, Fanny granted, was true; but tone and content seem also to have shown not only that Pierce had been philandering, but that the affair went back several years to a time when the marriage still had valid hopes of success. That gave the matter a particularly painful twist. Undeniably Fanny should not have read the letters, nor did she explain how she happened to find them. The charitable may attribute her thus behaving like Bluebeard's wife to the heavy strain she was under; few people always act in character.

What was in character was that, given the discovery, she took the matter up with Pierce with results so fierce on both sides that she consulted a lawyer about a formal separation.

Pierce, up on his high horse as safest place to be, persisting in his friable fiction about having put the letters away unread, refused to reply to the lawyer's request for leave to consult Fanny at the boardinghouse. Fanny told her story to Theodore Sedgwick; he came down from New York to try his hand with Pierce. In what Fanny described as "a moment of unguarded exasperation,"[14] Pierce admitted his infidelity to Sedgwick but pointed out that, after all, Fanny could not identify the lady and had given him back the letters, so she could not produce them as evidence . . . but in the end he agreed to a separation allowing Fanny twenty-five hundred dollars a year—then a comfortable income and representing, he averred, a third of his annual expectations—with separate quarters under the same roof as the children and the right to see them at will; all on condition that she stay off the stage and publish nothing against slavery or any other writing of which he disapproved. Through Sedgwick Fanny accepted. Pierce worked up pretentious quibbles and then reneged. His trusted ally, Elizabeth, came down from Stockbridge to try her hand and found him unreasonable. Personally rebuffed, aghast at the unsavory occasion of the crisis, she gave him both barrels: " 'I regard you as having deliberately and deeply injured the dearest friend that I have. . . . You . . . told me . . . last spring, that you had never sinned against Fanny in any way. . . . I have no feeling of unkindness towards you . . . nothing to prevent my praying God . . . to bring you back to him; but there can no longer be friendship, or even the appearance of it, between us.' "[15]

Pierce replied:

> Misguided herself, [Fanny] has misled you. . . . you will one day think . . . differently . . . when that day dawns . . . rely upon my regard for you being unchanged. For the monstrous wrong she does me, I freely forgive her. . . . I think of her with the deepest commisseration [sic] and weep;—oh! how I weep when she knows it not—that a heart so warm and true as hers, should be

> warped by a head so weak. . . . If in this life the head
> shall continue to oversway the heart, then must we look
> to the everlasting hereafter . . . rightly to feel, and
> rightly to know each other.

He had likely alienated the Sedgwicks anyway, for in such quarters those days adultery, even though some years stale and unprovable in court, was a cardinal matter. In the next round of negotiations Pierce could save face for himself only by insisting that Fanny renounce for life any communication whatever with any Sedgwicks, " 'those low-bred, vulgar meddlers,' "[16] quoth the major's grandson.

His wrath was the hotter as he came to suspect that Theodore Sedgwick was busy seeking proof of adultery for use in court, writing to London to get traces of misbehavior ferreted out there. The germ of this may have been well-meant offers from Charlotte Cushman to help. Her feelings were rather hurt when, for tactical reasons, neither Fanny nor her advisors now wanted the matter aggressively pursued. But Pierce firmly believed the hunt was up. As if to strengthen his persecutors' hand, the following March he got into a juicy scandal of unimpeachable freshness and conspicuousness.

He and a fellow Philadelphian, James A. Schott, Jr., were going to New York on business. Schott's wife, a daughter of the august Willing family of Philadelphia, and her sister, Mrs. John J. Ridgeway, went along to go to the opera. They all stayed at the Astor House, the new pride of the American hotel industry. At midnight, according to Schott, he found Pierce Butler in Mrs. Schott's bedroom in a compromising situation, nature never stated. He said that the ensuing row was aborted to avoid embarrassing the innocent Mrs. Ridgeway; but next day he sent Pierce a note renouncing all acquaintance and so on. He said he had previously noted and spoken to his wife about what he then took for "thoughtless imprudences"[17] between Pierce and his wife.

On the party's return home Schott was so violent toward his wife that he was bound over to keep the peace and she left his house, going to her parents. With some difficulty Schott found a friend to "act for him" in the conventional capacity as his second—Harrison Gray Otis, Jr., of the eminent Boston family that had entertained the

Kembles in 1835—and challenged Pierce to a duel. The occasion was ostensibly to be a quarrel unrelated to the lady, but no such pretext kept the whole town from knowing what it was all about. Mutual friends tried to convince Schott that he had not seen what he said he had—he was known for hair-trigger judgments—but failed. Doubtless at his second's suggestion, Pierce sent him a note: "On the oath of a Christian and of a man of honor, I tell you that you have strangely deceived yourself . . . if you will not accept this sacred pledge, God keep you."[18] When Schott rejected this, Pierce accepted the challenge. The parties met on the traditional out-of-state duelling ground at Bladensburg, Maryland. Each fired twice; all shots missed though both were considered good marksmen; then the proceedings were stopped. Sidney Fisher, the indispensable diarist, allowed that Schott's insisting on fighting "raised him a good deal in public opinion. Every one considers, however, that his accusation was totally without foundation, & [Mrs. Schott's] reputation is quite untainted."[19] That may reflect partly Schott's reputation for extravagantly going off half-cocked and partly the wife's family's impeccable standing. She sued for divorce and Schott let it go by default on the grounds that he had every reason to wish to be rid of her. Here is a strange mixture of archaic pistols-at-dawn (then dwindling but still a lively tradition both sides of the water) and a resort to divorce in a stratum of society where it was highly unusual.

It was set to Pierce's credit that on the ground he seemed to be the cooler of the two. All very well at the Philadelphia Club but unlikely to reconcile the Sedgwicks to him or, in view of previous findings, assuage Fanny's bitterness. A few weeks after the duel Sidney Fisher rode out to Branchtown with her:

> An agreeable companion, but . . . too prononcée, wants delicacy and refinement . . . the reverse of feminine in her manners and conversation . . . alluding constantly to her domestic troubles, which I believe are brought about by her want of tact and temper. She has talent, however, and converses well . . . has seen the best English society and her descriptions of men and manners are very interesting. . . . has published a volume of poems for the

purpose of paying for the horse she rode [poor Forrester]
. . . very fond of riding . . . could not live without it
. . . rides every day alone.

He bought the volume of poems, thought them no great thing—nor
are they—and justifiably faulted her for including in them "allusions
to her position and conjugal unhappiness that had better have been
omitted." [20]

At Mrs. McPherson's high-toned boardinghouse at 111 South
Sixth Street a special table was set apart for the Butler party. Day
after day the other boarders saw Pierce, Miss Hall, the two girl children, and Mrs. Butler dining glumly with only minimum pass-the-
salt-please between husband and wife. By agreement they saw no
more of each other than this. The emotional effect on the children
was naturally something to make a pediatric psychiatrist moan. That
either girl turned out fairly able to cope must mean that both were
sturdy stuff. Presently, however, Fanny could look back on Mrs.
McPherson's as the good old days.

In spring 1844 Pierce's finances were recuperated enough for
him to take a house on Walnut Street opposite brother John's, to be
occupied after refurbishing. Fanny got wind of the plan and through
her lawyer asked what it betokened for her. Pierce replied that she
could dwell therein on the old conditions, including boycott of the
Sedgwicks, plus some new ones: " 'That Mrs. Butler will not keep
up an acquaintance with any person that I may disapprove of; and
that, in her future intercourse with her friends . . . she will not
mention any circumstance which may occur in my house or family;
and that she will . . . cease to speak of me in terms of reprobation
and reproach.' " He demanded an answer in two days, for " 'arrangements for going into the house . . . will be modified by Mrs. Butler's determination.' " [21] Fanny refused these conditions. Learning
that Pierce was arranging to take the girls and Miss Hall to Newport
for two months while workmen were in the house—a clear breach of
previous agreement as to access—Fanny tried, apparently without
success, to get rooms for herself and a maid in the same Newport

boardinghouse. Soon Pierce had a note from the Reverend Dr. Furness offering of his own volition, without Fanny's knowing of it, to mediate as an old friend of the Butler family. Pierce professed gratitude but declined the offer: " 'I solemnly declare that my treatment of [Fanny] has been just and kind; and my conscience fully acquits me of one act towards her, of which a reasonable woman would justly complain.' " [22]

In the fall he settled Miss Hall and the children in the new house. Fanny went to live in a nearby boardinghouse convenient for the hour a day she was to see the girls. Breaches of agreement continued. By the end of the year Furness managed to get negotiations renewed, this time with Fanny's knowledge. Gradually, exploiting Furness's goodwill, Pierce beat Fanny down; or say that he used her eagerness to get back under the same roof with her children to blackmail her into accepting his conditions, including an offer of eight hundred dollars a year for personal expenses. Agreement was reached in mid-December. But on the pretexts of getting rooms ready for her and securing a signed copy of the conditions in her own hand, actual moving in was delayed until March 3, 1845, that is, after some ten weeks in limbo.

Even patient Dr. Furness grew testy about these delays. Some Philadelphians grasped the situation well enough to take Fanny's side. Rebecca Gratz, who was just getting to know Fanny well at this period, told her sister: "I have heard no one censure Fanny for the unhappy state she is reduced to except for extravagant expenditures in Europe but Pierce is accused of shameful dissipations. . . . they occupy the same house . . . but meet only as strangers—if they meet at all—This cannot last with any advantage to the children." And somewhat later: "[Fanny] is very sweet and lovely and most unfortunate—but she has one bright hour in every day when her children are permitted to visit her! . . . All her dearest duties transferred to another, and her anxieties about the training of the little girls tugging at her heart." Then after the capitulation: "She is going to Mr. Butler on his own hard terms as soon as he is ready—for the sake of living in the house with her children." And as to them, next year after both Fanny and Miss Hall had left the scene: "Her children spent Saturday with us . . . interesting little girls, but also need their poor mother's watchful care. There is not a female in the [Butler] family . . . able to counteract the injurious tendency of too much indulgence and the want of maternal direction."[23]

This lunatic arrangement, reflecting both Pierce's sadistic version of *paterfamilias* and Fanny's clinging to the role of *mater dolorosa,* guaranteed ructions to begin with. To make doubly sure, Pierce saw fit, within a few weeks of her coming in, to pass on to her an envelope enclosing a letter to her from what, with gingerly distaste, he termed "a Sedgwick." Fanny took this for permission to read it and did so. Pierce at once pounced on her for welshing: " 'You have lived in this house a little over a month, and you have already violated the principal condition which you bound yourself to observe. . . . address no more notes to me.' "[24] Not unnaturally Fanny saw this as entrapment, and struggle as Pierce might later to explain it, it is difficult to see it as anything else.

His unwillingness to have Fanny's overseas connections discussing his family affairs did not keep him from encouraging it when it might be useful. In the previous year's crisis he had sought advice from the Sartorises and Charles Kemble and got back cordial hopes that somehow matters would soon improve. Now, as soon as he agreed to admit Fanny to the new house, he wrote overseas about the arrangement, indeed presented it as a *fait accompli* months before it was effected. Charles Greville, once more summing up for masculine hegemony, replied that though it was impossible " 'to revive feelings . . . so wounded and crushed . . . there is no reason why you should not live together as friends' " and approved of Pierce's conditions and Fanny's acceptance of them. Sartoris was less satisfactory. As one man of the world to another, he approved the outlawing of the Sedgwicks—" 'people who . . . have always given [Fanny] the worst possible advice' "—but, he went on, maybe reflecting influence from Adelaide:

> however much . . . [Fanny] may have drawn misfortune
> on her own shoulders by . . . rashness . . . the penalty
> was so severe that we could not help feeling the greatest
> sympathy. . . . promote her comfort as much as possible,

and . . . allow her a fair share in the general care and
education of her children: this is a right, which, with all
her errors, she has done nothing to forfeit. . . . She has
generosity among her good qualities . . . a certain confidence . . . would do more towards softening her disposition, than severity and control, which only serve to
irritate her. . . . mothers have feelings with regard to the
children of their womb, which we men are hardly able to
realize.[25]

The governess proved a useful tool in the campaign to alienate
Fanny from her daughters, in which no subtlety was observed. During the time when Fanny was boarding nearby, Miss Hall had the
girls out for their daily walk; they encountered Fanny, who came up
to speak with them; following orders, with how much relish one
cannot know, the governess forbade it and marched them on. One
day Fanny came to Pierce about some permission granted or denied
Frances. In reply Pierce discussed the matter with the child only and
went back to his newspaper as if Fanny had not been in the room;
Miss Hall sat serenely by. When the girls' joint birthday was to be
celebrated at Butler Place, Miss Hall took them there in a carriage;
Fanny, forbidden to go along, "rode out alone on the public road,
listening to their voices and endeavouring to catch a glimpse of them
through the trees as they played on the lawn"—the trees of her
own planting eight years previously. For the next birthday Pierce
managed another twist of the thumbscrew: little Frances was sent to
tell her mother that her father, Miss Hall, Sarah, and she were again
celebrating at Butler Place, with no room in the carriage for Fanny
"but I could go on horseback or in a cab. The little creature saw the
shock which such a proposition gave and throwing her arms around
me, said 'Don't cry, mother, I'll go with you.' I could not, however,
condemn her to a sad drive with me . . . sent her with the others
and followed the carriage along in a hack cab," doubtless eating dust
all the way. Worse, Fanny believed, and in view of Miss Hall's apparent attitude, probably with reason, that "I was represented to [the
children] as the source of every inconvenience and disappointment
which they suffered."[26]

The inevitable consequence was deteriorating relations. In the case of young Sarah, for instance, Pierce's ill-concealed delight in this is clear in an intramural letter in June 1845:

> I must request that you will have nothing to say, or to do, with Sarah. . . . It is not in my power to control her behaviour to you; it is the reward you are reaping for your own past misconduct. . . . A mother who abandons her children, cannot expect to have the same hold upon their affections, when she returns, after a desertion of more than one year. Sarah's quick perceptions have enabled her to form her own opinions; she has judged you, and condemns you. . . . You have rendered my home wretched and miserable; and it will gratify you to know that you have completely destroyed my happiness in life. Forbear, for God's sake, and do not destroy the happiness of your child.[27]

That same spring saw salt vigorously rubbed into abrasions by rumors that Miss Hall and Pierce were on far better terms than Mrs. Grundy approved of. Such talk, Fanny pointed out at tactless junctures, was the predictable result of the governess's situation closer to Pierce than his own wife in such matters as quarters, meals, and access to the children. Indeed these prurient speculations grew strong enough to cross the Atlantic in force. Pierce was treated to expostulatory letters from England; from Mary Mackintosh: " 'I entreat you, if you have any wish (either for your children's sake, or your own comfort or respectability) that Fanny should remain in your house— to take some measures for appointing a successor to Miss Hall. I . . . consider her presence an insult to Fanny.' " From Adelaide Sartoris, hitherto able to see both sides of the Butlers' troubles: " 'Let me entreat you to modify that most unjust and intolerable arrangement by which Miss Hall (a *hired* instructress) supersedes my sister in her right and control over the children. *No* woman would bear such an *intolerable* insult. . . . There is but one opinion . . . here . . . that from the moment my sister returned to take her proper place, Miss Hall ought to have been dismissed . . . previous to Fanny's return to your house.' "[28]

Pierce was not unprepared. In the same mail Miss Hall heard

from her family in England. They were outraged because, as they had it from friends, Lady Byron and others had had from Fanny indirect reports of " 'a criminal connexion between her husband and you.' " The informants seem politely to have expressed faith that no daughter of such a family could thus have strayed; but did show " 'surprise . . . that [Miss Hall] remained under the circumstances.' "[29] And Miss Hall, taking it for granted that Fanny had thus traduced her, demanded that Pierce secure her written denial of the charge.

Pierce owed much of this irksome problem to his shady reputation as well as to his gradually depriving Fanny of access to the children. Shrilly he told Mary Mackintosh that if she thought him the kind of man who would seek " 'to degrade the mother of his children . . . [and] admits his wife into his house only for the purpose of insulting her,' " he wondered that she should try to reform such a monster, going on, " 'To whom I am indebted for painting my character in such colors, I am at a loss to conceive; the conception is worthy the mind of a Sedgwick.' " And though neither protester had explicitly gone beyond Miss Hall's usurpation of Fanny's place with the children, his reply to Mrs. Mackintosh showed awareness of the graver charge and demanded the names of those behind this " 'shameful . . . falsehood.' "[30] He also demanded from Fanny the retraction that Miss Hall sought. Fanny replied—in writing, for they were back at the game of intramural letters—that she did not reply to charges of scandalmongering concocted by strangers; that she had not instigated Adelaide or Mary to take him to task; and deftly: " 'I am sorry for the disadvantageous reports . . . about Miss Hall, but not at all surprised . . . they are the natural and inevitable consequence of her position in your family.' "[31]

Such nimble footwork sent Pierce into a spastic rage: " 'It is impossible to make any impression on one whose mental and moral obliquity blinds her to all the vices of her nature, whose reason is sophistry, whose religion is cant, and whose unbounded self-esteem renders her happy and satisfied in all her wrong doings. . . . clear yourself from an imputation that the vilest woman would be ashamed of.' " All he got in reply was a dexterous protest against being accused of " 'the guilt of propagating . . . falsehoods . . . in my

opinion, greater than that of a breach of chastity.' "[32] And in re-
quital for shouting he learned some days later that, without giving
him the satisfaction of knowing about it, Fanny had sent Miss Hall
a resounding written denial that she had ever " 'spoken, written, or
even *thought* . . . injurious things respecting her.' "[33] It was still
more awkward that Miss Hall too had failed to let him know. It was
Fanny's round. But the prize-ring metaphor itself betrays the destructive emotions involved. And to make a man feel like a fool is no way
to improve his conduct of disintegrating family relations.

When, late that year, Miss Hall resigned and went home, she
was armed with a fulsome letter from Pierce to her brother praising
her " 'gentleness, amiability, and kindness' " and vouching for " 'the
respect and esteem [for her] of every member of my family.' "[34] In
Pierce's view by then "my family" no longer included Fanny. Her
actual attitude toward Miss Hall is unclear. The woman's bad judgment in persisting in a situation sure to cause gossip was the only
specific charge Fanny leveled against her, but her views beyond that
must have been colored by the readiness with which Miss Hall had
allowed Pierce to use her. Taking oneself off one's relatives' hands
was the usual reason for well-bred girls' turning governess. Doubtless
this one needed the job in those terms and, three thousand miles
from home, was unlikely to refuse Pierce's orders. Whether he ever
gave her occasion to refuse—or acquiesce in—anything else one cannot know. Hearing of the matter, Will Thackeray told Adelaide that
his sympathy lay with Pierce; he too, he said, had suffered from such
malicious rumors about the governess he had to have for his two
motherless little girls. My own guess is that Miss Hall, though remaining *virgo intacta,* was not numb to Pierce's attractiveness. That
gravitational pull, probably masquerading as duty to one's employer,
would have helped greatly as she followed Pierce's wishes in walling
Fanny off from the girls' lessons, clothes, recreation, conversation.
. . . One senses a lively partisanship strengthened by the unfavorable
light in which this deliberate alienation put the difficult and impatient Mrs. Butler.

That last summer the matter of where to send the children to
keep them out of city heat led to confused, calamitous, and climactic

squabbles. Pierce let Miss Hall go to Yellow Springs as guest of a
Philadelphia matron who had taken a fancy to her; there she could
cool off in both senses. For the worst two months Sarah and Frances
were to board with the tenant's family on a farm the Butlers owned
near Darby, Pennsylvania, some miles out of Philadelphia. In charge
of them Pierce put Anne Martin, their former nurse, whom he sought
out because, he said, probably not in Miss Hall's hearing, only she
had ever been able to control them. Borrowing a bedroom at brother
John's, he turned his own house over to workmen for further redeco-
ration. Fanny was left therein to enjoy in the heat she dreaded the
noise and dismal debris of papering and painting, repairing, and so
on.

For Fanny going to and from the farm daily to visit the children
was so onerous that she persuaded the tenant, a kindly man who
cannot have feared his landlord much, to take her too as boarder.
Pierce burst in on this arrangement and furiously took the children
back to the city late one fittingly thunderstormy evening. The following day Fanny retrieved Anne and the children from city heat, restored them to the farm, and resumed her lonely life in that walled
and roofed desert on Walnut Street. She did not see Sarah and Frances
again for the next five years. The best she could do for the rest of this
summer was messages smuggled to and fro by the tenant farmer making his weekly trips to market with produce.

As the fall of the year came round, Fanny had lost all hope of
any success at playing Patient Griselda. The role did not suit her
talent to begin with, and the management had done little to make it
easier. She cut her losses, saying:

> I had now . . . sufficiently tested the experiment . . .
> [of] accepting the "conditions" imposed. My life had been
> all but intolerable in his house, my presence there had
> been the means of injuring my children; they had been
> removed from me for two months . . . I had finally been
> forbidden to see them. Thus my ministry toward them
> seemed in God's righteous dispensations, either to be
> ended utterly, or, for the present, utterly suspended. My
> friends and family in England . . . strongly urged me,

for my children's sake, to come away, and I perceived the
necessity.[35]

Not for the last time her genuine reverence for God's mysterious ways
helped her. To Samuel Gray Ward, a pillar of the Massachusetts bar
and great friend of hers in the Berkshires, she wrote that since Pierce
knew her family were urging her to come home, "he is less likely
than ever to make any concessions [obstructing] the object he has
pursued so steadily for the last three years . . . getting rid of me."[36]
She guessed, probably correctly as it turned out, that he planned to
force her to return to the stage for a living and then bring an action
for divorce.

Pierce had cut off her allowance because she had jibed at signing
a deed readjusting part of the Butler estate. She refused from anxiety
lest some of his antics impair her daughters' eventual financial interests. So when Fanny sailed for England, leaving children and ten
tumultuous years behind her, it was on borrowed money. It probably
came from those vulgar meddlers, the Sedgwicks.

XIV

Year of Consolation

THE THIRTY-SIX-YEAR-OLD WOMAN thus repatriating herself was swathed in defeat. Her ill-considered marriage had miscarried beyond repair. For its sake she had dismantled the professional career that she disliked. She had herself furnished two causes for failure by adopting recklessly, if with good conscience, cross-grained views on marriage and slavery. She had lost not only control of but even contact with her children. Having quarreled, however justifiably, with her chief source of income—her husband—she was practically penniless, which she resented the more because in her time she had much better than supported herself. And her husband's fierce resistance to her returning to the stage for livelihood because—this was always between the lines—her doing so would compromise his dignity and his daughters' reputations had now left her in effect blackmailed into a penurious exile. Her struggle up from this slough of despond was to take several years and leave her a changed woman. That she managed it she owed to innate advantages: she was a poor hand at self-pity, willing to take God's inscrutable purposes and her own shortcomings as ample accounting for what happened to her; and she had an unusual kind of imagination—the topographical. She once said that on the whole she valued places more than people. It was fitting that her realization of two topographical daydreams—the Berkshires and Italy—were important in her recovery from disaster.

Chief among those urging Fanny to take her losses and come home had been Sartoris and Charles Kemble. By the time she arrived, the Sartorises had gone to settle semipermanently in Rome. That left Charles chief emotional reliance of the embittered and confused daughter descending on his doorstep in 44 Mortimer Street, Cavendish Square. He seems to have given her all loyal sympathy and support. His resources for cherishing her were, if not ample, adequate for the time being. He had the income from those New Orleans bank deposits representing capital that had been Fanny's and would be again. The comfortable salary of the Examiner of Plays had been lost when son John Mitchell took over the post from his father. But Charles, though twice retired from the stage, was getting twenty guineas (twenty-one pounds) an evening from occasional public readings of Shakespeare in his own shortened—and cleaned up—versions.[1] It not only brought him a basic livelihood, it was also good for him, as he recognized, thus to stir round out of the Garrick Club, of which he had been a founder and was becoming its grand old man. He took so long there to read the *Times* that other members seldom saw it the same day. The secretary's solution was deferential and realistic: He supplied two copies, "Mr. Kemble's *Times*" and another for the membership generally.[2]

This workable situation was threatened, however, by a growing deafness that promised to cut him off from his cronies' gossip and hamper his readings by keeping him from hearing clearly what his voice did. Since he might have to discontinue readings, provision for distressed, dependent Fanny was indicated. As matters stood, she had only a small legacy from Aunt Victoire, recently deceased, whose will in effect returned some of the money originally meant for Aunt Dall. To safeguard this, it was thought advisable to secure from Pierce a waiver of his presumed right to all his wife's property. The delay thus caused was awkward; so was much else in Fanny's situation. Father and daughter discussed it with their knowledgeable friends and came out persuaded that she had best go back to America accompanied by Charles as father-legal champion and sue Pierce for separate maintenance.

The trip would be expensive but, if the courts found in Fanny's favor, a sound investment, and Charles hoped to finance it with readings in America. That was probably practical provided he was up to it physically. But he heeded that consideration so little that, always sanguine, he even contemplated returning to the stage, not just the reading platform, in the large American cities that had been so receptive ten years previously. Both he and Fanny may have had it in the back of their minds that, though she would be ill-advised to turn actress until after her suit was tried, in case it failed, Charles and she might again join forces to raid Yankee box offices from behind footlights. Say thirty thousand dollars thus acquired in a couple of seasons would make them permanently if modestly comfortable.

Fanny's readiness to hear of such a scheme fitted with her already burgeoning growing wish to return to America soon regardless. Her children were there, recently put into a boarding school in Germantown. They were allowed to write to her periodically but even so three thousand miles of turbulent salt water was a redoubtable barrier emotionally as well as physically. Nor was England's hold on her as firm as she had expected. Yes, the familiar routine was stimulating. Old friends like the Dacres and FitzHughs, newer ones like the Procters and Grotes; dining out twice a week or so with pleasant or strikingly interesting people helped shake off fits of gloom. She told Sarah Cleveland it was all "very brilliant, very amusing, and very kind." [3] To Harriet she wrote: "I ought to be infinitely thankful for my elastic temperament . . . never anything like it but the lady heroine of Andersen's story . . . who had 'cork in her body.' " [4] But she had also told Sarah Cleveland that "English life is not for those who have lived long in America." [5] And, as Henry Lee eventually wrote in a gallant obituary, "Whichever side of the ocean she sojourned, she was homesick for the other." [6] Thus, for all the slaking of her thirst for company worthy of her steel, she also yearned to settle in Lenox, building there a snug house with a beautiful view across a little lake to looming hills; on her desk was a watercolor sketch of the site she had in mind. Nor was it altogether scenery and the proximity of the Sedgwicks she had planned on. The laws of the Commonwealth of Massachusetts were, as American state codes then went, liberal about affording wives something like property rights.

Charles and she settled on a steamer sailing the first week in December. Harriet St. Leger, about to lose Fanny almost as soon as she had landed, protested that the North Atlantic in winter was notorious; they had much better wait till spring. With six crossings behind her, Fanny replied that in spite of the "strong probability of unfavorable weather . . . storms on that tremendous ocean are so *local* . . . that vessels . . . within comparatively small distances of each other . . . do not experience the same tempests. . . . the last time I came to England we sailed on the 1st of December, and had a long but by no means bad voyage."[7] Only this lamentable meteorology was never put to the test. Ten days before the sailing date Charles had an access of common sense and decided that the combined risks of the voyage, the legal contest, and American show business were too poor to venture on.

Almost at once an admirable alternative appeared: The Sartorises wrote affectionately urging her to come spend the winter with them in Rome. Nothing could better have reconciled her to giving up America and Lenox. For Italy was her other and earlier daydream. It went beyond her schoolgirlish yearning for the peninsula so lyrically recommended in Anna Jameson's *Ennuyée,* even beyond the residue of Byron in her tissues. Those were only tingles of an aestheticohistorical cult born some centuries earlier. Italy's topographical beauties were of unique quality; her language was uniquely mellifluous; her singers uniquely skilled, her atmosphere uniquely redolent of artistic virtues and inspirations, so that the sculptor or painter who had never breathed it long and gratefully could hardly qualify as seriously professional. In Fanny's time this was the Italy of Thackeray's *The Newcomes* and Hawthorne's *The Marble Faun;* of London art shows rich with paintings of *pifferari* and *contadine;* and of growing northern European colonies in Florence and Rome.

For along with cultural hegemony went a climate connoting festooned grapevines and *dolce far niente*. Not only Britons but also Scandinavians, Poles, Germans who could afford it took to wintering in these gracious cities where snow seldom came and one actually saw the sun for several days on end. Often physicians had sent them there. It was assumed, and sometimes was true, that those afflicted with tuberculosis, rheumatism, and the vaguely fashionable "delicate health" were better off in Rome than in Stockholm or London. Soon people took up extended residence in Italy because it was what those of means and cultivation often did, just as one went to French and German spas whether ailing or not. And Rome and Florence had urban and aesthetic flavors lacking in Homburg and Vichy.

Fanny had been reading a biography of Dr. Thomas Arnold, the tutelary genius of the Victorian public school, and its extracts from his Italian journals

> made me almost sick with longing . . . odd that this southern mania should return upon me so strongly . . . merely because there seemed to arise . . . a possibility of this long-relinquished hope being fulfilled. I know that I could not live in Italy and . . . should be dreadfully offended by the actual state of the people in the midst of all the past and present glory and beauty . . . a radiant halo round their social and political degradation. But I did once so long to live in Italy, and I have lately so longed to see it.

Now here was Charles not only approving the Sartorises' suggestion, so timely economically and emotionally, but considering going with her, for "he felt rather fatigued . . . would wish to protect me on my journey . . . and . . . never having been in Rome, would like to see it . . . I told him nothing he could do would give me greater pleasure." [8] Within two days, however, he decided to let her go alone and was deep in maps and guidebooks plotting out her best route. But soon he talked off and on of going himself after all, or coming down in the spring after a season of readings had fattened his purse. . . . Old age was tricking him into Pierce Butlerish vacillations.

The matter of the legacy was still holding up money that would now come in handy. *Blackwood's* magazine was taking some of Fanny's recent verses and would pay pretty well—any payment at all, Fanny said, was "good enough for such trumpery" [9]—but the cash in hand was still to come. Even more remote was revenue from the book about her encounter with Italy that she hoped to write. For a while it was disturbingly uncertain whether enough traveling money would be available. Not until December 20 did Fanny and her stolid maid, Bridget Hayes—it was unusual for a lady to make such a trip without male escort, it was almost unthinkable for her to do so altogether unattended—board the little Channel steamer at Southampton bound for *das Land wo die Zitronen blühn*.

Harriet St. Leger's doubts of the wisdom of sailing for America in December might have also applied to travel overland from England to Italy in the same month. Though France was building railroads here and there, through connections for major distances did not exist. The normal if relatively costly way to the warmer South was to choose a clement season and go as Charles Dickens and family had the previous year: in a private carriage drawn by post-horses secured in relays from the inn stables. Since Fanny could not afford that, she had to piece together fragments of several kinds of locomotion. The routing that Charles worked out, following copious advice from experienced friends, was: steamboat to Havre; stagecoach to Rouen; rail to Paris; rail to Nevers; stagecoach across a spur of the Massif Central to Chalon-sur-Saône; steamboat down the Saône to Lyons; more steamboats down the Rhone to Avignon; stagecoach to Marseilles; steamer to Civitavecchia (the port for Rome) via Genoa and Leghorn; stagecoach to Rome—as though it was Philadelphia-to-Darien all over again, even down to the dismalness of spending Christmas on the road.

In fair warning it began ruggedly. The steamer was pursued all the way across the Channel by a gale that Fanny, in the intervals of seasick misery, found as alarming as anything she had seen in mid-Atlantic. But it was reassuring that next morning her excellent French lubricated the confusions of customs and booking the seats she wanted to Rouen. From the old days she knew that remarkable instrument of public transport, the French *diligence,* so grotesque a contrast with both the trim British stagecoach and the well-engineered American Concord. It looked as if designed by a committee instructed to combine the peculiarities of several over-the-road vehicles. Fifteen passengers were packed into its two chief compartments; forward a third called the *coupé* had scant room for three; an indeterminate number occupied the roof; and just behind the high-perched driver was a sort of misplaced rumble seat with a hood called the *cabriolet* that rather airily held two. The whole was so clumsy and

cumbrous a war wagon that even on the good French highways it
needed five horses on level going and might require eight to ten on
upgrades. Fanny secured the whole *coupé* for Hayes and herself by
paying for all three seats, and hoped to manage the same in each
successive *diligence*. They were barely off for Rouen when a blinding
snowstorm came reminding travelers how foolish it was to have
chosen such a time. Eventually the rambling contraption found its
way to the railhead in Rouen where a piggyback arrangement blended
the archaic and the newfangled: a steamhoist lifted the *diligence* off its
wheels, luggage and all, and set it down on railroad trucks to complete the trip to Paris behind a locomotive. Of this, Fanny's first visit
there in twenty years, we know only that she saw some acquaintances;
whatever she did, she wasn't long about it, for by December 26 she
was in Nevers, presumably having spent Christmas in the train, and
impatiently awaiting the loosely scheduled *diligence* thence for
Chalon. There was no difficulty about securing the *coupé*—at that
time of year few cared to cross the Morvan heights, frequently snowbound, reputed still wild enough to harbor bandits and wolves and
at best primitive people and accommodations. The Kembles' friends
recommending this route had met it only in summer, when its
rugged beauties imply less risk.

In time a semi-*diligence* with only three horses dawdled in and
picked up Fanny and Hayes. Level ground for a while; then the horses
were laboring up gentle and then steeper slopes. At a roadside inn
where they stopped after dark to sup, the uncouth local people's talk
was all of impassable snows ahead. But the *diligence* went indomitably
forward, Fanny and Hayes with it, through woods and fields already
menacingly snowy. At the next hamlet reports of snow-choked highways were even firmer, but on they plodded, Fanny lying cold and
jostly on the transverse seat, Hayes possibly warmer but just as jostly
in the straw supplied to keep passengers' feet dry. At the next hamlet
there was no more to be said: they were well and truly snowbound
until shovels and possible thaws cleared the road ahead to let the
complementary *diligence* from Chalon come over; whereas Fanny had
been assured that there would be no change of vehicle all the way.

She was earning her beakers full of the warm south.

> My dismay and indignation were intense. The rain was
> pouring, the wind was roaring, and it was twelve o'clock
> at night. The inn . . . was the most horrible cutthroat-
> looking hole I ever beheld . . . a dirty, sleepy, stupid
> servant girl . . . ushered us into a kitchen as black as
> darkness itself and a single tallow candle could make it
> . . . now invaded by a tall brawny looking man in a sort
> of rough sporting costume . . . two sizable dogs that he
> had with him . . . running in and out . . . all but
> knocking us down . . . I . . . could have cried for very
> cowardice. I asked this person what was to be done; he
> answered that he was in the same predicament . . . I
> could do, if I liked, as he should,—walk over the moun-
> tains to Autun next day [a mere stroll of thirty miles—or]
> if the snow was no higher than the horses' bellies, or if
> the laborers of the district had been out clearing the roads
> . . . the master of the house might contrive some means
> of sending me on.[10]

And so it came to pass in the morning. Heavy rain had washed
off most of the snow overnight. The innkeeper, whose smallpox-
pitted face and lack of one eye lent him a disturbingly villainous air,
knew an opportunity when he saw it and exacted an enormous hire
for "a crazy, dirty, rickety sort of gig . . . and a crazy, dirty, rickety
pair of horses"[11] to transport to Autun this extraordinary *anglaise* who
looked like a Gypsy, behaved and spoke French like an indignant
duchess, and went traveling with only a maid for escort under conditions that would daunt most men.

Contrary to apparent probability, the gig and its sinister driver
made Autun without falling apart, the Hôtel de la Poste provided an
appetizing dinner in a comfortable room . . . things were looking
up. But next morning the *coupé* was unavailable. For ten hours Fanny
had to endure the atmosphere created by "a snuffy German, a French-
man reeking of stale cigar smoke . . . two India rubber cloaks [early
rubber garments were very smelly], and all our respirations,"[12] for,
of course, nobody else but Fanny would have dreamed of opening a
window and admitting a probably fatal *courant d'air*. At Chalon the
Saône was so high in flood that steamboats could not pass under the
bridges. That meant sixteen hours roundabout to Lyons in another
diligence instead of a comfortable eight hours by water.

Yet some compensations appeared: "I shall sleep in a bed for the first time tonight since last Wednesday . . . this is Monday. What a pity we make our luxuries things of every day and night. I positively look forward to my bed. Who that goes to bed every night does?" Add "the admirable perch from the Saône that I had for dinner . . . nearly two pounds . . . delicious . . . nothing could be better, but catching it," [13] said Thérèse De Camp's daughter. Next day the third passenger in the *coupé* was a bourgeois official from Lyons versed in medieval antiquities who was admirable company, squiring Fanny into the fine old church at Tournus and expertly discussing its architectural significance with the parish priest. Here she had pangs of conscience that might give thought to the many, many tourists for whom reverend churches are mere sightseers' trophies:

> It is extremely painful to me to come from a mere motive of curiosity into a temple dedicated to God; my conscience rebukes and troubles me the whole time, and all other considerations are lost in the recollection that I am in the house of prayer, consecrated by the worship of thousands of souls for hundreds of years. To gaze about, too, with idle, prying eyes, where sit and kneel my fellow-Christians with theirs turned to the earth in solemn contemplation or devotion, makes me feel sacrilegiously [*sic*] . . . I prayed as I stood before the altar in that dear little old church. [14]

Such ups and downs—the rapacious innkeeper of Château-Chinon and the cultivated Lyonnais antiquarian (who brought his pretty daughter to call on Fanny before she departed downriver); the delicious fish at Chalon and the squalor of the *diligences*—were at least good distraction from her traumatic past. To heighten stimuli, she was finding that her long stay in America lent crosslights, some rather ironical, on what she was now encountering: "If I had travelled more on the Continent," she told herself, "before I went to America, I should have been infinitely less surprised and annoyed . . . at the various unpleasant peculiarities of its inhabitants." The same sensibility that deplored American hotels' frowsiness and lack of privacy now marveled at French inns' serving attractive and toothsome meals on good china and yet letting the rest of the establishment range

from slatternly to filthy. Though tobacco chewing was not the cause
here, she was dismayed to find irresponsible spitting as much or more
of a scandal and menace among the run of Frenchmen:

> Oh, my poor, dear American fellow-citizens! how humbly
> . . . I do beg your pardon for all the reproaches I have
> levelled against your national diversion of spitting. Here
> I sit in the cabin [of the Lyons-Valence steamboat] sur-
> rounded with men hawking and spitting; and whereas
> spittoons have hitherto been the bane of my life in the
> United States, a spittoon here today . . . would have
> been the delight of my eyes. How I thought, too, of the
> honor and security, in which a woman might travel alone
> from Georgia to Maine . . . certain of assistance, atten-
> tion, the most respectful civility, the most humane pro-
> tection, from every man she meets . . . as though she
> were [his] sister or daughter.[15]

She was surprised to find herself defending America or at least
trying to convince several prosperous French businessmen-travelers
that they misinterpreted the defaults of American state securities that
seemed as much on the French as on Sydney Smith's mind:

> It is the most difficult thing in the world to make these
> people comprehend the complex [relation] of the federal
> and state governments . . . [or that] while in certain of
> the states . . . public securities have turned out no secu-
> rities at all, there exist others . . . whose credit, both
> financial and moral, is as solid . . . as any in the world
> . . . the general government appears to them responsible
> for the State insolvencies. The United States Bank is, to
> their apprehension, a government institution, instead of a
> private speculation; and President Polk and Nicholas Bid-
> dle, and Pennsylvania, Illinois, Massachusetts, and South
> Carolina, are all involved in one broad sentence of national
> dishonesty and want of faith.[16]

Even now there is no help for other versions of this familiar difficulty.

Fanny liked the courteous hospitality of the Avignon hotel;
thought Marseilles harsh and hideously expensive; deplored everything about the steamer out of Marseilles but admired Genoa so much
that she wished she could stay six months; at Leghorn probably got

more pleasure out of pacing the deck and watching the shipping and the heavens than her fellow passengers did out of their hurried excursion to Pisa; on landing at Civitavecchia found the *diligence* to Rome the filthiest and most decrepit yet. But as it lurched and creaked through the Campagna, she rejoiced in the "vast open expanse of yellow down" and "herds of beautiful iron-grey oxen." Toward sunset came indications that the city was near; then:

> Suddenly against the clear azure of the sky, a huge shadowy cupola rose up . . . rose higher and higher . . . and . . . St. Peter's stood over against us; towering into the violet-colored sky . . . I really saw it; I knew the whole form of the great, wonderful structure; I knew the huge pillars of the noble arcade, and the pale, ghost-like shining of the moonlit fountains . . . I was in Rome . . . the very Rome of my imagination.

Then "deep, dark, stinking streets" and a customs house to endure. A servant from the Sartoris household met and took her in an open carriage "up steep and slippery pavements to the Pincio, where, at a lighted window, I saw a woman's figure. I scrambled up three pairs of stone stairs, and so into my sister's arms, worn out, and ready to die with the fatigue of coming, and the emotion of being come." [17]

The views from the Sartorises' spacious apartment were admirable foretastes of "the very Rome of my imagination." Gradually, cordially, Fanny was taken to the Colosseum, the Vatican, and so on; treated to long rides in the Campagna; and, when Carnival came on, shown its traditional fooleries at the best times and places. She came out of that with her stays full of confetti and her head full of pungent detail that made several notable pages in the journal she kept with the eventual book in mind:

> I should certainly preserve no record whatever . . . but for the very disagreeable conviction that it is my duty to do so if there is, as I believe there is, the slightest probability of my being able by this means to earn a little money to avoid drawing on my father's resources. I have a great contempt for the barren balderdash I write but a

thing is worth what it will fetch, and if a bookseller will
buy my trash, I will sell it to him.[18]

As usual she was too hard on her casual writings. True, the
poems scattered through the eventual text are seldom distinguished,
interesting largely because some of them record her pining after her
children and plucky efforts to make peace with her recent history.
Her dutifully prolix accounts of her awe of the Apollo Belvedere,
Raphael's paintings, and so on differ from her contemporaries' prattle
about art only by using a slightly brisker idiom. (Even the best of
that sort of thing now sounds vapid and impertinent; God knows
what our great-grandchildren will think of what we now perpetrate
on such subjects.) The liveliest part of her book is the opening pages
dealing with that rattletrap scramble the length of France. But some
very good writing came from her joy in the loveliness of Roman gardens, the strange winter beauties of the Campagna and, the views
from the villa at Frascati whither the Sartorises shifted themselves
when warm weather came on. Her accumulating enjoyments made it
gracefully appropriate for her to entitle her book *A Year of Consolation*. Nor were scenery and the distractions of traveler's hardships the
only therapeutic agents. One is aware between the lines of her letters
as well as her book that the two sisters' serene hours together, laughing at the same things, singing folksongs together, immersing themselves companionably in the flowers and sunshine that meant much to
both, were generously healing. Sartoris too, for all his past suspicions
of Fanny's waywardness and her suspicions that he was too indolent
for his own good, was a background support so thoughtful and reassuring that she dedicated *Consolation* to him as "a most inadequate
token of gratitude, this record of the happy year I spent in Italy."

She had ample cause for that word *happy*. The omnipresence of
running water in formal courtyards and farmyards alike, the fanciful
cataracts at Tivoli, the streamlets threading through and down from
the forested mountains were, of course, her never-failing delight. She
is sitting by a watering trough made of an antique sarcophagus:

> Presently came two of the beautiful mouse-colored oxen of
> the campagna, slowly, through the arched gate of the

farm-yard, and, leaning their serious-looking heads upon
the stone basin, drank soberly with their great eyes fixed
on us . . . I, for the first time in my life, almost com-
prehending the delight of listless inactivity. As the water
ran lullingly by my side . . . between the gray shafts of
the pine trees . . . the distant landscape formed into separate and distinct pictures in incomparable beauty . . . I
think I could actually be content to sit on that fountain's
edge, and do nothing but listen and look for a whole summer's afternoon.[19]

The overt traits of this Italy she had yearned for—*dolce far niente*,
a surfeit of Great Art and landscapes making the backgrounds of famous portraits come true—were clichés not only proving real but
carrying rewarding quirks: the hoked-up waterworks at Tivoli were
coupled with the lurid, thundering pandemonium of the iron forges
powered by the falling water. In the dreamy, ruin-studded Campagna
she relished the "wide-awake determined air [of Italian daisies] which
would have made Burns' address to them absolutely ironical . . . the
most unhesitating white, with little stiff-necked stalks and faces all
turned up to the sky with a degree of self-possession quite astonishing
in a mere daisy."[20] Doubtless Italy shrugged off as something to be
expected of foreigners this woman taking her morning walks to no
particular goal in the paths round Frascati merely to work up a glow
and then souse herself in the cold water of the courtyard fountain.
Sometimes she soused Adelaide's children along with her and then
they all went to breakfast with good appetite. On one early ramble
she met a peasant girl who, reared to consider walking alone risky for
a woman, commented: " '*Ma come, siete sola?*' " to which, or maybe
to her own thoughts, Fanny replied, " '*Si, sola, sola,*' " and was answered: " '*E meglio sola che mal accompagnata!*' " "God keep her in
that mind,"[21] Mrs. Pierce Butler wrote in her journal. Having once
prided herself on liking to be alone, she was still finding that condition to be, though no positive good, a refuge from failure to find
happiness by staking it on others. The point was the clearer because
of occasional necessary correspondence to and from her Philadelphia
lawyers about Pierce's failures to live up to financial agreements.

The company she met at the Sartorises' large parties was often

English; when not, cosmopolitan, and conversation was in French. Fanny's book-fashion Italian had long enabled her to read Dante with respectful pleasure. Now in a few weeks, being nimble in languages, she could chat capably with shopkeepers, coachmen, et al. She had small use for the shopkeepers. Their insistent haggling in any and all transactions and their flat inability to accord foreigners anything near actual going price vastly irked her. She was dismayed as well as annoyed by the incessant begging, not merely among professional beggars and probable hardship cases, but common among well-fed laborers in the middle of their work, so that to her much of it seemed rather evidence of demoralization than of economic necessity. So did the almost universal obsession with the state lottery. These subjects of the pope were a pleasure to look at for not only "positive beauty of form and brilliancy of coloring, but a noble carriage, an ease, a grace, a dignity . . . above all, the grand style of their heads, that makes them pre-eminently subjects for artistic illustration . . . only in Italy . . . I have seen men's faces as positively beautiful as women's, and that frequently."[22] But her sense of fitness and northern morality led her to deplore the contrast between this nobility of form and lack of self-respect and devotion to gimcrackery.

Further disillusion was implicit in the hill villages round Rome that "delight the eye and invite the approach of the beholder, but . . . a nearer approach will only produce, in recompense for toiling up steep, stinking, slippery streets, lined with squalid habitations, and thronged with filthy inhabitants, the commonest of all earthly experiences—disappointment."[23] And in the vintage season, "when the entire population seems poured into the vineyards . . . the warm air is tipsy with the smell of the grapes, borne in tubs on the backs of mules . . . up every steep winding village path, to the huge vats, where the process of treading them is performed." But there ensues a change of tone "from the glory and the grace of the fragrant vine-bunches . . . under their fresh, glittering leaves, to the half-smashed dirty amalgamation of bruised discolored berries . . . jolted in nasty high narrow tubs . . . to the hideous-looking red-brown scum, in which a hairy, sweating, brawny peasant prances . . . his limbs be-smeared as though with blood."[24]

The ambivalence of her feelings about this Rome to which she would owe so much reminds one that the unification of Italy was then far in the future and the pope was still semifeudal sovereign of a broad belt of lands across the upper shank of the bootleg. These Papal States were not as hopeless as the Mezzogiorno below Naples. But Fanny saw them when they were no great credit to the social sensitivities of Gregory XVI. During her stay in Rome, he died and Pius IX succeeded him on Saint Peter's throne. For a short while, with amnesty for the throng of political prisoners in the papal jails and a loosening of censorship, it looked as if some breaths of politicosocial improvement might waft in from outside. Fanny's eventual book had a closing section, published as an article in magazines, reflecting the hopeful gossip then simmering among the foreign colony. But the windows soon closed again and in any case the end of her year had yet to show her much to modify her views of this festering little country of slipshod tyranny and institutionalized beauty. She had struck her keynote after the first week of her stay when they drove her up to a famous villa with "a most glorious view" over the city and the Campagna to the sea beyond: "Here (as everywhere) we were pursued by the shameless, wretched pauperism that disgusts and pains one the whole time . . . I would not live among these people for anything in the world; and when I think of England and America, I thank God that I was born in the one and shall live in the other."[25]

In that context it was significant that Italy—as well as the expectorating French—often brought America to her mind and that she often used American traits as touchstones for Italian things and ways. The climate of Rome in January she likened to that of the Sea Islands in that month—until the sirocco came along to vex her. A certain view in the hills beyond Frascati was "a perfectly ideal landscape, such as I have seen only once before in my life, at the twin lakes of Salisbury, in Connecticut." Her joy in the exuberant beauty of vegetables in Roman markets takes her into a rhapsody about midsummer in Philadelphia running over with tomatoes, sweet corn, watermelon, peaches. . . . Seeing a woman working an archaic handloom, she remarks that "so antiquated a machine . . . could hardly be found in Philadelphia."[26] And the cheapness of Italian provisions as compared to English leads to several pages about Americans' wastefulness of food, linking it ingeniously if not convincingly to the general economic flightiness that made speculation in land and business ventures as well as securities an abiding American vice.

Even in treating hopes of the new pope she contrasts his approaching troubles with reaction with the healthier position of the Roman Catholic Church in America where it

> thrives, and spreads, and flourishes, because it is separate from the political government . . . as religion it is the most pliant, malleable, insinuating, pervading, and powerful that has yet existed; as government, it is rigid, uncompromising, despotic. . . . The Bishop of Rome may yet be the powerful head of the most powerful sect of Christendom. I doubt if he can ever be the enlightened sovereign of a people with free institutions . . . the acclamations which precede and follow the present Pope's footsteps . . . seem to me to demand impossibilities, and to foretell disappointment.[27]

One cannot know how much of that crisp pessimism was her own thinking and how much of it was speculation heard across the dinner tables of Rome's foreign colony, but whatever its origin, it accurately prophesied what would befall Pio Nono as vehicle of liberal hopes. That political chapter in *A Year of Consolation* was properly hailed by the *North American Review* as "much the best account we have yet had"[28] of the Roman political climate. And its prescribing separation of church and state for the pope and his political holdings, however fantastic, showed how much experience in America—as well as passing years and still unresolved personal troubles—had contributed to the growing up of "dear good little me." Fanny Kemble was incapable of turning essentially American. But she had the psychological good luck to absorb into herself certain American essences that combined with her own salutarily—sometimes more so than she herself may have realized.

She could have stayed on more or less indefinitely with the Sartorises. Though in later life Adelaide and she occasionally disagreed, both being of definite ideas and great ability to express them, the relationship was on the whole harmonious. But as the end of the year that Fanny had apportioned for therapy neared, she was writing verses about the grateful grief of departure and made a deliberate visit to the Trevi fountain to take the sip of water that would bring her back sometime. Apparently the modern notion of throwing in a coin was yet to come. The elder method worked. Twice more in future years Fanny stayed long and fruitfully in Rome.

On December 8, 1846, 353 days after she had left England, she left Rome homeward bound.

XV

Footlights Again

THERE IS NO RECORD of Fanny's return from Italy to England in late
December 1846; we assume that she did not travel by way of the
Morvan heights. She was home before the holidays and staying with
the FitzHughs at Bannisters, pondering two ways to improve her
slender resources. Her projected book might bring some money; and
she was determined to free herself of dependency on her father and
work up a modest competence of her own by returning to the stage.

The first was cheeringly easy. She had written ahead to Edward
Moxon, a well-established publisher whom she knew from Rogers's
famous breakfasts; indeed Rogers had set him up in business.
Fanny—and no doubt Moxon too—understood that her resumption
of acting might help sell a book with her name on it. Even before he
saw the manuscript he offered a substantial advance and willingly
held off publication until an American edition was arranged; that was
advisable because transatlantic literary piracy not only flourished but
was still legal. So when Sarah Cleveland, reporting to Fanny about
having been to Philadelphia and finding the children getting along all
right, also offered to lend Fanny any funds she might need, the reply
was that there was no current emergency, thanks. She might yet sue
Pierce but meanwhile:

> I am about to return to my former profession. A few
> months of hard work at this distasteful trade will furnish
> me with present . . . independence and enable me to se-
> cure something for my girls hereafter—should Mr. Butler

or his creditors interfere . . . I shall either go to St. Petersburg and act where one tyranny will protect me from another or return to Massachusetts where under the protection of your own equitable laws I may hope to be permitted to keep the benefit of my own labour.[1]

For frontispiece *Consolation* had the engraving, not quite as insipid as some, of Sully's portrait of Fanny as Beatrice, all youth and merry charm. For a more pertinent portrait of the woman now setting out to wrest renewed recognition and badly needed money from the English-speaking theater, this is how a minor actor saw her at the Theatre Royal, Liverpool, during her reappearance tour:

> [She] walked upon the Liverpool stage (where we awaited the arrival with anxiety and curiosity) alone and unattended. We had expected to see a tragedy queen. We saw instead a quiet, unassuming lady of middle age . . . simply attired in a dark silk dress. Her pale, classic features were irradiated by a pair of dark, lustrous eyes which wore an eerie expression—imperious one moment, pleading the next . . . in vivid contrast to the abundant hair, even then slightly streaked with grey at the temples.

The men took off their hats, "she responded in one comprehensive and gracious courtesy, then . . . commenced the rehearsal."[2]

This decorous self-possession had been bolstered by a successful week at Manchester and two successful nights at Birmingham demonstrating that she could still reward an audience's attention. The way to that reassurance had not been altogether smooth. Soon after arriving, she had written to Bunn in a pretty regal tone: "It is my intention to return for the present to the stage. . . . You will oblige me by informing me whether it will suit you to enter into some arrangement."[3] He asked for her terms; she mentioned one hundred pounds a week; he offered fifty, and negotiations stopped there. Overtures made by the manager of the Princess' Theatre—new, permissive legislation now allowed more theaters into the London field—also petered out. Fanny had had no experience dickering with managers. Charles had always done that and well enough; her diffident awareness of this handicap made her a poor woman of business. She was also uneasily aware that

> a stout, middle-aged, not particularly good-looking
> woman, such as I then was, is not a very satisfactory rep-
> resentative of Juliet or Julia; nor had . . . nine years of
> private life improved my talent for acting such as it was.
> . . . While losing the few personal qualifications . . .
> the principal one was youth . . . [that] I ever possessed
> for younger heroines, I had gained none but age as a rep-
> resentative of Lady Macbeth, Queen Katherine, etc.

Things soon looked less bleak, however, when an offer of forty
pounds a week came in unsolicited from the theater in Manchester; a
break-in in the provinces before assailing London was a sound procedure and forty quid was forty quid. Hastily putting a touring wardrobe together, Fanny took to the road again attended by the faithful
Hayes, with not only Manchester but Birmingham, Liverpool, Dublin in prospect. It was like old times; only instead of Charles to steer
the ship, her sole support was Hayes who, having been whirled
through French blizzards and Italian carnivals, was now pitchforked,
unprepared but stubbornly calm, into the strange world of backstage
and "Overture, Mrs. Butler, overture!"[4]

Manchester proved better than promising. Its new Theatre Royal
was "one of the prettiest, brightest, and most elegant playhouses I
ever saw."[5] The owner-manager was enterprising and intelligent, his
stage manager pleasant and professional, the supporting company
"better than I shall probably find anywhere, even in London" in spite
of the usual slipshod attitude toward thoroughly learning lines. It
was rash of management and star to lead off with Fanny's well-re-
membered mainstay, *The Hunchback,* thus tempting comparison between her glowing, giddy Julia of sixteen years since and what she
might make of her now; probably only Juliet would have been riskier:
"I wondered at myself as I stood at the side scene . . . without any
quickening of the pulse."[6] The roar of applause as the house "rose to
her" in welcome was temporarily agitating and disconcerting; she had
been dreading its potential effects. But she soon got herself in hand
and after the final curtain could assure herself that "my physical
power of voice and delivery is not diminished, which is good for
tragedy; my self-possession is increased, which ought to be good for

comedy. . . . I may succeed . . . by going from one place to another, and returning to America, when I have worked out my public
favour here—say, in two years—to make what will enable me to live
independently."[7] Always that yearning to reach funded security; and,
as usual, that assumption that America was her eventual destination.

Thus bolstered emotionally, she had gratifying results as Juliana
in *The Honeymoon,* "a rather pretty, foolish part which I act accordingly; Lady Macbeth, which I never could, and cannot, and never
shall can act; and Juliet, which, I suppose, I play neither better nor
worse than formerly, but which, naturally, I am no longer personally
fit to represent."[8] The Liverpool *Guardian* spelled that out not altogether impolitely a few weeks later by noting that, while her work
was satisfactory enough, "her features bear traces of chequered health
and much thoughtfulness,"[9] as they had every reason to. There was
both tonic realism and regret in her lively sense of the changed relation between her physical equipment and the role that had launched
her on the road to fame if not fortune. Later that year a pushy young
actor asked her to recommend him to William Murray, in Edinburgh, where she was soon to appear, as a possible Romeo to her
Juliet. She replied that Murray already had a competent Romeo and
besides, "as I am quite old enough to be your mother . . . it would
be more advantageous to you to have a much younger Juliet and far
better for me to have an older Romeo."[10] Yet, to managers' dismay,
she refused to avail herself of new methods of stage makeup that
might mitigate the effects of time. She had never objected to the
heavy rouge that gaslight made necessary; but now actresses were
thickly whitening necks, arms, hands, "which I found it impossible
to accept." When Henry Greville, a loyally close friend in spite of a
stagestruck habit of offering advice on professional matters, told
Fanny that "what so beautiful a woman as Madame [Giulia, a great
operatic star] Grisi condescended to do, for the improvement of her
natural charm, was not to be disdained by a person so comparatively
ugly," she "steadfastly refused to make a whited sepulchre of myself
and continued to confront the public with my own skin, looking
. . . like a gipsy, or when . . . with any feminine coadjutor, like a
bronze figure vis-a-vis with a Plaster of Paris cast."[11]

Manchester's welcome included sundry invitations to dine. Soldier brother Henry, long stationed in Dublin, came over to visit the sister he had not seen for years and promised to mount her on a good horse when she played Dublin. There she was so successful that the Irish manager, like his counterpart at Manchester, talked return engagements. The lord lieutenant had her invited to the castle. . . . Then she went back to England for short-engagement trouping in the old fashion. It was simpler these days, for in the seventeen years since her memorable ride with George Stephenson, Britain had built a spider web of railroads and towns she played were accessible in commodious rail carriages. Fanny resented the new rail-line through the romantic ravine between Princes Street and Edinburgh's Castle Rock. But the vehicles that the iron horses drew were much preferable to the slower, if dashing, old stagecoaches. When she and Hayes were sole occupants of a ladies' compartment, she stretched out on the floor to sleep, with the clicking of the wheels only occasionally broken by the scream of the whistle.

The retirement hoard was slowly but steadily building up and the Princess's management was again showing signs of interest. In Liverpool Fanny found her cousin, Charles Kemble Mason, brother of the John Mason with whom she had acted in Bath and New York—a "lamentable actor"[12] but pleasant and wise in theatrical ways and willing to be her manager—an ally she greatly needed. She was working hard and not even showing signs of the impatience with footlights and stage jewelry that might have been reviving by this time. Now the Princess's manager came offering a mere fifteen pounds a week and, doubtless acting on Charles Mason's advice—for a London appearance for her was by now highly advisable—she accepted it. Her opening in *The Hunchback* was most cordially received by a crowded pit and full dress circle but the cheaper parts of the house were not so prosperous; and the *Illustrated London News* regretted that the supporting actors were not the sort of assistance she should have had. Fanny herself "is altered in appearance, as might be expected," but "her voice is . . . improved . . . evidences of care and intelligence—of matured judgment and acute perception—were visible throughout."[13]

Then a physical emergency intervened. Hemorrhoids consequent on the birth of Frances grew incapacitatingly painful and surgery had to be resorted to. Such an operation under conditions then prevalent—no knowledge of asepsis, no professionally trained nurses, oral morphine the best available analgesic—was grim. Fortunately ether and chloroform to anesthetize during the operation were newly available.[14] Fanny's dear friend, Fanny Longfellow, had had a very favorable experience with ether during childbirth. But Fanny Kemble, who always did things her own way, though well aware of the exquisite painfulness of what lay ahead, would have none of anesthetics on characteristic grounds: "Though torture is a serious thing, to lose all self government is a still more serious thing and I would rather know what I suffer than not know what I was saying or doing."[15]

As she recuperated from this Spartan-minded ordeal, another kind of trouble resumed: the trickle of letters from her children dried up. She had known that to resume acting risked Pierce's wrath but her empty purse left her no choice. Now she assumed, correctly, that as "the last and only cruel tyranny that remains for him to perpetrate,"[16] he had forbidden Sarah and Frances to write to her at all. He had long been acting his own character to perfection. Though Fanny had done her part in the settlement before leaving America by signing away her dower right to secure safeguards for the children's eventual interests, Pierce was dragging his feet on his part. Charles Sumner,[17] a warm friend of Fanny's who was her trustee in the approaching settlement, had not yet succeeded in cajoling or browbeating the final documents out of him; and Fanny's lawyer in Philadelphia was gloomily reverting to advising bringing suit for either separation or divorce—against which Fanny sometimes had scruples.

A gratuitous emotional wrench had come earlier that spring when the stagestruck Grevilles arranged a revival of that amateur performance of Lord Ellesmere's version of *Hernani* that had brought Craven and Fanny together in 1832. They asked her to play Donna Sol again; she consented; and again Craven played opposite! It had curious repercussions on her eventual reputation as actress. In the audience was Macready, with whom the Princess's management had been dealing as a costar to team with Fanny. He thought Henry Greville and a couple of others not bad for amateurs, but Mrs. Butler, he went home and told his diary, was "ignorant of the first rudiments of her art . . . affected, monotonous, without one real impulse—never in the feeling of the character, never true in look, attitude or tone. She can never be an actress and this I never ventured to think before."[18] One can understand that her performance may have suffered from crowding memories of not so long ago when Craven and she were engaged not in déjà vu but the real thing; nor can Macready have been aware of this probable drag on her. So when, a generation later, his diary was posthumously published, this resounding condemnation, reinforced by his blistering account of her acting as his costar later, made a great stir on the Rialto. Fanny herself contributed to that end by quoting the worst of it in her memoirs and adding wryly that there might well be something in it.

By early summer she was enough recovered from her operation and the associations of *Hernani* to go touring again with bookings Mason arranged in the west country and the midlands. In the autumn she trouped Scotland. Edinburgh was a delight and old friends invaluable, but sadness pervaded it all because Andrew Combe's long frailness had recently culminated in death. Her threnody for him helps one understand how salutary her religious bent could be:

> My first feeling was one almost of joy and congratulation . . . on first hearing of a good man's death . . . I have an instantaneous sense of relief . . . of infirmity, pain, sorrow, trouble, fleshly hindrance, and earthly suffering forever laid in the grave . . . and that glorious structure, a noble human soul, soaring into a purer atmosphere proper to it, and prompted to such higher duties as may well be deemed rewards for duties well fulfilled on earth. After a little while I began to cry, thinking of that sweet, beaming, intelligent, benevolent countenance, that I am never to see here again, but this was crying for myself, not for him.[19]

And now Fanny's second stage career was to culminate in London in a strangely turbulent, anticlimactic fashion.

The prelude was ominously agitating. A committee raising funds to buy and preserve Shakespeare's birthplace staged at Covent Garden an elaborate benefit with as many big names as possible doing scenes from the plays. Fanny disliked the scheme. She said a house in which Shakespeare had lived might have some point, but the mere building where he had been a mere baby doubtless behaving like other babies . . . Nevertheless she agreed to do Queen Katharine's death scene from *Henry VIII*. Thus again to match her voice and stage presence against the vastness of Covent Garden, built by Kembles, where so many Kembles had bidden the stage farewell, where she herself had so fatefully soared into fame, was necessarily a strain. It seems to have added to her effectiveness onstage as the distressed queen and then shatteringly backfired. The tumultuous applause after her scene built into an imperative demand for a curtain call. But she found the very notion of going back on the stage even momentarily intolerable: "I was seized with a perfect nervous terror . . . and left the house as quickly as possible. All the other actors will go on, and I shall incur unpleasant comments . . . for having, ungraciously withdrawn myself from the public call."[20]

And so it doubtless went. But she had been masterfully impressive. That may have helped to consummate a deal that had been blowing hot and cold and now, with Fanny half-distracted by conflicting advice from friends, was definite: She was to costar with Macready at the Princess' Theatre four nights a week. Rehearsals began.

Almost immediately both had reason to regret the engagement. Antagonism between Fanny and Macready should have been unlikely not only because of their previous friendly acquaintance, but because in several ways their stories were at least superficially similar. His father too was an actor-manager, albeit of only provincial status, who also had sought to keep his son from acting. Destined for the bar, William Charles was sent to Rugby, even then a renowned "public school."[21] In his case too the father's financial woes forced the son to go on the stage. First as cleverly precocious boy-manager, then as his own leading man, he saved the family day. As in Fanny's case his first appearance was in *Romeo & Juliet*—for once Romeo was and looked as young as the script implies. Mrs. Siddons observed him during a tour of the provinces and told him he had a future if he worked hard and did not marry before he was thirty. Sure enough, though his bright blue eyes and alert manner made women look kindly on him, he did not marry until his thirtieth birthday. He did not need the rest of Melpomene's advice. He was already fanatically diligent in studying roles and working out stage business, and soon he had skills enough for Charles Kemble to engage him for "second business" (Bassanio, say, Laertes, Macduff) at Covent Garden.

But for the most striking parallel with Fanny: Macready too despised the theater and its people. Though the family dramatics that his children staged for him moved him tenderly, he never let them see him perform until he was ready to retire and meanwhile was apprehensive lest they stray into acting. After a difficult rehearsal he snarls into his diary: *"What are these players? Are they not the veriest shams that ever disgraced manhood?* Have they a thought of purposes beyond escape from labour, the indulgence of their self-conceit and sensuality?" That is worse than anything that either Fanny or Wilhelm Meister ever said. He was even more impatient, savage indeed, about slovenly minor actors' neglect to learn their lines on the London as well as the provincial stage. And again like Fanny, he did not spare himself when he thought his night's performance did not ring true: "Acted Lord Hastings very ill indeed in the worst possible taste and style. I really am ashamed to think of it. . . . Whatever is good enough to play is good enough to play well. . . . I am worse than a common nightly drudge." [22] One likes him for that, no less because otherwise he was hard to like.

Now divergencies begin: Whereas Fanny never doubted she was a lady and to be received as such, she also took in stride the persistence of social onus for actors. Macready not only insisted on his status as gentleman and expected to be asked to dine at distinguished tables—as he sometimes was—but remained oversensitive about possible snubs and scornful innuendo. From great folks' amateur theatricals Fanny derived amusement and liked seeing them enjoying themselves. From such doings Macready, however, derived, says an admirable recent biography, a "conviction . . . well grounded, that the profession to which he was allied was . . . despised by the very

people who played at it [as patrician amateurs]. . . . the highest
commendation that several memorialists can find to make of Macready is that no one would ever guess him to be an actor. And Macready, while resenting these opinions, shared them." [23] Some of that
reminds one of Fanny's hope that she did not carry the "brand" of the
profession. But she arrived at that by a more self-respecting, not to
say haughtily Kembleish, route. Though none can doubt that her
having been an actress had something to do with her social troubles
in Philadelphia, she took that to be evidence of Philadelphia's cultural retardation.

Macready disliked and strongly mistrusted Charles Kemble,
which may have influenced his professional relations with Fanny. In
the old days at Covent Garden he had resented his employer's taking
all the leading roles in serious plays—as was, of course, Charles's
prerogative as company leading man. Reconciliation sometimes
seemed imminent but always aborted. Macready's diary calls Charles
"scoundrel" for using his daughter to solve the family financial problems. To make it up with such a man, Macready warned himself in
typically temperate terms, would amount to "alliance with fraud,
treachery, falsehood, the meanest and most malignant species of in-
trigue . . . vileness and profligacy of the most barefaced
character." [24] Bitterly he scolded himself for lacking courage to refuse
to contribute to the fund for the silver trophy celebrating Charles's
retirement from the stage. (Fanny, hearing of the scheme, said she
wished they'd skip the trophy and give him the cash it would cost.)
Deeply Macready resented the Crown's giving Charles the lucrative
post of Examiner of Plays; he had had an eye on it for himself. Complaining about it to his diary, he refused to allow a single "amiable
or estimable trait" [25] to this man whom most liked and many honored.

Even had the Kembles seen these journal entries, however, they
need not have taken them hard, for as Downer has written, Macready's "ill-concealed contempt for his calling" and "naturally violent temper" had left him "scarcely a friend in his profession, at any
rate of the masculine gender." [26] Had Fanny seen them, she would
probably have refused to act with him. As it was, the early phase of

their acquaintance was nothing ominous. It was Macready to whom she chose to send *An English Tragedy,* the play she considered the only worthy thing she ever wrote, from America in 1841; and no bad blood developed when, after properly scrupulous consideration, he rejected it as powerful but too gamy in substance for the stage of the time. During the Butlers' subsequent stay in London Macready, having met Pierce somewhere, called at Harley Street and, aware that Fanny had admired one of his performances, was prepared to like "her frank and genuine manner very much indeed. . . . rarely . . . have I seen a person I have been so taken with."[27] Two years later, as has been seen, the Butlers saw a good deal of him in New York and even let him somewhat into their confidence—separately—about their troubles. Now, however, for reasons hidden in his turbulent psyche, he had made up his mind that Fanny was personally brittle and professionally worthless. His only reason for consenting to her acting with him at the Princess must have been that her name on the billing would be a valuable supplementary "draw."

On her part she was apprehensive because of gossip about the physical hazards of acting with him, about "actors whose eyes had been almost thrust out by his furious fighting in Macbeth . . . others . . . nearly throttled . . . actresses whose arms had been almost wrenched out of their sockets . . . buffeted alike by his rage and his tenderness."[28] One of the causes, besides his high egocentricity, of his mauling his support like that probably was his notion that he could do a part justice only when in the complete, self-created illusion that he actually was the character involved in real events. Instead of complaining about bruises his Desdemonas should have been grateful that he did not strangle them in earnest. He brings to mind the conscientious young actor in *Nicholas Nickleby* who had to black himself all over, not just face and hands, in order to do himself justice as Othello.

He seemed aware of these tales. Calling on her when their co-starring was settled, he good-naturedly asked her not to take them too seriously, he was not as tough as usually painted. But she also found that she disliked his manners in the context of rehearsal: "not courteous or pleasant, or even well-bred; remains seated while one is standing talking to him; and a discussion having arisen as to the situation of a table . . . on the stage . . . he exhibited considerable irritability and ill-humour."[29] As no doubt he did. Obviously, throughout their few weeks together he thought of Fanny as just another leading woman hired to subordinate herself to the great tragedian's needs and wishes. He took over the best dressing room that Fanny thought should have been hers because she made a point of refusing to await stage calls in the greenroom. She may have owed that rudeness to Macready's annoyance at seeing "Mrs. Butler" in playbill type as large as "Mr. Macready." He refused to consider acting *Much Ado* and *King John* (he often played them elsewhere) which had roles for Fanny that she particularly fancied, insisting instead on plays that his roles dominated: *King Lear, Othello, Hamlet,* though she had never done Cordelia or Desdemona and had no wish to try. For *Macbeth* he insisted on setting the stage so that the whole banquet scene focused on him and left Lady Macbeth no room for maneuver while desperately seeking to reassure the guests. It is easy to understand how Fanny Kemble of all actresses, who had never played second fiddle to anybody (except once to Ellen Tree of her own volition) and had small use for most actors anyway, developed strong feelings about this rampant genius.

After reflection she acknowledged his great skill as producer-director and allowed that in certain tragic roles he excelled any of his contemporaries, but she thought his handling of Shakespeare's miraculous verse showed "want of musical ear . . . painful to persons better endowed in that respect . . . simply chopping it up into prose—a method easily followed by speakers who have never learned . . . that blank verse requires the same care and method that music does."[30] She, of course, was committed to deliberate refinements of rhythm as well as emphasis and pace to bring out the prosodic as well as the emotional values of the text. Whereas Macready was well into a "natural" or "domestic," as he sometimes called it, method that has since become dominant. Fanny's was the losing cause. Indeed things have now gone so far that Hamlet and his friends on the battlements mumble and slur like blue-jeaned youth on a street corner. Onstage at the Princess' Theatre in 1848, however, neither Macbeth nor his lady was inclined to concede and the clash of styles obviously greatly annoyed both.

As to physical damage, Fanny might have got off with the odd black-and-blue stigmata had she not broken a little finger some weeks previously. It had been rather neglected and now, even though she spoke of it several times to Macbeth or Othello, when Macready succeeded in really forgetting himself and grew regardlessly violent, it was all she could do not to scream with pain. In exasperation she concluded that "his artistic vanity and selfishness were unworthy of a gentleman" and found him particularly hard to act with because

> he growls and prowls and roams and foams about the stage . . . like a tiger in his cage . . . and keeps up perpetual snarling and grumbling like the aforesaid tiger, so that I never feel quite sure . . . it is time for me to speak. . . . I quail at the idea of his laying hold of me . . . I wish I was with you [Harriet St. Leger] instead of struggling here for my life—livelihood at any rate—with Macready . . . He can't touch me to-night, that's one comfort, for I am Queen Katharine.[31]

Macready vigorously set down his side of it in his eventually published diaries. He thought Fanny's notion of Desdemona's character sound but disliked the way she embodied it: "I have never seen any one so bad, so unnatural, so affected, so conceited. She proceeds not only *en grande artiste* but *en grande dame*. She is . . . living in an atmosphere of self-delusion . . . nothing genuine in her, poor woman! . . . if she would give herself up to the study of execution, she might yet become a very fine actress . . . but her many affectations prevent her."[32] Much of that, of course, comes of the gap between Fanny's elder school of acting, of formalized "points" and deliberate poses, and Macready's already much looser style. Five generations later it is almost comic to think of this mismatched pair dodging about a stage, each wedded to his and her own way, like a Roman gladiator trained to sword and shield pitted against one of those net-and-trident fighters. Yet this conflict of idioms was not inevitably invidious. What Macready found unendurable in Fanny was probably only one third that she worked in a tradition he had chosen to abandon; another third was that she got in his way onstage because her way was not his; and the other third that her resistance to his methods was *lèse majesté*.

Audiences were probably unaware of these disharmonies. But Macready's record of them has led to persisting doubts about Fanny's abilities; for instance, those of James Agate, the eminent English dramatic critic who—though he was far too young ever to have seen Fanny—called her a "simperer" and wrote: "I am convinced that she was always an amateur."[33] Was she so? For associated questions: Was she worthy of the great tradition behind her? Did her dislike for acting imply uneasiness about her own skills? Or, to put it another way, can one so malcontent with a given occupation be really good at it? Of that last issue she never made any bones. In Boston, for instance, she was so candid about her dislike of acting that her social acquaintances eagerly discussed its possible significance even as they praised her performances.

Since neither phonograph nor movie camera was then available, we have no objective evidence, only what people, Fanny included, wrote about her. Macready's comments are the prosecution's trumps. Add a much earlier witness, Walter Stirling, a friend of Mrs. Siddons's, telling an American friend of Melpomene's disapproval of Fanny's relying too much on "genius"[34] without proper study or reliance on others' advice. The defense can call a witness of equal stature, the great Mlle. Rachel, who was to French classic tragedy what Mrs. Siddons was to Shakespeare. Rachel attended one of the Ellesmeres' theatricals at Bridgewater House in 1841. The play was *The Hunchback,* Fanny in her favorite role. In Julia's great scene, "where the foolish heroine . . . is suddenly overcome by the remorseful recollection of her love for Clifford . . . I heard a voice out of the darkness . . . in a tone, the vibrating depth of which I shall never forget, 'Ah, bien, bien, très bien!' "[35] That voice might outweigh several Macreadys. On a less Olympian but professional level consider that young Fanny's rehearsals for *Venice Preserved* had the *stagehands* in tears. Alfred Bunn, dominant manager of the day and no great admirer of Kembles as such, called Fanny "highly gifted"[36] even though she was never under his management. Knowles, actor as well as playwright, said: "I owe [Miss Kemble] such a personation of [Julia] as . . . I did not think that heroine afforded scope for. Her Julia outstripped my fondest hopes."[37] Playing opposite her night after night in his own *Hunchback*, he was in a position to modify that opinion had amateurishness or unevenness marred her performances. It may have been that one reason her method so irked Macready was that it was not amateurish enough, instead reflecting a well-entrenched professionalism. That is, Thérèse De Camp was even more professional than Macready. Anybody whom she coached for three years, often with results she found acceptable, even laudable, had to be more than adequately versed in one school of "the rudiments of her profession."

Appraisal of Fanny's talent is blunted by her own impatience with her performances. She peppered letters and journals with comment on how she did on a given night, often disparaging: "I didn't play well [in *The Stranger*] . . . I acted like a wretch [in *Isabella*] . . . I played horribly [in *King John*]."[38] Self-approval was usually tepid: "I am much improved in my comedy acting [in *Much Ado*]."[39] Superlatives she saved for her father: "Played Bisarre [in *The Inconstant*] for the first time. Acted so-so, looked very pretty . . . my father incomparable."[40] Whereas, when she knew she was out of her depth: "I played like a very clever girl as I am; but it was about as much like Lady Macbeth, as the Great Mogul."[41]

Those ups and downs in performance quality can be cited against her professionalism. Dorothy Stickney's recent charming autobiography tells how she "passed a milestone . . . [when] I knew that I would be able to do [Molly Molloy in *The Front Page*] exactly the same the next night and the next and the next . . . my first intimation that I really knew something dependable about . . . acting."[42] But never forget that Fanny had acquired much of Thérèse's cutting tongue and was neither the first nor the last girl to sound like her mother when scolding herself. On many a night when she branded her performance as "atrocious," it probably wasn't. Add that in these informal jottings she had much of the schoolgirl's habit of saying "I'm frozen to death" when she feels a trifle chilly. Her "I played wretchedly" may mean merely that Euphrasia's business with the uplifted dagger hadn't felt quite as breathless as usual. And also that it is risky as well as mean to take temperamental self-criticism as clinching evidence. An old story has a visitor to a show of John Singer Sargent's work coming on the artist talking to himself in front of a fine example of his masterly charcoal sketch-portraits. Creeping up behind to pick up pearls of aesthetic wisdom, the visitor heard: "God dammit, I've got to learn to draw!" Fanny did tell Henry Lee late in her life, "I never was a good actress."[43] But she would not have said that coming off stage after hearing Rachel commend her.

Most leading ladies are too absorbed in what they are doing—in their colleagues' and their audiences' interests as well as their own— to harbor such general misgivings as Fanny's. She could never decide, as Macready obviously had, to what extent acting requires subjective commitment to the role. One evening Washington Irving and Edward Everett put that question to Fanny and her father. Charles told them that whereas "Miss O'Neill [his favorite Juliet] used to cry bitterly in all her tragedy parts . . . Garrick could be . . . playing tricks in the middle of his finest points." Fanny confessed that "sometimes I could turn every word I am saying into burlesque . . . at others my heart aches, and I cry real, bitter, warm tears, as earnestly as if I were in earnest."[44] She thought this two-level system had a degenerative effect on most actors. When J. W. Wallack, then delighting New York in *The Rent Day,* dined with the Kembles Fanny noted: "Oh! what a within and without actor. I wonder whether I carry such a brand in every look and limb . . . if I thought so, I'd strangle myself."[45] In her view Garrick damaged himself in making fun of the proceedings *sotto voce* while causing his audience to feel whatever he wished like a matador swinging the bull with the cape. She thought it unhealthy as well as difficult to "preserve one's feelings warm, and one's imagination excited, while one is aiming entirely at producing effects on others."[46] Nor did public acclaim reconcile her to the anomaly. After seven years away from the stage she told Lady Dacre that she still felt uncomfortable about people's having "[liked me] because I pretended to be a pack of Juliets and Belvideras and people who were *not* me. Perhaps I was jealous of my *parts;* certainly the good will obtained . . . always seemed to me quite as curious as flattering."[47]

She likened acting to dancing a hornpipe in fetters—no fancy of hers but a specialty sometimes interpolated in *The Beggar's Opera*—because so often at the mercy of impertinent details. Thus a given performance of hers was spoiled because "I'd a gown on that did not fit me, to which species of accident our *art* is marvellously subservient . . . too long or too short a skirt keeps one's heart cold in the balcony scene"[48]—that scene in which she so readily got airborne. One of her grandfather's upwardly mobile strollers might have thought that unprofessional. They could all recall when merely having a presentable gown to go on in, never mind its binding under the arms, was reason to thank heaven. They gave the same performance of Cora or Mrs. Millwood whether or not rain was dripping through the barn roof down on the makeshift stage. But as to Fanny's poor opinion of her calling, her great-grandfather, her grandfather, her father—not to mention Macready—all showed signs of sharing it without ever being accused of being unprofessional or of showing its ill effects in their performances.

Yet she felt it more strongly than any preceding Kemble. When she went to see Wallack act, only six weeks or so after she had been acting in Liverpool, "Mercy how strange I felt as I once more set foot in a theatre; the sound of the applause set my teeth on edge."[49] How many actresses feel that about applause even for somebody else? Fanny knew how to value cheers as useful in actor-audience symbiosis but was impatient of merely adulatory curtain calls. Indeed she held that it made little sense for actors to thank paying patrons for their generous support: "I never . . . saw, heard, or read of any set of people who went to a play-house to see what they did not like . . . our houses were full but as a necessary consequence of our own . . . exertions. I was glad . . . I wanted the money . . . and . . . glad the people applauded . . . because it is pleasant to please. . . . [But] in general I had [no] great *gratitude* towards my audiences."[50] Tactlessly she called acting the lowest of the arts or not art at all because it merely filled in "the outline designed by another . . . at best . . . a fine translation."[51] She may have caught the germ of that from Charles Lamb's "On the Tragedies of Shakespeare," which would so strongly influence her career as one-voice reader. But, though following Lamb, her vocabulary approached Macready's when she bewailed the dismal contrast between a great play as its creator completes it and what the stage inevitably does to it; she has just been acting Juliet with a Romeo even less competent than usual:

> How I do loathe the stage! these wretched, tawdry, glittering rags, flung over the breathing forms of ideal loveliness. . . . Pasteboard and paint, for the thick breathing orange groves of the south; green silk and oiled parchment, for the solemn splendour of her moon of night; wooden platforms and canvas curtains, for the solid marble balconies, and rich dark draperies of Juliet's sleeping chamber, that shrine of love and beauty; rouge, for the startled life-blood in the cheek of that young, passionate woman . . . a mimicker, a sham creature, me, in fact, or any other one, for that loveliest and most wonderful conception. . . . To *act* this! . . . horror! horror! how I do loathe my most impotent and unpoetical craft!
> . . . lying over [Romeo's] corpse, and fumbling for his dagger . . . I, Juliet, thus apostrophized him—Romeo being dead—"Why, where *the* devil *is* your dagger?"
> . . . What a disgusting travesty. . . . it's an absolute *shame* that one of Shakespeare's plays should be thus turned into a mockery.[52]

Ten years later, well after her marriage and retirement, Theodore Sedgwick asked her whether she ever felt like resuming acting and she answered: *"Never.* . . . My very nature seems to me dramatic. I cannot speak without gesticulating and making faces any more than an Italian can. . . . I am fond, moreover, of the excitement of acting, personating interesting characters . . . and *uttering the poetry of Shakespeare.* But the stage is much more that is not this, and that much more is positively odious to me, and always was."[53] Once she even suggested to Lady Dacre that she would welcome, mad as it sounded, legal ban on all theatricals except two annual productions as a national festival—one of a Mozart opera, one of a Shakespeare play.

The discrepancy between such feeling and Fanny's successes in the craft thus contemned so puzzled Brander Matthews, Columbia University's revered authority on and lover of the theater, that he tried to make genetics account for her. He said she was "proof positive of the strength of her hereditary endowment."[54] Until science finds a chromosome carrying the gene of histrionics—that will take a while—the case has only two alternatives: Either Agate's position that no problem exists, since she was no valid actress, only a simpering amateur; or the common sense of it, that it is not necessarily true that one can't do well what one dislikes doing. Many an able professional soldier has hated and deplored war.

For help in the general problem of how to judge Fanny as actress, I consulted Constance Cummings, a deeply versed Kemble-watcher as well as a brilliant modern actress. She replied:

> It is very difficult to assess actors of another age. The plays, the lighting, the theaters and the expectation of the audience were all so different from now that if one could plop down in a seat and see a performance of 150 years ago, one might find it laughable. But when you read criticisms of famous actors down the years . . . you find one theme constantly stated, that the actor in question who has just . . . taken the town by storm "has given the part a fresh interpretation . . . innocent of theatrical effects and old-fashioned fustian and has illuminated the part with a clear truth and reality with which it has never been invested before." Which means . . . that the good actors do not act a part as much as they act life . . . you feel you are not looking into a stage set but into the heart and soul of another human being. Fanny I am sure had this quality. . . . Sometimes one sees on the stage a young player with little or no experience . . . no technique, no conscious knowledge of how to obtain an effect, or secure a laugh with an unpromising line . . . yet he moves firmly and happily through the part he is playing and sets the audience quite at ease. "Ah," says one, "that young person belongs on the stage." . . . he has released and is riding on that mysterious current that carries actor and audience along together. . . . I think it unlikely that Fanny would have had such good notices all along had she not been first-rate, though of course it is possible. Critics

and audiences can be overenthusiastic for a variety of wrong reasons, but I think it was not so with her.

   . . . I just get through my skin . . . the information that she was the genuine thing. Impetuous, impatient, imperious . . . these qualities must have shown themselves from time to time in her work and always she would have been unstudied, emotional, and volatile, but the basic and unchanging quality would have been . . . a direct though implicit appeal to those realms of human awareness that operate beyond and without words. As when we hear a bit of music, or see a painting, or read a poem about which we . . . must be content with saying simply, "Yes, that's right."

XVI

High Priestess

ONCE HER TUG-OF-WAR with Macready was finished, Fanny left the stage for good. This was not cause and effect. The engagement had not much improved her opinion of the family profession, true. But long since she had determined to take advantage of her father's recent decision to discontinue readings, leaving the field obligingly free for her. Such a career as one-voice reader, chiefly of Shakespeare, promised and proved to be far less irksome to her temperament and, one may say, her prejudices. One feels the relief, almost cardiac and pulmonary, that she derived during the rest of her active life from finding that she could amply support herself without ever again having to march out on a garishly lighted stage hoping that just tonight, please, a dawdly company maybe bolstered by a competent colleague or two would support her well enough to do Shakespeare something like justice. Such a thing might happen now and again. But the odds against it were so high that it was infinitely preferable to use her disciplined single voice guided by her single worshiping, loyal intelligence to give hearers a consistently powerful *Richard III* or nimble *Midsummer Night's Dream*.

Occasional readings were a Kemble tradition. The first British exponent of one-voice dramatics seems to have been John Henderson, an actor of the late eighteenth century, who lent it tone, being "in every respect a gentleman . . . a welcome guest in the best society."[1] John Philip and Sarah went to his readings for both enjoyment and stimulus for their own remarkable verbal talents. Their subsequent readings sometimes included famous poems outside Shakespeare; Mrs. Siddons often deviated into Milton. Fanny recalled that "when Mrs. Siddons, in her mob-cap and spectacles, read *Macbeth* or *King John,* it was one of the grandest dramatic achievements that could be imagined." [2] Maria Edgeworth, who thought Melpomene a dull person, heard her read from *Henry VIII:* "I was more struck and delighted than I ever was with any reading. . . . I felt that I had never before fully understood or sufficiently admired Shakespeare, or known the full power of the human voice and the English language." [3] So it was a sort of apostolic succession, Henderson to Melpomene to Charles, when, reviving a relation begun in his younger days, the elderly Charles Kemble was invited to read for the royal family privately. It proved so enjoyable that there ensued a series of paid-admission readings in London "under the immediate patronage of the Queen and His Royal Highness Prince Albert." Then came bookings in London suburbs, at Brighton, Manchester, and so on. The fastidious care with which he studied the texts—the thing Fanny most admired in him—was her legacy from the occasions when, with or without an extrafamilial audience, her aunt did awesome justice to

> The raven himself is hoarse
> That croaks the fatal entrance of Duncan
> Under my battlements. Come, you spirits
> That tend on mortal thoughts, unsex me here . . .

or

> Sabrina fair,
> Listen where thou art sitting
> Under the glassy, cool, translucent wave.

As early as the Butlers' first London winter, Fanny read *Much Ado* one evening at Bowood and Tom Moore told his diary how delighted the Lansdownes' guests were. At Lenox she occasionally read for the Sedgwicks' cultivated circle. So she was well prepared when, in an Elijahlike gesture, Charles gave her the massive Shakespeare that he had marked up for emphasis and pacing and the cuts that a two-hour maximum required. For manager she enlisted Henry Mitchell, an old professional associate of the Kembles, who, after initial misgivings, eagerly arranged break-in bookings for her in the provinces. By late 1847 Fanny was thus sandwiching reading dates in between stage dates, even before the Macready episode. At Manchester, for instance, a town of good omen for her, they liked her new departure so well that at the end of a week she had six offers of engagements to read elsewhere.

The locus was not in theaters as such but usually in assembly rooms meant to accommodate balls, public meetings, and the mind-improving lectures on science, literature, and social problems that bulked large in Victorian culture. They could seat enough hundreds at a few shillings a head to cover the rent, Fanny's fee—she followed her father with twenty pounds an evening as a rule—and enough over to fatten the treasury of the local good cause or cultural association under whose auspices she read. These audiences were not altogether the same people who had recently flocked to applaud her at the Theatre Royal, Manchester. It was an advantage to her and readers after her that many well-to-do families who thought it sinful to enter a theater at all, no matter how innocuous the play or irreproachable the morals of the actors, nevertheless saw no harm in donning their good clothes to patronize a *reading* of Shakespeare. The Bard had become tutelary deity of the English-speaking world much as Homer had been for the Greeks of old, quoted from as storehouse of tribal wisdom second only to the Bible. In the smoke-smothered, bustling great industrial towns—Manchester, Birmingham, Leeds, and so on—where the pruderies of Dissent and Evangelicalism were strong, an able reader of this secular scripture had access to prospering pockets that stage players could not tap. True, expurgation and cutting were necessary: "All that is *merely* beautiful is sedulously cut out in my reading version," Fanny said, "in order to preserve the skeleton of the story; because the audience . . . are not familiar with the plays, and . . . they want . . . as much as possible of the excitement of a dramatic entertainment . . . without entering the doors of a theatre."[4] But, as has been seen, such surgery was already customary. The new editions of Shakespeare on the shelves of God-fearing midlanders were probably bowdlerized and Fanny's reading versions were based on those that her father had already cleaned up.

Had they cared to, her Methodist and Baptist patrons could have justifiably assured themselves that, by most accounts, Mrs. Butler's presentations of Shakespeare were more powerful and satisfactory than what the ungodly usually saw in immoral playhouses. Fanny's brilliance as reader seems to have come of several rightnesses in her new career. In Mitchell she had "the very kindest, most considerate, and most courteous of all managers," loyally making straight her way in spite of her Kembleish crotchets. He had assumed, of course, that he owed his client the usual overblown adjectives and subservience to the press. It took him a while to comprehend that Mrs. Butler would have none—none whatever—of either. Piteously he complained to Mrs. Sartoris that her sister wouldn't even let him refer to her performances as "these celebrated readings." "Why, ma'am," he said, "you know that even Morrison's Pills are always advertised as *these celebrated pills.*"[5] It also distressed him that Fanny never gave more than four readings a week (usually Monday, Wednesday, and Friday evenings and an odd afternoon) when local approval was usually strong enough to sell out six; and that though *The Tempest, A Midsummer Night's Dream, The Merchant of Venice, Macbeth, Romeo and Juliet,* and *Hamlet* were the most popular, she kept two dozen of the plays alive in her repertory lest she grow "hackneyed in my feeling or delivery of them."[6] She sometimes even implied that she preferred small houses, for she thought she read better to a few than to a crowd. Nor would she let Mitchell charge ten shillings a head in London, holding out for five and saying that actually half a crown would be more in keeping. In spite of these heresies, however, he knew integrity when he met it. He had seen them all, or most of them; he had managed the great Rachel in England and, though deploring the quantities of red wine that her staff absorbed and her *gamine* private manners, admired her. But "Mrs. Kemble," he said in retrospect, "Mrs. Kemble was my Hidol."[7]

An early reading at Hull under the auspices of the local Literary and Scientific Institute almost failed to be made because Fanny had been spending the afternoon "crying over the tender mercies of English Christians to their pauper population, till my eyes smart, and itch, and ache, and I shall have neither sight nor voice to read." With the mayor of Hull, a courtly and genial old gentleman, she had been taking a constitutional promenade in the huge train-shed of the railroad station and come on a bundle of rags in a corner that proved to contain a "live creature . . . a boy, whose attitude of suffering and weariness . . . was the most wretched thing you can imagine. I knelt down by him and asked him what ailed him. . . . Mr. Frost . . . began to ask him questions; and then followed one of those piteous stories which make one smart all over while one listens . . . parental desertion, mother marrying a second time, . . . beating, starving and final abandonment—they had gone away to avoid paying their rent, and left the boy to shift for himself." For some weeks of winter weather he had been living by begging, finding shelter where he could—occasionally the police picked him up and jailed him overnight—but his most articulate concern was the high probability that his mother and her man were mistreating his younger brother who had gone with them. In the station Fanny made it clear, he "had not been begging . . . with a pathetic appeal about his little starving brother; he was lying starving . . . stupefied, with his head covered over, buried in his rags."[8] He had been to the workhouse [poorhouse of the parish] where his mother had had him for two years; the people there knew him, thought him a good boy, but could not admit him for lack of some sort of certificate from officials he did not have accesss to.

Fanny and the mayor "carried the small forsaken soul to the workhouse, where we got him, with much difficulty, *temporarily* received. . . . I was in a succession of convulsions of rage and crying all this time, and . . . abjured and besought poor old Mr. Frost to take instant measures . . . we left him by the workhouse fire, the woman having gone to get him some food, and I returned blaspheming and blubbering to my inn."[9] Before leaving Hull, Fanny had the mayor promise to follow the case up and get the boy placed for a livelihood in some apprenticeship or the merchant marine; and pledged the proceeds of her next reading to take care of whatever fees, charges, or outfit he needed.

Then there was the small girl singing and begging in the streets of Glasgow whose plight Fanny took to the local authorities so vehemently that they rescued her from the drunken mother who thus sent her out daily to earn for both. And the miserable young woman whom Fanny saw being arrested for having spent the night on a park bench. She took her to her clergyman-friend, Harness, who applied for admission for her into a Magdalen institution [refuge for wayward girls], but the chaplain of the Mount Street workhouse where she was temporarily lodged saw fit to dispose of her by paying her way home to Bristol, where she had a sister barely managing a livelihood as a seamstress. Fanny reimbursed him but was grimly unhappy about the wisdom of his decision: "The poor unfortunate child is in the family way . . . it seems to me there has been some prejudice, or clerical punctilio, or folly, or stupidity, at work . . . thus to . . . send her back whence she came, no doubt to go through a similar experience as soon as possible again. God help her. . . . What a world it is!"[10]

Very likely Fanny's prolonged professional travels brought her other such generous episodes with no record surviving. All one knows further in this general context is that about one in five of her readings in Britain and America were fund raisers for local good works. That is, a fifth of her hard-earned income went to charity.

With Mitchell keeping the vexations of schedules and lodging at minimum, his Hidol could concentrate fruitfully for her audiences and herself on her great joy in what she was doing. This new career meant far more than mere freedom from lackadaisical rehearsals, stage-accidents, catering to the vanities of sulky colleagues. At last she was putting into action what she had learned years earlier from Lamb's devastating essay on "The Tragedies of Shakespeare Considered with Reference to Their Fitness for Stage Representation":

"The plays of Shakespeare are less calculated for performance on the stage than those of any dramatist whatever. Their distinguished excellence is a reason. . . . There is so much in them . . . with which eye, and tone, and gesture, have nothing to do." He has seen John Philip Kemble and Mrs. Siddons and gloried in their power, but:

dearly do we pay . . . for . . . this sense of distinctness
. . . instead of realizing an idea, we have only material-
ized and brought down a fine vision to the standard of
flesh and blood. . . . The Lear of Shakespeare cannot be
acted. The contemptible machinery by which they mimic
the storm he goes out in, is not more inadequate to represent the horrors of the real elements, than any actor can
be to represent Lear; they might more easily propose to
personate the Satan of Milton. . . . is The Tempest
. . . a subject for stage representation? It is one thing to
read of an enchanter, and to believe the wondrous tale
. . . but to have a conjurer brought before us in his con-
juring-gown, with his spirits about him, which none but
himself and some hundreds of favored spectators are supposed to see.[11]

This polemic must have sunk as deeply into Fanny's mind as
Goethe's low opinion of the personnel of show business. Now she was
privileged to strip away the buckram and tinsel that had accumulated
on the Bard, erase the memory of the have-at-thee hamminess and
gawky incompetence inseparable from staging him, and reveal the
authentic shape and subtle modulations.[12] Her only supplements to
words, words, words consisted of some use of facial expression, singing the little jewels of song provided for Ophelia, Ariel, et al., and
in A Midsummer Night's Dream, interpolating arrangements of Mendelssohn's music for it; this was particularly fitting because the com-
poser, recently deceased, had been one of Adelaide's and Fanny's good
friends. She reveled in these privileges the more because of the practically sacrilegious reverence she had felt for Shakespeare ever since
her budding career had persuaded her raptly to study all his works,
not just those she played in. It was eighteen years since she had
written Harriet: "The happiness of reading Shakespeare's heavenly
imaginations is so far beyond all the excitement of acting them (white
satin, gas lights, applause, and all) that I cannot conceive a time
when having him in my hand will not compensate for the absence of
any amount of public popularity."[13] While interpreting him aloud
to the very best of her considerable abilities, she must have felt like
a devotee revindicating the holiness and magic efficacy of a neglected

god's ancient rituals. To this devotion she ascribed her stubborn insistence on reading so many of his lesser acted works:

> For more than twenty years . . . [as] a wandering rhap-
> sodist, I never consciously sacrificed my sense of what was
> due my work . . . to my own profound feeling of the
> *virtue* of these noble works [I] owed whatever power I
> found to interpret them. My great reward has been, pass-
> ing a large portion of my life in familiar intercourse with
> that greatest and best English mind and heart, living al-
> most daily in that world, into which he lifted me.[14]

In one poem she thanked him as "Lord of the speech of my dear
native land!" for affording her so rewarding a livelihood. A sonnet
"To Shakespeare" ably expresses her devotion in verse of her better
quality:

> Oft, when my lips I open to rehearse
> Thy wondrous spells of wisdom, and of power,
> And that my voice, and thy immortal verse,
> On listening ears, and hearts, I mingled pour,
> I shrink dismayed—and awful doth appear
> The vain presumption of my own weak deed;
> Thy glorious spirit seems to mine so near,
> That suddenly I tremble as I read—
> Thee an invisible auditor I fear;
> Oh, if it might be so, my master dear!
> With what beseeching would I pray to thee,
> To make me equal to my noble task,
> Succor from thee, how humbly would I ask,
> Thy worthiest works to utter worthily.[15]

Practical regard to her audiences offered problems, of course.
Provincial sponsors wanted no part of her first proposal to solve the
attention-span problem by reading half a play one night, the other
half the next. She fell back on Charles's two-hour condensed versions
with a single intermission. They did preserve "the whole story . . .
and so much . . . of the wisdom and beauty as could well be kept
within the two hours . . . the reading [resembling] as near as possible in dramatic effect the already garbled and coarsely mutilated
stage plays the general public are alone familiar with. I was griev-

ously disappointed but could not help myself. . . . The readings were to be my livelihood; and I had to adapt them to the audiences who paid for them."[16] Presently, when doing her own surgery on plays that Charles had not worked over—*Antony and Cleopatra,* for instance, *Measure for Measure, Much Ado*—she ruefully appreciated the old veteran's skill in such matters.

It stirs the hair on the back of my neck to think of how she must have read Cleopatra's suicide, to my mind the greatest scene Shakespeare ever wrote. I wish she had left her reading version of *Measure for Measure* available to biographers, who would give much to know how she cleaned it up. To subject that powerfully gamy fable to what Fanny called "the omissions required by modern manners"[17] would hardly leave enough to run an hour and would shred the plot into vapid incoherence. Since she had a special fancy for the play, she seems to have left a good deal of it disturbingly intact. When a good Boston friend asked for a version suitable for reading to schoolgirls, she replied: "My dear Mary, the *story* of Measure for Measure is incorrigible and though I read the play because it is full of fine things and also the best sermon extant on the text 'let him that thinketh he standeth take heed lest he fall,' it is not suitable for babes but strong meat for men. . . . Shakespeare's plays were written neither for women nor for children."[18] That was, of course, historically true. That theater had no lunch-and-matinee public, no women's club cult of The Drama. It remains a miracle even less plausible than most that out of that stag amusement sandwiched between bear pit and brothel came so much portentous, dynamic honey and thunder. Almost ten generations later a devoted woman could still take it, even in truncated, expurgated form, and make it sweep and sing staid tradesmen out of their chairs in the Liverpool Institute.

For that is pretty much what she did. The apparatus was absurdly simple. Thanks to her tight hand on managers the preliminaries consisted of engaging a hall under proper local auspices—a little group of serious thinkers or a local bookshop trying to outshine the competitor—and posted-up bills promising that at such a time on such an evening Mrs. Butler (after the divorce in 1849, Mrs. Kemble) would read such and such plays. The consequent audience saw a platform equipped with a table, a chair, a lamp, a reading desk and a water flask and tumbler. The rest is typified in Fanny's reading in Baltimore for the benefit of the local Home for the Friendless:

> In the presence of a large and most brilliant assemblage
> . . . the spacious hall {had been] crowded to its utmost
> capacity for an hour. . . . Some two minutes before the
> exact time . . . a servant entered bearing two immense
> folio volumes of Shakespeare . . . {Fanny] came forward
> and made her bow. . . . Removing rather disdainfully
> a large bouquet of flowers that had been placed by the
> reading table, and announcing that she had the plea-
> sure of reading Macbeth . . . she presently opened one of
> the volumes, recited in a sweet voice the *dramatis personae*
> and suddenly became then and there transformed into a
> Hecate on a blasted heath . . . no need of scenic illusions
> . . . we were striding with Macbeth and Banquo across
> the desolate moor. . . . Never before have we been so
> much impressed with the needless character of theatrical
> accessories. . . . Here was a woman who became by turns
> every character . . . sitting palpably before us in laces
> and crinoline and under the blaze of gaslights, seemed
> faraway . . . in a remote past. . . . Baltimore Assembly-
> Room and Baltimore beauties disappeared utterly from
> our consciousness. . . . A lady at our right had never
> witnessed a play, another of a former generation had seen
> Sarah Siddons as Lady Macbeth . . . we watched . . .
> {they] were equally impressed.[19]

Most accounts make it clear that Fanny's grasp of her texts was so cogent, her techniques so flexible, and her spirit so imaginative that in even complicated scenes the separate characters were as well differentiated as though they had come on stage as real warm bodies; more clearly in fact. Intelligent auditors remarked in wonder how she lent the Gratianos and Malcolms, even the First Citizens and Second Gentlemen, usually so lamentably handled on stage, dramatic sub-stance and poignant interaction. Yet at the same time the characters' relations were manipulated with a consistency of tone such as no di-rector of a batch of actors, however willing and subservient, could hope ever to get.

Scores of voices, some eminent, some minor survivals, testify to the general effect. Thomas Wentworth Higginson, minister of the gospel, coconspirator with John Brown, colonel of a black regiment, transmission belt for Emily Dickinson—a man of versatile attitudes— heard her in 1850: "The tones of that unequalled voice . . . the immense animal spirits {in *Midsummer*}, the utter transformation of voice and gesture . . . and this in as portly a form as the country can produce . . . I cannot believe the play was ever given before . . . 'tis too airy for anything but the voice and *her* voice." [20] A minor London hostess told her diary: "The detail of each scene was given so naturally and with such entire simplicity that the audience were hardly aware they had not before them the whole mise en scène." [21] Old Rogers told Henry Crabb Robinson, one of London's most exigent cognoscenti, that Fanny read better than Mrs. Siddons; annoyedly skeptical, Robinson went to hear her and came away persuaded. Baron Bunsen, Prussian minister to the Court of St. James's, heard her do *Midsummer* with the Mendelssohn interpolations and pronounced her "the person of most genius in England." [22] Adelaide Ristori, a peerless Continental actress of the generation after Fanny's, heard her in London and kept saying over and over: "Che forza! Ma che forza!" [23] James Fenimore Cooper, America's most illustrious curmudgeon of the 1840s, went to hear Fanny do *The Tempest* prepared for boredom, but "from the first instant she spoke . . . I was wide awake. I have not been so much amused at a play since I was a boy." [24] But of all such data the most warming comes from Fanny Longfellow about how in early 1849:

> Mrs. Butler continues her readings to the delight and wonder of her crowded audiences. . . . her Queen Catherine was most touching—so much her own story, a stranger resisting her husband's divorce. . . . She wept and everybody else. Last night was *Macbeth* . . . [in] the second witch scene . . . the "hell broth" seemed boiling before your very eyes. . . . You can have no conception of the sonorous clangor of her voice, nor of its infinite compass and exquisite sweetness. . . . On Monday evening *The Merchant of Venice* . . . escorted upon the stage by Henry. . . . She came home [to Craigie House] with

us afterwards, and we had a very nice little supper. . . .
She was in great spirits, as she always is after reading.
. . . I presented her with a bouquet and Henry with a
sonnet, which he read. She was much over come. . . .
Her affectionate nature is easily touched by kindness, and
the tears flow at once." [25]

And Henry's sonnet, though not exactly Miltonic, has cordial virtues:

O precious evenings! all too swiftly sped!
    Leaving us heirs to ample heritages
    Of all the best thoughts of the greatest sages,
    And giving tongue unto the silent dead!
How our hearts glowed and trembled as she read,
    Interpreting by tones the wondrous pages
    Of the great poet who foreruns the ages,
    Anticipating all that shall be said!
O happy Reader! having for thy text
    The magic book, whose Sibylline leaves have caught
    The rarest essence of all human thought!
O happy Poet! by no critic vext!
    How must thy listening spirit now rejoice
    To be interpreted by such a voice!

It was implicit reciprocation that in later years when Fanny occasionally did evenings of other-than-Shakespeare, she often included Longfellow's "The Building of the Ship" among her selections.

    In the next generation came an important response to Fanny's
public cult: Horace Howard Furness, red-headed son of her good
minister friend, was only fourteen years old when hearing her read in
Philadelphia made him a lifelong addict of The Bard. He not only
insisted on hearing her whenever she read anywhere nearby, made
close nephew-style friends with her, became an admirable reader of
Shakespeare himself—but also spent his whole adult life creating the
immense New Variorum edition that is still one of the great monuments of scholarship. Here was a particularly gratifying side effect,
for there was no limit to her sense of intimate dedication. Henry Lee,
who, as a Harvard undergraduate, had sentimentally hired the horse
she had ridden, heard her read *Richard III* in 1867: "From the entrance soliloquy to the shrieking of the ghosts over the sleeping Rich-

ard, her reading was so inspired that we were all electrified; and the next morning I wrote: 'What was the matter with you last night? You never read so in your life . . . something extraordinary must have happened.' " Fanny replied that she had been practically beside herself because she had just learned that Cecilia Combe's will left her not only five priceless Kemble portraits but also a pair of gloves given by Garrick to Mrs. Siddons that were believed to have been Shakespeare's. "I had seen the flame," Lee wrote. "Now I had discovered the fuel." [26] The soundness of that attribution may have been dubious but through Fanny's will to believe the effect was superb. And it was highly fitting that she eventually passed the gloves on to Horace Howard Furness.

That winter of 1848–49 when the divorce tangle was at its worst Fanny's tumultuous success must have supplied invaluable buoying up. In New York as in Boston, Catharine Sedgwick noted with glee, she drew "the fashionable people, the old people, all the known clever people, the pious folk." [27] Philip Hone marveled at the way "delicate women, grave gentlemen, belles, beaux, and critics, flock to the [Stuyvesant Institute] and rush into such places as they can find two or three hours before . . . the lady's appearance." [28] Fanny's reading desk at the institute was specially designed and made for her engagement by John Ericsson, already famous as chief developer of the screw propeller, later for the momentous U.S.S. *Monitor*.

No such pandemic approval is ever unanimous, of course. Herman Melville who, as has been seen, sided with Pierce on the divorce matter, thought Fanny's Lady Macbeth "glorious" but her Desdemona "a boarding school miss." [29] Bronson Alcott, who had seen something of her round Boston and disliked her—she talked instead of listening to him—came away from her *Henry IV* alarmed by her unbecoming energy and "astonished at her brute power. . . . the depth of her voice is appalling . . . the hoarse notes the more particularly, and the grimace is in keeping. . . . a fearful creature, untamed, untameable . . . no rest, no company in her; no communion; impossible in any conversation." [30] His dismay may help toward understanding how Mrs. Charles Kean (formerly Ellen Tree of the Covent Garden company in Charles Kemble's time) felt about

Fanny's readings in New York: "marvellously good" except that her Falstaff in *The Merry Wives* was "though wonderfully clever . . . *disgusting . . . a coarse unsexing.*"[31] Beyond that actors' and actresses' surviving letters and journals say curiously little about this woman's impressive demonstrations that, though the theater in general needed their professional services, Shakespeare was better off without them. Macready, however, did make his opinion clear several times along the lines of "Went . . . to Mrs. Butler's reading of *Henry VIII* . . . too bad—I could not stay."[32] And Henry Irving, soon to be Macready's successor as incumbent chief of English tragedy, often elaborated on his disappointment when, as a stagestruck youth, earnestly studying *Hamlet,* he heard Fanny read it; he thought her style absurdly pretentious, her enunciation "fierce and sectional."[33]

For us, broken to microphones and method-mumbling, it is hard to gauge from hearsay how effectively—or pretentiously—her voice rang out with

> And gentlemen in England now abed
> Shall hold themselves accurst they were not here
> And hold their manhoods cheap whilst any speaks
> That fought with us upon St. Crispin's Day!

But we do know that her *Henry V* caused people to come round afterward saying, "Oh, it was all glorious but you *are* Henry V, my dear." Henry James thought this play, a particular favorite of hers, more successful in her handling "even than those that yielded poetry more various. It was gallant and martial and intensely English. . . . Her splendid tones and her face lighted like that of a war-goddess, seemed to fill the performance with the hurry of armies and the sound of battle . . . the illusion was that of a multitude and a pageant."[34]

Do not confuse what she did with the Ruth Draper sort of one-woman proteanism; or with Emlyn Williams as Dickens reading his own work. The best analogy is pretelevision radio drama. Now that that idiom is almost dead, deep thinkers sigh for the days when actors had only words (aided by sound effects) to stir hearers into imagining the perils, ecstasies, and conflicts of the script. Thus Fanny was doing for Shakespeare something he can never have contemplated for himself, abandoning the eye, trusting word and ear alone so to synergize that sight is never missed, indeed would hobble the listener's spontaneous contribution to the effect. (It is obvious from the above comments that though she did use some gesture and facial expression, she could have read from behind a screen and got the same effect; for her purposes these visible ingredients were like the golf swing's follow-through.) Actually she went further than radio in one respect. Broadcasters usually hired different voices; Fanny took all the parts in succession. She could, to Mrs. Kean's disapproval, be as gruff and coarse as Falstaff, as dewily ingenue as Ophelia in the next breath, and when necessary, turn herself into a whole mob-scene for Caesar's funeral. No wonder that when, after preliminary experience with reading in England, followed by her jangling weeks with Macready on stage, a New York manager offered to bring her to America for a star stage engagement, she replied with stately courtesy that "Mrs. Pierce Butler . . . presents her best compliments to Mr. Hackett . . . and begs to inform him that she has no intention of ever reappearing on the stage." [35]

Applause and prestige need not obscure economics and logistics. Summoned to America for the divorce proceedings, she found it true, as she had hoped, that readings would pay her living expenses with enough extra for either legal fees or nest-egg savings. And she already had three thousand pounds drawing a safe-as-houses three percent in the British "funds" (alias consols, that is, British consolidated sinking fund bonds); she had to make that investment in the name of her spinster English friend Emily FitzHugh because, being still a married woman, she could not otherwise protect assets from her husband. The divorce impinged on her career several ways. Reading was an activity less likely than stage acting to prejudice potential jurymen against her. But public awareness that she was a potential divorcee was bound to be somewhat damaging. A young son of the prominent and impeccable Wister family of Philadelphia—another Wister son eventually married daughter Sarah—applied to the University of Pennsylvania for permission for her to use a hall often devoted to just such cultural purposes. The request was declined on the obvious if unstated grounds that Fanny lacked the requisite respectability under the circumstances. Yet there was a more favorable side to it: the more the public learned of Pierce's case and Fanny's poignant rebuttal in the newspapers, the more persons less inflexible than the University of Pennsylvania's administrators veered toward sympathizing with her. That helped; and in any case all the noise about the divorce drew curiosity seekers to her audiences.

Her prosperity naturally led to its being exaggerated. Philip Hone managed to believe she was "making $2,000 or $3,000 a week, and never was money so easily earned—no expense except the room and the lights, and the performance is a 'labor of love.' Shakespeare was never paid for writing his plays as Mrs. Butler is for reading them." [36] That neglected agents' recompense, travel expenses, and the lady's prodigality in reading for good causes. Her reading in New York for the benefit of Saint George's Society (for the relief of down-on-their-luck Britons in America) brought them $1,100. Gratefully they gave her a solid gold replica of the badge of the Order of the Bath, showing Saint George killing his dragon; she wore it ever after when reading in public. In 1858 a return reading brought the society $800—another handsome sum that multiplied by four readings a week would come up to Hone's $3,000. But benefit tickets are always higher and gross is not net and we know that in late 1849 a very successful week in Cincinnati netted Fanny only $1,500. The most reliable gauge on her earnings is that after her first year reading in America she told Sidney Fisher, now a loyal supporter, that she had been able to hive up $20,000 at interest after taking care of her legal expenses for the divorce. Not bad at all in view of the far higher purchasing power of the dollar in those days.

As to money easily earned: True, in America as in Britain by 1849 trouping was less arduous. Railroads served most large cities, steamboats were still fast and commodious. Fanny's wardrobe was now only a few evening dresses and traveling costumes, far less cumbrous and troublesome than two or three elaborate dresses for each of half a dozen repertory plays in which the audience expected gorgeousness. But it was hard to find managers as able as Mitchell and as

meek as she trained him to be about reading only four times a week;
no nonsense in the handbills; admission never higher than a dollar;
and deplorable openhandedness about free passes, a trait that had
been one of Covent Garden's minor troubles about Charles Kemble.
The American factotum who served her best, Jedediah Barker, eventually grew too old for such exacting work and, to mutual regret,
resigned. Between managers it was Fanny herself who wrote those
innumerable letters—no telephones yet, and the electric telegraph
still in its infancy—about whether or not she would work in a reading in Ithaca the third week in May between tentative bookings in
Buffalo and Syracuse. The scores of these letters surviving show a
prolix courtesy that, for a woman of Fanny's impatient character,
must have come hard in so vexing a game with so many cards wild.

Add sporadic annoyances: In Milwaukee the hotel charges were
so high that she complained to the local newspaper. In Cincinnati her
admirers were insulted when they learned she was pushing on to her
next week's engagement instead of staying another week to savor the
elegancies of the Queen City of the West. The overheating of railroad
cars persisted. During her first western tour she was particularly
gloom-ridden because the menopause was making itself felt. Her
most valued companion was the ponderous, elaborately bound Bible
that Harriet St. Leger had given her, in which she read nightly,
without which she never traveled. "I have an antipathy to strangers,"
she wrote to young Charles Sedgwick, ". . . strange places strange
things & above all strange people—so that my present predicament
. . . an entirely strange one is utterly distasteful. . . . I was intended by nature for quite another sort of existence than this strolling
independence . . . a home where I would have been excessively
spoilt and petted would have suited me far better than this vagabond-
ing freedom and the general affections of a whole population."[37]

Yet such mutterings lack the vigor of her repugnance to stage-
trouping, which sometimes did lay her open to the reproach of quar-
reling with her bread and butter. Her joy in knowing she was serving
Shakespeare well kept her buoyant. Reporting that she took in
barely two hundred dollars in Rochester, New York, she goes on:
"However . . . the mere fact of reading Shakespeare is so agreeable

to me—I take such delight in my labour (so much more than any of my audience possibly can) that but for the necessity to make a trade of reading I should be almost ashamed of being paid at all for such pleasant work."[38] There is a serene glimpse of her in Sarah's account of a reading in Lenox for the Sedgwicks and a few friends: instead of the workaday lamp "massive silver candelabra, exquisite flowers, & her great quarto Shakespeare [Charles Kemble's] on the reading table, which stood before a window over which fell a crimson curtain which brought out her figure in her white dress & her beautiful head with its wreath of dark purple pansies. . . . She reads *As You Like It* most beautifully."[39]

High priestess of Shakespeare.

XVII

Put Asunder

LATE IN APRIL 1847, while Fanny was acting in London, Pierce Butler in Philadelphia sent a note to John Cadwalader, his lawyer and kinsman by marriage: "It is my wish and intention to secure a divorce from Mrs. Butler. She has left her home and children, & she has no intention of returning to them. Under these circumstances, I presume that I may ask for an absolute divorce as a matter of right. When you have a little leisure to devote to this subject, I shall be glad to attend you at your office."[1]

The presumption was correct. Pennsylvania was one of several American states with divorce statutes that, though seldom resorted to, were more liberal than those of some other states. Willful desertion for two years was one of several grounds admitted. Pierce probably did not hurry Cadwalader. Not until mid-September would it be the statutory two years since Fanny had left Philadelphia lest her presence further damage her children's emotional health. Six months later still and *Pierce Butler* vs. *Frances Anne Butler* had yet to appear on the docket of the court of common pleas. On March 28, 1848, however, there it was and a summons duly went overseas to the defendant.

Ostensibly cause and effect underlay Pierce's seeking "absolute divorce" instead of the mere formal legal separation that Fanny had often proposed. One of his cardinal points had been that she should never resume acting. He was aware that cutting off remittances, as he had done on the grounds that she had broken the agreement by leaving the country, would force her back on the stage for livelihood. Now he professed to believe that a complete break was necessary to spare the girls the shame of having a backslid actress as mother. Gossip hinted he was thus clearing the way for a new wife, a Miss Coleman, to wit. There may have been something in all that. But if the marriage scheme ever had substance, it evaporated.

As the divorce suit laggingly developed, Philadelphia had ample food for talk, however, and showed a tendency to well up in Fanny's favor. J. K. Paulding, the urbane humorist–politician–diner-out explained to ex-President Martin van Buren that the primary trouble was that Fanny had "married a Butler, a family which for three generations has been the curse of every woman connected with the name."[2] Though Pierce's reputation for loose living never got into the divorce proceedings, it certainly did Fanny's side no harm. On hearing that Pierce was suing on grounds of "wilful and malicious desertion," Sidney Fisher wrote: "As it is quite notorious that she was driven from his house by his own barbarous treatment, I think he can hardly succeed. . . . [Her] position is certainly a painful one. She is obliged to return to the stage . . . as Butler makes her no allowance."[3] Sidney had already come round to liking Fanny. More significant was his brother Joshua, a man of great weight in Philadelphia— the same who approved of his parents barring actors from their house—and Joshua's wife who now came down on her side. Before fleeing abroad, Fanny had also acquired a useful ally in Rebecca Gratz, the great lady of Philadelphia's small and powerful Jewish group, previously quoted as to the plight of Fanny's children.

In her time Rebecca was known as Philadelphia's most beautiful girl, and certainly Sully's portrait of her is startlingly lovely. It is probably true, though clinching proof is lacking, that Walter Scott modeled the winsome Jewish heroine of *Ivanhoe* on her from Washington Irving's description. Now elderly, she was spinster-chieftainess of the area's most respected Jewish family long entrenched in mercantile and landholding power. One of her brothers belonged to the City Troop, the silk-stocking militia cavalry in which John Butler was a captain; another was president of the Pennsylvania Insurance Company. . . . Several Gratzes married gentiles. . . . In sum, she was a prominent local symbol of personal integrity, good sense, charm, affluence, and devotion to good causes. And her liking for and defense of Fanny was invaluable.

When the court summons struck her, Fanny was in London, no longer working with Macready but still involved because, for all his contempt for her acting, he had recruited her for a great benefit to raise funds for a monument to Mrs. Siddons. At once she dropped benefit and plans for further readings in Britain. It was Liverpool and Cunard again in a cloud of anxiety and frustration. This time her savings supplied adequate traveling funds. Her lawyers in Philadelphia were eminent, able, conscientious, and already used to her peremptory temperament as well as her problems with Pierce. But she dreaded lest, once she reached America, Pierce would take the children to Europe to prevent "the possibility of my children's endeavouring to seek me." And otherwise she was ready for the worst: "For my beloved children's sake I shall disturb the peace of their minds with no further attempts to regain . . . mother's rights. . . . I do believe as God liveth that they will themselves return to me hereafter [that is, on coming of age free from Pierce's control]."[4] The bright spot this side of that remote hope—which did come to pass after a fashion—was the prospect of establishing herself among the Sedgwicks in her beloved Berkshire hills.

On landing she found that Pierce was trying to cloister the children out of reach in an Episcopalian girls' school in Georgia. (Then, however, he characteristically changed his mind and chose a school near Philadelphia that would allow them no visitors whom he did not personally accompany.) Soon settled in Lenox, Fanny had from the Sedgwicks not only affectionate moral support and good company, but also help in her legal problems from two generations of eminent lawyers. Probably at their instance, certainly with the approval of her Philadelphia counsel, she retained Rufus Choate, a renowned courtroom champion from Boston, for the final struggle. It was clear, however, that it would be a long, weary time before lances were actually couched in the lists before a Pennsylvania judge. Pierce's vacillations and the law's proverbial delays were well suited to each other. And for that matter, Fanny's resolution to make no antagonistic gestures, merely to do whatever was best for the children's emotional and economic interests, was confusingly difficult to apply.

Thus: Did that principle call for vigorously contesting the divorce because not to do so would saddle the children with the memory of a mother publicly convicted of willfully abandoning them? The Pennsylvania statute left plenty of room for contest on grounds that the spouse's conduct had been such as to render the defendant's life intolerable, forcing a flight from home. Such a defense would have to show that her conduct toward Pierce and the children, far from being abandonment of them and willful desertion of him, was consequent on his having in effect forced her out of his house by moral and personal pressures as cogent as if they had been a physical matter of blows and lock-and-key. To substantiate that, Fanny spent much of the summer drawing up an elaborate *Narrative* of what Pierce had put her through, particularly her frantic efforts to maintain with the little girls the parental contact that her heart yearned for and, she knew, God enjoined on her. The text included many letters that had passed between the spouses during their quarrels though, as has been seen, it scrupulously made no use of the anonymous lady-of-the-love-letters or of the maidservant seduced in London, whoever she was. Filed with the court late in 1848, it was widely reprinted verbatim in the newspapers and did much to increase public sympathy for Fanny far outside parochial Philadelphia. Some of the letters were highly personal, invoking earlier times when young love was real and, however factitiously, lyrical. When the children's and their mother's emotional futures were so critically at hazard that reticence was out of place, such exposure was unavoidable. For a Kemble, however, to have it all spread out in the New York *Evening Post* bulked large in what Fanny had already predicted would have to be "an inextricable web of wretched and wearisome misery."[4]

Or did the children's interests require her to bargain favorable practical terms against agreement not to contest? As summer dragged toward fall and Fanny flitted here and there to read for revenue and incidental distraction, Pierce threw out inconsistent signals of willingness to negotiate. He admitted no possibility of mere legal separation. Her effrontery in resuming acting in defiance of his stern orders may really have settled that in his stiff yet ill-anchored mind. But to rid himself of the vexations that Fanny had brought upon him, he was prepared to deal. She held some cogent cards. As his legal wife she had dower right to a third of his estate; nor could even the patrician old major's grandson afford altogether to discount the unmistakable esteem that Fanny had gradually acquired among such Philadelphians as Fishers, Furnesses, Biddles, Wisters, et al. True, his cards were better. His common-law right to all his wife's assets and his absolute control over her children were standing threats. The defense implicit in her *Narrative* would probably not be admitted in court without corroborative testimony that would be hard to come by and would throw the whole thing into the cultural uncertainties of a jury. Eventually came a tentative agreement. Fanny described it to Sarah Cleveland:

> I am to give up my right of dower . . . for an income of fifteen hundred dollars a year settled upon me to go to the children at my death and I am to withdraw my defense . . . and allow him to get his divorce provided the children are allowed to have two months of every year with me . . . and that I am permitted uninterrupted intercourse with them at all other times personally or by letter. . . . I am like Ceres in the lovely old world fable.[5]

Fanny gets some of the blame for the tortuous course of *Butler* vs. *Butler*. In some moods she hoped for an outright divorce that would restore her "to my own name, which I prefer & to the legal possession of my earnings." But then she also resented "the odious process by which the public disgrace of one of their parents must be the public justification for the other." She was reaching toward divorce by mutual consent with the adversary principle at least muted. In other moods, however, she could not efface from her moral sense a feeling born of the Book of Common Prayer that marriage was a positive sacrament and divorce its desecration. It was ironic that in their debate in print Pierce's one bull's-eye was theological: Fanny had rashly pleaded that Unitarians, such as she had become, sometimes omitted "obey" from the marriage ceremony, which absolved her of the duty to obey regardless. Her lawyer husband retorted that the marriage formula to which she had responded "I do" in 1834 was the "obey" form administered by an Episcopalian bishop. Otherwise it was inconvenient logically and emotionally that feminist notions went best with unencumbered individuals—a status she had lost if indeed she had possessed it since her late teens. Whenever she fumbled through these problems, she always circled back to the children. Considerations of personal emancipation could not "outweigh the placing Mr. Butler in a position to put a step-mother over my poor little girls."[6]

By late November it was very likely the case would go to trial early in 1849. Faced by preliminary pleadings, Fanny's emotions betrayed an unpromising flaw: she was "half crazy with the anticipated horror of having to make my appearance in a court of law to encounter the man who has destroyed my life and dragged me to this intolerable issue."[7] Once she reached Philadelphia, however, Pierce was unexpectedly obliging about allowing the girls to visit her at her hotel. After much legal juggling a date for a jury trial was definitely set for April 16, 1849. But meanwhile reflection on what Choate's forensic prowess and Fanny's ladylike stage presence might do to a jury caused Pierce to panic. He had already retained George M. Dallas, Vice-President of the United States, as Cadwalader's courtroom ace; in those simpler times major federal office was no bar to one's private career except seasonally. Now Pierce asked Dallas to give Daniel Webster, the nation's most renowned lawyer as well as perennial statesman, a retainer; for it had occurred to him the detestable Sedgwicks might try to pile Pelion on Ossa by putting Webster as well as Choate in Fanny's corner.

"On [this case] hangs my happiness, my peace of mind, and my existence itself," he wrote hysterically to Cadwalader. ". . . I have no wish to employ Mr. Webster in the trial before the jury, but I should be sorry to have his power against me." Dallas reported that Webster pocketed the retainer remarking "Mr. Butler could not possibly want him when he already had you and myself . . . he considered the retainer as merely intended to *buy his taciturnity*. I said that might or might not be."[8] Though Pierce was at least nominally a lawyer, it seems not to have occurred to him that this funk, strange in an imperturbable duellist, and the implied uneasiness about his legal representatives might annoy them. Dallas sought to withdraw from the case, relenting only after Pierce implored him not to abandon him defenseless. For Cadwalader had already withdrawn and refused to reconsider. He may have felt enough of the local atmosphere to develop a distaste first for the case and then for his client even if he was brother of a sister-in-law.

In the end neither Pierce nor Fanny had to undergo the strain of the witness stand and the hours in court fretting over the jurors' facial expressions. The trial was put off until fall. Well before then the tentative agreement was renegotiated with only minor changes. Fanny withdrew her defense. In return she got fifteen hundred dollars a year for life with reversion to the children secured by a mortgage on Butler Place and York Farm across the highway; two summer months with the girls; and by definition—and most welcome practically—her personal, social, and economic freedom. Divorce was granted by default November 21, 1849, only a few days before her fortieth birthday. Apparently she did not find it an unmixedly joyful birthday present, for only a few days later she was telling Harriet St. Leger about those spells of depression as she pursued a reading tour in the Midwest. But now she could bill herself for readings as "Mrs. Kemble." People sometimes wonder why, when reverting, she did not become "Miss Kemble." The reason probably was that in terms of her time it would be awkward to be a Miss, presumably unmarried, with two children often present and calling her "mother."

Her decision not to contest the divorce was probably good judgment on her and her advisors' part, particularly in view of her understandable horror of appearance in court and probably on the witness stand. Yet in one respect it was a pity. Rufus Choate was considered the ablest cross-examiner of the American bar. Think what he might have done to Pierce after Dallas said, "Your witness."

Six months after the divorce Pierce distributed among people who mattered to him an extensive rebuttal to Fanny's *Narrative*. He said his friends had urged him thus to vindicate himself by making available the materials he had prepared for his counsel. These 188

pages of handsome typography drew heavily on documents that Fanny
had already made public plus Pierce's files and memory. It is a valu-
ably clarifying document. Its opening lines state soundly that

> One reason, and perhaps the fundamental one, for the ill
> success which attended my marriage [was] the peculiar
> views . . . entertained by Mrs. Butler on the subject of
> marriage, and her unwillingness to abide by the express
> and inculcated obligations . . . of that contract. She held
> that marriage should be companionship on equal terms—
> partnership, in which, if both partners agree, it is well;
> but if they do not, neither is bound to yield—and that at
> no time has one partner a right to control the other.[9]

Fanny could have stated it no better herself.

This went far beyond her youthful analogy between marriage
and duet-playing in which the deeper-toned husband-performer contributed the elements holding the composition together and kept the
wife's higher frequencies from straying into flightiness. It was even
further beyond what the cultural caretakers of her day countenanced.
That was doubtless why Pierce opened with it. The case of a wife
maintaining such subversive folly was poor to begin with. Halfway
through his apologia he represented her consistent refusals to knuckle
under as wanton rejection of "the customary and pledged acquiescence
of a wife to marital control. . . . As it is unnecessary to argue a
point generally conceded," he told the hypothetical court he was ad-
dressing, "nothing is required to show the error of this principle of
equal rights in marriage . . . no one, who is not morally or intellectually astray, can fail to see the heartlessness and falsity of the preten-
sion." That is, mere statement of such a notion carries its own
refutation. Fanny had actually set it down for him on paper that she
doubted " 'whether one person can or ought to exercise control over
another. . . . there is no justice in the theory that one rational creature is to be subservient to another. . . . It is not in the law of my
conscience to promise implicit obedience to a human being fallible
like myself.' "[10] That, as Pierce knew society (and the judge) would
feel, was subversive of God's ordinance for Adam and Eve and contra-
dicted Saint Paul's "Wives, obey your husbands."

It is difficult now to grasp how shocking such doctrine then was, even though theory and practice were notoriously far apart. Wives flouted Saint Paul twenty times a day. Fanny was a strong person; Pierce wobbled precariously between stubborn and flighty. Another female temperament of the same strength could probably have well and truly henpecked him and left no bones broken, but she would not have consciously defended her doing so. Fanny, struggling for moral and personal elbow room, was candidly articulate about it; and too late. Pierce did have reason to complain that Mrs. Butler's notions as to the marriage contract and black slavery (a significant juxtaposition?) were either "not formed or not expressed before she became my wife; a knowledge of . . . either . . . must have proved an insuperable bar to our union."[11]

To some extent Mrs. Butler's views had certainly grown more definite in consequence of such firsthand experience as her war with Pierce over the *Journal* in their first few months. Add the innate impatience of restraint that had so perplexed her parents. Add hints infiltrating from the outside world where what books would eventually call the women's movement was trying to form out of fragmentary jostlings and outcries. Yet most high-strung, headstrong girls marrying into legal and moral serfdom circa 1834 and then feeling smothered probably failed to theorize about it, may not even have seen the husband-wife pattern as occasion for theorizing. Fanny's articulate speculations as to marriage even as spinster, identified her as one of the scatter of atoms likely to bond into the molecules making up feminism.

On reading Anna Jameson's book about venturing by horseback, canoe, and foot into the Canadian wilds, Fanny thanked the intrepid heroine "for the vindication of women's capabilities, both physical and mental, which all your books (but this perhaps more than all the others) furnish."[12] That was after her rough time with Pierce in Georgia but nine years before she ceased to be Mrs. Butler. It was good protofeminist talk from a maturing woman who had found marriage an ethical and emotional trap, saw lack of man-style education as one of women's grievances, and scornfully decried the hampering, body-deforming clothing that was part of women's bondage and made "dress reform" a lively aspect of the women's movement. Soon her donning trousers for outdoor activities would eye-catchingly qualify her for the feminist forefront.

Her acquaintance among protofeminists began with Anna Jameson and Caroline Norton in England. Presently Mrs. Norton, fired by disastrous experiences with a remarkably unsavory husband, would use her able pen, her formidable beauty, and her intimate knowledge of British politics—and politicians—to bring about the first substantial reform of British laws about child custody and women's property. In the next decade or two Fanny made good friends with such self-chosen guardians of woman-to-be as Lady Byron, Lucretia Mott, Frances Power Cobbe (a great friend and early neighbor of Harriet St. Leger), Harriet Martineau. Only Miss Martineau mistrusted Fanny, try as she might to accept her; and on her part, Fanny could never quite like Miss Martineau's kind of plodding sincerity, sound as she was on slavery. Young Harriet Hosmer's success in sculpture, an art almost exclusively identified with men, delighted Fanny; and in her later years she readily accepted suggestions that she call in one or another of the woman physicians coming into practice in London.

In the 1870s Elizabeth Cady Stanton, president of America's National Woman Suffrage Association, listed Fanny along with Mary Wollstonecraft, George Sand, Fanny Wright, and Victoria Woodhull as women "crucified"[13] by their fellow women still blindly observing man-made taboos and covenants. Mrs. Siddons's niece might not have cared for all those juxtapositions. She rather respected George Sand and quoted a description of her she had once heard—"unamiable, very emphatic, very dictatorial"—as "very like myself."[14] She was on more or less good terms with Mary Wollstonecraft's daughter, Mary Shelley. She may have met Fanny Wright in Lenox. But, unlike that ideologue namesake, she had never developed a schoolgirl crush on the Marquis de Lafayette and gone touring America with him. And she would certainly have been blisteringly eloquent about Victoria Woodhull's skill at blackmail and taste for red-flagged street demonstrations. Nor in any stringent way had her own sex "crucified" her. It was men who refused her use of that hall at the University of Pennsylvania, though their wives may well have influenced them. In view of the momentary hush that usually followed the word "divorce" in her day, it is also notable that though her *Narrative* was avidly discussed, it brought down on her nothing like the hail of abuse that the *Journal* had occasioned.

The *Narrative* not only secured her useful public sympathy, it was inadvertently good feminist propaganda. It dramatized her poignant case-history as implicitly typifying the married woman's plight as presumed subadult quasi-chattel, her children as inextricably their father's property as if she had been a slave-woman he owned. And her simultaneous career as reader showed that woman could stand firmly alone. The audiences to whom she read while *Butler* vs. *Butler* was in the court were mostly people who took for granted the traditional doctrines of husband's hegemony over wife and woman's inferiority to man in all but domestic skills. In that compact, intense, eloquent figure on the platform, however, they were exposed not merely to a woman struggling for freedom. She had the deeper significance of an unmistakable gentlewoman of serene independence supporting herself by giving society a generous money's worth of one of its great cultural by-products; a great lady accustomed to meet prime ministers, local committee chairmen, and stable hands with the same incisive give-and-take, borrowing from men's world whatever she found convenient, horses, trousers or oars or pungent language, while remaining as feminine as she wished.

Yet she was by no means the model women's-righter even in her day's terms. She was recurringly uneasy about woman-as-mother and woman-as-doer. When Sarah was fourteen months old, Fanny wrote to Harriet: "I shall never attempt [serious writing] again; I do not think nature intended mothers to be authors of anything but their babies. . . . though a baby is not an 'occupation' it is an absolute hindrance to everything else that can be called so."[15] She had no impulse to go preach women's rights like Frances Cobbe and Lucretia Mott. About the suffrage she was unorthodox, regarding it as secondary: "I have no doubt that women . . . will eventually obtain the right to vote, if they persist in demanding it. . . . what I covet more for them [is] a better, perhaps even a tolerably good, education. Fanny Cobbe always seems . . . misled by the very amiable modesty of supposing that other women are her . . . intellectual and moral peers; and I believe the women she talks to are conceited enough to take her at her word." After which sardonic view of the feminist rank and file, she is harping on education again a few months later: "I am quite willing that women should be allowed to do whatever they *can* . . . be politicians . . . doctors, divines, *soldiers if they can,* and vote by all means, if they like. My own . . . desire for them is a better, more thorough education."[16]

When Emma Willard, famous headmistress of a renowned girls' seminary in Troy, New York, sought to involve Fanny actively in organized feminism: "I sank myself for ever in her opinion, by . . . representing to her that as she had a perpetual stream of young womanhood passing through her hands . . . if she contrived to prevent her pupils from becoming desperately in love with . . . very contemptible men, she would do more for the emancipation of women than all the speeches, pamphlets, and 'platforms' in the world."[17] Yet forty years earlier she had the deft debater's answer to the antifeminist's presumption that women's capacities are inferior to men's, hence higher education is wasted on them: "If our capacities are inferior . . . let us not be overwhelmed with all . . . that foolish and vain bringing up can add; let us at least be made as strong in body and wise in mind as we can."[18] Yet she was unorthodox again when, as certain states revised their laws to give women sadly needed control over their own assets—of which Fanny had both general and personal reason to approve—she questioned the wisdom of doing so without equally freeing husbands from responsibility for a wife's debts and maintenance. Otherwise "this seems to me beyond all right and reason—the compensation of one gross injustice by another . . . almost *womanly* in its enthusiastic unfairness."[19]

But then nobody acquainted with Fanny Kemble had reason to expect her to follow the whole syndrome of any body of opinion. She was so unlikely *not* to do things her own way, wrongheaded or not. This, her own brand of feminism, at least showed that her heart was often in the right place and though she did not use her head to make speeches with, it usually fired on all cylinders. As it was, her very existence became feminist propaganda. Almost automatically public awareness of the circumstances of her divorce and the implications of her reading career made her a weighty factor. She was the woman who had been through divorce as gruelling as Victorian values could manage without erotic scandal to work with, and had come out the other side as much more of a person than ever. In view of how much of a person she had already been, that was saying a great deal.

Nowadays to refer to the Berkshires in general and Stockbridge, Lee, and Lenox in particular evokes Tanglewood, Jacob's Pillow, and Alice's Restaurant—shorthand for what happened when the well-off and then the trendy made a playground of a thrifty, quirky Yankee hill-region. Fanny Kemble had an inadvertent hand in that. She was, so far as I can learn, the first conspicuous outsider deliberately to immerse herself in the area's natural amenities. Until then one was born there or married a local person or came seeking livelihood, and there was very little of that last; indeed the economic trend was the other way. It is fitting enough that a minor highway leading out of Lenox skirts a clump of shrubbery masking a boulder bearing a plaque stating that this is officially

KEMBLE STREET
IN HONOR OF FANNY KEMBLE

a resident of Lenox for many summers after 1836. She purchased the knoll south of the oaks and thereon erected a residence which she called The Perch. It was demolished in 1905.

This and a similar memorial to Nathaniel Hawthorne, who made a limited but literarily prolific stay thereabouts in Fanny's time, were erected together in 1929. By then both celebrities were ancient history and the area was already past its prime as locus of gentlemanly estates.

At the dedication the speaker dutifully dredged up from old-timers and local archives anecdotes recording the impression the lady left on the community. She rode her big black horse all over the area. She used the rough side of her tongue freely. She neglected to add water to the ingredients of the punch at a large lakeside party she gave and many of the best people got tiddly; one of the gentlemen

who went off out of sight to swim was too much so to get his clothes
back on before returning to the party in a boat. So far it sounds like
a middle-aged interloper so throwing her weight about that lips
pursed and heads shook from Williamstown to Great Barrington.
Only after a while lips failed to tighten and smiles or grins often
went with whatever headshaking occurred, for gradually Lenox and
Fanny came pawkily to understand each other. Early in the acquaintance she hired a local youth to drive her round the countryside.
When he began glowing descriptions of the scenery she was to expect, she told him he was hired to drive, not talk. He buttoned his
lip but at the end of the day asked fifty cents over the settled fee.
What, she asked, was that for? "For sarce," he answered. She paid up
and laughed at him and herself and for the next forty years they were
good friends; he eventually became owner-manager of the local hotel
where Fanny and sometimes her friends spent many leisurely days. It
was in the lobby of the hotel that she told a mild little man to take
off his hat when he bade her good morning because "Gentlemen always do so in my presence." "But I'm not a gentleman, ma'am," he
said. "I'm a butcher," [20] which made her as good a story to tell on
herself as the fifty cents' worth of "sarce."

Lenox never knew what she would do next, of course. For a
reading at Stockbridge she chose *The Merry Wives*. Local sentiment
sought to have a less earthy text substituted and with some reason,
for Fanny's Falstaff was, as has been seen, pretty rowdy for a white-
steepled New England village. The evening of the reading she came
on the platform looking bleak and announced:

> Ladies and gentlemen, I have been met in my robing
> room by a committee . . . and requested not to read The
> Merry Wives of Windsor. . . . I have been met in my
> robing room by the clergymen of your town and they have
> requested me not to read The Merry Wives of Windsor.
> . . . I have been met in my robing room by a committee
> of the schoolteachers of your town and they have requested
> me not to read The Merry Wives of Windsor. Ladies and
> gentlemen, I shall have the honor of presenting to you
> this evening Shakespeare's immortal play, The Merry
> Wives of Windsor. [21]

The small lakes in the area afforded her peaceful fishing from skiffs. One of the local youths whom she hired as oarsman-escort remembered her as the most patient fisherman he ever encountered, alternating silent waiting for bites that never came with fits of singing or reciting to while away the time. For fishing she sometimes wore loose trousers and boots—a sensible innovation in which she had already caused a sensation in the Pennsylvania countryside. The very few women, such as Amelia Bloomer and Fanny Wright, who then wore visible versions of trousers did so as a militant feminist gesture. Fanny was merely being practical, she said. To Elizabeth Sedgwick's protest she replied that such bifurcated garments were better suited than voluminous skirts to what she was doing and "I won't listen to moralizing. . . . When I go on the stage I dress for the occasion; when I go into a drawing-room I dress for the occasion."[22] The same logic would have set her riding astride, but she seems to have resisted that temptation.[23] If she felt it, her not doing so hardly implies an uncharacteristic timidity, for she also occasionally wore trousers for rough rambling and scrambling with parties of both sexes in the local woods.

Lenox's acceptance of her must have been cordial by August 1844, when a Berkshire Festival celebrated the entry of railroads into the area. The interminable program included a speech by Mark Hopkins, Stockbridge-born president of nearby Williams College; a poem by Oliver Wendell Holmes, an occasional seasonal visitor and New England's master of occasional verse; verses from Mrs. Lydia Sigourney, eminent lady-poet from neighboring Hartford, Connecticut; and a 130-line ode from Fanny. It was read by Charles Sedgwick because she was then in Philadelphia entangled in the penultimate struggle over the divorce; it is a wonder she had the moral energy to write it. It welcomed home the hundreds of returning Berkshire-born who had gone thence to the greater opportunities of ocean and prairie; contrasted local freedoms with black slavery; mourned the recent death of Channing, who had been much in the Berkshires in his last years, but dwelt most on her delight in

> . . . rocky peak . . . wood-embowered dale . . .
> Oh welcome! from the meadow and the hill
> Glad greetings rise,

From flowing river and from bounding rill,
Smooth sunny field, and gloomy wood-depth still,
And the sharp thunder-splintered crag, that strikes
    Its rocky spikes
    Into the skies.[24]

It was a graceful repayment for the compliment of being thus treated as adopted daughter.

In further local goodwill Fanny did readings that paid for the Lenox town clock and helped finance the Lenox Library Association. Under the cultural conditions of the 1830s this acceptance by well-entrenched upcountry Yankees of a patently eccentric woman who had been an actress and was involved in divorce was really notable. Apparently Lenox and Stockbridge really were the signally special places that they claimed to be, what with Sedgwicks and all. Note that last: Matters might not have been so happy all round had Fanny not been sponsored by the Sedgwick clan, so numerous, influential, and respected that, according to amused outsiders, the Berkshire crickets in the fall chirped "Sedgwick, Sedgwick, Sedgwick." Most of their neighbors did not share the clan's Unitarian views or their strong feelings against black slavery. But if you had their approval— not to say the good fortune to become a family intimate—even your being an actress could be overlooked.

The complementary ingredient was, of course, what Henry Dwight Sedgwick called Fanny's "impetuous generosity . . . glowing sensibility . . . unfeigned religiousness."[25] In 1838 she and baby Sarah spent late summer and early fall at Lenox. The Appleton sisters, Brahmin girls so close to the Sedgwicks they called Catharine "Aunt Kitty," who had taken greatly to Fanny in Boston and then Newport, were also at the "staring brick hotel with Greek columns in front, looking forth . . . on a noble sweep of hill beyond hill."[26] Day after day the brilliant Mrs. Butler and Aunt Kitty's charming niece Kate and the Appleton girls and often Aunt Kitty herself sallied forth to enjoy themselves with a splendid innocence that has the flavor of an early Winslow Homer. Fanny described for Anna Jameson "the sort of life . . . lived here, the absence of all form, ceremony, or inconvenient conventionality whatever. We laugh and we talk, sing, play, dance, and discuss; we ride, drive, walk, run, scramble,

and saunter; and amuse ourselves extremely with little materials."[27]
"We" usually spent the evening at the Charles Sedgwicks' in Stockbridge: "Mrs. Butler in white," Fanny Appleton wrote, "bare arms
and neck if it be cold as November . . . singing old ballads with a
thrilling pathos . . . discoursing on deep topics with an earnestness
and far-reaching intelligence which kindles her face to wonderful
shiftings beyond any countenance I ever saw. Her soul seems always
boiling at fever heat."[28] One night an awesomely brilliant aurora
borealis set them discussing electricity (then ill-understood magic)
and "animal magnetism" (today "hypnosis," not much better understood for the change in label) with which, it appears, Pierce and she
and some of their Philadelphia acquaintances had been toying. Another night Fanny read them *The Tempest* in one of those just-among-
friends experiments that trained her for her later lucrative career.

These goings-on in what sounds like a completely decorous and
largely woman-directed Abbey of Thélème must have been a fine relief from sweltering in Butler Place during a July spent wondering
when Pierce would make up his mind to leave for the springs. One
day she is babbling with excitement about catching an eight-pound
pickerel, the next exulting in having been

> on the top of a mountain four thousand & seven hundred
> feet high with a [gentleman] who has been to the top of
> the pyramids & Mont Blanc & the Himalayas for aught I
> know & who said the view was the finest thing of the sort
> he had ever seen—& there I got my mouth full of clouds
> & my eyes & face full of clouds & nearly had the hair
> blown off my head & came down very much stupefied &
> have remained ever since very much exaltée.[29]

By the mid-1840s she had determined sometime to put down
roots in Lenox, her land of "splendid rosy sunsets over the dark blue
mountaintops . . . wild white-footed streams that come leaping
down the steep stairways of the hills."[30] For the next twenty-five
years she had some sort of stake in Lenox, owned or rented or projected, consequences of her own bow and spear giving her great satisfaction except when, plagued by leaky roofs, she referred to her
"wretched shanty."[31] This love affair, like others, had its tiffs. The

few times she tried wintering in the Berkshires were rugged, with snow in the dooryard sometimes up to the horses' bellies. Her letters to Frederick Leighton, the very rising young English painter, about autumn coloring in America were eloquent; but so was her description of the view from her Lenox window in the winter of 1860–61: "the abomination of desolation of the dready savage winter landscape of low black hills bristling with wintry woods and wide, bare, snow-covered valleys."[32]

Remember how many persons Fanny comprised. During her sojourns in the Berkshires reactions to her were particularly meaningful, some specious but some cogent. For symbol, the young woman with the pretty blond baby who wrote that rash book that was probably all right if the Sedgwicks defended her—anyway it was not disrespectful to New England—had grown too heavy for any but large, powerful mounts for her daily riding. A local lawyer acquaintance of hers observed with alarm an unmanageable horse that he had sold off because it kicked, bit and lay down on its rider tethered outside the Lenox hotel with a sidesaddle on and Mrs. Kemble about to mount. To his remonstrances she imperiously replied: "When you ride him, you're afraid of him. When I ride him, he's afraid of me";[33] so the well-meaning acquaintance held her stirrup and up and off she went. Though Charles Sumner was charmed with her when he met her in Lenox in 1844 and saw her put her arrow into the gold of an archery target and rode with her (at her suggestion), this tall, solemn, and archangelically handsome young man had also to describe her as "peculiar, bold, masculine, and unaccommodating."[34] For all that, he became a loyal and helpful friend. Whereas Herman Melville, who lived and wrote not far from Lenox in the same period, accused her of thinking it "honesty, to fling people's imputed faults into their faces"[35]—a crosslight no less interesting because Melville was prejudiced against her even before they ever met.[36]

As middle age nudged her toward something even less welcome, Fanny still joked and frolicked under her own conditions. She liked to hire the local four-horse "bus" to take congenial people, the Sedgwick-Sumner-Longfellow kind, on two-day, scenery-rich junkets across the Connecticut line. On Saturdays she often took half the girls of Elizabeth Sedgwick's school on a noon picnic up the mountain and an afternoon of open-air singing, dancing, and reading of Shakespeare; next Saturday the other half had the same treat; one assumes lemonade and sponge cake. On inclement Saturdays she went to the school, read half a play—probably not *Measure for Measure*—and had the girls over for dinner followed by the other half-play and dancing to her accompaniment on the piano. When Lenox heard she was coming back from her current reading tour, friends drove over in a body to the Albany steamboat to fetch her back to her happy land. Nobody ever called her Queen of the Berkshires, but she was one of the major local phenomena like Monument Mountain. Nearing her sixtieth year, still in love with the area, she wrote how good it was to know that "in spite of eccentricities or national peculiarities which may not always make me agreeable . . . the people of [Lenox] have some of the kind of regard for me which I shall ever bear to the inhabitants of a place which has afforded me the happiest days I have ever known in this land of my transplantation . . . and some of the sweetest and noblest men and women that I have ever known." [37]

XVIII

Extended Family

IN MID-1850 Fanny returned to England because again her father was failing ominously. That probably meant she would have to forgo being with her children that summer. At best the arrangement was embittering. The woman who thus repatriated herself had, since the divorce and likely in consequence of it, become rather a formidable person in terms enabling one to understand what led Melville and some others to be so harsh about her. Her compact, square-faced person accurately betokened pride in hardheaded independence and smaller than ever inclination to suffer fools gladly.

One symptom of this crisis-induced change was her apparently fairly successful effort to turn herself into an automaton-martinet, particularly as to clothes. Her evening-dress program was as rigid as the days of the week. In Rome in 1854 she apologized to Elizabeth Barrett Browning for making an informal evening call in "a fine dress and white satin shoes. In the first place [she said] she liked fine dresses—& in the second, she wore her dresses in rotation & nothing ever induced her to put on the Monday's dress on Tuesday. . . . I am told she is quite a creature of habit . . . lighting fires and putting on flannel on a given day of the year when cold weather ought to begin, whether it is as hot as a dogday or not."[1] Another rigid rule was to answer letters the day they arrived, a wildly impossible goal that she seems almost to have achieved. But when one or another very close friend did not write to her, she did not write either. Sarah Cleveland, for instance, was well aware that Fanny and she loved each other dearly; if it did not suit Sarah's convenience to write, what need for the implicit reproach of Fanny's writing to her? In such petty, dry logic she seems to have hoped to find continuing antidote for her natural temperament, which, reacting in its own way to other people's ways, had had such dismaying consequences. An ascetic impulse; a portrait of her at this period shows a deliberate, half-smiling calmness as of a still-handsome nun, committed to inner confidence but remote and wary of intrusion. This may imply that her ordeal had left her stronger, like a broken arm knitted well. But Pierce's choice of tactics had been well calculated also to leave scar tissue in the softer parts, tending to sensitize but also to insulate the tissues against anything else that would happen to her the rest of her life.

With this went an imperturbable outspokenness often as sharp as her mother's. It partook of impatience with sham or dullness and also of the quality that Mrs. Charles (Eliza Cabot) Follen had noted in 1835 when telling Sarah Perkins that Fanny had certainly liked her fiancé if she had been cordial to him, for "Fanny Butler cannot act off the stage."[2] In London some years later an aspiring young actress babbled on to her about the roles she had played and how she played them and the roles she hoped to play and so on and on; Fanny advised her to try Juliet's nurse—Shakespeare's most garrulous character. When the lovely Mrs. Scott-Siddons, a well-considered twig of the Kemble tree in the next generation, sought Fanny's opinion of one of her performances, Fanny told her she had just two things in her favor—her face and her name. Introductions from her favorite people were no protection. The Sedgwicks asked her to look after a young American clergyman friend of theirs in London; she did so dutifully but found him obsessed by an obvious dread that his speech and dress would identify him as an American, "a fear of trespassing against English usages [that] seemed to leave him hardly any other idea. . . . I was impelled to say, 'Sir, are you not a foreigner, an American? May I ask why it is . . . incumbent upon you, either by yourself or others, to dress and speak like an Englishman?' "[3] Her beloved Henry James brought a lady cousin of his into the box where Fanny and he awaited the great Tommaso Salvini's *Macbeth,* and Fanny warded off any possible distractions most imperiously: "I am *sorry* Mr. James has introduced you to me. I shall be obliged to tell you, *now,* that I shall not *speak* to you, or *look* at you, or be conscious of your existence, even, during the entire evening."[4]

And when she wanted to make a point in public, she could wield thunderbolts, enjoying it in a genuinely Olympian fashion. In Syracuse, New York, she was once persuaded to give an hour's readings before a local convention of schoolteachers whose physiques, as she studied them from the platform, she considered woefully typical of American neglect of fresh air and exercise: "two hundred young men and women, intelligent, conceited, clever, eager-looking beings, with sallow cheeks, large heads and foreheads, narrow chests and shoulders." She led off with Hamlet's soliloquy and instructions to the players and then pronounced: " 'The air of this room is pestiferous. You have here no ventilation, and two rusty sheet-iron stoves all but red hot.' " Then she gave them Imogen's brothers' lament over her dead body from *Cymbeline,* after which they got the second barrel: " 'You have now thrown open windows at the top and bottom, on opposite sides of the hall, producing violent draughts of cold air. . . . you . . . will get colds or the rheumatism.' " Then Mercutio on Queen Mab's arsenal of dreams and " 'There is a strong escape of gas . . . in this room; the screws in the gas-burners are none of them turned square; you are inhaling poison, and I am being choked.' " Then Othello before the Venetian senate, and bang she shut the book "and asked them of what use it was for them to listen to or learn poetical declamation while they were sitting there violating every principle of health . . . which concerns the physical well-being of themselves and their pupils."[5] Of all the thousands who came away from Fanny's readings deeply impressed those New York State schoolteachers were certainly among those least likely ever to forget her.

Settling down in the Sartorises' hospitable London house that summer of 1850, she had family vexations in prospect. Charles's health was soon on the mend, but his advanced age of seventy-six made it highly advisable to reinforce the arrangement that would return Fanny's nest egg to her on his death. And Pierce had neglected to pay the solicitor who drew the original papers his exorbitant fee for necessary copies of them. There was irksome delay while Fanny procured proper copies from Charles Sedgwick. Harness, her trustee in the matter, was willing but fumbly; as how should a fashionable, literary London clergyman not be? Her father's solicitor proved evasive and gradually it grew evident that Charles, never meticulous about finances, had somehow hypothecated at least part of his lifetime interest. To straighten it out after he died eventually required a prolonged Chancery suit. The old affection between father and daughter never lost validity. But old age was doing Charles Kemble no favors, which meant difficulties for his daughters.

To Fanny's scorn and indignation, for instance, a lady admirer was haunting his lodgings. The remedy he suggested was to take a house that Fanny would share. She consented though she was better off, and knew it, *chez* Sartoris. The earnings of her first reading season in Britain went into furnishing the house he chose. Then all too soon the occasionally perplexing case of brother Henry grew acute.

So far he has been seen only as a handsome, affable, desultory young army officer who owed his humdrum career in the Army to his sister's money and his family's inability to think of anything better to do with him. All were fond of him. So were many others, including John Mitchell's and Fanny's friend, Will Thackeray. And so was another Thackeray, no relation, whom we met as part of the family party in Germany in the 1830s—Mary Anne, whose father, George Thackeray, was not only an academic prince at Cambridge but possessed of a handsome private fortune. She seems to have been a pattern young lady of no special attractions but the potential four thousand pounds a year that she was to inherit. Henry was attracted. Their engagement met only one obstacle: her father forbade it, and when she demurred, made it clear that since she was of age, he could not keep her from marrying a glib, penniless paragon of charm and good looks; but if she did, no four thousand pounds a year.

The poor girl took her troubles to Fanny. Fanny seems to have told her that though Henry would "be kind enough as long as all goes well . . . if you were to be poor . . . your lot would be miserable . . . he would visit upon you his disappointments."[6] It was Henry who, after a season of hoping the old gentleman would relent in the face of a *fait accompli,* changed his mind and backed out. Some

years later he returned from overseas duty, learned that Thackeray
had died in 1850 and Mary Anne had her fortune. According to
Fanny, Adelaide Sartoris thought this occasion for rekindling the
match. So did Henry. Only Mary Anne, though still under his fascination, had the dignity and common sense to send him packing.
Off he went to Dublin to become adjutant of the Irish militia.

This sounds familiar? It should. One evening in 1879 Fanny
told Henry James that bit of Kembleana and out of it he made *Washington Square* and out of that Ruth and Augustus Goetz made *The
Heiress*. Several times James thus used Fanny's anecdotes from her
wide-ranging past. Henry Kemble's subsequent history was not, however, the sort of material suiting James's talent; rather that of the
Brontës. In the second winter of Fanny's stay in England Adelaide
and she were somehow apprised that they had a three-year-old
nephew of whom they were previously unaware, begotten by Henry
in a quasi-permanent liaison with a Dublin woman who had a mental
breakdown and then went to America, leaving the child's situation
forlorn. The Kemble sisters closed ranks. Fanny offered to take the
boy. Adelaide offered her household in England. Henry entrusted
him to Fanny, merely stipulating that he should occasionally visit his
offspring and that a Protestant rearing be given. The "gentlemanly
ease and indifference" with which the father took it all exasperated
Fanny, who was also uncertain of "my father's willingness to receive
the poor little creature into the house for men are severe upon their
sons' editions of their own favorite faults . . . but . . . God aiding,
I shall hope to save this poor little morsel of humanity from its present state of abandonment." [7]

They brought the boy to her in the London house she shared
with Charles, "literally in tatters, swarming with vermin, [but] I
never saw a finer child—tall stout straight well made as white as milk
and as firm as marble. . . . My father I am thankful to say has taken
to him very kindly." At first little Harry, so called to distinguish
him from his peccant father,

> had a violent antipathy to [Fanny] because when his
> grandfather [from Dublin who] brought him to London—
> left him—I was of course obliged to hold the poor little
> creature who would now be separated from him—he flew

into a perfect passion of rage and despair and has not been
able to endure my sight since but sets up the most ear
and heart piercing shrieks the moment he is brought into
my presence. . . . I must hope he will get over it.

Fortunately he did so, "gradually acquiring a taste for my society.
. . . I began to be afraid I was to be his bête noire for the rest of his
natural life." In a matter of weeks she reported to George Combe that
this was "an amiable healthy well conditioned little fellow"[8] and to
an American friend that she was "somewhat more cheerful lately" for
having acquired "a very beautiful well disposed child" for whom her
brother was "unable to provide . . . or even to educate him decently
. . . this little blue-eyed waif of almost four years old."[9] She was
already planning for him. Since he seemed a stable personality but
not sharply intelligent, a midshipman's berth in the Royal Navy
might be best—did this hark back to his father's having been denied
the only career he ever positively wished for?

Now came further light on Henry's home life in Dublin: the
same woman had borne him a baby girl whom he had apparently
preferred not to mention until the boy was provided for. Fanny was
highly indignant. But when Adelaide took complete charge of this
second occasion for family rallying round, Fanny pledged twenty
pounds a year to help, say half the cost of an extra nursery maid, on
top of full expenses for little Harry. Presently their father's insouci-
ance about such matters—and maybe his opportunism about heir-
esses—began to fall better into place. He was not only half-crippled
with inflammatory rheumatism consequent on a fall in the hunting
field, wearing leather breeches, no doubt, but he was going psy-
chotic. At least twice in the 1850s he had to make long stays in
private sanatoriums. Visiting him there, Will Thackeray reported
that the particular way he was out of his mind allowed him to be
foggily cheerful about his situation. A psychosis is always horrible,
and Fanny had every reason to speak of "poor Henry's dreadful condition."[10] But how like blithely egocentric Henry Kemble to imagine "himself staying at a gentleman's country seat . . . quite happy
[telling] himself long-bow stories all day."[11]

Further data about the baby girl are lacking. In the 1850s infant mortality was high even in such well-off households as the Sartorises'. In due time "little Harry" was sent to a school for middle-class boys in London, then in nearby Greenwich with vacations and occasional weekends at the Sartorises' country place. During Fanny's long absences in America, Harness and his family, and later W. B. Donne, august chief creator of the London Library and John Mitchell's successor as Examiner of Plays, a great friend of Fanny's since the Cambridge Apostle days, played uncle for him.

When he reached the age of fourteen, Fanny duly tried to get him into the Royal Navy; nothing came of it. Eventually she placed him in a gentlemanly bureaucrat's post in the Inland Revenue. But then history chose to repeat itself. Just like his grandfather Harry yearned to abandon pen pushing and turn actor, and at first Fanny felt about it much as her uncle John Philip had about Charles's rebellion. Her coming round on the subject was stiff but sensible:

> I am sorry for what you . . . tell me [she wrote to Frederick Leighton] about Harry's strong dramatic propensities. Of course, if he is fit for nothing else, or fitter for that than anything else, he had better become an actor, and his being so in England would not prevent his being a . . . respected member of society. I am, however, much reconciled to what at first disappointed me extremely— my not being able to bring him out to [America]; for if he should eventually take to the stage here, that is simply in most instances merely taking to the gutter.[12]

So, late in 1867 the Inland Revenue lost a nineteen-year-old clerk and Dublin saw the stage debut of another Kemble. Minor troupes at first, of course; Ellen Terry was vastly amused by an early performance of a comic butler entangled with a pet monkey. Then minor supporting roles in London's West End. Never starred, he was nevertheless a widely applauded specialist in several levels of comedy, a steady professional with much of his father's and grandfather's charm; indeed almost as firm a pillar of the Garrick Club as Charles Kemble had ever been. Once the issue of profession was settled, Fanny and he were pattern benevolent aunt and affectionate nephew. He consistently rallied round, coming in to lunch, taking her to plays he thought would amuse her, once spending most of a summer with her in Switzerland. "His Kemble face and voice . . . both very like his father's and my father's, are dear and pleasant to me,"[13] Fanny wrote to Harriet St. Leger. But in press interviews and such Harry never mentioned his father, the handsome young subaltern. He was solely, consistently "Charles Kemble's grandson."

In mid-1853 the Sartorises and Fanny went to Italy for a year free of major complications. Whatever arrangements they made for Charles and little Harry were adequate. They summered at Sorrento, where Fanny fell in love with Ravello, that paradisaical eagle's nest; in the fall they took a large lodging in Rome. Thackeray and his two growing daughters—their mother had become a hopeless mental case—were there, and Robert and Elizabeth Barrett Browning. Those were particular plums among the scores of Britons, some Americans, and sprinklings of French, Scandinavians and so on who, with health or art or fashion as reasons, made Rome-in-winter an institution. We owe Annie Thackeray and Mrs. Browning useful pictures of Charles Kemble's memorable daughters at this period. Annie's father now rather preferred Adelaide to Fanny, writing home that he had learned "to admire but not to endure"[14] Mrs. Kemble. Annie always remembered being taken to call on Mrs. Sartoris

> in a big Roman drawing-room with a great window to the west, and the colours of the room were not unlike sunset colours. There was a long piano with a bowl of flowers . . . soft carpets . . . a beautiful little boy in a white dress, with yellow locks all ashine from the light of the window, was perched upon a low chair looking up at his mother. . . . She was dressed (I can see her still) in a sort of grey satin robe, and her beautiful proud head was turned toward the child . . . she made us welcome then and all the winter.[15]

Sartoris evenings of good cosmopolitan talk and excellent music were deservedly famous, for not only was Adelaide a conversationalist as renowned as her sister, in a different style, but in her drawing room one could still hear her famous voice exquisitely singing everything that she liked best out of her impressive knowledge of music.

The other pivot of those evenings, the famous Mrs. Kemble,

> used to take [Thackeray's girls] out driving with her.
> . . . "Where shall I drive to?" asked the coachman. "An-
> date al Diavolo," says Mrs. Kemble gaily. "Go where you
> will, only go!" And away we drive through the streets and
> out by garden walls and garden gates to the Campagna,
> and as we drive along she begins to sing to us. I could
> box my own ears for wondering what the passers-by would
> think of it, instead of enjoying that bygone song.

Then here is Fanny in a black evening gown by the fire at Adelaide's
with her embroidery "gravely stitching on and on while all the brilliant company came and went." And one evening Annie is at the
Brownings' when Mrs. Kemble enters "the quiet little room, only lit
by a couple of tapers and by the faint glow of the wood fire . . .
Mrs. Browning dim in her dusky gown unrelieved; Mrs. Kemble,
upright and magnificent . . . in stately crimson edged with gold. It
happened to be the red dress day and she wore it."[16]

Mrs. Browning enjoyed having

> Fanny Kemble to come and talk to us with the doors shut,
> we three together. . . . I like her decidedly . . . mag-
> nificent still with her black eyes and radiant smile. A very
> noble creature indeed. Somewhat inelastic . . . attached
> to old modes of thought and conventions, but noble in
> quality and defects. . . . [the Kemble sisters] fail in
> nothing as you see them nearer—noble and upright
> women whose social brilliancy is their least distinction.
> Mrs. Sartoris is the more tender and tolerant, the most
> loveable and sympathetical.[17]

Robert Browning approved of both as much as did his wife, saying
of Fanny a little plaintively that he had often met her in London "but
she hardly noticed me though I always liked her extremely." In Rome
she most particularly noticed him during a picnic in the Campagna
when Mrs. Browning did not feel up to a further excursion to some
object of interest and her husband made nothing of staying behind
with her: " 'You are,' " the former Mrs. Pierce Butler told him,
" 'the only man I ever knew who behaved like a Christian to his
wife.' "[18]

Those winter picnics blended the values of the British country life with local traditions of *dolce far niente;* Boccaccio's house party with only a tinge of the menace of the plague latent in the poor health of some participants. Cheese and fruit and wine and cold dainties against a background of ruins here and there and laughter and singing among highly congenial persons of considerable cultivation. Sometimes they just talked, or somebody read poetry—his or her own or some master's —after the comestibles were discussed. On one such Kemble-centered outing near Lucca, where the Sartorises usually had some time at the baths, Adelaide, in view of its being Sunday, read a sermon of Channing's to them all. That might have struck Boccaccio as anomalous in the middle of a Tuscan landscape; but not anybody aware of the Kemble sisters' unaffected piety.

One frequenter of such occasions and the Sartoris evenings, Frederick Leighton, was a young English painter with a future. His brilliantly drawn, uncompromisingly explicit and incurably romantic paintings now have small communion with current values, but they made him eventually president of the Royal Academy and a peer of the realm. The Kemble sisters and he were the best of friends. Twice he painted May, Adelaide's daughter, and he did not hesitate to ask Fanny to sit for him in the character of Jezebel when he despaired of finding a suitable professional model.[19] Duly amused, she consented. Early in the 1860s Fanny, then in America, strained her moral credit with her cultivated friends in Boston and New York to get Leighton an American market for his work. Little came of it. He sent over a "Venus Disrobing for the Bath"—a slender but fully expressed, apple-breasted damsel with the right wrist barely obscuring the pudendum—that was a little too rich for American blood in those days. But Fanny's relative failure left them better friends than ever.

Harriet Hosmer, the pixieish Yankee girl studying sculpture in Rome—where else in 1852–53?—who had once been a pupil of Elizabeth Sedgwick's in Lenox, thought Adelaide "even more divine than her voice . . . there is only one woman like her . . . in point of goodness . . . Mrs. Sedgwick."[20] Little Hosmer seems to have become a sort of mascot for the harmonious mutual admiration society of which the Sartorises' inner circle in Rome consisted. Leighton called her "the queerest, best-natured little chap possible."[21] Even though dutifully regarding Rome as the fountainhead of sculptural wisdom, she called it the "land of the brave and the home of the flea"[22] and had fun donning men's clothes to get into a monastery to see some particularly choice works of art. Browning lent her the clothes and his company and the monks never knew the difference. Such brashness was a sure recommendation to Fanny, of course. For years Hattie and she kept up a briskly warm relation very pleasant for both, as the Hosmer talent prospered. Numerous replicas of her "Cupid" sold at handsome prices, the state of Missouri paid her ten thousand dollars for a heroic statue of Senator Thomas H. ("Old Bullion") Benton. . . . Over the years it was gratifying to see young people one liked—Leighton, Hosmer, young nephew Harry, Annie Thackeray, Henry James—shaping well. And many of them were associated with the healing amenities of Rome, of which sister Adelaide was crucial ingredient.

Adelaide Kemble Sartoris appears in this book because she was only sister of Frances Anne Kemble Butler, for whom the relationship was important. Yet that need not obscure sister's stature in her own right. In her few years of singing opera she shone about as brightly as Fanny had in spoken drama. Such musicians as Liszt, Mendelssohn, Dessauer, Sir Charles Hallé admired her professional knowledge of music and were also her warm and respectful friends. Her retirement and Sartoris's ample means widened her talent for social entertaining, so that her lodgings in Rome were intermittently a true salon of cosmopolitan renown. The Sartorises' occasional sojourns in Paris, with the same sort of social life, led a knowledgeable French lady to characterize the atmosphere *chez* Sartoris as "une Bohême exquise."[23] Sartoris was by no means always present. Once Adelaide was well established somewhere, he might spend longish periods in England presumably keeping up political and other connections as became a man of affairs. They had three children. An elder son, named Greville after the aristocratic brothers who were such good friends of the Kembles, was killed falling from a horse. The daughter, May, made an aristocratic marriage.[24] The younger son, Algernon, married Nellie,

daughter of President Ulysses S. Grant; the pair met during a transatlantic passage. It was not a happy union.

Since comparisons are inevitable: Adelaide was handsomer than
Fanny, her stage presence at least equally commanding. She had the
sisterly tact to gain weight to the same extent. When both were in
their sixties, Fanny calculated ruefully that between them they
weighed twenty-four stone four (340 pounds); and neither was tall
even in terms of their time. Adelaide's admirers sometimes regarded
her portliness as making her even more queenly. In private they often
sang duets most effectively in spite of the distance between Fanny's
rich if undertrained contralto and Adelaide's lovely and well-disci-
plined soprano. A number of their mutual acquaintances, as has been
seen, preferred Adelaide's serene goodwill and less percussive conver-
sational style to Fanny's. But that does not imply she was insipid.
Fanny relished her sister's "strong powers of ridicule and . . . union
of the sarcastic vein with a vivid imagination,"[25] and realized the
fitness of Adelaide's likening her to the nursery rhyme Dragon of
Wantley:

> . . . round as a butt,
> Full of fire from top to toe,
> Cock of the walk, to the village I strut,
> And scare them all wherever I go.[26]

Sisterly sparks often flew between them. Henry James vastly enjoyed
just sitting in Adelaide's drawing room in London or at Warnford or
Warsash and listening while these two—each in her distinctive style,
both witty and pithy—played a sort of scissors-cut-paper game of
conversation throughout the evening. The most vivacious passages in
Fanny's autobiographies probably give a good gauge on what her end
of the game was like.

Adelaide did some writing for publication, and the best of it, an
expanded sketch, A Week in a French Country House, utilizing her
firsthand knowledge of Continental social ways, gives useful clues to
the flexible, subtly ironic, winningly observant mind that Henry
James admired. About one minor character: "I . . . said that little
whitey-brown women with unsalient features always looked younger
than they really were." About a chief character:

I have never known but one other handsome woman
equally unoccupied with her own beauty. If you had told
her to put on her grandmother's nightcap, she would have
been quite content to do so, and to look like her own
grandmother in it. . . . The sunlight and the shadows
flit over her face according to her humours, just as they
brighten and darken the faces of uncontrolled childhood;
and in her and about her there is all the time a sort of
grand innocence which makes one laugh, and for which
one adores her.

Very perspicacious; sounds like George Eliot or Mrs. Gaskell. But
more to the point here, the pacing and diction show that Thérèse De
Camp's Gallic-edged dexterity with English rubbed off on her
younger as well as her elder daughter. They used it in different ways,
however. Fanny did her best writing in informal letters and diaries.
In verse or fiction she was seldom better than competent. Adelaide
published very little and her best consisted of one short fiction; if she
wrote flavorsome letters I don't know where they are.

This is not a case of Mycroft Holmes and better-known brother
Sherlock. Only one wonders whether Adelaide was not somewhat
more complicated than Fanny—which may or may not be a virtue
depending on the terms and contexts of the equations. She came out
of her prolonged operatic training in Germany and Italy with a
marked un-English accent—understandable but one doubts that
Fanny would have shown heavy oral stigmata; her manner of speech
was too peremptory to admit insidious influences. Certainly Adelaide
thought they "ordered things better in France"—and, for that matter, in Italy. Yet she spent most of her last twenty years in England
without apparent repining so long as she had available a country
house—Sartoris's place at Warnford, once for a long time a cozy
rented estate called Warsash on the water near Titchfield. When it
was indicated—with May's social future in view, for instance—she
took a house in London and entertained with her old skill.

Her social practicality had mixed results. It has been seen that,
regardless of what the effect on the bride might be, she rather approved of Henry's second attempt on Mary Anne Thackeray. From
distant Philadelphia Fanny strongly opposed Algernon Sartoris's mar-

rying Nellie Grant, calling her a "wild, uneducated Western girl."[27] Grant also objected, doubtless on other grounds, but was overruled presumably by the distaff side of the family. Fanny made rather a point of having nothing to do with the young couple before and after their grand White House wedding and much consequent foolish gabble about "the little American princess." Neither of Algernon's parents, however, seems to have felt strongly about it. And it must be said for them that when Algernon proved an idle, unreliable, and often absentee husband, they made no difficulty about absorbing Nellie and her eventual three children into their household where, as Henry James noted, the poor thing was a small fish out of water. Yet they do seem to have done what they could to make the alien corn nourishing and palatable to the exile. Nor are there any traces of Fanny's being tempted into "I told you so."

For, even though communications sometimes lapsed for longish periods, the sisterly relationship was consistently symbiotic and sympathetic. Fanny writes to Hattie Hosmer in Rome that she does well to be with Adelaide as much as possible: "You will seldom see a more amiable or a more charming person," she says. Not that Adelaide's chin-up serenity may not have masked emotional perplexities. "I have suffered so much from unkindness and neglect, that it makes me lenient to anyone who is kind,"[28] she once told Hamilton Aidé, a rising young writer in the Kembles' entourage. A few years later Henry Greville tells Fanny that he wishes Adelaide could "make a life for herself independent of Edward's pursuits and pleasure." He might as well wish she had a short nose, Fanny replied: "People who take life (and above all) love easy are twice blessed . . . the women of my mother's blood are not so and our affections seem to me among the foremost trials of our existences."[29]

Fanny might further have suspected "my mother's blood" in the talent for comedy that made Adelaide a delight in private theatricals and as Susannah in *The Marriage of Figaro*. Science now deplores such notions of genetics; but it remains true that through other means of influence Thérèse De Camp was written all over both daughters. Annie (Thackeray) Ritchie said they "had the rare power of stirring and stimulating one's sleepy, makeshift soul, suggesting, satisfying," and recalled "a great critic," not otherwise identified, who, hearing she was writing about them, said, " 'Use no conventional epithets; those sisters are beyond any banality of praise.' "[30]

It was just as well Fanny had two long respites in Rome during the 1850s, for otherwise the decade was rather rich in strains. Even during her first stay she was entangled in correspondence with her lawyers in Philadelphia over the settlement Pierce had to be chivied into making final. He seldom paid the quarterly $1,300; Fanny was inclined to let arrears accumulate without pushing protests home. A few months after her return from Rome in 1854 Charles Kemble died, seventy-nine years old. This relieved him of the miseries of old age, including deafness grown so severe that he could not hear the loudest thunder, was aware of it only by vibration in his knees, he said. Fanny's deep affection for him had survived his embarrassment about having nibbled at her money, but it did take several years of litigation to clear it for her. Her readings kept her solvent; and when brother John Mitchell died in 1857, leaving his children nearly destitute, she could contribute seven hundred pounds to the fund raised to provide for them. Fanny wrote bleakly to Henry Greville: "That root of kindred bore few blossoms and little fruit but its being wrenched away tore the heartstrings."[31]

In 1856 daughter Sarah had come of age, out from under Pierce's thumb, and Fanny returned to America for reunion with her and eighteen-year-old Frances at Lenox, beginning the arrangement of two months with their mother each summer. They had a lively and propitious season even though Pierce did what he could to spoil it by impulsively coming to Lenox for a week to impose himself on the girls' time, contravening the spirit if not the letter of the bargain. "The mere anticipation of his arrival made me ill," Fanny said. In the fall, when the girls returned to the shabby Philadelphia boarding-house that was all Pierce could then afford, she could tell herself that they "enjoyed their holiday with me . . . and speak of returning next year as of a pleasure in prospect." Yet "the delight of having them with me has been most cruelly allayed by all that I see of the unhappy result of the wretched influences to which they have been subjected . . . condemned to all sorts of ill habits."[32]

Particularly the lavish clothes allowances they were given in spite of Pierce's money troubles vexed her. She had no talent for cheese-paring herself, but in those last few years of the marriage he had been the prodigal. Now this overliberality seemed only part of a growing irresponsibility about finances, consistent with his continuing failure to pay the annuity. Then as summer ended came word that Pierce Butler, heir of the old major's famous fortune, had been wildly speculating in stocks and was well and truly insolvent. "An hereditary fortune . . . lost by sheer folly and infatuation,"[33] says Sidney Fisher's diary. Fortunately for Pierce most of the Butler assets were tied up in trusts with John's widow as part beneficiary. (In 1846 John Butler had gone off to the Mexican War and died of a particularly virulent form of Montezuma's revenge.) After prolonged confusion it was determined that sale of Pierce's half share of the slaves in Georgia—not included in the real property, hence available—would raise enough to pay his creditors. Circumstances mitigated the seriousness. Hampton Point, decreasingly fertile, was hardly paying for the maintenance of its several hundred black inhabitants. To put Hampton Point on a caretaker basis and concentrate the unsold half of the Butler slaves on profitable Butler's Island was, though involuntary, good management. And Pierce's half-title to the land of both plantations, protected by trusts, left him still worth nominally upward of $250,000.

Such things usually take time, so it was February 1859 before Pierce's slaves went on the block in the largest sale of such property America had ever seen—429 men, women, and children on display in the stables and carriage sheds at Savannah's racecourse. It rained throughout the several days of the sale, which must have deepened the depressing atmosphere of the affair. The rules of sale, following standing Butler policy, forbade separating wives and husbands or parents and children, but the sense of a community disintegrating was strong. Black slaves generally regarded such a disruptive necessity as a grim calamity; its usual cause was the master's death, requiring settlement of the estate, which was one reason why slaves were always very anxiously solicitous about the master's health.

Widely advertised, the event brought slave dealers and plantation owners from all over the South, filling Savannah's hotels, splashing in the rain from shed to shed examining the stock in trade, remarking on the relative lack of light skins—due, of course, to the isolation of the Sea Island operations—that meant heightened value, for admixture of white blood was taken to imply lowered tractability. A reporter from the antislavery New York *Tribune* posing as a buyer to get his story described the average raggedy slave as looking "as if he could shake himself out of his clothes with his hands in his pockets"; and the buyers as "of a rough breed, slangy, profane and boorish" and callously crude in inspecting and handling prospective purchases. In recovery from the national financial panic of 1857 the South's economy was booming. Slave prices were so high that certain enterprising Southerners were making a serious effort to revive the old slave-trade with West Africa. So the Butler slaves went high: $900 for average field-hands, up to $1,500 to $1,600 for such craftsmen as carpenters, blacksmiths, and coopers. The total net was an ample $303,850 and the auctioneer opened champagne for all; whites, that is. Pierce had come down to see the last of many of his long-standing possessions. Graciously he moved among them, speaking to many by name, sometimes shaking hands and, the reporter noted with wonder, "being recognized with seeming pleasure by all."[34] At the end he gave each alienated slave four shiny new quarter dollars to remember him by. "To give more would have been expensive," commented Sidney Fisher in Philadelphia. "They had masters and no wants & yet some token was proper on the occasion, no doubt a very sad one for Butler."[35] No doubt.

Fanny was outraged by "the ruin of my girls' prospects by their father's insane gambling in the stocks."[36] Between reading engagements she spent much of the next year seeking to salvage as much as possible for them. Not for herself, she insisted to old J. F. Fisher, her trustee in the deal with Pierce; she was proud of her ability to pay her own way and, now Pierce's munificence had dried up, take the girls to Lenox out of her own pocket. Now, however, she wanted the arrears of the annuity somehow collected and added to the principal of the trust for the eventual benefit of Sarah and Frances, which already held the mortgage on Butler Place and York Farm.

The urgency of thus safeguarding the house where they were

born was not all sentiment. The new railroads had Philadelphia growing out toward those properties; and an offer to buy York Farm had
come to seven hundred dollars an acre. Pierce offered to pay up the
arrears, now over twelve thousand dollars, if Fanny would relinquish
all legal hold on that mortgage in favor of the girls. She, however,
convinced that the extravagant way he had reared them—or let them
grow under destabilizing circumstances—had left both with little
sense of what to do with money, insisted on retaining control as
potential beneficiary of the trust until the girls married. For a wonder, in view of her lack of experience in such matters, she got her
way. And in the end it pleased her immensely to find that it was her
firmness in this respect that had kept the trust first creditor on
Pierce's insolvency, hence the two farms were untouchable for the
other creditors.

Now she could leave the girls in their boardinghouse—she
rather hoped it would begin their economic reeducation—and go on
an extended reading tour of the old Northwest to pile up some more
of the dollars that made her independent of lords and masters. Her
tour of that area two years earlier had been curiously tonic: "I have
been to the great West this winter," she wrote to Arthur Malkin,
another of her friends from John Mitchell's Cambridge days.

> The hurry of life . . . the rapidity, energy, and en-
> terprise with which civilization is there being carried for-
> ward, baffles all description. . . . Cities of magnificent
> streets and houses, with wharves, and quays, and ware-
> houses, and storehouses, and shops full of Paris luxuries,
> and railroads from and to them in every direction, and
> land worth its weight in gold by the foot, and populations
> of fifty and hundreds of thousands, where, within the
> memory of men . . . the forest grew and the savage wan-
> dered.
>
> I was at a place called Milwaukee . . . where they
> invited me to . . . read Shakespeare . . . an indication
> of advanced civilization, and one of the residents, a man
> not fifty years old, told me that he remembered the spot
> on which stood the hotel . . . a tangled wilderness
> through which ran an Indian trail. Does not all that sound
> wonderful? [37]

But later in the year the panic of 1857 moved her to not altogether nonsensical comments on the

> financial and commercial tornado which has swept over this country. . . . moral foundations are the only stable ones even for material prosperity . . . a man's faith in his neighbor is a more absolutely valuable thing than any amount of money either of them possess. The selfish cowardice which has caused the greater part of all this fearful smash is the most disgusting exhibition of the meanness of human nature that can be conceived.

Early the following year she had further good reason to lament the unreliability of the American economy when the trustees of the funds she was accumulating sold her New York-based securities that paid seven percent and put the proceeds into British consols at three percent, meaning three thousand dollars less income a year. She had the sense not to question her trustee friends' judgment but also wondered rebelliously whether "when those men die, shall I be able to get my money's worth again?" [38]

During that same reading tour's swing through New York State Fanny had Sarah along for a short vacation stay at Trenton Falls. In the twenty-four years since her first visit a sightseers' hotel had been built and flourished but the roaring, glittering waters had not changed and the forest hills round about were relatively untouched. But not even the full days of water watching and tramping in the woods, returning disheveled and soaked by occasional showers, could exorcise the vestigia of Pierce Butler. Some of the gloomiest—and most effective—verses Fanny ever wrote came out of this bit of emotional bad judgment. And to make sure it was a disaster Sarah contracted a large-scale case of poison ivy, no less miserable for her and indirectly for Fanny, because it was acknowledgedly nothing serious enough to carry any dignity.

In May 1859 Frances came of age, breaking Pierce's last substantial hold on Fanny. She immediately took the girl overseas for several months in England and on the Continent, doubtless with some notion of supplementing the disturbed and largely parochial rearing she had had. She never lost pride in the women her chicks grew into. "Oh, I wish I could show you [Sarah], she is so handsome and so clever," [39] she told Malkin. Frances was somewhat kittenishly pretty and sporadically vivacious. But it was a trial for Fanny that both were inclined to stay in the Philadelphia orbit that they knew best, which also implied persisting closeness to their father. Of the two Sarah was less firmly attached to him. After two years of vibrating between her parents' spheres of influence, she exorcised the issue by an admirable marriage—to young Dr. Owen J. Wister of a Germantown family very well placed among Philadelphians. Fanny and the Wisters were already cordial friends and son- and mother-in-law were never at odds; indeed over the years they got on better than Fanny and Sarah. But for the next two decades at least, until well after Pierce Butler was dead, Frances made it clear that she regarded herself as her father's daughter. Sometimes she was plucky about it, once very cruel; but always adhesive. It was a remarkable tribute to Pierce's renowned, indefinable but unquestionably redoubtable charm.

Nor were permanent effects lacking on Sarah. Her son, Owen Wister, the eminent novelist, wrote toward the end of his life:

> I was brought up to revere my grandfather. He did indeed make both his daughters adore him. . . . Only since I have been past middle life have I gradually made out that on the whole he couldn't have been a good person while Fanny Kemble, poor, tempestuous spirit . . . was noble and magnanimous. Butler was cold. Never forgave. That's the root of the trouble. Well, all dead & gone. The pale wraith [of the Kemble sisters] that lives in me . . . when I think of them, how vital and superb [they] were, how much they exceeded the average in their dimensions, glows for a moment in their light. [40]

XIX

ᵂ𝒻ᵉ

Irrepressible Conflict

For America that decade of the 1850s had been as eventful on the grand scale as for Fanny personally. It had begun with the momentous Compromise of 1850 that, hindsight now suggests, made the Civil War inevitable. In 1854 guerilla warfare created "Bleeding Kansas." In 1856 on the floor of the U.S. Senate a southern congressman beat Fanny's friend, Senator Charles Sumner, into insensibility for his violent attacks on slavery. In 1859, the year Frances Butler came of age and Sarah Butler married, John Brown was hanged for raiding Harpers Ferry. Fanny's young Shakespearean, Horace Howard Furness, was one of the abolitionist stalwarts who sneaked the corpse through Philadelphia to thwart threats to seize and dishonor it on its way north. The impending convulsion, already making such premonitory waves in American lives, would give Fanny her share of repercussions.

Most of the early ones came from Frances and her father. Now in her early twenties, the girl had some of her mother's style: " 'The puss!' " her admiring sister wrote, " 'with her short curling hair and baby mouth, she does not look eighteen & I believe she spoke her whole soul when she said: "There's nothing in the whole world I would like to be as much as a news-boy!" ' "[1] Sidney Fisher thought her "gay, graceful, thorobred, clever, cultivated, & more than pretty . . . a good figure & an expressive face, beautiful hair, & good features."[2] It amused her mother when, having danced with the Prince of Wales, the nation's most lionized visitor in 1860, at the ball given

him in New York, Frances shrugged him off as " 'a nice little fellow
and dances well.' Think . . . of the shock to my rather superstitious
. . . loyalty," Fanny wrote to Malkin, "at hearing my future sovereign . . . clapped on the shoulder by this monkey of a democratic
damsel of mine."[3] But that was before things heated up. Late in
1860 Pierce Butler had gone south on the annual inspection of the
plantations. The visit also enabled him to reconnoiter "the impending
crisis," to borrow a phrase from an antisouthern propagandist. He
was back the last week of the year, Sidney Fisher reported, "eager for
secession. . . . said he came only to buy arms and intends to return
immediately and join the army. He will take his daughter Fanny with
him and has bought a rifle for *her* too, for he says even the women in
the South are going to fight."[4]

That a man accustomed to responsible society, as Pierce was,
should have taken such talk seriously is hard but not impossible to
believe. One excuse, partial but sound, might be the failure of many
to understand at that juncture what secession and war would mean.
It took Pierce some months, of course, to get round to carrying out
his plan. Late in March 1861, however, he got away southward es-
corting not only Frances but also Fisher's Carolina-born sister-in-law
making a last-minute visit to her family. At the time Fort Sumter
was already under siege, President Lincoln had been inaugurated, federal government south of the Potomac was in abeyance. Incredulous,
Fisher tried to explain this genteel foray into chaos: For some years
Mrs. Fisher had been

> an intimate friend of Mrs. Kemble & [Joshua] Fisher [her
> husband] is the trustee of the latter and both . . . were
> not long ago loud in the denunciation of Butler, & Mrs.
> Fisher even went so far as to refuse to speak to him. But
> about a year ago, Fisher wished to invite [Sarah Butler] to
> a party, for her mother's sake chiefly. He did not like to
> do this without asking [Frances], and he could not ask her
> without including her father. . . . Butler went . . . and
> as he well knows how to do . . . made himself acceptable
> to Mrs. Fisher . . . secession I suppose has proved a bond
> of sympathy and when Butler heard that Mrs. Fisher was
> going to Carolina, as he also wished . . . to go to Geor-
> gia about the same time, he offered to be her escort.[5]

This demonstration of Pierce's way with ladies is the more impressive because Mrs. Fisher was one of the few in whom Fanny confided about the maidservant seduced in London. That he now encumbered his venture into a growingly disturbed region with the charge of two women, one elderly, may merely betoken his failing sense of reality. Frances, inexperienced, headstrong, and fond of her father, may not have appreciated how harebrained it was, but for a man approaching fifty it was surprising. He may have had a subtler reason. So late in March the plantations did not expect the owner's presence. In the previous December Pierce had presumably completed instructions for the coming year in rice. Daughter Sarah believed he was going south to enlist in the Confederate service as he had told Fisher he would. But since he eventually returned without having done so, Philadelphia's gossips' whispered theory may have been right—he was on some confidential mission involving financing or arms. And what better cover than chivalrously seeing Mrs. Fisher safe to Charleston with his pretty daughter along for company?

They reached Charleston early in April. Pierce was included in a patrician sightseeing party that General Pierre G. T. Beauregard himself showed over the batteries two days before Sumter surrendered. In a few days Frances in Darien wrote Sarah that the fall of Sumter surely would so impress the North with the South's dauntless determination that hostilities would be called off. After some weeks at Butler's Island Pierce escorted Frances by a necessarily circuitous route through the seceded states to Cincinnati, whence she came home: ". . . had not changed her clothes for six days until this morning," Sarah's diary says, ". . . . had not been in bed for six nights. Nevertheless she looks fat & fresh."[6] Pierce eventually relieved Sarah's mind by writing to her that, much as he valued the Southern cause, "as a born & bred Pennsylvanian he would never take up arms against his own country even were [his daughters] not . . . a restraining motive."[7] Such state loyalty was like Robert E. Lee's in reluctantly resigning from the U.S. Army to fight for his native Virginia. Nor is there any reason to suspect Pierce Butler of the white feather.

Either he had a specially acute fit of dawdling that summer or he still had some secret business in the South. For it was early Au-

gust, three months later, two weeks after Bull Run, before, greatly
to his daughters' relief, he reappeared in Philadelphia. The city's close
social and economic ties with the South probably assured him some
countenance at the Philadelphia Club. The copperheadish tendencies
of some of its members were one reason why well-placed Philadelphians hot for the Union soon founded the Union League Club as antidote. But Pierce's mysterious and prolonged absence on top of his
foolish remarks about arms buying the previous winter inevitably attracted attention. None had cause for surprise when, six weeks after
his return, Federal marshals came to Mrs. Jones's boardinghouse on
Walnut Street and arrested Pierce Butler on suspicion of trafficking
with the enemy. They let him consult George Cadwalader, his lawyer
brother-in-law, later a Union general, and then took him off to Fort
Lafayette, one of New York City's harbor defenses.

Mrs. Jones told Sarah how haughtily Pierce had bowed to the
officers "with slightly quivering lips & nostrils as is his wont when
at the highest pitch of anger."[8] Sarah's distress was great, Frances's
even greater. Hearing that Pierce would certainly be quartered with
the officers and given the run of the fort, Sarah planned to rush to
New York bringing him clean towels, fruit, and his flute, etc. But a
letter from him warned her bitterly that he was herded into a case-
mate with five others, no visitors, no use for either relatives or friends
to try to see him. Cadwalader was working toward eventual release
through personal influence; as to visiting, however, he said only President Lincoln or Lieutenant General Winfield Scott, Federal chief of
command, could grant that privilege. Sarah telegraphed to Frances, in
Lenox with her mother, to stay where she was and wrote to the President. Nothing happened. A few days later, after telling her husband
about it, she wrote again in different terms. He sent it to a friend of
his, G. V. Fox, recently become assistant secretary of the Navy, to
be handed personally to Mr. Lincoln. Then off Sarah went to Lenox
to comfort Frances.

To Arthur Malkin Fanny wrote calmly that "The charge against
him . . . that he acted as an agent for the Southerners . . . I think
. . . very likely to be true; whether it can be proved or not is another
question . . . [but] I think it probable that . . . [he] will be de-

tained until the conclusion of the war, as he is not likely to accept any oath of allegiance tendered . . . by this government."[9] After a week of Berkshire pleasures Sarah and Frances received presidential permission to visit Pierce—for only a short time and in presence of an Army officer, true, but for what it was worth they rushed to New York. Not long afterward he was released on condition of not an oath of allegiance as such but a sworn pledge to behave himself for the duration.[10]

Though Sarah's anxiety about him was as real as Frances's, her zeal for the Union was nearly as strong as her mother's. This is a pretty problem for psychologists gauging the effects of early environment, including parental relations. At the age of four elder daughter has five months of being a slave-coddled little princess on a model plantation and grows up rather more attached to her proslavery pro-Confederacy father than to her antislavery, pro-Union mother. Yet in the Civil War she is solidly pro-Union in a Philadelphia where copperheadism was socially admissible though by no means dominant. She rejoiced in Union victory, gloomed over Union defeat, readily swallowed anti-Confederate gossip, ministered to the boys in blue. Whereas the other daughter, too much the baby on the plantation to remember much about it, reared in the same jangled atmosphere as her sister, not only grew up obsessively fond of her father but from only a few weeks of the Sea Islands in early 1861 became utterly committed to his defense of slavery and the recalcitrant South.

I have insufficient data for hoping to understand the Butler sisters. It seems clear that of the three women, Fanny was best fitted for coping with life. Though they all had to struggle year after year with the problem, then so imperative, of keeping up an adequate staff of competent servants, white or black, native or exotic, only Fanny could and did often joke about it. Beyond that one can only wonder at the persistence of the unstable equilibrium of the group. Mother rather fears Pierce Butler as a once attractive manifestation of malice. Each daughter, in her own fashion, loves him dearly. Mother contemplates nothing but complete victory over the Confederacy. Elder daughter also wishes that but maybe not quite so intensely. Younger daughter, dedicated to Pierce's terms, dreads any such possibility.

The bond between elder daughter and mother is sometimes frayed because mother and daughter's husband get on tactlessly well and daughter is something of an unacknowledged hypochondriac. But the abiding sourness between mother and younger daughter comes not from cordiality between husband and mother at all, but from daughter's heedless extravagances and invidious cleaving unto Pierce.

Here, of course, the onlooker must stir in the chemical reactions more or less normal between mothers and daughters, the yeastier for all parties being high-strung. But how many of these strains were residue from the long years, when, as adolescents, the two were trained by spite and betrayed by affection for Pierce into mistrust and disapproval of Fanny? Those toxins must have persisted to an important degree, apparently more strongly in Frances. Yet the effects fluctuated, often falling short of critical severity. Both daughters were far closer to Fanny than to any of Pierce's female relatives. Each traveled with her mother far and long. Several years of close proximity to Sarah led to no major crises that one knows of. And though Fanny's final several years with Frances were not altogether peaceable, they worked out little worse than usual between aging matron-daughters and very old mothers. In spite of her wide swings of mood Sarah was unreservedly proud of Fanny as queenly reader and comrade of significant people. And Frances, though given to a flighty malice, admired and valued her mother's taken-for-granted relations with people with handles to their names.

One could wish that, having fought so hard for her chicks, then renounced them for their own good, then recovered them by grace of impersonal lapse of time, Fanny had not found their matured feathers sometimes disconcertingly stiff and their beaks capable of sharp pecking. But part of that may come of her scar tissue aforesaid, of a certain numbing of her salient points, so that reciprocal sympathies were somewhat dimmed. Consider that whereas Fanny's own records show her as a ready and persistent weeper well into the 1840s, after the ordeal of divorce was behind her, the incidence of tears is much lower. Fanny could still make warm new friends from both sexes and derive new exultation from the Alps, but there is reason to surmise that her personal feelings never again got as deep into her emotional marrow as when she was nursing Sarah or crying her heart out on Butler's Island over Psyche's plight. The episodes of violent weeping that one knows of were likely to be curiously impersonal; she almost flooded Henry James out of a theater box when he took her to see a sentimental play, and Bryan Procter's (Barry Cornwall's) clever wife and good friend of Fanny's felt impelled to warn Lord Houghton not to try to discuss the Civil War with her because she had "cried so terribly on Thursday"[11] when Procter spoke of it.

Ruefully Fanny recognized the coincidence of her private and America's public troubles. Late in 1864 she advised Henry Lee apropos of Anglo-American relations that "the two nations, mother and daughter though they be, can no more understand each other than I and my children can."[12] For the first year and a half of the war, she provided her British friends a running mail commentary. Its tenor shifted with events but always with the North's scale rising and the South's sinking in her esteem and hopes. Her beginning was less temperate than her later efforts. About the election of 1860 she tells Malkin: "The southern states are loud in vehement threats of secession . . . but their bluster is really lamentably ludicrous, for they are without money, without credit, without power, without character."[13] After the disaster at Bull Run that had the Federal cause floundering: "The United States schism . . . has become a wide yawning cleft . . . a mad tumult of folly and wickedness. . . . slavery has made the Southerners insane egoists, and the pursuit of gain has made the Northerners incapable egoists. . . . a grievous civil war, shattering their financial and commercial idols, and compelling them to find the connection between public safety and private virtues, may yet preserve them." Poor enough prophecy: certain results of the Civil War were beneficent but few historians would try to show that revulsion from corrupt materialism was one of them. Yet Fanny, bitter foe of slavery and firsthand observer of the South's ruling caste, could not hesitate as to which side to take:

> A short time ago I was in New York and Philadelphia, giving away, as tokens of female affection, swords and pistols to . . . soldiers, whom I remember boys in round

jackets. Up here [in Lenox] . . . the tap of a drum along
the village street at evening, calling the men to drill when
they have done work, is our faint echo of the great national stir, and the vivid stars and stripes flying from the
scattered farmhouses . . . [are] the only visible sign of
the strife . . . already begun.

For a while it looked as if, supposing Missouri seceded, her investments in St. Louis would go glimmering. She was game about it: "I
must be prepared for loss of property . . . certainly diminution of
income; but everybody will have to suffer more or less, and I may be
thankful that it will not be in the lives of those who are dear to me
that I can be touched." [14]

By mid-September 1861 she was further toward confidence in

the ultimate success of the North. . . . I hope to God
that neither England nor any other power from the other
side of water will meddle . . . after some bad and good
fighting, and an unlimited amount of brag and bluster on
both sides, the South, in spite of a much better state of
preparation, of better soldiers, better officers . . . and
. . . a much more unanimous and *venomous* . . . hostility, will be obliged to knock under. . . . slavery will be
swept from among the acknowledged institutions of
America. [15]

She was never an abolitionist in the formal sense even though sympathetic to such abolitionist stalwarts as Lucretia Mott and Charles
Sumner.

I have hitherto held the emancipation of the slaves to be
exclusively the business and duty of their owners [she now
wrote to Charles Greville], whose highest moral interest
I thought it was to rid themselves of such a responsibility,
in spite of the manifest worldly interests almost inextricably bound up with it.
. . . now, however, [I] heartily embrace [abolition-
ist views] . . . from the moment the United States government assumed an attitude of coercion . . . it was
bound . . . wherever it planted the standard of the
Union, to proclaim the universal freedom which is the
recognized law of the Northern United States. [16]

She had been aghast at the possibility, temporary but critical while it lasted, that the *Trent* affair[17] would bring Britain in on the Southern side, whither the cotton mills' need for raw material and the ruling classes' toploftical sympathy with "the Southern chivalry" seemed to be nudging Her Majesty's not altogether reluctant government.

For the next two years she was almost as apprehensive as if she were personally in charge lest that leaning should result in British recognition of the Confederacy, or worse. "Let there . . . be no war between England and America," she had written Charles Sedgwick in Washington. "The worthy old world totters on slowly enough toward general betterment without being set back . . . a hundred years by the folly and wickedness of two nations especially appointed to lead the progress of humanity."[18] It may have added immediacy to her feelings that she knew personally both Lord John Russell, the foreign secretary steering Britain's surly policy through these chancy waters, and Charles Francis Adams, U.S. minister to the Court of St. James's, cannily but sternly handling the American side. So far as I know she made no representations to either. But it was no mere love of gossiping that produced long letters from Lenox to the Grevilles about the risk of underestimating the North's strength and the folly of backing King Cotton and Jefferson Davis. The Grevilles knew any number of strategically situated persons on whom impression might be made.

Whether anything was thus effected, who knows? Certainly Fanny cannot be cast as budding stateswoman-advisor. And she certainly had no sibylline powers. She was wrong in assuming that Federal capture of New Orleans would substantially alleviate Britain's shortage of cotton; and that in consequence of the war cotton-production outside Dixie would make Manchester independent of America. She doubted that even if, as she wished, the North won, the two sections could be sutured together into eventual reunion; for years she had shared the long-standing European delusion that the United States was sure to split into two or three squabbling separate nations. Occasionally she advised American friends to use postwar readjustment to restrict the suffrage, particularly to disqualify recent immigrants. But much of that merely showed again that no matter how long Roger Kemble's granddaughter inhabited America, she remained ambivalently British about it. As Henry James so shrewdly said, her "love for the United States was a totally different matter from a liking . . . [they] commended themselves to her liberal opinions as much as they disconcerted her intensely conservative taste; . . . she never heard them eulogized without uttering her reserves or abused without speaking her admiration."[19]

It followed that on returning to Britain she was not at all infected by the pro-Confederatism of Mayfair, Belgravia, and the Dukeries. She rejoiced to hear that the Yankees had occupied St. Simon's Island, and for Henry Greville harked back to the time when she had spent days washing the babies who had now grown into adult field-hands marched into inner Georgia by perplexed overseers. She took the arrival of U.S.S. *Monitor* in Hampton Roads in time to checkmate C.S.S. *Virginia (née* U.S.S. *Merrimac)* as a clear act of divine providence. During a couple of weeks in Washington, she had not found its war-harried confusion edifying; but she met and admired Frederick L. Olmsted, a great man in the invaluable U.S. Sanitary Commission, and recommended to Greville Olmsted's books on slavery as the only really good ones. When staying with the Wisters in their comfortable stone house in Germantown, she was much in Philadelphia reading to the sick and wounded. Mid-May 1862 she assures Donne from Lenox that Yankee country folks are soberly giving "their lives for this struggle, about which they have at last become, after their own imperturbable fashion, horribly in earnest";[20] and tells him that Berkshire villages are now almost devoid of young men, so women are running things to an unprecedented and interesting extent!

On July 2, 1862, she sails for England in the Cunarder *China* in a change of scene planned for months though the surviving record does not show why. She was developing a habit of transatlantic vibration, America to Europe and vice versa every year or two. It kept her up with the Sartorises, young Harry, Harriet, Emily FitzHugh; and such old friends from among the Apostles as Donne, Malkin, Edward

FitzGerald; and in America with the Sedgwicks, Mary Fox, the Furnesses. Particularly now that at Uncle Sam's behest Pierce was immobilized with Frances as daughterly companion, and Sarah engrossed by war-related activity and a promising baby son named Owen after his father, Fanny's presence in America was less significant. And maybe more weightily she needed income. "I am slightly ruined by the sudden drying up of interest on capital invested alas! in St. Louis,"[21] she told young Charles Sedgwick as the financial repercussions of war now boomed in. Doubtless besides, war was distracting her potential audiences and fouling up travel arrangements, whereas her British public might well be ready for another reading tour after some years of respite. There were two sides to going "home": The slump in the exchange value of the dollar cut deeply into the purchasing power of her residual American income, if she went to the land of pounds, shillings, and pence. But she was confident—rightly, it proved—that over there she could "make my voice my purse once more."[22]

So she was in England during the latter half of the crisis in British-American relations that lasted far into 1863. The *Trent* affair was now history, but the British failure to keep commerce-raiding Confederate men-of-war (C.S.S. *Florida* and C.S.S. *Alabama*) from being outfitted and sailing from British ports looked like bad faith or worse. Next year the same thing was impending about more powerful vessels obviously being built for the Confederacy; and all through the rise of these actual or potential floutings of neutrality (as Washington necessarily saw them), British capital's need for cotton grew more critical, and London's influential diners-out more favorable to the Confederate cause. Lee's Army of Northern Virginia continued to make Federal armies look futile and Washington's official story—that the North's was a war for the Union, not a war against slavery—confused the considerable antislavery minority among influential Britons. Fanny found herself immersed in an elegantly gowned and coiffed, handsomely whiskered and white-waistcoated consensus, sure that Yankee dollar-chasers and counter-jumpers would never be a match for southern gentlemen; Lord John was quite right to take no insolence from that grotesque frontiersman in Washington;

and since it would be so awkward to get rid of it, slavery was as humane a way as any to provide for inferior races. "Daily and hourly," Fanny recalled, she was "hearing the condition of the slaves discussed, in a spirit of entire sympathy with their owners that nothing but the most absolute ignorance could excuse."[23]

From the beginning of the war antislavery feeling, hence anti-Confederacy sentiment, had been strong among Britain's large minority of Dissenters—the unfashionable but economically weighty religious groups outside the established Church of England. Mill hands put out of work by shortage of cotton showed remarkable sympathy with the North as an antislavery force even though years of joblessness might lie ahead. But from Sumter to Antietam neither of those elements had great leverage on public sentiment. The newspaper press early took and kept its tone from "Bull Run" Russell's contemptuous filings to the *Times* about Northern soldiers' incompetence. Nor was Fanny on the best terms with the antislavery patricians, chiefly women. The older among them were still mindful of the antislavery agitation that had freed the blacks in the British West Indies. Presently they, and their daughters, had been swept off their feet by the cataclysmic success of *Uncle Tom's Cabin* in the early 1850s. Led by the Duchess of Sutherland they had drawn up an "Affectionate and Christian Address of Many Thousands of Women of Great Britain and Ireland to their Sisters, the Women of the United States," adjuring them to set about immediate legalizings of slave marriages and outlawing of separation of slave families as preliminaries to abolishing slavery altogether. Just like that.

Following the lead of three duchesses, a countess, and the wives of several eminent writers, half a million British women signed in the winter of 1852–53. Fanny, then reading in Britain, declined to do so in spite of her vigorous and articulate hatred of slavery. She deplored the impertinent and self-righteous tone of the "Address": "I felt very sure that no other signer . . . knew more of the facts of American slavery than I did; but . . . no other knew, as I did . . . its absolute futility; and the bitter feeling that it could not fail to arouse, even in the women of the Northern States, by the assumed moral superiority that it would be thought to imply."[24] And much bristling did occur among American women abolitionists who had spent years trying somehow to influence the slave power toward even hints of meliorative action. Harriet Beecher Stowe herself, though an admiring protégée of the Duchess of Sutherland, expressed disapproval of this ill-conceived piece of condescension.

At the time Fanny thought seriously of striking what seemed to her a better-aimed stroke for the slaves by publishing the letter-diary she had kept for Elizabeth Sedgwick in the Sea Islands back in 1839. But to do so might goad Pierce into some harsh retaliation using the children as weapons to their detriment; and down there, besides, she had been in a confidential position with vulnerable persons, such as the Frasers. So every time she pondered the matter, Headman Frank and Jack and Psyche and the concupiscent and articulate Roswell King, Jr., went back into limbo. Now ten years later she was again in Britain, had her Georgian journal with her—may well have brought it just in case—and understood as well as anybody that what literate Britons thought of slavery in the South was as important as cotton supply or the interests of British shipbuilders. She went looking for a publisher.

That decision to print her *Journal of a Residence on a Georgian Plantation* made her as near immortal as bibliographies and libraries can arrange. It was and is the best available firsthand account of America's black slavery. After exhaustive exploration twenty years ago I made that judgment and find no reason to modify it. For authenticity and quality of observation it equals Olmsted's several accounts of his journeys through the South in the 1850s, and he never absorbed a single situation long enough for more than intelligent sketching. Fanny's findings were made "in depth"—often the depth of despair. Further, her book is not only indispensable to sudents of black slavery, it contains much very good writing—"easily the best"[25] of her prose, Henry James said.

Actually the text is incomplete. Its prelude should have been Fanny's account of that wild winter journey, so discreditable to Dixie, from Philadelphia to Butler's Island already published in *Bentley's Miscellany* in 1841.[26] But Bentley refused to release it, doubtless because Fanny had placed the project book with Longmans. This did not harm her later relations with the Bentley firm, and the omission made little difference to readers unaware of it. This Longmans narrative, hereinafter referred to as *Georgian Plantation,* is sandwiched between two letter-essays: for preface a statement of Fanny's view of slavery just before Pierce took her south; for tailpieces, a letter, never printed, to the London *Times* in 1853, on attacks on *Uncle Tom's Cabin;* and one to "C. G., Esq.," presumably Charles Greville, in late 1862, analyzing the situations of North and South in the light of Lincoln's post-Antietam promise of emancipation in 1863. The whole thus represents the evolution of Fanny's views of slavery and the South, expressed with unusual sensitivity, vigor, and clear logic.

The reader has already seen much of it quoted, but most of that was personal descriptions. On the side of comment: Her opening tells Elizabeth Sedgwick that "I *am* going [south] prejudiced against slavery . . . [but I promise] nevertheless to strive for accuracy and recognize mitigations when encountered, even [expect] to find them."[27] Apparently rebutting a defense of slavery recently shown her, she disposes in advance of the slaveholder's contention that slave status is appropriate for blacks because they are *"animals,* incapable of mental culture and moral improvement." In that case, why southern laws against teaching them to read and write? "We have no laws forbidding . . . our dogs and horses to learn as much as they can comprehend." Ably she fields the contention that economically the South's slaves are

> "better off than half the Continental peasantry" . . . [or] "the miserable Irish. . . ." Though the negroes are fed, clothed, and housed, and though the Irish peasant is starved, naked, and roofless, the bare name of freeman— the lordship over his own person, the power to choose and will—are blessings beyond food, raiment, or shelter. . . . ask the friendless, penniless foreign emigrant if he will give up his present misery, his future uncertainty . . . for the secure . . . dependence of the slave: the indignation with which he would spurn the offer will prove . . . his birthright as a man is more precious to him than the mess of pottage for which he is told to exchange it because he is starving.[28]

To the *Times*'s bland suggestion that good may exceed evil "in the practice, though not in the theory of slavery, or it would not maintain its existence," she responds by asking why the editor also holds out "the hope that it is surely . . . approaching its abolishment. Why . . . if good really has prevailed in it, do you rejoice that it is speedily to pass away?" Or, to move on into the main body of the journal:

> Southerners, you know, insist that [rank body odor] is inherent with the race, and it is one of their most cogent reasons for keeping them as slaves. [Yet] this very disagreeable peculiarity does not prevent Southern women from hanging their infants at the breasts of negresses, nor almost every planter's wife and daughter from having one or more little black pets sleeping like puppy-dogs in their very bedchamber, nor almost every planter from admitting one or more of his female slaves to the still closer intimacy of his bed. . . . A total absence of self-respect begets these hateful physical results. . . . Well-being, freedom, and industry induce self-respect . . . slavery is answerable for all the evils that exhibit themselves where it exists—from lying, thieving, and adultery, to dirty houses, ragged clothes, and foul smells.[29]

She had little of the propagandist's tactic of ignoring the client's shortcomings. She spoke frankly of shrinking from chatting with the slaves because of their "swarms of fleas . . . by no means the only or most objectionable companions one borrows from them; and I never go to the Infirmary . . . without coming away with a strong inclination to throw myself into the water, and my clothes into the fire." Unblinkingly she described these hapless blacks as horribly cruel to the plantation animals; savagely insolent to one another; the black "drivers" as often abusing their power to force themselves on slave women as callously as the white overseers; as subserviently accepting the white world's invidious notion that admixture of white genes, manifest in lighter skin color, betokened superiority to one's blacker fellows; as habitual liars and pilferers. The cook in charge when she arrived on Butler's Island made away with a whole ham and was flogged and put on field work. His brother, promoted to cook, pres-

ently failed to account for most of a mutton carcass, suggesting that
it had spirited itself away through a locked door. Shortly before
Fanny went North she "met Abraham, and thought that, in a quiet
tête-à-tête . . . I could get him to confess the truth . . . I was only
heaping sins on his soul with every lie I caused him to add. . . .
Dirt and lying . . . the natural tendencies of humanity . . . are
especially fostered by slavery. Slaves may be infinitely wrong, and yet
it is very hard to blame them."[30]

Brutal floggings, the callousness of case-hardened overseers, the
waste of valuable human material, neglect of the sick—all, as she saw
it, consequent on the inevitable inhumanity of slavery—have already
been cited from her book. But to stop there omits one of its
strengths. Periodically her horrified or ironic or glumly realistic accounts of some aspect of this nightmare environment break down into
lamenting wails that bring the poignancy home, show how it all
plowed up this plucky but thin-skinned woman. She has returned to
a Hampton Point infirmary to see if it has improved. No, two women
lie there filthy and neglected, one far advanced in pregnancy, the
other having been made to work in spite of chronic bleeding:

> What piteous existences. . . . I do wonder, as I walk
> among them, well fed, well clothed, young, strong, idle,
> doing nothing but ride and drive about all day, a woman,
> a creature like themselves, who have borne children too,
> what sort of feeling they have toward me. I wonder it is
> not one of murderous hate—that they should lie here al-
> most dying with unrepaid labor for me. . . . I feel as if
> I must tell them how dreadful and how monstrous it
> seems to me . . . how bitterly ashamed and grieved I feel
> for it all.[31]

Or, for the last time she has those slaves who care to come on Sunday,
their one free day, into her sitting room for a reading from the Bible
and the prayer book, and on promise of keeping utterly quiet, three-
year-old Sarah is present:

> Their eyes never wandered from me and my child, who
> sat close by my knee, their little mistress . . . my poor
> baby! Dear [Elizabeth], bless God that you have never

reared a child with such an awful expectation: and at the
end of the prayers, the tears were streaming over their
faces . . . [with] thanks so fervent in their incoherency,
it was more than I could bear, and I begged them to go
away and leave me to recover myself. . . . for quite a
while even [Sarah's] restless spirit was still in wondering
amazement at my bitter crying.[32]

Being shown where the inexorable river was eating away part of
St. Simon's Island:

A wild wish rose in my heart that the river and the sea
would swallow up and melt in their salt waves the whole
of this accursed property. . . . the horror of slavery with
which I came down to the South . . . has gained . . . a
morbid character of mere desire to be delivered from my
own share in it. . . . my zeal for the general emancipation of the slave has almost narrowed itself to this most
painful desire that I and mine were freed from . . . our
share in this huge misery; and so I thought ". . . Sweep
down and carry hence this evil earth and these homes of
tyranny . . . wash my soul and the souls of those I love
clean from the blood of our kind!" But I have no idea that
Mr. [Butler] and his brother would cry amen to any such
prayer.[33]

The "mitigations" that she had promised to recognize in slavery
proved very few. There was the stylish leadership of the southern
upper-class men:

The devil must have his due . . . men brought up in
habits of peremptory command . . . and under the constant apprehension of danger . . . acquire qualities precious to themselves and others. . . . The gentry of the
Southern states are pre-eminent in their own country for
that species of manner which, contrasted with the breeding of the Northerners, would be emphatically pronounced "good" by Englishmen. Born to inhabit landed
property, they . . . inherit . . . some of the invariable
characteristics of an aristocracy. The shop is not their element; and the eager spirit of speculation and the sordid
spirit of gain do not infect their whole existence. . . .

> The habit of command gives them a certain self-posses-
> sion, the enjoyment of leisure a certain ease.[34]

But with all that came also

> haughty, overbearing irritability, effeminate indolence,
> reckless extravagance, and a union of profligacy and cru-
> elty . . . a very different race of men from either Man-
> chester manufacturers or Massachusetts merchants . . . a
> remnant of barbarism and feudalism, maintaining itself
> with infinite difficulty and danger by the side of the latest
> and most powerful developments of commercial civiliza-
> tion . . . while the Boston men wrote and talked tran-
> scendentalism, and became the most accomplished of
> *aestetische* [*sic*] cotton-spinners and railroad speculators
> . . . and the New York men, owners of the fastest horses
> and finest houses in the land, having made a sort of Brum-
> magem Paris of their city, were the bankers and brokers of
> the Southerners . . . the latter were the legislators.
> . . . the government of the nation had become literally
> theirs.[35]

However much that might irritate the southerners she had in mind, Fanny at least made them out men of parts and style and showed why well-bred Britons home from America often allowed that southern gentlemen could almost be considered "one of us." No such emollient eased the abrasions caused by her picture of Georgian ladies and their setting. There might be "occasional marks of former ele-gance . . . in . . . a little carved woodwork . . . but all things have a Castle Rackrent air of neglect, and dreary, careless untidiness . . . the dirty, barefooted negro servants are in excellent keeping." Another such place is "large and not unhandsome, though curiously dilapidated, considering that people were actually living in it."[36]

As for the chatelaines thereof, the speech of Fanny's lady peers sorely troubled her with its resemblance to that of their black ser-vants, "in the women's case more marked than in that of their men because [the women's] avocations, taking them less from home, are less favorable to their throwing off this ignoble trick of pronuncia-tion. . . . the Yankee twang . . . is the harsher of the two, [but] the slave *slobber* . . . is the more ignoble in spite of the softer voices of the pretty Southern women who utter it."[37] Strangely indolent, the ladies marvel at Fanny's walking a quarter of a mile in the sandy streets of Darien and condole with her over the fatigue she must suffer from riding a few miles in a carriage on a sand road. It is all of a piece:

> the shaggy unkempt grounds . . . the ruinous, rackrent, tumble-down house itself; the untidy, slatternly, all but beggarly appearance of the mistress of the mansion herself. The smallest Yankee farmer has a tidier estate, a tidier house, and a tidier wife than this member of the proud Southern chivalry . . . the sameness and stupidity of my Southern female [neighbors'] . . . most vapid existence . . . would . . . render torpid . . . any amount of natural energy and vivacity. I would rather die . . . than live the lives of these Georgia planters' wives and daughters.[38]

It hardly needs saying that the post-Civil War South attacked the *Georgian Plantation* journal savagely. It was branded, like *Uncle Tom,* as Yankee propaganda born in prejudice and reared in spite and so on. Indeed, as generations passed, Dixie treated Fanny as a person even more roughly than it did Mrs. Stowe. Even so responsibly reconstructed a southern writer as Jonathan Daniels deduced that Fanny "must have been a woman both talented and evil-tempered in her righteousness so to sting the planters."[39] For where professional southerners can now sometimes take Mrs. Stowe's melodrama as irresponsible fiction converted to base uses, Fanny's book elicits an adrenal revulsion. True, Fanny wrote better, hit harder, covered a wider range of slavery's faults. . . . But all that is too logical to stir up the viscera so noisily. It was disrespectful to call southern gentlemen irritable, profligate, and indolent, but that could be let pass because Fanny had flatteringly likened them to British aristocrats. What was unforgivable was *lèse majesté* toward Mis' Magnolia. One simply *cannot* describe the southern lady circa 1840 as slatternly, stagnant, and boring without becoming an irredeemable hissing and byword wherever the Daughters of the Confederacy have chapters. It was even woundingly true that Fanny did not thus reject every lady she met in the

Sea Islands and vicinity. The Darien doctor's wife was acceptable, Mrs. Fraser on St. Simon's unimpeachable. Only the first was no southerner but New England-born and -reared, and the second, though southern-born, was daughter of an emigrant Scot and had had a social apprenticeship in good circles in London as wife of a British army officer.

One method of attacking Fanny's *Georgian Plantation* is to refer to accounts of certain British visitors to the Sea Islands a little later as showing conditions far better than she described. Thus Sir Charles Lyell, one of the fathers of geology, a witness of integrity, went ashore briefly at Butler's Island six years after Fanny left and approved of a new grove of orange trees and relatively good housing for the slaves. Amelia Murray, a former member of Queen Victoria's household, came to America in 1855 strongly against slavery, but what she saw in the South delighted her. She thought the slaves "the merriest, most contented people I ever saw" and said she would rather be a black slave on the Hamilton plantation on St. Simon's than "a grumbly, saucy 'help' [i.e., maidservant] in a Northern household." She was also persuaded that if southern slaveholders had reason to believe slavery "prejudicial to the Christian or temporal interests of the blacks, they have chivalry enough . . . to have cast aside mere motives of private interest." [40]

A more substantial indictment came twenty years ago when a Georgian specialist in Sea Islands lore, Margaret Davis Cate, published "Mistakes in Fanny Kemble's Georgia Journal," in the *Georgia Historical Quarterly*. She had already paid her respects to Fanny in a book of the 1920s, saying that since she came south "expecting to hear of . . . harsh treatment [of the local slaves], that is what she did hear." [41] Of the two errors treated in the later paper, the first, misstatement of the reason for the old major's giving his head driver a silver cup, is not significant. The second, however, is to the purpose: Fanny's book says a good deal about a quarrel and fatal brawl between two Sea Island planters as if it occurred during her stay; whereas Mrs. Cate shows clearly that the affair was over some weeks before Fanny ever saw Darien. It is a true bill. Setting down local gossip about the killing, Fanny is guilty of using the present instead of the past tense. Obviously, reworking this material for her copy for the printer in London twenty-three years later, she treated the lurid little bit as if it had gone on while she was in the area; from which Mrs. Cate eagerly deduced that "every statement in the *Journal* is open to suspicion. Can anyone know *fact* from *fiction* in Mrs. Kemble's *Journal?*" [42]

The short answer is that no such question arises. Barring a few risky uses of hearsay, Fanny was dealing in firsthand data, all factual as far as her rough diary and recollections could take her. Only a fanatic partisan could suspect that the bulk of her book, all flesh and blood and three dimensions, was woven out of whole cloth for propaganda effect—though the charge has been made. More formally, one can plead her guilty of postdating the Hazzard-Wylly affair and yet leave the court grounds for leniency. The killing was not at all fictional. Mrs. Cate's laboriously researched data substantiate most of what Fanny wrote; and the sordid manner of it was, as she implied, symptomatic of the unceremonious way in which southern gentlemen sometimes settled their disputes. She claimed no firsthand knowledge of the principals or the brawl they indulged in. Common sense must agree with John A. Scott, editor of the admirable modern edition of *Georgian Plantation* and a recent biographer of Fanny, that "the charge that the *Journal* contains fiction cannot be substantiated if Fanny's critics have no more formidable ammunition than the Wylly-Hazzard affair." [43]

Today's highway from Darien to Brunswick crosses Butler's Island. A historical marker off its southbound lane celebrates the Butler plantation as a pattern rice-operation and goes on: "During a visit here with her husband in 1839 Pierce Butler's wife the brilliant English actress Fannie [*sic*] Kemble wrote her Journal of a Residence on a Georgia [*sic*] Plantation, which is said to have influenced England against the Confederacy." [44] A pretentious book about antebellum Georgia's architecture of about the same vintage verges a little nearer reality; it credits *Georgian Plantation* with "diverting English sympathy from the cause of the Confederacy and helping to hasten the Surrender at Appomattox." [45] Even that is a dubious statement. But one of the things that keeps Fanny's memory, or at least that of her book, alive down among the magnolias is this theory that the Lost Cause owed some of its ultimate disaster to her effect on the vacillating British.

When *Georgian Plantation* appeared in London in May 1863, news of Lincoln's Emancipation Proclamation nominally freeing slaves held in seceded states was four months old. Historians agree that it did much to reassure antislavery Britons about the worthiness of the Union cause. John Bright, Britain's ablest maverick politician of the day, had been keeping the antislavery, hence pro-Northern, meaning of the American war in Britain's national consciousness. Henry Ward Beecher, brother of the author of *Uncle Tom* and America's most eloquently unctuous preacher, had recently been touring Britain expounding the iniquity of the South and the moral prowess of the North to audiences of mostly already persuaded workingmen or their Dissenter employers. But the diplomatic wrangling about building Confederate men-of-war was bubbling away, keeping the possibility of war alive in the newspapers at least, and the newest news tended to make Lincoln's Proclamation look absurd: the fresh Union disaster at Chancellorsville in early May topped the series persuading all too many Britons that whether or not Union soldiers had learned how to fight, their generals mishandled them. Not for two months yet would Britain hear of the simultaneous disasters to the Confederacy at Vicksburg and Gettysburg in early July. Not for two months more would the North's confidential threat that in case of war, Washington would deploy a swarm of Yankee privateers (in the more formal shape of letter-of-marque vessels) against British shipping finally give Russell cause to mind his international manners about keeping those new Confederate commerce-raiders from sailing. Well before that Britain had practically renounced recognition of the Confederacy while the war continued, insisting, however, that the North should eventually allow the South independence with slavery perpetuated within its new borders.

That May, in so precarious a juncture, Fanny's book was not ill timed. The situation still had a dismaying degree of fluidity. But that *Georgian Plantation* had a minor supplementary effect in strengthening the antislavery, hence pro-Northern elements in Britain is, though likely, indemonstrable. Fifty years ago a sound scholar, pro-Southern but responsible, diligently combed the British and American press of the time and concluded that, contrary to subsequent notions North and South, "the contemporary importance of the *Journal* was small. It was the anti-slavery historian and the Southerner outraged by the distortion of Mrs. Kemble's plantation picture who gave the *Journal* . . . a permanent place in the history of slavery." [46]

London's daily press, it appears, hardly noticed it. The important quarterlies mostly ignored it. Only weekly journals of opinion adequately reviewed it. Since its sales seem not to have been notably large, the above finding is probably fair as to Britain anyway. Even the most favorable treatment (in the *Athenaeum*) found it necessary to contrast its great merits with "the same writer's 'Journal' on America . . . a mistake and almost a scandal." But Fanny could readily have let that pass because of the reviewer's previous acid comments:

> The mealy-mouthed apologists [for the South] . . . to whom we could not refuse a hearing in answer to the exaggerations of the novelists [certainly meaning Mrs. Stowe], have of late had it all their own way. . . . we have heard more than enough about the chivalry of Southern gentlemen, the moral and physical graces of Southern women, the patriarchal character of [slavery], the devotion of slaves to their masters. . . . [This] description of [Southern ladies'] houses and ways of managing them will cause English ladies equal terror and amusement. The former are such as English farmers would disdain . . . while the latter would provoke adverse comment among gipsies. [47]

But for Fanny's purposes there was not enough of that sort of comment. This dismaying picture of the South's ruling whites may have been one reason for the relative snubbing that *Georgian Plantation* got. Editors committed to "the Southern chivalry" may have found it embarrassing thus to be told by a widely respected Englishwoman who knew many of the best people that, in effect, the John Bulls had been asking to dinner persons one really wouldn't care to know.

However that may be, the Northern states treated *Georgian Plan-*

tation rather better. Fanny had not contemplated bringing it out
there. But in London at the time was John Murray Forbes, a redoubtable Bostonian organizer of railroads and volunteer chief of war propaganda for the wartime governor of Massachusetts, on a secret
mission seeking to bribe the shipbuilders to abort the new Confederate commerce-raiders. Fanny and he were old acquaintances, and
hearing of her book, he urged her to let him place an American
edition where it would fan antislavery fire among war-weary Northerners. Thus it happened that Harper & Brothers, a house then
noted for skill in wide popular distribution, brought it out in the
triumphal week after Gettysburg and Vicksburg. That did happen
also to be the time of the catastrophic "draft riots"—actually anti-
black—that filled New York City for three days with homicide and
arson. Nevertheless *Georgian Plantation* went into a second large
printing and may be assumed to have attracted enough attention to
make Forbes's effort worthwhile. In what may have been not altogether a disinterested judgment *Harper's Monthly* called it "the most
powerful anti-slavery book yet written."[48] But the august and im-
partial *North American Review* agreed: "In some respects the most valuable of the recent publications on slavery . . . will be read and
pondered by those who have lent their too easy faith to mere transient
visitors in the land of bondage."[49] And the *Atlantic Monthly:* "the
first ample, lucid, detailed, faithful account from the actual head-
quarters of a slave-plantation where the slaves belonged to what are
called the most respectable people . . . a model plantation . . . not
a hard master, as masters go. . . . A sadder book the human hand
never wrote . . . a noble service nobly done."[50]

There the reviewer (probably George William Curtis) touched
on what is a flaw as well as an ornament. From one angle the reader
thinks, Yes, Butler's Island was known for good economic management and humane treatment of work-force; good Lord, if things were
this bad there, what was slavery like on average plantations?[51] Since
the Sea Islands were not typical, Fanny's book is no adequate answer
to that question. The datum-seeking historian would have preferred
that the Butlers' and their neighbors' holdings be nearer representative. For, outside the Mississippi Delta, the sugar country of Louisi-

ana, and the Alabama Black Belt, the South had few such large, mass-labor operations. As reporter Fanny should have had some months on an upcountry Georgia cotton plantation with fifty or sixty slaves; a few more on what Huckleberry Finn called "one of those little one-horse cotton plantations and they all look alike" in Arkansas, say; a few more on a family-style tobacco farm in North Carolina.

Such experiences might have spared her some of her few but regrettable errors. She would have learned, for instance, that it was not true that in Dixie "No white man . . . of any class puts hand to work of any kind."[52] She should not have generalized about differences between the gentry of the Deep South and those of the border states, for she had seen little of Maryland, Virginia, and Missouri, and of Kentucky knew only what was visible across the river from Cincinnati. She need not have taken seriously the theory then prevalent that admixture of white genes implies biological fragility, hence miscegenation would gradually extinguish blacks as a group. But none of that damages the fundamental significance of her book. Anybody who wants to know how black slavery in America necessarily smelled, sounded, and festered can find it all in these extraordinary pages—as it is available nowhere else in the literature.

The Ladies' Emancipation Society of London published as "The Essence of Slavery" a pamphlet of extracts from *Georgian Plantation*. Philadelphia put out a comparable compilation contrasting Fanny's account of slavery with rash statements defending it recently made by a couple of Pennsylvania's dignitaries. But there was nothing like the sales in the hundreds of thousands of copies, the competing stage-dramatizations that long kept *Uncle Tom* a worldwide miracle of communication. My poor opinion of both Mrs. Stowe and her most conspicuous work must already be clear. Hence, while pointing out flaws in Fanny's book, I deplore her generous defense of *Uncle Tom*. Though she thought Tom himself so implausibly perfect as to be grotesque, and "of the merits of [the] book as a work of art [had] no desire to speak," stoutly she endorsed its "general accuracy . . . with regard to . . . slavery."[53] She cannot have been aware—few are even now—that Mrs. Stowe's firsthand acquaintance with slavery was limited to a few days spent in Kentucky plus glimpses of a few runaways being smuggled through Cincinnati on the Underground Railroad. *Uncle Tom* goes disingenuously out of its way to conceal this lack. Yet, being red-hot against slavery and herself still inhibited from publication, Fanny might have forgiven that on the principle of *ben trovato*. Ten years later she included her sweeping endorsement in her own *Georgian Plantation* volume. And nowhere does she express regret at having been prevented from getting her explosive account of slavery published before *Uncle Tom* ran away with the potential public.

Yet there is reason to see that as bad luck historically. This is not mere literary comparison, simply juxtaposing a piece of writing usually genuine, often eloquent, sometimes superb with what I have elsewhere called Mrs. Stowe's "Sunday School superficiality,"[54] her claptrap melodrama of runaways and gimmicky doings on Legree's plantation and the ineffable mawkishness of Eva St. Clare and her Byronically gallant pa. More damaging were Mrs. Stowe's readiness to relegate the runaways to the freed slaves' settlement in an idealized West Africa conveniently distant; her rhapsodic delusion that religious gurgling could somehow dismantle slavery; and her implicit judgment that, however equal blacks' souls may be with those of whites in God's sight, absolute equality of mind and status in the white man's world, North or South, may be dubious. Indeed, as I indicated long since in *Goodbye to Uncle Tom* (1956), blacks are right—if for mistaken reasons—to use "Uncle Tom" as a pejorative. For in 1852 Mrs. Stowe posed a false set of blacks against a cheaply theatrical past and a precarious go-down-Moses future, whereas the blacks whom Fanny showed readers ten years later were flesh and blood—suffering, skewed, untruthful, sycophantic, almost always heartbreakingly underdeveloped victims of an archaic social system to which crass enterprise condemned them for the crime of having black skins; but for all that, potential peers of any other random group of human beings.

Maybe the substantial service that Pierce Butler did the South was not amateur gun-running but holding his daughters hostage until their majority, which tended to keep their mother from publishing. James Schott, Jr., was considered a crack pistol-marksman. At Bladensburg in 1844 he had a sore foot that hampered his ability to wheel and fire without flinching. Suppose that, instead of going wide, his first bullet had found his enemy's head or heart, not only vindicating his honor if not Mrs. Schott's virtue, but ridding Fanny of a calamitous husband. The Butler girls would have kept their interest in the family fortune while Pierce would have no longer been in a position to erode it. No guardians or trustees would conceivably have denied their mother custody. They had already flourished in London. Suppose Fanny had taken them to England, settled there, and gone into Shakespeare reading for her own livelihood. We know that she sometimes gave Lady Dacre and others opposed to slavery glimpses of her Georgia journal. Suppose they had said, My dear, in view of this dreadful possibility that the slave power will take over Texas, you should publish. Suppose she had done so some years before Mrs. Stowe obeyed God's behest and began, with His help, to write *Uncle Tom*. It is not unlikely that, in view of Fanny's corrosive, poignant, bleak picture of the Sea Island blacks, Mrs. Stowe would never have felt that overwhelming impulse, thus sparing the world the social and political side effects of her cardboard gospel.

Not that *Georgian Plantation* would ever have sold international millions. But had it appeared before *Uncle Tom* could blunt its effect, the English-speaking world might well have read it widely and profitably enough to be much better prepared for the slavery-related crises of 1845–75. This realistic briefing about slave owners' relations with their chattels might have critically strengthened opposition to the Mexican War; or got the South critically less of the lion's share in the Compromise of 1850. . . . Probably nothing could have prevented the eventual Civil War, but Fanny's dismaying and impressively British contempt for the southern gentry as a class might have helpfully cooled off pro-Southern sentiment in Parliament. God knows what would have been reasonable solutions for the postwar problems of Reconstruction. But a North soaked in *Uncle Tom*, under the illusion that it was dealing with Topsy and Eliza and chivalrous St. Clare and diabolical Legree, had unnecessarily small chance of making sense; nor could publication of *Georgian Plantation* in 1863 do much to realign matters too late. In 1845 . . .

But Schott had a sore foot.

XX

There's Rosemary . . .

DURING 1864 the war of destructive movement in the West and of
bloody attrition in the East was a gloomy ordeal for both sides.
Frances was somewhat isolated from such disquieting events, for she
had been traveling with her mother on the Continent and then settled
down with her in the rose-embowered cottage that the Sartorises put
at Fanny's disposal at Warnford. For a while Frances had been not
only upholding her father's hands but also doing what she could for
Confederate wounded prisoners. How she came to leave Pierce to face
the disintegration of the good cause alone I do not know. The reason
cannot have been slackening loyalty to him or the Confederacy, for in
Charleston in 1866, "people overwhelmed me [Frances] with thanks
for what I did for their soldiers . . . which really did amount to but
little. I say this and the answer invariably is, Oh yes, but your heart
was with us, which it certainly was."[1] When word of the fall of
Richmond reached England in mid-April 1865, Fanny recorded that
"[Frances] and I [wept] over the news, I with joy, she with sorrow."[2]

Fortunately for both women Fanny was temporarily alone when
news of the assassination of President Lincoln arrived. This public
grief got through her numbed tissues as few personal troubles now
could: "Yesterday . . . I scribbled in my pocket-book some very
indifferent rhymes about the fall of Richmond which it occurred to
me as I drove by the Spectator I would offer them." The staff there
apologized for the editor's keeping her waiting, explaining

all . . . terribly cut up by this dreadful news from America—what said I breathlessly—the murder of Mr. Lincoln
. . . I gave a loud scream . . . and burst into such passionate outcries and weeping that the poor man before me
seemed terrified and shocked beyond power of speaking.
. . . oh dear friend [Harriet St. Leger] it is too
horrible—that good up-right conscientious man. . . . I
fear every thing now for the present for the country with
its miserable Vice-President. . . . It is a southern deed—
it represents the spirit of slave-holding . . . the very
character of those cruel vindictive cowardly people—I fear
the northern people may be betrayed into some act of
fierce retaliation.[3]

Presently she is telling Frances Cobbe that she is glad Booth is killed,
for that forestalls a lynching. Even more temperately, she deplores
efforts to connect Jefferson Davis with the crime: "I wish to goodness
all the more prominent Southern leaders would get well away from
America and that the government would be wise enough to take no
more heed of them."[4] Thenceforth her contacts with the wreckage
left by the war were largely confined to awareness of Frances's stubbornly remaining unreconstructed. For within little more than a year
Pierce's devoted daughter went south with him to see what was left
of their principality. For the next ten years most of her considerable
energy and half her time went into occasionally promising efforts to
put Humpty-Dumpty back together again.

Federal occupation of St. Simon's had left deep physical scars
and, as former slaveholders saw it, demoralized the black inhabitants.
That was not crucial; Hampton Point had been phasing out before
the war. Butler's Island, however, had some basis for a future. When
the Federals approached in 1862, the overseer moved its several
hundred blacks upcountry. Many of them had drifted back through
chaos to the only home they had ever known, and were now ekeing
out a hand-to-mouth existence by hunting, fishing, and planting
small garden patches. The owner's cottage, in worse repair than ever,
was bare of furniture or cooking utensils, but Frances had brought
along basic necessities, a German maidservant, and a portrait of Robert E. Lee to hang over the mantelpiece. The old acquaintances she

had seen in Charleston on the way down had seemed "too sad to be bitter . . . the women live in the past, and the men only in the daily present, trying, in a listless sort of way, to repair their ruined fortunes."[5] With Frances as executive officer, there would be nothing listless about the Butlers' project.

Their quondam human property met Pierce and the daughter some had known as a baby in arms with so clamorous a welcome that it seemed to reflect relief at the prospect of authority in charge again. Fanny had sometimes suggested that somehow to pay the black slaves and make them look after themselves would heighten self-respect and maybe production. Now some such experiment was unavoidable. Its usual form in the immediately postbellum South was the "contract system"—the black signing up to work for a year for a share of the profits divided in proportion to work done; the employer supplying food, clothing, shelter, and maybe odd driblets of cash, all deducted from the year-end shares. This forerunner of the familiar sharecropper system was not cynically set up to create a disguised peonage. Under the conditions it was a commonsense approach, and at first Federal agents looking after the new freedmen's interests countenanced it. But virtual peonage was what it did create, for once the black was free and footloose, only restraint of the person could make such contracts enforceable. Otherwise the employer had to fall back on persuasion, bullying, subtle presumption on but never quite revival of the old relation—poor training for the black and utterly exasperating, of course, to anybody like Frances hoping to make the old place a going concern again.

Five years of neglect had half ruined the sluices and dikes essential to rice culture. It soon proved necessary to rely for restoring and maintaining the dikes on gangs of self-organized Irish who came down winters from the North to do what blacks had once done. Somehow father and daughter did manage to get a rice crop planted during their stay in 1866–67 and to take care of a few hundred promising new orange trees, for by now it was more than a generation since that devastating frost. Avidly Frances absorbed Pierce's knowledge of rice culture augmented by advice from veteran overseers. Within a few years the Sea Islands might have been gratified by the significant presence on a flourishing rice plantation of dear old Mr. Butler, still dapper and insinuating in spite of his sixty-odd years, lovingly steered and cared for by his bustling spinster-daughter. Only once again Mr. Butler's dilatory habits spoiled things. In spring 1867 Frances duly went north to get away from the oncoming "sickly season." Pierce stayed on to look after oddments, was delayed by this and that. . . . Before he was ready to leave, he quite unnecessarily came down with a massive attack of malaria, died of it and was buried at Darien.

Fanny did not record how it felt thus to be relieved of an at least potentially disturbing presence and its bitter connotations. One knows only that fifteen years later she still kept a bit of her wedding gown in her work basket. Pityingly she recorded Sarah's persistent, almost disabling sorrow. Frances's response was to double her devotion to what Pierce had, in her estimation, gallantly stood for. That winter she returned to Butler's Island to carry on single-handedly under conditions that would have daunted Scarlett O'Hara. Fanny, who had expected to take Frances to Europe presently, deplored this decision. At least Dr. Wister went South with her to help her get reestablished; and next year Sarah, now half owner, spent a month there with her son Owen, whom, to distinguish him from his father, everybody called Dan. In season house-guests sometimes thus gave Frances support. But most of the time this mistress of sixteen hundred exacting and vexatious acres was isolated among dislocated, sycophantic and yet resentful blacks with one or two hired white subalterns.

Sometimes one detects a backhanded pride in Fanny's mentions of how doggedly Frances is carrying on. The pair had some sympathies. Pierce had bought Frances a beautiful saddle mare "owned" by a man in Darien who had her from a Yankee deserter who had stolen her from a southern plantation during the war, "the dearest and most intelligent horse I ever had . . . would follow me about like a dog, and came from the farthest end of the pasture when she heard my voice." Intrepidly mare and mistress rode alone all over St. Simon's Island, to Frederica for the mail, visiting overnight at this or that plantation. When Frances was showing an elderly black stableman how to rub a horse down properly, he said: " 'Yis, so my ole missus taught me, and stand there to see it done.' . . . I generally found," wrote her mother's daughter, "that if I wanted a thing done I had first to tell the negroes to do it, then show them how, and finally to do it myself."[6] Whom does that sound like?

Some four years after Pierce died, marriage gave Frances an effective comanager. The lucky man was the Honorable and Reverend James Wentworth Leigh, a younger son of Lord Leigh whose Stoneleigh Abbey was a very stately home of England, but James had no more money than most younger sons in holy orders, depending on whatever livings family influence might provide. At Cambridge, where he was known as "Jimbo," he had been a noted horseman, a "muscular Christian" combining genuine piety with great zeal for shooting, cricket, water sports. As a young country parson he swore off alcohol to set a good example to soddenly inclined parishioners— and kept to it for life. On a first visit to America in 1869, fetched to Butler's Island as one of a house party, he was much struck by its "fair queen [residing] among her sable subjects and [entertaining] strangers with royal grace." And doubtless she appreciated his lively sympathy for the Lost Cause: "I considered the North had behaved shamefully. . . . they had a pretext, the abolition of slavery, but I have my doubt about their sincerity,"[7] he wrote much later in life.

Next spring Sarah and Frances were in England and visited one of Leigh's married sisters; in that propitious context he proposed and was accepted. Frances made close friends with Leigh's eldest niece, later the famously vivacious Countess of Jersey. In June 1871, after Frances's third season as doughty mistress of Butler's Island, the marriage took place at St. Thomas's, Portman Square, London, conducted by the Rev. the Lord Say and Sele, a kinsman of the groom; Sir Arthur Sullivan at the organ. Roger Kemble's granddaughter had done very well. And in due season Leigh was transplanted to the banks of the Altamaha to do the blacks and the rice fields as much good as in him lay.

Fanny countenanced the marriage cordially, going with Leigh to Queenstown to welcome his bride-to-be off the ship. That was as well, because in the long run Fanny owed this marriage a good deal.

In spite of his sympathy for the Lost Cause and willingness to believe good of slavery, his mother-in-law greatly liked Leigh's "great physical strength, activity, and dauntlessness, combined with his sweet face and voice, and the gentle tenderness of his manner . . . an especial charm for hard-working, rude, uncultivated people." [8] He was also a beloved "Uncle Jimmy" to all his young connections, including adolescent Dan Wister, and it always delighted Fanny when he came to stay at Butler Place or York Farm. She purred when he volunteered for Sunday duty in the local Episcopalian chapel that lacked a parson; also when he plunged into the doings of the Germantown Cricket Club. His emollient good nature unquestionably helped to keep relations between Fanny and Frances tolerable; and increased the cordiality of Fanny's fluctuating hopes that, now the moral curse of slavery was gone, Frances's ambitions for the plantation would be fulfilled. It was a great day when a barrel of excellent oranges, weighty proof of the success of the new plantings, arrived at York Farm from Butler's Island.

Leigh's first measure as prince consort—bringing white workmen over from England to supply the places of disappeared black craftsmen—proved a mistake. But within a few months he had learned a great deal about how to handle black field-hands, and soon he knew more than Frances about the engineering of the tides and waterways. The remains of Sea Islands "quality" took warmly to his gentlemanly ways. He was a good shot; he helped revive the prewar custom of boat racing, with a six-oared crew from each plantation. At the same time he was doing what a dedicated man of God could with Sunday morning sermons, confirmation classes, and Sunday afternoon schools to get something like religion into the work force; yet he had the sense not to try to compete or interfere with the blacks' own preachers' performances on Sunday nights. Like the younger sons who made able ranchmen when sent out to manage British properties in the cattle country West, Leigh was a striking cross-cultural adaptation.

Fanny could hardly have found her difficult younger daughter a more practicable husband than the one the girl chose herself. The same good luck held with her less difficult but not altogether well

adjusted elder daughter. The year Sarah came of age Fanny had told
Henry Greville that it would be difficult for her to find a man superior to herself, which was what she needed. She was well on target
with her Dr. Wister, a personably genial, intelligent, cultivated physician greatly respected by his patients in the high-chinned suburb of
Germantown only a few miles from Butler Place. Where Sarah inclined to impatience with Fanny's crotchets, he could be solicitous
and patently greatly admired his mother-in-law. And young Dan, by
now in prep school at St. Paul's destined for Harvard and Porcellian,
with a talent for music that professionals took seriously, had charmed
his grandmother ever since his birth in 1860.

    In her own way Fanny congratulated herself on two such sons-
in-law. But the connotations of the institution of marriage caused her
to feel and sometimes broadcast reflex warnings that in a matter so
fraught with perils it might be better to halt the marriage service at
the words "not to be entered into lightly or inadvisedly." During
Frances's second pregnancy her mother and she were guests at Stoneleigh Abbey. To Frances and Fanny enter the Honorable Margaret
Elizabeth Leigh. She was glowing with the news that the Earl of
Jersey, who had been backing and filling in a disconcerting fashion,
had finally proposed to her and been accepted. "Whereupon," Lady
Jersey wrote years later, "Mrs. Kemble demanded, with a tragic air
worthy of her aunt, Mrs. Siddons, 'And are you happy, young lady?'
I cheerfully answered 'Oh yes' and she looked as if she were going to
cry. My aunt said afterward that my marriage reminded her of her
own unfortunate venture." [9]

    Presently Fanny and Frances were at odds over another matter of
matrimony. When Algernon Sartoris's attachment to Nellie Grant
became matter for family deliberations and Fanny, as we have seen,
deplored the match, Frances went far out of her way shrilly to take
Algernon's side. A curious situation: She found herself defending the
intelligence and breeding of the daughter of the general who had
beaten down her Southern heroes. There was no avoiding a worse
storm later when Frances learned that Fanny planned to publish a
sequel to her *Records of a Girlhood* (1876), a large book of her letters
with passages of interpolated autobiography up to 1834. All it had
said about Pierce was only: "I was married in Philadelphia on the

7th of June, 1834, to Mr. Pierce Butler of that city." But Fanny's *A Year of Consolation* had already hinted at personal strains and *Georgian Plantation,* much more candid, had sensitized Frances to the possibilities of what Fanny might see fit to print. So far as those books showed, conflict over slavery and kindred issues was primary cause of a break not heavily discreditable to either party. But in 1848 Fanny's *Narrative* had got into the newspapers; nor did the judge's refusal to admit it as potential evidence diminish public interest in it. And two years later Pierce had circulated his printed *Mr. Butler's Statement* with so many details of highly personal family relations complementary to those Fanny had adduced. Now that Fanny was preparing an autobiography taking her story into God only knew what further details, Frances was frantically apprehensive. Mr. Butler's Statement was not widely known outside Philadelphia. But an old woman past her seventieth year might put before the lady patrons of Britain's circulating libraries a good deal about the revered dead father of the Honorable Mrs. Leigh! On May Day, 1881 she wrote to "My dearest Mother," syntax shaky, emotions surging:

> You have said over & over again that you thought people unjustified in writing personal reminiscences . . . painful to their relatives and friends—Then how can you think of writing about a person no longer alive whose memory is cherished and honored by his children & whom what you write would give the greatest pain, with those children yours too! Does being their Mother give you the right to wound and distress them? . . . to you his memory is only that of any ordinary person with whom your relations had been disagreeable but he is our Father, whose memory is sacred—I have never lost in the least degree the . . . bitterness I have always felt about the publication of your first Southern book—wh[ich] nothing would ever induce me to have in the house and now that my Father is dead, if you repeat those stories—I never can forgive it . . . I implore you not to alienate my affection from you entirely by doing it—Your loving daughter
>
> F.[10]

Fanny replied: "I can only acknowledge your letter. I cannot answer it otherwise than by saying that I must myself be the judge of what I think right to publish and of course accept the consequences of doing so." Frances sought support from Sarah: "If she repeats her Southern experiences or in any way alludes to her married relations I do not think I can ever see or speak to her again. . . . The success of her first book has so aroused her vanity and love of notoriety that the desire to keep herself before the public is irresistible—do get Owen to write to her."[11] Whether he did so does not appear; but Fanny's published text must have made Frances feel rather let down. It mentions Pierce only indirectly. Only those already familiar with Mr. Butler's Statement could discern some of the janglings Frances so dreaded. But it must vastly have annoyed her that it did contain the account of the trip to Georgia in 1838, which made the South sound like a lackadaisical rural slum seven hundred miles long.

That Frances really felt a "love of notoriety" in her mother is more than doubtful; set it down to harassed impatience. But another order of malevolence occasionally surfaced when conventional amenities wore thin. In two letters widely separate in time Fanny reminds Sarah of a violent outburst of "scorn and resentment" to which Frances once treated her mother when they were in Paris together, probably in the 1860s; Fanny recalled it "with horror for myself—and her." Very likely it was somehow connected with Pierce's memory. Ever since, Fanny wrote, she had refrained from speaking to Frances "with any freedom about anything . . . our intercourse is one of the tragic consequences of life."[12] As his wife's temperament consolidated, James Leigh too had to adopt evasive action, it appears. Fanny noticed "a painful dread on his part of the slightest subject of discussion or any thing that might create a collision between them—he spends habitually several hours in his own room smoking at night."[13]

When Frances bore a boy child in 1879, the temptation was too strong to resist. She named him Pierce Butler Leigh.[14] Unable to bring herself to attend the christening, Fanny could only "pray God to avert . . . the evil omen of such a name."[15] Ten months later her emotions were as strong as ever: "His name has not been uttered once in my hearing . . . I sometimes think I must make the effort to break the painful spell and call the boy by the name which I have not

pronounced for so many years & which will fill my mouth with the
bitterness of a poison that destroyed my life."[16] It is almost too pat
that the baby was calamitously afflicted with a skin ailment that doctors could do nothing for and died when he was only a year old.

Relations with Sarah were less high-keyed. During her last
American reading tours and on into the 1870s, Fanny's headquarters
were usually at York Farm. Most of that time the Wisters were oc-
cupying Butler Place over the way. That allowed a certain independence yet with family support nearby that a stout old lady nearing
her seventies might need in bad weather or emergencies. From York
Place she wrote young Dan at St. Paul's gay nonsense letters, spoiled
him when he came home during vacations, agreed to write the li-
bretto for a comic opera he had in hand. When all three Wisters
went to Europe for three years in 1871, Fanny showed Dan off to her
transatlantic connections as a most promising and attractive youngster. Sometimes it was sad to look across to Butler Place and recall
the high-strung, wasp-waisted young tangle of emotions who had
planted those large sugar maples and sat on the veranda watching
baby Sarah zigzag across the ill-kept lawn. But for all its associations—and searing summers and iced-up winters—it was a better haven than most and when Fanny left it for good in January 1877, she
wrote to an old friend in Boston: "I do not think I need tell you how
sadly and solemnly I close *that* chapter."[17]

Sarah's and her modus vivendi was a credit to the emotional
common sense of both, for neither was a pattern of easy going. In the
winter of 1872–73 Fanny and the Wisters were together in Rome
and met Henry James, soon a close friend of both mother and daughter. He saw Sarah as "almost beautiful . . . but . . . 'intensely conscious,' and diffident, and lacks a certain repose comfortable to herself
and others . . . [has] a fierce energy in a slender frame and . . .
always some social iron on the fire . . . rides, walks, entertains, has
musical rehearsals."[18] Fortunately for all concerned this relationship
remained merely enthusiastically friendly and mutually respectful for
life. Literary people took Sarah seriously. The *Atlantic Monthly* welcomed her anonymous pieces about travel and nature, and Dr. Silas
Weir Mitchell, Philadelphia's physician-novelist and pioneer in psy-

chiatry, leaned on her and her husband's cousin's wife, Mrs. Caspar Wister (née Furness) as indispensable critics of his plots and preliminary drafts.

Sometimes there is a glimpse of the mother-and-daughter relationship with its hair slipping down. Fanny is all packed up to leave York Farm for Lenox in the morning. At dinner Dr. Wister cordially suggests that she change her plans and stay on still longer, and Sarah, resenting thus being put in an ungracious position, has to make it clear that she wants her mother to leave. Seventy-year-old Fanny is reassuring about Sarah's gaining weight after one of the vague illnesses to which she was subject: "I am so glad you are growing fat my child because I am sure you are the handsomer for doing so & I like you to be as handsome as possible—when a woman is no longer young *slenderness* is apt to become *angularity* & goes too often into a withered looking leanness . . . you are tall enough to wear becomingly a certain amount of plumptitude, so may your shadow never be less."[19] The tone is motherly possessive as well as amusedly affectionate. Some years earlier she had told Malkin, who has asked about Frances: "The lady you call 'dear little Fan' is no more. She is represented by a portly personable body, little inferior to me in size and weight, and with a comely double chin, which I somehow . . . have avoided among my many signs of *elderliness.*"[20]

Note a slightly diminished benignity when Frances is the example of the Kemble women's "plumptitude." The same between-the-lines distinction is discernible in Sarah's recurring initiatives toward disposing of her interest in the Butler estate to Frances to end what Fanny termed "the torment of joint ownership"; whereas Frances insisted on retaining the original basis but with a freer hand: "I know too little of the affairs of the estate and too much of Fanny's character," commented her mother, "not to dread that she may be receiving more rope wherewith to hang herself."[21] And after the Wisters returned from Europe in 1874, Fanny felt a throb of special feeling for Sarah, resuming the role of suburban matron doomed to a never-ending procession of never satisfactory cooks and housemaids. She had fallen in love with the polyglot, elegant, cultivated, and socially stratified life that expatriates lived in Rome, and in a manner of speaking, never got over it. Fanny had less of that sort of cultural sweet tooth; but enough to make for sympathy.

In her sixtieth year Fanny Kemble gave up public reading. She had adequate winnings well invested. Her voice was failing, her strength for touring not what it had been. Until then, arduous though her tours were even on her rigid terms, they had certainly done her great emotional good. There was her joy in handling Shakespeare, as deep and real as a perpetual love affair; the regular relief from Sarah's prickliness or Frances's sulkiness; and the corresponding change of scene as well as the nature of vexations—late trains, bad weather, stupid arrangements at the reading hall, instead of stupid butchers and gossipy neighbors. And every hard-earned hundred dollars put away in securities suggested by William Rotch Wister, cousin of Sarah's husband and admiring younger friend of Fanny's, was another clause in her feminist-flavored declaration of independence. Thus to abandon a vocation of long standing obviously risked emotional dislocation. But she was not resourcelessly adrift, relegated to mere sitting by the fire writing longer and longer letters to such friends as were still alive. She had two valuable resources, Switzerland every possible summer, and the compiling and writing of her remarkable autobiographies.

Her first acquaintance with the Alps is hard to date; it must have been in the mid-1850s, maybe during a European trip she took with Mary Fox. Years later she recalled how they two had sat on the balcony of their hotel room "and I sang like a nightingale half the night through" and a year later "a woman in London society claimed my acquaintance upon the score of having been one of a crowd of listeners (unsuspected by me) underneath where I was warbling." [22] Her warm friend Arthur Malkin was a zealous Alpinist in a generation when the exploration of ways to break the neck at high altitudes was a passion among cultivated Britons and even riskier than now because mountaineering techniques were still being worked out. For the next several decades Fanny relied on Malkin for advice whether this or that pass would be open how early in the season and what obscure hostel would be starting point for hidden beauties that the tourist public had not yet discovered. Had she never heard of him, however, she would probably have exulted in the Alpine phenomenon anyway. Mont Blanc, the Jungfrau, the Matterhorn, Monte Rosa became her Olympians in a pantheon including as minor deities all the snow peaks of that serrated cluster of tortured geology. Here, of course, at the age of fifty or so, she was still Byron-taught. But again, the wealth of feeling thus attained was genuine. Now when she most needed diversions in a new context, she reaped the reward of developed skill in admiring nature's originalities. Spontaneously and raptly she could contemplate the Alps with the same order of joy as a Wagner-addict drowning in the "Liebestod."

Yet it was not a passive, opera-house-style affair. Being a woman disqualified Fanny from rope-and-ice ax work; in any case her increased bulk ruled out the indicated agility. But it did not impair her pedestrian powers enough to keep her from tramping wherever the guides would conceivably countenance her trying to go. For in that thickened body still lived the lithe young woman who had climbed the cataract at Cold Spring. At the age of sixty-eight she simultaneously congratulates herself on "The beautiful scenery, I am still, thank God, able to visit [lying] within easy reach by railroad and steamboat, and demands but little effort," and tells how the other day she

> [went] down to Brunnen *on foot* and by what may be called
> the back staircase of the mountain . . . the dry bed of an
> Alpine torrent, *fifteen hundred feet* down the steepest possi-
> ble hillside, by the irregular broken rocky steps of the
> mountain nymph—leaps and plunges. . . . rocky steps
> so round and smooth that my heavy mortal boots slipped
> and slid . . . threatening to make my descent headlong
> more than once. Arrived at the bottom, I took a carriage
> . . . and returned by the main road, resolving, until I
> become a centipede, nothing should tempt me to walk
> down fifteen hundred feet of perpendicular mountain side
> again.[23]

When the path to some vantage point was reputed impossible for her, she had herself carried up in a chair on poles by brawny-legged guides taking it in relays.

The exhilaration of new wonders often set her singing as she tramped. Guides knew her as *"la dame qui va chantant par les montagnes."* [24] She could not manage every summer, but after 1860 it was a better than even chance that July and August would see her somewhere in Switzerland with Sarah or Frances or young Harry or Henry James or Mary Fox or W. R. Wister or the Malkins or the Tyndalls, John Tyndall being an eminent Alpinist as well as a great scientist. In the dining room of the huge wooden hotel, guests would be told that the stocky, sternly handsome, shockingly sunburned lady was the famous Mrs. Kemble. It was rash to try to scrape acquaintance. A young British tourist who looked across from the next table and respectfully remarked, "I understand you also have fine hotels in America, Mrs. Kemble," got a glare from under formidable eyebrows and a snort and "Young man, I *have* no hotels in America." [25]

Her affinity with the Alps was so strong that she had jokingly to remind herself that her maternal grandmother had been Swiss, and granddaughter's blood might be glacier water. Yet this delight with snow peaks and wild flowers growing right up to the ice and the wild white horse-tail waterfalls did not curb her impatience with other people cluttering up the view and with the Swiss. She called them "the most disagreeable people in both worlds; but their country is my earthly paradise." [26] During her Alpine period international tourism underwent a massive expansion with Switzerland as flagship attraction. Eloquently Fanny deplored the "essentially watering-place character" of St. Moritz in the middle 1870s, "crowded with over-dressed dandies and equivocal or unequivocal ladies . . . a perfect fair of booths lined with rubbish, at extortionate prices, incessant *braying* of bands and ringing of bells, the eternal inrushing and outrushing of arriving and departing travelers." [27] She thought the Germans the "roughest most boorish and offensively ill mannered" among them but also gave Americans high marks for "want of tact, consideration and perception." [28] She was delighted with Alfonse Daudet's *Tartarin dans les Alpes* which, in 1885, devastatingly satirized amateur Alpinistics and the Swiss tourist industry and professed to have discovered that all its attractions and accommodations were synthetically arranged and managed by a single gigantic corporation—a sort of proto-Disney Enterprises. It tickled her so that in her seventy-seventh year she wrote and Bentley published an English adaptation of it—a five-act farce, *The Adventures of Mr. John Timothy Homespun in Switzer-land*. The courier character tells the hero "they have hired all the peasants, and the chamois, and the cows, . . . and at all the water-falls. . . . they have over each cascade a charmante young Swiss peas-ant . . . with one leg up (*attitudinizing*); and all her arms and eyes up to heaven, thus. . . . Ah, quel tableau! . . . You go up Mont Blanc with your cigar in your mouth, and your hands in your breeches pockets," and if a tourist does fall into a glacial crevasse, ". . . there, at the very bottom, you find the head-porter of the Grand Hotel . . . who says to you, 'Point out your luggage if you please, sare; and there is the omnibus who wait for you.' "[29]

The virtual heroine (whom Daudet did not supply) is an Amer-ican, a beautiful young heiress, Miss Scattergold, pursued by several absurd young Britons; and when, in spite of her admirable common sense, she decides to marry one of them, the closing scene has a lot of hands-across-the-sea. The thing was never acted nor meant to be, but as Fanny's one effort at business and dialogue for laughs—her other plays were all somberly serious—it is interesting and quite creditable. Thérèse De Camp, that clever hand at farce comedy, might have given some of its scenes good marks.

One hopes that Fanny's growing impatience with the Swiss and their methods made it easier for her to reconcile herself to having to give Switzerland up. Her arthritis now not only ruled out extensive walking, but took the enjoyment out of being carried over rough trails to places she wished to see. Even moderately high altitudes dangerously affected her breathing. By 1880 she tells George Biddle in Philadelphia that "the lady who goes singing all over the moun-tains . . . sits silent in the vallies now." Seven years later Sarah and she make what she fears will be her last visit even for looking up from the valleys: "It has been a blessing to me . . . to take leave of my dear Alps in her dear company."[30] So the same year that saw her japeries about Swiss tourism published also encountered in *Temple Bar* her formal farewell to "my dear Alps":

> The Angel walking with me took my hand,
>   And said: "No longer here mays't thou abide;
> To the soft valleys and low level land
>   Come down, and, humbly looking up, reside,

Till in thy lowest home thour't laid to dwell
  And I have come, thither to be thy guide."
"My mountains, oh, my mountains, fare ye well!"
  Weeping—"Oh, look on me once more!" I cried,
But thickest mist encompassed every head,
And darkness round each pinnacle was spread . . .
And here, disconsolate, I weeping lay,
Until the Angel on my shoulder laid
A tender pitying hand, and to me said—
"Look up once more—look!" And each awful head
In the departing light glowed ruby red.
"Now hast thou seen that last great glory well?"
My angel said, and at her feet I fell.
  My mountains, oh, my mountains, fare ye well![31]

Whether Fanny Kemble was the first author ever personally to prepare copy on a typewriter cannot be established. But it is likely, for she was doing so in the late winter of 1874 less than a year after Remington put on the market the first practical "printing machine," as they called it. She had bought it for Sarah; but it made her nervous, so Fanny took it over to York Farm and found it "a most delightful creature. . . . I sit upright to it, as I should to my piano, and it tires neither my eyes nor my back, as writing does, and I think must be an unspeakable comfort to my poor printers. [Such machines] are now very generally used in lawyers' offices and places of business . . . and with persons expert in their use are quite as rapid in writing as the pen."[32] She did not foresee what the delightful creature would do toward emancipating women. But she welcomed it with the ready approval that she had already accorded railroads and steamships. Now here she sat, her posture all that Sergeant So-and-so of the Foot Guards might have wished, hunt-and-pecking away on work of crucial personal significance—for the typewriter had come along just in time to help her prepare the first of her rich and waywardly ingratiating autobiographies.

Some years previously Harriet St. Leger, blind and far into her seventies, was arranging her affairs. Among her papers were most of the letters Fanny had written to her over the last fifty years. It was probably Frances Power Cobbe, close friend of both Harriet and Fanny, who got them shipped across the Atlantic. When they appeared on Fanny's ice-bound doorstep, it must have been like having one's previous life unroll in good earnest, for she had had few secrets from Harriet and had valued being able to unburden herself on paper addressed to Ardgillan Castle. To judge from the massive extracts published, sown with suspension points indicating excisions, the whole must have come to a million or so words covering anything and everything from Fanny's hopes of immortality to her liking for red gowns, and reflecting the changes of experience if not of ingredients that made vivacious Miss Fanny Kemble into broody Mrs. Pierce Butler and then into Mrs. Kemble, the massive sibyl of the reading desk.

Once Fanny sifted out of those extensive scribblings all that she wished to see printed, she burned the originals; only a few beginning "Dear Hal" survive in this or that library's manuscript room. God knows what went up the chimney—what vital details about the shipwreck of her marriage and what did go on between her and Craven; and how Charles and she got on with Uncle Vincent; and what Adelaide said when she learned of Harry's second byblow; and how her first sight of the Alps affected her . . . In view of the pungency of some things she did print, what she cut must often have been striking indeed for those times. As it was, her cutdowns of these letters are chief agents of the remarkable immediacy that her memoirs convey. Equally remarkable is the lack, specially notable in the first of the three books, of what teacher recommended as rhetorical virtues. This *Records of a Girlhood* has neither unity nor coherence. As for emphasis, its lightning flashes and abruptly beginning and ending showers are as disorderly as anything in nature. Its text must have driven copy and proof readers wild. Yet it also does come near giving an idea of why Fanny was renowned as conversationalist. And frequently for a paragraph or a page or two her writing goes airborne as true and clear and empathic as her sister's singing. For preliminary example she wrote that Adelaide's voice "haunts me like something precious that I have lost and go vainly seeking for; other people play and sing her songs, and then though I seem to listen to them, I hear *her* again . . . see again that wonderful human soul which beamed from every part of her fine face as she uttered those powerful sweet spells of love, and pity, and terror."[33]

Why she set about this *Girlhood* volume does not appear. Maybe delving into that box of letters subliminally renewed the process of forty years earlier when she made a book of her American *Journal,* and now, with no husband to say her nay, she could print what she pleased. Or it may merely be that, living now solely on income from savings, no more reading fees, with transatlantic comings and goings expensive, she always needed spare funds, and reverted to her long-standing presumption that practically anything she bothered to write would bring in money. The reliability of this means brings up the issue of how much her conspicuousness on the stage, then in the newspapers and then on the reading platform had to do with it.

Nobody could question that when John Murray brought out her *Francis the First* about the same time as her debut at Covent Garden, he had some such thing in mind. So did Carey when contracting for the American *Journal.* Similarly, when she wanted to buy Forrester back from the liveryman, her success in finding a publisher for an accumulation of tolerable—and markedly subjective—verses has the same connotations. And to assume that, though she left no hint of it, she did not understand much of that is to postulate a stupidity of which she was incapable. Not to acknowledge it to others could be part of the Kemble imperiousness of which she had her share all her life; any gesture she cared to make, literary or physical, merited consideration. That went with being a Kemble.

In the mid-1870s she had strong, affectionate connections in Boston and was, of course, personally acquainted with the successive editors of the *Atlantic Monthly;* and maybe even more to the point, with some hundreds of its most influential subscribers. The incumbent, William Dean Howells, readily agreed to pay $150 an installment for a series of articles to be called "An Old Woman's Gossip" (Fanny's title)—a sort of rambling fruitcake of higgledy-piggledy re-memberings relying heavily on her early letters to Harriet St. Leger, Anna Jameson, et al. In March 1875 the first consignment of it went to Howells with a letter adjuring him to send her no galleys to correct; another soon apologized for the loose syntax of her copy and gave him and staff full freedom to amend it as they liked, but in bafflingly ambiguous terms: "You are welcome to abridge or even entirely suppress my 'Gossip' provided you do not abridge or suppress

my payment for it. My motive in publishing is *purely sordid.* . . .
Do not *change* & do not *omit* anything . . . (I do not mean . . .
what you wish to curtail)."[34] Howells, a man likely to know spon-
taneity when he saw it, probably did little meddling. As Henry
James wrote years later apropos of Fanny's memoirs thus begun: "She
wrote exactly as she talked, observing, asserting, complaining, con-
fiding, contradicting . . . always effectually communicating . . .
uttered with her pen as well as with her lips the most agreeable,
uncontemporary, self-respecting English."[35]

Her "Old Woman's Gossip" ran twenty issues in the *Atlantic
Monthly* and also prospered when, retitled *Records of a Girlhood,* it
came out as a fat book in both America and England. Its looseness of
structure—rather lack of any such thing—admirably fits it for casual
picking up to open anywhere. Variety of subject matter combines
with Fanny's nimble mind and style to make the odds good that any
page—except those discussing religion—leads one to read on and on.
A few years later, as has been seen, Fanny dismayed Frances by em-
barking on a sequel, *Records of Later Life,* taking her up to 1848. *A
Year of Consolation* fitted into its middle. Then late in the 1880s she
again assembled letters into *Further Records 1848—1883.* This book
of mine shamelessly cannibalizes all four and a reader come this far
might conclude that he already knows them. No such delusion should
exist. These queerly bound old volumes must be explored in order to
meet on her own leisurely terms and in her own time the remarkable
woman who put them together.

One must, however, mention again the likelihood that thus
swimming backward through time to Edinburgh and Bannisters and
Butler's Island and the Perch with the demands of copying and pondering cuts providing counterpoint was valuable occupational therapy. Then there is the issue of Fanny's standing as writer. If
publishing an autobiography (ghosted or not) made a writer, there
would be standing room only on the literary slope of Parnassus. But
Fanny had not only hoped for a writer's career, publishers brought
out for her at their risk and expense two original and four adapted
plays; two volumes of verse; a short novel; a number of essays on
Shakespeare; at least one short story; and a scattering of pieces in

well-considered British and American periodicals—at least partial realization of her adolescent ambition. And though her critical sense as to painting, sculpture, and music was more or less that of her cultivated acquaintance, in writing she had a nose better than most. It means little that she shared her time's successive admirations for Goethe, Byron, Tennyson; or, on the down side, that early reading of Anna Jameson's *Ennuyée* forever after colored her attitude toward the contents of Italian galleries. She was polite, probably not insincerely, about Lady Dacre's accomplished daughter's inane little stories. But something, maybe her intimacy with Shakespeare—a formidable benchmark—made her see on her own that the noncomic British drama from the Restoration to her own time, Otway and Dryden to Milman and Knowles—even if the authors were friends of the family—was mostly stuff and nonsense.

As to novelists, she thought Balzac head and shoulders above the ruck at a time when the generic cultivated Victorian lady was seldom able even to breathe, let alone enjoy the vigorous breezes of the Comédie Humaine. *Barchester Towers* set her telling correspondents that Trollope was a man to watch. It is even more creditable that, heartily as she agreed with the world's verdict that *Vanity Fair,* brilliantly new, qualified its author as a genius, she had thought his *Barry Lyndon* had already demonstrated as much. Relatively few of her contemporaries had paid much attention to that grim little masterpiece. A woman thus able to relish the brushwork and draftsmanship as Mr. Lyndon progresses from impudent penury to blackleg success to bold affluence to chalkstones and prison may be forgiven for approving a good deal of watery-transient stuff. And it is a great pity that Henry James very probably never saw Fanny's explanation of his method to an acquaintance who had complained that his work was superficial: "His gift is . . . a very fine & refined delicate and suggestive treatment of surfaces—below which I think he allows you very well to see (without sounding them) depths of feeling and satire which a heavier plummet might disturb without any better effect than that of destroying the highly finished though lightly touched surface scenes and figures."[36]

Though it is risky to take seriously writers' judgments on the relative merits of their works, the bits of her verse quoted in this text show that Fanny was right to refuse to consider herself much of a poet. Her verses averaged on the whole rather better than those of, say, Felicia Hemans, Laetitia E. Landon or Lydia Sigourney, women versifiers of her day who managed to get consistently into print and develop consequent reputations. In unconscious tribute to the Bard a few of her sonnets follow Shakespeare's verbal patterns so closely that it seems a pity they lack the essential robustness of the prototypes. But her good friend, Robert Browning, was all too right to comment on her first volume of verse: "I had no idea Mrs. Butler could have written anything so mournfully mediocre . . . description without colour, songs without tune."[37] Over in America Fanny's good friend Fanny Appleton, soon to marry a considerable poet, thought the volume "less poetical than I expected from her geyser-like soul."[38] Her fictions, *Far Away and Long Ago,* and "The Rose Lily" are only respectable minor Victorian magazine work, making affectionate use of New England backgrounds after the manner of Catharine Sedgwick. The most notable thing about them is that Fanny wrote them in her late seventies, an age when talent, minor or major, seldom breaks out in a fresh place with any success.

And, having been right about her verses, she was at least half right about thinking her *An English Tragedy* worthwhile. This was the play that Macready, after consulting with Harness, Miss Martineau, et al., rejected as too rich for the Victorian audience's blood. Its ingredients are pandering, adultery, and crooked gambling. The protagonist, Lord Alford, once wooed and half won Anne, a lovely heiress; but because legal tangles encumbered her inheritance, he shied off. She has married the middle-aged barrister who righted her affairs, now a judge. With them lives his sister, Mary, lively and pretty. She is engaged to and loyally loves James Forrester, but their plans to marry are threatened by his gambling losses; he is one of several fleeced by Lord Alford, who uses cogged dice. Anne gets on bad terms with the judge because she fails to understand his professional scruples in a case in which she is interested. Alford reappears in her life, takes advantage of the rift, and seduces her. Soon tiring of his conquest, he arranges to pass her on as venal mistress to James's elder brother, Sir John Forrester. Alford secures Anne's consent to entertain Sir John by threats to expose her to her husband. Sir John is brought blindfold (to shield her identity) to Anne's window. She lets him in but at the critical moment refuses to go through with it. He departs moved by her beauty and her revulsion. Alford sends proof of her infidelity to the judge. He has a stroke and isolates himself for life in a single room. James, unaware of all this, again gaming with Alford, catches him cheating. During the ensuing quarrel Sir John appears, interferes, and gets killed by Alford, who is arrested. Anne, dying slowly of remorse with Mary looking after her, has a deathbed reconciliation with her husband. At the final curtain he faces a desolate life as grief-crippled invalid in charge of Mary, and, it is hinted, James.

Details in the script show that the setting is the postmedieval, trunkhose-and-ruff Neverneverland so dear to the stage of Fanny's day. Fittingly it is written in the workaday blank verse modeled on Massinger et al. that goes with that tradition. But the materials were contemporary. Fanny learned about a wife's thus rejecting the man her pandering lover sends her from Charles, who brought it home from a dinner at Lady Blessington's. In real life this lover was Baron de Ros, holder of one of the British peerage's oldest titles, and

> one of the most worthless men of his day . . . [but] well received by . . . the best English society. That he was an unprincipled profligate made him no less welcome to his male associates, or their wives, sisters, and daughters; but when Lord de Ros cheated his fellow-gamblers at the Club, no further toleration was possible . . . Lady Ellesmere, from whom I heard a story of his cold-blooded profligacy far more dreadful than that on which I founded my "English Tragedy" told me that her brother, Charles Greville . . . his most intimate friend . . . burst into tears when the fact of his cheating was discovered.[39]

De Ros sued his accuser for libel, lost the case and hence much of his elegant social connection. For Fanny the point was the irony that he (or her Alford) could destroy the peace and happiness of many by his particularly nasty tomcattings and go scatheless but the same connection could not for an instant tolerate his violating the gentlemanly taboo on cheating at the gaming table.

Macready was right to reject the play, of course. It was only a few years since the De Ros scandal and painful memories among the well placed made the subject matter hazardous. Nor did he probably feel prepared to ask any leading lady to pour out before a London audience such then outlandishly explicit lines as Fanny gave Anne to protest with when Alford makes his suggestion:

> Hear me, you man! I'm an adulteress,
> A branded thing for honest men to scorn,
> And true wives to cry out on . . .
> But if thou deem'st I am that shameless creature
> To turn from man to man, and sell my body
> For price of money, 'tis not so, I tell thee!
> I loved thee, idiot, idiot that I was!
> But I am not a common harlot yet.[40]

Nor was Fanny's point about the relative heinousness of promiscuity and cheating with dice, unmistakable if implicit, likely to be palatable. And the last unfavorable consideration—which seems to have occurred to nobody at the time—was that the Crown official who would pass on whether *An English Tragedy* could be performed on the English stage[41] was not only Fanny's father but the very man who had told her the story on which she based it.

Macready was also right, however, to call the thing "powerful . . . most painful, most shocking, but full of power, poetry, and pathos," and its author "one of the most remarkable women of the present day."[42] It is a pity it has never been acted. It reads as if it would catch fire on stage. Emotions build authentically in its straightforward dialogue, for which the blank verse is not the handicap it might be. The gaming scenes are lively, the sense of Anne's progress into reinfatuation with Alford is subtle and yet strong, and the bleakness of the last scene makes one shiver.

The important aspect of Fanny-as-writer remains, however, the limber, unpremeditated art of much of her autobiographical work. At its best her way with figures of speech can bring Emily Dickinson to mind: A swarm of fireflies "as if the Milky Way had gone mad and

taken to dancing";[43] "an enchanting, grey, soft afternoon, with now
and then a rain-drop and sigh of wind, like the last sob of a fit of
crying"; "the young moon came picking her way from the east, leading with her a dripping, draggled May."[44] Not long after telling her
American journal that "I can't write prose (query: can I write any
thing else?)," she records a stop to water the horses at a "lonely roadside house" in New York State: "We alighted, and without ceremony
strolled into the garden; a mere wilderness of overgrown sweetbriar,
faint-breathing dog-roses, and flaunting red poppies overshadowed by
some orchard trees,—from which we stole sundry half-ripe cherries.
The place was desolate, I believe; yet we lingered in it, and did not
think it so."[45] Or, for a total change of subject, from *Georgian Plantation:*

> In one miserable hut I heard that the baby was just
> dead . . . one of thirteen, many of whom had been, like
> itself, mercifully removed from the life of degradation and
> misery to which their birth appointed them; and whether
> it was the frequent repetition of similar losses, or an in-
> stinctive consciousness that death was indeed better than
> life for such children as theirs, I know not, but the father
> and mother, and old Rose, the nurse, who was their little
> baby's grandmother, all seemed apathetic and apparently
> indifferent to the event. The mother merely repeated over
> and over again, "I've lost a many; they all goes so;" and
> the father, without word or comment, went out to his
> enforced labor.[46]

In view of the content, it seems cold-blooded to go literary; but even
so, just let the cadences of that run over the consciousness.

She could also go beyond impressionistic record. Well outside
her valid religious bent, over her mind flickered small speculations
and ironies that, once encountered, are hard to forget because so well
expressed. At Trenton Falls, aware of the current beginnings of geology and doubts about cosmogony: "The strata are the most beautifully regular possible, and upon their broad smooth surfaces, a
thousand theories sit, which I hope I did not disturb, as I walked
over them in the plenitude of my ignorance admiring God's masonry."[47] Seven years later in limbo at Butler Place: "How many

things make one feel as if one's whole life was only a confused dream!
Wouldn't it be odd to wake at the end and find one had not lived at
all?" After which eerie suggestion it is reassuring—or is it?—to come
on this pronouncement the following spring:

> to misunderstand and be misunderstood is one of the in-
> evitable conditions, and, I think, one of the especial pur-
> poses, of our existence. The principal use of the affection
> of human beings for each other, is to supply the want of
> perfect comprehension, which is impossible. All the faith
> and love which we possess are barely sufficient to bridge
> over the abyss of individualism which separates one hu-
> man being from another; and they would, or could not
> exist, if we really understood each other.[48]

XXI

Embers Under Ashes

LATE IN JANUARY 1877 Fanny Kemble sailed with the Leighs—James, Frances, and baby Alice—from New York for England. Sixteen years still lay ahead of her but she never saw America again. The Leighs had given up Humpty Dumpty—at which they had made rather more sense than the United States had with cognate national problems—and now turned to the future appropriate to a well-born and widely liked Church of England clergyman. After confusions and false clues, Leigh secured a living in Stratford-on-Avon. The parsonage, a remodeled survival from a medieval monastery, had acres of grounds going down to the river. Even after working herself out a house and servants in London, Fanny spent much time with the Leighs and had their first Christmas there with them. At her and Sarah's suggestion Henry James was invited. He liked the venerable house and the children's doings and took an active part in decorating the Christmas tree. But he thought his host "not interesting . . . excellent, liberal, hardworking . . . but with the intellect and the manners of a boy of seven" and his hostess "inferior to both her mother and her sister . . . hating her position in England, detesting the English . . . rubbing it unmercifully into her good-natured husband. [But] she has a certain charm of honesty and freshness."[1]

The pertinence of Stratford was not likely to be lost on Fanny. Some years earlier on a previous visit she had sought and failed to get permission to spend the night in front of Shakespeare's tomb. Now it delighted her to see the son-in-law she liked conducting the stately old services she loved in the fine old church. But when the Leighs took her to visit the birthplace, already a tourist shrine, and the elderly gentlewoman in charge bored her with lame lore about the Swan of Avon and flowers mentioned in his plays, they took her impatience for numbness and one of them said testily: "Ah! No Shakespearean scholar, I perceive!"[2] Leigh's professional duties extended to Leamington, ten miles away. Presently, much to Frances's displeasure, they had to leave the quaint old monastery that she had been making more habitable and move to less notable quarters on Leamington Green. During their several years there Fanny made them extensive visits and poor little Pierce Butler Leigh was born and miserably died. Then Leigh was made rector of St. Mary's, Bryanstone Square, London, and took a house on Gloucester Place. Frances duly deplored this fresh uprooting.

Fanny had been failing to settle down comfortably. Indeed, with the possible exception of some of her stays in Lenox and one in London, that was a thing she seldom managed anywhere. Years of trouping and successive crises had accentuated her family restlessness of disposition. At her age the usual thing for a lady of adequate means lacking a husband and preferring not to live with married offspring was to set up housekeeping with a woman friend in similar circumstances in a permanent quasi-sisterly relation. Thus Harriet St. Leger shared quarters and resources with Dorothy Wilson, whom Fanny liked; Frances Cobbe with Mary Lloyd whom, Fanny said, she liked even better . . . But it is doubtful whether, given her temperament, such an arrangement would have suited month in, month out. Instead she kept shifting from a given house to lodgings, then to another house, and so on, her long stays in Switzerland and the scarcity of satisfactory servants, even in England, keeping the pattern unsettled.

One of her longer stays was in Queen Anne's Mansions, an early apartment house. Very up-to-date, it boasted what Fanny had heard Irish servants in America calling an "alleviator," an improvement almost as new and quite as influential as the typewriter. Then for some years she rented Mary Lloyd's neat small house in Hereford Square, but eventually difficulties with smelly drains seemed to threaten unbecoming frictions with Miss Lloyd—having a friend for landlord is often awkward. The redoubtable Mrs. Kemble, facing her eighty-first birthday, gave up her struggle to fend for herself and took refuge with the Leighs in Gloucester Place.

Arthritis and gastritis had been plaguing her for some time. Now other ailments of old age were taking toll. Loss of quality in the voice as well as stiffness of the hands forced her to give up the singing and playing that had whiled away so many of her evenings. She was going deaf and developed a derisive scorn for the ear trumpet supplied her. It was worse than vexing to have either to ask people to shout at one or put up with having to repeat; feelingly she described a meeting after many years with Lord Houghton (once Dicky Milnes) in which the deafness of both and his poor articulation due to missing teeth made conversation all cross questions and crooked answers. In spite of the best dentist in London, her teeth were deserting her. The remains of her famous heavy, glossy-dark hair, now thin and white, were cut short. Her eyes, though still usable, had weakened to where she was as likely to play a game of patience as to read a book. And as for the exercise she had always craved: "A half mile *crawl* when the pavement is dry is my utmost on foot,"[3] she told Sarah in 1889.

Toward all this she felt, or anyway expressed, an ironic stoicism. Every day at five o'clock "I rest myself from the *exertion* of doing nothing all day & prepare myself by changing my dress for the *exertion* of doing nothing all night." Returning from the Continent to hear of the deaths of several old friends: "If one will persist in living to seventy-five, one surely will find one's *intimacy* is with death, not life,"[4] and here was a note from Alfred Tennyson, her exact contemporary, grumbling that his recent elevation to the peerage was "surely a chaplet on a skull."[5]

Adelaide was already gone in 1879. Fanny was taking birthdays with the resolution of a steeplechase rider taking successive fences. On the seventieth to George Biddle:

> I used to love the winter cold but am beginning seriously
> to reflect upon the hygienic uses of *heat* and incline to
> think that all people over seventy [should] . . . either go
> to the south or to *bed* & stay there from the 1st of Decem-

ber till the 28th of February . . . what a dutiful woman
I am . . . going this afternoon to hear my friend Miss
Cobbe report the "duties of the women of England at the
present time"—My own intimate conviction is that *my*
duty . . . would be to sit and doze in my chimney corner.

On her seventy-fifth birthday, to Biddle: "God bless you for your
dutiful and affectionate birthday greeting. . . . You say old age is
sad & so it is in some of its aspects but not at all in all—the loss of
power, of activity, of enjoyment is also loss of power of suffering
. . . peace . . . is . . . welcome to one whose life has been scattered battered shattered & spattered like mine." On the seventy-
eighth, to Sarah: "It seems incredible to me that I was once young—
& equally incredible that I am so no longer." On the eightieth: "As
I was hobbling down to my eight o'clock dinner [the servants]
warned me . . . a surprise awaited me . . . round a bright table
with a splendid birthday cake lighted with eighty candles stood eight
of my youngest relations . . . they ate ice cream & cake & I couldn't
eat my dinner."[6] But the inexorability of the calendar also gave her
a private "chief day of rejoicing"—the winter solstice, "the turning
of the year to the light"[7] when, with a quasi-pagan sense of sun and
reprieve, she sometimes put on a special dress and a wreath of flowers
all by herself. It was a resilient spirit.

Though by now less mobile, Fanny was not so isolated as she
had been in Branchtown off and on. Mary Anne Thackeray, the spin-
ster-heiress who rejected young Harry while staying friends with his
sisters, took her to concerts and out to her country place near Wind-
sor. Annie Thackeray, Will's elder daughter, married to Richmond
Ritchie, a civil servant, lived next door for a while. Harry Kemble,
now well established, rallied round. So did Hamilton Aidé. Once
came calling a retired military man impressively named Sholto Douglas who had been one of Juliet's avid admirers fifty years previously
and now, learning she still existed, sought her out; every few weeks
thereafter lavish quantities of exquisite flowers from his greenhouses
in Hampshire came to Hereford Square. But out and away the most
gratifying element in Fanny's last two decades was the glowing
friendship, as of aunt and favorite nephew, with Henry James.

It began in Rome the winter of 1872–73 at Sarah Wister's weekly evening party where James "met everyone, including the terrific Kemble herself, whose splendid handsomeness of eyes, nostril and mouth were the best things in the room." It had already deepened when he spent Christmas with the Leighs at Stratford in 1877. His letters home were rich in praise of Mrs. Kemble:

> People . . . seem to me . . . nothing but *surface*. . . . Mrs. Kemble has no organized surface at all . . . is like a deep cistern without a cover . . . into which . . . one must tumble without a splash. . . . her conversation is strong meat. . . . Her book [*Girlhood*] . . . has been a quite *immense* success [in London] but she cares no more for [that] than for the sole of her shoe. . . . She always talks as if she were going to die next month [1880] but fortunately her previsions are not realized, and every now and then she has explosions of vitality (I don't mean merely of temper) which ought completely to reassure her. I took her last night to the St. James' Theatre . . . and she wept with such ferocity during the last act that I was glad we were in the seclusion of a box.[8]

"Your mother . . . the last time I saw her," he reports to Sarah Wister, "went through the whole gamut of her talents . . . gave imitations, spouted Shakespeare, represented a ballet we had just seen, said 50 good things a minute." And when assuring Sarah that rumors he is about to marry are false: "Your mother is the only woman I am in love with, but she has repeatedly refused my hand."[9]

He advised her to read *Treasure Island*—thus introducing a highly admired close friend *in absentia,* for Robert Louis Stevenson was then a house-bound invalid—and must have been gratified by her pleasure in "the robust simplicity of it . . . almost as good as Robinson Crusoe for its perfect tone of plain narrative."[10] He sent her everything of his own that saw print; she read it all at least three times and then he listened with a sort of obliged pleasure to her comments, which were not always unmitigated praise. For she took the fond aunt's privilege of seeing her favorite nephew warts and all. She thought his reading aloud was atrocious; and his visit of some days in Switzerland a little long because he was "in his usual gently

lugubrious spirits . . . he's always kind & good & pleasant & agreeable but I would give much to stiffen his *limp* despondency."[11] She
thought him better off in her snug little drawing room in Hereford
Square mildly glowing with affectionate interest while she held forth
imperiously and hyperbolically, amused by her own vehemence:
"Aren't you glad you aren't an empress?" he once asked in a letter to
her. "But you are, God save your Majesty!"[12] And in due course she
signs herself for him: "Goodbye—in the old velvet gown & sables.
Your affectionate, Katharine of Russia."[13]

Long since she had advanced him from "My dear Henry James"
to "Dear Henry." She calls him back from America with "I think of
you almost as if you belonged to me. . . . get all the good you can
from your native land & come back to your adopted one of smoke &
fog & damp & dark & many friends." Some weeks later: "You are a
Puppy!—no I am not languishing for you . . . unless a sore throat
& obstructed bronchial tubes & a heavy drowning cold in the head
are symptoms of sentimental sorrow . . . I have my pocket handker-
chief in my hand oftener than I could wish but it is to blow my nose
& not wipe away regretful tears." He has written in some whimsical
context that he wished she had a cage; this, she writes, "presented
me with a funny image of myself as an elderly Parrot—heaving myself clumsily sideways up my perch—staring at my friends with a
dreadful immovable inexpressive eye & repeating every five minutes
the same dry dictatorial sentiment . . . 'That's bad!' Me voyez
vous?"[14] So shrewd an auditor cannot have failed to understand how
good it was for her thus to launch herself on extravagant banter and
self-caricature. When she had to renounce travel, it was highly appropriate that it was to Henry James she gave her traveling clock,
like the old warrior handing his sword to the young one, for thenceforth he was her widest window on the outside world—a younger
Cyrano bringing the minutiae of Paris to Roxanne in the convent
garden. Curious that, so far as I know, he never used either of the
Kemble sisters as raw material for his fictions, though Sarah may have
been thus utilized once. Maybe Fanny and Adelaide carried too heavy
a charge for his well-engineered but light wiring. On the other hand,
his extended obituary of Fanny in *Temple Bar* was lovingly brilliant.

* * *

Age increased Fanny's dependence on servants, usually her own but in the last years Frances's too. It had, of course, always been greater than is usual nowadays. In 1981 even persons of large economic resources may not understand how utterly women a hundred years ago were committed to wage-earning hewers of wood and drawers of water. Victorian novels make it clear that above a domestic level almost to be classed as poverty, at least one slatternly, dimwitted and abjectly ill paid "slavey" emptied chamberpots, hauled water upstairs in pails, laid the fires, took out the ashes, washed the dishes, scrubbed the floors . . . In middle-income circumstances, like Fanny's, both sides of the water, one assumed a multiple domestic staff—in England, say, a cook, two housemaids, a nursemaid, maybe a "boy in buttons" to answer the door, run errands, clean the knives . . . In their by no means pretentious houses both Fanny and Frances usually had also at least one manservant.

Thus, reared as she was, even imaginative Fanny Kemble could hardly have conceived of a housekeeping situation in which meals would not be cooked and served for her, beds made, linen washed and ironed, errands run, slops disposed of, and so on, by her own employees leaving her free to practice music or write as much as she chose, or receive visitors until it was time to change for dinner into an evening gown laid out for her on the bed by a maid who helped her into it. When unable to recruit such a cadre she went into lodgings or (in America) a boardinghouse where some of the same conveniences, though often poorly managed, were available collectively. Her letters sputter about the high wages one must pay incompetents who think nothing of leaving one in the lurch whenever it suits their fancy, and the strange difficulty (in America especially) of finding any persons who really seem to want servants' berths to begin with. In Lenox she was once reduced to employing a married couple who were "convicted thieves . . . partly because I knew not where to turn for others, and partly in the hopes of reforming them, as they were . . . young offenders."[15] (It is the biographer's curse that bits like that sometimes turn up with no further clue as to how it worked out.) Her best resource in America was the European professional servant coming overseas for the higher wages allegedly paid there. Thus her last staff at York Farm included an English personal maid, an English cook, and an Irish manservant, all of whom planned to return home when Mrs. Kemble closed the place.

Not only in her own house but in lodging house or hotel, steamer or stagecoach, a personal maid was almost as essential a part of the outfit as her hairbrush. And it probably speaks well for her essential good nature and considerateness that several such incumbents stayed with her year after year in trying circumstances; for instance, Marie, a German maid who traveled with Fanny for fifteen years of the discomforts and vexations of reading tours. Thus developed warm and touchingly valuable, familylike ties, as of chieftain to clansman. Hayes, the stolid girl who accompanied Fanny on that wild winter pilgrimage across France, became, Fanny said, "more than a servant . . . a friend. . . . I cried some tears at the thought . . . of parting with her."[16] Now it does not always follow that a servant's long tenure with mutual attachment developing means that either employer or servant is a good sort. The unswervingly loyal and admiring secretary of long standing is sometimes just as nasty and crooked as her boss, and each values the other for predatory skills. But Fanny's long-term servants were loved in generous terms; thus she went far out of her way to help Margery O'Brien after the former nursemaid's disastrous marriage, divorce, and illness. In 1877 Fanny took with her on her summer's travels a promising Swiss maid who had been five years in her previous situation in Scotland. Mrs. Kemble spent a full week at tourist-infested Montreux, a place she detested, just so the girl could daily visit her parents, who lived nearby.

The most rewarding such relationship began in the early 1870s when Fanny acquired as personal maid an English girl, Ellen (surname never given) and as manservant a northern Italian, Luigi Brianzone. Both were likable and capable; eventually they determined to marry. Neither Ellen's family nor Fanny objected in principle. Luigi's people, it appeared, were respectable farmers in the hills between Como and Maggiore, and the differences in nationality and religion were taken more in stride than might have been expected. But Fanny was about to go to America for some two years and the bond between mistress and maid was already strong enough to postpone the marriage. While Ellen spent the two years with Fanny, Luigi would return to Varese to prepare eventually to bring Ellen there to settle among his own kin.

So she crossed the ocean to look after her lady in the house on Rittenhouse Square rented while York Farm was got ready; and at York Farm two winters; and at Lenox seasonally; with alarums and excursions as the Leighs' comings and goings marked their seasons in the Sea Islands. In Rittenhouse Square Ellen met the resident ghost and devotedly forbore to mention it until long afterward lest it alarm and inconvenience Mrs. Kemble. Fanny was well aware how precious Ellen's loyalty was: "[she] has been friend, helper, adviser, housekeeper, maid, servant, everything to me . . . has sacrificed her own health . . . comfort, convenience, and happiness, to her devotion to me." As the years stretched toward three, because the Leighs' plans kept changing, "I have felt the responsibility of keeping her here, even involuntarily as I have done, weighing upon me more and more . . . with a great sense of relief . . . [I hear] she has promised her mother not to prolong her stay in America beyond the autumn. . . . What will become of me without her I do not know . . . mean time it is a comfort to me to think that she . . . is going home . . . to the worthy fellow to whom she is engaged . . . and . . . a home of her own, which she so richly deserves."[17]

Late in the spring of 1877 Fanny attended the Brianzones' wedding in Italy. Next year she attended the christening of their first child and could congratulate them also on their future now being more secure, for the nobleman who had been commander of the regiment of dragoons in which Luigi had done his military service now made him supervisor of one of his estates. Aware that the family's upland quarters were simple, Fanny stayed in Stresa, where the christening took place, and had Ellen and the baby with her for a week's visit. Otherwise, with her lady for guest, Ellen "would have worried and exerted herself to make me comfortable, English fashion, and the effect would have been very bad for her."[18]

Doubtless letters and further visits kept the connection warm. Thirteen years later Fanny's new life with the Leighs and its consequent loss of independence became less irksome because Ellen, at whose instance I do not know but obviously with Luigi's loyal consent, came back to England to take over again. It must have been all labor of love, for her wages of two pounds a week, though ample for that time, cannot have made up for prolonged absence from husband and family. Fanny's relations with the Leighs' servants were harmonious enough, indeed better than Frances managed. But a devoted maid already expert in her special ways was sorely needed. Fanny now could use the pen herself only when writing to Sarah, and even then might need her hand guided. Otherwise Ellen took her dictation replying to affectionate inquiries from such distant old friends as S. G. Ward and John Murray Forbes or thanking "Dear Willy" Wister for his reports on his management of her finances, which she studied, she once told him, "with becoming attention and gravity . . . feeling a little at the same time like a three year old baby *pretending to read."* A minor happy acquisition was a Scotch terrier bitch whom Fanny named Romp, "highly descriptive of her manners and morals . . . general favourite with all the household . . . extremely bright vivacious eyes & a very intelligent countenance & general resemblance to Sir Walter Scott." [19] By then few enough persons in Britain were qualified to know how the living Sir Walter had looked; it had been sixty years since he praised Miss Kemble's seat in the saddle there on Princes Street where now stood the pseudo-Gothic memorial to him that Fanny did not much care for.

By then saddles were only a long-dimmed memory. Early in 1892 an enterprising writer for the American *Ladies' Home Journal* came reconnoitering the Leighs' country place in hopes of interviewing Fanny. That was impossible, of course. But he did pick up from gossip, probably at the local pub, certain crumbs: she was never seen socially anymore and outsiders intending to pay their respects were never admitted. Sometimes she had an outing in a closed carriage or, in the best weather, a pony cart masterfully driven by her daughter, Mrs. Leigh. She now read little, they said, but her Bible and a few religious books. Out of these scanty data came a flowery little piece entitled with inadvertent irony "A Glimpse of Fanny Kemble" that was on sound ground at least in saying that she had "vanished into a world of shadows."[20] When at the Gloucester Place house in London, she wrote to S. G. Ward, the routine was: "I go out every day in a wheeled chair, see a view, old and attached friends, read a little and knit a little. . . . My health . . . is good enough for the machine of three and eighty years wear."[21]

Frances, as usual, had things to complain of, with what justification it is hard to gauge. Human beings as old as her mother was in 1892 very often develop irresponsible quirks. On the other hand Frances was of a harsh, rigid, and petulant disposition that makes it unfortunate we have only her as lens through which to view the situation. Well, here she is writing to W. R. Wister that an alarming gastric episode in midwinter fully persuaded Fanny she was near death, and now that she is fully recovered, she nevertheless persists, in spite of doctors' reassurances, in acting on that belief. She insists she cannot feed herself, Ellen must do it. Having arranged (at whose instance we do not know) that Frances take over all her incoming money and dole it out to her on request, Fanny is now asking for and giving away money by handfuls: "£100 to Ellen on top of £200 at Christmas, £50 to the footman, who does her many services; £25 to the butler, whose duties seldom affect her"[22] Some months earlier, it appears, Fanny had instructed William Minot, Catharine Sedgwick's husband, who handled the Boston segment of her finances, to consolidate the securities in his charge with those in Wister's into a trust, income to Fanny for life, Sarah and Frances as eventual beneficiaries. Maybe those substantial sums for the servants, Ellen particularly, were confusedly intended to express gratitude in lieu of or as supplements to legacies in a will. Yet it *was* rather flighty and one can understand some of Frances's uneasiness. Such outlays might compromise Fanny's ability to pay whatever her regular contributions to household expenses may have been; they were probably not light, since Frances was always short of money. And since the trustee of the new trust was empowered to cash in up to five thousand dollars in case of need, Fanny's new demands might somewhat erode the principal.

Frances seems to have asked Dr. Wister to take up with Minot the possibility that Fanny's failing memory as to recent events and so on meant serious senile disability. Minot replied that the letters she wrote to him showed no signs of mental incapacity. The same holds good, in my judgment, of most of Fanny's letters surviving from this period. But she herself was complaining of lapses of memory, and now and again possibly symptomatic confusions afflict her. For one small matter, she issued a series of bewilderingly conflicting instructions to Sarah as to how to get a certain important black shawl fetched to her from America. . . . Her notes to W. R. Wister requesting special remittances are warmly affectionate but also pay little heed to whether the substantial amounts sought are readily available. . . . And when Sarah enters a long-range expostulation about the largesse to the servants, the reply (signed by Fanny but dictated to Ellen, as Sarah suspiciously noted) is simply: "My dear child: Pay Ellen a year's wages for me. Neither you nor I can ever repay her devotion."[23] and then goes into family news: Alice Leigh, now a grown girl, is soon to be presented at court.

Thus even Sarah, the more generous sister, had reason to wonder whether Ellen was deliberately exploiting her mistress's gratitude. The terms were there. The three hundred pounds already in hand was an important sum in the Brianzones' world. It was a great pity that this miserable tangle arose to trouble the potential peace of Fanny's ninth decade. How much she fretted over it cannot be known. The vagaries of minds encountering the biochemical effects of aging are by no means well understood. But at least the case for believing that the Brianzones were crassly making a good thing out of Fanny is badly damaged by the loving sincerity of what Ellen wrote to Frances Cobbe when, on January 5, 1893, her lady died, literally in Ellen's arms. It is good to know that she went out supported by this middle-aged servant who had twice reoriented her own life for Fanny's sake:

> My dear mistress . . . passed away peacefully on Sunday
> night as I was putting her to bed. . . . that night week
> when coming up stairs she had a sort of fainting fit yet it
> did not seem like a faint, her dear hands were warm all
> the time. We got her to bed, and she never went down
> stairs again, never was dressed, but every day walked from
> her bed to the sofa and laid there several hours, then back

to bed. The Doctor, nor any of us thought there was immediate danger, although she refused all nourishment, it
was with great coaxing that I got her to take any thing,
and never more than three spoon fulls . . . water, water
was all her cry day and night. My poor darling, I wish
you could see her, she looks so peaceful and so handsome.
No one ought to wish it otherwise, she was so tired of life
and longed so to go, even I can not wish her back. . . .
I sat by her rubbing her hands for a long time, then a
little after 11, she said, My dear, I will go to bed. . . .
I put my arm around her and she walked quite well to the
stool at her bedside, I began undoing her dressing gown
when she said I must get up she looked up quick . . .
her dear head dropped on my arm, not a groan, not a
struggle, her spirit must have flown straight up to God,
if you saw how peaceful she looks you would say so.
. . . I shall go to the funeral, perhaps that will start my
tears. . . . I am truly thankful to God for allowing me
to come back, and care for my dear mistress to the end.[24]

Telegraph and railroad brought Luigi in time for the funeral. At
the graveside Henry James noted Ellen "with a very white face and
her hands full of flowers." Fanny, he wrote Sarah, "was very touching
. . . these last months—and yet with her wonderful air of smoul-
dering embers under ashes, she leaves a great image, a great memory."[25]

They buried her in her father's grave in Kensal Green cemetery
in the suburbs north of London. I went out there. In 1893, no doubt,
the place was well kept up. Now it is a frowsy wilderness of weeds
and brush masking mausoleums and monuments. Even with plot and
grave numbers as guides, the obliging man in charge had difficulty
finding where the right grave should be; and it took him ten minutes'
hard work with a sickle as large as Father Time's to clear the briers
and sprawling shrubs from the recumbent gravestone. No epitaphs—
only the requisite names and dates.

In the three years since my visit the low-grade jungle must have
grown back over the stone, and the moldy grime that we scuffed
away with our feet in order to read the lettering must again obscure

"Frances Anne Kemble/1809–1893." On one of the surviving briers hung a ripe berry glowing so red in the sunshine that I felt impelled to pick and eat it. I did not do so, not caring to risk Mrs. Kemble's thinking it disrespectful. But now I wish I had.

NOTES

Mrs. Kemble's letters and other memorabilia are scattered in some fifty-odd libraries and other repositories in the United States and Britain. This book's debt to those institutions is acknowledged elsewhere in its pages. In the following notes those collections most heavily drawn on will be identified by the following abbreviations:

Berg   Henry W. and Albert Berg Collection, New York Public Library, Astor, Lenox and Tilden Foundations.
B-Col.   Butler Library, Columbia University
Folger   Folger Shakespeare Library
HSP   Historical Society of Pennsylvania
HTC   Harvard Theatre Collection
Houghton   Houghton Library, Harvard University
Huntington   Huntington Library, San Marino, California.
LC   Library of Congress
NLS   National Library of Scotland

Those of Mrs. Kemble's books heavily drawn on are identified by the following:

Consolation   *A Year of Consolation*
Further Records   *Further Records 1848–1883*
Georgian Plantation   *Journal of a Residence on a Georgian Plantation in 1838–1839*
Girlhood   *Records of a Girlhood*
Journal   *Journal of Frances Anne Butler*
Later Life   *Records of Later Life*

Minor uses of her other published writings are identified in the Notes and the Sources.

I *Footlight Patricians*

1. Kemble, *Georgian Plantation*, p. 21.

2. Quoted in Edel, *Henry James*, Vol. II; pp. 352, 360.

3. Wister, *That I May Tell You*, p. 205.

4. Hazlitt, *Characters*, p. 14.

5. *Blackwood's* magazine, April 1832.

6. Quoted in Kemble, *Girlhood*, p. 162.

7. *Ibid.*, p. 10.

8. Hunt, *Dramatic Criticism*, p. 9.

9. *Blackwood's* magazine, April 1832.

10. *Dictionary of American Biography*, "Gouverneur Kemble."

11. *Appleton Cyclopedia of American Biography*, Vol. III, p. 510.

12. Kemble, *Journal*, Vol. II, p. 1.

13. The new arms were: "Azure on a bend cotised argent a rose gules between two leopards' heads sable." "Caboshed," by the way, means an animal's head with everything back of the ears cut away, like a Halloween mask. None of the above discussion necessarily negates the hairdressing Kembles' claim. As Thomas Hardy's *Tess of the D'Urbervilles* implies, many an august English family had an ill-fated offshoot that, though legitimate, sank into social oblivion while retaining the prestige-bearing name.

14. Ray, *The Age of Wisdom* p. 124.

15. Fanny's mother had a recollection apropos: She was discussing with a knowledgeable Parisian "the career and circumstances of the young ballet women at the Paris Opera and asked: '*Et y en a-t-il qui sont filles de bonne conduite? qui sont sages?*' '*Ma foi*,' was the reply, '*elles auraient grand tort: personne n'y croirait.*' " (*Girlhood*, p. 65).

16. This situation was utilized in *Humphrey Clinker* and John O'Keeffe's *Wild Oats*, or the Strolling Gentleman, a lively if lengthy comedy of the late eighteenth century.

17. This dodge crossed the Atlantic with British actors and was used to get round law and public disapproval in New England and Pennsylvania.

18. For precedent, John Ward, father of Roger's wife, had forbidden her ever to marry an actor. When she insisted on marrying Roger, the old gentleman grumblingly averred that actually she had not disobeyed him for Kemble was not professionally competent enough to be properly considered an actor.

19. In the pre-Victorian theater a "benefit" was usually much simpler than today's multistar clambake raising funds for charitable purposes. It was a special performance toward the end of an engagement with proceeds going to the leading man or leading lady as a bonus over salary. The beneficiary personally sold and often autographed the tickets as an added inducement. Sometimes, however, as in this case, one or more eminent performers would join the beneficiary to do him a good turn.

20. Kemble, *Girlhood*, p. 17.

21. Moore, *Memoirs*, Vol. II, p. 769.

22. Eastlake, *Journals*, Vol. I, p. 123.

23. Kemble, *Girlhood*, pp. 223, 396.

24. Clayden, *Rogers and His Contemporaries*, p. 66.

25. In a recent biography (*Sarah Siddons*, 1970) Roger Manvell's final paragraph says, "On the evening following Sarah's death, Fanny Kemble played

Lady Macbeth, Sarah's greatest part, at Covent Garden," using this piece of disrespect, which it certainly would have been, to strengthen his previous indictment of Fanny as "unsympathetic and overbearing" and "a pert young girl." Only Fanny did nothing of the sort. On June 8, the evening of the day Mrs. Siddons died, Fanny and her father were billed to play *The Provoked Husband* but they did not do so, turning their roles over to Ellen Tree and Mr. Warde. Next night, June 9, the bill was the opera *Cinderella* and a spectacle about Napoleon, no Kemble in either. All next week Fanny and her mother were at Oatlands. Manvell's error probably comes of misinterpreting a passage in Fanny's journal: *"Thursday, June 9th.—*. . . And so I am to act Lady Macbeth" (*Girlhood,* p. 42), taken to mean she was to act it on that date; whereas it is likely she had merely just learned from her father of his decision eventually to add that role to her repertory.

26. Kemble, *Girlhood,* p. 417.

27. *Ibid.,* p. 35.

28. Quoted in Baker, *John Philip Kemble,* p. 192.

29. Downer, *Eminent Tragedian,* p. 240.

30. No namesakery here. Fanny's "Anne" with an *e* came from her godmother, "Daughter of a Staffordshire banker, [my mother's] dear friend" (*Girlhood,* p. 92) and her "Frances" from her aunt, Frances (Kemble) Twiss.

31. Fitzgerald, *The Kembles,* Vol I, pp. 99–107.

32. Kemble, *Girlhood,* p. 2.

33. Frances Anne Kemble, "On the Stage," *Cornhill Magazine,* December 1863.

34. Jane Porter, MS journal, Folger.

35. Johnson, *William Bodham Donne,* p. 40.

36. Kemble, *Girlhood,* pp. 5–6.

37. *Ibid.,* pp. 3, 4, 5.

38. Garrick Club, *Original Letters,* Folio 110.

39. Kemble, *Girlhood,* p. 7.

40. Doran, *Annals,* Vol 3., p. 218.

41. *Girlhood,* p. 450.

42. *Ibid.,* p. 24.

II *"Cette Diable de Kemble"*

1. The story roughly: the new Covent Garden opened September 18, 1809, with John Philip and Mrs. Siddons in *Macbeth.* The management, daunted by the first riot, closed it again to prepare a financial statement issuance which would, it was hoped, cool things off. The reopening October 4, with *The Beggar's Opera,* showed things were hotter than ever. Management persisted, however, in billing and performing various pieces until December 15, when Kemble's public capitulation ended the war. The eighteenth century often saw theater riots. Ostensible causes were usually an unpopular actor or, as here, resentment of raised prices. But the O.P. affair was uniquely well organized and long-lasting. It had, one understands, hidden subsidiary causes: The new building suppressed a third (popular-priced) gallery to make room for a larger number of private boxes with anterooms; this was taken (maybe justifiably) as an attempt to increase revenues by catering to immorality in these hideaways. Add growing resentment of the semimonopoly on theatrical enterprise that royal charter afforded Drury Lane and Covent Garden. Some commentators mention a

generalized class-conscious sentiment.

2. An adaptation of August Friedrich Ferdinand von Kotzebue's *Die Spanier in Peru,* which was very popular on the English-speaking stage for fifty years; the heroine was named Cora, hence probably the numerous Coras in the nomenclature of the nineteenth century.

3. Kemble, *Girlhood,* p. 26.

4. This quotation reminds me that I must acknowledge how heavily, for lack of other data, this book relies on Fanny's autobiographical writings. Attention should be called to Eleanor Ransome's recent *The Terrific Kemble,* an admirable compilation from them. Fanny's accuracy is fortunately very high. No doubt some dressing up of anecdote is there; few can resist that. But the better one knows her, the likelier it seems that a given thing she tells of went pretty much as stated.

5. Thus called to distinguish him from his father, first Baron Lyttelton, "the good Lord Lyttelton." Son's "libertinism was exceptional even in his age and rank," says the *Dictionary of National Biography.* His death was as notable as his morals: He dreamed a bird flew into his room, changed into a woman and told him he had only three days to live. The evening of the third day he died.

6. Kemble, *Girlhood,* p. 42.

7. *Ibid.,* p. 57.

8. *Ibid.,* p. 64.

9. These Continental burlesques and their British and American imitations were elaborate travesties of conspicuous dramas of the day or hackneyed classical legends. There actually was a close connection between these pieces and the now almost defunct "burlesque" of the Minsky era of forty or so years ago; but the line gradually attenuated and little likeness remained.

10. Kemble, *Girlhood,* p. 66.

11. *Ibid.,* p. 80.

12. *Wilhelm Meister,* Boylan translation, pp. 405–6.

13. Kemble *Girlhood,* p. 85.

14. *Ibid.,* pp. 79, 86.

15. *Ibid.,* p. 293.

16. Henry James, *Temple Bar,* May 1893.

17. Frances Power Cobbe, *Life,* p. 160. She implies that this costume may have been modeled on that of "the Ladies of Llangollen," a pair of aristocratic spinsters who chose to live as recluses in Wales for fifty years—and attracted much attention.

18. Kemble, *Girlhood,* p. 92.

19. Harriet St. Leger to Cecilia Combe, undated, NLS.

20. Kemble, *Girlhood,* p. 273.

21. Today's hyperawareness of erotic deviations may tempt readers to look for lesbianism in this friendship. Harriet's dress was semimasculine; Fanny made many cuts in her letters to Harriet before printing them; the tone of what got printed is often eloquently affectionate and no doubt Harriet responded the same way. But an open mind studying the surviving data—notably some of Fanny's comments to friends about Harriet—is likely to conclude that not even cryptolesbianism is involved: thus to George Combe, whose wife was close to Harriet, in 1833: "Harriet is my very dearest friend but there is much in her that I see with sorrow and anxiety as well as very much that I love and admire and respect" (Combe Papers, NLS). Five generations ago cultivated women wrote to women friends in terms of explicit love and longings to embrace and endearing epithets actually meaning no more than deep, explicit affection suffusing a comradely interdependence. To my mind the St. Leger/Kemble relation is best understood as something between a

flighty, keen, generous girl and an elder sister playing psychopomp-governess out of spontaneous affection. For a helpful discussion of the issue, giving potential lesbianism about its proper weight, see Carl N. Degler, *At Odds!* (1980), pp. 144–58.

22. Usually applied to intellectual, particularly literary, women and so used here. The original context was masculine. It betokened the blue (worsted, not elegantly silken) stockings presumably worn by unfashionably dressed literary men attending parties given by high-minded ladies to supplant the dancing and card-playing that dominated social life in the mid-eighteenth century. The transition from these doings to women's writing careers was easy, and the "blue stocking" reference crossed over with it.

23. Brookfield, *Cambridge "Apostles,"* p. 262.

24. Henrietta Le Mesurier to Mary Ann Hardwyke, Perkins Library, Duke University, Bandinel Family Papers.

25. Kemble, *Girlhood,* pp. 139, 142, 141.

26. *Ibid.,* p. 141.

27. Combe Papers, NLS.

28. Kemble, *Girlhood,* pp. 144, 145, 400.

29. *Ibid.,* p. 150.

30. Eastlake, *Journals,* Vol. I, p. 31.

31. *Dictionary of National Biography.*

32. Kemble, *Girlhood,* p. 411.

33. Created by Dr. Franz Joseph Gall in Vienna—yes, Vienna—circa 1800, phrenology spread famously. Americans taking it seriously included Horace Mann, the great educationist; Henry Ward Beecher, renowned preacher of the mid-nineteenth century; Dr. Samuel Gridley Howe, pioneer educating the blind; Allan Pinkerton, founder of the famous detective agency. . . . See my *The Americans,* pp. 445–49 for a sketch of the movement. Novels, magazines and newspapers of the period abound in references to the "bumps" and phrenology's system of discernible human traits such as Amativeness, Philoprogenitiveness, and so on.

34. Combe Papers, NLS.

35. *Consolation,* Vol. II, p. 8.

36. Kemble, *Girlhood,* p. 151.

37. *Ibid.,* p. 158.

38. Combe Papers, NLS.

39. Kemble, *Girlhood,* pp. 165–67.

40. *Ibid.,* pp. 331, 333–34.

41. Folger.

42. Lady Byron to FK, Folger.

43. Littell's *Living Age,* Feb. 29, 1849.

III *"Miss Kemble Called for the Stage!"*

1. Kemble, *Girlhood,* pp. 305–06.

2. Ray, *The Uses of Adversity,* p. 175.

3. Brookfield, *Cambridge "Apostles,"* LL.

4. Kemble, *Girlhood,* p. 188.

5. *Ibid.,* pp. 123, 136, 138.

6. Fanny's first Romeo was a middle-aged, competent member of the Covent Garden Company whose routine performance did not hamper her triumph but got him ungenerously sneered at by her multiplying admirers. She often had Romeo trouble, which was too bad, for Juliet was one of her best roles. Looking back, she said that the only Romeo she ever had who looked the part was Ellen Tree, who, playing opposite her some years later in tights and tunic, was tall enough, aquilinely handsome, young,

and by all accounts a most intelligent performer.

7. This did not mean a return to her profession for Thérèse. When Fanny repeated Juliet two nights later, Miss Lacy of the Covent Garden troupe did Lady Capulet. Thérèse never trod the boards again.

8. Talfourd, *Critical and Miscellaneous Writings,* pp. 117–18.

9. Moore, *Memoirs,* Vol. II, p. 712.

10. Thackeray, *Letters,* Vol. I, p. 105.

11. Kemble, *Later Life,* Vol. II, p. 363.

12. *Examiner,* October 11, 1829.

13. *Ibid.,* November 1, 1829. Presently Hunt wrote that Fanny's Juliet had a "robustness" that kept it inferior to certain other readings of the part (*Dramatic Criticism,* p. 284); he sometimes sniped at her handlings of other roles. One can only surmise how much

of this came of the ups and downs that she herself noted and deplored in her performances; see Chapter XV.

14. Kemble, *Girlhood,* pp. 221, 565.

15. *Ibid.,* pp. 21–22.

16. It is probably bad news for horses that a trend toward reviving the sidesaddle exists among today's lady riders; or so say the firm of Miller's, New York's famous merchants of saddles, etc.

17. Kemble, *Girlhood,* p. 241.

18. *Ibid.,* p. 488.

19. Folger.

20. Kemble, *Girlhood,* pp. 209–10.

21. Manvell, *Sarah Siddons,* p. 312.

22. Combe Papers, NLS.

23. Kemble, *Girlhood,* pp. 243, 411.

24. *Ibid.,* p. 415.

IV *Youth like Summer Morn*

1. This seems anomalous to us; it did not to our ancestors. An almost modern parallel was the movie theater's running a short slapstick comedy and a newsreel between showings of a Hollywood tearjerker. The Regency/Victorian afterpiece was connected with the curious custom of half-price admission: after say the third (central) act of the main attraction, paying half price at the box office admitted one to see the rest of it *and* the complete afterpiece. Thus, empty places, when available, were filled and produced some revenue; and even when no places were available during the main attraction, the half-price patron

could count on those left by patrons going home after the fifth act, too serious or too early-rising for the afterpiece.

2. Kemble, *Journal,* Vol. I, p. 152.

3. Kemble, *Girlhood,* pp. 208–09.

4. *Ibid.,* pp. 249–50.

5. *Ibid.,* p. 315.

6. Andrew Combe to FK, Folger.

7. Kemble, *Girlhood,* p. 288.

8. *Ibid.,* pp. 281–83.

9. *Ibid.,* pp. 283–84.

10. *Ibid.,* pp. 295, 447–48.

11. *Ibid.,* p. 448.

12. Combe Papers, NLS.

13. Kemble, *Girlhood,* p. 301.

14. *Ibid.*, p. 296.

15. *Ibid.*, pp. 455–56.

16. *Ibid.*, pp. 306, 301–02.

17. Add subtleties in the Regency attitude toward women writers: Lady Dacre published under her own name; but when her daughter published two volumes of vapid stories (*Recollections of a Chaperone; Tales of the Peerage and the Peasantry*) they came out anonymously "edited by Lady Dacre," which led many to believe the mother was the writer. The only reason I can think of for this inane subterfuge is that daughter's husband was a clergyman.

18. Clayden, *Rogers and His Contemporaries*, p. 125.

19. A friend told him that since he could well afford it, he should set up a private hearse. At Lord Byron's funeral, they said, Theodore Hook, a most ruthless jokesmith of the day (and original of Mr. Wagge in *Vanity Fair*), advised Rogers to stay out of sight of the undertakers (*Maclise Portrait Gallery*, pp. 180–89). But Rogers seems to have taken it all very much in stride, and in any case had his own tongue for sword and shield; for sample: "Mr. Rogers," his vis-à-vis at an august dinner-table said to him, "I'm sure you're talking some mischief about me." "Oh, Lady Davy," he replied, "I spend my life defending you." I have already cited his insisting that John Philip Kemble, in retirement in Switzerland, sulked when people paid more attention to Mont Blanc than to him.

20. Roberts, *Rogers and His Circle*, p. 109.

21. Kemble, *Girlhood*, pp. 391, 357.

22. "Jordan" was then a euphemism for chamberpot. Regency caricaturists made great play with this in their usually vicious satirizings of the duke's irregular establishment.

23. Kemble, *Girlhood*, pp. 227–29.

24. *Ibid.*, p. 365.

25. *Ibid.*, p. 374.

26. *Ibid.*, pp. 418–19.

27. *Ibid.*, p. 423.

28. *Ibid.*, pp. 436–37.

29. *Ibid.*, p. 439.

30. *Ibid.*, p. 442.

31. The one exception I know of (I hope there were more) was the marriage in the 1780s of a widowed daughter of Lord Sandwich to a popular comedian, "Gentleman" Smith. Doran's *Annals* (Vol. III, p. 126) says that her family considered it a disgrace. Smith offered to quit the stage if the family would secure him an annuity equal to his theatrical earnings. This was refused and he continued his career in order to make provision for his wife. The problem disappeared when she died in 1762.

32. Among the didactic tales that Miss Martineau wrote as *Illustrations of Political Economy* was "For Each and All," about a successful actress quitting the stage to marry a peer and being unpleasantly treated by his relatives and friends. Fanny recalled late in life that Miss Martineau had told her that it was Fanny's venture into matrimony that inspired the plot. The attribution is implausible because the story was published before Fanny went to America and married; indeed also before she ever met Miss Martineau. Fanny did express approval, however, maybe because it reflected the author's opinion of acting as an irksome, discreditable and insecure profession.

33. Folger.

34. Kemble, *Girlhood*, p. 531.

35. Kemble, *Journal,* Vol. I, p. 72.

36. Kemble, *Later Life,* Vol I, p. 77.

V *White Elephant, Red Ink*

1. Only one amusing thing came of this fumbly affair: Forty years later, when a book of Fanny's named Trench as a participant, he was annoyed, for he had never told his wife and family about this chapter in the youth of an archbishop-to-be. He was still touchy about it when Fanny's daughter, the Honorable Mrs. J. W. Leigh, brought it up as she sat next to him at a dinner party (*Further Records,* p. 168).

2. Kemble, *Girlhood,* pp. 356, 363.

3. Little more than a hundred years later . . . The parallel is tempting but treacherous. The young Britons and others who went to Spain to aid the Loyalist government against Franco were part of an organized Marxist-ideological demonstration; whereas Sterling's band were intellectually and emotionally responsible to nobody, merely reacting to an international climate then yeasty with barricades but romantically eclectic about it.

4. Kemble, *Girlhood,* p. 405.

5. Brookfield, *Cambridge "Apostles,"* p. 164.

6. Kemble, *Girlhood,* pp. 294–95.

7. Combe Papers, NLS.

8. Combe Papers, NLS. For the details of Westmacott's attacks, see *Fraser's Magazine,* November 1830.

9. Kemble, *Girlhood,* p. 314.

10. *Ibid.,* pp. 416, 322.

11. *Ibid.,* p. 416.

12. *Ibid.,* pp. 359, 361.

13. *Ibid.,* p. 361. "Mrs. Norton." Melbourne's liking for the lovely bluestocking got him sued by her feckless husband for "criminal conversation" (i.e., adultery) as preliminary to suit for divorce. The suit failed but some of the consequent strains had a part in making the lady an effective campaigner for broadening of women's rights.

14. *Ibid.,* pp. 491–92.

15. *Ibid.,* p. 385.

16. *British Drama,* Vol. I.

17. In 1804 Crabbe Robinson wrote home from Germany: "To express what we should call Puritanism in language, and excess of delicacy in matters of physical love, the word Engländerei has been coined" (quoted in George S. Young, *Victorian England,* p. 43 fn.).

18. Kemble, *Journal,* Vol. I, p. 197.

19. Kemble, *Girlhood,* p. 503.

20. To some extent the play hangs on a strange custom of the day—that of referring to a hunchback (usually a result of scrofula) as "my lord" or "your lordship." Charles Lamb wrote a small essay about this and confessed himself unable to account for it. It remains as puzzling as the other custom of touching the hunchback's hump for luck.

21. Kemble, *Girlhood,* p. 427.

22. *Ibid.,* pp. 427, 512–29.

23. *Ibid.,* p. 512.

24. *Ibid.,* p. 521.

25. *Ibid.,* p. 525.

26. *Ibid.,* p. 527.

27. *Ibid.*, pp. 370, 82.

28. R. E. Lee to John Mackay, *Regional Review*, March 1941.

29. Armstrong, *Five Generations*, p. 210.

30. Kemble, *Later Life*, Vol. I, pp. 68–69.

31. Longfellow, *Mrs. Longfellow*, p. 14.

32. Kemble, *Journal*, Vol. I, p. 153.

33. Kemble, *Girlhood*, pp. 200, 240.

34. *Ibid.*, pp. 419, 505.

35. Kemble, *Later Life*, Vol. I, p. 278.

36. Kemble, *Girlhood*, p. 291.

37. Kemble, *Journal*, Vol. I, p. 201.

38. Kemble, *Girlhood*, pp. 254, 287.

39. *Ibid.*, p. 103.

40. Folger.

41. Kemble, *Girlhood*, p. 413.

42. Kemble, *Journal*, Vol. II, pp. 77–78.

43. Kemble, *Girlhood*, p. 218.

44. Kemble, *Journal*, Vol. I, p. 227.

45. *Ibid.*, pp. 213, 71.

46. Kemble, *Further Records*, p. 66.

VI *That Dreadful America*

1. Kemble, *Journal*, Vol I, p. 16.

2. When such relative squalor prevailed for cabin passengers, think what it was like for the *Pacific*'s ninety emigrants in steerage. The atmosphere there, when rough weather required battening down, was said to be about as bad as that of the Middle Passage for black slaves in the old Guinea trade. Fanny's *Journal* mentions the steerage passengers only once: she had a sympathetic chat with a woman hopefully bound for something better than she had known in England. Note too that though the cabin-passengers listed in the New York papers as arriving in the *Pacific* also included a certain Sarah Garner and a certain Sarah Sharpe (neither of which names corresponds with that of any male passenger) Fanny mentions on the distaff side only herself, Aunt Dall, and Hodgkinson's sister. (See New York *Evening Post*, September 4, 1832.)

3. Kemble, *Journal*, Vol. I, pp. 14–5, 22.

4. John Bartlett, *Familiar Quotations* (1940), p. 314.

5. Kemble, *Journal*, Vol. I, p. 13.

6. *Ibid*, pp. 17–18.

7. *Ibid.*

8. *Ibid.*, pp. 23–24.

9. *Ibid.*, p. 25.

10. *Ibid.*, p. 27.

11. *Ibid.*, p. 34.

12. *Ibid.*, pp. 41–43.

13. *Ibid.*, p. 48.

14. *Ibid.*, p. 49.

15. *Ibid.*, pp. 52–53; *Girlhood*, p. 539.

16. Bunn, *The Stage*, Vol. II, p. 27.

17. New York *Evening Post*, September 17, 1832.

18. Kemble, *Girlhood*, p. 536.

19. Kemble, *Journal*, Vol. I, pp. 95–96.

20. New York *Evening Post*, September 18, 1832.

21. Hone, *Diary*, p. 77.

22. Kemble, *Girlhood*, p. 551.

23. Kemble, *Journal,* Vol. I, p. 99.

24. Kemble, *Girlhood,* p. 545.

25. *Ibid.*, p. 563.

26. Kemble, *Journal,* Vol. I, p. 54. "Canezous and pelerines," were not exotic songbirds or new perfumes but short capes of fine materials primarily for evening wear.

27. Kemble, *Girlhood,* pp. 536, 548.

28. Kemble, *Journal,* Vol. I, p. 97.

29. *Ibid.*, Vol. II, pp. 19–21.

30. *Ibid.*, Vol. I, pp. 52, 56, 60.

31. L'Estrange, *Literary Life of William Harness,* p. 68.

32. The new canals had not yet brought coal to Manhattan, which still heated and cooked with wood barged and slooped down the Hudson. When coal did come in somewhat later, it was anthracite, hence relatively clean-burning. So the large cities of the Northeast were never so calamitously smoked up as London, which used bituminous coal, as also did Pittsburgh, St. Louis . . .

33. Kemble, *Journal,* Vol. I, p. 109 fn.

34. *Ibid.*, p. 96, 106.

35. *Ibid.*, pp. 131–32.

36. *Ibid.*, p. 134.

37. Kemble, *Girlhood,* p. 550.

38. Kemble, *Journal,* Vol. I, p. 138 and fn.

39. *Ibid.*, pp. 5–7.

40. *Ibid.*, p. 167.

41. *Ibid.*, p. 155 and fn.

42. *Ibid.*, pp. 139, 143.

43. Kemble, *Later Life,* Vol I, p. 400.

44. Kemble, *Journal,* Vol. I, p. 149.

45. L'Estrange, *op. cit.*, p. 68.

46. Charles Wikoff, *Idler,* pp. 36–38.

47. Kemble, *Later Life,* Vol. I, p. 140.

48. Kemble, *Later Life,* Vol. I, p. 132.

49. In 1849 a John Kemble Mason, obviously the same in view of the blood kinship, signed as witness to a power of attorney that Fanny gave during her divorce formalities. He is identified as "physician," and appears as such in Philadelphia directories of the time. One assumes he had quit the stage and gone in for medicine, training for which was not then as arduous and time-consuming as now. His brother, Charles Kemble Mason, also came to America and did well enough in supporting roles; eventually he had the privilege of playing the Ghost opposite Edwin Booth's Hamlet. Fanny liked them both, and had found Charles obliging and useful while he managed her return to the stage in 1847; but he was, she thought, "a lamentable actor" (*Later Life,* Vol. III, p. 191).

50. Durang, *History of the Philadelphia Stage,* Vol. II, p. 205.

51. Before settling in Philadelphia De Camp managed and acted minor roles in troupes in the Southeast, where, towns being few and small, show business was rather precarious. James E. Murdoch, a workmanlike leading man in his time, learned much of his craft trouping with De Camp and had considerable respect for him as well as for his versatile talents. Did he have a more staid disposition in earlier life? Well, even Murdoch had to write: "He was a gentleman of somewhat eccentric habits" (Murdoch, *The Stage,* p. 202).

52. Kemble, *Journal,* Vol. I, p. 173.

53. Nicholas Biddle was then president of the Bank of the United States. It was at a small dance at the Willings' that Fanny's Gypsylike air caused remark, as previously noted.

54. Kemble, *Journal,* Vol. I, p. 184 fn.

55. *Ibid.,* p. 153.

56. Berkeley to Pierce Butler, HSP.

57. Story, *Life and Letters,* pp. 116–17.

58. Howe, "Young Fanny Kemble," *Atlantic Monthly,* November 1944.

59. Kemble, *Girlhood,* p. 572.

60. "*Philadelphia Scrapple,*" pp. 74–75.

61. Mitchell, *Mitchells and Days,* p. 114.

62. J. F., Fisher, *Diary,* p. 197.

63. Mitchell, "Autobiography," Typescript HSP.

64. Emily FitzHugh to George Combe, NLS.

65. FK ms. note on annotated copy of *Journal,* B-Col.

66. Emily FitzHugh to George Combe, NLS.

67. The above should not be taken to mean the writer takes phrenology seriously. It was, as Dr. Oliver Wendell Holmes described it, the pattern pseudoscience—a monument to the foolishness of which the human mind is capable. But a man as able as George Combe could, after experience with many subjects, often discern (maybe subliminally) the stigmata of genuine personality traits and, though using the jargon of phrenology, make some rough and ready sense. More cynically, fortunetellers do the same sort of thing.

VII   *Man Is Fire*

1. In Philadelphia a potential difficulty came of gossip that in Washington Fanny had insulted Robert Fulton's nephew by offering to pay horse-hire for a mount he had borrowed for her. It was only a sharp joke to express her irritation at his being included in the riding party without her knowledge. Washington buzzed with it, however; leaflets about it circulated in Philadelphia. Charles brought one of them on stage, then got Fanny out before the curtain with him, which, she said, made her wish she had been "a caterpillar under a green gooseberry bush." His candor and her confusion brought them a tumultuous ovation such as they had not yet had in Philadelphia, and Fanny wrote: "I love the whole city of Philadelphia from this time

forever more" (Kemble, *Journal,* Vol. II, pp. 106–7).

2. Kemble, *Journal,* Vol. II, p. 129.

3. Kemble, *Girlhood,* p. 153.

4. L'Estrange, *Literary Life of William Harness,* pp. 67–68.

5. MHS.

6. Dartmouth College Library.

7. Howe, "Young Fanny Kemble," *Atlantic Monthly,* December 1944.

8. The Massachusetts Historical Society has a very Fannyish note showing that A. H. Everett, the statesman's brother, later an editor of the *North American Review,* and the Kembles were soon on cordial terms: "As Mr. Butler is somewhat indisposed and Miss Kemble feels a strong desire to refresh herself

with the cooling sea breeze before the fatigues of the evening, will Mr. Everett obligingly accompany Miss Kemble and Miss De Camp on horseback as their preux chevalier tomorrow morning about 12 o'clock? Chelsea Beach will be charming at present."

'Come hither, come hither, come hither,
There shall we see
No enemy
But winter and rough weather.'
Note its being taken for granted that normally her escort would be Pierce Butler.

9. MHS.
10. MHS.
11. Henry Lee, "Fanny Kemble," *Atlantic Monthly,* May 1893.
12. *Adams Papers,* Vol. V. p. x.
13. Kemble, *Journal,* Vol. II, p. 152.
14. Kemble *Georgian Plantation,* p. 86.
15. Kemble, *Journal,* Vol. II, p. 152.
16. *Adams Papers,* Vol. V, pp. 84–85.
17. Kemble *Journal,* Vol. II, pp. 154–55.
18. MHS.
19. Kemble, *Journal,* Vol. II, p. 121.
20. Robert Rushmore (*Fanny Kemble,* p. 90) surmises that Pierce proposed and was accepted at Trenton Falls in July 1833. But Fanny's note in her copy of the printed *Journal* (opp. p. 186, Vol. II) at Columbia says: "We were engaged before we left Boston."
21. Quoted in Armstrong, *Five Generations,* p. 217.
22. HSP.
23. Kemble, *Journal,* Vol. II, pp. 178, 173, 160.
24. *Ibid.,* p. 175.
25. Trelawny, *Adventures,* p. vii.
26. See Anne Hill, "Trelawny's Family Background and Naval Career," *Keats-Shelley Journal,* Winter 1956; also William St. Clair's 1974 edition of *Adventures* and *The Incurable Romancer* (1976). Until those studies appeared, even recent biographers (names charitably omitted) took *Adventures* as largely authentic.
27. Apparently some of Trelawny's literary friends, such as Walter Savage Landor and Mary Shelley, took a hand in advising and maybe suggesting revisions of *Adventures.* If so, too many cooks again. Incidentally, unless my ear for quirks of style fails me, a good deal of Herman Melville reads as if he had read and enjoyed *Tom Cringle,* or *Adventures,* or both.
28. Kemble, *Journal,* Vol. II, p. 182.
29. Grylls, *Trelawny,* p. 187.
30. Kemble, *Journal,* Vol. II, p. 183.
31. *Ibid.,* p. 161.
32. *Ibid.,* pp. 162–65.
33. Folger.
34. Quoted in St. Clair, *The Incurable Romancer,* p. 156.
35. Kemble, *Journal,* Vol. II, pp. 188–89.
36. *Ibid.,* p. 215.
37. *Ibid.,* p. 176.
38. Ibid., pp. 189, 194–95.
39. *Ibid.,* p. 213.
40. Kemble, *Girlhood,* pp. 580, 584.
41. *Ibid.,* pp. 580, 586.
42. Folger.
43. FK MS. note on annotated copy of *Journal,* B-Col.
44. Kemble, *Girlhood,* p. 586.
45. There is a persistent story that

Pierce followed whithersoever the Kembles went that winter and even often played his flute in the local theater orchestra of the evening. *Appleton's Cyclopedia of American Biography* (Vol. III, pp. 510–11) has it thus; but too much of its other detail about Fanny is inaccurate to make it a reliable authority. It is also given without attributed sources in the *Germantown Crier*, April 1959.

46. Kemble, *Girlhood*, pp. 588–89.

47. NLS.

48. Kemble, *Girlhood*, p. 24.

49. *Ibid.*, p. 589.

50. NLS.

51. L'Estrange, *op. cit.*, p. 72.

52. Kemble, *Girlhood*, p. 559.

53. Grammar and syntax, both shaky, reflect agitation; but a close reading makes it clear that the only interpretation of this ambiguous statement must be that it was Pierce who had not only behaved nobly but had come to dislike Charles and feel that his prospective father-in-law had been unfair to him—a favorable tactical position to assume.

54. LC.

55. *Germantown Crier*, May 1958.

56. Philadelphia *Daily Advertiser*, June 9, 1834.

57. HSP.

58. Murray, Vol. II *Memoirs*, p. 403.

59. Huntington.

VIII *Love, Honor, and Obey*

1. Berg.

2. Longfellow, *Mrs. Longfellow*, p. 14.

3. Kemble, *Later Life*, Vol. I, p. 4.

4. *Ibid.*

5. Kemble, *Later Life*, Vol. I, p. 18. Carey's haste to get the text into type and printed off before the whole manuscript was in may signify awareness that Pierce might attempt suppression through legal proceedings, in which case investment in production costs already incurred could be part of a defense.

6. Butler, *Mr. Butler's Statement*, p. 22.

7. *Ibid.*, pp. 22–23.

8. Kemble, *Later Life*, Vol. I, p. 1.

9. New York *Commercial Advertiser*, January 3, 1835. "rumors say . . . soon enough." Incorrect, if it matters. Fanny did not offer the book to Murray until later and sent it to England not in manuscript but in sheets for Murray's printers to reset from.

10. Murray, *Memoirs*, Vol. II, p. 400.

11. Trollope, *Domestic Manners*, pp. vi–vii.

12. Marryat, *Second Series*, p. 293.

13. Trollope, *Domestic Manners*, pp. 20, 99, 137.

14. NLS.

15. Folger.

16. The Reverend Isaac Fidler's *Observations on Professions, Literature, Manners and Emigration in the United States and Canada* (1833). This Church of England clergyman brought his family to America hoping for an Episcopalian pulpit or a teaching post in a secondary school. When he secured no such thing, he wrote his book to warn Britons that America was a swindle; even still-crude Upper Canada (now Ontario) was better.

The thing so blatantly intends to discourage emigration that it rouses suspicions that British conservatives encouraged him.

17. Those who had first seen Boston or New York always said this about Washington. But Mrs. Trollope, who landed at New Orleans and came up the rivers to reach it the other way thought it elegantly charming after Cincinnati; and New York, thus approached, was delightful, hogs and all. What she would have said of Washington had she been there first would assuredly have been another matter.

18. Kemble, *Journal,* Vol. pp. 40, 41 fn, 43 fn.

19. In 1830 over-exploitation of oyster beds had not yet reduced American oysters to their present dainty size, little larger than that of their European cousins. Encountering a sizable Chincoteague in Baltimore in the 1850s, Thackeray said he felt as if he had swallowed a baby.

20. Kemble, *Journal,* Vol. I, pp. 234, 235 and fn.

21. *Ibid.,* pp. 90, 43.

22. *Ibid.,* pp. 87, 89–90.

23. Hone, *Diary,* MS, New-York Historical Society, January 5, 1835.

24. Hone, *Diary,* p. 76.

25. *Ibid.,* pp. 340–41.

26. Kemble, *Journal,* Vol. I, pp. 59, 84.

27. *Ibid.,* Vol. II, p. 12 fn.

28. *Adams Papers,* Vol. VI, p. 132.

29. *Southern Literary Messenger,* May 1835.

30. A. H. Everett, then managing the *Review,* is usually identified as the reviewer here. Since he was a cordial acquaintance of Fanny's in Boston, as has been seen, he probably knew—as the reviewer obviously did not—that reference to greenroom manners was impertinent.

31. *North American Review,* July 1835.

32. Adkins, *Fitz-Greene Halleck,* p. 256.

33. *Edinburgh Review,* July 1835.

34. Kemble, *Journal,* Vol. I, pp. 154–55 fn, 245.

35. MHS.

36. Clark and Clark, *Letters,* pp. 88–89.

37. So far as I know the author has never been identified. The references in the text make it clear he or she was British, and sound very much as if she were no lady—indeed can have been nothing of the sort in the Victorian sense—but was likely a man posing as a woman.

38. Kinney, *Description,* pp. 4–7.

39. *Edinburgh Review,* July 1835.

40. London *Times,* February 10, 1835.

41. *Athenaeum,* May 30, 1835.

42. *Quarterly Review,* July 1835.

43. Queen Victoria, *Girlhood of Queen Victoria,* Vol. I, pp. 126, 132.

44. Catharine Sedgwick, *Life and Letters,* p. 240.

45. Murray, Vol. II *Memoirs,* pp. 402–04.

46. Kemble *Journal,* Vol. II, pp. 103–04 fn.

47. *Atlantic Monthly,* August 1863.

IX *The Creaking Door*

1. Kemble, *Girlhood,* p. 573.
2. LC.
3. Clark, and Clark, *Letters,* p. 36.
4. Cecilia Combe, "Twenty Months in the United States," MS. NLS.
5. Kemble, *Later Life,* Vol. I, pp. 9–10.
6. *Ibid.*
7. *Ibid.,* pp. 10–11.
8. *Ibid.,* pp. 24, 3–4, 43.
9. Kemble, *Journal,* Vol. I, p. 196 fn.
10. Butler, *Mr. Butler's Statement,* p. 24.
11. Kemble, *Far Away and Long Ago,* p. 252.
12. Butler, *op. cit.,* pp. 24–25.
13. Kemble, *Girlhood,* pp. 135, 498.
14. Berg.
15. Those attacking Fanny's account of slavery often accuse her of lying, or anyway of bad faith, in representing that she married Pierce insufficiently aware that his heritage included slaves. Thus in *Georgian Plantation:* "When I married . . . I knew nothing of these dreadful possessions . . . and even if I had I should have been much puzzled to have formed any idea of the state of things [on the Butler's Island plantation]" (p. 104). To settle this calls for more evidence than is available of what Pierce did and did not tell her before marriage. The likely situation is sketched above. At home in England Fanny knew many young men whose ample money came from economic abstractions—"the funds," "estates in the north," "East India stock"—and it might not come home to her that the second might involve the horrible quasi-slavery of the coal mines and the last slavery in India. The phrase "plantations in the South" could have been similarly bloodless.

16. Kemble *Journal,* Vol. II, pp. 81, 24.
17. Kemble, *Later Life,* Vol. I, pp. 31, 159.
18. *Ibid.,* p. 35.
19. Murray Archives.
20. Whether Pierce went with Fanny to Lenox this first time, and if so how long he stayed, I wish I knew. He certainly met at least the elder Charles Sedgwicks early in Fanny's relation with them; but beyond that (from internal evidence) there is little to go on. My unsupported surmise is that he went to the Berkshires with Fanny and the baby, stayed a short while, got on well with the Sedgwicks, then left, returning weeks later to escort his family home again.
21. Kemble, *Later Life,* Vol. I, pp. 48–51.
22. Kemble, *Girlhood,* p. 498.
23. Butler, *op. cit.,* p. 9.
24. New York *Mirror,* November 15, 1836.
25. Internal evidence ascribes this to Nathaniel P. Willis, of the *Mirror's* staff, journalist and versifier.
26. Kemble, *Later Life,* Vol. I, pp. 78, 81.
27. *Ibid.,* pp. 162–63.
28. *Ibid.,* pp. 74–75.
29. *Ibid.,* pp. 80–81, 89–90.
30. Butler, *op. cit.,* pp. 9–11.
31. Kemble, *Later Life,* Vol. I, pp. 145–46.
32. *Ibid.,* p. 115.
33. Berg.
34. NLS.

35. Thomas, *Love and Work Enough*, p. 122.
36. Butler, *op. cit.*, pp. 26–27.
37. Kemble, *Later Life*, Vol. I, p. 149.
38. *Ibid.*, pp. 151, 159–60.

39. *Ibid.*, p. 158.
40. *Ibid.*, p. 172.
41. *Ibid.*, p. 161.
42. Butler, *op. cit.*, p. 48.
43. Butler, *op. cit.*, pp. 27–29.

X   *Peculiar Institution*

1. Kemble, *Later Life*, Vol. I, p. 169.
2. Berg.
3. Berg.
4. King did not mention that this measure, by reducing chance of miscarriage, promised the owner a larger number of new black babies likely to grow into valuable field-hands. Even when the owner renounced sale away from the plantation, as a few did, this was welcome increment. Hence one wonders why more slaveowners were not more generous about time off for pregnant women.
5. *Southern Agriculturist*, December 1828.
6. Kemble, *Later Life*, Vol. I, p. 176.
7. Kemble, *Georgian Plantation*, pp. 15–16.
8. Kemble, *Later Life*, Vol. I, p. 183.
9. *Ibid.*, pp. 189–90.
10. *Ibid.*, p. 194.
11. *Ibid.*, pp. 199, 201.
12. *Ibid.*, pp. 201–02.
13. *Ibid.*, pp. 203–04.
14. *Ibid.*, pp. 207, 213.
15. *Ibid.*, pp. 217–18.
16. *Ibid.*, p. 218.
17. *Ibid.*, p. 222.
18. *Ibid.*, pp. 219–20.

19. *Ibid.*, pp. 215–16.
20. Today one sees little Spanish moss thereabouts. Its disappearance is thought to have come from air pollution by a pulp mill in Brunswick. Fanny was wrong about its being parasitic, by the way.
21. Kemble, *Later Life*, Vol. I, p. 223.
22. Kemble, *Georgian Plantation*, pp. 48–49.
23. *Ibid.*, p. 173.
24. *Ibid.*, pp. 127–28.
25. *Ibid.*, pp. 106–07, 58.
26. *Ibid.*, p. 56.
27. Holmes, *"Dr. Bullie's Notes,"* p. 150. Holmes wrote that he was "attending physician on the estates of Mr. Butler . . . for many years before and after [Fanny's stay]." Yet Roswell King, Jr., wrote in 1828 that "physicians are of little use, except in surgical cases" (see note 5) on slave plantations, and maintained that experienced slave nurses could handle everything else. That leaves little room for Holmes. Holmes also wrote, as to Fanny's descriptions of conditions in the Butler infirmaries: "I was cognisant of all that happened in the hospitals or among the sick in their own quarters. I plead innocent of any complicity in or knowledge of any such things" (p. 150)—a denial of Fanny's

findings, if it means anything. On such points the reader must make up his or her own mind which to believe.

28. Kemble, *Georgian Plantation,* pp. 32–34, 38.

29. *Ibid.,* p. 34.

30. *Ibid.,* pp. 35, 40.

31. *Ibid.,* p. 122.

32. Russell, *My Diary,* p. 133.

33. Daphne Alexander to Amelia M. Watson, Lenox Library Association.

34. Kemble, Georgian Plantation, p. 52.

35. *Ibid.,* pp. 22, 41.

36. *Ibid.,* pp. 44–45.

37. *Ibid.,* pp. 77–78.

38. Many years later King's daughter Julia wrote down elaborate recollections of her elders' gossip about Butler's Island and Fanny, on whom she was hysterically harsh. Reading these papers at the Georgia Historical Society, I assumed at first that this was just the usual indignation against Fanny's book on slavery. But there soon weighed in a special reason for vituperation: The lady took it as an insult that Fanny wrote of her father as "overseer" instead of "supervisor," which put him in a despised category. She did not seem to mind, explicitly anyway, Fanny's identifying him as father of several mulattos and brother of another. Then she developed a grotesque belief that Fanny fell in love with King and when he rejected her advances, she vented her rage by writing harsh lies about him, slavery, and the Sea Islands.

39. Kemble, *Georgian Plantation,* pp. 131, 78.

40. Naming black slaves out of classical lore was a widespread custom kept up by contemptuous awareness of the amusing absurdity of calling a lean little pickaninny Venus or a docile field-

hand Pompey or Caesar. The British and French in the West Indies did it too; so did the ancient Romans. See my *Goodbye to Uncle Tom,* 120 and fn.

41. Kemble, *Georgian Plantation,* pp. 101–02.

42. *Ibid.,* pp. 102–03.

43. *Ibid.,* pp. 103–05.

44. *Ibid.,* pp. 105–06.

45. *Ibid.,* pp. 224, 79–80.

46. *Ibid.,* pp. 124–5.

47. Kemble, *Later Life,* Vol. I, p. 236.

48. *Ibid.,* p. 236.

49. *Ibid.,* pp. 240–56.

50. Kemble, *Georgian Plantation,* pp. 176–77.

51. *Ibid.,* pp. 161, 177.

52. *Ibid.,* p. 178.

53. Higginson, *Letters and Journals,* p. 218.

54. Kemble, *Georgian Plantation,* p. 241.

55. *Ibid.,* pp. 278–80. "conspiracy . . . slaves." This episode must have been common knowledge round Darien; Pierce once gave Fanny some details as he had them from fellow planters. One wishes she had set down something about it. I can find nothing at all about it in compendia of slave uprisings. Malcolm Bell, Jr., a highly knowledgeable Kemble-watcher in Savannah, thinks it was somehow connected with the Royal Navy's raids on the Sea Islands during the War of 1812 with accompanying efforts to persuade slaves to escape.

56. *Ibid.,* p. 168.

57. *Ibid.,* pp. 170–72.

58. *Ibid.,* pp. 230–31.

59. *Ibid.,* p. 234.

60. *Ibid.,* pp. 229, 256.

61. Butler, *Mr. Butler's Statement,* p. 34.

XI   A Sea of Troubles

1. The northward voyage usually had prevailing winds behind it and by mid-spring conditions at sea were more favorable. For particular evidence: In his *Statement* (p. 30) Pierce says, "We returned . . . in April, 1839 . . . to our home in the vicinity of Philadelphia." We know from *Georgian Plantation* that they were still at Hampton Point on April 20, which hardly leaves time for the cumbrous land routing of the previous winter to get them to Philadelphia by May 1. Yet on April 30 Fanny writes a letter to Lady Dacre from New York (*Later Life*, Vol. I, p. 244). She certainly had not had time to reach Philadelphia and get on to New York by that date. The only reasonable explanation is that she was just off a Savannah-to-New York packet after a fair weather voyage of a week or less.

2. Butler, *Mr. Butler's Statement*, pp. 30–1.

3. *Ibid.*, p. 35.

4. *Ibid.*, p. 41.

5. *Ibid.*, pp. 32, 38.

6. *Ibid.*, p. 33.

7. *Ibid.*, pp. 33, 34, 36.

8. *Ibid.*, pp. 36–9. The able rhetoric of Pierce's *Statement*, as in this and many other persuasive letters, may rouse suspicion that he had help from a clever lawyer or a professional writer. Certainly they are better done than might be looked for from a rather inactive young lawyer of limited education. The few other letters of Pierce's I have seen are, though coherent, too brief to show much else. So this possibility must be let go with mere mention.

9. *Ibid.*, p. 39.

10. *Ibid.*, pp. 40–43.

11. *Ibid.*, pp. 43, 45.

12. *Ibid.*, pp. 45–47.

13. Melchiori, *English Miscellany,* 1969.

14. Kemble, *Later Life,* Vol. I, pp. 259, 258.

15. *Ibid.*, pp. 276–77.

16. The meaning of this cannot be determined. In my opinion it refers to some feeling of Fanny's that Pierce had been negligent about keeping the children free of their parents' quarrels—not to definite threats to their veracity, obedience or whatever.

17. Butler, *op. cit.*, pp. 48–9.

18. *Ibid.*, pp. 49–50.

19. Kemble, *Later Life,* Vol. I, p. 285.

20. *Ibid.*, Vol. II, pp. 4–5.

21. Sidney Fisher, *Diary,* April 19, 1840.

22. Butler, *op. cit.*, pp. 2–3.

23. *Ibid.*, pp. 53–54.

24. *Ibid.*, pp. 55–56.

25. Kemble, *Later Life,* Vol. II, p. 25.

26. *Ibid.*, pp. 23, 30.

27. *Ibid.*, p. 42.

XII   Oh, to Be in England

1. Butler, *Mr. Butler's Statement*, pp. 58–59.

2. Kemble, *Later Life,* Vol. II, pp. 74–75.

3. *Ibid.*, p. 68. Fanny's choice of whose names to blank out and whose to print in full was bafflingly arbitrary. Identification of the blanks is often im-

possible. In such a context as this it hardly matters.

4. *Ibid.*, pp. 95–96.

5. *Ibid.*, pp. 141, 186.

6. A minor contribution of Fanny's to social history: During this visit to Belvoir in 1841 she encountered the germ of a crucial British social institution that one thinks of as having always existed: On the first wet afternoon she had a "private and rather mysterious invitation to the Duchess of Bedford's room, and found her with a small and select circle of female guests . . . brewing and drinking tea, with her grace's own private tea-kettle. I do not believe that this now universally honored and observed institution of 'five o'clock tea' dates further back . . . than this very private and, I think, rather shamefaced practice of it" (*Later Life*, Vol. II, p. 187).

7. Kemble, *Later Life*, Vol. II, pp. 73, 170, 75.

8. *Ibid.*, pp. 117–18.

9. *Ibid.*, pp. 123–24.

10. *Ibid.*, p. 211.

11. *Ibid.*, p. 217.

12. Berg.

13. Butler, *op. cit.*, p. 60.

14. *Ibid.*, p. 61.

15. Kemble, *Later Life*, Vol. II, p. 223.

16. *Ibid.*

17. *Ibid.*, p. 255.

18. *Ibid.*

19. *Ibid.* pp. 255, 253.

20. HSP.

21. Jameson, *Letters and Friendships*, pp. 200–01.

22. Kemble, *Later Life*, Vol. II, pp. 264–65.

23. *Ibid.*, p. 277.

24. *Ibid.*, pp. 278–9.

25. *Ibid.*, p. 257.

26. *Ibid.*, pp. 285, 270.

27. *Ibid.*, p. 289

28. Greville, *Memoirs*, pp. 198–99.

29. *Ibid.*, p. 200.

30. Butler, *op. cit.*, pp. 66–7.

31. *Ibid.*, pp. 67–68.

32. *Ibid.*, pp. 68–70.

33. *Ibid.*, pp. 70–71.

34. *Ibid.*, p. 64.

35. *Ibid.*, pp. 73–75.

36. "I have twice separated myself . . ." Note discrepancy: Here Pierce speaks of his separating himself from Fanny twice when all through the rest of his defense pamphlet he represents Fanny's escapades as occurring at her own willful instance. If this implies that he suppressed some incidents, there is no hope of recovery, for Fanny burned the letters in which trace of them might be found.

37. Butler, *op. cit.*, pp. 81–86.

38. *Ibid.*, p. 90.

39. *Ibid.*

40. Kemble, *Later Life*, Vol. II, p. 283.

41. Folger.

42. Kemble, *Later Life*, Vol. III, p. 5.

XIII *Impatient Griselda*

1. Kemble, *Later Life*, Vol. III, pp. 7, 9.

2. *Ibid.*, pp. 9–10.

3. *Ibid.*, pp. 10–11.

4. *Ibid.*, pp. 38, 45.

5. It appears that Pierce had al-

ready sold Forrester and Fanny had not yet bought him back, as already told of, with the proceeds of her first volume of verse. His death occurred in July 1844.

6. Kemble, *Later Life,* Vol. III, p. 15.

7. Berg.

8. Kemble, *Later Life,* Vol. III, pp. 17–18.

9. *Ibid.,* p. 32.

10. *Ibid.,* p. 40.

11. See below for more on Macready's crosslights on Fanny. Meanwhile one should mention that he was occasion of one of the most disgraceful episodes in American theatrical history: Edwin Forrest, "the American Tragedian," chose to regard Macready as a deadly rival and made so much anglophobic noise about it that political thugs in New York City found it worthwhile to take up his cause. Hence the Astor Place riots, in which several dozen members of a mob were killed when the militia fired into them.

12. Macready, *Journal* p. 204.

13. Macready, *Diaries,* pp. 233, 241, 242, 243.

14. HSP.

15. Butler, *Mr. Butler's Statement,* p. 104.

16. *Ibid.,* pp. 105–6, 134.

17. James A. Schott, Jr., *Statement,* p. 2.

18. HSP.

19. Sidney Fisher, *Diary,* p. 162.

20. *Ibid.,* May 15, 1844.

21. Butler, *op. cit.,* p. 125.

22. *Ibid.,* p. 127.

23. Miriam G. Moses Papers, Southern Historical Collections, University of North Carolina, Chapel Hill. ". . . expenditures in Europe." Fanny spent indiscreetly on clothes during the Butlers' stay in London. But most of their heavy expenses for rent, entertaining, and so on were incurred at Pierce's instance and unduly prolonged by his vacillations about returning home.

24. Butler, *op. cit.,* p. 154.

25. *Ibid.,* pp. 141–43.

26. New York *Evening Post,* December 2/4, 1848.

27. Butler, *op. cit.,* pp. 168–69.

28. *Ibid.,* pp. 161–62.

29. *Ibid.,* p. 160.

30. *Ibid.,* p. 158. The former Mary Appleton knew the Sedgwicks well, of course. Pierce also suspected Anna Jameson of spreading rumors about him.

31. *Ibid.,* p. 163.

32. *Ibid.,* pp. 163–64.

33. *Ibid.,* p. 165.

34. *Ibid.,* p. 167.

35. New York *Evening Post,* December 2/4, 1848.

36. Houghton.

XIV *Year of Consolation*

1. Whether the initial reading was at the Queen's instance is dubious. As Princess Victoria, age seventeen, she had failed to admire Charles in Joanna Baillie's *The Separation* when he was sixty-one: "I . . . like Macready far better. Kemble whines so much and drawls the words in such a slow peculiar manner . . . makes terrible faces . . . looks old and does not carry himself well" (*Girlhood of Queen Victoria,* Vol. I, p. 146). The Dowager Queen Adelaide, however,

sometimes had Charles in to read informally; my guess is that it was she who thus brought about sponsorship from on high.

2. Garrick Club, *Original Letters.*

3. Berg.

4. Kemble, *Later Life,* Vol. III, p. 82.

5. Berg.

6. Henry Lee, "Frances Anne Kemble," *Atlantic Monthly,* May 1893.

7. Kemble, *Later Life,* Vol. III, p. 65.

8. *Ibid.,* pp. 87–88.

9. *Ibid.,* p. 109.

10. Kemble, *Consolation,* Vol. I, pp. 10–11.

11. *Ibid.,* p. 15.

12. *Ibid.,* p. 23.

13. *Ibid.*

14. *Ibid.,* p. 26.

15. *Ibid.,* pp. 6, 33.

16. *Ibid.,* p. 37.

17. *Ibid.,* pp. 57–59.

18. Kemble, *Later Life,* Vol. III, pp. 123–24.

19. Kemble, *Consolation,* Vol. I, p. 64.

20. *Ibid.,* p. 104.

21. *Ibid.,* Vol. II, p. 103: "Why, you're alone!" . . . "Yes, alone, alone." . . . "Better to be alone than in the wrong company."

22. *Ibid.,* p. 115.

23. *Ibid.,* p. 111.

24. *Ibid.,* pp. 104–5.

25. *Ibid.,* Vol. I, p. 65.

26. *Ibid.,* Vol. II, pp. 98–99, 106.

27. *Ibid.,* p. 166.

28. *North American Review,* July 1847.

XV *Footlights Again*

1. Berg.

2. Coleman, *Fifty Years,* Vol. II, p. 414.

3. HTC.

4. Kemble, *Later Life,* Vol. III, pp. 140, 165.

5. *Ibid.,* p. 165.

6. *Ibid.,* p. 168.

7. *Ibid.,* p. 164.

8. *Ibid.,* p. 165.

9. HTC, undated clipping.

10. Players Club.

11. Kemble, *Later Life,* Vol. III, p. 141.

12. *Ibid.,* p. 191.

13. *Illustrated London News,* May 1, 1847.

14. Fanny thought it lamentably "imprudent and wrong" of certain aristocratic London ladies of the day to be learning to "take chloroform as a pastime" (*Later Life,* Vol. III, p. 369).

15. Berg.

16. Berg.

17. This became a lasting and valuable friendship but not of the sort justifying a recent lady-novelist in depicting Sumner as in love with Fanny and proposing marriage. Supposing he had done so, she would certainly have been wise to reject him kindly. Charles Sumner was rangily handsome, able and conscientious as U.S. senator and outstanding leader of abolitionism; but far too rigid and humorless for any chance of close compatibility with Fanny.

18. Macready, *Diaries,* Vol. II, pp. 365–66.

19. Kemble, *Later Life*, Vol. III, p. 210.

20. *Ibid.*, pp. 306–07.

21. The English "public school" was then and still is, of course, a privately endowed and operated secondary school for boys of preeminent social prestige; nothing like the American meaning of the term. Our nearest equivalent (though not altogether like) is the Groton, St. Paul's sort of thing.

22. Macready, *Diaries*, Vol. I, pp. 384, 369.

23. Downer, *Eminent Tragedian*, pp. 277–78.

24. Macready, *Diaries*, Vol. I, p. 241.

25. Macready, *Journal*, p. 86.

26. Downer, *op. cit.*, p. x.

27. Macready, *Diaries*, Vol. II, p. 125.

28. Kemble, *Later Life*, Vol. III, p. 378.

29. *Ibid.*, p. 375.

30. *Ibid.*, p. 376.

31. *Ibid.*, pp. 386–87.

32. Macready, *Journal*, p. 248.

33. Agate, *These Were Actors*, p. 26.

34. HSP.

35. Kemble, *Later Life*, Vol. II, p. 100.

36. Bunn, *The Stage*, Vol. I, p. 18.

37. Matthews and Hutton, *Actors*, Vol. Kean-Booth, p. 250.

38. Kemble, *Journal*, Vol. I, p. 238; Vol. II, pp. 117, 25.

39. *Ibid.*, Vol. I, p. 220.

40. *Ibid.*, Vol. I, p. 117.

41. *Ibid.*, Vol. II, p. 31.

42. *Ibid.*

43. Dorothy Stickney, *Openings and Closings*, p. 84.

44. Henry Lee, "Frances Anne Kemble," *Atlantic Monthly*, May 1893.

45. Kemble, *Journal*, Vol. II, p. 95.

46. *Ibid.*, Vol. I, p. 61.

47. *Girlhood*, p. 288.

48. Folger.

49. Kemble, *Journal*, Vol. II, p. 117.

50. *Ibid.*, Vol. I, p. 52.

51. *Ibid.*, Vol. II, pp. 109–10 fn, 59.

52. *Ibid.*, p. 16.

53. B-Col.

54. Matthews and Hutton, *op. cit.*, p. 245.

XVI *High Priestess*

1. Doran, *Annals*, Vol. III, pp. 149–52.

2. FK, "On the Stage," *Cornhill Magazine*, December 1863.

3. Fitzgerald, *The Kembles*, Vol. II, p. 215.

4. Kemble, *Later Life*, Vol. III, p. 418.

5. Kemble, *Girlhood*, p. 224.

6. Kemble, *Later Life*, Vol. III, p. 228.

7. Henry James, *Temple Bar*, May 1893, p. 180.

8. Kemble, *Later Life*, Vol. III, pp. 264–68.

9. *Ibid.*, p. 268.

10. *Ibid.*, p. 259.

11. Lamb and Lamb, *Works*, Vol. I, pp. 99, 98, 107, 108.

12. George Vandenhoff, a prominent leading actor, took to the reading platform in his elderly years in the 1860s on the same basis as Fanny: "as an Interpreter of Shakespeare's inspired page without the aid or drawback . . . of stage accessories, costumes, scenery, and a company of actors. I never stand at the reading-desk, in my plain evening toilette, that I do not congratulate myself on being freed from the pomp and circumstances of the theatre" (*An Actor's Note-book*, pp. 328–29).

13. Kemble, *Girlhood*, p. 247.

14. Kemble, *Later Life*, Vol. III, pp. 273–74.

15. Kemble, *Poems* (1859), pp. 61, 59.

16. Kemble, *Later Life*, Vol. III, p. 371.

17. *Ibid.*, p. 369.

18. Houghton.

19. *Southern Literary Messenger*, January 1859.

20. Higginson, *Life and Letters*, p. 192.

21. Byrne, *Gossip*, Vol. II, p. 348.

22. Bunsen, *Memoirs*, Vol. II, p. 278.

23. Henry James, *Temple Bar*, May 1893.

24. Cooper, *Correspondence*, Vol. II, p. 609.

25. Longfellow, *Mrs. Longfellow*, pp. 148–49.

26. Henry Lee, "Frances Anne Kemble," *Atlantic Monthly*, May 1893.

27. Catharine Sedgwick, *Life and Letters*, p. 313.

28. Hone, *Diary*, March 13, 1849.

29. Melville, *Letters*, pp. 77–78.

30. Houghton.

31. Kean and Kean, *Letters*, p. 37.

32. Macready, *Journal*, p. 260.

33. Terry, *Story of My Life*, pp. 193–94.

34. Henry James, *Temple Bar*, May 1893.

35. Huntington.

36. Hone, *op. cit.*, p. 272.

37. B-Col.

38. B-Col.

39. Wister, *That I May Tell You*, p. 60.

XVII *Put Asunder*

1. Quoted in *Pennsylvania Magazine of History and Biography*, January 1955.

2. Paulding, *Letters*, pp. 501–02.

3. Sidney Fisher, *Diary*, p. 210.

4. Berg.

5. Berg, FK to Sarah Perkins Cleveland, August 19, 1848. The chronology of off again, on again in Mr. Butler's Statement is confused. Some of Fanny's pertinent letters are undated and the surviving legal papers on Pierce's side provide only scanty help. The text is as near as I can come to a coherent account. Somebody else might work out a somewhat different continuity but the general story was, I believe, pretty much as given here.

6. HSP.

7. Berg.

8. Quoted in *Pennsylvania Magazine of History and Biography*, January 1955.

9. Butler, *Mr. Butler's Statement*, p. 9.

10. *Ibid.*, pp. 75–77.

11. *Ibid.*, p. 18.

12. Kemble, *Later Life*, Vol. I, p. 280.

13. Sachs, *The Terrible Siren*, p. 79.

14. Ritchie, *Friend to Friend*, p. 43.

15. Kemble, *Later Life*, Vol. I, p. 54

16. Kemble, *Further Records*, pp. 24, 64.

17. *Ibid.*, p. 65.

18. Kemble, *Journal*, Vol. II, pp. 122–23fn.

19. Kemble, *Later Life*, Vol. III, p. 65.

20. Birdsall, *Berkshire County*, p. 333.

21. Sedgwick and Marquand, *Stockbridge*, pp. 212–13.

22. HTC.

23. A letter of Fanny Appleton's in 1838 can be read to mean that Fanny did ride astride in trousers: "her riding costume—white pants (tout à fait à la mode des messieurs) and habit, with a black velvet jacket and cap" (Longfellow, *Mrs. Longfellow*, p. 52). But mention of "habit" as well as jacket must mean the trousers were worn under the conventional long riding skirt, maybe to simplify hooking the knee over the pommel. Certainly if Fanny had ridden astride, Fanny Appleton would have conspicuously recorded it.

24. Kemble, *Poems*, (1859), pp. 17–24.

25. H. D. Sedgwick, *Century Magazine*, August 1895.

26. Longfellow, *op. cit.*, p. 53.

27. Kemble, *Later Life*, Vol. I, p. 165.

28. Longfellow, *op. cit.*, pp. 59–60.

29. Berg.

30. Kemble, *Later Life*, Vol. II, pp. 101–02.

31. Berg.

32. Barrington, *Frederick Leighton*, p. 73.

33. HTC, undated clipping.

34. Sumner, *Memoir and Letters*, Vol. II, p. 319.

35. Melville, *The Confidence-Man*, p. 78.

36. No direct evidence but they probably did. Fanny often called at the Hawthornes' during their stay in the Berkshires, and Melville saw much of them. Apropos of the above from *The Confidence-Man:* Egbert S. Oliver (*New England Quarterly*, October 1945) contends that its Goneril character was based on Fanny as Melville saw her and her history. The reader should be cautioned that in 1848–49 Melville went to some of her readings in Boston, found her repugnant, called her "so unfemininely masculine that had she not . . . borne children, I should be curious to know the result of a surgical examination. . . . The Lord help Butler. I marvel not he seeks being amputated off from his matrimonial half" (*Letters*, pp. 77–78). And that, though Oliver fails to mention them, in several respects the case of Melville's Goneril differs from Fanny's: It is Goneril as wife who sues her long-suffering husband for divorce, gains custody of the child whom she has been tormenting, and leaves the man a penniless outcast suspected of insanity. Yet the case for intended identification is plausible. If Melville did mean Goneril to be recognized as Fanny, this was viciously malicious.

37. Lenox Library Association.

XVIII *Extended Family*

1. Browning and Browning, *Letters to George Barrett*, p. 87.

2. Eliza Follen to Sarah Perkins Cleveland, Berg.

3. Kemble, *Later Life*, Vol. III, pp. 250–51.

4. Quoted in Edel, *Henry James*, Vol. III, p. 306.

5. Kemble, *Further Records*, p. 323.

6. Matthiessen and Murdock, *Henry James' Notebooks*, February 11 [1879].

7. NLS.

8. NLS.

9. Houghton.

10. Folger.

11. Ray, *Thackeray*, Vol. I, p. 165.

12. Barrington, *Frederick Leighton*, Vol. II, p. 84.

13. Kemble, *Further Records*, p. 225.

14. Ray, *Age of Wisdom*, p. 226.

15. Ritchie, *Friend to Friend*, pp. 57–58.

16. Fuller and Hammersley, *Thackeray's Daughter*, pp. 79–81.

17. Elizabeth Barrett Browning, *Letters*, Vol. II, pp. 154, 159, 167.

18. Robert Browning, *Learned Lady*, p. 133.

19. As part of a revival of interest in Victorian painting, unfortunately condescending in tone, Leighton has had a good deal of attention recently, maybe more than he actually deserves. But his London house, built to his ideas, is an interesting museum of his works now; he was the first painter elevated to the peerage; and even at worst, he was a splendid draftsman.

20. Hosmer, *Harriet Hosmer*, p. 142.

21. Quoted in Barrington, *op. cit.*, Vol. I, p. 146.

22. Hosmer, *loc. cit.*

23. HSP.

24. I understand that there is some reason to believe that niece May was the original of the Lucia of E. F. Benson's series of stories about Riseholme and Tilling.

25. Kemble, *Girlhood*, p. 332.

26. Kemble, *Further Records*, p. 298.

27. LC.

28. Quoted in Ritchie, *op. cit.*, p. 59.

29. Folger.

30. Ritchie, *op. cit.*, p. 59.

31. University of Texas, FK to Henry Greville. For the record, John Mitchell's wife was Natalie Augusta, daughter of Professor Amadeus Wendt of Göttingen; the couple's children were Henry Charles, colonel of the 2nd Bengal Cavalry; Gertrude, married to Charles Santley, the great singer; and Mildred, married to the eldest son of W. B. Donne, her father's Cambridge crony.

32. Houghton.

33. Sidney Fisher, *Diary*, p. 279.

34. Thomson, *What Became*, pp. 6, 4.

35. Sidney Fisher, *op. cit.*, p. 319.

36. Berg.

37. Kemble, *Further Records*, pp. 316–17.

38. *Ibid.*, pp. 319, 321.

39. *Ibid.*, p. 324.

40. Wister, *That I May Tell You*, p. 3.

XIX *Irrepressible Conflict*

1. HSP. The "newsboy" was a figure credited by folklore with precocious shrewdness and gamin-style charm—a sort of Sam Weller in short pants.

2. Sidney Fisher, *Diary*, p. 470.

3. Kemble, *Further Records*, p. 334.

4. Sidney Fisher, *op. cit.*, p. 375.

5. *Ibid.*, p. 383.

6. Wister, *That I May Tell You*, pp. 37–38.

7. *Ibid.*, p. 46.

8. *Ibid.*, p. 63.

9. Kemble, *Further Records*, p. 335.

10. So far as I know, Pierce kept a low profile until after the Civil War, but he does seem to have got mixed up with a dubious business enterprise again. Late in 1864 a dispute over titles and exploitation of a budding oil field in western Pennsylvania in which he had an interest set him challenging a fellow shareholder to a duel. The affair ended in his opponent's having him bound over to keep the peace and Pierce's promising to expose him as coward and no gentleman to their fellow members of the Philadelphia Club. See Butler, "Statement and Correspondence in Regard to His challenge to A. Mehaffey to Fight a Duel," Philadelphia, 1864.

11. Wemyss, *Life of Milnes*, Vol. II, p. 85.

12. HTC.

13. Kemble, *Further Records*, p. 334.

14. *Ibid.*, pp. 330–31.

15. *Ibid.*, pp. 335–36.

16. Kemble, *Georgian Plantation*, p. 322.

17. Commodore Charles Wilkes, U.S.S. *San Jacinto*, took from a British mail-steamer, *Trent*, on the high seas two Confederate envoys going to take up posts as emissaries to the governments of Britain and France. After bluster on both sides the United States released them with apology enough to let the matter be patched up.

18. B-Col.

19. Henry James, *Temple Bar*, May 1893.

20. Donne, *Donne and His Friends*, p. 262.

21. B-Col.

22. Cornell University Library.

23. Kemble, *Later Life*, Vol. I, pp. 260–61.

24. *Ibid.*, p. 260.

25. Henry James, *Temple Bar*, May 1893.

26. *Bentley's Miscellany*, Vol. XII, pp. 1, 141. The same material is more accessible in Kemble, *Later Life*, Vol. I, pp. 170–217.

27. Kemble, *Georgian Plantation*, p. 15.

28. *Ibid.*, pp. 7–8.

29. *Ibid.*, pp. 319, 23–24.

30. *Ibid.*, pp. 133, 283.

31. *Ibid.*, p. 233.

32. *Ibid.*, p. 252.

33. *Ibid.*, p. 193.

34. *Ibid.*, pp. 295, 305.

35. *Ibid.*, pp. 305, 301, 326–27.

36. *Ibid.*, pp. 116, 147.

37. *Ibid.*, pp. 211–12.

38. *Ibid.*, pp. 236, 156.

39. Daniels, *A Southerner Discovers the South*, p. 314.

40. Amelia Murray, *Letters*, pp. 195, 214, 312.

41. Margaret Davis Cate, *Our Todays and Yesterdays*, p. 142.

42. Margaret Davis Cate, "Mis-

takes in Fanny Kemble's Georgia Journal" *Georgia Historical Quarterly*, Vol. XLIV, 1960.

43. John A. Scott, *Journal of Negro History*, October 1961. Scott's paper makes the suggestion that Fanny updated the killing to make it sound as if she had been in the islands at the time because her revulsion against Pierce's duelling with Schott made her wish thus to state a "fundamental truth" about duelling "without revealing the secrets of her personal life." I don't follow this, but Professor Scott knows a great deal about Fanny, and my failure to understand may be my fault. My own theory, for what it is worth, probably not too much, is that Fanny's final preparation of the *Georgian Plantation* manuscript was very hurried and the emotional repercussions from the material were deep and distracting, so that, as she went back over what she had heard from local gossip and recalled seeing Wylly's fresh grave in the local churchyard, she developed an illusion of having been there while the affair was going on and wrote it down accordingly as-if.

44. Not too bad in view of the local attitude toward Fanny. The other marker's tone is different: "Famous Butler Authors. Pierce Butler and his daughter Frances, who shared his interest in the South, returned to Butler's Island in 1866 and worked to rehabilitate the plantation. Pierce Butler died in 1867, but Frances continued for several years to manage the island acreage. She wrote a book, *Ten Years on a Georgia*

Plantation, an interesting and valuable account of life in this section during the reconstruction. Owen Wister, author of *The Virginian*, and other novels was the son of Sarah Wister, sister of Frances. He often visited the plantation."

45. Parkerson, *White Columns in Georgia*, p. 127.

46. Lombard, *Georgia Historical Quarterly*, No. 4, 1961.

47. *Athenaeum*, June 6, 1863.

48. *Harper's Monthly*, August 1863.

49. *North American Review*, October 1863.

50. *Atlantic Monthly*, August 1863.

51. For an answer to this question I may refer the interested reader to, for a short version, pp. 394–415 in my *The Americans;* for a longer one, pp. 67–194 in my *Goodbye to Uncle Tom.*

52. Kemble, *Georgian Plantation*, p. 76.

53. *Ibid.*, p. 300.

54. Furnas, *Goodbye to Uncle Tom*, p. 37. Mrs. Stowe seems to have had a high opinion of Fanny; she said to James Leigh, "I guess that mother-in-law of yours would make six clever women and then there would be a remnant" (*Other Days*, p. 215). The two ladies' one recorded meeting, in Lenox when Mrs. Stowe was very well along in years and given to delusionary ideas, seems to have consisted largely of expanding on her firm belief in the occult powers of the "planchette"—later known as the Ouija board.

XX   There's Rosemary . . .

1. Frances Leigh, *Ten Years*, p. 13.

2. Folger. "[wept]." This word is hopelessly illegible in the original but the sense must be as here supplied.

3. Morgan Library. "Spectator."
The London *Spectator*'s editorial policy
had been less pro-Confederacy than that
of most of the London press.

4. Folger.

5. Frances Leigh, *op. cit.*, p. 12.

6. *Ibid.*, pp. 62–63, 57, 140.

7. J. W. Leigh, *Other Days*, pp.
114, 111.

8. Kemble, *Further Records*, p.
195.

9. Powell, *Margaret*, pp. 29–30.

10. HSP.

11. HSP.

12. HSP.

13. HSP.

14. A letter from Leigh to Dan
Wister in the Library of Congress, dated
January 28, 1876, indicates that that
winter at Butler's Island Frances bore a
son; and that he died soon after birth but
had already been christened Pierce. The
indication is strengthened by the note in
Further Records, p. 133, that, as the
Leighs sail for Georgia in mid-November
1875, Frances was "near her confinement." So apparently Frances had
planned from the beginning that her
first boy child should be named Pierce.

15. Berg.

16. Berg.

17. Houghton.

18. Wister, *That I May Tell You*,
p. 8.

19. HSP.

20. Kemble, *Further Records*, p.
361.

21. HSP.

22. HSP.

23. Kemble, *Further Records*, p.
275.

24. Henry James, *Temple Bar*, May
1893.

25. J. W. Leigh, *op. cit.*

26. Kemble, *Further Records*, p.
267.

27. *Ibid.*, p. 269.

28. Folger.

29. Kemble, *Adventures of Mr. John
Timothy Homespun*, pp. 27–29.

30. Berg.

31. Henry James, *Temple Bar*,
January 1890.

32. Kemble, *Further Records*, p.
151.

33. Kemble, *Later Life*, Vol. I, p.
163.

34. Houghton.

35. Henry James, *Temple Bar*, May
1893.

36. Berg.

37. Browning and Browning, *Letters*, p. 925.

38. Longfellow, *Mrs. Longfellow*, p.
111.

39. Kemble, *Later Life*, Vol. I, pp.
119–21.

40. Kemble, *Plays*, pp. 110–11.

41. So far as I know there is not
even any expression of disappointment
because *Georgian Plantation* did not receive as much attention in Britain as it
might have. Fanny was not much given
to the Maud Muller complex.

42. Downer, *Eminent Tragedian*, p.
180.

43. Kemble, *Later Life*, Vol. I, p.
58.

44. Kemble, *Girlhood*, pp. 395,
403–04.

45. Kemble, *Journal*, Vol. II, pp.
186–87.

46. Kemble, *Georgian Plantation*,
p. 95.

47. Kemble, *Journal*, Vol. II, p.
194.

48. Kemble, *Later Life*, Vol. II,
pp. 28, 67.

XXI *Embers Under Ashes*

1. Edel, *Henry James,* Vol. III, pp. 147–48.
2. J. W. Leigh, *Other Years,* pp. 142–43.
3. HSP.
4. Folger.
5. HSP.
6. HSP.
7. Folger.
8. Edel, *Henry James,* Vol. II, pp. 318, 212, 225, 311.
9. HSP.
10. Houghton.
11. HSP.
12. Edel, *Letters,* Vol. II, p. 353.
13. Houghton.
14. Houghton.
15. Kemble, *Further Records,* p. 330.
16. Kemble, *Later Life,* Vol. III, pp. 201–02.
17. Kemble, *Further Records,* p. 154.
18. *Ibid.,* p. 280.
19. HSP.
20. Dolmann, *Ladies' Home Journal,* April 1892.
21. Houghton.
22. HSP.
23. HSP.
24. Folger.
25. Edel, *Henry James,* Vol. III, pp. 267–68.

SOURCES

This list identifies the books and pamphlets (no periodicals) from which come the direct quotations in the preceding text. To include other sources consulted but not directly quoted would inordinately have increased its bulk. At the end I list previously published books about Fanny Kemble. The Driver and Wright items there mentioned have good and fairly full bibliographies.

Adams, Charles Francis, *Diary of Charles Francis Adams,* Vol. 5, ed. Marc Friedlander and L.H. Butterfield. Cambridge, Mass.: Harvard University Press/Belmont Press, 1974.

Adkins, Nelson Frederick. *Fitz-Greene Halleck: An Early Knickerbocker Wit and Poet.* New Haven, Conn.: Yale University Press, 1930.

Agate, James, ed. and comp. *These Were Actors: Extracts from a Newspaper Cutting Book 1811–1833.* London: Hutchinson & Co., n.d.

Armstrong, Margaret. *Five Generations: Life and Letters of an American Family 1750–1900.* New York: Harper & Bros., 1930.

Baker, Herschel. *John Philip Kemble: An Actor in His Theatre.* Cambridge, Mass.: Harvard University Press, 1942.

Barrington, Mrs. Russell. *The Life, Letters and Works of Frederick Leighton.* New York: Macmillan Co., 1906.

Birdsall, Richard D. *Berkshire County: A Cultural History.* New Haven, Conn.: Yale University Press, 1959.

The British Drama: A Collection of the Most Esteemed Tragedies, Comedies, Operas, and Farces, in the English Language. London: Jones & Company, 1824.

Brookfield, Mrs. Charles. *The Cambridge "Apostles."* New York: Charles Scribner's Sons, 1906.

Browning, Elizabeth Barrett, *The Letters of Elizabeth Barrett Browning.* Edited, with biographical additions, by Frederic G. Kenyon. London: Smith, Elder & Co., 1897.

Browning, Elizabeth Barrett and Robert Browning. *Letters of the Brownings to George Barrett,* eds. Paul Landis and Ronald E. Freeman. Urbana: University of Illinois Press, 1958.

Browning, Robert. *Learned Lady: Letters from Robert Browning to Mrs. Thomas Fitzgerald, 1876–1889,* ed. Edward C. McAleer. Cambridge, Mass.: Harvard University Press, 1968.

Bunn, Alfred. *The Stage: Both Before and Behind the Curtain, from "Observations Taken on the Spot."* N.p.: Richard Bentley, 1840.

Bunsen, Frances, Baroness. *A Memoir of Baron Bunsen: Late Minister Plenipotentiary and Envoy Extraordinary of His Majesty Frederic William IV, at the Court of St. James.* London: Longmans, Green, & Co., 1868.

Butler, Pierce. *Mr. Butler's Statement.* Philadelphia: J. C. Clark, printer, 1850.

Byrne, Julia Clara Busk. *Gossip of the Century: Personal and Traditional Memories—Social Literary Artistic &c.* London: Ward & Downey, 1892.

Cate, Margaret Davis. *Our Todays and Yesterdays: A Story of Brunswick and the Coastal Islands,* rev. ed. Brunswick, Georgia: Glover Bros., 1930.

Clark, Willis Gaylord and Lewis Gaylord Clark. *The Letters of Willis Gaylord Clark and Lewis Gaylord Clark,* ed. Leslie W. Dunlap. New York: New York Public Library, 1940.

Clayden, P. W. *Rogers and His Contemporaries.* London: Smith, Elder, & Co., 1889.

Cobbe, Frances Power. *Life of Frances Power Cobbe.* Boston: Houghton Mifflin & Co., 1894.

Coleman, John. *Fifty Years of an Actor's Life.* London: Hutchinson & Co., 1904.

Cooper, James Fenimore. *Correspondence of James Fenimore Cooper,* ed. James Fenimore Cooper, grandson. New Haven, Conn.: Yale University Press, 1922.

Donne, William Bodham. *William Bodham Donne and His Friends,* ed. Catherine B. Johnson. London: Methuen & Co., 1905.

Doran, F. S. A. *Annals of the English Stage from Thomas Betterton to Edmund Kean.* London: John C. Nimmo, 1888.

Downer, Alan S. *The Eminent Tragedian: William Charles Macready.* Cambridge, Mass.: Harvard University Press, 1966.

Durang, Charles. *History of the Philadelphia Stage Between the Years 1749 and 1855,* 6 vols. Philadelphia: University of Pennsylvania Library, 1868.

Eastlake, Elizabeth. *Journals and Correspondence of Lady Eastlake,* ed. Charles Eastlake Smith, nephew. London: John Murray, 1895.
Edel, Leon. *Henry James,* 5 vols. London: Rupert Hart-Davis, 1953–72.

Fisher, Joshua Francis. *Recollections of Joshua Francis Fisher,* written in 1864, arr. Sybil Cadwalader. N.p., privately printed, 1929.
Fisher, Sidney George. *A Philadelphia Perspective: The Diary of Sidney George Fisher Covering the Years, 1834–1871,* ed. Nicholas B. Wainwright. Philadelphia: Historical Society of Pennsylvania, 1967.
Fitzgerald, Percy. *The Kembles: An Account of the Kemble Family, Including the Lives of Mrs. Siddons, and Her Brother John Philip Kemble.* London: Tinsley Brothers, 1871.
Fuller, Hester Thackeray and Violet Hammersley, comps. *Thackeray's Daughter: Some Recollections of Anne Thackeray Ritchie.* Dublin: Euphorion Books, 1951.
Furnas, J. C. *Goodbye to Uncle Tom.* New York: William Sloane Associates, 1956.

Goethe, Johann Wolfgang. *Wilhelm Meister's Apprenticeship,* trans. R. Dillon Boylan. London: George Bell & Sons, 1910.
Greville, Charles. *The Greville Memoirs,* ed. Roger Fulford. New York: Macmillan Company, 1963.
Grylls, R. Glynn. *Trelawny.* London: Constable & Co., 1950.

Hazlitt, William. *Characters of Shakespeare's Plays.* New York: Wiley & Putnam, 1846.
Higginson, Thomas Wentworth. *Letters and Journals of Thomas Wentworth Higginson,* ed. M. T. Higginson. Boston: Houghton Mifflin Co., 1921.
Holmes, James. *"Dr. Bullie's Notes": Reminiscences of Early Georgia and of Philadelphia and New Haven in the 1800s.,* ed. and comp. Felma Eugene Presley. Atlanta: Cherokee Publishing Co., 1976.
Hone, Philip. *The Diary of Philip Hone,* ed. Allan Nevins, new enl. ed. New York: Dodd, Mead & Co. 1936.
Hosmer, Harriet. *Letters and Memories,* ed. Cornelia Carr. New York: Moffat, Yard & Co., 1912.
Hunt, Leigh. *Leigh Hunt's Dramatic Criticism 1808–1831,* ed. Lawrence

Huston Houtchens and Carolyn Washburn Houtchens. New York: Columbia University Press, 1949.

James, Henry, *Letters of . . .* , ed. Leon Edel. Cambridge: Harvard University Press, 1974.

Jameson, Anna. *Letters and Friendships,* ed. Mrs. Stewart Erskine. New York: E. P. Dutton & Co., n.d.

Kean, Mr. and Mrs. Charles. *Letters of Mr. and Mrs. Charles Kean Relating to Their American Tours,* ed. William G. B. Carson. St. Louis: Washington University, 1945.

Kemble, Frances Anne. *The Adventures of Mr. John Timothy Homespun in Switzerland: Stolen from the French of Tartaron de Taroscon[sic] aux Alpes.* London: Richard Bentley & Son, 1889.

―――. *Far Away and Long Ago.* New York: Henry Holt & Co., 1889.

―――. *Further Records 1848–1883.* New York: Henry Holt & Company, 1891.

―――. *Journal of Frances Anne Butler,* 2 vols. Philadelphia: Carey, Lea & Blanchard, 1835.

―――. *Journal of a Residence on a Georgian Plantation in 1838–1839.* New York: Harper & Bros., 1863.

―――. *Plays: An English Tragedy. Mary Stuart,* trans. from the German of Schiller. *Mademoiselle de Belle Isle,* trans. from the French of Alexandre Dumas. London: Longmans, Green: Longmans, Roberts, & Green, 1863.

―――. *Poems.* Boston: Ticknor & Fields, 1859.

―――. *Records of a Girlhood.* New York, Henry Holt & Co., 1889.

―――. *Records of Later Life,* 3 vols. London: Richard Bentley & Son, 1882.

―――. *A Year of Consolation.* New York: Wiley & Putnam, 1847.

[Kinney, Lucy Markoe]. *Description of a Visit to Washington.* N.p., n.d.

Lamb, Charles and Mary Lamb. *The Works of Charles and Mary Lamb,* Vol. I, *Miscellaneous Prose,* ed. E. V. Lucas. New York: G. P. Putnam's Sons, 1903.

Leigh, Frances Butler. *Ten Years on a Georgia Plantation Since the War.* London: Richard Bentley & Son, 1883.

Leigh, J. W. *Other Days,* New York: Macmillan Co., 1921.

L'Estrange, A. G. *The Literary Life of the Rev. William Harness, Vicar of All*

Saints, Knightsbridge, and Prebendary of St. Paul's. London: Hurst & Blackett, 1871.

Longfellow, Fanny Appleton, Mrs. *Longfellow: Selected Letters and Journals of Fanny Appleton Longfellow (1817–1861),* ed. Edward Wagenknecht. New York: Longmans, Green & Co., 1956.

Macready, William Charles. *The Diaries of William Charles Macready, 1833–1851,* ed. William Toynbee. New York: G. P. Putnam's Sons, 1912.

———. *The Journal of William Charles Macready 1832–1851,* abr. and ed. J. C. Trewin. London: Longmans, Green & Co., 1967.

Manvell, Roger. *Sarah Siddons: Portrait of an Actress.* New York: G. P. Putnam's Sons, 1970.

Marryat, Capt. Frederick. *Second Series of a Diary in America, with Remarks on Its Institutions.* Philadelphia: T. K. & P. G. Collins, 1840.

Matthews, Brander and Laurence Hutton, eds. *Actors and Actresses of Great Britain and the United States from the Days of David Garrick to the Present Time.* New York: Cassell & Co., 1886.

Matthiessen, F. O. and Kenneth B. Murdock, eds. *The Note Books of Henry James.* New York: Oxford University Press, 1947.

Melville, Herman. *Works of Herman Melville,* Vol. XII, *The Confidence-Man: His Masquerade.* London: Constable & Co., 1923.

———. *The Letters of Herman Melville,* ed. Merrell R. Davis and William H. Gilman. New Haven, Conn.: Yale University Press, 1960.

Mitchell, S. Weir, Helena Mary Langdon (Mitchell), and Kenneth Mackenzie Day. *The Mitchells and Days of Philadelphia.* N.p., George Valentine Murray II, 1968.

Moore, Thomas. *Memoirs, Journal and Correspondence of Thomas Moore,* ed. John Russell. New York: D. Appleton & Co., 1862.

Murray, Amelia M. *Letters from the United States, Cuba and Canada.* New York: G. P. Putnam's Sons, 1856.

Parkerson, Medora Field. *White Columns in Georgia.* New York: Rinehart & Co., 1952.

Paulding, James Kirke. *Letters of James Kirke Paulding,* ed. Ralph M. Alderman. Madison: University of Wisconsin Press, 1962.

"Philadelphia Scrapple": Whimsical Bits Anent Eccentricities of the City's Oddities by Several Anonymous Philadelphians. Richmond, Va.: Dietz Press, 1952.

Pierce, Edward L. *Memoirs and Letters of Charles Sumner,* 4 vols. Boston: Roberts Brothers, 1877–93.

Powell, Violet. *Margaret Countess of Jersey.* London: Heinemann, 1978.

Ray, Gordon N. *Thackeray: The Age of Wisdom, 1847–1863.* New York: McGraw-Hill Book Co., 1958.

Ritchie, Lady [Anne Thackeray]. *From Friend to Friend.* New York: E. P. Dutton and Company, 1920.

Roberts, R. Ellis. *Samuel Rogers and His Circle.* London: Methuen & Co., 1910.

Russell, William Howard. *My Diary North and South.* Boston: T. O. H. P. Burnham, 1863.

Sachs, Emanie. *"The Terrible Siren," Victoria Woodhull (1838–1927).* New York: Harper & Bros., 1928.

St. Clair, William. *Trelawny: The Incurable Romancer.* New York: Vanguard Press, 1977.

[Schott, James, Jr.] *A Statement By . . .* [Baltimore, 1844].

Sedgwick, Catharine M. *Life and Letters of Catharine M. Sedgwick,* ed. Mary E. Dewey. New York: Harper & Bros., 1872.

Sedgwick, Sarah Cabot and Christina Sedgwick Marquand. *Stockbridge 1739–1939.* Great Barrington, Mass.: Berkshire Courier, 1939.

Stickney, Dorothy. *Openings and Closings.* New York: Doubleday, 1979.

Story, Joseph. *Life and Letters of Joseph Story,* ed. William W. Story, son. Boston: Charles C. Little & James Brown, 1851.

Talfourd, T. Noon. *Critical and Miscellaneous Writings of T. Noon Talfourd,* 2nd Amer. ed. Philadelphia: A. Hart, 1852.

Terry, Ellen. *The Story of My Life: Recollections and Reflections.* New York: Doubleday, Page & Co., 1919.

Thackeray, William Makepeace. *The Letters and Private Papers of William Makepeace Thackeray,* 4 vols., ed. Gordon N. Ray. Cambridge, Mass.: Harvard University Press, 1945–46.

Thomas, Clara. *Love and Work Enough: The Life of Anna Jameson.* Toronto: University of Toronto Press, 1967.

[Thomson, Mortimer]. *What Became of the Slaves on a Georgia Plantation: A Sequel to Mrs. Kemble's Journal.* N.p., 1863.

Trelawny, Edward John. *Adventures of a Younger Son,* ed. William St. Clair. London: Oxford University Press, 1974.

Trollope, Frances. *Domestic Manners of the Americans.* New York: Dodd, Mead & Co. 1901.

Victoria, Queen. *The Girlhood of Queen Victoria: A Selection from Her Majesty's Diaries between the Years 1832 and 1840,* ed. Viscount Esher. New York: Longmans, Green & Co.

Whitman, Walt, *Specimen Days of Walt Whitman: Complete Prose Works.* Boston: Small, Maynard & Co., 1898.

Wikoff, Henry. *The Reminiscences of an Idler.* New York: Fords, Howard & Halbert, 1880.

Wister, Fanny Kemble. *That I May Tell You.* Wayne, Pa.: Haverford House, 1979.

Books About Frances Anne Kemble

Armstrong, Margaret. *Fanny Kemble: A Passionate Victorian.* New York: Macmillan Co., 1939.

Bobbé, Dorothy De Bear. *Fanny Kemble.* London: Elkin Mathews & Marot, 1932.

Buckmaster, Henrietta. *Fire in the Heart.* New York: Harcourt, Brace and Company, 1948. Fiction.

Driver, Leota S. *Fanny Kemble.* Chapel Hill: University of North Carolina Press, 1933.

Gibbs, Henry. *Affectionately Yours Fanny: Fanny Kemble and the Theatre.* London: Jarrolds, 1947.

Kerr, Laura. *Footlights to Fame: The Life of Fanny Kemble.* New York: Funk & Wagnalls, 1962. Juvenile.

Marshall, Dorothy. *Fanny Kemble.* London: Weidenfeld and Nicolson, 1977.

Ransome, Eleanor, ed. *The Terrific Kemble: A Victorian Self-Portrait from the Writings of Fanny Kemble.* London: Hamish Hamilton, 1978.

Rushmore, Robert. *Fanny Kemble.* New York: Crowell-Collier Press, 1970.

Scott, John Anthony. *Fanny Kemble's America,* Women of America Series. New York: Dell Publishing Co./Laurel Leaf Library, 1973.

Stevenson, Janet. *The Ardent Years.* New York: Viking Press, 1960. Fiction.

Wister, Fanny Kemble. ed. *Fanny The American Kemble: Her Journals and Unpublished Letters.* Tallahassee, Fla.: South Pass Press, 1972.

Wright, Constance. *Fanny Kemble and the Lovely Land.* New York: Dodd, Mead & Co., 1972.

INDEX

Adams, Charles Francis, 160, 161, 387
Adams, John Quincy, 127
Adventures of a Younger Son, 132-33, 136-37
Adventures of Mr. John Timothy Hopkins in Switzerland, 420
Afterpieces, 63
Agate, James, 315, 320
Age, the, 81-82
Aglaë, Pauline Marie Armande, 25
Aidé, Hamilton, 372, 434
Alabama, 178
Albans, Duke of, 77
Albany, N.Y., 133
Albert, Prince, 249, 323
Alcott, Bronson, 334
Allston, Washington, 127
Alps, the, 417-21
Alvanley, Lord, 72
America, 88-89ff., 97-180, 187-243, 266-84, 286ff., 293-94, 305, 336-58, 373-88, 406-30 (See also specific cities, residents); Civil War, 379-405, 406-7; Italy compared to, 299-300; servants, 437-38
American Notes, 153
Anglais pour Rire, Les, 30
Antony and Cleopatra, 330
Appletons, the, 125, 355. *See also* Longfellow, Fanny Appleton; Mackintosh, Mary Appleton
Ardgillan Castle, 35
Arkwright, Frances Kemble, 21

Arkwright, Sir Richard, 21
Armstrong, Margaret, 165
Arnold, Thomas, 289
As You Like It, 339
Athenaeum, The, 164, 401
Atlantic Monthly, 165, 402, 415, 423-24
Austen, Jane, 24, 37
Avignon, 294

Baillie, Miss, 62
Balls and dancing, 58-59, 95-96
Baltimore, 95, 118-19, 174, 199, 331
Bannisters, 184, 185, 302
Barbauld, Mrs., 37
Baring, Lady Harriet, 246
Barker, Jedediah, 338
Barrett, Mrs., 124
Bath, 20, 23-24, 86
Beauregard, G. T., 381
Beaux' Stratagem, The, 63
Becher, Sir William, 77
Bedford, Duke and Duchess of, 246
Beecher, Henry Ward, 400
Beggar's Opera, The, 18, 22, 77, 318
Belvoir, 246
Bentley, R. H., 250, 391, 392, 419-20
Bentley's Miscellany, 250, 251, 391
Benton, Thomas H., 369
Berkeley, Francis H. F., 117
Berkshires, 175-76, 243, 342, 352-58. *See also* Lenox, Mass.
Berrys, the Miss, 183
Bessborough, Countess of, 38

483

ABOUT THE AUTHOR

J. C. Furnas has had a long and distinguished career in American letters, first as a journalist and later as the author of a number of respected books on American social history, as well as the definitive biography of Robert Louis Stevenson. Furnas graduated from Harvard College.